PUBLIC SECTOR ECONOMICS

Also by Richard W. Tresch:

Public Finance: A Normative Theory

Public Sector Economics

RICHARD W. TRESCH
Boston College

palgrave
macmillan

First published 2008 by
PALGRAVE MACMILLAN
Houndmills, Basingstoke, Hampshire RG21 6XS and
175 Fifth Avenue, New York, N.Y. 10010

Companies and representatives throughout the world

PALGRAVE MACMILLAN is the global academic imprint of the Palgrave Macmillan division of St. Martin's Press, LLC and of Palgrave Macmillan Ltd. Macmillan® is a registered trademark in the United States, United Kingdom and other countries. Palgrave is a registered trademark in the European Union and other countries.

ISBN-13: 978–0–230–52223–7
ISBN-10: 0–230–52223–8

This book is printed on paper suitable for recycling and made from fully managed and sustained forest sources. Logging, pulping and manufacturing processes are expected to conform to the environmental regulations of the country of origin.

A catalogue record for this book is available from the British Library.

A catalog record for this book is available from the Library of Congress.

10 9 8 7 6 5 4 3 2 1
17 16 15 14 13 12 11 10 09 08

Printed and bound in China

To my loving family,
Alayne, Sara, Kim, Jim, Sophia,
and my mother.
And in loving memory of my father.

Contents

Preface

Public Sector Economics is a textbook designed for the one-semester, upper-level under-graduate economics course commonly referred to as public finance. It presents the main-stream economic perspective on the public sector, divided into five parts: introduction, public expenditure theory and policy, tax theory and policy, cost–benefit analysis, and fiscal federalism. The standard topics in each area are covered, although the empha-sis may vary somewhat from any of the other mainstream undergraduate textbooks. I have included separate chapters on applying the social welfare function, decreasing cost services, public assistance, social insurance, and taxes and transfers under asymmetric information, as well as three chapters on fiscal federalism. I also conclude the text with an Epilogue on behavioral public sector economics, which appears to be the new frontier in the economic analysis of the public sector.

Incorporating the Internet

The book's main difference relative to existing texts is not in its emphasis, however. It is in its use of the Internet. Anyone who sets out to write a textbook on the economics of the public sector cannot help but feel overly constrained. Ideally, the book should provide a comprehensive treatment of a field that contains an enormously wide range of topics, with an appropriate mix of theory and examples for each topic. At the same time, the book cannot be too long. This is a daunting task.

My solution is not to attempt all this in one book. Instead, I have chosen to use the Internet to separate the theory from the examples. The textbook provides a unified treat-ment of the economic theory of the public sector with a limited number of examples, just enough to help students understand the theory. I believe students will benefit from an uncluttered presentation of the mainstream theory that shows them how it informs and ties together the many economic issues that governments wrestle with.

To complement the text, I have developed a large number of topical examples and placed them on the book's website, www.palgrave.com/economics/tresch, for students and instructors to access. I see a number of advantages in having the examples on the Internet. One is relevance and currency. Examples have been commissioned from economists throughout the world to ensure the broadest possible student interest. The concise and clearly expressed examples presented online are taken from a wide range of topical issues. In addition, the list of examples and the examples themselves will be continually revised and refreshed so that they always remain relevant and up to date. Another advantage is flexibility. Instructors can direct students towards a subset of examples that is tailored to their particular course, rather than feeling bound to cover the specific examples that appear in a textbook. Still another advantage is that, if warranted, an example can be more fully developed than would be possible if it were included within the textbook.

The Internet serves other purposes as well. The material placed there includes: occasional elaborations of the theory and additional topics that appeal to some instructors but do not fit easily into the main flow of the text; learning aids for the student such as chapter summaries and questions; and chapter-by-chapter guidelines for instructors that provide an overview of the main points in each chapter and suggestions for integrating the Internet examples with the theory presented in the text.

I firmly believe that the combination of a theoretical textbook and examples on the Internet is an effective way to approach a broad discipline taught by instructors who undoubtedly have different preferences about the topics they wish to cover.

A Mainstream Perspective

That said, the book is not for everyone. It is firmly grounded in the mainstream economic theory of the public sector. The theory of public choice is discussed in the first chapter and developed on those occasions when it has had a substantial impact on the mainstream theory. Examples include Pareto-optimal redistributions to explain motives for public assistance, the mechanism design problem for nonexclusive goods, and incentives for people to engage in tax evasion. But this is definitely not a textbook in the public choice tradition. The same holds true for political economy. Political considerations receive some attention, for example Arrow's General Impossibility Theorem in the discussion of the social welfare function and the median voter model in the chapters on federalism, but those seeking an undergraduate textbook on political economy will not find it here. That would be quite a different book.

Level of Presentation

Finally, the textbook assumes that students have taken intermediate microeconomic theory. For the benefit of students who have had only the introductory course, Chapter 3 presents the standard two-good, two-factor, two-person general equilibrium model. The model introduces these students to the fundamental analytical concepts that are used throughout the text. They should have no difficulty understanding the economic theory of the public sector with these concepts in hand.

Acknowledgements

I welcome the opportunity to thank a number of people, and I will begin with two economics professors who had a profound influence on me at the beginning of my career, Peter Diamond and Nan Friedlaender. Peter taught the public sector sequence when I was a graduate student at MIT. He delivered a series of lectures whose insights and originality we students could not possibly fully comprehend and appreciate until a number of years later. Peter sparked my interest in the subject and gave me an enormous head start as a public sector economist. Nan then served as a wonderfully supportive mentor during my first years at Boston College, especially as I began teaching in the PhD program. It has been many years since Nan passed away, yet I still acutely miss her as a professional colleague and a friend.

Regarding the book itself, I am deeply grateful to the Boston College students who assisted me in researching and developing the Internet examples: graduate students Matteo Cacciatore, Shoghik Hovhannisyan, Pallavi Seth, and Andrei Zlate, and undergraduate Lauren Kiely.

My heartfelt thanks go out to Jaime Marshall, my editor, and Neha Sharma, his assistant, for their unwavering enthusiasm and encouragement. I also wish to thank Linda Norris, my production manager, Maggie Lythgoe, my copy editor, their colleagues at Aardvark Editorial, and Catherine Travers, my development editor, for their considerable efforts on my behalf. Their work has significantly improved the book and the Internet material. I am also deeply grateful to the superb marketing and sales staff at Palgrave Macmillan for their support of this project. And a final thank-you goes out to the many economists who wrote examples for the Internet.

Introduction

The Foundations of Public Sector Theory

Two watershed presidential elections in the United States during the 20th century were the election of Franklin Roosevelt in 1932 in the depths of the Great Depression and the election of Ronald Reagan in 1980 at a time of double-digit inflation and unemployment. These two elections framed the ongoing liberal–conservative debate over economic policy.

President Roosevelt expanded the federal government's role in promoting freedom in the economic sphere. The traditional notion of economic freedom at the time was the classical definition of freedom as liberty – the freedom *to do* what one wants to do so long as others are not harmed. To this Roosevelt added the commitment to protect people so that they enjoyed freedom *from* fear and freedom *from* want. Roosevelt's two new freedoms gave rise to the Social Security Act of 1935, under which the federal government for the first time provided public insurance to prevent people from falling into poverty and public assistance to the poor. A willingness to have the government promote freedom from fear and want by combating poverty and assisting the poor is generally what people most closely associate today with the label "liberal" in the United States. Conservatives, in contrast, hold fast to the older definition of freedom as liberty and are far less willing to support public transfers to the poor.

Ronald Reagan's election was the conservatives' response to Roosevelt. Reagan campaigned on the premise that the government was the problem for the nation's economic malaise at the time, and promised to get the government "off our backs." He proposed the largest tax cut in the nation's history, to be balanced with massive reductions in the public insurance and public assistance programs. Congress gave him the tax cut but preserved the social programs. Furthermore, despite the conservative leanings of the next three presidents following Reagan – George H. W. Bush, Bill Clinton, and George W. Bush – the shift to a more conservative Congress in 1994, and the increasingly strident debate between conservative and liberals in the media, federal social welfare spending has continued to grow rapidly since 1980. It was 10% of GDP when Reagan took office and 13% of a much larger GDP in 2005. In truth, there appears to be far less practical difference between liberals and conservatives in the United States than the public rhetoric would suggest, even on the question of social welfare. This point should be kept in mind as you begin your study of public sector economics.

Public sector economics is the study of government economic policy, which has both positive and normative dimensions. Examples of the positive dimension are such questions as the improvement in national security that results from developing and financing a new jet fighter aircraft and the effects of taxes and transfer programs on people's incentives to work and to save. The normative dimensions focus on the questions of the appropriate economic role of the government and how government policies should be designed to promote a society's economic objectives. The normative questions are the battleground between the liberals and conservatives, and the natural place to begin. As suggested above, there happens to be a broad consensus in the United States on the answers to these questions. The liberal–conservative debate centers on the details, as we shall see.

THE THREE MAIN DIVISIONS WITHIN PUBLIC SECTOR ECONOMICS

The normative analysis of the public sector naturally divides into three main parts: public expenditure theory, the theory of taxation, and the theory of fiscal federalism.

The fundamental normative question on which all others turn is the question of legitimacy: What economic functions should the government perform or otherwise become involved in? This question points to the expenditure side of government budgets: What expenditures do we expect to see in government budgets, and why?

Once the appropriate government functions have been determined, a subsidiary question is how the government should carry out its functions. What are the appropriate means of proceeding within each function? These are the central normative questions of public expenditure theory.

Government expenditures have to be financed, so the next question relates to the problem of raising taxes. What principles should guide the design of the government's tax policy? In other words, what makes a good tax good and a bad tax bad? Describing the appropriate design of taxes is the essence of the theory of taxation.

The final normative questions arise because the United States, and many of the other developed economies, have chosen a federalist structure of government. Federalism refers to a tiered system of governments in which each government has some jurisdiction over the governments in the tier immediately below it. The fiscal hierarchy in the United States consists of the national government, the 50 state governments, and over 89,000 local governmental bodies – cities, towns, metropolitan district commissions, regional school boards, and the like. An inherent feature of federalism is that every person in the United States is a citizen of at least three governmental bodies, and similarly for other countries. This gives rise to a fundamental sorting question: Once the legitimate economic functions of government have been determined, which governments should perform these functions? Properly sorting the functions among the three tiers of governments is necessary to ensure that governments do not work at cross-purposes with one another. An example would be the national government trying to redistribute income from person A to person B while the state government in which the two people live is simultaneously trying to redistribute income from person B to person A. Inconsistent policies cannot possibly promote society's economic interests.

A subsidiary question is how the people should sort themselves within each tier of government below the national government. This question has economic implications because people choose to live in particular states and localities in part because of their tax and expenditure policies. Competition among governments to attract people can restrict the options available to any one government. The analysis of how to sort the economic functions of government and the people throughout the fiscal hierarchy is called the *theory of fiscal federalism.*

HUMANISM, CAPITALISM, AND CONSUMER SOVEREIGNTY

Let's begin with the fundamental question of the legitimate economic functions of government. This question clearly has no one answer. A society's view of the legitimate role of the government largely depends on the economic system it has chosen, with the choices occurring along the spectrum from centrally planned socialism on the one end to a decentralized capitalist economy on the other end. Centrally planned socialism in its purest form is characterized by: having all important economic decisions made by a bureau of the central government; the use of a national plan to coordinate all relevant economic information and allocate resources; public ownership of capital and land; and the use of moral incentives such as encouraging citizens to perform certain economic functions for the good of the state. The government is virtually all-controlling and all-encompassing. A decentralized capitalist economy in its purest form is characterized by: decentralized decision making by individuals and business firms for nearly all economic transactions; the use of markets and prices to coordinate all relevant economic information and to allocate resources; private ownership of all factors of production; and the exclusive use of material incentives to guide economic decisions. The economic role of the government is limited to providing a legal system that establishes property rights to resources and ensures that contracts are enforced. The government might also issue the nation's currency, although this role is not essential.

All nations have chosen economic systems well within the end points of the spectrum, so that the role of the government typically ranges far beyond its minimum functions under pure market capitalism but is much less than the all-encompassing government under centrally planned socialism. For example, government expenditures in the United States are about 30% of GDP, which places the United States near the low end of the developed market economies. Nonetheless, the normative theory of the public sector as it evolved in the West has remained quite close to the capitalist end of the spectrum. It is most definitely a theory of government in the context of a decentralized market economy.

The tying of public sector theory to the market economy has its roots in *humanism*, a philosophical revolution that swept through Europe during the 14th century and was the intellectual foundation for the Renaissance that lasted from the 14th to the 16th centuries. Humanism changed the focus of mankind's quest from the service of God to the intellectual, cultural, and economic development of the individual. It led, in turn, to the fundamental value judgment that underlies all of Western economics, *consumer (producer) sovereignty*. Consumer (producer) sovereignty is often stated as a positive principle in economic textbooks, that the consumers (producers) are the kings in a decentralized market economy because they make all the economic decisions. This is true enough, but the normative interpretation of consumer (producer) sovereignty is equally important, that consumers (producers) *ought* to make the economic decisions because they know best what promotes their own economic well-being. Once consumer (producer) sovereignty took hold, it provided the normative foundation for the rise of market capitalism. In addition, mainstream Western economists were all children of humanism and took the normative interpretation of consumer (producer) sovereignty as a first principle. This naturally led them to tie public sector theory to decentralized market capitalism. The belief in consumer sovereignty dictated not only the *legitimate functions* of government, but also the *goals* of government economic policies and the *legitimate methods* for achieving those goals.

LEGITIMACY THROUGH MARKET FAILURE

Since decentralized market capitalism honors the principle of consumer (producer) sovereignty, the question of what gives the government legitimacy in the context of a market economy has a natural answer: market failure. The government should provide those economic functions that the market cannot perform at all, or that the market economy performs sufficiently badly to warrant government intervention. People can reasonably disagree over the meaning of "sufficiently badly" and also whether the government can be expected to improve upon the market in any case. Indeed these are the details over which liberals and conservatives do battle, and the details are often important. But liberals would agree with conservatives that the burden of proof is always on government intervention, that is, on market failure. No one would argue for government intervention into any economic activity that the market economy is handling well. Liberals and conservatives agree on rendering unto the market what is the markets to do.

THE GOVERNMENT'S ECONOMIC OBJECTIVES

A humanistic society would presumably want to pursue the broad goal of promoting the economic well-being of its citizens. But what exactly does this mean? Humanists would no doubt like to define the goal as maximizing everyone's well-being or, at least, allowing each person to achieve his or her maximum economic potential. As nice as these goals may sound, however, neither can be the economic goal of a society. They are not simply unattainable; they are meaningless because they violate one of the fundamental principles of economics, the Law of Scarcity. Resources are scarce, and those used to make some people better off, or to enhance their economic potential, are not available to make other people better off, or to enhance their economic potential.

A society, instead, has to choose proximate goals that relate to economic well-being, and the two most common economic goals are *efficiency* and *equity (fairness)*. People often refer to "the public interest," especially in regulatory settings. In an economic context, the public interest is understood to be the public's interest in efficiency and equity. The objectives of the government's economic policies, therefore, are to promote efficiency and equity (fairness).

EFFICIENCY

Economics majors are aware that efficiency has a standard meaning in economic analysis, the concept of *Pareto optimality*. Since promoting individual well-being or utility is the ultimate social goal, the notion of Pareto optimality defined in terms of people applies. *An economy-wide allocation of resources is efficient if in order to increase any one person's utility at least one other person's utility must be decreased.* The common picture of Pareto optimality in terms of people is the *utility possibilities frontier* defined in terms of the utilities of two people, persons #1 and #2. Refer to Figure 1.1.

Person #1's utility is on the horizontal axis and person #2's utility is on the vertical axis. At point A, person #1 has zero utility and person #2 enjoys the maximum possible utility, and vice versa at point B. The frontier AB need not have a smooth shape but it must slope continuously from northwest to southeast so that more utility for one implies less for the other, such as in the move from C to D. That is, the Law of Substitution holds along the efficiency frontier. Conversely, all points beneath the frontier, such as E, are attainable but inefficient. By reallocating resources, it is possible to make person #2 better off without sacrifice to person #1 (move north from E to F), or make person #1 better off without sacrifice to person #2 (move east from E to G), or make both people better off (move northeast from E to a point such as H). All such moves are called Pareto-superior reallocations. Points beyond the frontier, such as J, are unattainable, given society's scarce resources.

Striving for efficiency has a compelling element of justice or equity to it. A humanistic society interested in promoting individual well-being would not want to be at inefficient points such as E, from which Pareto-superior moves to points such as F, G, and H are possible. There is, after all, no opportunity cost to these reallocations. Put differently, any point under the frontier is always dominated by some points on the frontier. Society cannot maximize everyone's well-being simultaneously, but it can strive to reach a trade-off situation in which more utility for someone means less utility for someone else. This is all one can ask for in the name of efficiency.

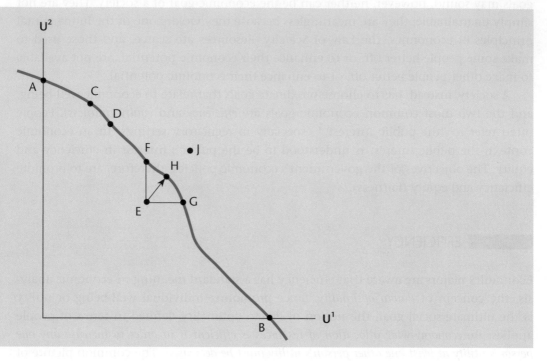

Figure 1.1

EQUITY

Striving for equity or fairness is a much more slippery quest than striving for efficiency. The main problem is that, in contrast with efficiency, there is no consensus on the meaning of equity. Philosophers, theologians, economists, other social scientists, indeed people in all walks of life have thought about the meaning of equity or fairness without arriving at a convincing definition. The best we can do is present the most common notions of equity that exist in the economics literature, notions that do appear to have some influence with the general public when applied to economic issues.

Economists typically divide equity into two separate components, end-results equity and process equity. *End-results equity* asks whether the outcomes of economic decisions or events are fair. *Process equity* judges whether the rules of some economic endeavor are fair, independently of the outcomes. Some discussion of each of them is in order.

End-results equity

Capitalist societies have a natural interest in end-results equity because capitalism tends to produce large disparities in income and wealth, leading to nations made up in part of haves and have-nots. At some point people have to ask themselves how much inequality in income or wealth they are willing to tolerate. This is especially true regarding the extremes of poverty and wealth, which can tear apart the social fabric of a nation. The United States is a good example. The United States has always tolerated wide disparities in income and wealth. It has never articulated a policy regarding the overall distribution of income (or wealth). At the same time, President Johnson declared a war on poverty in 1964 with the goal of eradicating poverty in the United States, and many have expressed concern about the increasing concentration of income that started in the mid-1970s and accelerated in the early 1990s. Today over half the income generated in the United States goes to the 20% of households at the top of the income distribution, and much of the increase in income since the mid-1970s has gone to households in the top 1% of the distribution (Gordon, 2005).

Suppose a society decides that the distribution of income is too unequal and is willing to redistribute income by taxing the rich and transferring the tax revenues to the poor. All societies have made this decision to some extent. The problem becomes knowing when to stop: What is the right amount of redistribution? Alternatively, what is the optimal distribution of income? These are the fundamental questions of distributive justice in economics and their answers are by no means clear. They involve comparing the losses suffered by the rich who are taxed with the gains to the poor who receive the transfers, and no consensus has ever developed on how to do this. Most economists are skeptical that such interpersonal comparisons of utility gains and losses can ever be determined in a convincing way. Still, societies are willing to redistribute so they presumably have concluded that an extra dollar is worth less to a rich person than to a poor person at the initial distribution. But once the distribution narrows, is an extra dollar still worth more to the poorer person? Apparently not at some point, since all societies stop short of redistributing to the point of equality. How the decision to stop is made, however, is never obvious. As a consequence, the notion of achieving an optimal distribution of income or wealth, that is, of achieving distributive justice, remains at best problematic.

Two principles within end-results equity have gained widespread acceptance in economics, horizontal equity and vertical equity. *Horizontal equity* calls for equal treatment of equals. Two people who are equal in every relevant economic dimension – motivation, ability, productivity – should have the same economic outcomes. Whether or not any two people are ever equal in every respect is debatable, but the principle is clear enough. *Vertical equity* says that it is permissible to treat unequals unequally, for example asking higher income people to pay more in taxes than lower income people. But the question of just how unequally society may treat unequals is a difficult one. The quest for vertical equity is, after all, just a different way of stating the quest for distributive justice.

Process equity

Process equity is most closely associated today with the Harvard philosopher Robert

Nozick. Nozick (1973, pp. 45–126) argues that process equity is the only form of equity that matters. His view is that any outcome of a fair game is inherently fair, so that the only requirement is to ensure that the rules by which the economic "game" is played are fair. If they are, then there is no need to make a separate judgment about the end results. Sporting events provide an obvious analogy: Who wins or loses is ultimately irrelevant so long as everyone plays by the same rules.

Nozick's view is not entirely applicable in the economics sphere, however, if only because the rules of the economic game strike many people as inherently unfair. It is as if people begin the economic "race" to success at very different starting lines. An obvious example is children born to wealthy parents and children born to poor parents. The wealthy children have a much greater chance of enjoying economic success as adults than do the poor children. A subtler example is that children are born with different gene packs that give them different chances of succeeding in a market economy. The market tends to favor those who are bright and somewhat aggressive over those who are dull and timid. Genetic differences are somewhat less troubling than differences in parental wealth because considerable effort is required to realize inherent genetic advantages. Nonetheless, certain genetic traits do give some people an enormous advantage in the economic race. Once society concludes that the economic rules may not be fair, then it may be willing to make separate judgments about the end results. Or, some people may be willing to help the poor regardless of why they are poor. In any event, all societies do make separate end-results judgments and, as we shall see, end-results equity is a central component of public sector theory.

The quest for process equity is important in its own right, however. Two principles of process equity are widely held in the United States, equal opportunity and social mobility. *Equal opportunity*, or *equal access*, says that all people should have the right to do whatever they are willing and able to do. The "able to do" part of the principle is important; society need not guarantee to everyone the right to do anything they please. Some attention must be paid to what people are reasonably capable of doing. Equal opportunity is the economic equivalent of equality before the law. It rules out inappropriate discrimination against people in economic affairs, such as on the basis of their gender, race, and religious beliefs. It also calls for the elimination of barriers to entry in product and factor markets to promote competition.

Equal opportunity provides the one direct link between end-results and process equity in a market economy. Equal opportunity leads to horizontal equity, the equal treatment of equals, as a condition for equilibrium in the long run. For example, if a product market has equal access because there are no barriers to entry, then the entry (exit) of firms in response to profits (losses) continues until all economic profit (loss) is competed away. All investors in that market ultimately earn the same rate of return in the long run. The same would be true across markets absent barriers to entry. Investors everywhere would earn the same rate of return in the long run (standardizing for risk). Similarly, absent discrimination and other barriers in labor markets, workers will seek higher paying or more desirable jobs, and leave lower paying and less desirable jobs until identical workers receive the same level of utility no matter where they work. Any differences in wages in the long-run equilibrium are equalizing differences – they exactly compensate workers for the relative desirability of different jobs. Equals are treated equally in terms of wages plus job satisfaction. As these examples indicate, horizontal equity is the only possible equilibrium outcome in the long run in markets with equal access or opportunity.

Social mobility

Social mobility refers to the ability of households or individuals to move through the income distribution over time. Today they are in the middle of the income distribution; tomorrow they may be in the lower fifth or the top fifth of the distribution. Social mobility and equal opportunity are closely related. Social mobility is impossible in a caste system. People are destined to remain where they started out in life because economic opportunities are determined strictly by caste. Once access to opportunities becomes possible, then people are able to move through the distribution. Indeed, the so-called American dream is to create a better life for oneself and one's children by being able to take advantage of economic opportunities as they arise. The chance for success appears to far outweigh in people's minds the distressing fact that many people also move downward in the distribution over time. Maintaining the opportunity for improvement, for social mobility, is a dearly held principle of process equity in the United States.

THE GOVERNMENT AS AGENT

The third implication of the belief in consumer (producer) sovereignty relates to the appropriate methods for the government to follow in carrying out its legitimate economic functions. Consumer sovereignty implies that, to the extent possible, the government is to act strictly as an agent on behalf of the citizens. If the market should fail in some way that requires the government to step in, the government officials should ask only what the citizens would like them to do to correct the failure. The individuals' preferences are the only preferences that matter, just as in the market economy itself. Abraham Lincoln, in his Gettysburg Address, spoke of government as being of, by, and for the people, and this is exactly how government is viewed in the mainstream theory of the public sector. The preferences of the president or the Speaker of the House are irrelevant per se, beyond the single voice they each have as one of the nation's citizens.

The view of government as agent has its strengths and weaknesses. On the positive side, it tends to make the theory of government a more interesting and compelling undertaking from a narrow economic perspective. A theory in which the president's preferences are dominant could become nothing more than another exercise in consumer theory. One would simply ask what economic problem the president wishes to solve: What are his objectives? What does he view as his choices or alternatives? His constraints? Then the standard techniques of consumer theory can be used to solve his problem. Relying instead on the economic preferences of individual citizens adds much more complexity and subtlety to the government's economic problem, especially when the citizens happen to disagree on some issue. It also gives the theory much more normative clout, precisely because it pursues the economic objectives of efficiency and equity from the individuals' perspectives.

On the negative side, the government-as-agent point of view is almost entirely devoid of political content. There is only one exception. We will see in Chapter 3 that the theory requires a political solution to the problem of achieving end-results equity. Otherwise, the mainstream theory is as far removed as possible from an organic theory of the state in which the government is seen as an entity in its own right with an entire set of institutional idiosyncrasies and agendas. As such, the normative mainstream public sector theory has virtually no predictive power about how governments might actually behave or, importantly, how political considerations might influence economic outcomes when the government does intervene in the economy. The mainstream theory remains narrowly economic in scope; it is most definitely not a theory of political economy.

The government-as-agent view has one other implication. Whenever the government has to intervene in some area, public sector economists always ask whether the government policy is decentralizable. By this they mean can the government permit the failed market to continue to function and merely tweak it through some kind of tax or subsidy to achieve the desired efficiency or equity outcomes. Decentralizing government policy is not always possible, however. Sometimes a complete takeover with government provision of the service is the only viable alternative. Even so, government provision is always the option of last resort. The strong presumption is that individual preferences are more likely to be decisive in guiding government policy if the decentralized market can continue to function.

JAMES BUCHANAN AND THE THEORY OF PUBLIC CHOICE

The principal competitor to mainstream public sector theory is the theory of public choice, whose founding father is considered to be Nobel laureate James Buchanan. Public choice remains a minority view, but it is a very important minority. Buchanan set out the underlying principles of his public choice theory in his Nobel address (Buchanan, 1987, pp. 243–50).

According to Buchanan, the mainstream theory is inherently flawed at the outset because it views people as essentially schizophrenic. They are assumed to be entirely self-interested in their private economic affairs, yet when thinking about government policies, they suddenly become other-interested, concerned with the public interest in efficiency and equity. Buchanan thinks this is nonsense. In this view people do not change their stripes when moving from the economic to the political sphere. They remain as narrowly self-interested in public matters as they are in their own economic affairs. They view the government as just another venue that allows them to pursue their economic self-interests.

This is true whether they are employed by the government or are simply affected by government spending and tax policies. Buchanan refers to people's interactions with the government as fiscal exchanges to underscore their close relationship with market exchanges.

Buchanan's second main criticism of mainstream theory is its lack of political content. He believes that to be useful an economic theory of government must have an underlying political foundation. For Buchanan, the necessary political content is process oriented, concerned primarily with establishing the appropriate rules under which economic policies are formulated. In particular, the notion of efficiency in people's fiscal exchanges with the government takes on a special meaning: The government is efficient if it establishes rules that allow people to get from the government what they want. This is potentially a very different meaning of efficiency from that of Pareto optimality.

In thinking about the political rules in this way, Buchanan followed the late 19th century Swedish economist Knut Wicksell, who thought about how the government establishes a legitimate economic link with its citizens. Wicksell argued that this could occur under only one political system: a one-person, one-vote pure democracy in which unanimity is required to pass any government policy. No one can lose under unanimity, so that the people get only the government policies that they want. This establishes the legitimate link between the government and the people. Furthermore, voting by unanimous consent is consistent with Pareto optimality since it would approve all Pareto-superior policies and only those policies. That is, voters would approve all policies that made some people better off without making anyone else worse off (those who would be no better off would presumably abstain). Once all such Pareto-superior policies were approved, society would be on its utility possibilities frontier.

The problem with a unanimous voting policy is that it is impractical. It leads to paralysis once the group of voters becomes large because virtually any government policy is bound to cause some people to suffer losses, and any potential loser has effective veto power. Pareto-superior policies are very hard to come by in practice. Wicksell recognized this limitation but nonetheless thought that unanimity was the only sure path to economic legitimacy for the government.

Buchanan understands the impracticality of unanimous voting, so he argues for solving the legitimacy problem with the following compromise. He would require unanimity, but only once, when the nation's constitution is being drafted at the constitutional convention. He argues that the rules and procedures established by a government are legitimate if and only if they have been agreed to unanimously by the members of the constitutional convention. Again the focus is on process, on establishing the rules and procedures that govern or guide economic policies; the end results or outcomes of government policies are less important in and of themselves.

As time progresses, economic situations arise that could not have been foreseen by the founding members. In these cases, an as-if test is substituted: The resulting economic policies are legitimate if people believe that the founding members would have agreed to them unanimously had they been able to foresee them. Buchanan offers as a counter-example the large federal budget deficits that existed at the time of his address. He cannot believe that such

13

large budget deficits would have been approved by the founding members. They would have instead supported annual balanced budgets had the problem occurred to them. Buchanan has long proposed a balanced budget amendment to the Constitution for this reason.

The government's economic policies following the constitutional convention are of two kinds, either amendments to the Constitution or the ordinary, annual tax and spending decisions that all governments make. An example of the former is the 16th amendment to the U.S. Constitution ratified in 1913, which permitted the taxation of income. Constitutional amendments would presumably require a super majority if not unanimity to pass, as they do in the United States. Proposed amendments to the Constitution must be approved by a two-thirds majority in the House and Senate, and then ratified by three-quarters of the states. The ordinary tax and spending decisions may require only a simple majority to pass, as they typically do. But they must always be consistent with the intentions of the founding members to be legitimate.

ASSESSING THE PUBLIC CHOICE CHALLENGE

Buchanan's theory of public choice does not represent a complete break from the mainstream public sector theory. Both theories share the fundamental belief in consumer sovereignty and the primacy of individual preferences as a guide to government decision making. They agree that democracy (or a representative form of government for large societies) is the political system that is most consistent with a decentralized market economy since each honors the principle of consumer sovereignty. And both theories assume that individuals are self-interested in their own economic affairs.

These similarities notwithstanding, public choice is sufficiently different from the mainstream theory to pose a serious challenge to it. There are three main differences. First, public choice has a much richer political content. It gives essentially equal billing to political and economic concerns, whereas the mainstream theory tends to ignore political issues whenever possible. As a result, public choice is a theory of political economy, whereas the mainstream theory is more narrowly an economic theory of the public sector. A central research question for public choice economists is how political institutions influence economic policy decisions. Second, the normative thrust of public choice is narrowly focused on process, on establishing appropriate rules and procedures, whereas the normative mainstream theory is directly concerned with outcomes as well as process. In fact, mainstream public sector theory has tended to pay much more attention to outcomes than to process. Third, public choice assumes that people are narrowly self-interested in both their public and private economic affairs, whereas the mainstream theory assumes that people are narrowly self-interested only in their private affairs. When turning to public matters, they are willing to pursue the public interest in efficiency and equity, even if it might conflict with their own narrow economic self-interest.

Public choice has become an important minority viewpoint in the public sector literature and understandably so. Each of its main differences with the mainstream theory is appealing. Because of its focus on political issues, the public choice perspective is much better able to explain and predict actual government policy decisions than is the mainstream theory. The latter necessarily remains more normative than positive in its thrust. The public choice focus on process is also attractive. People may well be more concerned about process than about outcome in many if not most areas of their lives. We saw this in the discussion of equity. U.S. citizens almost certainly care more about equal opportunity than equality per se. For example, they clearly care about ensuring equal access to labor markets but willingly accept fairly broad disparities in wages and salaries. Finally, the insistence that people are narrowly self-serving in all their economic affairs is bound to be appealing to economists, given the almost universal assumption in economic analysis that people are always trying to maximize their own utilities. If they are not self-serving utility maximizers, what then is their objective? No obvious answer comes to mind. Furthermore, politicians' motives are often self-serving, and many people do try to turn government policies to their own personal advantage in inappropriate ways, such as by cheating on their taxes.

The assumption that people are self-interested utility maximizers in their public affairs cuts both ways, however. It produces a theory of the public sector with a very thin normative base. Since governments intervene when markets fail, an economic theory of government requires a solid normative foundation to guide policy decisions. The mainstream view that people are other-interested at times, that they have a sense of community and care about the public interest in efficiency and equity, does provide a solid normative foundation for the design of public policies. Not so the public choice presumption that people view the government as just another venue for maximizing their self-interests. Self-interested behavior may be okay in a market context but it is much less attractive in a social context. It leaves out any sense of community, of shared purpose, of good citizenship, from which the norms for public behavior normally arise. It is especially wanting if government employees themselves are entirely self-interested. One might add that good citizenship and a sense of community would seem to be necessary elements for a good society. A society populated with nothing but aggressively self-interested maximizers sounds very much like a society that no one would want to live in.

The mainstream view has received support lately from a new field of economics called *behavioral economics*, which attempts to understand how people form their preferences rather than simply taking preferences as given. Researchers in this field rely heavily on conducting experiments to discern people's preferences in different situations, often with undergraduate economics majors as the subjects. Some experimental settings are market oriented, such as a game played between subjects acting as oligopolists. Other settings are public sector oriented. One common experiment gives people tokens that they can use to purchase either a publicly provided good such as defense or a private good. Spending a token on the public good benefits everyone; spending a token on the private good benefits only the purchaser. The subjects play one token each round. The payoffs of the two goods are set such that everyone is best off if all the tokens are spent on the public good, but that each person gains the most personally each round by purchasing the private good. That is, if the subjects follow only their narrow self-interests, they will purchase only the private good each round, and pass up the larger gains to everyone by purchasing the public good. (This game will be described more fully in Chapter 8.)

The experiments show that subjects tend to follow their self-interests in the market experiments but not in the public good experiments. In the latter, most subjects buy at least some units of the public good, which goes against their narrow self-interests. They appear to exhibit two kinds of reciprocal behavior: conditional cooperation and willingness to punish. The conditional cooperation is that subjects are more likely to purchase the public good in a given round the more that others have contributed to the public good in previous rounds. Conversely, they are more likely to purchase the private good (punish the others) the less that others have contributed to the public good in previous rounds. This kind of reciprocal behavior is other-interested in the spirit of the mainstream theory, especially the tendency for conditional cooperation (Fehr and Gachter, 2000).

Whatever the truth about people's preferences may be, this textbook presents the mainstream theory of the public sector. As such, it focuses narrowly on the economic analysis of government spending and taxation, without much attention to political considerations. It also assumes that the economic goals of government policy are the public interest in efficiency and equity. Public choice perspectives are not featured, but not ignored either. They are discussed on those occasions when they have been particularly influential in the analysis of public policy.

CHAPTER 2

Market Failures

If government intervention in a market economy is justified by market failure, in what ways do markets fail? What kinds of activities should governments become involved in?

THE WELL-FUNCTIONING MARKET ECONOMY

A useful way to answer these questions is to approach them from the opposite direction. Imagine that you are asked to design a market economy that functions as well as it possibly can. This exercise would require you to make two sets of assumptions about the economy. One would be a set of market assumptions about the structure of the individual product and factor markets. The other would be a set of technical assumptions about the nature of individual preferences and production technologies. What market and technical assumptions would you make?

THE MARKET ASSUMPTIONS

Regarding the market assumptions, markets work best if they are perfectly competitive. Therefore, you would choose the four assumptions that are required for perfect competition. Every product and factor market would have: (1) large numbers of buyers and sellers, so that the actions of any one consumer or producer have no noticeable effect on the market; (2) homogeneous products (factors) – wheat is wheat (unskilled labor is unskilled labor); (3) perfect information, in the sense that each buyer and seller has access to all the relevant information needed to confidently engage in exchange; and (4) no barriers to entry or exit, so that all buyers and sellers have equal access to market opportunities. Assumptions (1), (2), and (3) imply that every buyer and seller is a price taker. They have no influence over the equilibrium price, which is determined by the interaction of all buyers and sellers in a market. (Nor do individual buyers or sellers have any influence over any other market outcome.) Assumption (4), equal opportunity, is a defining characteristic of a competitive market in the long run. As we saw in Chapter 1, it assures horizontal equity – equal treatment of equals – as a condition for equilibrium in the long run. All investors earn the same rate of return on their capital, standardized for risk, and identical workers receive the same utility, no matter where they work.

THE TECHNICAL ASSUMPTIONS

A number of technical assumptions are required to assure that preferences and production are well behaved. Regarding preferences, each consumer has the standard indifference map, as depicted in Figure 2.1.

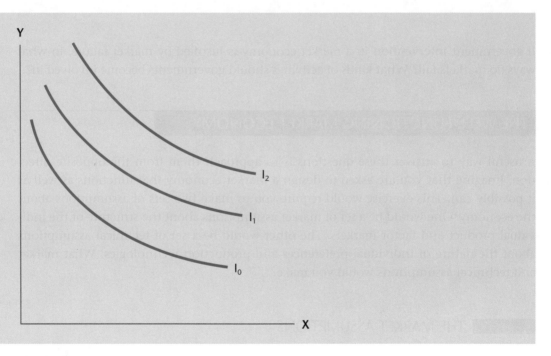

Figure 2.1

The indifference curves are continuous and represent a complete ordering of the two goods X and Y. A complete ordering means that consumers, when presented with any two bundles A and B containing amounts of X and Y, can determine that they prefer A to B, or B to A, or that they are indifferent between A and B. Also their preference ordering is transitive. For example, if A is preferred to B, and B is preferred to a third bundle C, then A must be preferred to C. Finally, the slope of each indifference curve, the marginal rate of substitution between Y and X ($MRS_{Y,X}$) diminishes as X increases. That is, the willingness to trade Y for X diminishes the more X and less Y a person has. It turns out that the economy functions best if the Law of Scarcity also applies to all consumers, meaning that everyone would consume more of at least one good if they were given additional resources. These are all standard assumptions of consumer theory and are assumed to hold in virtually all public sector applications.

Regarding production, the conditions on the isoquants in the production of any one good are much the same as those for consumers' indifference curves. Figure 2.2 shows the isoquants of capital (K_Y) and labor (L_Y) in the production of good Y. For example, isoquant q_0^Y shows the different combinations of K_Y and L_Y that can be used to produce the quanity of Y equal to Y_0. The isoquants exhibit a diminishing marginal rate of technical substitution between K_Y and L_Y ($MRTS_{K_Y,L_Y}^Y$), the rate of trade between K_Y and L_Y on the margin that keeps the production of Y constant. The important point is that under these conditions, the aggregate production possibilities frontier between any two goods, say X and Y, exhibits increasing or constant (opportunity) cost, as illustrated in Figure 2.3(a). The frontier that is bowed outward from the origin is increasing cost and the straight line frontier is constant cost. The frontier in Figure 2.3(b) that bows inward to the origin is decreasing cost, and it is decreasing costs that must be avoided for the competitive economy to function properly.

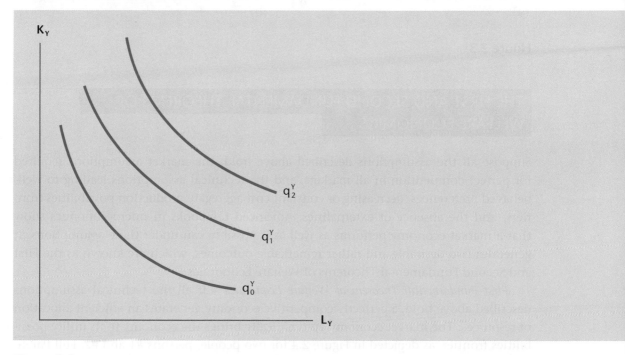

Figure 2.2

A final important technical assumption is that there are no externalities in consumption or production. This is true if consumers' utility functions depend only on their own consumption and firms' production functions depend only on the factors of production that they purchase to produce their goods. An *externality* exists when the consumption by some consumer or the production by some firm directly affects (alters) the utility function or production function of at least one other consumer or firm. Competitive market economies do not produce efficient allocations of resources in the presence of externalities.

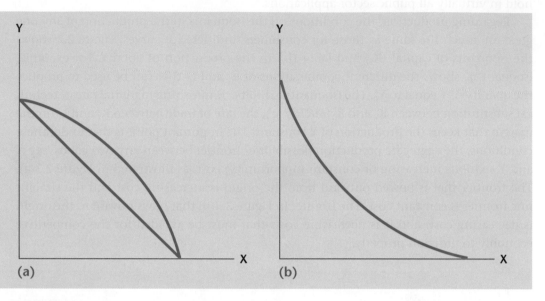

Figure 2.3

THE FIRST AND SECOND FUNDAMENTAL THEOREMS OF WELFARE ECONOMICS

Suppose all the assumptions described above hold: the market assumptions required for perfect competition in all markets, and the technical assumptions leading to well-behaved preferences, decreasing or constant cost aggregate production possibilities frontiers, and the absence of externalities. Advanced textbooks in microeconomics show that a market economy performs as well as it possibly can under these assumptions. It generates two desirable and rather remarkable outcomes, which are known as the First and Second Fundamental Theorems of Welfare Economics.

First Fundamental Theorem of Welfare Economics – If all the technical assumptions described above hold, a perfectly competitive economy generates an efficient allocation of resources. The market economy automatically brings the economy to its utility possibilities frontier, as depicted in Figure 2.4 for two people, persons #1 and #2. Full Pareto optimality holds in terms of people, which is one of the two main economic objectives of all humanistic societies. Adam Smith marveled at how the market economy, as if directed by an "invisible hand," appears to generate the proper allocation of resources. The First Fundamental Theorem of Welfare Economics shows that Smith's conjecture was correct, providing all the market and technical assumptions described above hold. No other economic system can do any better in satisfying the efficiency criterion.

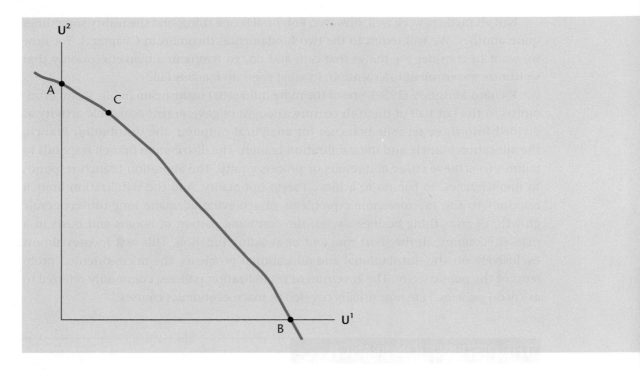

Figure 2.4

Second Fundamental Theorem of Welfare Economics – If all the technical assumptions described above hold, a perfectly competitive economy can generate any of the feasible efficient allocations of resources with a suitable distribution of initial resources. Refer again to Figure 2.4, and assume that the feasible efficient allocations lie between points A and B, so that at worst one person has zero utility. The First Fundamental Theorem guarantees that the perfectly competitive market economy will bring the economy somewhere on the frontier, say at point C. The Second Fundamental Theorem says that the perfectly competitive market economy can bring the economy to any other point on the frontier between A and B, inclusive, simply by redistributing the initial resources given to persons #1 and #2. For example, point A can be achieved by giving person #2 all the resources; point B by giving person #1 all the resources.

These two theorems describe the potential of a market economy, a potential that is truly remarkable given that: markets are decentralized – no one directs the millions of individual buyers and sellers as they make their decisions; most economic exchanges are anonymous – the buyers and sellers usually do not know one other; and the rules of the market are entirely self-serving – consumers enter the market to maximize their utilities, producers to maximize their profits, with no thought given to the other buyers or sellers in the market. Indeed, the prior miracle is that markets form at all, yet markets do form very easily. If a demand for some product or service develops, someone will start a firm and supply it. And most markets work exceedingly well. Small wonder that capitalism has won the day over centrally planned socialism throughout most of the world.

Not all markets work well, however. Potential is one thing, and the reality sometimes quite another. We will return to the two fundamental theorems in Chapter 3. For now we want to consider the things that can, and do, go wrong in a market economy that legitimize government intervention. In what ways do markets fail?

Richard Musgrave (1959), one of the more influential mainstream public sector economists in the last half of the 20th century, thought of government economic activity as divided into three separate branches for analytical purposes: the distribution branch, the allocation branch, and the stabilization branch. The distribution branch responds to failures to achieve either end-results or process equity. The allocation branch responds to inefficiencies, to failures to achieve Pareto optimality. And the stabilization branch responds to the macroeconomic problems of achieving adequate long-run economic growth, of smoothing business cycles, the continual pattern of booms and busts in a market economy, in the short run, and of avoiding inflation. This text focuses almost exclusively on the distributional and allocational problems, the micro-oriented problems of the public sector. The government's stabilization policies, commonly referred to as "fiscal policies," are now usually covered in macroeconomics courses.

THE DISTRIBUTION BRANCH

Suppose all the market and technical assumptions described above do hold. Would there be anything for the government to do? There would be no inefficiencies for the allocation branch to solve because by the First Fundamental Theorem, the economy would achieve a full Pareto-optimal allocation of resources in terms of people. Society would be on its utility possibilities frontier; it would be impossible to make someone better off without making someone else worse off.

The difficulty relates to the Second Fundamental Theorem. Although any point on the utility possibilities frontier can be achieved by a suitable initial distribution of resources (income), in fact the market takes the initial distribution of resources (income) as a given and brings the economy to one point on the frontier, such as point C in Figure 2.5.

Point C is realistic in the sense that capitalist economies invariably produce a highly unequal distribution of income, with some people (here, those represented by person #2) being far better off than others. Society has a distributional judgment to make relating to end-results equity: Is point C acceptable, or is some more equal distribution preferred? Suppose society prefers a more equal distribution. It then has no choice but to make a collective decision through some kind of political process to have the government redistribute resources, presumably by means of a tax and transfer program. In terms of Figure 2.5, the decision might be to tax person #2 and transfer the revenues to person #1 to move to a more equal point such as point D. The market will not undertake this redistribution for society. As noted, it takes the initial distribution of resources as a given. Go back to the beginning, run the economy again, and it will again generate point C. Only by redistributing resources through taxes and transfers and then running the economy again can society reach point D.

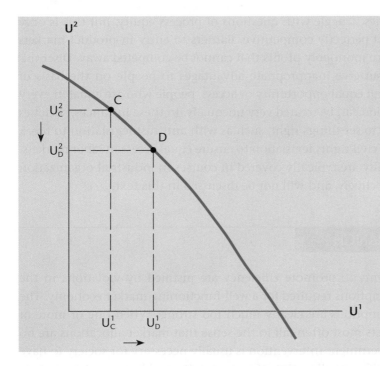

Figure 2.5

Notice that the quest for end-results equity is a fundamental problem that all societies must confront. It cannot be assumed away. A decision has to be made regarding the initial distribution of resources even if the economy performs as well as it possibly can, with all the market and technical assumptions above holding.

One possible choice is to accept point C simply because it is the point generated by the well-functioning, perfectly competitive economy. But that itself would be a choice that a society would have to make collectively through a political process and, in fact, societies never make that choice. They are always willing to redistribute income to some extent from the haves to the have-nots.

Another point to stress is that the fundamental distributional problem is only one of end-results equity, not process equity. Equal opportunity or access is achieved if, as assumed, all markets are perfectly competitive because equal opportunity is a defining property of a perfectly competitive market in the long run. Equal opportunity in turn guarantees horizontal equity, the equal treatment of equals. An economy with complete equal opportunity is also likely to exhibit a high degree of social mobility as people seize opportunities available to them and move through the income distribution. The only equity problem with all the assumptions above holding is vertical equity, the problem of distributive justice. Unequals can be treated very unequally even with equal opportunity, and society has to decide how much inequality it can tolerate.[1]

All other market problems or failures that justify government intervention arise because the market and technical assumptions needed for the economy to function as well as possible are too strong. They are often violated in actual markets.

For example, all societies struggle with questions of process equity, but this is only because all markets are not perfectly competitive. Barriers to entry in product markets allow some investors to earn monopoly profits that cannot be competed away. Discrimination in labor markets can give inappropriate advantages to people on the basis of their race or gender. Without equal opportunity or access, people who are equal in every relevant economic dimension can be treated very unequally. In these instances, societies often call on governments to set things right, such as with antitrust legislation to break down barriers to entry and civil rights legislation to ensure equal access in labor markets. These issues of process equity are typically covered in courses in industrial organization and labor economics, respectively, and will not be discussed in this text.

THE ALLOCATION BRANCH

All attempts by governments to promote efficiency are justified by violations in the market and technical assumptions required for a well-functioning market economy. The market and technical assumptions are clearly much too strong. When one or more of them does not hold, markets most often fail in the sense that market allocations are no longer Pareto optimal. Government intervention is usually necessary for society to have any hope of achieving an efficient allocation of resources. We will begin with violations of the technical assumptions in order to present the allocational or efficiency problems as they are discussed in the text.

VIOLATIONS OF THE TECHNICAL ASSUMPTIONS

EXTERNALITIES

The assumption that no activities give rise to externalities is obviously a disservice to reality. Many consumption and production activities generate substantial externalities, both beneficial and harmful. Examples related to consumption activities include: inoculations against disease, which provide some protection for those who are not inoculated; receiving the high level of general education necessary for informed participation in a democratic society; and contributing to congestion or smog by choosing to drive on a congested highway. Examples related to production activities include: research and development efforts that generate new products or cheaper ways to produce existing products; and industrial water and air pollution that fouls beaches and causes a number of health problems.

Markets are generally unable to allocate resources efficiently in the presence of externalities, especially if the external effects are widespread. Consider, for example, the market for paper products. Consumers have a demand for a variety of paper products that producers are quite willing to supply. Suppose that the market for paper products is perfectly competitive, with the market supply and demand curves given by D and S^{priv} in Figure 2.6. The market demand curve D represents the marginal value (MRS) of the paper to consumers at each output Q. Similarly, S^{priv} represents the private marginal cost to the paper companies of supplying paper at each output Q, the cost of using labor, capital, land, and material inputs to supply an additional unit of paper. The market equilibrium without government intervention is (Q_c, P_c), at the intersection of D and S^{priv}. At Q_c, the marginal value and marginal cost of supplying paper are equal. Absent externalities, Q_c would be the efficient quantity of paper to be exchanged.

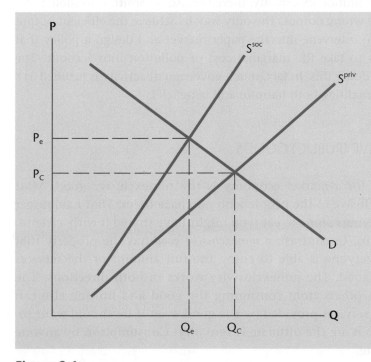

Figure 2.6

The production of paper generates an externality, however, in the form of air pollution from the factory smokestacks. The air pollution damages buildings and causes health problems for many people. At each output of paper, Q, the marginal cost of the pollution is the additional harm to all people combined from the additional pollution generated by producing one more unit of paper. The marginal cost of pollution must be added at each output to the firms' private marginal cost of producing paper to account for the full, or social, marginal cost of producing paper, represented by the supply curve S^{soc}. The efficient equilibrium given the pollution is (Q_e, P_e), at the intersection of D and S^{soc}.

The problem is that no producer has any incentive to take the costs of pollution into account. Worse, a market economy is a recipe for maximizing air and water pollution. Air and water are common use resources; no one owns them. As a result, firms are able to treat clean air and water as free resources, which they then use in place of other inputs whenever possible, such as for the disposing of industrial waste products through smoke-stacks or into the water. They will never receive a bill for the harm done in polluting the air or water. Therefore, they base their production decisions on their private marginal cost, S^{priv}, and supply Q_c to the market. Even if the managers of some firms were civic-minded and considered producing in a nonpolluting way, they would soon think better of it. The firm's cost would rise relative to its competitors, and if it is the only firm that is not polluting it might not have a noticeable effect on the overall amount of pollution. Its efforts to protect the environment would be futile.

In the presence of the pollution externality, therefore, Adam Smith's invisible hand automatically generates the wrong output. The only way to achieve the efficient output Q_e is for the government to intervene into the paper market and design a policy that forces the paper producers to take the marginal cost of pollution into account. The market itself has no way of doing this. In fact, much government activity is justified as a response to important externalities, both harmful and beneficial.

██████ NONEXCLUSIVE (PUBLIC) GOODS

Another serious problem for a market economy is the nonexclusive good. Most goods and services are exclusive to the people who purchase them. That hamburger you bought for lunch was yours alone to eat (you might have shared it with a friend, but that was your decision). In contrast, a *nonexclusive good* has the property that once someone buys it, everyone is able to enjoy the full amount of the services (utility) provided by the good. The nonexclusivity works in both directions. The purchaser cannot exclude others from consuming the good and no one else can exclude himself from the services provided by the good even if he should want to. As such, nonexclusive goods are the ultimate externality: Consumption by anyone necessarily affects everyone.

Nonexclusive goods pose such difficulties for a market economy that it would be nice if they were simply a theoretical possibility, and unimportant in practice. But the classic example of a nonexclusive good is defense, the provision of national security. If someone in a country were to purchase a nuclear missile to deter aggression by foreign nations, all citizens in the country would necessarily receive whatever protection that missile provides whether they want it or not.

Markets cannot allocate nonexclusive goods because they fall prey to a phenomenon known as the *free-rider problem*. Suppose you are a member of a small island nation that is continually bothered by surrounding nations. One day a salesperson comes by offering a missile that she claims is so destructive that the mere threat of using it will scare off the other nations from ever bothering you again. Moreover, the missile is not too expensive – anyone can afford to buy it. The woman is persuasive; you and all your fellow citizens want to buy the missile. But when she asks who will buy it, no one is likely to say "I will." The best outcome for you is for someone else to buy it, in which case you enjoy the full protection provided by the missile and it does not cost you a dime. You get to free ride on the purchase by someone else. Unfortunately, everyone else thinks the same way and no one buys the missile, even if everyone wants it and can afford to buy it. The market completely fails in this case. Society has no choice other than to have a government agency purchase the missile (generally, provide for national security) through some kind of collective decision process. Notice that the free-rider problem is absent for exclusive goods. If you want to eat a hamburger, you have to purchase it yourself.

Lighthouses are another example of a nonexclusive good. No shipping company wants to pay for a lighthouse, since the protection it provides is automatically available to all the competing shipping companies as well. This is why most lighthouses are built and serviced by the public sector.

VIOLATIONS OF THE MARKET ASSUMPTIONS

PROPERTY RIGHTS AND ENFORCEABLE CONTRACTS

Some government intervention is necessary for a market economy to function even reasonably well, much less to be perfectly competitive. At a minimum, the government must establish a legal and judicial system that defines the rights to private property and ensures that contracts are enforced. Otherwise people will be reluctant to engage in market exchanges. Virtually everyone concedes this minimum function of government in a market economy. The question, then, is what market problems justify a need for further government intervention and the answer lies in the assumptions for a perfectly competitive market.

DECREASING COSTS/ECONOMIES OF SCALE

In the first place, the assumption that all markets have a large number of firms as required for perfect competition is far from true. Less than 3% of markets in the United States are perfectly competitive, almost none outside the agricultural sector. Many markets are dominated by a few firms (oligopoly), or in some cases a single firm (monopoly), and when they are, the market outcomes are usually inefficient. The emergence of large firms is in turn largely due to a violation of the technical assumption that there are no significant decreasing costs. In fact, the production of some goods exhibits considerable economies of scale, which causes the average cost of production to decline up to a substantial portion of market demand.

Figure 2.7 illustrates the various degrees of economies of scale. Each panel shows the average cost curve of a single representative firm (AC_f) and the entire market demand curve (D) for the product.

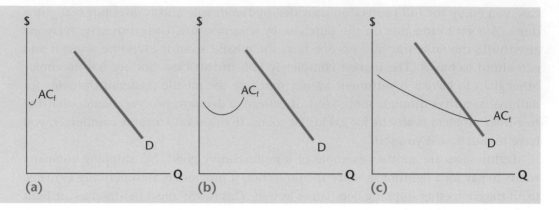

Figure 2.7

In Figure 2.7(a), the economies of scale are quickly exhausted; the firm's average cost curve begins to increase well short of the market demand. In this case, the market will support a large number of firms, so that it is likely to be at worst monopolistically competitive. Although monopolistically competitive markets are not completely efficient, they work fairly well. Government intervention is unlikely to improve on the market outcomes, so that governments in capitalist economies typically leave these markets alone.

In Figure 2.7(b), the economies of scale are substantial, large enough that the minimum efficient scale for a single firm (the point at which the average cost curve reaches its minimum) is a large proportion of the overall market demand. Industries with these production characteristics are likely to set up as oligopolies, with the few dominant firms setting prices well above average and marginal costs and enjoying a maintained profit position. When this happens, the owners of the firms rather than the firms' customers enjoy the advantages of the lower costs made possible by large-scale production. Society may ask the government to establish antitrust laws or regulations that prevent firms from exploiting their market power. Government policies aimed at the oligopolies are typically covered in courses in industrial organization and will not be discussed in this text.

Figure 2.7(c) depicts the most extreme case of economies of scale, in which the average costs of a single firm declines all the way to the market demand curve. This is referred to as a *natural monopoly*, because the market has to be supplied by a single firm to capture the full benefits of the economies of scale or decreasing costs. Requiring more than one firm in the name of competition would force the firms to produce on a higher portion of their average cost curves and simply waste resources. At the same time, though, if a monopolist is given control of the market, it might use its market power to charge a high price, keep output too low, and earn an excessive profit. Only government regulation or government provision of the service can prevent the exercise of market power.

Natural monopoly is not a rare phenomenon. It happens whenever providing a service requires high initial set-up costs to provide any service at all combined with relatively low operating costs of supplying customers once the production facilities are in place. A number of important goods and services have these cost characteristics. The so-called public utilities – electricity, water, sewage – are one example, with the scope of the natural monopoly being regional. It is costly to string wires on poles to all the houses and businesses, or run the water and sewage pipes to them. Once the network of wires and pipes are in place, however, sending the electrons over the wires or the water or sewage through the pipes can be done very cheaply. As a result, the average costs of providing the utilities continuously decline.

Transportation provides many examples of natural monopolies, including highways, bridges and tunnels, and mass (rail) transit. In each instance a large percentage of the total cost are set-up costs. They are all very expensive to build. Once they have been constructed, however, the (marginal) costs of an additional person driving on a roadway or riding on the subway are very low so long as there is no congestion. (Congestion is an externality problem.) As a result, average cost continues to decline up to market demand.

Recreational facilities such as beaches and parks have much the same cost characteristics – once the facilities have been established, the total cost of these facilities does not increase very much, no matter how many people use them, up to the point that they become congested.

Broadcasting and telecommunications are still other examples of natural monopolies. Think of watching TV. There are considerable costs associated with producing television programs, generating the signals, and stringing cables and purchasing TVs to receive the signals. But the cost of an additional viewer turning on a TV to watch a program is essentially zero, whether one or one million other people are also watching the program.

Finally, the advent of desktop computing and software has greatly increased the importance of the natural monopoly case, because software is an example of a global natural monopoly. Virtually all the costs associated with producing a software program occur in the writing and testing of the program. Once a software program is ready to go to market, it can be downloaded at no cost over the Internet, whether to six or six billion people. (Software companies do not allow free downloads because they would not be able to make a profit, but the lowest cost method of distributing software is clearly over the Internet.)

Not surprisingly, governments typically become involved in the natural monopolies either as regulators or providers of the service. Left to their own devices, these markets would almost certainly misallocate resources and generate monopoly profits, in violation of the public interest in efficiency and equity. We will analyze the natural monopoly case in this text because it is the justification for much government activity in the United States and elsewhere.

PRIVATE OR ASYMMETRIC INFORMATION

Private or asymmetric information refers to economically relevant information that people or firms have about themselves which others do not or cannot know, at least not without devoting considerable time, effort, and resources to discover the information. One of the requirements of perfect competition is that people do not have such private information.

They clearly do, however, and private information has three very important implications for an economic analysis of the public sector. It causes many different kinds of efficiency problems that increase the economic role of the government; it seriously threatens the government-as-agent ideal; and some economists argue that it is the ultimate source of all inefficiencies that governments respond to.

Market failures

Private or asymmetric information is an important source of market failure that has led to many kinds of government intervention. One example relates to people's willingness to engage in exchange. Market exchanges may not be even-handed if buyers or sellers have information about products that is not available to those on the other side of the market. People sense this, and become reluctant to engage in exchange for fear of being cheated.

Producers often know some things about their products and services that the buyers do not. For instance, when you drive into a service station and pump 10 gallons of gasoline, how do you know that you have actually received 10 gallons? The truth is you do not know – you never even see the gasoline as it enters your tank. To avoid being cheated, people turn to the government to provide independent certification that when the pump says 10 gallons it really is 10 gallons. They do not trust the oil companies to certify the pumps. Note the government's inspection sticker on the pump the next time you buy gas. Asymmetric information about products is the justification for such government agencies as state Bureaus of Weights and Measures, the Federal Drug Administration to test new drugs, and the federal Occupational Safety and Health Administration (OSHA) to protect workers from dangerous working conditions. In addition to providing independent certification, government agencies can monitor firms and test products on behalf of all citizens much more cheaply than if consumers conducted the monitoring and testing themselves. There are considerable economies of scale in testing and monitoring products.

Another important example of market failure resulting from private information occurs in insurance markets. People want to insure themselves against the misfortunes of life but private companies are not always willing to supply the insurance. Insurance markets are said to be incomplete because the demand for insurance is only partially satisfied, and may not be satisfied at all. People often turn to the government in these instances to provide the insurance that they want. Insurance provided by the government is called "social insurance."

A number of conditions have to hold for insurance companies to be willing to provide insurance against some event. The first is that the probabilities of the event happening to individuals have to be independent of one another. The independence allows the insurance company to pool the risk among a large group of people. The probabilities are independent for life insurance: The probability that you will die today is independent of the probability that I will die today. The probabilities are not independent for becoming unemployed, however. When the economy goes into a recession, millions of people simultaneously lose their jobs. Were companies to offer unemployment insurance, they would suffer huge losses every time a recession occurred. They would lose the advantage of pooling independent risks. Therefore, if people want unemployment insurance, the government has to provide it.

Another requirement is that the insurance companies must have good information about the people they are insuring. Absent good information, they are vulnerable to the problems of adverse selection and moral hazard, both of which can undermine the formation of insurance markets. Notice that, unlike our first examples, the problems in insurance markets arise from the private information of the buyers, not the sellers.

Adverse selection can occur if the insurance companies are unable to determine the relative riskiness of the people they are insuring. They have to be able to distinguish the high-risk individuals from the low-risk individuals to write profitable policies. Automobile insurance is an example. Accident records indicate that young people, especially young males, have a much higher incidence of accidents than other drivers. Knowing this, the automobile insurers charge higher premiums to young female drivers and still higher premiums to young male drivers. Suppose, however, that the insurance companies had no way of assessing the relative riskiness of the insured. That is, the insured have private or asymmetric information about themselves. The insurers would then have to charge everyone the same premium. But at a single premium, the lower risk individuals are subsidizing the higher risk individuals, so they drop out. The insurance companies are left with a pool of higher risk individuals, hence the term adverse selection. They have to raise their premiums to avoid losing money. Eventually the premiums might rise above what the highest risk individuals are willing to pay, and even they are left uninsured. The market could break down entirely even though everyone wants the insurance.

Private information also exposes the insurance companies to the possibility of *moral hazard*, in which those being insured can influence the probability of the event occurring unbeknownst to the insurance companies. Unemployment insurance would certainly be subject to the problem of moral hazard. The insurance is meant to be paid only if people are fired, not if they voluntarily quit. But people could easily cheat the insurance companies. Suppose someone wanted to quit his job. He could go to his employer and ask the employer to say that he was fired so that he could collect unemployment insurance. In return, the employee would agree to give the employer a percentage of the insurance payment. Insurance companies would have difficulty protecting themselves against this kind of moral hazard, which is another reason why they do not offer unemployment insurance.

Medical insurance is also vulnerable to adverse selection and moral hazard because it is difficult to know who has good genes and who has bad genes in terms of susceptibility to disease, and who maintains healthy and unhealthy eating habits and lifestyles. The problems of private information have not prevented private markets for medical insurance from forming, but all governments in the developed market economies are also large providers of medical insurance. Private information is one reason why. Another reason is distributional. Insurers know that the risk of illness increases with age, so they charge higher premiums for medical insurance as people grow older. The problem is that the required premiums become so high that many elderly cannot afford them, so the government provides the insurance for the elderly – Medicare in the United States. The primary motivation for Medicare is distributional, not information based.

In summary, private or asymmetric information leads to a number of important market failures that justify government intervention or provision of services.

The government as agent

Private or asymmetric information is also an extreme threat to the mainstream view that governments should respond to market failure by acting strictly as an agent of the people. If a market fails for some reason, the government is supposed to ask first and foremost what the citizens would want it to do. What are the people's preferences? This presumes, however, that people will tell the government the truth about their preferences and any other things about them that the government may need to know. Unfortunately, people with private information often have strong incentives to hide the information from the government for their own personal gain. Common examples are concealing income on which they ought to pay taxes or obtaining transfers that were not meant for them. How can the government possibly act as an agent for the people if they will not necessarily tell the truth about themselves?

The desire to retain the government-as-agent perspective has led mainstream public sector economists to the study of the *mechanism design problem*, which refers to the design of mechanisms – policies – under which the self-interested or utility-maximizing strategy for people is to tell the truth about themselves. We will take a look at some specific truth-telling mechanisms that economists have devised later on in the text. Suffice it for now to say that the search for such mechanisms has been disappointing. The truth-telling mechanisms that work in principle tend to use up scarce resources and introduce an unwanted element of coercion by forcing people to participate in the mechanism. They also tend to be highly unrealistic, not at all the kinds of policies that governments would actually engage in. Private information is truly damaging to the government-as-agent ideal.

The ultimate justification for an allocation branch?

Finally, some economists argue that private or asymmetric information is the ultimate justification for government intervention involving any efficiency-based market failure. Their argument is as follows.

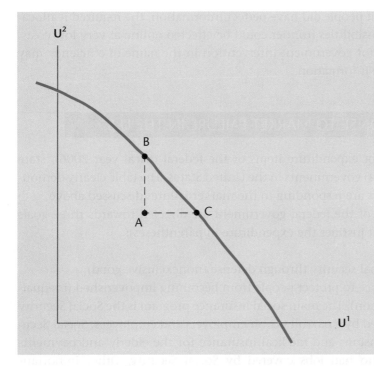

Figure 2.8

The problem with any source of inefficiency – externality, nonexclusive good, decreasing costs, private information – is that it places society beneath its utility possibilities frontier, such as at point A in Figure 2.8. But at inefficient points such as A, it is always possible to reallocate resources to make someone better off without making anyone else worse off. In Figure 2.8, all points from B to C, inclusive, on the frontier are Pareto superior to A. Suppose people had perfect information about everything. Then it would be in their mutual self-interest to interact through every possible means – markets, one-on-one bargains, side payments, whatever is necessary – to reallocate resources among themselves to exploit all the Pareto-superior possibilities and end up somewhere between B and C on the utility possibilities frontier so that everyone is better off. To exploit utility-improving opportunities is the very definition of rational economic behavior. Rational individuals armed with perfect information will move to the utility possibilities frontier on their own; there is no need for government intervention to correct for inefficiencies.

The standard counterargument is that once societies become large, transactions costs would prevent people from interacting as required to reach the frontier even if they had perfect information, or at least would make such interactions prohibitively expensive. The government can generate the efficient outcomes much more cheaply by acting as an agent on behalf of the people. The counterargument has merit. Transactions costs are an insurmountable obstacle to effective private solutions for many real-world allocational problems. Still, in today's world of high-speed computing and the Internet, it is not unreasonable to argue that the transactions costs themselves are the result of imperfect information. For if people did have perfect information, the required reallocations to reach the utility possibilities frontier could be effected online at very low costs. Therefore, the justification for government intervention in the name of efficiency may ultimately be due to private information.

GOVERNMENT RESPONSE TO MARKET FAILURE IN THE U.S.

Table 2.1 presents the major expenditure items of the federal (fiscal year 2006), state (FY 2004), and local (FY 2004) governments in the United States. The table clearly demonstrates that the governments are responding to the market failures discussed above.

The main expenditures of the federal government are directed towards three goals (with the market failure that justifies the expenditure in parentheses):

1. Providing for the national security through defense (nonexclusive good).
2. Providing social insurance to protect people from becoming impoverished (inequality and private information). The main social insurance program is the Social Security system, which is financed by a payroll tax on employers and employees. Social Security provides public pensions and medical insurance for the elderly and payments to disabled workers who had jobs covered by Social Security. Other important social insurance programs are the separate pension program for federal civil service employees and the military, unemployment insurance, income and price support programs for farmers, and a variety of support programs for veterans of foreign wars.
3. Providing public assistance – welfare – to the poor through a variety of in-kind and cash support programs (inequality). The largest public assistance program by far is Medicaid, which provides medical insurance to the poor and other medically needy people with low incomes. Medicaid is larger than all the other major public assistance programs combined. Food Stamps and Housing Assistance are the other large in-kind programs. The main cash support programs are Temporary Assistance to Needy Families (TANF) (aid to poor single parents with children), Supplemental Security Income (SSI) (aid to the elderly, blind, and disabled who are poor), and the Earned Income Tax Credit (EITC) (a tax credit that supplements the wages of low-income workers).

The federal government also addresses various allocational problems by means of regulatory agencies that do not appear in the table. Examples include the Environmental Protection Agency, OSHA, and the Bureau of Standards (externalities and private information). The grants-in-aid to state and local governments also have distributional and allocational motivations, such as the Medicaid and TANF public assistance grants (distribution), and grants to support highway construction and maintenance and mass rail transit (decreasing cost).

The state and local governments respond equally broadly to instances of market failure. They administer two of the public assistance programs to the poor, Medicaid and TANF, with financial support from the federal government, and they operate general

TABLE 2.1 Expenditures by federal, state, and local governments in the United States

	$ (billions)	Percent of subcategory	$ (billions)	Percent of subcategory
A. *Federal Government (fiscal year, 2006)*				
Government Expenditures on Goods and Services			$679	(26%)
Defense and defense related[1]	$576	(85)		
Non-defense expenditures	103	(15)		
Domestic Transfers to Persons (Direct Expenditures			1,315	(50)
Social Insurance				
Social Security benefits (OASDI)	549	(42)		
Medicare	376	(29)		
Civilian and Military Retirement	99	(9)		
Unemployment Insurance	32	(2)		
Agricultural support payments	21	(2)		
Veterans benefits[2]	64	(5)		
Public Assistance				
Food Stamps	30	(2)		
Housing Assistance	32	(2)		
Supplemental Security Income (SSI)	34	(3)		
Earned Income Tax Credit (EITC)	36	(3)		
Net interest payments			227	(9)
Grants-in-aid			434	(16)
Payments to individuals	277	(64)		
TANF	21	(8)		
Medicaid	181	(65)		
Other	157	(36)		
Total Expenditures			2,655	(100.0)
B. *State Governments (fiscal year, 2004)*[3]				
Direct Expenditures			819	(68)
Public welfare	292	(36)		
Education	181	(22)		
Highways	72	(9)		
Health and hospitals	70	(9)		
Other	204	(25)		
Grants-in-aid			390	(32)
Total General Expenditures			1,209	(100.0)
C. *Local Governments (fiscal year, 2004)*[3]				
Education			474	(44)
Housing and community development			33	(3)
Health and hospitals			90	(8)
Public safety			111	(10)
Public welfare			43	(4)
Highways, airports, other transportation			67	(6)
Other			265	(24)
Total General Expenditures			1,083	(100)

NOTES
1. Includes national defense; general science, space, and technology; and international affairs.
2. Includes education benefits, medical benefits, insurance benefits, and compensation, pension and burial payments.
3. Data for state and local governments were available only through fiscal year 2004.

SOURCES: *Budget of the United States Government, Fiscal Year 2008,* February 2007, (Washington, D.C.: U. S. Government Printing Office, 2007), Part Five: Historical Tables, Tables 1.3, 3.1, 3.2, 6.1, 11.1, 11.3, 12.1, and 12.3. U.S. Census Bureau, *State and Local Government Finances 2002–04,* U.S. Summary, available on the Census Bureau website.

and psychiatric hospitals for the benefit of patients with low incomes (distribution and private information). They also address a variety of allocation problems. These include: public education at all levels and public safety (externalities); transportation and recreational facilities – highways, mass transit, beaches and parks (decreasing cost); and the public utilities – electricity, water, and sewage (decreasing costs). In short, governments in the United States do exactly what one would expect them to do to promote the public interest in efficiency and equity in the context of a capitalist market economy; they respond to market failures.

The chapter so far has discussed public expenditure theory, the legitimate role of the government in a market economy. We conclude with some brief observations on the other two main themes of public sector analysis, the theory of taxation and fiscal federalism.

THE THEORY OF TAXATION

The theory of taxation is not always distinct from public expenditure theory. The solutions to some allocational problems require certain kinds of taxes. For example, students who have studied externalities in their other economics courses know that externalities can be corrected by a set of taxes or subsidies that depend on the form that an externality takes. In this case, the taxes are subsumed with the theory of externalities.

At other times, however, the link between the expenditures and the taxes to finance them is not so direct. In these instances, governments have to resort to general taxes to finance a broad range of expenditures. The five most important general taxes in the United States are, in order of importance: personal income taxes (federal, 43 states, some cities); the payroll tax to finance the Social Security system (federal); corporation income taxes (federal, 45 states); general sales taxes (45 states, some cities); and property taxes (local, some states).

These general taxes require their own set of design principles. The two main economic goals in levying taxes are the same as the goals for public expenditures, to promote the public interest in equity and efficiency. General taxes are clearly part of the pursuit of end-results equity since redistribution is essentially a tax and transfer operation. The equity goal is to decide on the fairest way to tax the "haves" to raise revenue to transfer to the "have-nots." Transfer policy can also be considered as part of the theory of taxation in the broadest sense, since it is the second half of the tax-transfer program in the pursuit of end-results equity.

The pursuit of efficiency in taxation takes a special twist with respect to general taxes. General taxes are a necessary evil in the sense that they invariably give rise to some inefficiencies. Therefore the efficiency goal for general taxes is to minimize the amount of inefficiency per dollar of tax revenue collected. This is the best one can ask for as a practical matter. The same point applies to transfers to the have-nots; they, too, generate inefficiencies. But minimizing the inefficiencies of taxes and transfers is likely to reduce some of their desired redistributional effect. Consequently, in thinking about taxes and transfers to promote end-results equity, society has to determine the proper balance between the gains to equity from redistributing and the efficiency losses of the taxes and transfers themselves. We will analyze general taxes in Part III of the text.

FISCAL FEDERALISM

As noted in Chapter 1, societies that choose a federalist system of government have two economic sorting problems to resolve, one related to the functions of government and the other to the sorting of people and capital across jurisdictions. Having determined the legitimate functions of government, society must then decide which governments should perform each of the functions so that governments do not work at cross-purposes to one another in the pursuit of equity and efficiency. Included in the sorting of functions is the allocation of the major taxes among the different levels of government. The sorting of people relates primarily to the lowest level of government, that is, how people decide which locality to reside in. This sorting issue can also apply to the allocation of capital among jurisdictions, however, in which case it becomes national and even international in scope. The proper sorting of people and capital among jurisdictions is essential for achieving both equity and efficiency.

Table 2.1 indicates that the United States has chosen to split the distribution function between the federal and state and local governments, while allowing the state and local governments to provide most of the allocation functions, with the single exception of national defense. Similarly, the federal and state governments have chosen to levy personal and corporate income taxes, but the general sales tax is used primarily by the states and the property tax primarily by the localities. We will discuss the economic principles behind these choices in Chapter 21 and elsewhere in the text.

The sorting of people among localities is an economic issue because people choose localities in part on the basis of their taxes and public services. In the United States, for example, the quality of the local public school system is particularly influential in determining which communities people would like to live in.

Charles Tiebout conjectured that the ability of people to choose among localities with different public services would improve the efficiency of the government sector in two ways. First, the ability of people to move, to "vote with their feet" as he put it, would avoid the free-rider problem that otherwise plagues externalities and nonexclusive goods. If people like the services better in another town, they can move there. This in turn improves the efficiency of the public sector by providing a better match between the public services people desire and the public services provided to them. Second, the provision of public services at the local level allows for experimentation so that people can discover more effective ways of educating their children or ensuring the public safety, to give just two examples.

While Tiebout's hypothesis has its merits, subsequent analysis has shown that the ability of people, and capital, to move across jurisdictions itself opens up avenues for inefficiencies that would not be present with a single government. For example, a major issue in the European Union (E.U.) today is the potentially inefficient movement of capital throughout the member nations in response to differences in how each nation taxes income from capital. Capital is so mobile across borders that capital taxes may have to be standardized throughout the E.U. In general, whether the movement of people and capital promotes or hinders the public interest in equity and efficiency remains an open question. We will explore these issues in Chapter 22.

A final comment on fiscal federalism is that grants-in-aid are an important fiscal device. A *grant-in-aid* is a transfer payment from one government to another, most commonly from a government to the governments immediately below it in the fiscal hierarchy, such as U.S. federal grants-in-aid to the states and state grants-in-aid to the localities within a state. Chapter 23 considers various motivations for grants-in-aid.

The Fundamental Theorems of Welfare Economics

Chapter 3 concludes the introduction to public sector economics with a description of a simple model of an entire economy that is useful for illustrating a number of principles of public expenditure and tax theory. Our more limited purpose here, however, is to develop the two Fundamental Theorems of Welfare Economics that result when all the technical and market assumptions of a well-functioning market economy hold. These two theorems are the baseline results that economists use to begin thinking about virtually all economic issues relating to the government sector. An example comes immediately in Chapter 4 when we turn to the government's attempt to achieve end-results equity, which is the natural place to begin the study of public sector economics. Recall that society might judge the distribution of income to be inequitable even if the economy functions as well as it possibly can. If so, then the government has to intervene with taxes and transfer payments to redistribute income. An inequitable distribution of income is the one potential market failure that cannot be assumed away.

THE STRUCTURE OF THE MODEL

Modern capitalist economies are incredibly complex. The United States, which is by far the largest economy, generates over $13 trillion of output and income during the year, about 30% of the total output and income generated in markets throughout the world. It has more than 300 million individuals, about half of whom are in the labor force; 27 million private business firms that produce tens of thousands of goods and services; a capital stock in excess of $35 trillion; 89,000 federal, state, and local governmental bodies that spend $4 trillion each year; and over $2 trillion of international trade with virtually all the nations of the world.[1] Individuals, firms, and government agencies engage in billions of economic exchanges with one another every day.

Fortunately, we do not need to confront the size and complexity of the U.S. economy to understand the basic principles of public sector economics. They can be illustrated with an extremely simple model consisting of just two people, two goods, and two factors of production.[2] Label the two people persons #1 and #2, the two goods X and Y, and the two factors of production K and L for capital and labor.

The three fundamental elements of any model describing an entire economy are the preferences of the individuals, the production technologies for producing the goods, and market clearance for the goods and the factors. These are as follows in the simple $2 \times 2 \times 2$ model:

1. *Individual preferences:* The two people derive utility from consuming X and Y. Their utility functions are: $U^1 = U^1(X_1, Y_1)$ and $U^2 = U^2(X_2, Y_2)$, where X_i, Y_i are the consumption of X and Y by person i, i = 1,2. The two people also supply all the capital and labor that firms use to produce X and Y. We assume initially that the supplies of capital and labor are absolutely fixed, with the total supply of capital and labor equal to K* and L*. In other words, the individuals view their labor and capital as endowments for which no decisions have to be made. This is why capital and labor do not appear in the utility function.

2. *Production technologies:* X and Y are produced with capital and labor according to the production functions: $X = X(K_x, L_x)$ and $Y = Y(K_y, L_y)$, where K_i, L_i are the capital and labor used in the production of good i, i = X,Y. The production functions are assumed to be constant returns to scale (CRS), for example a doubling of the capital and labor used in the production of X doubles the production of X, and similarly for Y.

3. *Market clearance:* The markets for both goods and both factors of production have to clear for the economy to be in a general equilibrium. Since the two individuals consume all the X and Y produced by the firms and supply all the capital and labor used by the firms, the four market clearing equations are:
   - *Goods:* $X_1 + X_2 = X$; $Y_1 + Y_2 = Y$, where X and Y are the total production of goods X and Y. (Think of the production of X as taking place in one firm, and similarly for Y. Adding many firms is an unnecessary complication for our purposes.)
   - *Factors:* $K_X + K_Y = K^*$; $L_X + L_Y = L^*$, where $K^* = K_1^* + K_2^*$ and $L^* = L_1^* + L_2^*$. K_1^* and K_2^* are the fixed supplies of capital from persons #1 and #2, and similarly for their labor supplies L_1^* and L_2^*.

The assumption of CRS in production is extremely useful in the context of a market economy. It implies that if all markets are competitive, then the revenue received by the firms from selling X or Y must equal their costs of production, their payments to the capital and labor that they use. There are no pure economic profits that have to be accounted for. The equivalent statement from the individuals' perspectives is that the income they receive from supplying their capital and labor is their only source of income, and it just equals their expenditure on X and Y.

THE FIRST FUNDAMENTAL THEOREM OF WELFARE ECONOMICS

Suppose that all the technical and market assumptions necessary for a well-functioning economy that we described in Chapter 2 do hold. Under these assumptions, the First Fundamental Theorem of Welfare Economics says that a competitive economy can achieve a Pareto-optimal allocation of resources that places society on its utility possibilities frontier. The demonstration of this theorem in our simple $2 \times 2 \times 2$ economy consists of two steps. The first step is to show that three rules are necessary for the economy to achieve a Pareto-optimal allocation of resources: a consumption rule; a production rule; and a combined consumption-production rule. The second step is to show that each of the three rules do hold if all markets are perfectly competitive.

THE NECESSARY CONDITIONS FOR A PARETO OPTIMUM

The three necessary conditions for a Pareto-optimal allocation of resources are:

1. *Consumption:* The marginal rate of substitution (MRS) between the two goods X and Y must be equal for both people:

   $MRS^1_{X_1,Y_1} = MRS^2_{X_2,Y_2}$.

2. *Production:* The marginal rate of technical substitution (MRTS) between the two factors capital and labor must be equal in the production of X and Y:

   $MRTS^X_{K_X,L_X} = MRTS^Y_{K_Y,L_Y}$.

3. *Consumption-production:* The (equal) marginal rate of substitution between X and Y in consumption must be equal to the marginal rate of transformation (MRT) between X and Y in production:

   $MRS_{X,Y} = MRT_{X,Y}$.

Let's consider each of them in turn.

THE CONSUMPTION CONDITION

The marginal rate of substitution is a slope of an indifference curve. As such, it is the consumer's *willingness to trade* small amounts of Y for X, willing to trade in the sense that the consumer would be indifferent to the trade. Utility remains constant as the consumer moves along any indifference curve. Refer to Figure 3.1. Person #1's MRS at point A on indifference curve I_1 is 5 to 1: $MRS^1_{X_1,Y_1} = (-)\frac{5}{1} = (-)\frac{\Delta Y_1}{\Delta X_1}\Big|_{U^1 = \bar{U}^1}$. She would be willing to give up 5 units of Y_1 to receive an additional unit of X_1 (or vice versa).

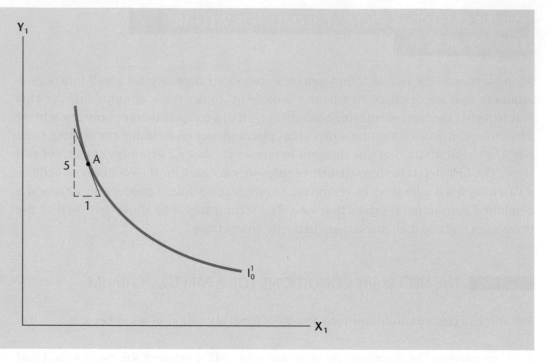

Figure 3.1

To see why the marginal rates of substitution between the two goods have to be equal for all people for Pareto optimality, suppose that at a given allocation of X and Y, the marginal rates of substitution are unequal, say 5/1 for person #1 and 1/1 for person #2:

$$MRS^1_{X_1,Y_1} = \frac{5}{1} \text{ and } MRS^2_{X_2,Y_2} = \frac{1}{1}.$$

Any trade of X and Y between the two individuals at any ratio between 5/1 and 1/1 would make both people better off. For example, arrange a trade at 3/1 – have person #1 give 3 units of Y to person #2 in exchange for 1 unit of X. Person #1 is better off, since she is willing to trade 5 units of Y in exchange for the 1 unit of X. Person #2 is also better off, since he is willing to give up 1 unit of X in exchange for 1 unit of Y, but he receives 3 units of Y. Since both people are made better off by the exchange, the original allocation is not Pareto optimal. Only when the marginal rates of substitution are equal for the two people is no such mutually beneficial trade possible. Exchanges of X and Y between the two individuals when their MRSs are equal can only make one person better off by making the other person worse off. The Law of Substitution holds, as required for Pareto optimality.[3]

The Pareto-optimal allocations of X and Y are illustrated by the so-called Edgeworth Box in Figure 3.2. The sides of the box represent the total production of X and Y, equal to $\overline{X}$ and $\overline{Y}$. Person #1's indifference curves for X_1 and Y_1 are drawn with point A as the origin. Her utility increases along the higher numbered indifference curves in the northeast direction. Person #2's indifference curves for X_2 and Y_2 are drawn with point B as the origin. His utility increases along the higher numbered indifference curves in the southwest direction. Similarly, person #1's consumption of X_1 and Y_1 is measured along the axes east and north from A, and person #2's consumption of X_2 and Y_2 is measured along the axes west and south from B. At point C, for example, person #1 consumes X_1^C and Y_1^C and person #2 consumes X_2^C and Y_2^C, with $X_1^C + X_2^C = \bar{X}$ and $Y_1^C + Y_2^C = \bar{Y}$.

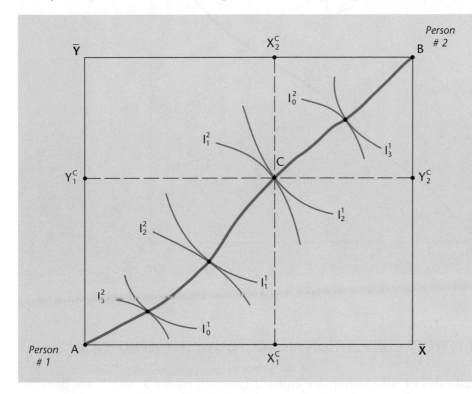

Figure 3.2

The line AB is the locus of points at which the indifference curves for the two people are tangent, that is, their marginal rates of substitution are equal, as required for Pareto optimality. AB is referred to as the "contract curve."

To see that the contract curve AB is the Pareto-optimal set of allocations of X and Y between the two people, refer to Figure 3.3. Consider a point off the contract curve such as D, at which person #1 has utility represented by I_4^1 and person #2 has utility represented by I_2^2. Exchange X and Y between the two people to move to the contract curve at a point such as E between I_4^1 and I_2^2. After the exchange, person #1 achieves indifference curve I_5^1 and person #2 achieves indifference curve I_3^2. Both people are better off. Therefore points off the contract curve cannot be Pareto optimal because such mutually beneficial exchanges between the original indifference curves to the contract curve are always possible. Conversely, any movement along the contract curve AB can only make one person better off by making the other person worse off. Therefore, the points on the contract curve are Pareto optimal.

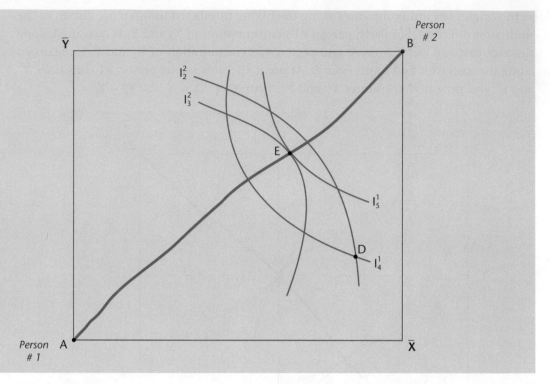

Figure 3.3

PERFECT COMPETITION AND CONSUMPTION EFFICIENCY

The marginal rates of substitution are equal if the markets for X and Y are perfectly competitive. This result follows from the assumption that consumers purchase X and Y to maximize their utility. Consider person #1. Her objective is to maximize her utility function, $U^1 = U^1(X_1, Y_1)$, subject to her budget constraint that her total expenditures on X and Y must equal her total income from her fixed supplies of capital and labor. The budget constraint is $P_X \cdot X_1 + P_y \cdot Y_1 = I_1$, where I_1 is her total income.[4] Consumers have no control over prices under perfect competition – they take P_X and P_Y as given.

Refer to Figure 3.4. The budget constraint is represented by the line AB, whose slope is (the negative of) the ratio of the prices, $(-)\dfrac{P_X}{P_Y}$.[5] The price ratio indicates the *ability to trade* Y for X in the consumer's budget. For example, if $P_X = \$2$ and $P_Y = \$1$, $\dfrac{P_X}{P_Y} = \dfrac{2}{1}$. With \$2 of income, person #1 can purchase 2 units of Y_1 or 1 unit of X_1. Her ability to trade Y_1 for X_1 is $\dfrac{2}{1}$. The indifference curves represent the levels of utility attainable with different combinations of X_1 and Y_1 as given by the utility function $U^1 = U^1(X_1, Y_1)$. Person #1's objective is to reach the highest indifference curve possible on the budget line. This occurs at point C, at which indifference curve I_3^1 is tangent to the budget line AB. At the point of tangency, the slopes of the indifference curve and the budget line are equal: $MRS_{X_1,Y_1}^1 = \dfrac{P_X}{P_Y}$. In other words, person #1 maximizes her utility by purchasing the combination of X_1 and Y_1 such that the *willingness to trade* Y_1 and X_1 (the MRS) equals the *ability to trade* Y_1 and X_1 $(\dfrac{P_X}{P_Y})$. In general, the MRS between any two goods must equal the ratio of their prices to maximize utility.

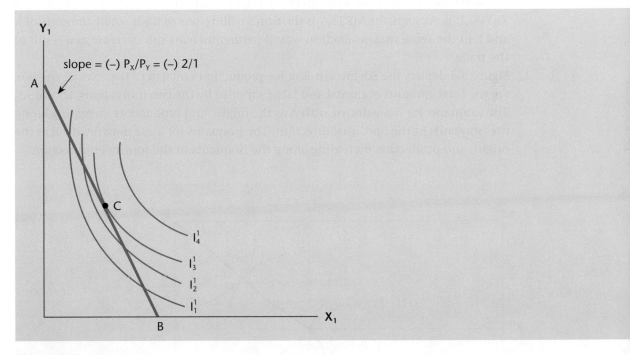

Figure 3.4

What is true for person #1 is true for everyone. Person #2 also maximizes his utility by purchasing X_2 and Y_2 such that $MRS_{X_2,Y_2}^2 = \dfrac{P_X}{P_Y}$. Under perfect competition, person #2 faces the same prices, P_X and P_Y, as does person #1. Therefore, since they are both setting their $MRS_{X,Y}$ to the same price ratio, their $MRS_{X,Y}$ must be equal, as required for Pareto optimality. In other words, their own self-interests automatically lead them to one of the points on the contract curve AB within the Edgeworth Box in Figure 3.2. People may consume different amounts of goods and services if their tastes and their endowments of L and K differ. But if they are maximizing their utilities, then their MRS between any two goods, their willingness to trade small amounts of the goods, must be equal. This principle holds for any number of people, and any number of goods. That we are considering only two people and two goods makes no difference.

THE PRODUCTION CONDITION

The analysis of the production condition that the marginal rates of technical substitution between capital and labor must be equal in the production of X and Y for Pareto optimality is virtually identical to the analysis of the consumption condition. Therefore we will only sketch the demonstration of this condition in the corresponding steps:

1. The marginal rate of technical substitution between capital and labor, $MRTS_{K,L}$, is the slope of an isoquant, which gives the combinations of K and L that can produce the same amount of X (or Y) as given by the production functions $X = X(K_X, L_X)$ [or $Y = Y(K_Y, L_Y)$]. As such, the $MRTS_{K,L}$ is the firm's willingness to trade small amounts of K and L in the sense that production would neither increase nor decrease as a result of the trade.
2. Figure 3.5 depicts the Edgeworth Box for production efficiency. The axes of the box are the total amounts of capital and labor supplied by the two individuals, L* and K*. The isoquants for X are drawn with A as the origin, and production increasing along the isoquants in the northeast direction. The isoquants for Y are drawn with B as the origin, and production increasing along the isoquants in the southwest direction.

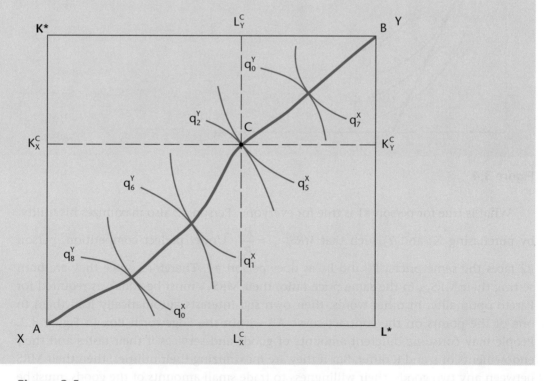

Figure 3.5

3. The isoquants are tangent along the contract curve AB, the locus of efficient allocations of capital and labor between X and Y. The $MRTS_{K,L}$ are equal for X and Y at the points of tangency, as required for Pareto optimality. All points off the contract curve are inefficient. By reallocating K and L between X and Y to move to the contract curve somewhere between the isoquants at the original allocation, society can produce more of X and of Y. Along the contract curve, increasing the production of X requires decreasing the production of Y, and vice versa. The Law of Substitution holds, as required for Pareto optimality.

4. Points on the contract curve in K-L space correspond to points on the production possibilities frontier in X and Y space. The production possibilities frontier gives the combinations of X and Y that the economy can produce if X and Y are produced efficiently. In other words, points on the frontier correspond to the isoquant numbers along the contract curve AB, since these numbers indicate the amounts of X and Y produced. For example, point C in Figure 3.5 is at the isoquants q_5^X and q_2^Y. The corresponding point on the production possibilities frontier would be the quantity of X represented by q_5^X and the quantity of Y represented by q_2^Y. Similarly, any points off the contract curve in Figure 3.5 correspond to points below the production possibilities frontier. The combinations of X and Y below the production possibilities frontier are possible, but inefficient.

5. Notice that the assumption of fixed supplies of capital and labor are required to set the boundaries of the production Edgeworth Box and therefore the end points of the production possibilities frontier. If capital and labor were not fixed, then the total amount of each supplied would depend on the wages (P_L) and interest rates (P_K) that the individuals receive for their capital and labor. As the wages and interest rates change, so too would the boundaries of the Edgeworth Box and the end points of the production possibilities frontier. Nonetheless, the $MRTS_{K,L}$ would still have to be equal for X and Y for production efficiency. We discuss the case of variable factor supplies in the Appendix to this chapter.

6. The $MRTS_{K,L}$ are equal for X and Y if the markets for capital and labor are perfectly competitive. This result is based on the assumption that firms try to maximize the output that they produce for any given expenditures on their factors of production. For the firm producing X, the total cost of production is $TC_X = P_L \cdot L_X + P_K \cdot K_X$. Given total cost of TC_X^*, the total cost line is AB in Figure 3.6, whose slope is (the negative of) the price ratio $\frac{P_L}{P_K}$. The ratio $\frac{P_L}{P_K}$ indicates the firm's ability to trade K for L in production and hold total cost constant. The firm's goal is to reach the highest possible isoquant on the TC_X^* line, which is point C in the figure. At C, the $MRTS_{K_X,L_X}^X = \frac{P_L}{P_K}$: the willingness to trade K_X for L_X equals the ability to trade K_X for L_X. What is true for the firms producing X is true for the firms producing Y, or any firms. Therefore, since all firms face the same prices P_K and P_L for K and L when factor

markets are perfectly competitive, the $MRTS_{K,L}$ is equal for all firms, as required for Pareto optimality in production. In general, the MRTS between any two factors must be equal across all firms that use the factors for production efficiency, and they are equal if factor markets are perfectly competitive.

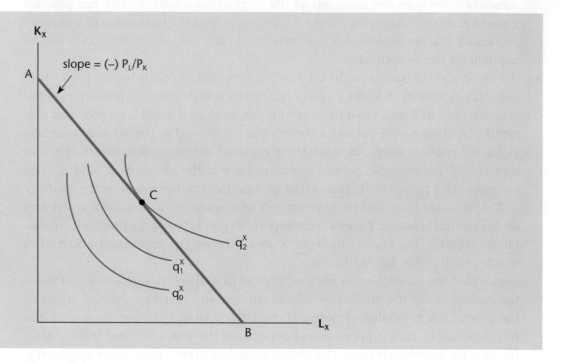

Figure 3.6

THE CONSUMPTION-PRODUCTION CONDITION

THE CONSUMPTION-PRODUCTION CONDITION

The consumption condition requires that the MRS between any two goods be equal across all consumers for efficiency in consumption. The production condition requires that the MRTS between any two factors be equal in the production of all goods so that the economy operates on its production possibilities frontier. The consumption-production condition combines the two previous conditions by requiring that the (equal) MRS in consumption between any two goods be equal to their marginal rate of transformation (MRT) in production. The MRT is the slope of the production possibilities frontier, in terms of our model the trade-off on the margin between Y and X assuming that the goods are always produced efficiently (that is, that the $MRTS_{K,L}$ remain equal in the production of X and Y). This consumption-production condition ensures that the economy reaches its utility possibilities frontier, along which it is impossible to make one person better off without making someone else worse off. This is the definition of full Pareto optimality in terms of individuals.

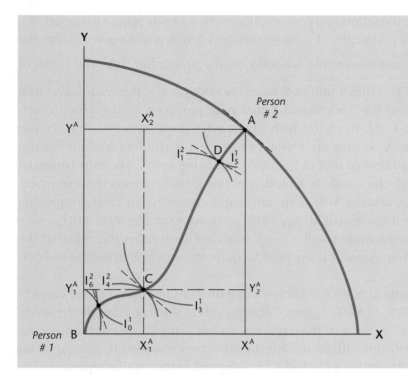

Figure 3.7

Figure 3.7 illustrates the consumption-production condition. Suppose the economy is operating on point A on its production possibilities frontier (pp-frontier), producing output X^A and Y^A. (Because the economy is on the frontier, the production condition of equal $MRTS_{K,L}$ between X and Y is satisfied.) Let point A define the boundaries of the consumption Edgeworth Box. Place person #1 at point B, the origin of the pp-frontier, with her indifference curves increasing in the northeast direction. Place person #2 at the opposite end of the Edgeworth Box, with point A serving as the origin and his indifference curves increasing in the southwest direction. The line AB is the consumption contract curve along which the $MRS^1_{X_1,Y_1} = MRS^2_{X_2,Y_2}$, as required for consumption efficiency. The $MRT_{X,Y}$ is the slope of the pp-frontier at A. The consumption-production condition requires that, among all the points on the consumption contract curve, society chooses point C at which the (equal) $MRS_{X,Y}$ equals the $MRT_{X,Y}$ at point A. Person #1 must receive (X^A_1, Y^A_1), and person #2 (X^A_2, Y^A_2) of the total quantities produced, X^A and Y^A.

This would appear to be a distributional condition since it indicates how the total quantities produced have to be divided among the consumers. But it is an efficiency rule, and one that is satisfied if the goods markets are perfectly competitive. To see the efficiency implications, suppose society chose a different point such as D on the consumption contract curve, at which the (equal) $MRS_{X,Y}$ differs from the $MRT_{X,Y}$ at A. Let the

$MRT_{X,Y} = \dfrac{3}{1}$ and the equal $MRS_{X,Y} = \dfrac{1}{1}$. When these two margins are unequal, it is always possible to rearrange production and consumption to make both people better off. For example, move up the pp-frontier at A by producing 1 less X and 3 more Y. Since the $MRT_{X,Y}$ at A is $\frac{3}{1}$, this move keeps the economy on the pp-frontier. Take the 1 unit of X from person #2 and give him 1 unit of Y. Since his $MRS_{X,Y} = 1/1$, this trade leaves him indifferent. It also leaves the 2 additional Y that were produced to distribute to each of the individuals, say 1 unit to each, which would make them both better off. Person #2 receives 2 Y for the X he gave up instead of just the 1 Y required for indifference. Person #1 receives an additional unit of Y without sacrificing any X. Mutually beneficial rearrangements of production and consumption of this kind are always possible whenever the (equal) $MRS_{X,Y}$ and the $MRT_{X,Y}$ are unequal. Conversely, no Pareto-improving exchanges are possible if the (equal) $MRS_{X,Y} = MRT_{X,Y}$. In our example, if the $MRT_{X,Y}$ were also 1/1, then producing 1 more Y and 1 less X could not help either individual. If the unit of X were taken from person #1, she would require the unit of Y to remain indifferent, and no one gains.

Assume that the optimal point C is chosen along the consumption contract curve in Figure 3.7. With the $MRS_{X,Y} = MRT_{X,Y}$, point C corresponds to some point C' on the utility possibilities frontier in Figure 3.8. If the economy reaches point C', then it is impossible to make one person better off without making the other person worse off, as required for full Pareto optimality. The utilities $U^1_{C'}$ and $U^2_{C'}$ correspond to the utilities represented by the indifference curves I^1_3 and I^2_4 at point C in Figure 3.7.

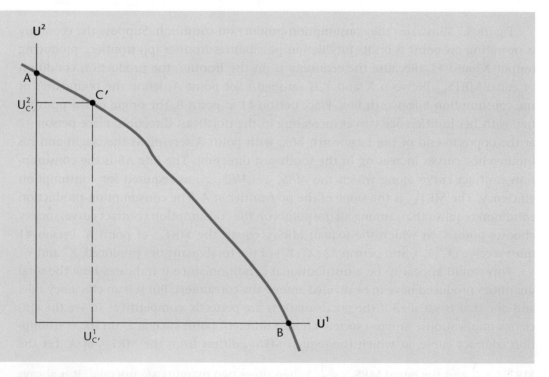

Figure 3.8

Notice that reaching points on the utility possibilities frontier is more exacting than reaching points on the pp-frontier. Points on the pp-frontier require only production efficiency, that the $MRTS_{K,L}$ be equal for X and Y. Points on the utility possibilities frontier are attainable only if all three conditions hold. The economy must be on its pp-frontier, and consumption must be at just the right point on the consumption contract locus, point C in Figure 3.7.

PERFECT COMPETITION AND PRODUCTION-CONSUMPTION EFFICIENCY

We have seen that the self-interests of consumers and producers ensure that the consumption and production conditions are satisfied if the economy is perfectly competitive. The consumption-production condition is satisfied as well. This follows from the proposition that competitive, price taking firms set price equal to marginal cost (MC) to maximize profit. Thus, $P_X = MC_X$ and $P_Y = MC_Y$ from profit maximization. But the $MRT_{X,Y}$ is the ratio of marginal costs, $\dfrac{MC_X}{MC_Y}$. $MC_X = \dfrac{\Delta TC_X}{\Delta X}$ and $MC_Y = \dfrac{\Delta TC_Y}{\Delta Y}$. Therefore, $\dfrac{MC_X}{MC_Y} = \dfrac{\Delta TC_X}{\Delta X} / \dfrac{\Delta TC_Y}{\Delta Y}$. Suppose $\Delta TC_X = (-)\Delta TC_Y$, that equal dollars of resources (capital and labor) are transferred between X and Y. Then $\dfrac{MC_X}{MC_Y} = \dfrac{\Delta Y}{\Delta X}$, given $\Delta TC_X = (-)\Delta TC_Y$. But this is the $MRT_{X,Y}$, the trade-off on the margin between Y and X when equal dollars of resources are transferred between the two goods.

Therefore, with X and Y firms setting price equal to marginal cost, $\dfrac{P_X}{P_Y} = \dfrac{MC_X}{MC_Y}$ = $MRT_{X,Y}$. But each consumer purchases X and Y such that $MRS_{X,Y} = \dfrac{P_X}{P_Y}$. Therefore, $MRS^1_{X_1,Y_1} = MRS^2_{X_2,Y_2} = MRT_{X,Y}$ as required for the consumption-production condition.

In summary, a perfectly competitive economy reaches its utility possibilities frontier when all the assumptions for a well-functioning economy hold. This is the First Fundamental Theorem of Welfare Economics.

One important implication of the First Fundamental Theorem for a market economy is worth noting: All agents must face the same prices for the goods and factors to achieve an efficient allocation of resources. In the context of our model, the two consumers have to face the same goods prices P_X and P_Y for the consumption condition to hold, the producers of X and Y have to face the same factor prices P_K and P_L for the production condition to hold, and the individuals and firms have to face the same goods prices P_X and P_Y for the combined consumption-production condition to hold. This implication becomes important in the analysis of tax policy. Commonly used taxes, such as income, sales, and excise taxes, introduce inefficiencies into the economy because they drive a wedge between the prices paid by buyers and sellers. To see this in the context of our simple model, consider an excise tax on good X (for example a tax on gasoline or cigarettes). The price of X that consumers base their decisions on is the price including the tax. The price that the producers of X base their decisions on, however, is the price net of the tax because they have to send the tax on each unit of X to the government. Only the revenue remaining after paying the tax is available to pay the operating costs of producing X and generate a return to the owners' capital. A moment's reflection on our analysis of the combined consumption-production rule above indicates that the (equal) $MRS_{X,Y}$ would not equal the $MRT_{X,Y}$ if the consumers and producers face different price ratios $\dfrac{P_X}{P_Y}$ because of the excise tax on X.

THE SECOND FUNDAMENTAL THEOREM OF WELFARE ECONOMICS

The Second Fundamental Theorem of Welfare Economics points to a question that all societies must resolve, the question of end-results equity. Will society be satisfied to achieve a point such as C' on its utility possibilities frontier in Figure 3.8? Point C' does have much to recommend it. It results from an efficient allocation of society's scarce resources of capital and labor. Also, because markets are perfectly competitive, it satisfies the process equity criterion of equal opportunity or equal access; recall that equal opportunity is a defining characteristic of a competitive market. Equal opportunity in turn is likely to produce a reasonable degree of social mobility, another important criterion of process equity.

All these properties notwithstanding, a society may reject C' on the grounds that it violates its sense of end-results equity. At C' person #2 ends up being quite a bit better off than person #1. This outcome is suggestive of the outcomes in the actual developed capitalist economies, which tend to produce the extremes of wealth and poverty along with a large middle class. A society could decide that C' is acceptable because of all its other desirable qualities or simply because it is the outcome that the market has generated. But societies never make that choice. They react to inequality of outcomes, especially large inequalities, by choosing to redistribute income from the well-off haves to the less well-off or impoverished have-nots. These redistributions are justified in the name of end-results equity.

This is where the Second Fundamental Theorem of Welfare Economics comes into play. The second theorem says that all the feasible Pareto-optimal points on the utility possibilities frontier, those between A and B in Figure 3.8, are attainable with a suitable distribution of resources, in this case a suitable distribution of the fixed capital and labor. Presumably the economy reached C' because person #2 had the majority of the fixed labor and capital. Point A would be the outcome if person #2 had all the fixed capital and labor, and point B would be the outcome if person #1 had all the fixed capital and labor. By redistributing the income from the fixed capital and labor between the two people, the market economy can, in principle, generate any of the other points on the utility possibilities frontier. The intuition is that none of the three conditions necessary for a Pareto optimum depends on how capital and labor are distributed between the two people.

The market will not make the required redistributions, however. C' resulted from a given distribution of the fixed capital and labor between the two people, and the market takes this distribution as given. It does not judge whether the outcome at C' is fair. Run the economy again with the same distribution and it will again generate C'. The required redistributions must be undertaken by the government in response to a collective decision that society makes regarding the appropriate distribution of income or well-being. This is why the problem of distributive justice is a fundamental problem that cannot be assumed away or left to the market to resolve. We turn to the quest for end-results equity in Chapter 4 as the natural starting point for the study of public sector economics.

Variable Factor Supplies

The assumption in our $2 \times 2 \times 2$ model that the supplies of capital and labor are fixed is clearly inaccurate. Factor supplies are variable, not fixed. Many people adjust the hours that they work to changes in the wages they receive and their savings to changes in interest rates. These factor supply adjustments turn out to be very important in the study of the public sector.

We ignored these variations in factor supplies in this chapter because they significantly complicate the $2 \times 2 \times 2$ model without changing its basic implications. In particular, the First and Second Fundamental Theorems of Welfare Economics continue to hold with variable factor supplies.

The complications arise because if labor and capital can be varied, then they enter individuals' utility functions and become two more decisions that individuals have to make. As such, they introduce five additional marginal rates of substitution that consumers must equate with price ratios to maximize their utility: the MRS between X and L, Y and L, X and K, Y and K, and L and K. For example, each person now has to equate the $MRS_{X,L}$ with the price ratio $\frac{P_L}{P_X}$ to maximize utility, and so on for the other MRSs. These new MRSs become part of an expanded consumption condition that have to be equalized across all consumers to achieve a Pareto-optimal allocation of resources. Similarly, these five new MRSs have to be equated to the firms' margins for the same goods and factors in an expanded consumption-production condition. For a firm, the trade-off on the margin between a good and a factor is a marginal product, for example the marginal product of labor in the production of X, MP_L^X. This marginal product has to be equated to each individual's $MRS_{X,L}$ as part of the expanded consumption-production condition, and similarly for the other four new margins.

We will analyze variable factor supplies with their expanded set of margins at various points in the text. They are especially relevant for the analysis of taxes and transfers. For now, however, it is sufficient to note that the First Fundamental Theorem of Welfare

Economics continues to apply with variable factor supplies. So long as individuals and firms face the same prices for all the goods and factors, and individuals maximize utility and firms maximize profit, then the expanded set of consumption, production, and consumption-production conditions holds and the economy reaches a point on its utility possibilities frontier.

To give just one example, if all consumers face the same prices P_X and P_L for X and L, then each one will consume X and supply L such that $MRS_{X,L} = \dfrac{P_L}{P_X}$, thereby satisfying the expanded consumption condition that $MRS_{X,L}$ must be equal across all consumers. Regarding the consumption-production condition, the relevant margin for the firm is the marginal product of labor in producing X, MP_L^X. The condition that $MRS_{X,L} = MP_L^X$ is satisfied if each X producing firm sets MP_L^X equal to $\dfrac{P_L}{P_X}$ to maximize its profit. That this is the profit-maximizing solution for the firm can be seen by rearranging $MP_L^X = \dfrac{P_L}{P_X}$ in two ways:

$$P_X \cdot MP_L^X = P_L$$

and

$$P_X = \frac{P_L}{MP_L^X}.$$

The first equation says that the firm hires labor such that the price of labor equals the value of labor's marginal product, which is the profit-maximizing rule for hiring labor. In the second equation, P_L is the additional cost of hiring one more unit of labor and the marginal product is the extra output from hiring one more unit of labor. Therefore,

$$\frac{P_L}{MP_L^X} = \frac{\Delta TC_X}{\Delta L_X} \Big/ \frac{\Delta X}{\Delta L_X} = \frac{\Delta TC_X}{\Delta X},$$ the marginal cost of producing X. Therefore, the second

equation gives the profit-maximizing rule that the firm should supply X such that the price of X equals the marginal cost of producing X. But if $MP_L^X = \dfrac{P_L}{P_X}$ to maximize profit, and $MRS_{X,L} = \dfrac{P_L}{P_X}$ to maximize utility, then $MRS_{X,L} = MP_L^X$ as required for Pareto optimality so long as the consumers and firms face the same prices for X and L.

The same argument applies to the equality of $MRS_{X,K}$, $MRS_{Y,L}$, and $MRS_{Y,K}$ across consumers to satisfy the expanded consumption condition, and to the equalities of $MRS_{X,K} = MP_K^X$, $MRS_{Y,L} = MP_L^Y$, and $MRS_{Y,K} = MP_K^Y$ to satisfy the expanded consumption-production condition. Finally if all these conditions are satisfied, then $MRS_{K,L}$ $(= \dfrac{P_L}{P_K})$ must also be equal across all consumers and the (equal) $MRS_{K,L} = MRTS_{K,L}$

$(= \dfrac{P_L}{P_K})$.[6] In conclusion, the expanded consumption and consumption-production conditions required for Pareto optimality are all satisfied so long as consumers and firms face the same prices for the goods and factors. The First Fundamental Theorem of Welfare Economics applies to the model with variable factor supplies.

Public Expenditure Theory and Policy

CHAPTER 4

The Social Welfare Function and the Quest for Distributive Justice

Our study of public sector issues begins with one of the more difficult problems that societies have to resolve, the quest for distributive justice or end-results equity. Recall from Chapter 3 that the distribution problem is fundamental in the sense that it cannot be assumed away. Society would have to make a judgment about the distribution of individuals' well-being even if all the technical and market assumptions for a well-functioning market economy happened to hold.

To focus on the distribution problem, assume that all the required technical and market assumptions for a well-functioning market economy do hold, so that the economy achieves an efficient allocation of resources. It reaches point A on the utility possibilities frontier, as pictured in Figure 4.1, at which person #2 receives utility of U_A^2 and person #1 receives utility of U_A^1.

Person #2 has much the better of it at point A. We chose such an unequal outcome to reflect that fact that capitalist economies usually generate a highly unequal distribution of income, with extremes of wealth and poverty. All capitalist societies have responded to inequality to some extent by taxing the rich and transferring to the poor. But how exactly should a society respond to an unequal point such as A in the name of distributive justice? What principles should guide its redistributional policies?

In the late 1930s, Abram Bergson and Paul Samuelson invented an analytical construct that they called the *individualistic social welfare function* to solve the distribution question. Written W= W(U^1, ,U^h,....U^H), its arguments are the utility functions of the H individuals (or households), h = 1,....,H. The social welfare function W indicates the amount of welfare (utility) from a social perspective that results from the utilities received, the well-being, of each individual in the society. This is the sense in which the social welfare function is individualistic. The Bergson–Samuelson individualistic social welfare function has proven to be extremely useful to mainstream public sector theory, yet at the same time it is highly problematic as a guide to public policy. We will begin with its role in public sector theory.

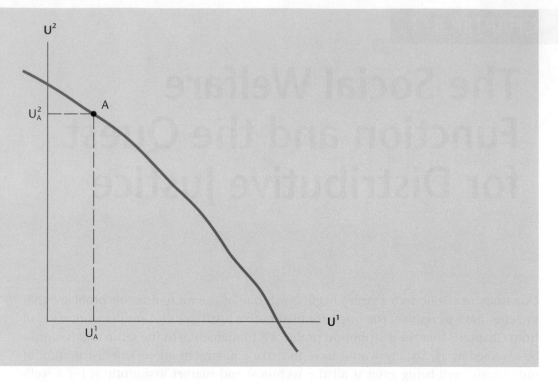

Figure 4.1

THE SOCIAL WELFARE FUNCTION AND DISTRIBUTIVE JUSTICE

In keeping with the humanistic tradition and the principle of consumer sovereignty, the Bergson–Samuelson social welfare function judges or ranks social outcomes in terms of how well off all the people are at each outcome as they themselves view their well-being. The utility functions are their own utility functions. Nothing else matters to social welfare. The social rankings implied by W can in turn be thought of as ethical rankings of the different individuals that are analogous to individuals' ranking of goods and services according to their own preferences as they decide what to buy. In particular, the ethical rankings lead to a set of social welfare indifference curves in Figure 4.2(b), W_0, W_1, W_2,..., that are analogous to person #1's indifference curves for goods X and Y, I_0^1, I_1^1, I_2^1 in Figure 4.2(a).

Society is indifferent to the combinations of utility for persons #1 and #2 along any social welfare indifference curve, such as points A and B on W_0, but prefers all combinations on a higher social welfare indifference curve to any combination on a lower social welfare indifference curve. For example, point C on W_1 is preferred to either A or B in Figure 4.2(b). In addition, the slope of a social welfare indifference curve gives society's willingness to trade off one person's well-being for the other person's well-being on the margin. At point C, society is willing to sacrifice 5 utils of satisfaction for person #2 in exchange for giving person #1 one more util of satisfaction. This social marginal rate of substitution of individuals' well-being is analogous to person #1's marginal rate of substitution between X and Y, $MRS_{X,Y}$, the slope of an indifference curve in Figure 4.2(a). Finally, the rankings of the individuals' well-being given by the social welfare indifference curves can be represented by some social welfare function W, just as the rankings of the goods and services given by the consumers' indifference curves can be represented by some utility function U.

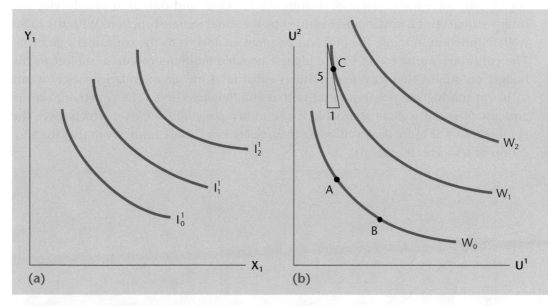

Figure 4.2

Another property of social welfare that Bergson and Samuelson proposed is that everyone's well-being should count. This property is referred to as honoring the *Pareto principle*: If any one person's utility should increase (decrease), with everyone else's utility held constant, then social welfare should also increase (decrease). Analytically, $\frac{\Delta W}{\Delta U^i} > 0$, holding constant the utilities of all other people h = 1,...,i − 1, i + 1,....H, for any i.[1] According to Nobel laureate Wassily Leontief (1966, p. 27), the twin principles that social welfare should be individualistic and honor the Pareto principle are the only principles that all economists can agree upon when thinking about the problem of distributive justice.

Note, finally, that the social welfare function is not a market concept. It must be determined collectively by society through some kind of political process. As such, it is the one point in the mainstream theory of the public sector that the government must do more than simply act as an agent for the people, trying to determine what their preferences are for the problems that market failures leave for the government to solve. The ethical rankings represented by the social welfare function are the one piece of information that government officials must add to individuals' preferences to solve the distribution question and, as we shall see, to settle on final solutions for the various efficiency problems that arise from market failures. Richard Musgrave's distribution and allocation branches are inherently interrelated.

▨ THE BLISS POINT

Society can solve the problem of distributive justice if, and only if, it can develop the interpersonal ethical rankings represented by the social welfare function. With the social welfare function in hand, the problem becomes analogous to the consumer's problem. The consumer wants to get to the highest possible indifference curve, subject to the budget constraint that total expenditures equal total income. Similarly, society wants to be on the highest possible social welfare indifference curve. The constraint on the amount of social welfare attainable is the utility possibilities curve, which gives the combinations of individual well-being that society can choose from, given that the allocation of resources is efficient.

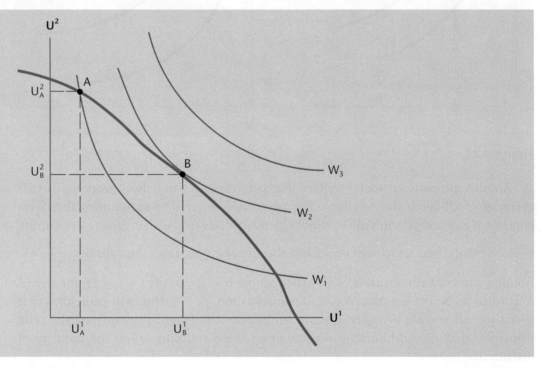

Figure 4.3

Refer to Figure 4.3. Social welfare is maximized at point B along the utility possibilities frontier U^2-U^1, with the amount of social welfare represented by the social welfare indifference curve W_2. Francis Bator (1957) called point B the "bliss point," a term that has stuck among economists. The *bliss point* is distributionally the best of all the efficient combinations of U^2 and U^1 attainable on the utility possibilities frontier. The distribution of individual well-being is optimal at B, with person #2 receiving utility of U_B^2 and person #1 receiving U_B^1. In contrast, the distribution U_A^2 and U_A^1 at the original point A is on a lower social indifference curve W_1 – it does not yield as much social welfare as the bliss point.

THE INTERPERSONAL EQUITY CONDITION

What condition has to hold to be at the bliss point, point B? Economists usually describe it in terms of the individual's social marginal utilities of income. The concept of a social marginal utility of income comes from thinking of individual utility as a function of an individual's income, which is used to buy goods and services. Under this interpretation, the social welfare function becomes

$$W = W(U^1(Y_1),...,U^h(Y_h),....,U^H(Y_H))$$

where Y_h is the income of person h.

Suppose person h's income changes, with no change in the income of anyone else. The change in social welfare is given by

$$\Delta W = [(\Delta W/\Delta U^h) (\Delta U^h/\Delta Y_h)]\Delta Y_h.$$

The second term inside the brackets is person h's marginal utility of income. It gives the change in the utility of person h per unit change in person h's income. When multiplied by ΔY_h, the amount that person h's income changes, it gives the change in person h's utility. The first term inside the brackets is called the *marginal social welfare weight*. It gives the change in social welfare per unit change in the utility of person h. When multiplied by the change in person h's utility (the product of the last two terms on the right-hand side), it gives the amount that social welfare changes.

The entire term inside the brackets is the *social marginal utility of income* for person h, SMU_Y^h, the product of the marginal social welfare weight for person h ($\Delta W/\Delta U^h$) and person h's marginal utility of income ($\Delta U^h/\Delta Y_h$). The marginal utilities of income come from the individuals themselves, based on their own preferences for goods and services. The marginal social welfare weights, in contrast, must be determined collectively by society through some kind of political process. They indicate the (marginal) ethical worth of each person from society's point of view.[2] The social marginal utility of income for person h indicates the increase in social welfare per unit increase in person h's income.

The social marginal utilities of income must be equal for all individuals for social welfare to achieve its maximum value. To see why this is so, return to the two-person economy of Chapter 3, for which the social welfare function would be $W = W(U^1(Y_1), U^2(Y_2))$. The movement from A to B in Figure 4.3 is achieved by taxing person #2 and transferring the revenue to person #1, such that $\Delta Y_1 = -\Delta Y_2$. The total effect on social welfare of this redistribution from person #2 to person #1 is

$$\Delta W= [(\Delta W/\Delta U^1) (\Delta U^1/\Delta Y_1)] \Delta Y_1 + [(\Delta W/\Delta U^2) (\Delta U^2/\Delta Y_2)] \Delta Y_2.$$

But with $\Delta Y_1 = -\Delta Y_2$,

$$\Delta W = \{[(\Delta W/\Delta U^1)\,(\Delta U^1/\Delta Y_1)] - [(\Delta W/\Delta U^2)\,(\Delta U^2/\Delta Y_2)]\,\}\Delta Y_1$$

or,

$$\Delta W = [\,SMU_Y^1 - SMU_Y^2\,]\Delta Y_1.$$

Presumably person #1 had the higher social marginal utility of income at the initial distribution A in Figure 4.3 simply because he is worse off. Whatever the reason, the government can increase social welfare by redistributing income from person #2 to person #1 because $SMU_Y^1 > SMU_Y^2$. The increase in social welfare from giving person #1 additional income ΔY_1 exceeds the loss in social welfare from forcing person #2 to give up that same amount of income. Moreover, the government should continue to redistribute income so long as $SMU_Y^1 > SMU_Y^2$. Once enough income has been transferred, however, the social marginal utilities eventually become equal and $\Delta W = 0$. Social welfare can no longer be increased, which means that social welfare is at its maximum. Society has reached Bator's bliss point B in Figure 4.3.

What holds for two people holds for any number of people. If the social marginal utilities of any two people are unequal, social welfare can be increased by transferring income through taxes and transfers from the person with the lower social marginal utility of income to the person with the higher social marginal utility of income. Conversely, when the social marginal utilities of income are equal across all the people, no social welfare improving redistributions are possible. Social welfare is at its maximum at the bliss point. The equality of the social marginal utilities of income is referred to as the *interpersonal equity condition* for a social welfare maximum.

Interpersonal equity condition: the SMU_Y^h must be equal, all h = 1,...,h,..,H.

The interpersonal equity condition and the Pareto-optimal conditions from Chapter 3 are the two sets of conditions that are necessary for social welfare to attain its maximum value at the bliss point. The Pareto-optimal conditions are the efficiency conditions that guarantee that the economy is on its utility possibilities frontier. Recall that one such condition is the consumption condition, that the marginal rate of substitution in consumption between any two goods must be equal for all individuals. Then the interpersonal equity condition brings the economy to the bliss point on the utility possibilities frontier.

POLICY IMPLICATIONS – LUMP-SUM TAXES AND TRANSFERS

As we have just seen, society moves along the utility possibilities frontier by a series of taxes and transfers until the interpersonal equity condition is satisfied. Not just any taxes and transfers will do, however. The taxes and transfers must be non-distorting, meaning that they do not introduce any inefficiencies into an economy.

The properties that make a tax or transfer non-distorting can be expressed in a number of ways. Begin with Figure 4.3, which assumes that the economy is efficient and operates somewhere on its utility possibilities frontier. The redistribution of income from person #2 to person #1 is non-distorting and preserves efficiency if it allows the economy to remain on the utility possibilities frontier. The economy has to remain on its utility possibilities frontier in order to reach the bliss point. In contrast, a distorting tax or transfer is one that moves the economy below the utility possibilities frontier to an inefficient allocation of resources. Another way to describe a non-distorting tax or transfer, therefore, is that it permits all the Pareto-optimal conditions to hold that bring the economy to its utility possibilities frontier, for example the three Pareto-optimal conditions described in Chapter 3 for the simple two-person, two-good, two-factor economy. But as we have seen, these conditions hold in a market economy only if all economic agents face the same prices for the same goods and factors of production. Therefore, a third way to describe a tax or transfer as non-distorting is that it continues to allow all agents to face the same prices for the same goods and factors. These are three equivalent ways of defining a non-distorting tax or transfer.

How can the government design its taxes and transfers so that they are non-distorting? The answer is that they must be *lump sum*, meaning that the amount of tax paid or transfer received cannot be changed by any economic decision that an individual or firm might make in reaction to the tax or transfer. An example would be a tax (transfer) based on a person's age. An age tax (transfer) would not cause any two individuals or firms to face a different price for any good or factor involved in a market transaction.

A final point is that the government can redistribute lump sum any good or factor that is commonly used or supplied by consumers to move the economy along the utility possibilities frontier. In thinking of the transfer in terms of income, economists make use of the property that only relative prices matter for the allocation of resources. Therefore, the price of the good or factor transferred can arbitrarily be set at one, with all the other prices adjusted accordingly to maintain the same relative prices. Redistributing units of a good or factor whose price is one is equivalent to redistributing units of income.

SUMMARY: THE MAINSTREAM THEORY OF DISTRIBUTIVE JUSTICE

The two great questions of distributive justice or end-results equity are:

1. What is the optimal distribution of individual well-being?
2. If society is not at the optimal distribution, how should it redistribute to reach the optimum?

We have just seen that the mainstream theory of distributive justice provides very simple answers to these questions.

If society can establish an ethical ranking of individuals' well-being that can be represented by a Bergson–Samuelson individualistic social welfare function, then:

1. The optimal distribution of well-being occurs when the social marginal utilities of income are equal across all individuals. This is the interpersonal equity condition for a social welfare maximum and it holds at the bliss point B in Figure 4.3. The bliss point is the optimal distribution of well-being along the utility possibilities frontier.
2. If the initial distribution is not optimal, then the government should tax and transfer lump sum until society is at the bliss point and the social marginal utilities of income are equal for all.

In short, the Bergson–Samuelson social welfare function provides economists with a complete theory of end-results equity or distributive justice. It describes both the optimal distribution and the optimal redistributional policy. Mainstream public sector theory has nothing more to say about the quest for distributive justice.

In contrast, if society cannot establish an ethical ranking of individuals' well-being that can be represented by a Bergson–Samuelson individualistic social welfare function, then the two great questions of distributive justice can never be completely answered.

A final point to stress is that the lump-sum taxes and transfers redistribute the initial distribution of resources and then the workings of the economy bring society to the bliss point. The emphasis on the initial distribution of resources is important, because the initial distribution of resources is likely to be a major determinant of society's ethical judgments of individuals embodied in the marginal social welfare weights. Consider two scenarios leading to unequal outcomes. In the first, two people make equal efforts but earn different incomes because they start with different amounts of resources. One has more innate ability or receives a large inheritance. In the second, they both begin with the same resources but one person earns more income because she works much harder. A society is likely to react more strongly to the unequal incomes in the first scenario, especially if the different outcomes are the result of differences in inherited wealth.

DETERMINING THE ALLOCATION OF RESOURCES

The social welfare function does far more than answer the distribution question. It also chooses the final allocation of resources for the economy among all the possible efficient allocations. Refer again to the two-person, two-good, two-factor economy in Chapter 3. By choosing the bliss point on the utility possibilities frontier, the social welfare function chooses a corresponding point on the production possibilities frontier, and therefore the aggregate quantity of X and Y. Once X and Y have been chosen, the three Pareto-optimal conditions of that model determine how much capital and labor are allocated to the production of each good and how much of the aggregate X and Y is consumed by each person. Musgrave's distribution and allocation branches of government are tightly interrelated. The efficiency criterion of Pareto optimality ranks all efficient allocations along the utility possibilities frontier as equally good; it cannot choose among them. The final allocation is determined only when the social welfare function resolves the distribution question.

In summary, the importance of the social welfare function to mainstream public sector economics theory can hardly be overstated. It is clearly one of the linchpins of the mainstream theory.

PROBLEMS IN APPLYING THE MAINSTREAM THEORY OF DISTRIBUTIVE JUSTICE

The social welfare function provides the government with a simple guideline for achieving the optimal distribution of income, but it is a guideline fraught with practical difficulties. The problems begin with the call for lump-sum taxes and transfers and extend to the social welfare function itself. In truth, the social welfare function is one of the more problematic constructs in all of economic theory. This is just another way of saying that any society is likely to have great difficulty in agreeing on a set of ethical rankings of individuals to guide its distribution policies.

LUMP-SUM TAXES AND TRANSFERS?

Simply put, taxes and transfers that are used to redistribute income are unlikely to be lump sum. The problem is not that lump-sum taxes and transfers are difficult to imagine. Quite the contrary. It is easy to design a lump-sum tax or transfer and governments have actually used them. One common example in U.S. history is the poll tax, levied when people vote. The decision to vote or not does affect the amount of tax paid, but voting can be considered a political decision not an economic decision. On the transfer side, any transfer based on something the recipient did in the past would be lump sum. An example would be a one-time transfer to families of $500 for each child that the family had as of two years ago.

The problem, rather, is that lump-sum taxes and transfers are unlikely to have the redistributional bite required to satisfy the interpersonal equity condition. Redistributional taxes and transfers are motivated in capitalist societies by the disparity in income and consumption between the haves and the have-nots. To effectively reduce the inequality, both the taxes and the transfers have to be related to some extent on how much income or consumption people have. But taxes and transfers based on either income or consumption are generally not lump sum. They almost always drive a wedge between the prices for goods or factors that are relevant for individuals and firms. Under an income tax, for example, the wage that is relevant to the employers in making their hiring decisions is the entire wage that includes the income tax. The wage that is relevant to employees in making their labor supply decisions is their take-home pay, the wage net of the income tax. With employers and employees looking at different wages for the same labor, any Pareto-optimal efficiency condition relating to the supply and use of labor cannot hold. The income tax forces the economy beneath its utility possibilities frontier. Bator's bliss point may be an ideal to strive for, but it is unlikely to be a practical target for the government.

PROBLEMS WITH THE SOCIAL WELFARE FUNCTION

The social welfare function is an extremely problematic construct. In truth, economists cannot provide satisfactory answers to any of the following questions: What is a nation's social welfare function? What should the social welfare function be? Can there be a social welfare function? This is not a pleasant state of affairs for one of the linchpins of public sector theory. We will consider each question in turn.

WHAT IS THE SOCIAL WELFARE FUNCTION?

An economist would have great difficulty in trying to estimate the operative social welfare function for any nation at some point in time. Since economists always want to know what is true on the margin, they would be particularly interested in the slopes of the social welfare indifference curves at the current distribution of income. What is the ethical social marginal rate of substitution between any two people, the willingness to sacrifice the well-being of one person to increase the well-being of the other person? The ethical social MRS is the ratio of their marginal social welfare weights.

The problem here is not that a marginal rate of substitution is some abstract theoretical construct that cannot be observed. Quite the contrary. A consumer's MRS between any two goods is easily estimated. Suppose you know that some person regularly eats both Caesar salads and tacos, but that is all you know about her. You also know that the prices of Caesar salads and tacos are $P_{CS} = \$8$ and the $P_T = \$4$. If you were asked to estimate her marginal rate of substitution between Caesar salads and tacos, you would say that her $MRS_{CS,T} = \$8/\$4 = 2/1$. Why? Because you assume she is rational and tries to maximize her utility, and consumer theory tells us that people maximize utility by consuming goods and services such that the MRS between any two goods is equal to the ratio of their prices. We may all have different tastes and different incomes and consume different amounts of the same foods, but on the margin we are all identical.

No such theory guides us in estimating the social MRS along a social welfare indifference curve. The social welfare function is determined collectively by a society through the political process, and politics is often extremely muddied. One is never quite sure how political decisions are made. Furthermore, the desire to redistribute can often change over time as different political parties come into power.

To give one example of the difficulty here, suppose we ask: How heavily are U.S. citizens willing to tax the people with the highest incomes? The U.S. federal personal income tax uses a system of graduated or increasing tax rates on brackets of income as income increases. Consider the tax rate levied on the highest income bracket. In the early 1960s, the highest tax rate was 91%. Since then it was changed to 50%, then to 28%, then again to 39.6%, and most recently to 35%. U.S. citizens cannot seem to decide how heavily they want to tax the rich.

In truth, it is extremely difficult to know what a nation's social welfare function is.

WHAT SHOULD THE SOCIAL WELFARE FUNCTION BE?

Since the social welfare function is so central to their theory, mainstream public sector economists would certainly like to be able to say with some confidence what the social welfare function should be. But this is not to be. Economists, other social scientists, philosophers, theologians, natural scientists, people from all walks of life have thought about what the ethical social rankings of individuals should be, without anyone ever making a convincing case. All we can say is that most economists believe that the reasonable limits of the rankings are the utilitarian and the Rawlsian social welfare functions.

UTILITARIAN SOCIAL WELFARE

The utilitarian social welfare function is attributed to Jeremy Bentham, a political economist who wrote in the late 18th and early 19th centuries. Bentham argued that the goal of society should be to maximize aggregate satisfaction, which implies that the social welfare function is just the sum of the individual utility functions,

$$W^B = \sum_{h=1}^{H} U^h.$$

W^B is referred to as either the *utilitarian* or the *Benthamite social welfare function*. The social welfare indifference curves are 45° straight lines, as pictured in Figure 4.4 for persons #1 and #2.

They indicate that society is indifferent to inequality. So long as society is on W_1, it is indifferent whether the outcome is at point A in which person #2 has all the well-being, at point B in which person #1 has all the well-being, or at point C in which the distribution of well-being is equal. Societies have never been so indifferent to inequality, however, which sets Bentham's indifference to inequality as a reasonable lower limit for society's concern for inequality.

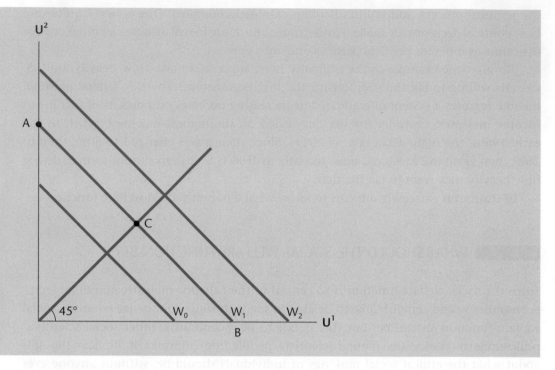

Figure 4.4

The Benthamite social welfare function does incorporate one property of ethical rankings that is widely held, the property of impersonality. *Impersonality* says that society has no right to give different ethical social welfare weights to individuals based on their personal characteristics, and the Benthamite social welfare function does not do so. All the marginal social welfare weights, $\Delta W/\Delta U^h$, are equal to 1. Impersonality rules out such policies as affirmative action in the United States, under which public policy has given special consideration to women and minorities in labor market settings from the mid-1960s to compensate for past discrimination against them. Many people opposed affirmative action from the outset and the opposition to affirmative action appears to be increasing. One senses that U.S. citizens do embrace impersonality as a general principle, and are willing to grant extra ethical weight to certain groups only under special circumstances, such as to help right the wrongs of previous labor market discrimination.

RAWLSIAN SOCIAL WELFARE

At the other end of the ethical spectrum stands John Rawls, a Harvard philosopher who proposed that social welfare should be highly egalitarian (Rawls, 1971). Rawls' view of distributive justice is grounded in part on a philosophical notion called the "veil of ignorance." The idea is that we are handicapped in thinking about distributional policies because we know where we currently stand in the distribution and what our future prospects are likely to be, and so we have some idea how these polices might affect us. This self-knowledge biases our thinking about distributive justice. Therefore, the only way to be entirely objective is to pretend that we stand behind a veil of ignorance that prevents us from seeing our own position in the distribution. The ignorance is meant to be profound in the sense that both the present and future is one of true uncertainty.

Economists distinguish between risky and truly uncertain situations. In the former, we face uncertainty about future outcomes but we can attach probabilities to the possible outcomes. Our goal, then, is to maximize our expected utility in the face of the risks. In a truly uncertain situation, we may have a sense of what the future possibilities are, for example that we and our descendents could be very well off, have about average income, or be quite poor. But we have no idea how to attach probabilities to the various outcomes. This is the situation the veil of ignorance refers to. We have no idea now where we stand in the distribution and also no idea how well off we are likely to be in the future. The question, then, is what kinds of distributional policies we would favor when faced with true uncertainty.

Economists have not been able to develop a theory of behavior under true uncertainty. All we have are some suggestions. Rawls argues that we would be extremely risk averse in thinking about the distribution. We would focus on the worst-case scenario, the prospect of becoming impoverished, and ask society to adopt a so-called maximin policy. Society should always pursue policies that maximize the well-being of those who are worse off. This provides the maximum protection against the worst-case (the minimum) possibility. The maximin policy leads to a social welfare function of the form

$$W^R = \min (U^1, , U^h, ..., U^H)$$

where min refers to minimum. Social welfare equals the utility achieved by the person who has the lowest level of utility, that is, the person who is the worst off. Since only that person's utility counts, the level of social welfare is set equal to that person's utility level.

The min social welfare function generates right-angled social welfare indifference curves, as illustrated in Figure 4.5 for persons #1 and #2. The curves are drawn along the equal utility 45° line as a frame of reference. They are right-angled because, starting from a position of equal utility, a movement from A to B on W_1 makes person #2 better off without affecting person #1. But now person #1 is the worst off and since person #1's utility has not increased, social welfare cannot increase either. A and B must lie on the same social welfare indifference curve. The same argument applies to making person #1 better off without affecting person #2; the social welfare indifference curves are right-angled. Notice also that using the 45° line as a frame of reference makes sense because society would want to promote the well-being of whoever is worse off until the utilities of the two people are equal. This is why the *Rawlsian social welfare function* is considered the most egalitarian, the limiting case at the opposite extreme from Benthamite indifference in terms of society's aversion to inequality.

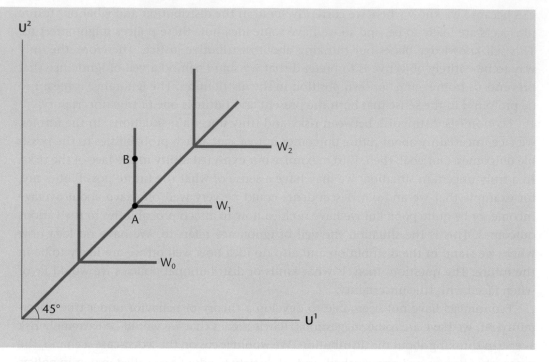

Figure 4.5

Economists are generally unconvinced by Rawls' proposal. First of all, there is no reason to suppose that people would be so extremely risk averse when faced with true uncertainty about their incomes. Again, there is no accepted theory of behavior under true uncertainty. Second, the Rawlsian social welfare function violates the Pareto principle as we have just seen. A policy that makes one person better off without affecting the worst-off person does not increase social welfare. Economists generally believe that everyone should count, not just the poorest group. Along the same lines, Rawls would have society reject a policy that brings huge gains for everyone but the worst-off group, if the worst-off group is made just slightly more worse off. This possibility is especially troubling in a dynamic growth context. The essence of growth is a now-versus-the-future trade-off. The first generation is asked to save and invest to promote long-run economic growth for the benefit of future generations. If the growth process takes, however, then the first generation would be the worst-off generation. Therefore, despite the potentially huge gains to future generations from economic growth, the first generation should not be asked to sacrifice. It should consume all its resources, which makes growth impossible. Without growth, the second generation would now be the worst off if it saved and invested for the benefit of future generations. It, too, should consume all its resources. And so on, into the future. The Rawlsian social welfare function is a prescription for no economic growth, clearly an uncomfortable outcome.

Most economists would argue that the social welfare indifference curves should have the standard shape, as pictured in Figure 4.2(b), with diminishing social marginal rate of substitution. The willingness to trade off the well-being of the two people would vary depending on how well off each person is. The Benthamite/utilitarian social welfare function represents one extreme that flattens the curves to a straight line in being indifferent to the distribution. The Rawlsian egalitarian social welfare function represents the other extreme that steepens the curves to right angles in being the most egalitarian. The truth should undoubtedly lie somewhere between these extremes, but the extremes are too wide to be useful as a guideline to policy. To say that the quest for distributive justice should lie somewhere between indifference to inequality and a striving for complete equality is not to say very much at all.

CAN THERE BE A SOCIAL WELFARE FUNCTION? ARROW'S GENERAL IMPOSSIBILITY THEOREM

The humanistic tradition that has propelled the nations of the world towards capitalism as the best way of promoting consumer sovereignty in the economic arena would just as naturally favor one-person, one-vote democracy or a representative form of government in the political arena. The final question about the social welfare function, then, is whether a democratic society can be expected to develop a consistent set of ethical rankings to solve the problem of distributive justice. In 1951, Kenneth Arrow showed that the answer is no, in general. Arrow's result, which he called the General Impossibility Theorem, is considered by many to be the greatest intellectual achievement in political economy of the twentieth century. It shook the belief in democracy to the core, because it is not just related to the problem of developing a social welfare function. It applies to the ability of democracies to make consistent social decisions about anything at all (Arrow, 1951).

In fact, Arrow was not thinking about distribution issues when he developed his theorem. He had been asked by the Department of Defense to analyze how decisions are made in a democratic society about nonexclusive goods such as defense. Arrow approached the problem as an exercise in cooperative game theory. Think of partners in a law firm trying to determine how to divide the profits of a firm. The idea behind cooperative game theory is to develop a set of fundamental principles that the partners would all agree should apply in a division of the profits. Then the partners agree to abide by those principles in distributing the profits, whatever division they might imply. Ideally, the number of fundamental principles should be few in number and not at all controversial.

Along the same lines, Arrow thought about the fundamental principles that should apply to social decision making in a democracy. He proposed the following five principles that he felt most people would agree to:

1. *The social decision process must provide a complete ordering of social outcomes.* The need for a complete ordering of outcomes is necessary in any decision-making

context that involves people's preferences. It has two components. First, when confronted with any two alternatives A and B, society can determine that it prefers A to B, or B to A, or that it is indifferent between A and B. The one possibility that must be ruled out is that society does not know what it thinks about A and B; this is when preference-based decision making breaks down. The second component is that society's preferences must be transitive. Let SP stand for "socially preferred to." Transitivity requires that if A SP B, and B SP C, then A SP C. Indifference can be substituted for preference in the transitivity relationship. Transitivity is the meaning of consistency in decision making.

2. *Any individual preferences over social outcomes must be allowed.*[3] Democratic voting must lead to consistent social decisions for any and all preferences that the individuals might have regarding social outcomes that they are asked to consider.

3. *Social decisions must honor the Pareto principle.* If everyone agrees that A is preferred to B, then A SP B.

4. *The independence of irrelevant alternatives.* Suppose the social decision process decides that A SP B and B SP C. Then society changes it mind about B and C, deciding now that C SP B. This change cannot affect the ranking between A and B, or any between any other alternatives. This is the only truly controversial principle that Arrow proposed because it could be that three or more social decisions are somehow interrelated. Still, this assumption greatly simplifies social decision making in a democracy, and decisions are often made on a pair-wise basis in democracies. Suffice it to say that many people have tried to relax this assumption in the hope of overturning Arrow's theorem but without success.

5. *Non-dictatorship.* It cannot be that one person is always decisive, in the sense that society's preferences always turn out to be the same as the preferences of that one person, no matter what the preferences of the other people might be. That person would in effect be a dictator if this were the case.

Arrow proved that, in general, these five principles cannot all hold simultaneously. The usual proof of the theorem is to show that if principles 1 through 4 hold, then one person is a dictator. Another variation is to show that if principles 2 through 5 hold, then 1 does not hold. The social decisions are not consistent, in general. This is the variation that is most often used to show the difficulties with democratic decision making.

The qualifier "in general" is important. Arrow's theorem says that social decisions under democracy might not be consistent, not that they necessarily must be inconsistent. Social decision making under democracy would almost certainly be consistent on issues for which there is broad agreement. The difficulty comes when there is considerable disagreement, as there is likely to be about issues such as national defense and the appropriate distribution of income. We will consider a distributional example to illustrate the problems that can occur.

Suppose society consists of three people who are voting on three different ways to split $100 among them, policies A, B, and C. (The three people could be legislators representing their constituencies.) Assume that the people are entirely self-serving; they rank the policies according to the income they receive under each policy. The choice of policies is decided by majority rule. The policies are as follows:

	1	2	3
A	$50	20	30
B	30	50	20
C	20	30	50

The individual preferences for A, B, and C are:

Person #1: A P B P C
Person #2: B P C P A
Person #3: C P A P B

Consider social preferences determined by majority vote:

A vs. B: 2 of 3 prefer A (persons #1 and #3) A SP B
B vs. C: 2 of 3 prefer B (persons #1 and #2) B SP C
C vs. A: 2 of 3 prefer C (persons #2 and #3) C SP A

The social preferences are inconsistent (intransitive): Since A SP B and B SP C, transitivity requires that A SP C. But C SP A.

Inconsistent preferences lead to indifference curves that cross, and generate all kinds of anomalies. Refer to Figure 4.6. According to the social welfare indifference curves, society would be indifferent if the distribution changed from A to B, since both are on W_1. Society would again be indifferent if the distribution changed from B to C, since both are on W_2. This should imply that society is also indifferent between A and C, but C SP A. It is on a higher social welfare indifference curve. In addition, society prefers D to A according to this ranking, even though both people are better off at A than at D. Social preferences of this kind are in total opposition to the humanistic quest for promoting individual well-being. These examples illustrate why indifference curves representing preferences cannot cross.

A further difficulty for democratic societies when social preferences are inconsistent is that any policy can win depending on the order that the vote is taken. To see this, consider the follow voting orders. The example reflects the pair-wise voting that often occurs in legislatures.

A vs. B, the winner vs. C. A wins the first round, C the second round. Winner: C.

A vs. C, the winner vs. B. C wins the first round, B the second round. Winner: B.

B vs. C, the winner vs. A. B wins the first round, A the second round. Winner: A.

Controlling the voting agenda is crucial when preferences are inconsistent.

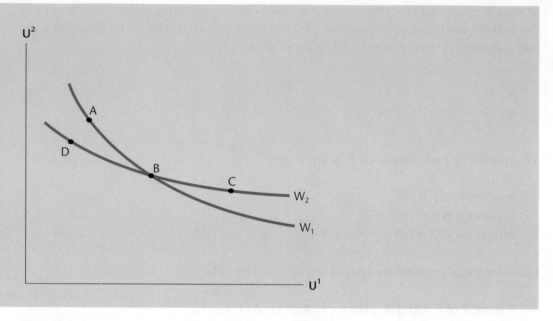

Figure 4.6

REACTIONS TO ARROW'S THEOREM

Public sector economists tended to react in one of three ways to Arrow's General Impossibility Theorem, along with the other two problems with social welfare functions discussed above:

1. *The technocratic reaction.* Some mainstream economists, most notable among them MIT's Paul Samuelson, concluded that there was no use in economists thinking anymore about what the social welfare should be and how it might evolve in a democracy. Economists can do little more than revert to being technicians who advise public officials on how to solve their economic problem, which consists of objectives, alternatives, and constraints. The objective is presumably to maximize a social welfare function. The officials who are currently running the government do have some social welfare function in mind that corresponds to their thinking about distributive justice or end-results equity. All economists can do is ask the officials what that social welfare function is. Then they can help the officials understand the nature of their alternatives and the constraints they operate under. Once all the elements of the economic problem are in place, they can advise the officials what to do. Economists know how to solve the economic problem.

2. *The flexible form reaction.* The majority of mainstream economists have chosen to retain the social welfare function in their analyses of economic issues. They choose flexible form social welfare functions that allow for the full range of possibilities

for society's aversion to inequality, from Benthamite/utilitarian indifference to inequality to Rawlsian egalitarianism. This allows them to determine how different views of inequality affect policy recommendations on public sector issues, which is presumably of interest to policy makers. We will take this approach in Chapter 5 when we demonstrate some policy applications using a flexible form social welfare function.

3. *The public choice reaction.* Public choice economists are completely unconcerned about the difficulties surrounding the social welfare function because they do not believe in social welfare functions in the first place. A social welfare function can evolve in a democratic society only if people think in an other-interested manner about the problem of distributive justice, and in their view people do not think that way. As noted in Chapter 1, public choice economists assume that people are entirely self-serving in all their interactions with the government. It would never occur to people to register ethical rankings of other individuals through some political process, rankings that then could be represented by a social welfare function. The social welfare function simply does not exist. Furthermore, it is also unnecessary. One can explain transfers to the poor and other public redistributional programs without reference to a social welfare function. We will return to the public choice perspective on redistributional policies in Chapter 10.

CONCLUDING COMMENTS ON THE DISTRIBUTION QUESTION

Chapter 4 has told a fairly depressing tale about the quest for distributive justice in democratic, humanistic societies. Its main message is that all societies must solve the distribution question of end-results equity or distributive justice, but that they can do so only if the citizens can agree upon a set of ethical rankings of individuals that can be represented analytically by the Bergson–Samuelson individualistic social welfare function. Unfortunately, a majority rule, democratic voting process is unlikely to select a particular social welfare function and, even if it could, no one can advise the citizens with any confidence about what the social welfare function should be. In truth, the quest for distributive justice is likely to be a source of unending debate and disagreement in a democracy, as indeed it has been in the United States.

CHAPTER 5

Applying the Social Welfare Function

As noted at the end of Chapter 4, the most common reaction among mainstream economists to the difficulties surrounding the social welfare function is to maintain the social welfare function in policy analysis but give it a flexible form that admits the full range of ethical rankings, from utilitarian indifference to Rawlsian egalitarianism. The idea is to see how different reactions to inequality might influence policy recommendations.

The pioneer of the flexible form approach was Anthony Atkinson of the London School of Economics. Shortly after World War II, the United States and Great Britain began conducting annual surveys of the personal characteristics and incomes of households. The surveys asked questions on such things as the number of people in the household and their ages, the household's income, and the education of the head of household.[1] One of the main purposes of the surveys is to provide information on the degree of income inequality, and the governments publish various summary statistics of the distribution of household incomes. By 1970, when Atkinson began his research on the social welfare function, economists had devised a number of numerical measures of the effects of various kinds of inefficiencies on social welfare. Atkinson wanted to develop corresponding numerical measures of the effect of income inequality on social welfare. In order to do so, he had to find a way to link the social welfare function to the surveys' household income data.

THE ATKINSON ASSUMPTIONS

Atkinson needed a number of assumptions to make the social welfare function operational. Since his concern was the distribution of income, Atkinson first assumed that each household's utility is a function only of its income, and defined the social welfare function as $W = W(U^h(Y_h))$. We will refer to household h and person h interchangeably, in keeping with the development of the social welfare function in Chapter 4. Recall for future reference that the social marginal utility of income for person h under this specification is $SMU_Y^h = (\Delta W/\Delta U^h)(\Delta U^h/\Delta Y_h)$, the product of the marginal social welfare weight $\Delta W/\Delta U^h$ and the private marginal utility of income $\Delta U^h/\Delta Y_h$. The interpersonal equity condition for a social welfare maximum requires that the social marginal utilities of income be equalized across all individuals (households).

THE THREE MAIN ASSUMPTIONS

Atkinson added three more very strong assumptions about the social welfare function, assumptions that have been almost universally adopted by economists using the flexible form approach. They are: (1) equal marginal social welfare weights; (2) everyone has the same tastes or preferences; and (3) diminishing marginal utility of income. Each assumption is controversial, even heroic, and requires some comment.

Equal marginal social welfare weights – The first assumption is that the marginal social welfare weights, $\Delta W/\Delta U^h$, must be equal for two people who have the same income. This assumption appeals to many people because it honors the principle of impersonality, which says that society's ethical rankings of individuals should take into account only their economic circumstances, in this case their incomes. The rankings should be independent of any other personal characteristics such as race, gender, and creed, hence be impersonal. This assumption is controversial, however, because it would rule out the U.S. affirmative action policies that have been in effect since the 1960s. These policies give other-things-equal preference in hiring to women and non-white minorities to compensate for past discrimination against them. In defense of impersonality, one could say that even if affirmative action policies are viewed as sensible in the context of labor markets, they are less compelling for the government's redistributional policies. People's economic circumstances, not their personal characteristics, should probably be the decisive factor in designing the government's tax and transfer policies.

Atkinson happened to make the most extreme impersonality assumption by adopting the Benthamite/utilitarian social welfare function, $W = \sum_{h=1}^{H} U^h$. Under utilitarianism, everybody's marginal social welfare weight is identical and equal to one, regardless of their economic circumstances. This may seem like an odd choice to bring to the study of inequality, but as we shall see below, it is simply a matter of convenience. Atkinson introduces a concern for inequality through his specification of the individuals' utility functions. Many economists following Atkinson have adopted more general social welfare functions with varying marginal social welfare weights, but they maintain the basic assumption that two people with equal incomes have the same marginal social welfare weights. It turns out that all the results we discuss below follow under this more general specification.

Identical tastes or preferences – Atkinson's second assumption is that everyone has the same preferences, the same utility function $U^h = U(Y_h)$, so that any differences in the utility attained by any two people result entirely from differences in their incomes. This assumption is clearly false, but it can be defended in the context of designing government policies. Perhaps the most basic defense is that it is simply an assumption by default. Suppose we assume, realistically, that people's preferences do differ. How, then, should we model the differences? No obvious method comes to mind. A related question is whether the government should base its redistributional policies at all on differences in people's preferences, or only on differences in their economic circumstances, as suggested above. If you believe that only economic circumstances should matter, as many people do, then a sensible modeling strategy is to assume identical preferences to take preferences out of play. Finally, it could be argued that people's preferences are quite similar, at least in the United States, if one looks at people over their entire lifetimes. Most large differences in preferences are the result of people being in different stages of their lives. For example, 40-year-old parents with children have quite different preferences from those of 20-year-old college students. But the preferences of the parents when they were in college were undoubtedly similar to the preferences of today's college students, and the college students' preferences are likely to be similar to the parents' preferences when they are 40 years old with children. Preferences surely even out somewhat over our lifetimes. Whether these justifications appeal to you or not, Atkinson's assumption of identical tastes has been widely adopted in the social welfare analysis of inequality.

Diminishing marginal utility of income – Atkinson's third assumption is that the common individual utility function exhibits diminishing marginal utility of income, as illustrated in Figure 5.1. Income is on the horizontal axis and utility is on the vertical axis.

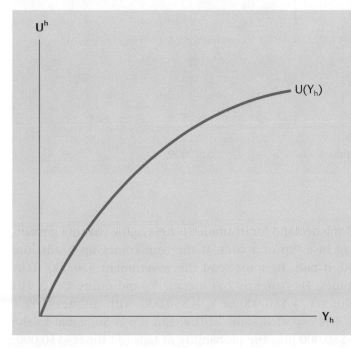

Figure 5.1

The utility function, $U(Y_h)$, bows downward toward the horizontal axis. The marginal utility of income, $\Delta U^h / \Delta Y_h$, is the slope of the utility function at each level of income, and the slope diminishes (gets flatter) as income increases.

The assumption of diminishing marginal utility of income is particularly troubling to economists because the assumption is neither necessary nor sufficient for any result in the theory of the consumer. The marginal rate of substitution (MRS) for any two goods along an indifference curve must decrease. But the MRS is the ratio of the marginal utilities of the two goods, and the MRS can diminish even if the marginal utilities are both increasing.

The best defense for the assumption of diminishing marginal utility is that people take out insurance to protect themselves against life's misfortunes such as sickness or a fire in their homes. By insuring themselves against these events, they behave as if they have diminishing marginal utility of income. Refer to Figure 5.2.

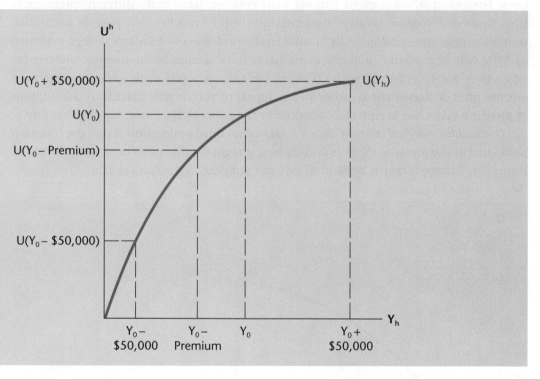

Figure 5.2

An easy way to think about the demand for insurance is to imagine that the government forces a person to engage in a flip of a coin. If the coin comes up heads, the government gives him $50,000; if tails, he must send the government $50,000. Tails represents one of life's misfortunes. He currently has income Y_0 and utility $U(Y_0)$. His income after the coin flip is either $Y_0 + \$50,000$ or $Y_0 - \$50,000$, with utilities $U(Y_0 + \$50,000)$ and $U(Y_0 - \$50,000)$. The expected value of the coin flip is $0, equal to the probability of heads (.5) times $50,000 plus the probability of tails (.5) times –$50,000: $\left[.5 \cdot \$50,000 + .5 \left(-\$50,000 \right) \right] = \$0$. If he were indifferent to risk, what economists call risk neutral, he would be willing to accept the coin flip. But most people do not like risky situations involving substantial amounts of money; they are said to be *risk averse*. If the person is risk averse, he would be willing to pay some amount of money, a premium, to an insurance company that offered to take the coin flip for him. He accepts less income, (Y_0 – premium), to avoid the coin flip. In doing so, he is behaving as if the gain in utility from winning $50,000 is less than the loss in utility from losing $50,000: $[U(Y_0 + \$50,000) - U(Y_0)] < [U(Y_0) - U(Y_0 - \$50,000)]$. The gains and losses of income are equal, but not the gains and losses of utility. The person acts as if he has diminishing marginal utility of income.

There is a problem, however, with accepting the insurance analogy in the context of income inequality. Given Atkinson's second assumption – identical preferences – the assumption of diminishing marginal utility of income implies that a dollar transferred from a richer person to a poorer person gives the poorer person a greater increase in utility than the utility lost by the richer person. Comparing utility gains and losses across people is quite different from describing how any one person reacts to increases or decreases in his or her own income. Indeed, many economists would argue that inter-personal comparisons of utility gains and losses are impossible. If so, they would reject Atkinson's flexible form approach to social welfare analysis. Yet one has to be willing to engage in interpersonal comparisons of utility to infer the social welfare implications of a given degree of inequality or any tax-transfer policy that redistributes income. And, for what it is worth, there is a centuries-old tradition in political economy of accepting the notion that an extra dollar is worth less to a rich person than it is to a poor person. This proposition appears to appeal to many people's intuition. In any event, the assumption of diminishing marginal utility of income is central to the flexible form social welfare analysis of inequality and redistribution.

IMPLICATIONS OF ATKINSON'S ASSUMPTIONS

Equality?

The widespread acceptance of Atkinson's three assumptions by mainstream economists is surprising because together they produce a startling and unattractive conclusion: the complete equality of income. Figure 5.3 illustrates. Suppose society consists of two groups of people, the rich and the poor, with incomes Y_R and Y_P. All people within a group have the same income. Note that the private marginal utility of income, $\Delta U/\Delta Y$, the slope of U, is lower for the rich people, in keeping with the assumption of diminishing marginal utility of income.

Assume that the government can tax and transfer lump sum, so that any redistributions from rich to poor keep society on its utility possibilities frontier. The interpersonal equity condition for a social welfare maximum requires that the government tax and transfer to equalize the social marginal utilities of income across the two groups:

$(\Delta W/\Delta U^R)(\Delta U^R/\Delta Y_R) = (\Delta W/\Delta U^P)(\Delta U^P/\Delta Y_P)$. Under Atkinson's three assumptions, this implies that everyone must have the same income, Y_M, the mean level of income! This follows because if everyone has the same income, they have the same private marginal utility of income $\Delta U/\Delta Y$, from the second and third assumptions. With everyone's income equal, they would also have the same marginal social welfare weight $\Delta W/\Delta U$, by the first assumption.[2] Therefore, the interpersonal equity condition would be satisfied. The conclusion is that if redistribution is costless, then the government should tax all income above the mean and transfer it to all people with income below the mean until everyone has the mean level of income after tax and transfer. This conclusion is clearly unattractive – one would be hard-pressed to find anyone who would support such a policy. Even so, most mainstream models of redistributional policy generate this leveling to the mean if taxes and transfers are lump sum.

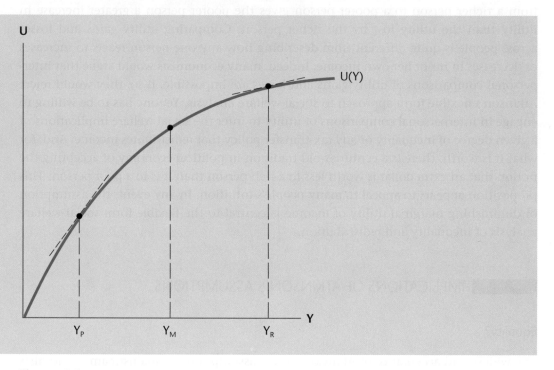

Figure 5.3

As unattractive as this conclusion may be, Lester Thurow (1975, pp. 26–7) argues that it is the appropriate baseline conclusion for redistributional policy, at least in the United States. Public policy decisions are often highly complex. As such, we always need a baseline policy result developed under strong simplifying assumptions to begin thinking about a policy problem, a baseline from which we can begin to add more realistic assumptions. Thurow notes that equality is deeply embedded in the American psyche – Americans place a high value on equality. The Declaration of Independence, one of the U.S. founding documents, would begin if written today: "All [people] are created equal," and it is often said that we all have inherently equal worth as human beings. Why, then, should economic outcomes be unequal? Thurow says this is the right question to ask. Equality is the appropriate baseline norm for end-results equity or distributive justice in the United States. Allowing inequality to exist always has to be justified. That is, the burden of proof is always on inequality when a society values equality.

Okun's leaky bucket

Mainstream economists, along with most people, offer a ready justification for allowing inequality: Redistributing income is not costless because lump-sum taxes and transfers are not feasible. Suppose, to take the limiting case, that the government announced a policy of taxing and transferring everyone to the mean income. Any incentive to work (or save) would cease, since everyone would wind up with the same income whether they worked (saved) or not. The economy would shrink to nothing.

Less dramatically, taxing and transferring entails efficiency costs that have to be weighed against the gains from making the distribution of income more equal. Arthur Okun (1975, pp. 91–100) proposed an image of a leaky bucket that has stuck in the public sector literature. He asked us to think of the rich placing their tax dollars in a bucket, which is then carried to the poor to be distributed to them. The bucket has holes in it, so that some money leaks out of the bucket on its journey to the poor. The leaks represent the efficiency costs of taxing and transferring. The leaks in Okun's bucket are of three kinds: deadweight loss, administrative costs, and compliance costs.

Deadweight loss – This is the loss in the marketplace when distorting taxes or transfers are based on goods or services, including factor services, exchanged in the market. We showed in Chapter 2 that everyone must face the same prices for goods and services for the Pareto-optimal conditions to hold that place society on its utility possibilities frontier. Distorting taxes and transfers violate this condition because buyers and sellers face different prices in their market transactions. If taxes or transfers generate different sets of consumer and producer prices, then the MRS ≠ MRT, and society is forced inside its utility possibilities frontier. This is a deadweight loss in utility because no one can recapture the lost utility. Total consumer utility is always higher at some point on the utility possibilities frontier than at any point under the frontier. We will explore the deadweight loss from taxes and transfers in Chapter 15.

Administrative costs – These are the costs to the government of administering the various taxes and transfer programs. The administrative costs of the major taxes in the United States are quite small, in the order of 0.5% of the revenue raised. The administrative costs of transfer programs can be considerable, however. This is especially true of in-kind programs such as Medicaid, public housing, and other social services, which require hiring people to deliver the services and to monitor the recipients to determine if they qualify for the aid.

Compliance costs – These are the costs from the point of view of the taxpayers and the transfer recipients, equal to the time, money, and effort required of them to compute their tax liabilities and mail tax checks to the governments or to register for various transfer programs. These costs are often quite high.

Okun's leaky bucket is the standard justification for inequality. Return to the initial situation in Figure 5.3 with the two groups of people, the rich and the poor, reproduced in Figure 5.4.

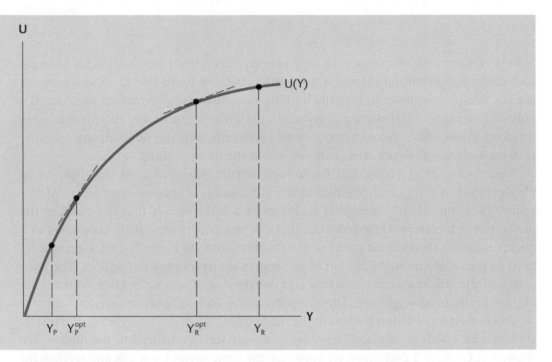

Figure 5.4

Think of taxing and transferring in terms of the economist's standard marginal benefit (MB) and marginal cost (MC) calculations, in which redistribution occurs until the marginal benefit and marginal cost of redistribution are equal. For simplicity, assume as Atkinson did that the social welfare function is utilitarian, with the marginal social welfare weights always equal to one $[\Delta W/\Delta U = 1]$. Under costless lump-sum taxes and transfers, the marginal cost of taking a dollar from one of the rich people is the private marginal utility of the rich, MU_Y^R. The rich count in social welfare, so that social welfare decreases when the rich are taxed. The marginal benefit of transferring that last tax dollar to one of the poor people is MU_Y^P. Redistribution occurs until MB = MC, or $MU_Y^P = MU_Y^R$, which obtains when everyone has the same mean level of income.

Under distorting taxes and transfers, the marginal cost of taxing and trans-ferring is now the MU_Y^R *plus* the efficiency losses of Okun's leaky bucket, which we will call MC$_{OLB}$. The MB of redistributing is still MU_Y^P. As with lump-sum taxes and transfers, redistribution should continue until the MB = MC. Therefore, at the optimal redistribution MB = MU_Y^P = MU_Y^R + MC$_{OLB}$ = MC. Since MC$_{OLB} > 0$, at the optimal redistribution $MU_Y^P > MU_Y^R$, as illustrated in Figure 5.4.

Equivalently, $Y_R^{opt} > Y_P^{opt}$; some inequality remains, justified by the efficiency costs of taxing and transferring, Okun's leaky bucket. Society must weigh the benefits of making the distribution of income more equal, given by the difference in marginal utilities of income $MU_Y^P - MU_Y^R$, with the efficiency costs of redistributing, MC_{OLB}, and people are likely to disagree on when the proper balance between equity and efficiency is reached.

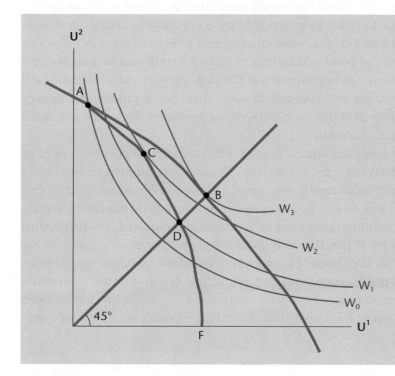

Figure 5.5

Figure 5.5 represents the equity–efficiency trade-off in terms of the model developed in Chapter 3. Assume that the economy is currently at point A on the first-best utility possibilities frontier for individuals #1 and #2. If lump-sum taxes and transfers are feasible, then the bliss point is at B on the frontier under the Atkinson assumptions, with each person receiving the same income and therefore the same utility. B is on the 45° line from the origin, the line of equal utility. With costly taxes and transfers, the attempt to redistribute from A introduces inefficiencies and forces the economy to be on a lower frontier AF, which economists refer to as the *second-best utility possibilities frontier*. The highest level of social welfare is reached at point C, at which the social welfare indifference curve W_2 is tangent to the second-best frontier. Remaining on the 45° line of equality and moving to point D is too costly in terms of inefficiency relative to C. Similarly, maintaining efficiency on the first-best utility possibilities frontier and staying at A is too costly in terms of inequality relative to C. Point C is the best compromise between equity and efficiency.

▨▨▨▨ REDISTRIBUTION AS A NEGATIVE-SUM GAME

Notice that the mainstream view of redistribution with costly taxes and transfers sees redistribution as a negative-sum game: The amount of utility gained by the transfer recipients is less than the utility lost by the taxpayers. Or, as it is often stated, the attempt to redistribute the economic pie reduces the overall size of the pie. This was not always the view of redistribution. Two hundred years ago political economists tended to view redistribution as a positive-sum game. Most economies were at a very low stage of economic development, so low that the poorest members of society were living at a subsistence level of income, with just enough food to survive. The idea was that transfers to the poor would improve their nutrition and energy and make them more productive, thereby increasing their productivity and the overall size of the economy. This view still holds today for the less developed economies.

Some economists have now applied the view of redistribution as a positive-sum game to the industrialized market economies, at least through education. Modern growth theory stresses the importance of human capital, education, to long-run economic growth. One implication is that society should ensure that everyone receives a good education, including the poor, so that talented individuals can be identified and nurtured, no matter what their family income may be. If this theory is correct, and society values equality as the United States appears to do, then there is a compelling argument for education subsidies to the poor. The benefits of education notwithstanding, it is fair to say that mainstream public sector economics continues to view redistribution as a negative-sum game because of the efficiency costs of taxing and transferring. Education subsidies are at best an exception to the general view.

THE AVERSION TO INEQUALITY

The first three Atkinson assumptions are in the nature of general principles for applying the social welfare function. The final step in bringing the social welfare function to the survey data on the distribution of income is to specify the individuals' common utility function. Atkinson had the additional requirement of expressing society's concern for inequality within the utility function since he had chosen the utilitarian version of the social welfare function. Atkinson borrowed a utility function that was common to the literature on risk taking. He assumed that

$$U^h = \frac{1}{(1-e)} Y_h^{(1-e)} \quad e = [0, \infty]$$

where e represents society's aversion to inequality. The value of e is to be determined collectively by the citizens through some kind of democratic political process. As we shall see in a moment, e = 0 represents utilitarianism in terms of income, no concern for inequality, and $e \to \infty$ represents Rawlsian egalitarianism, the strongest aversion to inequality of income. Aversion to inequality increases as e increases (Atkinson, 1983, pp. 53–9).

A number of properties of Atkinson's utility function are worth noting. First, the marginal utility of income is the derivative of the utility function with respect to income: $MU_Y^h = \dfrac{dU^h}{dY_h} = Y_h^{-e} = \left(\dfrac{1}{Y_h}\right)^e$. MU_Y^h decreases as income increases, in keeping with Atkinson's third general assumption. Second, the marginal utility of income is the concept needed to determine whether the distribution of income is optimal, and it turns out to be a simple function of income. Atkinson wanted a utility function that was easily brought to the income data. Third, return to our example of the rich and poor and note that the ratio of their marginal utilities is equal to the inverse ratio of their incomes raised to the power e:

$$\frac{MU_Y^P}{MU_Y^R} = \left(\frac{Y_R}{Y_P}\right)^e.$$

Suppose e = 0. Then $\dfrac{MU_Y^P}{MU_Y^R} = 1$, or $MU_Y^P = MU_Y^R$. Since their marginal utilities are always equal (to 1), there is never a gain from redistributing from rich to poor, no matter how unequal their incomes might be. This is the utilitarian social welfare function in terms of income. Alternatively, notice that $U^h = \dfrac{1}{(1-e)} Y_h^{(1-e)} = Y_h$ when e = 0. Atkinson assumed that $W = \displaystyle\sum_{h=1}^{H} U^h$, that the social welfare function was utilitarian in terms of utilities. When

e = 0, $W = \displaystyle\sum_{h=1}^{H} Y_h$; social welfare is utilitarian in terms of income. There is no concern for inequality; social welfare depends only on the aggregate amount of income.

Suppose, next, that $e \to \infty$. Then $\dfrac{MU_Y^P}{MU_Y^R}$ goes to infinity if Y_R is even a penny above

Y_P. Those with lower incomes get infinite weight in a redistribution relative to those with higher incomes, which reflects the Rawlsian concern only for the poorest members of society. Thus $e \to \infty$ reflects the greatest possible aversion to inequality.

Between e = 0 and $e \to \infty$, $\left(\dfrac{Y_R}{Y_P}\right)^e = \dfrac{MU_Y^P}{MU_Y^R}$ increases as e increases. The poor receive

an ever higher weight on the margin relative to the rich, reflecting an increasing aversion to inequality. Therefore, Atkinson's utility function is flexible enough to consider the full range of aversion to inequality from utilitarian indifference to Rawlsian egalitarianism.

Finally, $MU_Y^P > MU_Y^R$ if $Y_R > Y_P$ for all e except e = 0. The difference in MU_Y^P and MU_Y^R is the value that society places on making the distribution of income more equal, a value that depends on e, its aversion to inequality. With costless redistribution, marginal utilities of income and thus incomes should be equalized, at the mean income. Atkinson's utility function establishes equality as the baseline distribution, in line with Thurow's argument.

THREE APPLICATIONS OF THE ATKINSON SOCIAL WELFARE FUNCTION

As noted in the introduction, Atkinson wanted to measure the social welfare implications of income inequality from the annual household surveys. This is easily done once the common utility function has been specified. Atkinson's specific social welfare function is

$$W = \sum_{h=1}^{H} \frac{1}{(1-e)} Y_h^{(1-e)} \quad e = [0, \infty].$$

All one need do is plug in the incomes from the household surveys into the equation and compute the resulting level of social welfare for any given value of e. As incomes change, so too does the level of social welfare. Both the level and the changes in social welfare depend on society's choice of e.

We will consider three applications based on Atkinson's social welfare function.

SOCIAL WELFARE, THE LORENZ CURVE, AND THE GINI COEFFICIENT

The most common method of representing the degree of income inequality is by means of a diagram called the Lorenz curve, along with its associated Gini coefficient. Both concepts are named after the people who invented them. To graph the Lorenz curve, first order all the households in the survey from lowest income to highest income. Divide the population into equal groups, say quintiles (fifths), and compute the proportion of the total income received by each fifth of the population. The data for households in the United States in 2005 are given in Table 5.1.

TABLE 5.1 Personal distribution of income in the United States: households (2005)

Percentage of households	Bottom 20%	2nd 20%	3rd 20%	4th 20%	Top 20%
Percentage of total income	3.4	8.6	14.6	23.0	50.4

SOURCE: U.S. Census Bureau, *Current Population Survey*, March 2006, Historical Income Tables, Table H-2. The associated Gini coefficient is reported in Table H-4.

The *Lorenz curve* is a graph of the cumulative percentage of the total income against the cumulative percentage of the population. It is usually presented within a square, as in Figure 5.6. The vertical sides of the square represent the cumulative percentage of income received by the cumulative percentage of the households along the bottom of the square. The Lorenz curve must begin and end at the end points of the diagonal, since 0% of the households have 0% of the total income, and 100% of the households have 100% of the income. The diagonal within the square is the line of perfect equality. If every household had the same income, then the first 20% of the households would have 20% of the total income, the first 40% of the households would have 40% of the total income, and so forth up the diagonal. The Lorenz curve would coincide with the diagonal. The Lorenz curve lies below the diagonal if the distribution is at all unequal. The farther the curve is below the diagonal, the more unequal the distribution, which is a convenient visual representation of the degree of inequality.

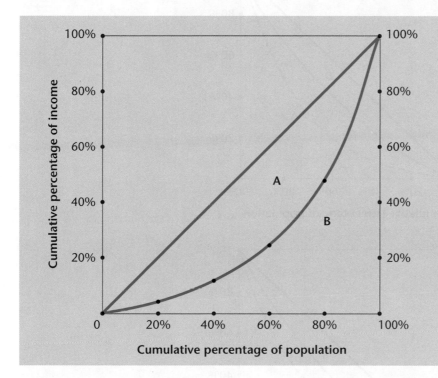

Figure 5.6

For example, the Lorenz curve in Figure 5.6 is a graph of the distribution of income from Table 5.1. The four points computed from the table are noted and a smooth line has been drawn through them to complete the curve. The distribution of income in the United States was quite unequal in 2005. The poorest 20% of the households had only 3.4% of the income, the poorest 40% had only 12.0% (= 3.4 + 8.6). Conversely, the richest 20% of the households earned more than half the total income.

The *Gini coefficient* is the ratio of the area between the Lorenz curve and the diagonal of the square to the total area under the square, or

Gini = area A/area (A + B)   Gini = [0,1]

Gini = 0 represents perfect equality. The Lorenz curve lies on the diagonal and A = 0. Gini = 1 represents perfect inequality in the sense that one household has all the income. The Lorenz curve lies along the horizontal axis until the last household is added, at which point it jumps to the top of the diagonal, so that B = 0. Between the limits of 0 and 1, the larger the Gini coefficient, the greater the inequality. The Gini coefficient for the data in Table 5.1 is .469. The Gini coefficient was .397 in 1975, an indication that the distribution of income had become much more unequal since 1975.[3]

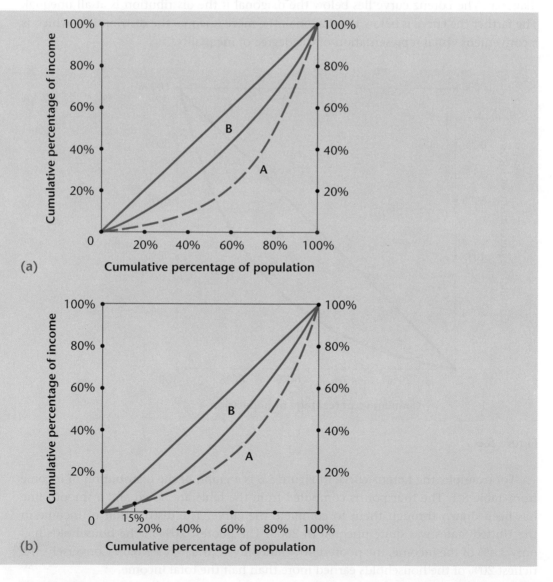

Figure 5.7

Atkinson was interested in the social welfare implications of changes in the Lorenz curve over time. Consider two distributions of income that have the same mean level of income: $Y^A = (Y_1^A, ..., Y_h^A, ..., Y_H^A)$ and $Y^B = (Y_1^B, ..., Y_h^B, ..., Y_H^B)$.[4] Atkinson (1970) proved that if the Lorenz curve for distribution Y^B lies everywhere inside the Lorenz curve for distribution Y^A, as in Figure 5.7(a), social welfare is higher for distribution Y^B under Atkinson's three assumptions for any aversion to inequality e (other than e = 0, the utilitarian indifference case). This was one of the first results linking the social welfare function to data on the distribution of income. The intuition is that the more equal distribution Y^B can be obtained from the distribution Y^A by top-down redistributions from higher income to lower income people. Given diminishing marginal utility of income, and assuming that marginal social welfare weights are never larger for higher income people than for lower income people, then the social marginal utility of income also diminishes with income. Therefore, top-down redistributions must increase social welfare because they always redistribute from those with lower SMU_Y to those with higher SMU_Y. We can say unambiguously that Y^B is the better distribution.

The problem with comparing two distributions of equal mean over time, or across countries in a given year, is that their Lorenz curves are likely cross, as in Figure 5.7(b). Now the aversion to inequality parameter e matters. According to the figure, distribution Y^A gives a higher percentage of the overall income to the bottom 15% of the population, and distribution Y^B gives the higher percentage to the top 85% of the population. A high aversion to inequality closer to the Rawlsian end of the spectrum might well judge Y^A to have the higher social welfare since it gives higher weight to low incomes. Conversely, a low aversion to inequality closer to the utilitarian end of the spectrum might favor distribution Y^B. In any event, all one need do is plug the individual incomes from each distribution into Atkinson's social welfare function to determine which has the higher social welfare. The difficulty is that the answers can change for different values of e, and society may not have reached a clear-cut decision on what its aversion to inequality is. If not, then one cannot be sure which is the better distribution.

◼ THE SOCIAL COST OF INEQUALITY AND THE EQUALLY DISTRIBUTED EQUIVALENT INCOME

Given that society values equality, one would like to have a sense of the social cost of inequality. Another innovation by Atkinson was to develop the first income measure of the social cost of inequality, similar to the income measures of inefficiency that had long been in existence and that we will meet in Chapter 15. Consider again distribution Y^A above, and assume that plugging the individual incomes Y_h^A into Atkinson's social welfare function yields a value of social welfare equal to W^A. Ask what level of income, if given equally to everyone, would yield the same level of social welfare W^A. Atkinson called this the *equally distributed equivalent income*, Y_{ede}. Since Y_{ede} is given equally to all H people, it is the solution to the equation

$$W^A = H \frac{1}{(1-e)} Y_{ede}^{(1-e)}.$$

Compute the ratio of Y_{ede} to the mean level of income Y_M^A, and suppose it is 0.7. Then society could have the same level of social welfare with only 70% of the total income if everyone had the same level of income. Therefore, the cost of the existing inequality is 30% of total income.

Notice that Y_{ede} depends on e, the aversion to inequality. Y_{ede} is always less than Y_M unless: (1) everyone has the same level of income – there is no inequality; or (2) e = 0, society is indifferent to inequality. There is clearly no cost to inequality in either case.[5]

Atkinson was also the first economist to develop a Gini-style index of inequality that incorporated the aversion to inequality. His index is

$$I(e) = 1 - \frac{Y_{ede}}{Y_M} \quad I(e) = [0,1]$$

for any distribution of income such as Y^A. $I(e)$ depends on e because Y_{ede} depends on e. $I(e)$ is zero if there is no inequality or if society is indifferent to inequality. The index increases as inequality increases or e increases because either causes the Y_{ede} to decrease. It reaches one in the limit if one person has all the income or the aversion to inequality is infinite (Rawlsian). Atkinson's index of inequality has spawned a large number of inequality indexes that depend on the aversion to inequality. Note that the original Gini coefficient is independent of e. It is purely a measure of inequality with no link to social welfare.

DOES THE UNITED STATES CARE MUCH ABOUT INEQUALITY?

One of the earliest applications of Atkinson's social welfare analysis is due to Arnold Harberger and it will serve as our final example. Writing in the 1970s, Harberger (1983, pp. 107–10) used the Atkinson framework to suggest that the United States does not care much about inequality. In the 1970s, the average income of the people in the top quintile of the U.S. income distribution was nine times the average income of the people in the bottom quintile. Let the top quintile represent Y_R above and the bottom quintile represent Y_P. Therefore $\left(\frac{Y_R}{Y_P}\right) = \frac{9}{1}$. Under Atkinson's framework, $\left(\frac{Y_R}{Y_P}\right)^e = \frac{MU_Y^P}{MU_Y^R}$.

Suppose, said Harberger, that the aversion to inequality in the United States is only 0.5, very close to the utilitarian indifference end of the spectrum. If so, then $\left(\frac{Y_R}{Y_P}\right)^{\frac{1}{2}} = \left(\frac{9}{1}\right)^{\frac{1}{2}}$

$= 3 = \frac{MU_Y^P}{MU_Y^R}$. The United States has stopped redistributing income even though MU_Y^P is three times MU_Y^R. This suggests that the leaks in Okun's bucket are huge, because society is assuming that for every dollar taken from the rich, only 33 cents arrive to support the poor. Fully two-thirds of each dollar transferred is lost to the combined inefficiencies of deadweight loss, administrative costs, and compliance costs. Harberger believed that the inefficiencies of taxing and transferring were much less than 67 cents on the dollar, which led him to conclude that the aversion to inequality in the United States was even less than 0.5, very close to utilitarian indifference. The United States does not care much about inequality.

Whether Harberger's conclusion is correct is difficult to say. At the time that Harberger developed his example, the conventional wisdom among public sector economists was that the efficiency costs of taxing and transferring were quite low, well below 67 cents per dollar. Most of the efficiency cost analysis at the time was on the tax side, and the tax most often studied was the federal personal income tax. The administrative costs of the income tax were known to be less than 0.5% of tax revenues, no one gave a thought to compliance costs, and the accepted deadweight loss of the personal income tax was in the order of 7% of tax revenues. Efficiency costs of 67 cents per dollar would have seemed absurdly high, as they did to Harberger.

Things have changed considerably since the 1970s, however, again mostly on the tax side. The administrative costs of collecting income tax revenues are still assumed to be negligible, but subsequent analysis of the compliance costs of the personal income tax suggests that they may be as high as 10% of revenues collected. Estimates of the deadweight loss from the personal income tax are now all over the map, but there has been a decided upward drift since the 1970s. The consensus estimate is now in the range of 30–40% of tax revenues. These newer estimates suggest that 67 cents on the dollar may not be too far from the true value of the efficiency costs, which would raise the Harberger view of e in the United States. At the same time, the distribution of income has become much more unequal. The ratio of the mean incomes in the top and bottom quintiles now exceeds 14/1, which would lower the Harberger view of e in the United States. One can hazard a guess that Harberger had it about right, that the United States does not care very much about overall inequality. Whatever the truth may be, Harberger's analysis is yet another indication of how useful the Atkinson framework can be for thinking about issues of inequality.

SOCIAL MOBILITY AND SOCIAL WELFARE

Social mobility, the ability of people to move through the distribution of income over time, is a process-equity concept, whereas the social welfare function is concerned with end-results equity. Yet it would be remiss to end a chapter on applications of the social welfare function without paying some attention to social mobility, because the degree of social mobility in a nation can have a profound effect on the government's ability to redistribute income.

Economists describe the pattern of social mobility by means of a transition probability matrix. Suppose people are divided into one of five income classes or quintiles, as in the data in Table 5.1. Then the transition probability matrix, P, would be a 5 × 5 matrix

$$P = t \begin{bmatrix} t+1 \\ p_{ij} \end{bmatrix}$$

whose 25 elements p_{ij} give the probability that a person who is in income class i at time t will be in income class j at time t + 1. For example, p_{14} is the probability that a person who is in the bottom income class 1 at time t will be in the next-to-the-highest income class 4 at time t + 1, and so forth. The time periods t and t + 1 would likely be 5–10 years apart at a minimum, to give people enough time to move through the distribution.

The limits on the transition probability matrix are:

1. A caste system, in which people are born into a particular income class and are not allowed to move to any other income class. In this case, the diagonal elements of P are all equal to 1 (p_{ii} = 1) and the off-diagonal elements are all equal to zero (p_{ij} = 0, i ≠ j).
2. Complete mobility, in which everyone has an equal chance of being in any one income class at time t + 1 regardless of what income class they are in at time t. With five income classes, all the elements of P equal .2, or 20% (p_{ij} = .2). Actual transition probability matrices are somewhere between these two extremes.

Economists do not know what determines the particular transition probability matrix that any nation has. It is the result of a huge number of factors – economic, social, cultural, religious, and political. What is the distribution of wages for different kinds of jobs? Are women discriminated against in taking certain jobs? Are marriages fairly random across abilities and education levels, or do men and women tend to sort themselves when marrying by ability and education? Are the income tax rates on some people so high that they stifle the incentive to work hard? The answers to questions such as these affect the degree of social mobility within a nation.

Whatever determines a nation's transition probability matrix, its effect on social welfare can be monumental. To see why, suppose the elements of the matrix have the following three properties:

1. All p_{ij} > 0. This says that starting from any income class in time t, there is some probability that a person will be in any of the five income classes in t + 1. Movement between any two income classes is never blocked, even top to bottom. There is, for example, some probability that a person in the lowest income class will move in one period to the highest income class and, unfortunately, vice versa.
2. The p_{ij} are a complete description of the movement of people through the income classes over time. That is, the probability of a person being in income class j at time t + 1 depends only on which income class he is in at time t. All previous history is irrelevant, such as what income class the person was in at time t – 1.
3. The p_{ij} are constant over time.

Under these three properties, the transition probability matrix P eventually brings the economy to the same distribution of income *no matter what the initial distribution of income happens to be*. The intuition is as follows. Suppose everyone starts in the middle of the distribution, income class 3. This could be because the government can tax and transfer income lump sum and therefore follows the prescription of leveling everyone to the mean income, under Atkinson's three assumptions in applying the social welfare function. In any event, by time period t + 1 the distribution will no longer be equal. The people will have distributed themselves into all five income classes, according to the elements of the transition probability matrix p_{31}, p_{32}, p_{33}, p_{34}, and p_{35}. By time period t + 2 they will have spread themselves even more, according to the elements p_{ij} that apply to the income class each person happens to be in at time t + 1. Time period t + 3 leads to still more spreading throughout the distribution, and so on, into the future. After enough time periods pass, it clearly does not matter that the distribution started off entirely equal, or at any other distribution for that matter. The matrix P homes in on a particular distribution as time marches on.

An important implication of this result is that the underlying social mobility in the economy is always trying to undo whatever redistributional policies the government has undertaken. If the government wants to maintain a particular distribution, it may have to continually redistribute to offset the march of the transition probabilities over time. In this sense there is a trade-off between end-results equity and social mobility. A higher degree of social mobility is desirable in and of itself in terms of process equity, but at the same time higher social mobility causes the government's redistributional policies to unravel more quickly.[6] In terms of end-results equity, society would prefer a lower degree of social mobility.

This rather dramatic implication can only be suggestive because the three assumptions on the p_{ij} are very strong. For example, if the government did level everyone to the mean income, then the p_{ij} would almost certainly change because of the effects of that policy on work and saving incentives. Redistributions are not lump sum. Still, society's preferred redistributional policies do have to contend with an underlying pattern of social mobility that is not well understood and may be difficult to change even if it were well understood. For instance, if marriage patterns turned out to be important to social mobility, would society be willing to enforce a different pattern of marriages – say, random marriages – in the name of promoting distributive justice? This would be difficult to imagine in the United States.

Externalities: Theoretical Issues

Chapter 6 begins the discussion of the various allocation problems that cause difficulties for a market economy. Allocation problems are efficiency issues. Recall from Chapter 2 that they arise because the technical and market assumptions required for a well-functioning market economy are too strong. When one or more of the assumptions fails to hold, the essence of the economic problem for society is always the same: The market economy is driven below its utility possibilities frontier, and government intervention is almost always required to bring the economy back to the frontier. The market cannot be expected to restore efficiency on its own.[1]

One of the technical assumptions is that there are no externalities associated with market transactions. Broadly speaking, externalities are third-party effects. In the standard market transaction, the consumers and firms directly engaged in the transaction receive all the benefits or bear all the costs associated with the transaction. Occasionally, though, third parties receive some benefits or bear some costs even though they are not part of the transaction. The inefficiency arises in a market economy because the direct transactors have no incentive to consider the third parties' benefits or costs. The government has to intervene to ensure that the full benefits and costs of the market transaction are accounted for, which is a fundamental requirement for achieving an efficient allocation of society's scarce resources.

Externalities are fairly common, so much so that by themselves they could justify a broad scope for government intervention in a market economy. Therefore, one practical question that all capitalist societies have to address is how extensive and important must the externalities be in a particular market to justify government intervention in that market. There is no easy answer to this question.

PRELIMINARIES: THE TERMINOLOGY OF EXTERNALITIES

Externalities take so many forms that some preliminary discussion of their characteristics is in order before analyzing their effects. Here are four of the more important characteristics for policy purposes.

Pecuniary versus technological externalities – A good place to start is to realize that some kinds of third-party effects require government intervention and some do not. Consider the following examples:

1. With gas prices above $3.00 a gallon, you decide that you want to buy a small, fuel-efficient car. Unfortunately, so do millions of other people, with the result that the average price of a small car rises by a few hundred dollars. The other people's decisions to buy a small car cause you harm because they increase the price of the car you want to buy.

2. Factories in the industrial Midwest spew pollutants from their smokestacks that damage the paint on houses and cars and cause respiratory and other health problems. The pollutants may also harm other businesses, such as commercial fishing in lakes whose fish populations have been affected by acid rain. The damage from the pollutants affects people and firms independently of whether they choose to purchase the products that these factories produce.

Your intuition tells you, correctly, that the first kind of externality is not a problem at all for a market economy. It represents nothing more than supply and demand at work. The increased demand for small cars drives up the prices of these cars. The higher price is the signal to automobile producers to produce more of the small cars that consumers want. And the producers do respond, because small cars are now more profitable at the higher price. Prices and profits are the signals that a market economy uses to make producers responsive to the desires of consumers. Economists call these kinds of third-party effects *pecuniary externalities*, meaning that they operate entirely through the prices that consumers and producers face. As such, they affect consumers' budget constraints and firms' profits, but nothing more. Pecuniary externalities do not require government intervention.

The same is not true for the second example, however. The pollution damage differs from the small car externality in two respects. First, the pollution directly affects consumers and firms in the sense that it enters or alters their utility functions and production functions. The damaged houses and cars reduce the amount of utility that consumers receive from these goods, and the utility that consumers receive generally from all their purchases diminishes if they suffer respiratory diseases and other forms of ill health. Commercial fishing firms need more resources to catch the same amount of fish when the fish population declines, a direct change in their production functions. Second, neither the factories nor their customers have any incentive to take the pollution damage into account. Economists call externalities with these two characteristics *technological exter-*

nalities: They directly affect consumers and producers and they are not accounted for by the market system. The second characteristic is essentially redundant since technological externalities are almost never accounted for in the market system. From now on we will mean technological externalities whenever we refer to externalities, since they are the only externalities that require government intervention to achieve efficiency.

Economies and diseconomies – Technological externalities can be beneficial or harmful. Economists refer to beneficial externalities as *external economies*, and to harmful externalities as *external diseconomies*. Examples of external economies include: primary and secondary education (each person in a democracy benefits when any other citizen receives a basic general education because then people's votes are likely to be better informed. This is why the United States mandated a minimum level of public or private education for all citizens in the 1800s); the purchase of computers (the value of email service to any one person depends on how many other people have computers and can send and receive emails. This type of externality is called a "network effect." It applied equally to the telephone in the early 20th century); research and development (new products or methods of producing existing products are ideas that can be used by anyone once they are discovered by one firm's R&D team. This is why inventions are protected by patents to preserve the incentive to invent); and vaccinations (vaccination against a contagious or infectious disease lessens the chances of those who are not vaccinated of contracting the disease once a substantial percentage of the population has been vaccinated).

The most common examples of external diseconomies are the various kinds of pollution, one example of which we described earlier. Other important examples are congestion on highways (all drivers on a congested highway are affected when one more car enters the highway); and airport noise (people living near airports get less enjoyment out of their homes). We will use industrial air and water pollution as our primary example to analyze externalities in this chapter and Chapter 7. Fortunately, the principles that apply to pollution also apply with only minor and obvious modifications to all other external diseconomies and economies.

Consumer and producer externalities – Externalities can arise from both consumption and production activities, and economists tag the externalities as consumer or producer externalities depending on their source. Examples of consumer externalities include the congestion and smog that result when people drive on urban highways, as well as the examples of a general education, the purchase of computers, and vaccinations noted above. Industrial air and water pollution and research and development are examples of producer externalities. Furthermore, consumer and producer externalities can each affect either other consumers or other producers, or both. As noted above, industrial air and water pollution is likely to affect consumers generally and certain other producers such as commercial fisheries. The smog that results from congested urban highways is more likely to affect other consumers than producers, but the congestion itself affects both consumers and producers.

Aggregate versus individualized externalities – A final important distinction to keep in mind when analyzing externalities is the difference between an aggregate and an individualized externality. In an *aggregate externality*, the identity of the individual sources of the externality does not matter. Only the aggregate or combined activity of the sources matters to those affected by the externality. In an *individualized externality*, the identity of the individual sources does matter to those affected by the externality. The distinction is best illustrated by an example. We will select one that we will use throughout the chapter – industrial air pollution.

The prevailing winds in the United States flow from west to east. As a result, most of the damage from a factory sending pollutants into the air occurs to households and individuals living to the east of the factory. (This explains in large part why the western suburbs of U.S. cities usually have higher incomes than the eastern suburbs. The western suburbs are the more desirable because they receive much less pollution from the manufacturing plants in the cities, so that is where those with higher incomes choose to live.) Assume for the sake of illustration that *all* the damage from pollution occurs to people living east of a factory.

Consider two scenarios, illustrated by Figure 6.1. In Figure 6.1(a), there are four factories emitting pollutants, F1, F2, F3, and F4, and they all lie to the west of the population, P, that is harmed by the pollutants. In Figure 6.1(b), the four factories and the population groups affected by the pollutants are partially intermingled. Factories F1 and F2 lie to the west of both population groups P1 and P2. Factory F3 lies to the east of population group P1 and to the west of population group P2. Factory F4 lies to the east of both population groups P1 and P2, and we will assume that those who live to the east of F4 are so far away that they are unaffected by the pollution from any of the factories.

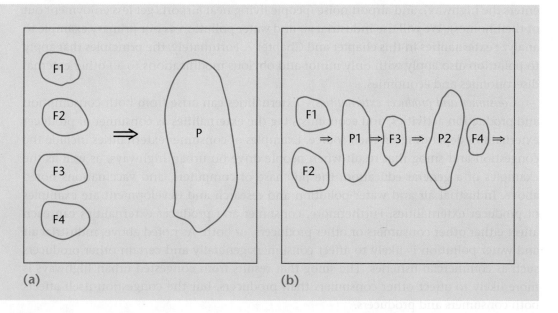

(a)   (b)

Figure 6.1

In the first scenario, the damage to the population P of the pollution emitted by the four factories can be assumed to depend on the aggregate amount of pollution emitted by the four factories combined. The identity of the factory emitting the pollution does not matter to anyone in the population. This is an example of an aggregate externality. In the second scenario, the identity of the factories matters. The pollutants from factories F1 and F2 harm both population groups P1 and P2, whereas the pollutants from factory F3 harm only those in population group P2, and the pollutants from factory F4 harm no one. The people affected by the pollution care very much indeed which factory is emitting the pollutant.

This distinction between aggregate and individualized externalities matters because the aggregate case is much easier for the government to try to correct than is the individualized case. The policy needed for an efficient solution to an aggregate externality is simple and straightforward, enough so that the government often has a reasonable chance of greatly improving upon the uncorrected market outcome. In contrast, the policies needed to provide an efficient solution to an individualized externality are often so complex as to be impracticable. The government is unlikely to be able even to approximate the efficient solution.

Fortunately, many important externalities are of the aggregate kind. For example, the identities of the drivers on congested urban highways do not matter. The congestion and smog depend only on the total number of drivers on the highways at any one time. The same is true of network externalities and vaccinations. The total number of people in the network or being vaccinated is what matters, not who these people happen to be. The same is often not true for industrial air and water pollution, however. Industrial pollutants come from factories located at specific sites, and their location often matters. Nonetheless, we will begin our analysis of pollution with the aggregate case described in Figure 6.1(a), since it is the easier of the two cases and it also happens to be broadly applicable to many forms of externalities.

AGGREGATE EXTERNALITIES

The cleanest way to analyze a particular externality, or any other efficiency problem, is to assume that it is the only problem in the otherwise well-functioning economy described in Chapter 2. This allows us to focus on the nature of the inefficiency arising from the externality and its solution without adding such potential complications as having a number of efficiency problems simultaneously or taking into consideration practical and political limitations on government policy responses. These are best added later after the nature of externalities is fully understood. Beginning in this way also implies that the government can return the economy to its utility possibilities frontier if it can provide an efficient solution to the externality.

One of the requirements of a well-functioning economy is that the markets for goods and services are perfectly competitive. Therefore, to allow for a large number of suppliers, we will adopt a variation of the scenario in Figure 6.1(a) and assume that a large number of factories are located next to each other in some industrial zone and are all producing the same product. The product could be anything – steel, electricity, paper – assume paper. The market for paper is perfectly competitive and these factories comprise the total number of factories producing the paper. No people live between the factories, so that all people affected by the air pollutants from the factories live to the east of the factories as in Figure 6.1(a). The pollution any one person suffers depends on the total pollution from all the factories combined, an aggregate externality. Finally, to keep our first example as simple as possible, assume that the amount of pollution emitted from a factory varies in direct proportion to the amount of output produced by the factory. Therefore, units of output can be thought of as equivalent to units of pollution. (We will relax this assumption later on in the chapter.)

THE SOCIAL OPTIMUM

The market for paper, including the pollution damage that it causes, is depicted in Figure 6.2. The market demand curve D is the sum of the demand curves of all buyers of paper. At each output Q, D represents the marginal value (MV) of paper, the value to each consumer of the last unit of paper purchased. The market supply curve S^{priv} is the sum of the supply curves of all the paper factories. At each output Q, S^{priv} represents the private marginal cost (MC^{priv}) at each factory, the cost of the last unit of paper supplied to the market. The private marginal cost reflects the standard production costs of producing paper arising from the firms' purchase of factors of production, such as labor, materials, and capital equipment. Left to its own devices, the market for paper would reach a competitive equilibrium (Q_c, P_c) at the intersection of D and S^{priv}. The equilibrium price P_c equates the marginal value of consuming paper with the private marginal cost of producing paper in the usual manner.[2]

The usual competitive allocation is not the right allocation in the presence of externalities, however. The problem is that S^{priv} misses the damages to consumers of the pollutants that are the byproduct of producing paper. The appropriate supply curve from society's perspective is S^{soc}, which includes at each output Q the full social marginal cost (MC^{soc}) of producing paper. MC^{soc} adds to the private marginal cost at each Q the aggregate marginal damages (MD) from the pollutants suffered by all the people affected by the pollutants.

Figure 6.3 shows how the aggregate marginal damages are constructed on the assumption that only two people are affected by the pollution. Figure 6.3(a) shows the marginal damages suffered by the first person at each unit of paper production, MD_1, and Figure 6.3(b) shows the marginal damages suffered by the second person, MD_2. MD_1 and MD_2 could be quite different depending on where the two people live. The aggregate marginal damages at each unit of output, shown in Figure 6.3(c), are the vertical summation of MD_1 and MD_2 at each output, $MD_1 + MD_2$. In general, the aggregate marginal damage at each output is $\sum_{h=1}^{H} MD_h$, where h = 1,..., H are all the people affected by the pollution.

Therefore, $S^{soc} = MC^{soc} = MC^{priv} + \sum_{h=1}^{H} MD_h$. The difference between S^{priv} and S^{soc} could be

quite substantial if large numbers of people are affected by the pollution, as is often the case with industrial pollution.

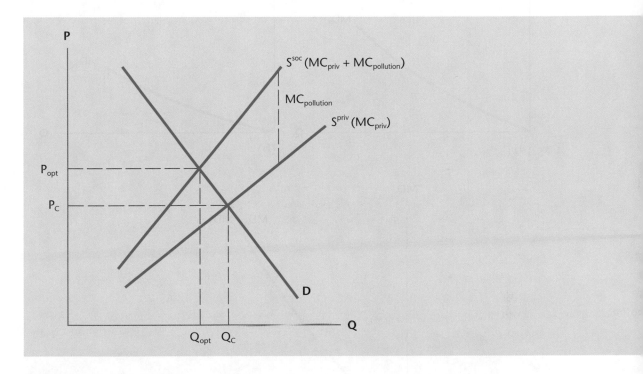

Figure 6.2

The optimal quantity and price in the market for paper is (Q_{opt}, P_{opt}) in Figure 6.2, at the intersection of D and S^{soc}. Q_{opt} is the output at which the marginal value of paper to consumers is equal to the full marginal cost of producing the paper, as required for Pareto optimality. Because of the pollution externality, the market for paper requires a higher price and a lower output than the standard competitive outcome for the economy to be on its utility possibilities frontier. Any output of paper beyond Q_{opt} has less value to consumers than the full social cost of producing it. Therefore, the resources saved by producing less paper are better used in the production of other nonpolluting goods, and the higher prices of paper induce consumers to redirect their expenditures towards the nonpolluting goods. The same general principle applies to all polluting goods.

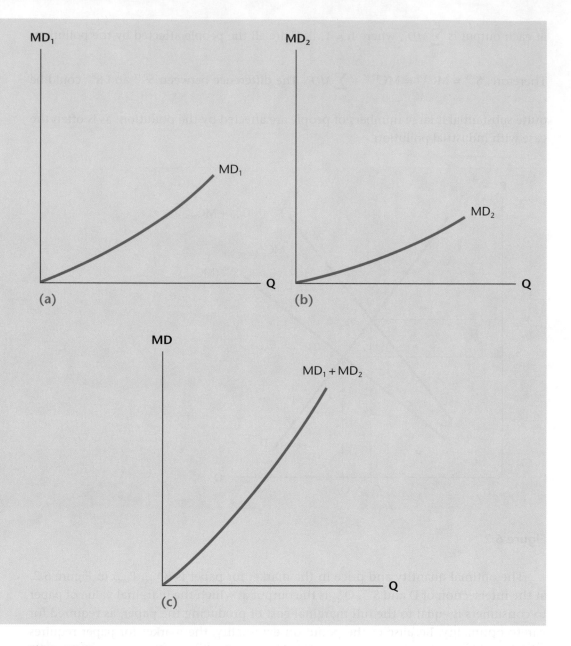

Figure 6.3

THE PIGOVIAN TAX

The question is how to reach the social optimum (Q_{opt}, P_{opt}) and the answer turns out to be quite simple, at least in principle. All the government need do is levy a per-unit tax on the producers of paper and let the market for paper continue to operate. Figure 6.4 illustrates. A per-unit tax t increases each firm's private marginal costs by the amount of the tax because the firms must now send t dollars to the government for each additional unit that they produce. Therefore the tax shifts S^{priv} up parallel by t at every Q, so that S_t^{priv} becomes the relevant market supply curve. The new market equilibrium occurs at the intersection of D and S_t^{priv}. If, as pictured, the tax t equals the sum of the marginal damages at Q_{opt}, the vertical distance between S^{soc} and S^{priv} at Q_{opt}, then the equilibrium is (O_{opt}, P_{opt}) as required for efficiency. After paying the tax, the firms have only P_N left per unit to cover their production costs, which is why they reduce their market supply to Q_{opt} along S^{priv}.

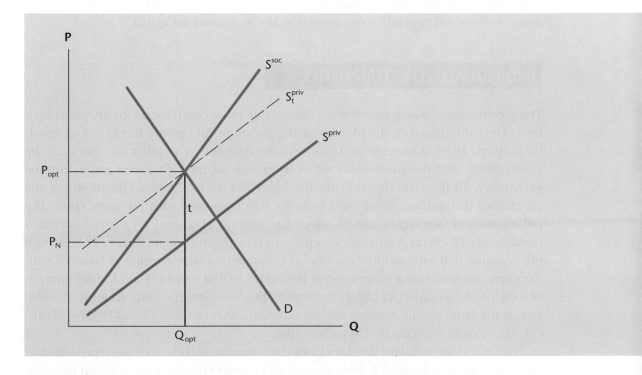

Figure 6.4

One might well ask whether a single tax is appropriate for all firms. At the original competitive equilibrium, each firm is supplying the output at which P_c equals its own MC^{priv}. If individual firms' marginal costs (supply curves) differ, then they are supplying different amounts of paper to the market and are therefore contributing more or less to the overall level of pollution. Should not a tax reflect each firm's contribution to the pollution? The answer is "no"; a single tax is appropriate. The reason is that it is each firm's *marginal* contribution to the pollution, not its total contribution, that matters. Each firm may supply different amounts of paper to the market, but the next unit of paper (pollution) has the same aggregate marginal impact on the people affected by the pollution, no matter which firm supplies it. Thus each firm should face the same tax, equal to the aggregate marginal damage at the optimum.

A tax equal to the aggregate marginal damages at the optimum is called a *Pigovian tax* after the economist A.C. Pigou, who first proposed the tax. There is nothing special about our paper example in the design of this tax. A Pigovian tax is the optimal policy prescription for any aggregate external diseconomy. Conversely, a Pigovian subsidy equal to the aggregate marginal benefits at the optimum is the optimal policy prescription for any aggregate external economy. An example might be an educational subsidy to children in a democratic country without a public education system. The subsidy accounts for the external benefit to all citizens of ensuring that each citizen has a certain minimum level of education so that they can make informed decisions when voting. (A single subsidy is appropriate if the external advantages of having a minimum level of education in a democracy do not depend on the abilities of the individual students.)

INDIVIDUALIZED EXTERNALITIES

The government's policy response is considerably more complicated for an individualized externality in which the identity of the person or firm giving rise to the externality matters. The proper response to an external diseconomy is still a tax, but now the government must design an entire set of taxes, one tax for each source generating the externality. To illustrate the individualized case, return to Figure 6.1(b) in which the geographic distribution of polluting factories is intermingled with the population. The pollution from factories F1 and F2 affects the entire population P1 + P2; the pollution from factory F3 affects population group P2; and the pollution from factory F4 affects no one. Assume that each factory type F1,…, F4 represents a large number of factories with the same cost structure and emission of pollutions so that we can retain the assumption of a competitive market for paper, and that all factories emit the same amount of pollution at the same output. Assume, also for simplicity, that factories F1 and F2 have identical private costs of production at each output.

The marginal pollution damages from the output of each factory are represented in the three panels of Figure 6.5. Even though all factories emit the same amount of pollution at each output of paper produced, the marginal damages at each output are highest for F1 and F2 in Figure 6.5(a) because their pollution affects the entire population. Their aggregate marginal damages curve from either F1 or F2, $MD_{1,2}$, is the vertical sum of the marginal damages to each member of the population at each total output of paper, q_1 + q_2, from these two factories. The aggregate marginal damages curve from F3, MD_3 in Figure 6.5(b), is the vertical sum of the marginal damages to each member of population group P2 at each output of paper from F3. The aggregate marginal damages curve from F4, MD_4 in Figure 6.5(c), is zero at each output of paper from F4 because that factory's pollution affects no one.

The four panels of Figure 6.6 depict the optimal tax policy along with the optimal price and quantity of paper. In the case of an individualized externality, social supply curves have to be defined separately for each polluting firm. Refer first to Figure 6.6(a). The private supply curve for factories F1 and F2 is $s_{1,2}^{priv}$, representing the private marginal cost of producing paper at each output in these factories. The social supply curve $s_{1,2}^{soc}$ is obtained by adding the marginal damage curve $MD_{1,2}$ from Figure 6.5(a) vertically to $s_{1,2}^{priv}$ at each output. It represents the full marginal cost of producing paper in factories F1 and F2. In Figure 6.6(b), the social supply curve s_3^{soc} is obtained by adding the marginal damage curve MD_3 from Figure 6.5(b) vertically to s_3^{priv} at each output. It represents the full marginal cost of producing paper in factory F3. In Figure 6.6(c), the social supply curve s_4^{soc} is the same as s_4^{priv} since the pollution from factory F4 affects no one. The full marginal cost of producing paper in F4 is just the private marginal cost of the paper.

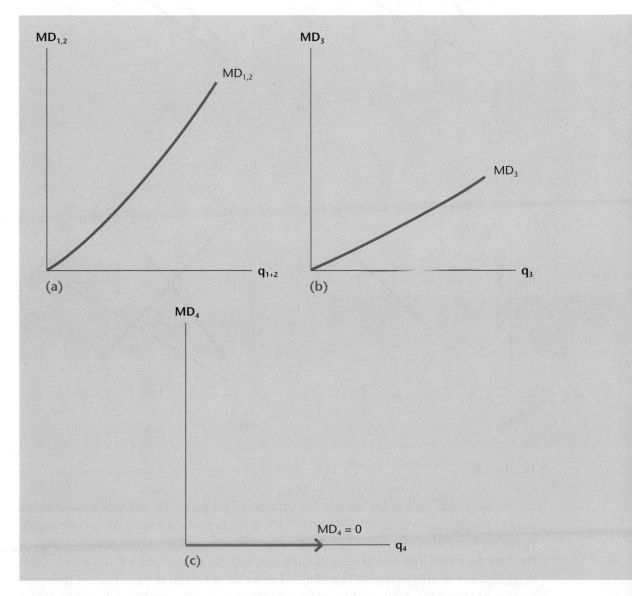

Figure 6.5

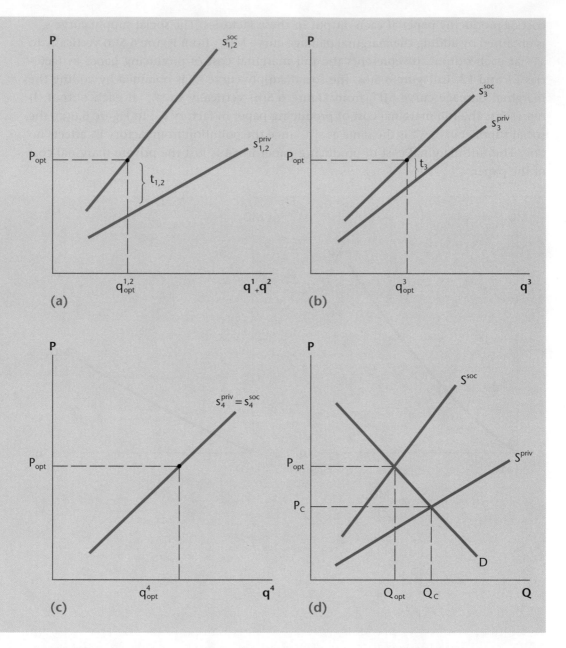

Figure 6.6

Figure 6.6(d) depicts the market demand curve for paper, D, and private and social market supply curves for paper, S^{priv} and S^{soc}. S^{priv} is the horizontal sum of the private supply curves of the four factories and S^{soc} is the horizontal sum of the social supply curves of the four factories. The competitive equilibrium without accounting for the externalities is (Q_c, P_c), at the intersection of D and S^{priv}. The social optimum is (Q_{opt}, P_{opt}), at the intersection of D and S^{soc}. Factories F1 and F2 contribute $q_{opt}^{1,2}$ to Q_{opt} as shown in Figure 6.6(a).

This output is achieved by levying a tax, $t_{1,2}$ on F1 and F2, equal to the aggregate marginal external damages caused by the pollution of F1 and F2 at $q_{opt}^{1,2}$. Factory F3 contributes q_{opt}^3 to Q_{opt} as shown in Figure 6.6(b). This output is achieved by levying a tax, t_3 on F3, equal to the aggregate marginal external damages caused by the pollution of F3 at q_{opt}^3. Factory F4 contributes q_{opt}^4 to Q_{opt} and pays no tax, as shown in Figure 6.6(c). It receives the full price P_{opt} and simply produces along its private marginal cost curve.

Notice that the individual taxes have the effect of reducing output at each factory in proportion to the marginal external damage caused by their pollution. The biggest reduction (highest tax) occurs at F1 and F2 and the least reduction at F4. Also, the taxes remain Pigovian in design, in the sense that they equal the aggregate marginal external damage caused by each factory. But there is no tax on paper production at the market level as in the case of the aggregate externality, which is the case Pigou had in mind with his single-tax policy.

Needless to say, designing the appropriate set of taxes for individualized externalities is likely to be a daunting task if there are a large number of sources of industrial pollution. Unfortunately, industrial air pollution is almost certainly an example of an individualized externality because the pollutants from any two sources are likely to affect different groups of people even if the emissions are the same at each source, as in our examples. For instance, a factory emitting air pollutants is likely to cause much more external damage if it is located to the west of a major U.S. city than if it is located in the northern woods of Maine somewhere near the coast. We will return to this point in Chapter 7 when we discuss U.S. antipollution policy.

TAX POLLUTION AT ITS SOURCE

We assumed in the previous examples that the amount of pollution emitted by the paper factories varies in direct proportion to the output produced at the factory. We did so to illustrate as simply as possible a number of fundamental principles associated with externalities, such as how taxes should be designed to properly account for externalities. But pollution-proportional-to-output happens to be a terrible assumption. Firms can often produce their output in many different ways, choosing from a variety of production technologies that require different kinds and combinations of factors of production. In fact, similar products are produced quite differently in different countries, reflecting the relative scarcities of various factors of production. For example, production in India tends to favor labor-intensive techniques and production in the United States tends to favor capital-intensive techniques, reflecting the relative abundance of labor (lower wages) in India and the relative abundance of capital (lower cost of capital) in the United States. What is true of capital and labor holds as well for the use of air and water to dispose of industrial waste products. Firms could instead use capital and labor to dispose of their waste products by collecting them in containers and shipping them to sites where they would do no harm. In truth, the amount of pollution emitted by a factory does not necessarily have to vary in direct proportion to the output produced in the factory, and an effective antipollution policy must take this into consideration.

An important principle that our previous examples miss is that a Pigovian-style tax for air and water pollution should be levied as closely as possible to the source of the pollution. If a particular pollutant discharged into the air or water is causing the external damage, then monitor and tax the amount of that pollutant discharged. If the problem is simply the use of water or air as disposals for industrial wastes, then tax the use of water or air. The goal is to induce firms to produce their output in a less polluting manner and this can only be achieved by taxing the source of the pollution directly.

Economists view industrial water and air pollution as a direct consequence of firms' desires to maximize profit. Part of the requirement for maximizing profit is that a firm hires its inputs efficiently so that it achieves the output–total cost combinations on its total cost curve. Recall that the quantity–cost combinations on the textbook total cost curve are the best combinations the firm can hope to achieve. Refer to Figure 6.7, which pictures a firm's long-run total cost curve. The combination (q_1, TC_1) can be interpreted in one of two ways: (a) if the firm spends TC_1 on its factors of production, then output q_1 is the *maximum* possible output the firm can produce; or (b) if the firm produces output q_1, then TC_1 is the *minimum* possible total cost of producing that output. Quantity–price combinations above and to the left of TC are possible but inefficient, and points below and to the right of TC are unattainable, given existing factor prices and technology. The TC curve is thus an efficiency frontier for the firm, the result of the firm efficiently solving its input or how problem.

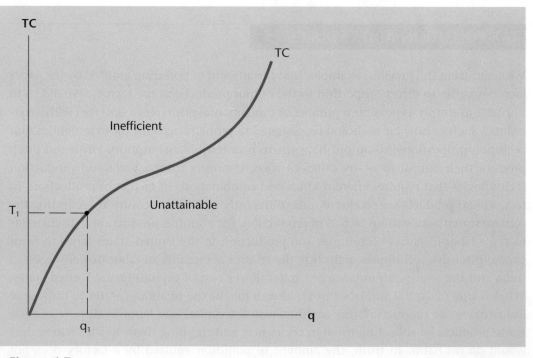

Figure 6.7

Recall, also, that the principles for efficiently using factors of production to be on the total cost curve are very simple. All the firm needs to do is compute the ratio of the marginal product (MP_f) to the price (P_f) of each factor that it uses or might consider using, $\dfrac{MP_f}{P_f}$. The ratio gives the extra output per dollar from using one more unit of the factor.[3] Then apply the following two principles:

1. Equalize $\dfrac{MP_f}{P_f}$ across all the factors of production. The firm is on its total cost curve when the extra output per dollar is equal across all factors.
2. If the ratios between any two factors are unequal, substitute in favor of the factor with the higher ratio (higher output per dollar on the margin) until the ratios are equal. By substituting in this way, the firm can obtain more output without any additional cost. If the ratios never equalize, then do not use the factor with the lower ratio. It is too costly, given its productivity to the firm.

Now apply these principles to a firm that can use water or air as a convenient disposal for its industrial wastes. As such, the water or air becomes one of the factors of production that the firm takes into consideration when trying to reach its total cost curve. Think of one of our paper factories producing its output (q) using capital (K), labor (L), and air (A), according to the production function $q = q(K, L, A)$.[4] Efficient production requires that the firm use capital, labor, and air such that

$$\frac{MP_K}{P_K} = \frac{MP_L}{P_L} = \frac{MP_A}{P_A}.$$

The essence of the industrial pollution problem for a capitalist economy is that air is a common use resource. No one owns the air, so there is no market for air and therefore no price for air that reflects the value society places on clean air. P_A is zero to any firm that wants to use it to dispose of its waste products. Place a value of zero in the denominator of $\dfrac{MP_A}{P_A}$ and the ratio becomes large without limit:

$$\frac{MP_K}{P_K} = \frac{MP_L}{P_L} < \frac{MP_A}{P_A = 0} \to \infty.$$

The extra output per dollar from using air always exceeds the extra output per dollar from using capital or labor for disposing of wastes or anything else the firm might use air for. The cost-minimizing/profit-maximizing incentive is to substitute away from capital and labor in favor of using air. The firm would want to drive the MP_A down to zero if it could, exploiting its free resource until it literally has no further use for it. The ratio 0/0 is undefined, but it is the best the firm can do to minimize its production costs. In this sense, the profit motive of the firms, combined with the common use resource feature of air, is a recipe for maximizing industrial pollution.

This example is a specific instance of another important principle of economics, that a quantity complaint – there is too much pollution – is most often a symptom of a pricing problem – P_A is zero. The implication of the principle is that the best way to respond to the quantity complaint is to solve the pricing problem. Responding to a quantity complaint with a quantity solution is not the way to proceed. Industrial air pollution is a good example.

The best way to respond to air pollution by the paper factories is to place a tax, t_A, on the use of air that reflects the value of clean air to society. Suppose the owners of the factory have driven $MP_A = 0$ before the levying of the tax. With the tax imposed, the value of $\dfrac{MP_A}{P_A}$ goes from $0/0$ to zero, so that the ratio is now less than $\dfrac{MP_K}{P_K}$ or $\dfrac{MP_L}{P_L}$:

$$\frac{MP_K}{P_K} = \frac{MP_L}{P_L} > \frac{MP_A}{P_A(=0)+t_A} = 0.$$

Now the firm's incentive is to substitute away from air in favor of capital and labor to dispose of its waste products or whatever else it was using air for. The advantage of reducing its reliance on air is that it reduces the taxes it pays. As it substitutes, the marginal products of capital and labor fall and the marginal product of air rises. The firm continues to substitute in favor of capital and labor until

$$\frac{MP_K}{P_K} = \frac{MP_L}{P_L} = \frac{MP_A}{P_A(=0)+t_A}.$$

The amount of pollution emitted from the factory naturally falls as its reliance on air is reduced, for any amount of paper the firm may choose to produce in the factory.

The advantages of taxing firms for their use of air are fourfold. First, the tax policy appeals to the same profit motive that led to the pollution in the first place. Firms have to consider substituting capital and labor for now taxed air to dispose of waste products and other purposes to continue to produce their output at the lowest possible cost. Only by restoring the three $\dfrac{MP}{P}$ ratios can the firm be on its new total cost curve that now includes any taxes paid for the use of air.

Second, the burden of reducing pollution falls on firms, not the government. Firms have to prove that they have reduced their use of air to justify a reduction in their tax burdens. Presumably the amount of smoke passing through chimneys can be monitored in a verifiable manner, and it is up to firms to ensure that it is monitored correctly.

Third, each firm responds to the tax in the way that is least costly for it, and the responses could vary widely among them. Some firms may find it least costly to put scrubbers on smokestacks to purify the air; others may switch to a cleaner burning fuel; still others may find that simply paying the tax and producing as before is its least-cost strategy.[5] The varying responses of the firms are not a problem for the tax strategy, however. Quite the contrary. The government's goal is to achieve a given reduction of pollution at the lowest possible cost. All the government need do is adjust the tax until it achieves the aggregate reduction of pollution that it seeks. Since each firm is responding to the tax in its least-cost way, the government is assured that it has reached the targeted pollution reduction at the lowest possible aggregate cost. It need not concern itself at all with the individual firms' responses.

Finally, the tax strategy receives some help from the output market even though the tax is on the use of air (water). Refer to Figure 6.8, which pictures the market for paper.

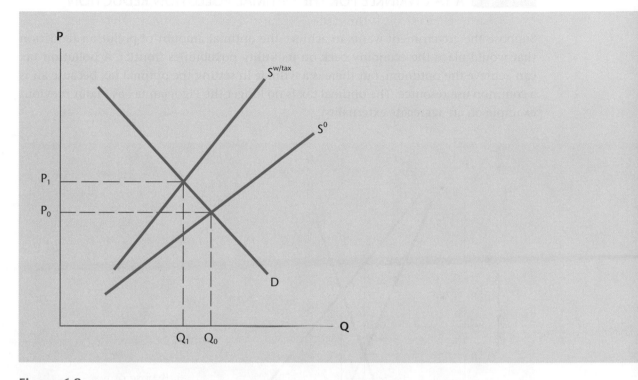

Figure 6.8

Each firm's total and marginal costs of producing paper increase as a result of the tax on air simply because the firms are now paying for an input that used to be free to them. By substituting in favor or capital and labor and returning the $\dfrac{MP}{P}$ ratios to equality, the firms can lower their costs below what they would be if they did not substitute, but they cannot return to the original cost curves. And costs obviously increase for those firms that simply choose to pay the tax and produce paper as before. With marginal costs rising at every output, the supply curve in Figure 6.8 increases from S^0, the supply curve (marginal cost) before the tax, to $S^{w/tax}$, the supply curve (marginal cost) after the tax and the firms' least-cost substitution away from air. The equilibrium changes from (Q_0, P_0), at the intersection of D and S^0, to (Q_1, P_1), at the intersection of D and $S^{w/tax}$. There is no tax on paper, however, unlike our first examples. Nonetheless, by raising the firms' cost of production, the tax on air increases the price of paper and induces consumers to switch some of their purchases to other nonpolluting products. Note, importantly, that a tax on paper that brought to market the same quantity of paper Q_1 would not result in the same reduction in pollution as the tax on air because it gives the firms no incentive to use more capital and labor and less air in producing the paper. Only a tax on air can induce the substitutions away from using air and reduce pollution for each unit of paper produced.

A TAX WRINKLE FOR THE OPTIMAL POLLUTION REDUCTION

Suppose the government wants to achieve the optimal amount of pollution reduction that would place the economy back on its utility possibilities frontier. A pollution tax can achieve the optimum, but there is a wrinkle in setting the optimal tax because air is a common use resource. The optimal tax is no longer the Pigovian tax as in our previous example on an aggregate externality.

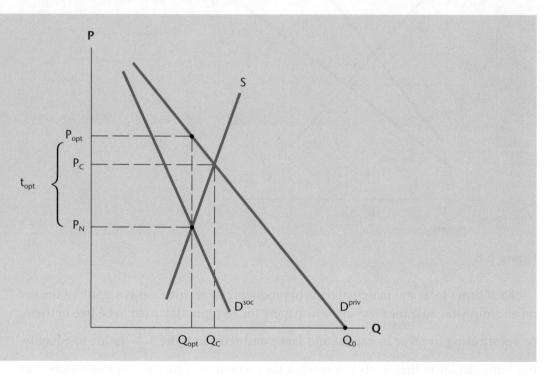

Figure 6.9

We need to describe the market for air to demonstrate the optimal pollution tax. Refer to Figure 6.9, in which the amount of air is on the horizontal axis. Since air is a factor of production, the roles of supply and demand are reversed relative to the market for paper. The supply curve S in the figure reflects the marginal disutility that society places on air, the amount it must receive at each quantity of air on the horizontal axis to sacrifice one more unit of air (just as the supply curve of labor reflects the marginal disutility of supplying labor). The private demand curve for air, D^{priv}, indicates the private marginal value to any one firm of using another unit of air, equal to the value of air's marginal product (VMP_A) in producing paper. The $VMP^A = MP_A \cdot P_P$, where P_P is the price of a unit of paper. The social demand curve for air, D^{soc}, is the social marginal value of using air. It subtracts from D^{priv}, at each unit of air used by the paper firms, the sum of the marginal damages of the air pollution to all the individuals affected by the pollution. The social marginal value of using air is, therefore, the firms' private marginal value of using air minus the sum of the marginal pollution damages. The optimal amount of air exchanged between society and the firms is Q_{opt}, at the intersection of S and D^{soc}. At Q_{opt}, the marginal disutility to society of supplying air equals the social marginal value of using the air, as required for the efficient use of air.

If air were owned and supplied as any ordinary good, then the standard analysis would apply. The equilibrium without a pollution tax would be (Q_c, P_c) at the intersection of S and D^{priv}. The optimum would be achieved by a Pigovian tax on the use of air equal to the sum of the marginal pollution damages at the optimum, t_{opt} in Figure 6.9. The price to the firms of using air would rise to P_{opt}, and the price received by the owners of air would be P_N. But since air is a common use resource, the price of air without a pollution tax is zero and the firms use an amount of air equal to Q_0, at which D^{priv} intersects the horizontal axis. Therefore the optimal tax must be the entire price P_{opt}, equal to the Pigovian tax, t_{opt}, plus P_N. t_{opt} reflects the sum of the marginal pollution damages at the optimum and P_N reflects the marginal disutility to society along S of supplying air.

ZERO POLLUTION?

The final question to address regarding pollution is: How much pollution is too much pollution? Many people might say that *any* pollution is too much pollution, but economists would disagree with this view for the majority of pollutants. Reducing pollutants does bring benefits but it also entails costs. In our example above, the costs take the form of increasing the paper firms' costs of production, which in turn increases the price of paper to consumers and pushes them towards other nonpolluting products.

The proper goal in reducing pollution is to strike a balance between the benefits and costs by maximizing the net benefit of reducing pollution, the difference between the total benefit and total cost. This point is reached when the marginal benefit and marginal cost of reducing pollution are equal, as pictured in Figure 6.10. Equalizing marginal benefit and marginal cost is the general prescription for maximizing the net benefit associated with any economic activity.

The horizontal axis of Figure 6.10 indicates the percentage reduction in pollution, PR, from 0%, the initial condition when pollution is at its highest, to 100%, zero pollution. The vertical axis measures the marginal benefit (MB) and marginal cost (MC) of further reducing pollution at each amount of pollution reduction. The patterns of MB and MC are the standard ones. At the initial situation, with maximum pollution, the marginal benefit of reducing pollution is high. The marginal benefit declines as the amount of pollution is reduced, eventually becoming quite low near 100% pollution reduction, when few pollutants remain in the air. Conversely, the marginal cost of reducing the first amounts of pollution is typically quite low, and then rises as the amount of pollution is reduced. The marginal cost of removing the remaining pollution when pollution is already near zero may be very high. The optimal amount of pollution reduction is PR*, at the intersection of MB and MC, not zero pollution. With MB = MC, the net benefit from reducing pollution is at its maximum, which is the best society can achieve.

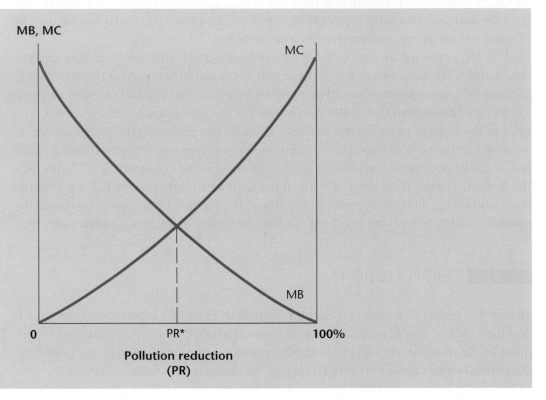

Figure 6.10

MB and MC are measured with reference to Figure 6.9. The marginal benefit of reducing pollution is the negative of the marginal harm of increasing pollution. In Figure 6.9, it is the vertical difference between D^{priv} and D^{soc}, the sum of the marginal damages of the pollution at each level of air use. As less air is used and pollution is reduced, the sum of the marginal damages from a further reduction of air use diminishes; the vertical distance between D^{priv} and D^{soc} decreases. The marginal cost of reducing pollution is the net private loss on the margin of using less air, which is the negative of the net private benefit from using more air. The private benefit of using air is the value of air's marginal product in using air, which is given by D^{priv}. The private cost of using air is the disutility of supplying more air, which is given by S. Therefore, the net private benefit from using air is the vertical difference between D^{priv} and S, which is the negative of the marginal cost of using less air. The marginal cost rises as less air is used; the vertical distance between D^{priv} and S increases. At the optimum amount of air use in Figure 6.9, the vertical distance between D^{priv} and D^{soc}, the marginal benefit of reducing the use of air (reducing pollution), just equals the vertical distance between D^{priv} and S, the marginal cost of reducing the use of air (reducing pollution).

Some pollutants may be so harmful that the marginal benefit of reducing pollution remains higher than the marginal cost of reducing pollution right up to 100% pollution reduction. Examples might be known carcinogens such as asbestos and mercury, or the chlorofluorocarbons that deplete the ozone layer. In these instances, zero pollution is the optimal amount of pollution. But the vast majority of industrial air and water pollutants are not nearly so harmful. For these pollutants, such as sulfur dioxide emissions in factory smoke or fertilizer runoff into waterways, the pattern of the marginal benefits and costs of reducing the pollutants is as pictured in Figure 6.10 (or 6.9). Efforts to reduce these pollutants should stop well short of zero pollution. Beyond PR* in Figure 6.10, the extra costs in the form of lost private sector value exceed the extra benefits of any further reduction in the pollutant.

CHAPTER 7

Externalities: Policy Considerations

The government's response when marketed activities give rise to externalities is easy enough to describe in principle: The government should levy a Pigovian tax (subsidy) on the externality-generating activity equal to the sum of the marginal external damages (benefits) at the optimum. Applying the Pigovian tax runs into a number of difficulties, however. Chapter 7 discusses a selection of these difficulties, along with some other relevant policy considerations in correcting for externalities.

We will focus on aggregate externalities because they require only a single tax and give the government the best chance of accurately accounting for the externalities. The multiple taxes required by individualized externalities are obviously going to be difficult for governments to implement. We begin with the simplest case from Chapter 6, in which the external pollution damage to people caused by the paper factories is proportional to the aggregate output they produce. This case is sufficient for illustrating a number of practical problems the government faces in trying to restore Pareto optimality in the presence of externalities.

THE COASE THEOREM

The first requirement in correcting for externalities is that some decision maker has to internalize the externality, to see the full extent of the damage (benefit) that it generates. The government performs that role in the Pigovian tax (subsidy) solution. In our pollution example, the government sees the aggregate external marginal damage that the paper firms cause to people when they increase the production of paper and levies a tax that forces the firms to pay for the damage.

A Pigovian tax might not be necessary, however. Suppose that all the people affected by the factories' pollution were also the owners/managers of the paper companies. They would then have an incentive to internalize the externality themselves. Since the people experience the pollution damage caused by producing the paper, their goal now as owners/managers is not to maximize the firms' profits. Instead they would want to maximize their net benefit or utility from the production of paper, where the net benefit equals the combined profits of the firms less the pollution damages that the production of paper inflicts upon them. To achieve this goal, they would compute the full social marginal cost of producing the paper at each of the factories, equal to the private marginal cost of producing the paper plus the aggregate marginal pollution damages. Then they would produce the output at each factory such that the price of paper equals the full social marginal cost of production, which is exactly the solution required for Pareto optimality. Having internalized the externality by owning the firms, the people's private interest in maximizing utility coincides with the public interest in efficiency. The pollution damage is no longer an external, third-party effect and no government intervention is required to achieve the utility possibilities frontier.

In a well-known article published in 1960, Ronald Coase argued that Pigovian taxes to correct for externalities are unnecessary even if the damages (benefits) remain external to the agents generating the externality (Coase, 1960). All the government has to do to ensure efficiency is establish ownership of property rights to the externality so that the externality can be bought and sold in the marketplace. Once a market for the externality exists, private parties have incentives to negotiate the efficient amount of the externality, just as markets generate incentives for the efficient exchange of any good or service. This result is known as the *Coase Theorem*. A corollary to the Coase Theorem is that the side of the market to which the property rights are given is irrelevant to achieving an efficient allocation. The rights may be given either to the generators or the recipients of the externalities.

Our pollution-proportional-to-output example from Chapter 6 can be used to illustrate the Coase Theorem. Figure 7.1(a) partially reproduces Figure 6.4, which illustrates the Pigovian tax solution to the pollution externality. The competitive allocation without government intervention, and without assigning the property rights to clean air, is (Q_c, P_c), at the intersection of the market demand curve D and the private supply curve S^{priv}, which includes only the private marginal cost of producing paper. The efficient allocation is (Q_{opt}, P_{opt}), at the intersection of D and the social supply curve S^{soc}, which includes both the private marginal cost of producing paper and the aggregate marginal external damage from producing paper. The optimum is achieved with the Pigovian tax t, equal to the aggregate marginal external damages at Q_{opt}.

Figure 7.1(b) displays the marginal benefit (MB) and marginal cost (MC) of reducing pollution based on Figure 7.1(a), with the horizontal axis recording the amount of pollution reduction from zero to 100%. Zero represents the initial situation at the competitive equilibrium, (Q_c, P_c). MB is the vertical distance between S^{soc} and S^{priv} in Figure 7.1(a), and MC is the vertical distance between D and S^{priv}.

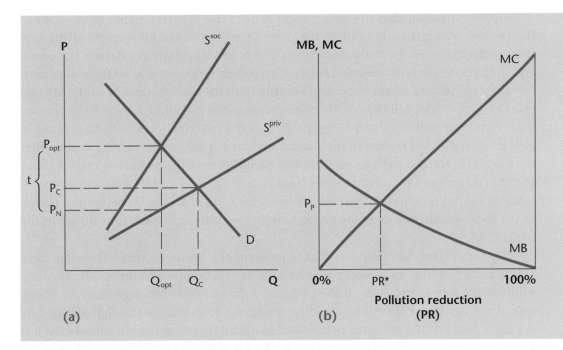

Figure 7.1

Can the market reach the efficient equilibrium (Q_{opt}, P_{opt}) without benefit of the Pigovian tax? Coase's answer was "yes," simply by having the government assign the property rights to clean air. He is almost certainly correct if the scope of the externality is quite limited. To see this, consider the simplest possible case in which there is only one factory generating pollution and one person affected by it.

Suppose the government assigns the property rights to clean air to the factory owner, which is equivalent to the owner having the right to pollute. The owner would select output Q_c at the price of paper P_c if he considered only the private marginal cost of producing paper. Once the rights to pollute have been assigned, however, the owner has the option of selling the rights in the marketplace. Moreover, the person has an incentive to purchase some of the rights to pollute from the owner to reduce the amount of pollution. Refer to Figure 7.1(b). At the existing competitive equilibrium with PR = 0, the benefit to the person of reducing pollution by one unit is MB, whereas the cost to the owner is only MC in terms of lost sales of output in the paper market. Therefore, it is mutually beneficial to both parties for the owner to sell the right to one unit of pollution to the person for any price between MB and MC, and thereby reduce pollution by one unit. The same is true for the second unit of pollution, and so on, up to the intersection of MB and MC. Suppose the person offered the owner the price P_p for the rights to units of pollution, at the intersection of MB and MC. The owner would sell PR* rights to pollute. Since P_p is equal to the Pigovian tax, the reduction of pollution to PR* is equivalent to the reduction of paper output from Q_c to Q_{opt} in Figure 7.1(a), and the efficient output of paper and pollution is achieved.

123

Suppose, instead, that the government assigns the property rights to clean air to the person, which is equivalent to the person having the ability to prevent the firm from polluting. Now the natural starting point of any negotiation between the owner and the person is at zero pollution because to produce any output at all the owner must buy rights to pollute from the person. Starting from the right-hand side of the MB and MC in Figure 7.1(b), MB ($S^{soc} - S^{priv}$) is interpreted as the marginal *damage* to the person from *increasing* pollution and MC (D $- S^{priv}$) is the marginal *benefit* to the owner of *increasing* production from zero production. As above, suppose the factory owner offers the person P_p for the right to each unit of pollution and the pollution market clears at PR*. The output of paper increases from zero to Q_{opt} in Figure 7.1(a) and again the efficient output is achieved, without the need for a Pigovian tax. Whether the person or the factory owner receives the property rights to clean air is irrelevant for achieving efficiency.[1]

The Coase Theorem becomes highly problematic, however, when there are large numbers of factories and people involved, as in our original example. The theorem would still apply in principle. If the pollution rights to clean air were assigned to one side of the market or the other, then the incentives to exchange the rights to pollute at a price between the marginal benefit and marginal cost of pollution would exist just as in the one-factory, one-person example. And it is in everyone's mutual interest to develop a market for the rights. The essence of an uncorrected externality, or any allocational efficiency problem, is that it drives the economy below its utility possibilities frontier, such as at point A in Figure 7.2. All points to the north, east, and northeast of A on the line segment BC are Pareto superior to A: They make one person better off without making anyone else worse off, or both people better off. Rational individuals should try to move from A to some point on the line segment BC and exploit these potential gains however they can, and the market exchange of pollution rights is one way to do it.

Nonetheless, establishing a market for pollution rights is likely to encounter severe practical difficulties, especially when a large number of people are affected by an externality as is often the case with air pollution. The transactions costs alone of bringing everyone together would be formidable. Also, people would have an incentive to free ride on the goodwill of other people if firms owned the pollution rights. (The same incentive to free ride would apply to the factory owners if the people owned the pollution rights.) The problem is that each person affected by pollution has to consume the same aggregate amount of pollution, unlike a normal market in which people can consume whatever quantities of a good or service that they want. These difficulties lead most economists to conclude that the Coase Theorem is inapplicable when externalities are widespread, which are precisely the kinds of externalities that governments become involved in. A Pigovian tax (or equivalent government policies – see below) is required to correct for externalities in these instances.

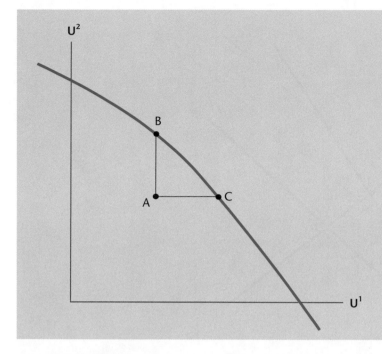

Figure 7.2

MEASUREMENT PROBLEMS IN DESIGNING PIGOVIAN TAXES

The government faces two difficult measurement problems in trying to set the optimal Pigovian tax for any aggregate pollution externality. The first is that the Pigovian tax has to be equal to the aggregate marginal damages *at the optimum*. The second is that there are severe gaps in our scientific knowledge about the benefits of reducing pollution.

ITERATING TO THE OPTIMUM

Suppose the government can measure the marginal damages of pollution accurately. Even so, when it first attempts to measure the marginal benefits to establish the Pigovian tax, it will be measuring them at the wrong level of pollution. Refer to Figure 7.3, which builds on Figures 6.4 and 7.1(a) for our pollution-proportional-to-output case.

The Pigovian tax is t_{opt}, equal to the distance gh between S^{soc} and S^{priv} at Q_{opt}, the aggregate marginal damages at the optimum. But the market is at the competitive equilibrium (Q_c, P_c) before the government places a tax on the paper firms. Therefore, when the government first measures the aggregate marginal damages, it will measure them as ab, the distance between S^{soc} and S^{priv} at Q_c. If Q_c is far from Q_{opt}, ab could far overstate the aggregate marginal damages at Q_{opt}, which is what the government would like to know.

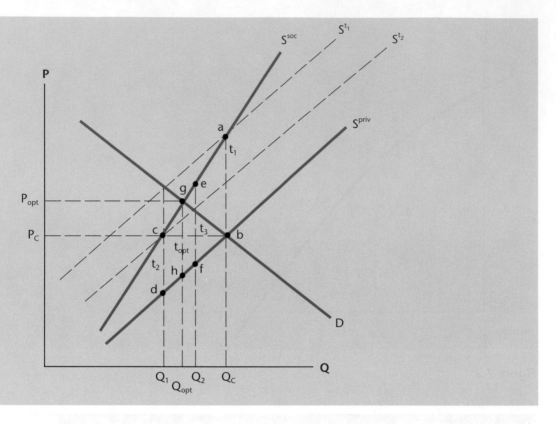

Figure 7.3

The government may be able to iterate close to the optimum with a series of taxes, however, as illustrated in Figure 7.3. It begins by setting a tax t_1 equal to ab, knowing that t_1 is too large. The market overshoots Q_{opt} and establishes a new equilibrium at Q_1, at the intersection of D and S^{t_1}. The government again measures the aggregate marginal damages and finds them to be cd, the distance between S^{soc} and S^{priv} at Q_1, and resets the tax to t_2 (= cd). The tax t_2 is too low, and the market overshoots Q_{opt} again in the other direction, establishing a new equilibrium at Q_2 at the intersection of D and S^{t_2}. The aggregate marginal damages are now ef, the distance between S^{soc} and S^{priv} at Q_2. Resetting the tax again to t_3 (= ef) overshoots again in the other direction, but the market is homing in on the optimum Q_{opt}. Since the series of taxes overshoots the optimum on both sides, the government may be able to obtain a reasonably good estimate of what the aggregate marginal damages are at the optimum with only a few iterations and establish a tax that is approximately correct. For instance, t_2 is close to t_{opt} in Figure 7.3. This is the probably the best one can hope for in any practical application.[2]

THE BENEFITS OF REDUCING POLLUTION

The assumption in the preceding section that the government knows the marginal damages of pollution at each level of pollution is an heroic one, to say the least. There are huge scientific gaps in our knowledge of the damages caused by many different kinds of pollutants. The U.S. government has recognized eight substances as definitely carcinogenic and banned their use. Another example is the ban on fully halogenated chlorofluoroalkane, which had been used in aerosol spray cans and refrigerants, because of its known destruction of the ozone layer in the atmosphere. But the dangers of the nearly 200 substances that the government recognizes as pollutants – sulfur dioxide, particulate matter, nitrous oxide, carbon dioxide, and so forth – are far less certain and the subject of strenuous debate within the scientific community. For these substances, any attempt to measure a marginal benefit curve, such as in Figure 7.1(b), at different levels of the pollutant would involve a great amount of guesswork and be highly controversial. As a result, most governments do not even try to measure the damages. Instead, they arbitrarily set a target or standard of reducing the pollutant by some percentage and then design policies to meet the target.

The efficiency objective in this approach is simply to meet the pollution target at the lowest possible cost. Fortunately, the principles that apply to the optimal Pigovian tax apply for the most part to efficiently meeting a pollution target. As we saw in Chapter 6, the least-cost way to meet the target is to tax the pollution at its source, and as close to the pollutant as possible. All the government need do is adjust the tax until the target is met. The outcome is not Pareto optimal – the economy remains below its utility possibilities frontier – unless by chance the pollution target happens to be the pollution level at which the marginal benefit and marginal cost of reducing pollution are equal. In other words, the tax is not a Pigovian tax. But it is efficient in the sense that it meets the pollution target at the lowest possible cost.

THE COMMAND AND CONTROL (CAC) APPROACH

Unfortunately, governments often respond to quantity goals with quantity policies rather than pricing policies such as pollution taxes, and the quantity policies can be excessively inefficient and costly. The United States is particularly guilty of this. The federal government used marketable pollution permits in 1991 to meet a targeted reduction of sulfur dioxide emissions from electric utility plants, and we show below that these are essentially equivalent to taxes. But this remains the only important example of a pricing strategy for combating either air or water pollution since the federal government directly entered the fight against industrial source pollution in 1970 (air pollution) and 1972 (water pollution). The government has overwhelmingly favored a so-called *command and control (CAC)* approach, in which all firms are required to adopt specific technologies to reduce their emissions of pollution. The mandated pollution control equipment on automobiles is another familiar example of the CAC approach.

The two models of pollution that we developed in Chapter 6 can be used to illustrate the excessive costliness of the quantity approach. Consider once again the pollution-proportional-to-output model and refer to Figure 7.4(c). Suppose the government wants to reduce aggregate pollution by 45%, which is the reduction in the quantity of paper produced from Q_c in the original, competitive equilibrium to Q_1. The tax solution would be a tax on paper equal to t_1, a tax that reduces the quantity of paper demanded to Q_1 and establishes Q_1 as the new equilibrium. Figure 7.4 assumes that the firms producing paper are of two types, 1 and 2, distinguished by their individual supply curves, that is, by their private marginal costs of producing paper. The firms in Figure 7.4(a) have individual supply curves s^1 and the firms in Figure 7.4(b) have individual supply curves s^2. At the original competitive equilibrium (Q_c, P_c), the type-1 firms each supply q_c^1 to the market and the type-2 firms each supply q_c^2 to the market. At the target equilibrium under the pollution tax, each firm maximizes its profit by supplying the output at which the price net of tax, P_N, equals its private marginal cost. This implies that the type-1 firms supply q_1^1 to the market and the type-2 firms each supply q_1^2 to the market.

The easiest quantity policy to compare with the tax outcome is an even-handed approach in which the government mandates that each firm reduce its output by 45%. The 45% reductions are represented by $q_{45\%}^1$ and $q_{45\%}^2$ in Figures 7.4(a) and (b). Relative to the tax solution, output in the type-1 firms has increased from q_1^1 to $q_{45\%}^1$ and output in the type-2 firms has decreased from q_1^2 to $q_{45\%}^2$, and therein lies the excessive costliness of the even-handed quantity approach. Every unit of output added to the market at the type-1 firms has a higher marginal cost (MC > P_N) than every unit of output removed from the market at the type-2 firms (MC < P_N).

The example illustrates that the tax policy is less costly whenever firms have different costs of production, as is likely the case. The tax implicitly takes these differences into account by imitating the cost-effectiveness of competitive markets. The way to minimize the total cost of supplying output to a market is to equalize the marginal cost across the firms. At a competitive equilibrium, firms with different costs supply different quantities to the market, but the cost of supplying the last unit is the same at all firms because they all supply the output at which the market price equals their marginal costs. With marginal costs equal across firms, any substitution of output to the market between firms must increase the total cost of supplying the market. The tax solution follows the same principle, which is why it is least cost. The example illustrates a fundamental principle in fighting pollution: When pollution can be reduced at many sources, the marginal cost of reducing pollution should be the same at each source. This guarantees that any pollution target is met at the lowest possible cost.

In summary, even-handed quantity approaches may well appeal to a sense of equity along the following lines: Since all firms are contributing to the aggregate pollution, they should all reduce their pollution by the same amount or in the same manner. This may explain the popularity of the federal government's CAC policies. But fighting pollution is an efficiency problem, not an equity problem. The goal is to meet a pollution target at the lowest possible cost, and this is better achieved by a pricing strategy such as a pollution tax or other equivalent pricing strategies.

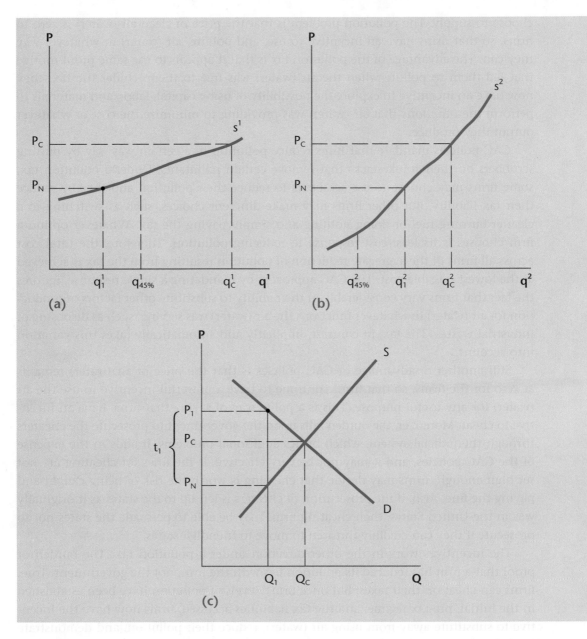

Figure 7.4

The second, more realistic model of air or water pollution in Chapter 6 yields additional insights on the deficiencies of CAC policies relative to a pollution tax. Recall in that model that firms view clean air, or water, as a productive resource. As such, air (water) becomes one of the factors of production that firms consider as they try to equalize the ratios $\dfrac{MP_{factor}}{P_{factor}}$ in order to minimize the total cost of producing whatever output they choose to supply. The pollution problem is that the price of clean air (water) is zero to firms, so that firms have an incentive to use, and pollute, air (water) in whatever way they can. The advantage of the pollution tax is that it appeals to the same profit motive that led them to pollute when the air (water) was free to them. Under the tax, they now have an incentive to explore the possibility of using capital, labor, and materials to perform the functions that air (water) was providing to minimize the cost of whatever output they produce.

CAC policies mandate that firms reduce pollution in a certain way, say by putting scrubbers on their smokestacks that remove certain pollutants. Under a pollution tax, some firms may choose to use scrubbers to reduce their pollution and thereby reduce their tax liability. But other firms may make different choices, such as switching to a cleaner burning fuel or doing nothing and simply paying the tax. Whatever option a firm chooses is its least-cost response to reducing pollution. Therefore, the total cost across all firms of the aggregate reduction of pollution resulting from the tax is achieved at the lowest possible cost. The CAC approach, by mandating a single response, ignores the fact that firms vary considerably in their ability to substitute other factors of production for air (water) in whatever functions the air (water) was serving, such as disposing of industrial wastes. The tax, in contrast, implicitly and automatically takes this variation into account.

Still another disadvantage of CAC policies is that the price of air (water) remains at zero for the firms, so that firms continue to have a powerful incentive to use the air (water) for any useful purpose. This is a polite way of saying that firms have an incentive to cheat. Moreover, the burden falls upon the government to prosecute the cheaters through the judicial system, which brings additional problems. It adds to the expense of the CAC policies, and it may not be very effective. If the fines for cheating are not set high enough, firms may decide that cheating is worth the risk of being caught and paying the fine. Also, if the prosecution of cheaters is left up to the states as it originally was in the United States, then cheating firms may be able to persuade the states not to prosecute if they can credibly threaten to move to friendlier states.

The incentives work in the other direction under a pollution tax. The burden of proof that a firm has reduced its pollution lies with the firm, not the government. True, firms can cheat on their taxes. But once firms' levels of pollution have been established in the initial, pre-tax regime, and the tax liabilities accessed, firms now have the incentive to substitute away from using air (water), reduce their pollution, and demonstrate to the government that their tax liabilities should be reduced. Having made the factor substitutions and reduced their taxes, they are unlikely to switch back to their original production techniques. In summary, the different incentives to firms under a pollution tax versus the CAC approach are yet another powerful argument in favor of a pricing strategy over a quantity strategy for combating industrial air (water) pollution.

ALTERNATIVE PRICING STRATEGIES: SUBSIDIES AND PERMITS

Taxes are not the only pricing strategies available to governments for reaching pollution reduction targets, optimal or otherwise, at least cost. Two other possibilities are subsidies to firms to reduce pollution and marketable pollution permits. They have the same marginal properties as pollution taxes and therefore the same least-cost properties for meeting pollution targets. But they differ in other respects that may make them more or less attractive than taxes in certain instances.

THE MARGINAL EQUIVALENCE OF POLLUTION TAXES, SUBSIDIES AND MARKETABLE PERMITS

To see that taxes, subsidies, and permits are equivalent on the margin, return to the simple pollution-proportional-to-output model and consider how a profit-maximizing, perfectly competitive paper firm would react to each of them.

Tax

The firm's profit under the tax strategy is:

$$\text{Profit} = pq - C(q) - tP(q)$$

where: p is the market price of paper; q is the quantity of paper produced; C(q) is the total cost of producing paper; t is the per-unit pollution tax; and P(q) is the amount of pollution as a function of the firm's output. The firm maximizes profit by producing the output at which marginal profit is zero:

$$\frac{d\text{Pr}ofit}{dq} = p - \frac{dC}{dq} - t \cdot \frac{dP}{dq} = 0, \text{ or}$$

$$p = \frac{dC}{dq} + t \cdot \frac{dP}{dq}.$$

This is the familiar competitive supply rule to maximize profit: produce the output at which price equals marginal cost. Here the marginal cost of increasing output consists of the private marginal cost $(\frac{dC}{dq})$ plus the increase in the pollution tax liability $(t\frac{dP}{dq})$. Regarding the second term, the tax t is levied on each unit of pollution and $\frac{dP}{dq}$ indicates how much pollution increases when output increases by one unit.[3] Therefore the product of the two terms is the marginal increase in the firm's pollution tax liability.

Subsidy

Under a subsidy to reduce pollution, the firm's profit equation would be:

$$\text{Profit} = pq - C(q) + s\,[\bar{P} - P(q)]$$

where: s is the per-unit subsidy and $\bar{P}$ is the level against which the reduction of pollution is measured, presumably the initial, no-subsidy amount of the firm's pollution. Alternatively,

$$\text{Profit} = pq - C(q) - sP(q) + s\bar{P}$$

The competitive supply rule is

$$\frac{d\,\text{Profit}}{dq} = p - \frac{dC}{dq} - s \cdot \frac{dP}{dq} = 0 \text{ , or}$$

$$p = \frac{dC}{dq} + s \cdot \frac{dP}{dq}$$

which is identical to the competitive supply rule under the pollution tax if s = t. Therefore the incentives to firms to reduce output under the tax and subsidy are identical. The only difference is that the subsidy is kinder to firms because they are subsidized in total rather than taxed. Profits to firms are higher in the short run under the subsidy.

Marketable pollution permits

Under a *marketable permit* system, the government issues permits to firms that allow them to emit a given quantity of pollution under each permit. Suppose that the government auctions the permits to firms and a price of a permit P_p is established through the auction. Assume also that firms buy only the permits that they need, and that each permit allows one unit of pollution. Then a competitive firm's profit equation under the permit system would be

$$\text{Profit} = pq - C(q) - P_p P(q)$$

where P(q) represents both the total amount of the firm's pollution and the total number of permits it buys in the auction.

The competitive supply rule is

$$\frac{d\,\text{Profit}}{dq} = p - \frac{dC}{dq} - P_p \cdot \frac{dP}{dq} = 0$$

which is identical to the competitive supply rule under the tax if the price of the permits P_p equals the tax rate t. But if the tax policy and the permit policy lead to the same aggregate reduction in pollution, then the two must be equal. Refer back Figure 7.4(c). Under the tax policy, the government sets a tax rate t that generates the output Q_1. Suppose, instead, the government issued Q_1 permits and put them up for auction. Since the competitive supply rule for firms is identical under the two policies, the auction price of the permits P_p would have to equal t to generate Q_1 as the competitive equilibrium. The firms' cost per unit of polluting on the margin must rise by the same amount under the two policies for firms to supply the same outputs to the market.

The United States used a variation of the permit system just described to reduce the sulfur dioxide (SO_2) emissions of the public utilities. It first established the number of permits that would allow the targeted amount of SO_2 emissions. Then it distributed the permits to the utilities according to an arbitrary formula and allowed them to buy and sell the permits among themselves. The market for permits reached an equilibrium within a matter of months.

As above, let P_p be the equilibrium price of the permits and assume that one permit allows one unit of pollution, and assume that the firm receives an initial distribution of permits equal to $\bar{P}$. Then the firm's profit equation under the marketable permit scheme is

Profit = pq − C(q) − P_p [P(q) − $\bar{P}$], or

Profit = pq − C(q) − P_pP(q) + P_p·$\bar{P}$.

If the firm wants to pollute more than its original allocation of permits allows, then it purchases permits in the permit market. If it has excess permits, it sells them. In either case, the firm's competitive supply rule is

$$\frac{d\,\mathrm{Pr}\,ofit}{dq} = p - \frac{dC}{dq} - P_p \cdot \frac{dP}{dq} = 0$$

which is identical to the government auction case and therefore identical to the tax policy with P_p = t.

DIFFERENCES IN TAXES, SUBSIDIES AND PERMITS

The three policies are not identical in every respect, however. One obvious difference has already been mentioned, that the subsidy and marketable permit strategies are kinder to firms and may therefore have political advantages over the tax. There are more subtle differences as well.

Subsidies

The difference between the tax and the subsidy lies in the overall effect on firms' profits, that their profits are reduced in the short run under the tax but increased under the subsidy. This difference is likely to matter in terms of the effect of the two policies in reducing pollution, especially if pollution is at all related to output, and it argues against the subsidy policy.

Figure 7.5(a) shows the average (AC) and marginal costs (MC) of a representative paper firm and Figure 7.5(b) shows the overall market for paper. AC^0 and MC^0 are the curves before government institutes a tax or subsidy, and the market supply curve is S^0, the sum of the firms' marginal cost curves. The original long-run equilibrium is at (Q^0, P^0). Each firm produces q^0 and earns zero economic profit.

The per-unit tax shifts up the average and marginal cost curves to AC' and MC', and the market supply curve shifts up by the amount of the tax. Since P does not rise by the amount of the tax, the firms are now making losses. Some paper firms exit the market in the long run until the short-run supply curve reaches S' and the remaining firms are once again just breaking even, at price P'. Price rises to the minimum of AC' and output in the long run is reduced to Q'. Since pollution is related to output, the exit of some of the paper firms helps to reduce the aggregate amount of pollution.

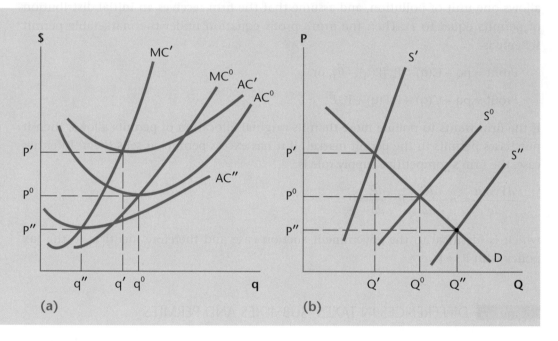

(a)   (b)

Figure 7.5

The per-unit subsidy for reducing pollution also shifts the marginal cost curve to MC' since the cost of producing output rises on the margin. But since firms are subsidized overall, the average cost curve shifts *down* to AC''. Firms are making profits under the subsidy policy, which encourages the entry of new firms. Entry occurs until price falls to P'', the minimum of AC'', and the paper firms are once again breaking even. Output in the long run increases to Q''. Each firm produces less output under the subsidy, q''. But the entry of new firms increases aggregate output and also aggregate pollution, if pollution is related to output.

In effect, new firms enter the industry to obtain the subsidy. This property argues strongly against offering firms subsidies to reduce pollution. The only way to prevent the aggregate entry effect is to offer the subsidy to existing firms but not to new firms, but this has the disadvantage of allowing the existing firms to earn economic profits in the long run. And it still does not reduce aggregate output and pollution as much as the tax policy does because no firms exit the industry. The tax policy is clearly the better policy.[4]

Pollution permits

Marketable permits have an obvious advantage over pollution taxes if the government sets a pollution reduction target. It can simply issue the number of permits equal to the pollution target and let the market for permits establish the price of the permits that leads to the least-cost properties of this pricing strategy. There is no need to iterate to the target as in the tax case. Also, taxes would have to be adjusted periodically if the economy is experiencing general inflation, whereas the market price for the fixed number of permits would adjust to inflation automatically.

There are some disadvantages relative to the tax, however. The biggest fear among economists is that existing firms could turn the permits into a barrier to entry by purchasing more permits than they need and hoarding them, thereby increasing the entry costs for new firms or precluding entry entirely. This was not an issue in the case of the electric utilities because the utilities are regulated, but it could be a problem if permits were used more generally.

Another potential drawback is that a permit market is likely to be national in scope and establish one price for the permits nationwide, as was true of the permits for sulfur dioxide emissions. The problem here is that a national market implicitly assumes that the emissions of firms constitute a nationwide aggregate externality, when in fact the damages of air (water) pollution are almost always regional in scope. As such, pollution emissions are an example of an individualized externality and require separate prices for the permits in each region. For example, suppose an electric utility located in a sparsely populated area of Maine sells a permit in a nationwide market to a public utility located in densely populated Los Angeles. The implicit assumption of this transaction is that the marginal benefits of reducing pollution in Maine are equal to the marginal costs of increasing pollution in Los Angeles, which could hardly be true. It may well be easier to levy a set of differentiated regional taxes for some pollutants than to establish a set of regional markets for the permits.

▬▬▬▬ TAXES, PERMITS, AND UNCERTAINTY

A final issue in the choice between taxes and permits turns on the inherent uncertainties involved with the measurement of the benefits and costs of reducing pollution. We have already noted the uncertainties surrounding the marginal benefits of reducing many kinds of pollutants. The marginal costs of reducing pollution, which are the difference between market demand and (private) supply curves, are obviously not going to be known with certainty either. The question is whether policy makers are more concerned about the uncertainties surrounding the marginal benefits or the marginal costs. This matters because permits are better at controlling the amount of pollution, whereas taxes are better at controlling the increase in the costs to firms of reducing pollution.

Figure 7.6 illustrates the nature of the policy choices under uncertainty. It assumes that policy makers do not have very precise knowledge about either the marginal benefits or the marginal costs of reducing pollution. Nonetheless, they do have an intuitive sense about the shape of each curve.

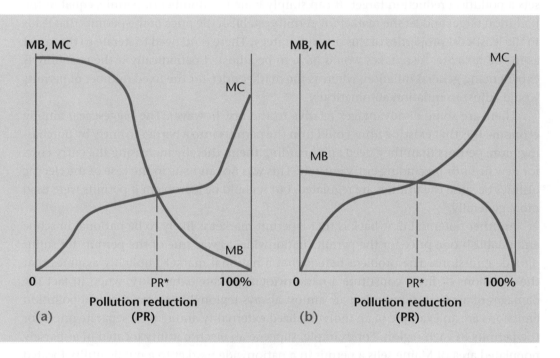

Figure 7.6

In Figure 7.6(a), policy makers sense that the marginal benefit curve is very steep below the optimal level of pollution reduction, whereas the marginal cost curve is fairly flat over a wide range of pollution reduction. In this case, permits are the better option. Recall that the marginal benefits at any level of pollution reduction are the same as the marginal damages of the remaining pollution. By controlling the amount of pollution reduction, the government can ensure that the marginal damages of the remaining pollution are fairly low. If the permits are too few so that the market is far to the right of the optimal amount of pollution reduction where MB and MC intersect, at least the extra costs are not expected to be very large. The fear with using taxes in this case is that the taxes might be set too low, with too little pollution reduction. They definitely do not want the market to be far to the left of the optimum because then the damages from the remaining pollution could be very high.

The situation is reversed in Figure 7.6(b). Policy makers sense that the marginal bene-

136

fits of reducing pollution are fairly flat, but the marginal costs are fairly steep above the optimal level of pollution reduction. They want to be able to control costs in this case, for which the tax is the better option. The fear now is winding up far to the right of the optimal amount of pollution reduction, a region in which the costs of reducing pollution far exceed the benefits. If the tax happens to be too low and the market is to the left of the optimum, at least the damages from the remaining pollution do not increase very much.

The best policy choice has to be determined on a case-by-case basis. One suspects that for most air and water pollutants, the marginal benefit curve declines quickly at first and then remains fairly flat as the amount of pollution reduction approaches 100%, whereas the marginal cost curve remains flat at first until the majority of pollution has been reduced, at which point it increases rapidly. If this is true, then the choice between taxes and permits depends on their point of intersection. If MB and MC intersect in their flat portions and the flat regions are fairly wide, then permits and taxes are equally good. The decision will turn on some of the other issues mentioned above. If they intersect in the steep portion of the MB curve, then permits are preferred; if they intersect in the steep portion of the MC curve, then the tax is preferred.

WASTE TREATMENT AND OTHER DEFENSIVE STRATEGIES

WASTE TREATMENT

The U.S. federal government's first serious attempt to reduce pollution occurred in the 1950s when it established a grant program to subsidize municipalities for the construction of waste treatment plants for bodies of water within their jurisdictions. This is essentially a defensive strategy toward pollution, designed to clean up the pollution after the fact rather than trying to reduce the pollution at its various sources.

Waste treatment after the fact is certainly an option worth considering. Imagine that scientists develop a magic pill that costs only pennies and when dropped in a lake or a river cleans out all the impurities and renders the water suitable for drinking. Using these pills would clearly be the least-cost strategy for combating pollution. Waste treatment is not so cheap, of course, but there are substantial economies of scale in cleaning up pollution, enough so that it is likely to be an important component of any antipollution strategy.

The question remains whether it should be the only strategy for combating pollution, and the answer is almost certainly "no." At best, it should be combined with pollution taxes (or marketable permits) on the firms that generate the pollution, for two reasons. The first is the principle developed above that the marginal costs of reducing pollution should be equalized across all the ways of reducing pollution. A pollution tax imposes (equal) marginal costs of reducing pollution on the firms. Waste treatment after the fact comes with its own marginal costs. If waste treatment alone is used, then the marginal costs to the firms of reducing pollution are zero and the marginal costs of waste treatment are necessarily greater than the marginal costs of reducing pollution at the source. Conversely, without waste treatment, the marginal costs of reducing pollution at the source (the firms) are maximized and the marginal costs of cleaning up pollution after the fact are zero. The least-cost strategy is likely to be to use both options, such that the marginal costs of reducing pollution at the sources equal the marginal cost of reducing pollution through waste treatment.

The second reason for a dual tax/waste treatment strategy is that by not taxing firms at the source, efficient exchanges in their markets cannot occur. Consider again our pollution-proportional-to-output case. Without a pollution tax, the market for paper reaches its equilibrium at the intersection of the demand and private market supply curves, the original equilibrium in Figure 7.1(a) above. Efficiency requires that the equilibrium be at the intersection of the demand and the social market supply curve, and this can be achieved only if firms face a cost for polluting, either through taxes or permits. So a pricing strategy to reduce pollution at its source should be a part of any optimal strategy.

SUBSIDIZING THE VICTIMS

Another defensive strategy is to subsidize the victims of pollution for all or part of the harm they have suffered. One example would be to subsidize the purchase of paint by those people whose homes have been discolored by air pollution. This turns out not to be a good idea. Paint is a standard good that does not give rise to any externalities. We saw in Chapter 2 that the Pareto-optimal condition for such a good is that the marginal rate of substitution in consumption between paint and some other reference good be equal across all consumers of paint and also equal to their marginal rate of transformation in production. For this condition to hold, all consumers and producers of paint and the reference good must face the same prices because consumers and producers set their marginal rates of substitution and marginal rates of transformation to the ratio of the prices of the two goods. Consumers would not face the same prices, however, if people whose homes are discolored by pollution are allowed to buy paint at a subsidized price, whereas all other consumers pay the full price. The condition that the marginal rate of substitution between paint and some reference good must be the same for all consumers would fail to hold. Therefore, subsidizing the victims in this way moves the economy inside its utility possibilities frontier in and of itself.

The only way to subsidize the victims of external diseconomies such as pollution and avoid introducing another inefficiency into the economy is to subsidize the victims in a lump-sum manner, such as by a per-person payment of some amount. We saw in Chapter 3 that lump-sum transfers allow all the Pareto-optimal conditions to hold.[5] Also, the pollution would still have to be taxed at its source to reach the utility possibilities frontier.

RESISTANCE TO POLICIES

A final practical difficulty with policies designed to correct for externalities is that they are often resisted by the very people they are trying to help. A good example is automobile congestion on urban highways. Congestion is an example of an aggregate external diseconomy. When drivers enter a congested highway, they impose costs on all the other drivers (and themselves) in the form of increased travel time. But the congestion depends on the total number of drivers on the highway; the identity of the individual drivers is irrelevant.

The optimal response to congestion is a toll equal to the aggregate costs across all drivers of the increased travel time when one more driver enters the highway. The congestion tolls would vary by time of day, highest during the rush hours and zero in the middle of the night and at other uncongested times. Congestion tolls have been used with considerable success in some cities – Singapore, Toronto, London – but they have been resisted in the United States. U.S. drivers want the reduced congestion that the tolls would bring yet they apparently believe that the congestion tolls would make them worse off.

Figure 7.7 illustrates the problem from the drivers' perspective. It represents the market for driving on a particular highway. The horizontal axis shows the number of drivers on the highway. The horizontal supply curve S assumes that additional road capacity can be provided at constant marginal cost. This assumption takes the supply side out of consideration so that we can focus on the demand side of the market, where the congestion occurs. The demand curve D^{priv} reflects the value to the drivers from using the highway, the value of being able to drive from one place to another. This is why they are on the highway in the first place. D^{soc} reflects the full value to the drivers from using the highway. At each level of road use, it subtracts from D^{priv} the aggregate marginal costs to all drivers of time lost from the congestion, the additional costs from one more car entering the highway. The marginal congestion costs presumably rise as more cars use the road, which is why the distance between D^{priv} and D^{soc} increases with road use.

The equilibrium without a congestion toll is (Q_c, P_c), at the intersection of D^{priv} and S. (P_c covers the costs of supplying and maintaining the road and is assumed to be paid by the drivers.) The optimal amount of road use is Q_{opt}, at the intersection of D^{soc} and S. It is achieved by a congestion toll, t, which raises the total price to the drivers to P_{opt}.

We will use consumer surplus to show how well off drivers are with and without the congestion toll. Consumer surplus is the area between D^{soc} and S (= MC) up to any given output. At the no-toll equilibrium, the consumer surplus is the sum of areas 1 + 2 – 4. The idea of the toll is to remove negative area 4 by reducing the road use to Q_{opt} (tolls = $t \cdot Q_{opt}$). But the drivers have to pay tolls equal to the sum of areas 2 + 3 to achieve Q_{opt}. If the tolls could be returned to the drivers lump sum, they would clearly be better off because their consumer surplus would be the sum of areas 1 + 2. They would avoid the negative surplus area 4, which is the intent of the congestion toll.

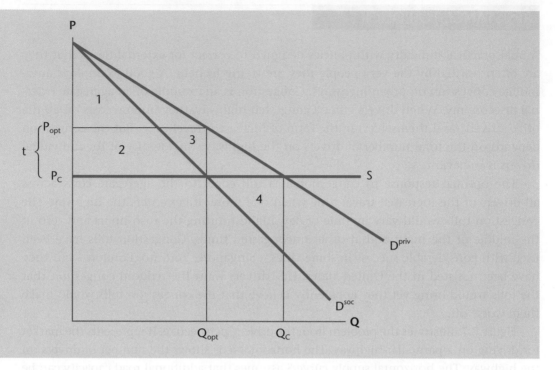

Figure 7.7

The tolls are not returned lump sum, of course. They are used to finance some government services. Suppose, however, that the drivers believe they receive no benefit from the state government in return for the congestion tolls collected from them. They would then view their consumer surplus with the toll as the sum of areas 1 – 3. The part of the toll equal to area 2 is a transfer of part of their former surplus to the government, which the drivers view as lost surplus without any offsetting gain. The part of the toll equal to area 3 was never part of their original surplus, so it represents a pure loss. The drivers will oppose the toll if the area 1 – 3, their surplus with the toll, is less than area 1 + 2 – 4, their surplus without the toll.

Resist if: 1 – 3 < 1 + 2 – 4, or

4 < 2 + 3.

The congestion tolls collected from the drivers exceed the gains to them of avoiding the negative surplus arising from the congestion without the toll. This may well be the view that the majority of drivers have.

Figure 7.8 illustrates the nature of the problem from the perspective of the utility possibilities frontier. U^2 on the vertical axis represents the utility of the drivers and U^1 on the horizontal axis represents the utility of all other people. The economy is below the frontier at point A at the original no-toll equilibrium Q_c in Figure 7.7 because the congestion externality is not properly accounted for. The optimal congestion toll brings the economy to the frontier. But if the drivers see no benefit from the congestion tolls they pay, then they may view the tolls as bringing the economy to a point such as B on the frontier, at which they are worse off than at A. The resistance to the toll is essentially distributional in nature, that the gains from the toll revenues go to other people, not the drivers. Whatever the case may be, externality policies are going to be difficult to implement if they are resisted by the people whom they are designed to help.

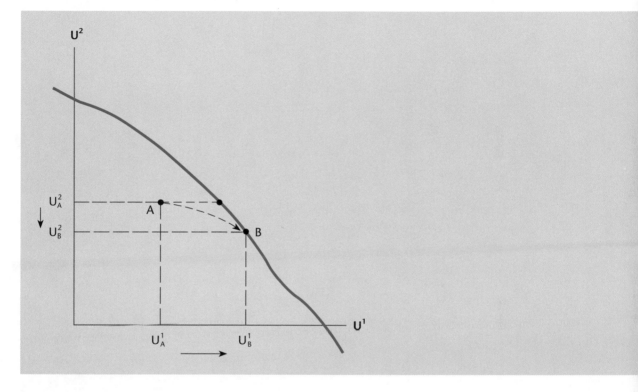

Figure 7.8

CHAPTER 8

Nonexclusive Goods

Nonexclusive goods such as national defense are a particular kind of externality. Recall from the discussion of Chapter 2 that a *nonexclusive good* has the property that if one person consumes the good, then everyone receives the full consumption services provided by that good. The nonexclusivity runs in both directions. A purchaser of the good cannot exclude anyone from consuming the services of the good and nonpurchasers cannot exclude themselves from consuming the services even if they want to. Nonexclusive goods, therefore, are the ultimate consumer externality: Purchase of the good by anyone affects everyone.

Nonexclusive goods deserve a separate chapter, however, because there is a fundamental difference between them and the externalities considered in Chapters 6 and 7. The externalities in those chapters all arose from some ongoing private market activity such as producing paper or driving downtown to work. In contrast, nonexclusive goods cannot reasonably be expected to be provided in the private sector because of the incentive people have to free ride on others' purchases of them. Standard exclusive goods such as paper and hamburgers can be marketed because if you want them, you have to be willing to pay for them, thereby registering your demand for them. But this is not true for nonexclusive goods such as defense. Even if you very much want a nonexclusive good such as a ballistic missile, the best option for you is to remain silent and hope that someone else buys the good. If someone does, then you enjoy the full services of the missile and it does not cost you anything. You free ride on the purchases of others. Since everyone has the same incentive to free ride, people's demands are not registered in the marketplace and a market cannot form. Society has no choice but to have the government purchase defense and other nonexclusive goods on their behalf. This is why nonexclusive goods are commonly referred to as public goods, in contrast to the standard exclusive goods, which are referred to as private goods.

Bringing a nonexclusive good like defense into the government sector is hardly the end of the story. Government officials have two difficult questions to answer:

1. How much defense should the government provide? What is the efficient amount of defense spending?
2. How should people be asked to pay for defense (presumably through some kind of tax)?

HOW MUCH DEFENSE?

In thinking about how much defense to provide, mainstream public sector economists assume that government officials act as agents on behalf of the citizens. The question is not how much defense certain government officials such as the president or secretary of defense might want. Rather, the question is how much defense the people want the government to provide. As in all public sector issues, the people's preferences are what matter.

The government-as-agent perspective assumes that government officials think about how much defense to provide as a pseudo-market problem. The question becomes: What would be the level of defense if it could be determined in a perfectly competitive market? There are market supply and demand curves for defense (or any other nonexclusive good). The goal is to discover what they are and then find the supply and demand equilibrium that they imply. The equilibrium quantity in this pseudo-market is the optimal or efficient amount of defense to provide.

There is nothing special about the supply side of the defense market in relation to the nonexclusive property of defense. The market supply curve S represents the marginal cost of producing defense at each output, the usual interpretation of a supply curve. Military hardware and equipment are mostly supplied by private sector firms, and we will assume that the government officials know the marginal cost of supply.

The difficulties lie on the demand side of the market. Figure 8.1 illustrates. Interpret the output Q as an index commodity representing all the components of defense spending, simply called defense, whose price is P. The figure assumes that there are only two individuals, with demand curves d^1 and d^2. The market demand curve D is, as always, the summation of the individuals' demand curves for defense, but with this twist. It is the *vertical* summation of the individual demand curves for defense rather than the horizontal summation as for standard exclusive goods. Therefore, D is the vertical sum of d^1 and d^2 at every output. The reason for the reversal in summing the demand curves is that for the private exclusive goods, all consumers face the same price and buy whatever quantities they want. Therefore, at each price, the total quantity demanded is the sum of the quantities demanded by each individual – the market demand curve is the horizontal summation of the individual demand curves. For nonexclusive goods like defense, in contrast, the government selects a single quantity of defense that every individual is forced to consume. At the given quantity, an individual demand curve gives the individual's demand price for that quantity, the amount he or she is willing to pay to consume the last unit of defense. Since individual demand curves differ, so too do the individual demand prices. At Q_1, person #1 is willing to pay P_1^1 for the last unit and person #2 is willing to pay P_1^2. The price P_1^D on the market demand curve at Q_1 is $P_1^1 + P_1^2$, the sum of the individual demand prices. It is the called the "market demand price," the aggregate amount that the two individuals are willing to pay for the last unit of defense at Q_1. The market demand price is determined the same way at every output, the sum of the individual demand prices each time. At each output, therefore, the market demand curve is the vertical summation of the individual demand curves.

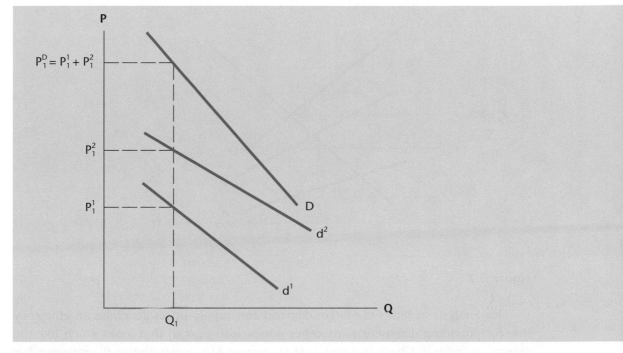

Figure 8.1

Figure 8.2 adds the market supply curve, S, to the demand curves from Figure 8.1. The equilibrium is Q_e, at the intersection of S and D. Of all the outputs that the government could select, Q_e is the only one with the property that the market supply price, P_e^S, equals the market demand price, P_e^D. The equality of the market supply and demand prices establishes Q_e as the optimal or efficient amount of defense by the standard efficiency principle of market exchange: The optimal output to be exchanged is the output at which the marginal value to the buyers equals the marginal cost of the suppliers. At Q_e, and only at Q_e, the aggregate value to individuals of the last unit of defense exchanged ($= P_e^D$) is equal to the cost of supplying the last unit ($= P_e^S$). At any output to the left of Q_e, the market demand price exceeds the market supply price; D lies above S. Consumers in the aggregate are willing to pay more for the next unit of output than it costs to supply it, so output should be increased. At any output to the right of Q_e, the market supply price exceeds the market demand price; S lies above D. The cost of supplying the last unit of output exceeds the amount that consumers in the aggregate are willing to pay for it, so output should be decreased. Q_e is the efficient amount of defense.

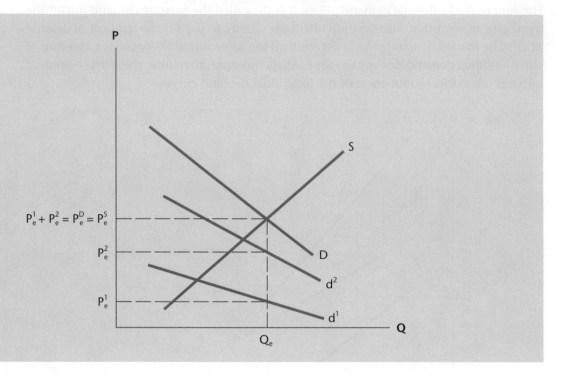

Figure 8.2

Our analysis in terms of market demand and supply prices generates an efficiency rule for providing defense (or any other nonexclusive good) that looks much like the externality rules in Chapters 6 and 7. At Q_e, person #1's demand price P_e^1 represents her marginal value of consuming defense MV_e^1, and person #2's demand price P_e^2 represents his marginal value of consuming defense, MV_e^2. The market supply price, P_e^S is, as noted, the marginal cost of defense, MC_e. Therefore, at the optimum

$$MV_e^1 + MV_e^2 = P_e^1 + P_e^2 = P_e^D = P_e^S = MC_e.$$

In general, for any number of individuals (households) H,

$$\sum_{h=1}^{H} MV_e^h = MC_e.$$

The sum of the marginal values over all individuals equals the marginal cost of defense at the optimum. This is essentially the same rule as the Pigovian tax (subsidy) for market-generated externalities, in which the tax (subsidy) equals the sum of the marginal damages (benefits) over all the people affected by the externality. The only difference is that the entire value of defense to consumers is in the form of an externality, whereas goods such as paper have a private use to consumers that is separate from their external effects.

THE SAMUELSON RULE

The most common representation of the rule for the efficient provision of a nonexclusive good is in terms of marginal rates of substitution and transformation defined relative to a representative private good whose price and marginal cost are equal to 1. Label the private good as good 1. MV_e^1 above is the same as person #1's marginal rate of substitution between defense and good 1, $MRS_{defense,1}^1$. $MRS_{defense,1}^1$ indicates the amount of good 1 that person #1 is willing to give up to consume another unit of defense, willing to give up in the sense that utility does not change. With the price of good 1 equal to 1, this is also the amount of income person #1 is willing to give up to consume another unit of defense, which is the standard way of representing the marginal value of any good. Similarly, $MV_e^2 = MRS_{defense,1}^2$. On the supply side, the marginal rate of transformation between defense and good 1 is the ratio of their marginal costs. With $MC_1 = 1$, $MRT_{defense,1}$ = $MC_{defense}$. Therefore, defense is provided efficiently when

$$\sum_{i=1}^{2} MRS_{defense,1}^i = MRT_{defense,1}.$$

In general, for H individuals (households),

$$\sum_{h=1}^{H} MRS_{defense,1}^h = MRT_{defense,1}.$$

This is known as the Samuelson Rule after Paul Samuelson (Samuelson, 1954), who first developed it. It is the Pareto-optimal rule for the provision of nonexclusive goods.

Contrast the Samuelson Rule to the Pareto-optimal rule for private exclusive goods that we developed in Chapter 3: MRS = MRT. Both rules say that goods and services should be exchanged to the point at which the marginal benefit and marginal cost of the exchange are equal. The difference is that when people buy one more unit of an exclusive good, the only benefit is to themselves, measured by their MRSs for the good. When the government provides one more unit of defense, everyone is affected, so that the marginal benefit is the sum of their individual MRSs for defense.

LINDAHL PRICES

Swedish economist Erik Lindahl carried the pseudo-market idea one step further. He noted that the efficient amount of defense, or any nonexclusive good, could be determined in an auction involving all the citizens (Lindahl, 1971). Lindahl's public goods auction is analogous to the Walrasian auction that economists use to describe how perfectly competitive markets operate for private goods, named after French economist Leon Walras.

In the private goods auction, an auctioneer calls out a price and notes the quantities demanded and supplied at that price. If the quantities are unequal, no sales occur. Instead the auctioneer calls out a different price and keeps adjusting the price until the quantities demanded and supplied are equal, at which point the market is in equilibrium. Some highly competitive markets operate much as Walras described, such as the markets for stocks, bonds, agricultural produce, and other commodities.

Lindahl's public goods auction is much more complex. The auctioneer calls out a quantity that the government might supply, and notes the marginal cost or supply price P^s at that quantity. Call the quantity Q_0. He then assigns a tax share or price to each citizen such that the individual tax shares sum to P^s and notes whether every person wants to purchase Q_0 at the assigned tax shares. Suppose they do not. Then the auctioneer keeps adjusting the tax shares, trying to find an assignment of tax shares such that every person does want to buy Q_0. If this proves to be impossible, the auctioneer calls out a second quantity, notes the new supply price, and tries again to find an assignment of tax shares that sum to P^s and induce everyone to want to buy the second quantity. The process continues until the auctioneer calls out the efficient quantity, Q_e in Figure 8.2. At that quantity, it is possible to find an assignment of tax shares that add to P_e^s such that everyone wants to purchase Q_e. The tax shares are the individual demand prices in Figure 8.2 (as a proportion of P^s, the supply price). At that point, the auction is finished and the efficient provision of the public good has been determined.

Notice from Figure 8.1 that there is always an assignment of taxes or individual demand prices at any given quantity that the auctioneer calls out such that every person wants to purchase that quantity. These prices sum to the market demand price P_e^D on the market demand curve D. Only at Q_e, however, is the auctioneer's second requirement also met, that the individual demand prices or tax shares of P^s add to the supply price P^s on the market supply curve S. The individual demand prices, or tax shares, at the efficient equilibrium have forever after been known as *Lindahl prices*.

What should we make of the pseudo-market equilibrium approach with its Lindahl auctioneer? It is a convenient and familiar analytical device for determining the properties of the efficient provision of nonexclusive public goods such as defense, and that is worth something. Yet it is hardly practicable as a guideline to policy makers. For starters, the Lindahl auction is clearly hopelessly complex in any realistic setting, especially since all citizens would have to participate. The complexity of the auction is not even the most serious problem, however. A more fundamental issue with the entire pseudo-market analysis is the free-rider problem. The incentive for citizens to free ride on others does not disappear simply by having the government provide nonexclusive goods. People participating in Lindahl's auction have no incentive to reveal their demands for the public good at their assigned tax shares or prices, especially if they believe that they might actually have to pay that price for the good should the auction end. Better to lie and say that only a zero tax share would lead them to want to purchase whatever quantity the auctioneer calls out and hope that others pay for the good. Unfortunately, everyone reasons the same way and would not be willing to pay for it, and the auction falls apart. The sad truth is that the government needs to know the individual demand curves of citizens to provide the efficient amount of the public good when acting as the citizens' agent, yet citizens have no incentive to reveal their demands. Determining the efficient provision of a nonexclusive good as important as defense is an insurmountably difficult problem in practice.

HOW TO PAY FOR DEFENSE

Lindahl prices are often held up as an ideal to strive for, notwithstanding the difficulties in trying to determine them. They are seen as having two desirable properties. First, they provide a simple test of whether the provision of defense, or any other nonexclusive good, is efficient, as described above: Do the Lindahl prices sum to the supply price, or marginal cost, at the given quantity? Second, they are viewed as a fair way of paying for defense, because they are in accordance with the benefits-received principle of taxing to pay for publicly provided goods and services.

LINDAHL PRICES AND THE BENEFITS-RECEIVED PRINCIPLE OF TAXATION

The benefits-received principle originated in the feudal societies of Europe in the 13th and 14th centuries, when noblemen would pay a tax or tribute to the Crown in return for protection of their fiefdoms from foreign invaders. These payments for the benefits of defense led to the broader conception of the *benefits-received principle of taxation* that has survived to this day. It says that, to the extent possible, users of any publicly provided good (or service) should pay in proportion to the benefits they receive from the good. In addition, the users should pay for the full costs of the good. Non-users of the good should not have to pay anything. The benefits-received principle is a widely embraced principle of equity or fairness in paying for government expenditures in the United States and many, if not all, of the other industrialized capitalist countries.

The benefits-received principle cannot be applied to all government expenditures, an obvious exception being transfer payments to the poor. Presumably the benefits of transfers programs go to the recipients of the transfers. If they are then taxed to pay for the benefits they receive, there would be no net transfer to them. But the principle could possibly be applied to all the resource-using government expenditures that wind up in the public sector because of the various efficiency or allocation problems described in this section of the text. And the idea is that if it can be applied, it should be applied, as a matter of fairness. The belief in the benefits-received principle is the motivation behind recent tax reforms in the United States in which local governments are now commonly charging fees for services such as garbage collection and the use of public beaches rather than paying for them out of the local property tax. The fees more closely tie the payment of services to their use by citizens.

The appeal of the benefits-received principle of taxation in capitalist countries is hardly surprising because markets themselves operate on a benefits-received basis. If you want a particular good or service, you pay for it, and the more you want it, the more you pay. If you do not want it, you do not have to buy it. The only matter of contention in paying for publicly provided goods and services relates to the question of what benefits our taxes should be based on. Should people pay in proportion to the total benefits they receive? to the average benefits? to the marginal benefits?

A natural answer is marginal benefits because that is how we pay for private goods in the marketplace. Although we may have different incomes and tastes and purchase different amounts of a good, on the margin we are all identical. We consume to the point at which the price we pay, which is the same for everyone, equals our marginal value of the good, or our MRS in terms of some reference private good. If we buy many units of the good, we do so at a price that reflects the value of the last good we purchase.

Return now to the pseudo-market representation of defense in Figure 8.2. The prices that reflect the marginal values or MRS of defense for the two individuals are their demand prices at Q_e, P_e^1, and P_e^2, the Lindahl prices. It is the Lindahl prices or tax shares that most closely mimic the way that we pay for private goods and services, and for this reason they are widely considered to be a fair way to pay for defense.

SOME DIFFICULTIES WITH LINDAHL PRICES

Would people embrace Lindahl prices simply because of their correspondence to competitive market prices? The answer is "probably not." Figure 8.3 illustrates a potential difficulty with Lindahl pricing for defense. Here the two people are called Hawk and Dove, with Hawk much more enthusiastic about defense spending. Their individual demand curves are d^{Dove} and d^{Hawk}. As above, D is the market demand curve, the vertical summation of d^{Dove} and d^{Hawk} at each output, and S is the market supply curve.

In Figure 8.3(a), Dove's support of defense has run out right at the efficient quantity Q_e. Her demand curve hits the horizontal axis at Q_e; the value she places on the last unit of defense spending is zero. Consequently, when the curves are added vertically, Hawk's demand curve intersects the market demand curve D at the intersection of D and S. The Lindahl prices are $P_e^{Dove} = 0$ for Dove, and $P_e^{Hawk} = P_e^D = P_e^S$, the market demand and supply prices, for Hawk. Hawk pays the full costs of defense, even though Dove gets some total benefit from defense as indicated by her demand curve. Hawk may well object to this "sharing" of defense spending.

Unfortunately, the situation is likely to be even worse for the Hawks of the world, as illustrated in Figure 8.3(b). In this case, Dove's support for defense has run out well before Q_e. She places a negative value on additional defense spending on all units past the point at which her demand curve hits the horizontal axis. Defense is a bad, not a good to her on the margin. Now when the two demand curves are added, Hawk's demand curve is above the market demand curve D at Q_e by the same distance that Dove's demand curve is below the horizontal axis. The Lindahl prices are $P_e^{Dove} < 0$ and $P_e^{Hawk} > P_e^D = P_e^S$. Hawk must pay the full costs of defense at Q_e *plus* subsidize Dove for the harm that defense causes her on the margin. Hawk would surely object to this, yet the situation is entirely realistic. Think of the debate over the merits of the war in Iraq. Some people (Hawks) wish the United States had been more aggressive and sent even more troops to Iraq; other people (Doves) do not believe the United States should have gone to war in the first place. Should the former subsidize the latter for the war?

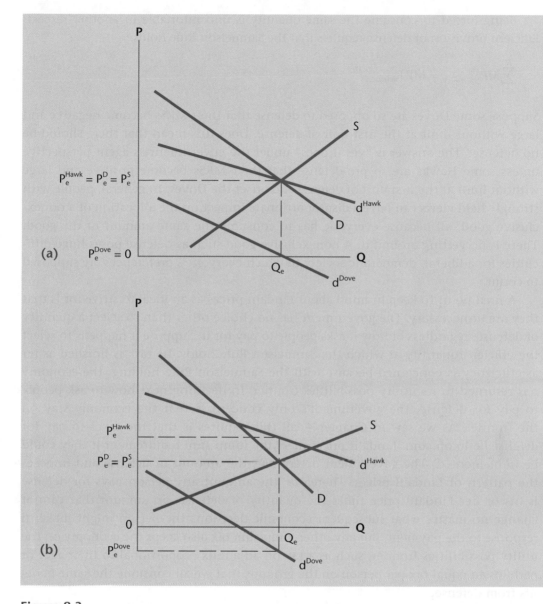

Figure 8.3

The problem with the competitive pricing analogue for nonexclusive goods is that it is only partially accurate. True, Lindahl prices equal individuals' marginal values or MRS for defense just as for private goods. But the market process is reversed, and this matters. Unlike private goods, we are all forced to consume the same amount of defense, and at that one quantity our marginal values (MRSs) are likely to differ. A pattern of different payments for the same amount of a good is not at all analogous to competitive pricing, in which the price is the same for everyone.

Being forced to consume the same quantity is uncomfortable in another respect. Efficient provision of defense requires that the Samuelson Rule holds:

$$\sum_{h=1}^{H} MRS_{defense,1}^{h} = MRT_{defense,1}.$$

Suppose some Doves are so opposed to defense that their MRSs become negative and large without limit at the first unit of defense. Does this mean that there should be no defense? The answer is "yes it does" under the government-as-agent perspective unless some Hawks are so pro-defense that their MRSs become positive and large without limit at the first unit of defense and offset the Doves. In general, people with strongly held views can have a disproportionate impact on the allocation of a nonexclusive good, all because everyone has to consume the same amount of the good. There is no getting around it: A nonexclusive good such as defense poses huge difficulties for a liberal, democratic society in which everyone's preferences are supposed to count.

A final point to keep in mind about Lindahl prices as an ideal to strive for is that they are unnecessary. The government has no choice other than to select a quantity of defense, regardless of how it asks people to pay for it. Suppose it happens to select the efficient quantity at which the Samuelson Rule holds. Its task is finished as far as efficiency is concerned because with the Samuelson Rule holding, the economy has returned to its utility possibilities frontier. In deciding next how to ask people to pay for defense, the government's only concern is that the economy stay on the frontier. As we saw in Chapter 4, all this requires is that the taxes to pay for defense be lump sum. Lindahl prices meet the lump-sum requirement if they could be implemented. The government determines the amount of defense and imposes the pattern of Lindahl prices. Therefore, the amount any person pays for defense is his or her Lindahl price times the quantity of defense, an amount that cannot change no matter what subsequent economic decisions the person might make in response to the payment. But any other lump-sum tax also keeps the economy on the utility possibilities frontier, such as a tax on all adults proportional to their ages or perhaps an equal tax per person on the grounds that we all consume the same benefits from defense.

An age tax would undoubtedly strike people as a terribly unfair method of paying for defense, but it does not matter. The distribution branch would take into account the lump-sum taxes that people pay for defense when designing its redistribution policy. Recall that its goal is to design a set of lump-sum taxes and transfers that bring the economy to the bliss point on the utility possibility frontier, the point that maximizes social welfare. The taxes and transfers achieve the bliss point by satisfying the interpersonal equity condition, that the social marginal utilities of income be equal across all people. Suppose many poor elderly people end up being charged a disproportionate amount for defense under an age tax. Poorer people presumably have higher than average social marginal utilities of income and the age tax would lower their incomes and increase their social marginal utilities of income even more. The distribution branch would simply offset their taxes with extra transfers until their social marginal utilities of income have been lowered to the same value as everyone else's social marginal utilities of income. In the end, the payment for defense depends on people's relative social marginal utilities of income, not their preferences for defense. Those with higher incomes – lower social marginal utilities of income – end up paying a disproportionate share of the defense spending. The same argument applies to an equal per-person tax.

In truth, *the benefits-received principle of taxation has no role to play in the mainstream theory of the public sector as a principle of equity or fairness in paying for publicly provided goods*. The general public and public sector economists no doubt part company on this point. In the mainstream theory, all matters of equity are contained within the social welfare function and the resulting interpersonal equity condition, no place else. The usefulness of Lindahl prices if they could be implemented is their efficiency property. They would provide a simple test of whether the Samuelson Rule holds, that is, whether the government has achieved the efficient provision of defense. Simply compare their sum with the supply price, the marginal cost of defense. Their fairness as a means of paying for defense is irrelevant. The distribution branch has the final, and only, say in matters of end-results equity as it redistributes to reach the bliss point on the utility possibilities frontier.

THE MECHANISM DESIGN PROBLEM

When all is said and done, the nastiest problem with defense remains the free-rider problem. It is a specific instance of a more general problem that the government faces: People have private information that the government as agent needs to know in order to make an efficient decision about a publicly provided good or service, but people have a self-interested incentive to hide their information from the government. As we have seen in the case of defense, the government needs to know the individual demand curves to select the efficient amount of defense but people have an incentive to conceal them in the hope of free riding on the goodwill of others.

The natural response to private information of this kind is to try to solve the so-called *mechanism design problem*: Design a mechanism or procedure under which the dominant or utility-maximizing strategy for individuals is to reveal the truth about themselves. This turns out to be a very difficult assignment. Economists have proposed solutions to the mechanism design problem in various contexts, but none so far that are practicable for nonexclusive goods.

Edward Clarke (1971) proposed the first solution to the mechanism design problem in the early 1970s in the context of providing a nonexclusive good such as defense. Clarke's mechanism is illustrated in Figure 8.4.[1]

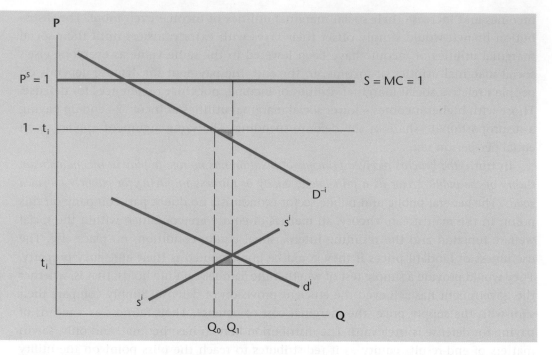

Figure 8.4

Suppose the nation consists of N individuals. The government begins by asking all N individuals how much defense they would demand at various prices, in other words, what their demand curves look like. The data on the demand curves are collected, even though the people could be lying through their teeth. They have no incentive at this point to reveal their true demand curves. The government also arbitrarily assigns a tax share, t_i, $i = 1,...,N$, to each individual to pay for defense. The tax shares bear no necessary relationship to the stated demand curves. Suppose for simplicity that the marginal cost of supplying defense is constant and equal to 1, as indicated by the supply curve S in the figure. Then the tax shares sum to 1, the supply price of defense.

The mechanism is as follows. The government singles out one individual, say person i, whose tax share is t_i. It then adds vertically all the stated demand curves of the other N-1 individuals to form the market demand curve for these people labeled D^{-i} in Figure 8.4. (The superscript –i means "all but person i.") The sum of the tax shares of the other N-1 individuals is $(1 - t_i)$, as indicated by the upper tax share line in the figure. The government selects as a starting point output Q_0 at the intersection of D^{-i} and the tax share line $(1 - t_i)$.

Person 1 is then given a choice of accepting Q_0 or any other output that she prefers, with the following provision attached. If she chooses some other output, she must pay a tax to compensate the other N-1 individuals for the losses they suffer in moving from Q_0. Using the standard consumer surplus measure, their aggregate loss is the area between the demand curve D^{-i} and the tax share line $(1 - t_i)$ from Q_0 to the output she chooses.

This tax is in addition to person i's tax share t_i and is known as a "Clarke tax." The Clarke tax is paid so that the other N-1 individuals remain willing to participate in the mechanism and accept a different output. The line $s^i s^i$ duplicates the area between D^{-i} and $(1 - t_i)$ as the area between $s^i s^i$ and person i's tax share line t_i.

Suppose for the moment that d^i represents the true demand curve for person i. Person i's best choice is output Q_1, at the intersection of d^i and $s^i s^i$ by the standard marginal benefit = marginal cost argument. The marginal value to person i of each additional unit of defense beyond Q_0 is given by the demand curve d^i, and the marginal cost is $s^i s^i$, equal to the per-unit tax share t_i plus the Clarke tax on each additional unit. Therefore, the marginal benefit and marginal cost of defense are equal at Q_1, so that Q_1 maximizes the consumer surplus to person i among all her possible choices. Moreover, selecting the best output along her true demand curve gives person i more consumer surplus than she would receive by selecting the intersection of $s^i s^i$ and some false demand curve. Therefore, person i has an incentive to reveal her true demand curve, and Q_1 is established as the new level of defense.

Having discovered the true demand curve for person i, add her to all the other individuals, select a second person, say person j, and offer the same choice to him: Output Q_1 chosen by person i or any other output subject to paying a Clarke tax. This choice induces person j to reveal his true preferences and perhaps select a different output from Q_1. Now add person j to the N-1 individuals and select a third person. Continue in this way until everyone has been selected. Eventually everyone's true demand curves are revealed and the mechanism selects the efficient level of output. To see this, suppose that person i above is the last person selected rather than the first. Then D^{-i} is the vertical sum of the N-1 true demand curves of all the other people. Once person i reveals her true demand curve and selects Q_1, then adding d^i to D^{-i} generates the true market demand curve. Also, adding t_i to $(1 - t_i)$ generates the supply price of 1 on S. Therefore, the intersection of D^{-i} and the vertical line from Q_1 is equivalent to the intersection of the market demand and supply curves at Q_1. Q_1 is the efficient level of defense.

The essence of the Clarke tax is that it induces people to reveal their true preferences by basing the cost of their decisions on the preferences of others rather than on their own preferences. This feature is common to solutions of the mechanism design problem in any context. Nonetheless, Clarke's mechanism is not very realistic. It does not approximate any procedure that governments have ever used and there is no reason to believe that all people would be willing to play Clarke's game. Some may decide that the potential gains are less than the costs to them of participating. The government may have to force people to participate. Unfortunately, impracticality and the need for coercion are common features of solutions to the mechanism design problem. The truth of the matter is that private information is often an enormous obstacle to a government that wants to act on behalf of citizens and base its decisions on their preferences.

DO PEOPLE FREE RIDE?

A final question that naturally arises for nonexclusive goods is whether people will actually free ride if given the opportunity to do so. Economists have explored this question by conducting computer laboratory experiments with college students, most often economics majors because they presumably understand incentives. The standard form of the experiments is a game among the students played as follows. Each student is given a fixed number of tokens, W, which can be used to purchase either a private good, X, or a public good, G: W = X + G. The reward for purchasing X is R per unit of X and the reward for purchasing G is V per unit of G, with R > V. The direct reward to each student for purchasing a private good is greater than the reward for purchasing a public good. But the public good is nonexclusive, so that a purchase of G by any student yields the reward V to all the students in the experiment. Assuming that there are N students, the total reward for each purchase of G is NV, with NV > R. The total reward across all students for each purchase of a public good exceeds the direct reward to a student from purchasing a private good. The game may be played once, or over many rounds, with students receiving W new tokens each round. At the end of the experiment, the students receive the total monetary rewards due them from all the purchases made during the game.

With NV > R for each purchase of G or X, the Pareto-optimal solution to this game is for students to purchase only the public good G. Purchasing only G each round would maximize the total profits available to each student, an amount equal to WNV, whereas purchasing only X yields WR for each student. But the game is structured such that purchasing G is not in the students' narrow self-interest. The self-interested play is to purchase X and free ride on the purchases of G by the other students. To see why, consider the profits earned by one of the students, student i, each round:

$$\text{Profit}_i = RX_i + VG_i + V \cdot \sum_{j \neq i} G_j \,,$$

with $W_i = X_i + G_i$. The profit consists of the rewards based on her own purchases of X_i and G_i plus the rewards received from the purchases of the public good by all the other students. Student i can control only her own purchases X_i and G_i, however. The purchases of G by the other students are whatever they will be, a given from student i's point of view. Suppose the game is played only once. Then student i has an incentive to purchase only the private good no matter what the other students do. Purchasing X_i yields a reward of R and purchasing G_i yields a reward of V. With R > V, purchasing X_i instead of G_i increases student i's profit by R – V. (Conversely, purchasing G_i instead of X_i decreases student i's profit by R – V.) What is true for student i is true for all the other students. So the expected outcome of a one-shot game is that every student purchases only X, and attempts to free ride on the other students. The Pareto-optimal outcome of everyone purchasing only G cannot be achieved. Each student earns WR instead of WNV had everyone purchased only G.

Playing the game for many rounds does not change the expected outcome. Suppose the game is played for 10 rounds. The rational, self-interested student solves the game by a process that game theorists refer to as "backward induction." The idea is to think first about purchases in the last round, the 10th round. Once the game has reached that point, the 10th round is equivalent to a one-shot game, for which the strategy is to purchase only X. All students realize this, so they assume that only X will be purchased in the last round. That round has, in effect, become predetermined, so think next about the 9th round. With the 10th round predetermined, the 9th round is now equivalent to a one-shot game, for which the strategy again is to purchase only X. Therefore the 9th round is also predetermined, so think next about the 8th round, which is now equivalent to a one-shot game with the last two rounds predetermined. This process of backward induction continues to the first round, which is then also equivalent to a one-shot game. So the expected outcome of the experiment is that students purchase only X, no matter how many rounds the game is played. The self-interested incentive is to attempt to free ride on the other students.

The actual outcomes of these experiments are quite different from the expected outcome, however. Most experiments are conducted over more than one round. The usual outcome is that the students allocate a large percentage of their tokens to the public good in the early rounds, 50% or more. Purchases of the public good diminish as the game proceeds, but not to zero as expected. Students still allocate a substantial percentage of their tokens to the public good in the later rounds, as much as 25% in some of the experiments. The pattern of significant, if diminishing, purchases of the public good stands up against all variations of the game, such as the number of rounds played, the number of students, whether the students know each other, and whether the outcomes are announced after each round. There is some variation across the individual students in each experiment, but the pattern of outcomes is as represented above.

The cooperative rather than narrowly self-interested behavior that the students exhibit is no doubt pleasing to mainstream public sector economists, who believe that people have some interest in promoting the common or social good. They are not entirely self-serving. Still, the behavior of the students is puzzling, given the structure of the game. Economist James Andreoni, who has conducted many of these experiments, posits that people receive a separate warm glow from behaving cooperatively and contributing to the rewards of others. In one test of his hypothesis, he conducted two experiments that differed only in the way that the instructions to the students were written. In the first experiment, students were told that each purchase of the public good G would yield a reward of V for every other student. In the second experiment, the students were told that each purchase of a private good X would cost each of the other students a reward of V.

The first experiment is an example of a positive framing of the game. It leads the students to assume that their endowment of tokens W are all in the form of the private good X and that they can do a good deed by sacrificing some of their endowment to the common good by purchasing G. The second is an example of a negative framing of the game. It leads the students to assume that their endowment of tokens W are all in the form of the public good G and that they do harm to others by sacrificing some of their endowment to increase their personal gains by purchasing some X. Other than the instructions, the games are identical to the standard game described above. The outcomes are quite different though. Students allocate a significantly higher percentage of their tokens each round to the public good in the positive frame game. They appear to get more personal satisfaction from doing a good deed than from avoiding doing a bad deed. Andreoni (1995) sees these results as offering some support to his warm glow hypothesis.

CHAPTER 9

Decreasing Cost Services: the Natural Monopolies

Capitalist economies would work best if all markets were perfectly competitive, but some markets are not going to be even highly competitive, much less perfectly competitive. The impediment to competition most often lies on the supply side of the economy. The production of some goods and services exhibits substantial economies of scale, enough so that the average or unit costs of a single firm do not reach their minimum until the firm's output is a significant percentage of the overall market demand. The markets for these goods are likely to be structured as oligopolies, with a few large firms dominating the market. Oligopolies may or may not be reasonably competitive. If not, they are likely to attract the attention of the government's antitrust or regulatory agencies.

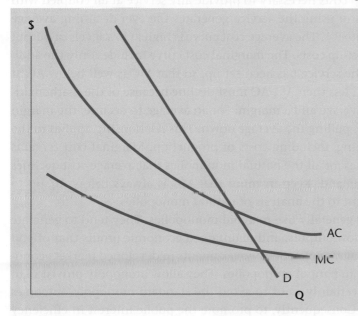

Figure 9.1

The economies of scale can be so large that a single firm's average costs continue to decline all the way to the market demand, as illustrated in Figure 9.1. The average cost (AC) and marginal cost (MC) curves are those of a single firm, and D is the overall market demand curve. The relevant market could be regional, national, or even global, depending on the nature of the good or service. Economists refer to markets with this characteristic as a *natural monopoly*, because having a single firm produce the good at a low average cost is much cheaper than having many small firms each producing small quantities in the region of high average cost. Allowing a monopoly conserves the use of society's scarce resources.

As noted in Chapter 2, instances of natural monopoly are hardly rare. A number of very important goods and services have the cost characteristics of a natural monopoly, including: the public utilities such as electricity, water, and sewage; transportation – highways, bridges, tunnels, and mass (rail) transit; recreational facilities such as parks and beaches; all forms of telecommunication – radio, TV, and wireless communication; and the production of computer software, for which the economies of scale are essentially global. Production in each instance is characterized by very high set-up costs relative to the marginal operating costs. There are considerable costs to constructing and maintaining electric lines, water and sewage pipes, highways and mass transit, and parks; to producing, transmitting, and receiving television programs; and to writing and testing software programs. But once these set-up costs have been incurred so that consumers can use the services, the cost of one more person turning on a light bulb or a faucet, driving on a road, visiting a park, turning on a TV set, and downloading a software program are minimal to near zero (short of congestion in the case of the public utilities and transportation and recreational facilities; congestion is an externality and a separate issue).

The pattern of high set-up costs necessary to provide any service at all coupled with low marginal operating costs of using the service generates the ever-declining average cost curve. Refer again to Figure 9.1. The average cost curve is high at low levels of output because it includes the high set-up costs. The marginal cost curve includes only the additional operating costs once the service has been set up, so that MC is well below AC at low units of output. With MC less then AC, AC must decline because of the mathematical relationship between an average and a margin: For an average to decline, the margin must be less than the average, pulling the average down. This relationship applies to the average and margin of anything, including costs of production. Marginal cost remains low enough as output increases for all the natural monopolies that average cost declines all the way to the market demand. Keep in mind that MC is always below AC up to market demand; it is important to the analysis of natural monopolies.

Capitalist societies would generally like to avoid monopolies. They tend to generate inefficiently high prices and low outputs, and maintained economic profits that offend people's sense of equity. This may explain why governments in developed market economies almost always intervene in natural monopolies. They allow monopoly provision to save on costs but they most certainly want to avoid the standard monopoly outcomes for these important services. Consequently, to promote the public interest in efficiency and equity, they usually either operate the service themselves or grant private investors a monopoly franchise to provide the service and then regulate the firm.

Achieving efficiency and equity when a market is a natural monopoly is easier said than done. The government is faced with difficult pricing and investment decisions that differ in kind from the pricing and investment decisions of private firms and happen to generate a lot of controversy. As we shall see, the main difference is that profitability cannot guide the government's decisions as it does in the private sector, which in turn is the source of much of the controversy. The government must resort to other principles that are unfamiliar to private investors and managers. We will consider the pricing and investment decisions in turn.

THE PRICING DECISION

The goods and services of the natural monopolies draw the attention of governments because of their production characteristics. From the consumers' point of view, however, they are just like any standard private good that they purchase in the marketplace. As such, the Pareto-optimal condition for efficient exchange between the consumers and the natural monopoly firm is the same as that for any private good that we developed in Chapter 2: MRS = MRT. The consumers' common marginal rate of substitution between the product of the natural monopoly and another reference private good is equal to the marginal rate of transformation between the two goods in production. As we also saw in Chapter 2, this condition can be satisfied only if the natural monopolist sets its price equal to its marginal cost. The argument is as follows. Select as the reference private good a good whose price and marginal cost equals one. Then the consumers set their common MRS to the price charged by the natural monopolist. In addition, the MRT, which is the ratio of the marginal costs of both goods, is the natural monopolist's marginal cost. Therefore, to achieve MRS = MRT requires that P = MC. Figure 9.2 illustrates. It reproduces the market demand curve and the firm's average and marginal cost curves from Figure 9.1.

The requirement that P = MC for efficient exchange is satisfied at the intersection of the demand and marginal cost curves, as it is for any monopolist. The efficient output is Q_{eff} and the efficient price is P_{eff} (= MC). Q_{eff} is the output that maximizes the net value of the exchange, the total value of the good to consumers minus the total cost to the producer of supplying the good. As always, net value is maximized when the marginal value to consumers, their common MRS, is equal to the firm's marginal cost of supplying the good.[1]

There is a problem with the efficient solution for the natural monopoly, however. Since marginal cost is below average cost at Q_{eff} the price P_{eff} is not sufficient to cover the total cost of production. At (Q_{eff}, P_{eff}), the firm's total revenue is $P_{eff}Q_{eff}$ and its total cost is $AC \cdot Q_{eff}$. The firm makes a loss equal to $(AC - P_{eff})Q_{eff}$, the rectangular area $ACabP_{eff}$ in Figure 9.2. The government must raise additional revenues to cover the loss whether the firm is privately or publicly owned – the factors of production have to be paid their opportunity cost. The usual statement is that the loss has to be covered "out of general tax revenues," but we can say more than that in the context of mainstream public sector theory.

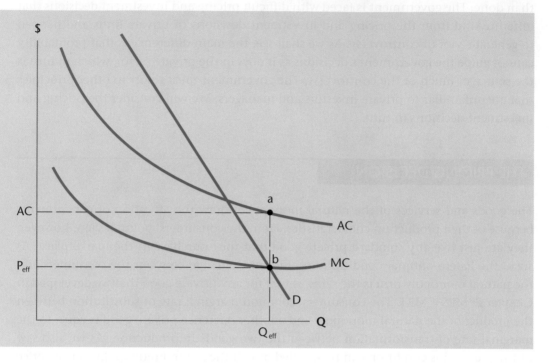

Figure 9.2

Setting price equal to marginal cost for a natural monopoly satisfies the first requirement of government policy for all allocational or efficiency problems: It keeps the economy on its utility possibilities frontier because it satisfies the Pareto-optimality condition for efficient exchange, that MRS = MRT. The only other requirement is to ensure that the economy remains on its frontier, which implies that the subsidy to cover the firm's losses at the efficient price must be lump sum. If the payment is lump sum, however, it effectively becomes part of the distribution branch's lump-sum taxes and transfers that bring the economy to the bliss point on the utility possibilities frontier, the social welfare maximum among all the possible efficient allocations. Recall that the bliss point is reached by taxing and transferring lump sum to satisfy the interpersonal equity condition, that the social marginal utilities of income be equal across all individuals. The distribution branch takes the subsidies to the natural monopolies into account when determining the optimal pattern of lump-sum taxes and transfers, just as it would any lump-sum tax used to pay for defense. (Refer to the discussion in Chapter 8 if you are unclear on this point.) The only difference the natural monopolies make in the quest to achieve the interpersonal equity condition is that the taxes collected lump sum from people must be sufficient to pay for the transfers given lump sum to the people plus the lump-sum transfers required to cover the losses of the natural monopolies. In other words, the lump-sum subsidies to cover the losses of the natural monopolies do more than preserve efficiency. They become subsumed within society's effort to achieve distributive justice, end-results equity.

To summarize, the efficient provision of the output of a natural monopoly has two distinct parts:

1. Set price equal to marginal cost, the standard prescription for the efficient exchange of any private good or service.
2. Cover the resulting losses to the monopolist with a lump-sum subsidy. The government's distribution branch then takes the required subsidy into consideration when determining the pattern of lump-sum taxes and subsidies that satisfy the interpersonal equity condition for a social welfare maximum, that the social marginal utilities of income be equal across all individuals.

U.S. POLICY – AVERAGE COST PRICING AND THE BENEFITS-RECEIVED PRINCIPLE

Governments in the United States universally reject the economist's call for marginal cost pricing of the natural monopolies in favor of average cost pricing. The reason appears to be that marginal cost pricing violates the benefits-received principle of taxation in paying for public goods and services that we introduced in Chapter 8.[2] The natural monopolies are perfect candidates for the benefits-received principle because users can be distinguished from non-users, and more intensive users from less intensive users. As such, the principle says that users should pay the full cost of the services, non-users should pay nothing, and more intensive users should pay more than less intensive users.

The marginal cost price P_{eff} from Figure 9.2 partly satisfies the benefits-received principle. Users pay P_{eff}, non-users pay nothing, and more intensive users pay more than less intensive users because P_{eff} is a per-unit price. The problem, though, is that P_{eff} does not cover the full cost of the service, and the subsidy to cover the losses "out of general tax revenues" breaks the link between use and payment. For example, people in the western part of a state may end up subsidizing the users of an electric utility serving people in the eastern part of the state if they pay a higher share of the state's sales and income tax revenues.

Governments could give the appearance of adhering to the benefits-received principle by setting the efficient price P_{eff} and then charging all users and potential users an annual fee for the privilege of using the service, with the annual fees set at a level to cover the losses with efficient pricing. The fee would be lump sum, as required, but it would also be taken into account by the distribution branch when designing its set of lump-sum taxes and transfers. For example, low-income students and the elderly are frequent users of a city's subway system and the one-time fees may be difficult for them to afford. The distribution branch would note this, and give them extra transfers to offset the fees as part of its redistribution. In terms of public sector theory, therefore, those with high incomes (low social marginal utilities of income) ultimately pay for the subsidies to cover the losses of the natural monopolies as the distribution branch taxes and transfers to equalize the social marginal utilities of income. This is so no matter how much they use the services of the natural monopolies, or even if they do not use them at all. This underscores a point made in Chapter 8, that the benefits-received theory is useful only as an efficiency principle, not as an equity principle in public sector theory. The benefits-received price P_{eff} is a price set for efficiency reasons; the subsidy to cover the losses is subsumed within the interpersonal equity condition, the only condition relevant to the government's quest for end-results equity. In any event, governments have rejected marginal cost pricing and one-time fees for the natural monopolies.

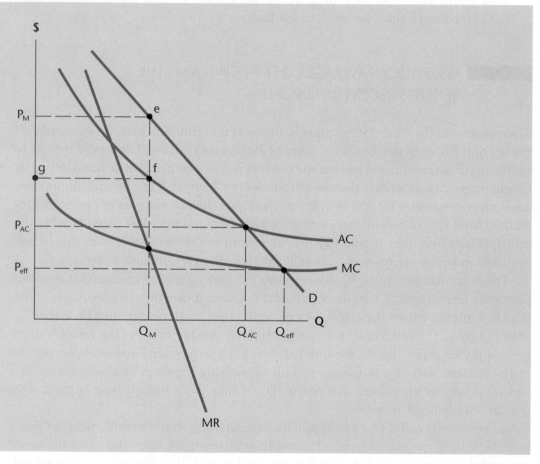

Figure 9.3

Having rejected marginal cost pricing, governments apparently see themselves as having essentially two options, monopoly pricing or average cost pricing. They are both illustrated in Figure 9.3, along with the efficient solution (Q_{eff}, P_{eff}). MR is the marginal revenue curve associated with the market demand curve D.

One option is to grant private investors a monopoly franchise and let them do what they want. This has the advantage of avoiding the costs of regulating firms. But the fear is that the investors will behave as textbook monopolists and maximize profits. If so, they produce the output Q_M at which MR intersects MC, and set the price P_M on the demand curve. The maximum profit is $(P_M - AC)Q_M$, the rectangular area $P_M$efg. This is a terrible outcome from the point of view of the public interest. It keeps prices much too high, and output much too low relative to the efficient outcome. The whole point of allowing a monopoly is to achieve the cost savings possible with the decreasing average costs. But if the monopolist sets the price at P_M, the cost savings accrue narrowly to the owners of the firm as profit rather than to the general public in the form of lower prices to match the lower costs.

Nobel laureate Milton Friedman argued that private investors would understand the outcry against maximizing profit and accept much lower profits to maintain their monopoly position.[3] This may be. For example, the NFL raises ticket prices for the Superbowl but nowhere near the profit-maximizing prices. We know this because ticket scalpers receive many times the price of the tickets. Nonetheless, government officials reject the unregulated solution out of hand. Cost overruns on public projects, such as the $15 billion Big Dig in Boston that was originally estimated to cost $2 billion, arouse the public's ire. But if firms were seen to be *profiteering* at the public's expense, the public outcry would be deafening. Governments do not want to risk that possibility with the natural monopolies.

The other option is the one chosen: Set the price equal to average cost, and supply the output Q_{AC}. Average cost pricing is viewed as a reasonable compromise between equity and efficiency. The average cost price P_{AC} covers the full cost of the service and thus meets all the requirements of the benefits-received principle. Non-users never have to subsidize the users as with marginal cost pricing. Furthermore, although Q_{AC} is not the efficient output, the nature of the natural monopolies' cost is such that (Q_{AC}, P_{AC}) is much closer to (Q_{eff}, P_{eff}) than to (Q_M, P_M). At P_{AC} consumers gain most of the cost advantages of establishing a natural monopoly.

The average cost pricing solution is almost universal in the United States. Electric utility regulators try to set prices that cover the private utilities' operating costs plus allow a fair return on investors' capital. Tolls on highways, bridges, and tunnels are set to cover the costs of the metropolitan commissions that are responsible for their construction and upkeep. Parking and entrance fees at parks and beaches are set to cover the costs of these recreational facilities. And so forth. The perceived fairness of the benefits-received principle appears to be very strongly held in the United States. This is clearly an instance in which mainstream public sector theory is at odds with the public's view of equity.

THE INVESTMENT DECISION

There is an all-or-none quality to the investment decision of a natural monopoly that is absent in almost all private investment decisions. We refer here to a decision by private investors to enter a perfectly competitive market. The decision of a single firm to enter a market is typically viewed as representing a marginal addition to overall industry output, so small that the entrant would have no noticeable effect on output or input prices. Therefore, private investors can appropriately measure the costs and revenues to them of entering the market at the existing market prices. If entry would be profitable at the existing prices, it occurs; if it would lead to losses, it does not.

The fundamental investment decision is quite different for a natural monopoly, for two reasons. First, it represents a decidedly non-marginal, all-or-none addition to the market – either the entire service will be provided by one firm or there will be no service at all. Second, if the government were to choose the efficient price and quantity, the service would be provided at a loss. Profitability is not the guide to the investment decision that it is in the private sector. The fundamental investment question then is: Should the service be provided even if it is to be operated at a loss? And the answer is: "It depends."

Economists distinguish between two possibilities, the easy case and the hard case. In the *easy case*, pictured in Figure 9.4(a), a private monopolist charging a single price could at least break even. In the figure the solid line demand curve D cuts the average cost curve from above. There are many prices on D, all those above its intersection with the average cost curve AC, at which the monopolist would do better than break even; it would make a profit. The limit to the easy case is the dotted line demand curve D', which is just tangent to the AC curve. By producing at the point of tangency, the monopolist would break even (all other points on D' would generate a loss). The easy case is easy because it is a sufficient condition for providing the service. Fortunately, many of the natural monopolies fall within the easy case, including: all the public utilities; urban highways, bridges, and tunnels; the more popular recreational facilities; radio, television, and most other forms of telecommunication; and much of the software industry.

In the *hard case*, pictured in Figure 9.4(b), a private monopolist charging a single price cannot break even. The demand curve lies everywhere below the average cost curve, so that the monopolist would make a loss at any price. Society may still want the service though, the key insight being that even though the demand curve lies below the average cost curve, it may be enough above the marginal cost curve to justify having the service. At low enough demand, however, the service should not be provided.

The necessary condition for providing the service comes out of the hard case. It is called the hard case because it is difficult to obtain the information needed to determine if the service should be provided. Unfortunately, there are number of important examples of the hard case, notably transportation and recreational facilities in rural areas and possibly even mass rail transit. Regarding rail transit, every system in the United States runs at a deficit despite repeated efforts by city officials to raise fares to close the deficit.

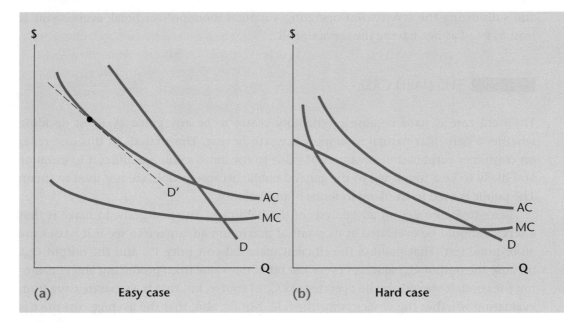

Figure 9.4

THE EASY CASE

The easy case is easy because it passes the standard profitability test. So long as any good can collect enough revenue to earn a profit or break even, it should be provided. The reason is that total cost in economic analysis refers to total opportunity cost. Therefore, if the firm is breaking even or earning a profit, then all the factors of production are earning as much or more in this firm than they can earn anyplace else, including, importantly, the capital invested in the firm. The owners are receiving a return to capital at least as large as they can earn in their next best opportunity, standardizing for risk (riskier investments require a higher return to offset the increased risk). Since all factors are receiving payments equal to or exceeding their opportunity cost, they are being used where they have the most value. Society is making the best use of these scarce resources. Reallocating them to their next best use would entail an efficiency loss.

The only wrinkle for the natural monopoly is that the monopolist should not be allowed to break even or earn a profit. As argued in the previous section, the efficient solution that maximizes the net value from producing and consuming the good is to set the price at marginal cost and earn a loss that is covered by a lump-sum subsidy. The possibility of at least breaking even justifies having the service, but does not imply that the service should actually break even. At the same time, it does imply that the preference for average cost pricing in the United States does no gross harm. Pricing at average cost and breaking even does sacrifice some net value relative to pricing at marginal cost and subsidizing the service. But operating a natural monopoly at break even is still at least as good as not having the service at all.

THE HARD CASE

The hard case is hard because profitability ceases to be any guide at all in deciding whether a particular natural monopoly is worth having. The analysis in this case relies on consumer surplus-style measures of value to consumers that are difficult to estimate and likely to be a tough sell to the general public because people are not used to them. The public is used to thinking in terms of profitability.

Refer to Figure 9.5 for an analysis of the hard case. The first point to make is that a service should be evaluated at its point of maximum advantage to see if it passes the all-or-none test. That point is the efficient marginal cost price P_{eff} and the output Q_{eff}, because the output Q_{eff} squeezes every last bit of net value from producing and consuming the good. It should also be operated at Q_{eff}, of course, but that is a separate issue from evaluating whether the service is worthwhile. Notice, also, that the average cost price is not an option in the hard case.

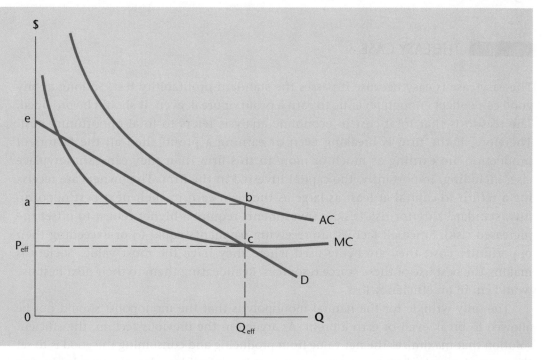

Figure 9.5

Is operating the service at Q_{eff} better than having no service at all? A common analysis is to see if it passes the following consumer surplus test. The total cost of the service at Q_{eff} is $AC \cdot Q_{eff}$, the rectangular area $0abQ_{eff}$. The revenue collected at the marginal cost price is $P_{eff}Q_{eff}$, the rectangular area $0P_{eff}cQ_{eff}$, which is used to offset some of the cost. The firm's loss is $(AC - P_{eff})Q_{eff}$, the rectangular area $P_{eff}abc$. The consumer surplus is the area under the demand curve D and above the price line P_{eff} to Q_{eff}, the triangular area $P_{eff}ec$. The all-or-none test compares the consumer surplus with the loss. If the consumer surplus exceeds the loss, then the service is worthwhile: area $P_{eff}ec > P_{eff}abc$. The consumers receive more surplus from the service than the subsidy they have to pay to cover the loss. Conversely, no service is preferred to Q_{eff} if the consumer surplus is less than the loss: $P_{eff}ec < P_{eff}abc$. The required subsidy to cover the loss exceeds the surplus the consumers receive from having the service. Therefore, the point of indifference between having no service and operating the service at the efficient output is that the consumer surplus just equals the loss: $P_{eff}ec = P_{eff}abc$.

Unfortunately, knowing the consumer surplus at the efficient output is a demanding requirement, far more so than knowing that the service could at least break even, as in the easy case. It requires an estimate of the entire demand curve, which is highly problematic because the higher prices on the demand curve may never have been observed. The entire demand curve has to be extrapolated from estimates of the curve within a narrow range of prices, and no one can be sure how accurate any proposed method of extrapolation might be.

There is yet another difficulty. The consumer surplus measured under a market demand curve is not a valid measure of consumers' willingness to pay for the good unless there is no income effect associated with the good. That is, changes in consumers' income would have no effect on the quantity of the good demanded. This is unlikely for most of the goods and services provided by the natural monopolies. Assuming that changes in consumers' incomes do affect their demands for these goods, the proper willingness to pay measure is the corresponding area behind the compensated demand curve, which is illustrated in Figure 9.6 along with the market demand curve. D^C is the compensated demand curve and D^A is the actual market demand curve.

The issue is the value to the consumer of having the price of the service provided by a natural monopoly drop in price from P_0 to P_{eff}. The price P_0 is so high that the quantity demanded is zero. It is equivalent to the situation of having no service at all. Points along the actual demand curve are determined by lowering the price of the product, with consumers' incomes held constant. Points along the compensated demand curve are determined by lowering the price of the product and having the consumers give up some of their incomes lump sum so that their utility remains unchanged. If there are no income effects, the two curves are the same. One would expect, however, that sacrificing income would lower the demand for the product. If so, then the compensated demand curve lies to the left of the actual demand curve, as pictured. (See Chapter 15 for further discussions of compensated demand curves.)

At each point on the compensated demand curve, the price equals the MRS, the amount of the reference good the consumer is willing to give up to be able to consume another unit of the natural monopolist's good. With the price of the reference good equal to 1, the MRS is the income the consumer is willing to pay to consume another unit of the natural monopolist's good. As the price decreases unit by unit along the compensated demand curves, the various MRSs are comparable because the consumer is being held on the same indifference curve, the same level of utility, the level of utility without the service when the price is P_0. Therefore, the area behind the demand curve to the price axis from P_0 to P_{eff}, area $P_{eff}P_0a$, gives the total amount the consumers are willing to pay to have the price decrease from P_0 to P_{eff}. This measure of their willingness to pay is what should be compared with the loss (area $P_{eff}abc$ in Figure 9.5) in deciding whether the service passes the all-or-none test. In contrast, as the price decreases along the actual demand curve, it still equals the MRS at each price, but the MRSs are measured along different indifference curves, and thus different utility levels. Therefore, areas behind the actual demand curve as the prices change unit by unit are not comparable.

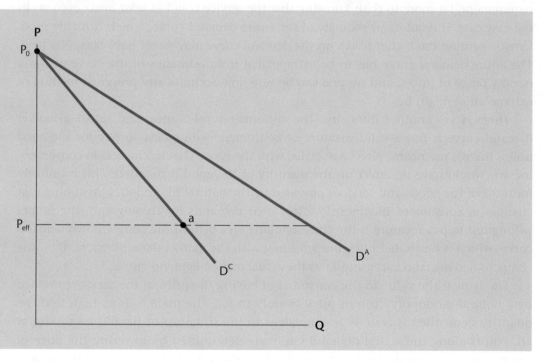

Figure 9.6

Fortunately, economists now have numerical techniques at their disposal to calculate compensated demand curves from estimated actual demand curves. But the point still stands that the actual demand curves for most of the services offered by the natural monopolies are going to be difficult to estimate except perhaps within a very narrow range of prices.

◼◼◼◼◼ MINIMIZE THE DEFICIT?

Suppose the actual demand curve could be estimated. Even so, it would be difficult to imagine a public official trying to convince the public that a service that always operated at a deficit is worthwhile because the consumer surplus behind the corresponding compensated demand curve exceeds the subsidy required to cover the losses. People understand profit and loss, not consumer surplus and compensated demand curves. Skeptical, hard-nosed business types are likely to grumble that they cannot run their businesses at a loss, so why should the government be allowed to.

The answer is that natural monopolies are different in kind from the standard business because their average costs decrease all the way to the market demand. In fact, the insistence on a profit and loss perspective can be extremely damaging in the hard case. In the easy case, governments attempt to break even and establish an average cost price, which, as we have noted, does no gross harm. Average cost pricing is out for the hard case, so people often petition government to do what they perceive to be the next best option: If you must run the city's rail transit system at a deficit, at least try to minimize the deficit.

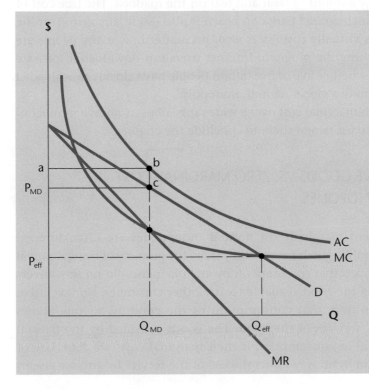

Figure 9.7

The common call to minimize the deficit can do gross harm, however, as illustrated in Figure 9.7. MR is the marginal revenue curve associated with the market demand curve D. Minimizing the deficit is the same as maximizing profit, even though the profit is negative. Therefore, the deficit is minimized by producing the output at which MR = MC, output Q_{MD}, and charging the price P_{MD} on the demand curve. The minimum deficit is $(AC - P_{MD})Q_{MD}$, the rectangular area $abcP_{MD}$. The efficient output, the output that maximizes the net value of having the service, is Q_{eff} at the intersection of D and MC. By minimizing the deficit, the government sacrifices net value equal to the area between D and MC from Q_{MD} to Q_{eff}. (We are assuming no income effects here.) It is possible, therefore, that the service passes the all-or-none test at Q_{eff} but fails the all-or-none test at Q_{MD}. At the price P_{MD}, the trains run too empty, too often and the transit system is not worth having. The impulse to think in terms of profit and loss is simply wrong for the hard case natural monopolies.

NATURAL MONOPOLIES WITH ZERO MARGINAL COSTS

The marginal costs of many of the natural monopolies are virtually zero from the first user onward. Once a road, tunnel, or bridge has been constructed, the cost of one more person driving on the road is virtually zero up to the point of congestion, the only additional cost being a minuscule amount of wear and tear on the roadbed. The true cost of one more person using an uncongested park or a beach is also essentially zero. Turning on a radio or TV program is virtually costless as well, no matter how many people are already listening to or watching the program. Internet users can download a software program at virtually no cost whether five or five billion people have already downloaded the program; software is literally a global natural monopoly.

The pattern of (near) zero marginal cost over a wide range of users raises a number of interesting issues. We will discuss two of them to conclude the chapter.

NONEXCLUSIVE GOODS VS. ZERO MARGINAL COST NATURAL MONOPOLIES

Nonexclusive goods and zero marginal cost natural monopolies are often lumped together and referred to as public goods because they share the property of being nonrival in consumption. Nonrival means that consumption by any one person in no way affects or diminishes the amount of the good available to any other consumer. Nonexclusive goods are nonrival by definition, that consumption of the good by anyone allows everyone to receive the full services of the good. The goods provided by the natural monopolies are also nonrival in consumption if their marginal costs are zero. Use of the service by any one person in no way limits the use of the service by anyone else or raises the costs to them.

One is free to lump both kinds of goods together and call them public goods, of course, but we prefer to limit the designation "public good" to the nonexclusive goods. One reason is that nonexclusive goods almost certainly have to be provided by the public sector because of the free-rider problem, whereas the natural monopolies could be provided by the private sector and sometimes are, for example most of the electric utilities, television, software. Another reason is that although both sets of goods are nonrival, their efficient allocation is quite different. They really are distinct types of goods. Figure 9.8 illustrates the difference.

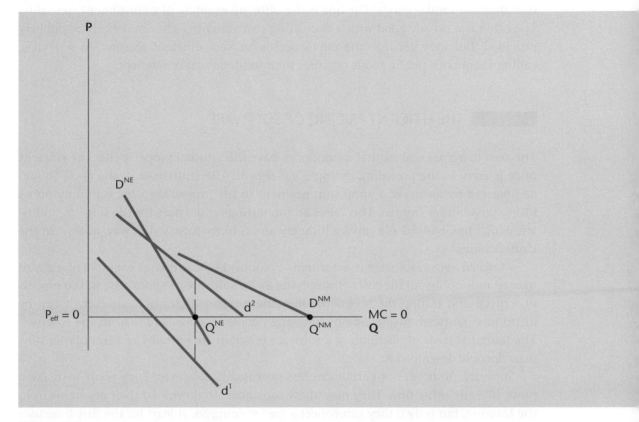

Figure 9.8

Figure 9.8 makes two assumptions so that the two goods are as similar as possible. The first is that the marginal cost of supplying the nonexclusive good is also zero at every output, which is certainly not true of defense, lighthouses, and any other important nonexclusive good. The second is that there are only two consumers of the goods. Person #1 has different demands for the goods from person #2, but each person has the same demand for both goods, represented by d^1 and d^2 in Figure 9.8. Since the demands for the goods are the same and their marginal costs are zero, is the efficient output of each good the same? The answer is "no."

The market demand curve for the nonexclusive good, D^{NE}, is obtained by *vertically* adding d^1 and d^2, since the government has no choice but to select a single quantity of the good. The efficient output is Q^{NE}, the point at which D^{NE} hits the horizontal axis; the sum of the two demand prices on d^1 and d^2 equals the supply price of zero.

The market demand curve for the natural monopoly good, D^{NM}, is obtained by *horizontally* adding d^1 and d^2, as it would be for any private good. The two people can use

173

the service as much as they want to at each given price. The efficient output is Q^{NM}, the point at which D^{NM} hits the horizontal axis: $P_{eff} = MC = 0$. With MC equal to zero, the two people should be allowed to use the service until their marginal values are zero.

In summary, the nonrivalry property shared by the two goods should not suggest that they are similar goods. The one is the ultimate example of a consumer externality. The other is a private good with a decreasing cost structure. They may both be publicly provided, but they get into the public sector for very different reasons. In our view, calling them both public goods obscures their fundamental differences.

THE EFFICIENT PRICING OF SOFTWARE

The zero marginal cost natural monopolies have the unusual property that the efficient price is zero, as the preceding example has shown. The entire cost of the good should be financed by means of a lump-sum payment to the firm to keep the economy on its utility possibilities frontier. This raises an interesting set of issues for the software industry, which has evolved as a private industry and is likely to stay that way, at least in the United States.

As noted above, software is a distinctive product because it is an example of a global natural monopoly. All the costs of supplying a new software program arise in the process of writing and testing the program. Once the program is ready to market, it can be distributed costlessly worldwide by allowing people to download it from the Internet. The marginal costs of distributing a software program are virtually zero no matter how many people download it.

Software firms cannot permit costless downloads, however. They want to make a profit like any other firm. They may allow consumers to download their programs from the Internet, but only if they can collect a fee for doing so, at least for the first-time user (existing users can often download updates at no charge). More often, though, they package the program on a CD and sell it. Creating and distributing CDs is far more costly than allowing consumers to download the programs from the Internet, but it is a simple way for firms to make a profit on their software.

The profit motive leads to an inefficient allocation of software, as illustrated in Figure 9.9. D and MR are the market demand and marginal revenue curves for a particular software program that only one firm supplies. AC and MC (= 0) are the firm's average and marginal cost curves. The efficient allocation is $(Q_{eff}, P_{eff} = 0)$, at the intersection of D and MC, the horizontal axis. The firm is presumed to maximize profit. It produces Q_M programs at the intersection of MR and MC, sets a price of P_M, and earns profit $(P_M - AC)Q_M$, the rectangular area $P_M abc$.[4]

There is a way for the firm to achieve the efficient output Q_{eff}, however. It could adopt the library model. Libraries make all-or-none offers to consumers. If you want to use a library, you obtain a card that is usually renewable each year. Private libraries typically charge an annual fee for the card; public libraries may or may not charge a fee. Once you have the card, you can then borrow all the books you want at no charge throughout the year. You cannot use the library at all without the card.

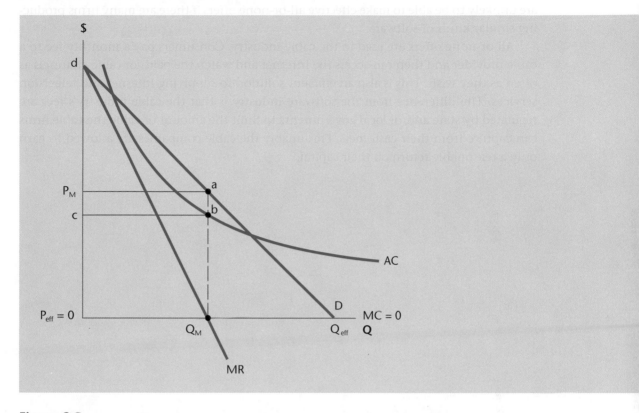

Figure 9.9

Private firms would love to make such all-or-none offers to consumers. Our software company above does well by charging a fee for each download of its software. But suppose it could make a library-like offer to its customers: Pay us an annual fee and you can download the software program for nothing, and all its future updates. In fact, you can download our entire inventory of software for nothing. If you do not pay the fee, you can never have any of our products.[5] How much would consumers be willing to pay to download each software program for free? The answer is an amount up to the total value they receive from each software program, which we can represent as the entire area under D up to Q_{eff}, triangular area $0dQ_{eff}$. Area $0dQ_{eff}$ far exceeds the revenue $P_M Q_M$ obtained from the single price, profit-maximizing solution, the rectangular area $0P_M a Q_M$.

The good news is that the all-or-none offer is efficient. It generates the efficient price and output (Q_{eff}, $P_{eff} = 0$), and the annual fee is lump sum, as required to keep the economy on its utility possibilities frontier. The bad news is that the all-or-none offer transfers all the value that consumers receive in the market exchange to the firm in the form of higher profits. This is not an especially attractive way to achieve the efficient outcome.

The policy implication of this example is that the government must be vigilant about breaking down barriers to entry in the software industry to maintain competition. Firms are unlikely to be able to make effective all-or-none offers if there are many firms producing similar kinds of software.

All-or-none offers are used in the cable industry. Consumers pay a monthly fee to a cable provider and then can access the Internet and watch the paid-for cable channels as often as they wish. This is also an efficient solution to supplying Internet and television services. The difference from the software industry is that the cable industry's fees are regulated by state and/or local governments to limit the amount of value the cable firms can capture from their customers. Presumably the cable companies are allowed to earn only a reasonable return on their capital.

CHAPTER 10

U.S. Transfer Payments: the Public Choice Perspective

The next three chapters turn to the analysis of transfer payments, the last major item of expenditure for the federal, state, and local governments. We begin with a brief history of the evolution of the major transfer programs in the United States that are targeted to either aiding the poor or preventing people from becoming poor.

THE MAIN U.S. ANTIPOVERTY TRANSFER PROGRAMS

In 1601, during the reign of Queen Elizabeth I, the British established a Poor Law that set down three principles for helping that nation's poor:

1. People who are poor and cannot reasonably be expected to help themselves escape poverty, such as disabled adults, orphaned children, and the elderly, are deserving of the nation's sympathy and aid.
2. Able-bodied people should work. They should not expect aid from the state. The only exceptions are able-bodied people who are looking for work and unable to find a job – the involuntarily unemployed, to use today's terminology.
3. Aid to the poor should be administered at the local level because local officials would know who is truly deserving of aid and who is shirking, attempting to live off the public dole.

The impulses behind these principles are both charitable and hard-nosed. Society is willing to support the poor who are helpless through public charity, but at the same time it does not want to play the sucker by supporting people who are fully capable of helping themselves. The charitable impulse was dulled somewhat in the application of the Poor Law, however. England established almshouses for poor adults and their families and orphanages for unattached children. They were run by overseers appointed by local officials who had full responsibility for the poor in their care without much effective governmental oversight. The overseers were often brutal and inhumane to their charges, treatment that was most famously chronicled in the novels of Charles Dickens.

The American colonies adopted the principles of the 1601 Poor Law in their approach to public charity, along with the almshouses and orphanages. Nothing changed following the American Revolution and independence from England; indeed, very little changed at all for the next 150 years. Public assistance remained the responsibility of the states and their local governments, and the almshouses and orphanages continued under conditions that were hardly better than those Dickens had described in England. The federal government had absolutely no role in the provision of public assistance to the poor. The only piece of federal social legislation was the Child Labor Act of 1912, which was aimed at preventing the exploitation of children in the workplace.

The Great Depression of the 1930s was the catalyst that forced the federal government into contributing to efforts to aid the poor. The states and localities were simply overwhelmed as millions of people were thrown out of work. The unemployment rate reached 25.2% in the depths of the Depression in 1933 (Gordon, 2000, p. A2). These people were out of work and quickly becoming impoverished, obviously through no fault of their own. At first Congress responded with hundreds of millions of dollars of subsidies to the states in the early 1930s to help support the unemployed. Then the Congress passed, and President Roosevelt signed, the Social Security Act of 1935, the single most important piece of antipoverty legislation in U.S. history. The federal government would forever after be a major player in the nation's fight against poverty.

THE SOCIAL SECURITY ACT OF 1935

The Social Security Act, and supporting legislation passed between 1935 and 1937, established a two-pronged approach to poverty, consisting of social insurance on the one hand and public assistance ("welfare") on the other hand. It remains to this day the central strategy in the federal government's war on poverty that President Johnson declared in 1964 following the assassination of President Kennedy. The social insurance component was meant to be preventive, to prevent people from ever falling into poverty. The public assistance component was symptomatic, to give aid to people who had become poor.

The centerpiece of the Act was the social insurance component, which bore its name. The Act established the Social Security system, the nation's first public pension program for private sector employees.[1] Employees contributed to the system throughout their working lives by means of a payroll tax on their wages, half of which was paid for by employers and half by employees. The employees and their spouses were then entitled to a public pension during the employees' retirement years for as long as they lived, the so-called Social Security benefit. The pensions are disproportionately higher for lower income workers, but they are not means tested by income. Any employee who paid into the system, rich or poor, is entitled to a pension. The goal of the Social Security system is to prevent people from falling into poverty after they retire and becoming wards of the state. It is also entirely administered by the federal government, both the payroll tax and the pensions.

The Social Security Act also established three new public assistance programs for the poor, Old Age Assistance (OAA), Aid to the Blind (AB), and Aid to Families with Dependent Children (AFDC). The design of these programs was consistent with the first and third principles set down in the 1601 Poor Law. They were means tested – people had to be poor to receive benefits – and, as their names suggest, they were also categorical. Being poor was not sufficient grounds for support in and of itself. People had to be poor *and* elderly, or blind, or in families with a single parent, all categories of people who were deemed unlikely to be able to help themselves escape poverty.[2] The target group for the AFDC program was widows with children. The nuclear family was intact in the 1930s, far fewer women worked than today, and few people had life insurance. Therefore, the death of a husband could leave a woman with children in desperate straits, and the prevailing view in those days was that women with children should be at home raising the children rather than working.

In addition, in line with the third principle of the 1601 Poor Law, the three public assistance programs were to be administered by the state governments, not the federal government, and many of the states required their local governments to administer the programs. The states also determined the benefit levels per recipient. The federal government's contribution was strictly financial but it was substantial, between 50% and 83% of the benefit payments under these programs. The percentages in the original formulas varied by level of payment and state per capita income; they were higher the lower the monthly payments to recipients and the lower a state's per capita income.

Finally, the original public assistance programs offered both cash and in-kind benefits. The cash benefits were in the form of monthly benefit checks to the recipients and the in-kind benefits were payments to medical vendors – physicians, hospitals, and so forth – who provided services to the recipients. In contrast, the Social Security pensions were strictly cash; they provided no in-kind benefits.

The federal government instituted a number of other social insurance and public assistance programs between 1933 and 1937. On the insurance side of the ledger were four major programs. Unemployment Insurance was established in 1935. It is a state-administered program financed by payments by employers that provides temporary support to workers who become involuntarily unemployed, and is subject to narrow federal guidelines. This program was consistent with the second principle of the 1601 Poor Law. The federal government also passed the first price support program for the major agricultural crops in 1933 and instituted a federal minimum wage in 1937. One other important public assistance program came out of the Great Depression, Housing Assistance, in 1937. At first the expenditures were directed toward building and operating public housing projects for low-income families. As the program evolved and the public housing projects fell out of favor, the assistance became more in the form of rent subsidies for apartments provided by landlords in the private sector.

During the last half of the 20th century, the federal government made some significant changes to the social insurance and public assistance programs and added a few new programs. But the dual preventive and symptomatic approach to fighting poverty set down in the Social Security Act of 1935 has remained intact. The major changes and additions by decade were as follows.

1950s – In 1951, the federal government instituted a new categorical public assistance program, Aid to the Disabled (AD). As with the initial public assistance programs, AD was administered by the state governments (the local governments in some states), the states determined the monthly cash payments and medical vendor support, and the federal government paid between 50% and 83% of the monthly payments to the recipients. In 1956, the federal government added benefits to disabled workers to the Social Security system.

1960s – The 1960s brought the single biggest reform to the Social Security Act. In 1965, in response to President Johnson's declared war on poverty, the federal government instituted two new medical programs, Medicare and Medicaid. Medicare was an entirely new program, financed by an addition to the payroll tax that was targeted to Medicare. Its basic component was hospital insurance to the elderly beginning at age 65. For an additional premium, the elderly could also elect insurance coverage for physicians' visits and related services.

Medicaid was also a new program, but quite different in intent from Medicare. Its purpose was simply to consolidate all the medical vendor payments in the four public assistance programs under one administrative body. In the beginning, therefore, only poor people who were receiving monthly cash payments under one of the four public assistance programs of the Act were eligible for medical coverage under Medicaid. Also, as with the four programs, Medicaid was administered by the states and the states determined the amount and breadth of the medical coverage in their states. The federal government offered financial assistance between 50% and 83% of total state payments each month that varied (inversely) only with states' per capita incomes, and allowed a state to choose the Medicaid reimbursement formula for the other four public assistance programs if it provided more federal aid to the state. Once it came into existence, Medicaid developed a life of its own and was continually expanded, mostly in the 1990s (see below). With the rapidly rising costs of medical care since 1965 and the occasional expansions of its coverage, Medicaid has become larger than all the other public assistance programs combined. This was certainly not the original intent of the program in 1965.

1970s – There were three major changes in the 1970s, two in the form of new programs and the third a reorganization of existing programs. They were part of a reform movement to increase the federal presence in the public assistance effort. One new program was Food Stamps (1971), which offered coupons to poor families and individuals that allowed them to buy food at a discount. The Food Stamp program was noteworthy because it was the first break with the principles of the 1601 Poor Law. The program was entirely federal and also noncategorical. All poor families and individuals qualified for Food Stamps regardless of their other personal characteristics.

The second new program was the Earned Income Tax Credit (EITC, 1976), which was linked to the federal personal income tax and administered by the U.S. Internal Revenue Service (IRS). It offered a wage subsidy to low-income workers that was designed to offset somewhat the negative incentives to work that were built into the other public assistance programs, which we will discuss in Chapter 11. As with Food Stamps, it was entirely federal and also essentially noncategorical beyond the requirement that a person be employed. The wage subsidy was available to all workers with low incomes regardless of their other personal characteristics.

The major reorganization was a new program, Supplemental Security Income (SSI, 1972, effective in 1974), which combined the existing OAA, AB, and AD programs. The federal government also took over the administration of SSI and set a level of monthly benefits that was much higher than the benefits offered by the poorer states under the three replaced programs. States could supplement the federal payments if they wished and the higher income states did. Consequently, the new SSI program represented no substantial change for them or for their poor citizens who had been supported under the replaced programs.

The call for a larger federal presence was based largely on the huge variation in support levels across states in the original programs. Reformers wanted more uniform treatment of the poor nationwide. SSI was a move in the direction of uniformity but, as noted, only a partial move. Also, benefit payments under AFDC and Medicaid remained state determined and thus continued to vary widely across the states.

1980s – There were no major changes in this decade, only some modest expansions of support under Medicaid and the EITC.

1990s – This was another important decade for public assistance reform. The most important structural reform was the replacement of AFDC with Temporary Assistance to Needy Families (TANF) in 1996, a reform that President Clinton hailed as ending welfare as we know it. This was an exaggeration because AFDC was only one component of public assistance, and one of the smaller ones at that. But AFDC had become associated with welfare in the public's mind and viewed with great skepticism ever since the 1960s, when the nuclear family began to break apart. The caseloads under AFDC exploded by the late 1960s, helped to a considerable extent by socially minded lawyers who showed recently separated and divorced, low-income parents with children (overwhelming women) how they could apply for the benefits they were now entitled to. AFDC replaced OAA as the largest public assistance program at the time, and the public became suspicious that they were being taken advantage of. Divorce and separation are conscious decisions, unlike the death of a spouse. People worried that they were supporting women who could be working or at least should be supported by their separated husbands or the fathers of their children, in violation of the first principle of the 1601 Poor Law.

TANF finally ended the entitlement to public assistance for single parents by allowing states to remove them from the rolls if they had received assistance for two consecutive years, or if they had received public assistance intermittently over a five-year period. States who continued to support single parents after five years had to do so entirely out of their own funds. TANF also changed the form of federal support from a matching payment per recipient to a block grant that states could use as they saw fit, either for monthly payments or to pay for such services for recipients as job training, education, and childcare support. The original block grant each state received was equal to the average of the federal payments to the state over the three last years of the AFDC program. It was to be reviewed by Congress and adjusted, if necessary, every six years.

TABLE 10.1 Income support programs in the United States federal, state, and local governments (fiscal year 2006)

	Expenditures ($ billions)
Social Insurance	
Social Security[1]	549
Medicare	376
Military and Civil Service Retirement	99
Unemployment Compensation	32
Veterans Benefits	64
Agricultural Support Programs	21
Subtotal: Social Insurance	1,141
Public Assistance (means tested)	
Cash Assistance	
Temporary Assistance to Needy Families (TANF)	34
Supplemental Security Income (SSI)	57
Earned Income Tax Credit (EITC)	36
In-kind Assistance	
Medicaid	301
Food Stamps	30
Housing Assistance	32
Other public assistance[2]	88
Subtotal: Public Assistance	578
Total Income Support	1,893[3]

NOTES:
1. Social Security includes old age, survivors, and disability benefits.
2. Includes 50–60 small programs in the areas of food, education, job training, medical care, and other social services. Most of the aid in these programs is in kind.
3. Includes $174 billion of federal payments to persons that are not in either category.

SOURCES: *Budget of the United States Government, Fiscal Year 2008* (Washington D.C.: U.S. Government Printing Office, February 2007), Part Five: Historical Tables, Tables 3.1 and 11.3. Also, author's estimates of the state and local portion of public assistance for fiscal year 2006 based on data from previous years.

There were two other important changes during the 1990s. One was a significant increase in the wage subsidies under EITC. The other was a substantial expansion of Medicaid. The federal government extended its financial support to a number of new services for pregnant woman and children. In addition, states were now allowed to offer Medicaid to families with up to twice the poverty line level of income, so-called medically needy families.[3] These expansions of EITC and Medicaid helped ease the transition of low-income women from TANF to work. Without them, the loss of entitlement to public assistance under TANF would have been very harsh for these women.

2000s – The one major change since the turn of the century was the addition of a prescription drug benefit for the elderly under Medicare that took effect in 2006.

Table 10.1 lists the expenditures under the major U.S. social insurance and public assistance programs for fiscal year 2006. A few points are worth noting. One is that the social insurance programs account for nearly two-thirds of the total transfer payments. Keep in mind that the vast majority of these payments go to the nonpoor; their purpose is to prevent the nonpoor from falling into poverty.[4] A second point is that Medicaid accounts for 52% of total public assistance transfers, a percentage that is likely to increase as medical costs continue to rise more rapidly than inflation generally. Because of the rise of Medicaid, the majority of public assistance to recipients is now in kind rather than cash. Finally, the rapid increase in medical costs has turned Medicare into a huge program. Medicare will overtake the pension and disability payments as the largest component of the Social Security system within the next 10–20 years as the prescription drug benefit matures and members of the baby boom generation reach 65.

THE PUBLIC CHOICE PERSPECTIVE ON PUBLIC ASSISTANCE

At the most fundamental level, what impulses lie behind the social insurance and public assistance programs? The mainstream view is that people put on their other-interested hats from time to time, thought about the problem of end-results equity or distributive justice, and arrived at collective, majority rule democratic decisions that led to the current transfer programs. The public's sense of end-results equity that evolved from this process is summarized in the mainstream theory by the ethical rankings of the social welfare function.

Nonsense, say the public choice economists. People don't wear separate self-interested economic and other-interested societal hats, they don't think in terms of end-results equity beyond perhaps the narrow confines of their own families, and there is no such thing as a social welfare function. The transfer programs that we see must have evolved from entirely self-interested behavior. The only question is what form that behavior took.

Recall the viewpoint of James Buchanan, described in Chapter 1, that legitimacy in government ultimately extends back to a nation's constitutional convention: A government program is legitimate if it would have been approved unanimously by the framers of the Constitution. And Buchanan assumes that the framers were entirely self-interested in their economic and political affairs. Buchanan argues that the social insurance programs, and perhaps even the public assistance programs, that have evolved from the Social Security Act of 1935 could have received the unanimous support of the framers of the U.S.

Constitution even though they were almost all extremely wealthy. Suppose they view the future as Rawls had suggested people should view the future when thinking about matters of equity, through a veil of ignorance. The veil is so opaque that people assume they have no idea what their future prospects and those of their descendents might be. If so, then even if the framers were entirely self-interested and not thinking at all about equity, they may support social insurance, and even public assistance programs, on the grounds that even though they are well-to-do today, they and/or their descendants may not been so well off in the future. If not, then they would be protected by the existence of these kinds of public transfer policies and would be willing to pay for them. They would think of the taxes as premium payments for a public insurance policy against the possibility of becoming impoverished.

This argument is more convincing for the social insurance programs, because if these programs do protect people against becoming impoverished, then there is no need for the public assistance programs from a self-interested perspective. But this does not matter, according to the public choice economists. The public assistance programs can also be justified by self-interested behavior by the following argument.

People may be self-interested, but they also clearly have altruistic or charitable impulses that contribute to their own utility. We know this because many people contribute to private charities and their contributions are entirely voluntary. These contributions obviously increase the donors' own utility or they would not be given. Public assistance can be viewed as an extension of private charity that arises simply because of a technical problem associated with private charity – the free-rider problem.

Before looking at the free-rider problem associated with charitable giving, note the subtle difference in the mainstream and public choice views of public assistance. The mainstream, social welfare view of public assistance sees it as a win–lose proposition. When wearing their other-interested hats and thinking about distributive justice, people conclude that public assistance is appropriate. They would rather not pay the taxes to support public assistance from their narrow self-interested economic perspective, but they reluctantly do so to support the public interest in end-results equity. Under this line of thought, public assistance is viewed as a win–lose proposition: the poor beneficiaries of public assistance gain utility but the nonpoor lose utility when they pay their taxes. Not so under the public choice perspective. Voluntary gifts to private charities are clearly a win–win proposition: The donors gain utility along with the beneficiaries of their gifts. Since public assistance is just an extension of private charity, it too is a win–win proposition.

Win–win propositions sound more like issues of efficiency than of equity. Recall that inefficiencies place society below its utility possibilities frontier. Correcting an inefficiency and returning to the frontier leads to the possibility that everyone gains. In contrast, the mainstream view of redistributional policies is that they move society along the utility possibilities frontier, with the result that some people gain and others lose.

The win–win redistributional policies in the public choice perspective are indeed a matter of efficiency. The impulse to give to a private charity arises because there is something about the beneficiaries supported by the charity that bothers the potential donors.

The donors believe that they might not be properly fed, or have adequate housing, or, more generally, not have enough resources to provide themselves with a minimally acceptable standard of living. If so, then the charitable impulse is just another kind of consumption externality: Something about one person, the beneficiary, affects – enters the utility function of – another person, the donor. According to this view, the private donations are simply correcting for this externality. For this reason, private charity and, by extension, public assistance are referred to by public choice economists as *Pareto-optimal redistributions*. Their purpose is to return society to its utility possibilities frontier, not to move society along its frontier. In mainstream terms, they are allocation policies designed to correct for an inefficiency in the form of a consumption externality, not redistributional policies designed to promote end-results equity.

PARETO-OPTIMAL REDISTRIBUTIONS

We will begin with the simplest possible model of private charity to see the public choice perspective. Suppose there are just two goods: Food (F), and one other commodity that serves all other purposes (Y). Assume that the price and marginal cost of Y are equal to 1. (We can do this because only relative prices matter to the allocation of resources.) There are also just two people, a rich person, R, and a poor person, P. P gets utility from her own consumption of the two goods: $U^P = U^P(Y_P, F_P)$. R likewise receives utility from his own consumption of the two goods, Y_R and F_R. But when R thinks about P, he is troubled because he believes P does not have enough food to eat. Therefore, his utility depends as well on F_P, the food consumption of P: $U^R = U^R(Y_R, F_R, F_P)$. The food purchased by P confers an external economy on R. Assume, finally, that Y and F are produced in competitive markets, so that the prices P_F and $P_Y(= 1)$ equal the marginal costs of producing F and Y.

If there were no externality, we know from Chapter 2 that the Pareto-optimal or efficiency condition for the production and consumption of Y and F would be

$$MRS^R_{Y_R,F_R} = MRS^P_{Y_P,F_P} = MRT_{Y,F} = P_F = MC_F$$

with $P_Y = MC_Y = 1$. The MRS for each person measures the units of Y they would be willing to give up to consume one more unit of F. They each would set their MRS to P_F. Moreover $MRT_{Y,F}$ is the ratio of the marginal costs of producing F and Y, or just the MC_F with $MC_Y = P_Y = 1$. Therefore, P_F would also be equal to the $MRT_{Y,F}$ the additional Y that must be sacrificed along the production possibilities frontier to produce one more unit of F. Perfect competition would generate the Pareto-optimal conditions, with both people purchasing F and Y at the market prices P_F and $P_Y = 1$.

When R decides on his purchases of Y and F, his decision is entirely private to him. Therefore the Pareto-optimal condition for his purchases is the standard

$$MRS^R_{Y_R,F_R} = MRT_{Y,F} = P_F,$$

and he should buy F and Y from the producers at the marginal cost prices P_F and $P_Y = 1$.

185

When P decides on her purchases of Y and F, however, there are two margins to consider. One is the standard $MRS^P_{Y_P,F_P}$, the amount of Y she is willing to trade for another unit of F. The other is $MRS^R_{Y_R,F_P}$, the amount of his own Y that R is willing to sacrifice to have P consume one more unit of F. Therefore, the Pareto-optimal condition for P's consumption of F is

$$MRS^P_{Y_P,F_P} + MRS^R_{Y_R,F_P} = \text{MRT}_{Y,F} = \text{MC}_F = P_F.$$

As we just saw, this condition would not be satisfied by having each person purchase Y and F in competitive markets.

Someone has to intervene to take account of the externality. If there were literally just one rich person and one poor person, it is likely that the two people would engage in a Coase-style bargain to achieve the optimum because it is in their mutual interests to do so. R would be willing to transfer some of his food to P because his $MRS^R_{Y_R,F_P}$ indicates that he is willing to sacrifice some of his own purchasing power to have P consume more food. And P would certainly accept the transfer of food. It is a win–win transfer, which is the basis for voluntary charitable contributions.

WHY PUBLIC ASSISTANCE?

The problem with relying on voluntary private charity, however, is not that there are many poor people to support but rather that there are many nonpoor people willing to support them. Suppose we adjust our simple model to include N rich people, but still have only one poor person. As before, the consumption of Y and F by the rich are private events that can be handled efficiently by the competitive markets for Y and F. Now, however, when P consumes F, all the rich people are affected. The Pareto-optimal condition becomes

$$MRS^P_{Y_P,F_P} + \sum_{R=1}^{N} MRS^R_{Y_R,F_P} = \text{MRT}_{Y,F} = \text{MC}_F.$$

Attempting to achieve this Pareto-optimality condition through voluntary contributions of F by each rich person to P runs up against the free-rider problem. Each rich person benefits if he gives some food to the poor person. But he benefits just as much if some other rich person gives the same amount of food to the poor person. Better, therefore, to let someone else transfer food to the poor person and get the full benefit of the transfer without making any sacrifice whatsoever. Unfortunately, all the rich people think alike. They all try to free ride on the charitable impulses of the other people and no one ends up transferring food to P.

The solution is to have the government transfer the food to P through a public assistance program such as Food Stamps, and tax the rich to pay for the public transfers so that they all share in the costs.[5] In this way, all the rich gain as well as P, and society moves to its utility possibilities frontier. It is a win–win efficiency policy.

Having studied private activities that give rise to externalities in Chapter 7, we know what the policy should be, a Pigovian subsidy. The government should subsidize P's purchase of food, with the subsidy equal to the aggregate value to the rich people of having P consume one more unit of food. But the aggregate marginal external value to the rich is the $\sum_{R=1}^{N} MRS_{Y_R,F_P}^{R}$, the aggregate amount of Y all N rich people would be willing to give up to have P consume one more unit of food.

The reason the Pigovian subsidy works in this case is as follows. Faced with a subsidy s, the net price of food to P is $P_F - s$, which she sets equal to her MRS_{Y_P,F_P}^{P}:

$$P_F - s = MRS_{Y_P,F_P}^{P}$$

But $P_F = MC_F = MRT_{Y,F}$. With $s = \sum_{R=1}^{N} MRS_{Y_R,F_P}^{R}$,

$$P_F - s = MRT_{Y,F} - \sum_{R=1}^{N} MRS_{Y_R,F_P}^{R} = MRS_{Y_P,F_P}^{P}$$

or

$$MRS_{Y_P,F_P}^{P} + \sum_{R=1}^{N} MRS_{Y_R,F_P}^{R} = MRT_{Y,F}$$

the Pareto-optimal condition.

Suppose that there are a large number of poor people. This makes no difference so long as the rich view each of the poor as equally needy. In that case, the consumption of an additional unit of food by any poor person has the same effect on each rich person. Therefore, the same Pareto-optimal condition applies to each of the poor as in the case of the single poor person and is achieved by the same Pigovian subsidy as above. Every poor person should be allowed to purchase food at the net-of-subsidy price $P_F - s$.

There may instead be different classes of poor, say the near poor (NP), the poor (P), and the very poor (VP), that the rich view differently. In that case, the utility of each rich person is $U^R = U^R(Y_R, F_R, F_{NP}, F_P, F_{VP})$, and the government needs to design separate Pigovian subsidies for each class of poor:

$$S_{NP} = \sum_{R=1}^{N} MRS_{Y_R,F_{NP}}^{R}$$

$$S_P = \sum_{R=1}^{N} MRS_{Y_R,F_P}^{R}$$

$$S_{VP} = \sum_{R=1}^{N} MRS_{Y_R,F_{VP}}^{R}$$

Presumably $S_{VP} > S_P > S_{NP}$.

The same analysis applies to any good that the rich believe the poor are lacking, whether it be food, housing, medical care, or anything else. In each instance, the government should design a Pigovian subsidy equal to the aggregate marginal effect on the rich of the poor's consumption of the good and allow the poor to purchase the good at the subsidized price. These subsidies correct for the external effect of the poor's consumption of the good on the rich and in doing so bring the economy to its utility possibilities frontier.

CASH OR IN-KIND ASSISTANCE?

The model in the preceding section calls for in-kind aid, a food subsidy, but is it the correct model? It may not be. Return to the case of many rich people and one poor person, P. Suppose the rich look at P and conclude that she has inadequate amounts of all the necessities: food, housing, clothing, medical care, and so forth. Her problem is simply that she lacks the income necessary to enjoy a minimally adequate standard of living. That is, the rich worry about P's entire utility or well-being. Their utility function is $U^R = U^R(Y_R, F_R, U^P(Y_P, F_P))$.

In this case, the best response of the government is to give a cash transfer to P. The intuition is that for any given amount of aid, P can achieve either the same or higher utility with a cash grant than with a subsidy on one of their goods, and the expectation is that she will have higher utility. Therefore, since the rich want P to be as well off as possible, both the rich and P prefer the cash transfer.

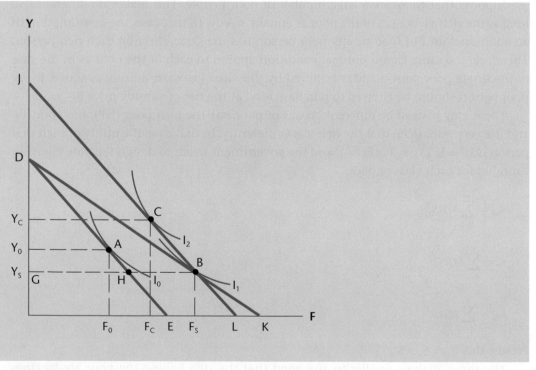

Figure 10.1

Figure 10.1 illustrates the advantage of a cash grant from the point of view of the poor. I_0, I_1, and I_2 are three of P's indifference curves for Y and F. Her budget line without any assistance is DE, and its slope is $(-)P_F/P_Y = (-)P_F$. The original equilibrium is at point A, at which the indifference curve I_0 is tangent to the budget line, and she consumes (F_0, Y_0).

A food subsidy of s rotates the budget line to DK. Her new equilibrium is at point B, at which the indifference curve I_1 is tangent to the new budget line DK. She consumes (F_s, Y_s) with the subsidy, spending GH on food out of her own resources and receiving a subsidy of HB from the government for the remainder of her food expenditure.

Suppose, instead, she receives a cash transfer of HB from the government, the same amount as the food subsidy. The cash shifts the budget line out parallel to DE in amount HB. The new budget line is JL. Her equilibrium with the cash transfer is at point C, at which the indifference curve I_2 is tangent to the budget line JL. She consumes (F_C, Y_C). Notice that she consumes more food with the food subsidy than with the cash transfer yet is better off with the cash transfer. This is the expected result. She consumes more food with the food subsidy because the subsidy changes the relative prices in favor of food. As such, it contains both a substitution effect and an income effect in favor of food. In contrast, the relative prices of F and Y remain the same under the cash transfer so that it has only an income effect. The income effects are designed to be the same, so the extra substitution effect with the food subsidy induces her to consume more food.[7]

P is better off with the cash subsidy, however, as can be seen by what economists refer to as a "revealed-preference argument." When she bought (F_C, Y_C) on budget line JL with the cash transfer, she could have bought (F_s, Y_s), but when she bought (F_s, Y_s) with the subsidy on budget line DK, she could not have bought (F_C, Y_C). Therefore, (F_C, Y_C) is revealed as preferred to (F_s, Y_s). The intuition is that the subsidy constrains P in a way that is absent under the cash transfer. She had to bias her purchases toward food under the subsidy to generate a transfer of HB, whereas under the cash transfer she receives HB no matter what she buys. The extra freedom makes her better off with a cash transfer. The lesson is clear: If the rich care about the overall well-being of the poor, public assistance should be in the form of cash.

Which is the correct model? The United States has apparently always been ambivalent regarding the answer. The public assistance programs have been a mixture of cash and in kind from the very beginning (recall that the three original public assistance programs, OAA, AB, and AFDC, gave recipients monthly cash benefits and paid for some of their medical expenditures). And the programs that were added since 1935 have been both in kind – Housing Assistance, Food Stamps, Medicaid – and cash – EITC. Some taxpayers undoubtedly believe that the poor simply lack resources and are willing to give them cash. Their impulses are purely altruistic toward the poor. Others, though, are skeptical, and somewhat paternalistic. They are willing to help the poor but worry that the poor might not spend cash transfers wisely on the goods and services they and their families truly need. They like the accountability that in-kind aid appears to give, that the poor really are spending the assistance on necessities such as food, medical care, or housing. The mixture of cash and in-kind transfers appears to be a compromise to both views.

IN-KIND TRANSFER LIMITS AND ACCOUNTABILITY

The in-kind model calls for allowing the poor to purchase as much of the aided item as they wish at the (Pigovian) subsidized price. The United States does not usually do this, however. It often imposes limits on the amount of the subsidized aid, for two good reasons. One is that Congress and the state legislatures like to know how much money they are committing to a particular program when they legislate it. But under an unlimited subsidy, the legislators cannot know how much the program will cost until the recipients have made their consumption choices. For example, in Figure 10.1, the amount of the subsidy HB becomes known only after P chooses consumption point B on budget line DK. One way to gain some control over the budget in advance is to set a limit on how much each person can receive. Another reason for setting limits on in-kind aid is to avoid the possibility of resales of the aid. If the poor were allowed to buy unlimited Food Stamps worth one dollar of food for only 70 cents, a 30% discount, they would have an incentive to purchase the Food Stamps as fast as the government could print them and sell them to the nonpoor for, say, 80 cents. A limit on the amount of Food Stamps each recipient can buy removes this incentive.

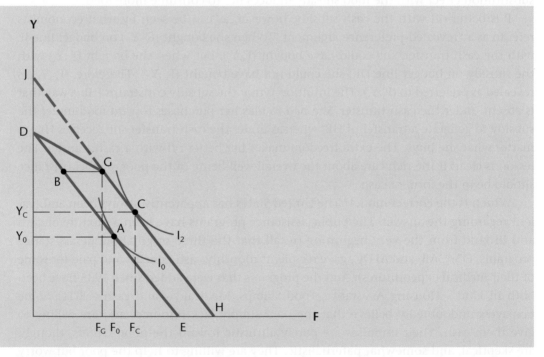

Figure 10.2

Setting limits on in-kind aid can remove its apparent accountability, however, as illustrated in Figure 10.2, which reproduces the original budget line DE and the original equilibrium A on indifference curve I_0 in Figure 10.1. Suppose the government issues Food Stamps to P that allow her to buy food at a 30% discount, up to a limit of F_G. The new budget line rotates out from point D by 30% until it reaches point G, the limit. Beyond G, P receives a transfer of BG in Food Stamps, no matter how much food she purchases. Therefore, the budget line becomes parallel to DE beyond G. The parallel segment is GH. Her new equilibrium is point C, at which indifference curve I_2 is tangent to the line segment GH.

Suppose, instead, that P receives a cash transfer in the amount BG, the limit of the Food Stamp transfer. The cash transfer shifts the budget line parallel to the original budget line DE in the amount BG, and the new budget line is JGH. Her new equilibrium under the cash transfer is point C, identical to the equilibrium under the Food Stamp program. The cash transfer differs from the food discount with a limit only in the regions JG and DG. If, as here, P is not in the region DG under the Food Stamp subsidy, then the original discount does not matter. She is indifferent whether she receives the amount BG as a discount on some of her food purchases or as a cash transfer. Her options are the same in either case and generate the same equilibrium.

The test of whether the limit is binding is simple. If P buys more food than is subsidized by Food Stamps, then she is beyond the limit and the subsidy is irrelevant. This is true of almost all families and individuals who receive Food Stamps, which is why economists view Food Stamps as essentially another cash transfer program. Notice that the apparent accountability of the Food Stamps is also destroyed once the limit has been exceeded. The poor person could spend less on food if she wished by moving to a point on line segment GH that had less food than at the original equilibrium A, although she does not do this in Figure 10.2. The figure assumes that food is a normal good, as it is likely to be for the poor.

ARE PARETO-OPTIMAL REDISTRIBUTIONS ENOUGH?

If cash and in-kind public assistance are motivated by the altruism of the nonpoor as the public choice economists believe, are the resulting Pareto-optimal redistributions enough? Can a theory of the public sector do without the social welfare function after all? Mainstream economists would answer "no" to both questions. They point out that Pareto-optimal redistributions restrict the utility possibilities frontier somewhat but they do not select the distributionally best point on the restricted frontier. Only the social welfare function can do that. Figure 10.3 illustrates for the two-person case, with the utilities of the two people on the axes.

Refer first to Figure 10.3(a). Suppose that person #2 has all the resources, so that the economy is initially at point A. If person #2 is altruistic, he will want to transfer some resources to person #1. The transfer makes both people better off, so the economy moves to the northeast from A. At some point, say at point B, person #2's altruism ends because person #1 now has enough resources from person #2's point of view. Further transfers from person #2 to person #1 would make person #2 worse off. The economy would move southeast along its utility possibilities frontier.

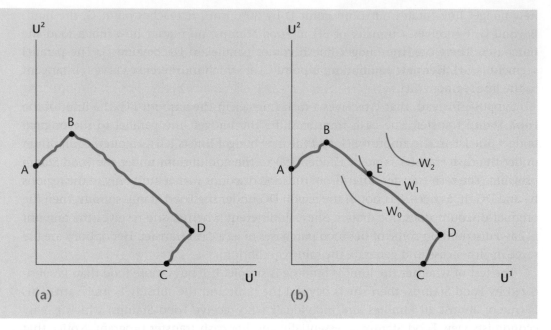

Figure 10.3

The same argument applies if person #1 has all the resources, so that the economy is initially at point C. If person #1 is altruistic towards person #2, transfers from person #1 to person #2 make both people better off, and the economy moves to the northeast from C. Person #1's altruism ends at point D when she decides that person #2 now has enough resources. Further transfers from person #1 to person #2 make person #1 worse off, and the economy moves northwest along its utility possibilities frontier. The restricted utility possibilities frontier is BD.

If the economy were initially beyond B or D in either direction, then the Pareto-optimal redistributions should take place on efficiency grounds. Efficiency requires that all win–win reallocations be exploited so that the economy achieves a Pareto optimum: In order to make someone better off, someone else must be worse off. The Pareto-optimal points are those from B to D, the points on the restricted utility possibilities frontier.

To say that Pareto-optimal redistributions are also enough to satisfy end-results equity or distributive justice is to argue that points B or D are necessarily socially optimal. Main-stream economists would dispute this view. For instance, it could happen that relatively few people control most of the nation's resources and that they are not very altruistic. The result would be a highly unequal distribution of income that many people might find objectionable. Accepting Pareto-optimal redistributions as sufficient also completely disenfranchises the poor in determining the optimal distribution of income, and this may not seem fair.

Mainstream economists argue that society cannot avoid making a collective decision about the initial distribution of resources, and that decision requires developing a set of ethical rankings that the social welfare function and its associated social welfare indifference curves represent. Only the social welfare function can determine the distribution-ally best point on the restricted utility possibilities frontier, Bator's bliss point, point E in Figure 10.3(b). Point E achieves end-results equity, given the social welfare indifference curves in the figure, not points B or D.

In conclusion, mainstream economists agree with the public choice position that Pareto-optimal redistributions are necessary to reach the utility possibilities frontier if people are privately altruistic toward others. But they believe that the lump-sum taxes and transfers that satisfy the interpersonal equity condition for a social welfare maximum are what ultimately resolve the question of distributive justice. One implication of the mainstream view is that if the lump-sum taxes and transfers were to eliminate poverty and make the distribution of income more equal, then the private altruistic impulses behind the Pareto-optimal redistributions may well disappear. The interpersonal equity condition is necessary to achieve a social welfare optimum; the Pareto-optimal redistri-butions may or may not be.

CHAPTER 11

Practical Issues in Designing Transfers to the Poor

There are three practical questions of particular interest to economists in designing transfer payments to the poor:

1. Should the transfers be cash or in kind?
2. If the transfers are in kind, can they be decentralized? Decentralized means that the poor receive subsidies to purchase particular goods such as food in already functioning, decentralized markets. The alternative is centralized provision, meaning that the transfers are distributed by a government agency. The preference is for decentralized provision since it minimizes the government's intervention in the economy.
3. Should the transfers be broad based or targeted? Broad based means that the transfers are available to everyone, in the spirit of the U.S social insurance programs. Targeted means that they are targeted to the poor. They could be targeted to all the poor such as the Food Stamp program, or be categorical and more finely targeted to the poor with certain personal characteristics such as TANF, which is targeted to poor families headed by a single parent.

The mainstream and public choice theories of transfer payments that we have developed in Chapters 4 and 10 provide guidelines for answering each of these questions, but not always definitive guidelines. We will begin by reviewing briefly what the theories have to say about them, and then turn to more narrow and practical issues associated with the third question, the choice between broad-based and targeted transfers.

MAINSTREAM AND PUBLIC CHOICE PERSPECTIVES: WHAT DOES THEORY TELL US?

MAINSTREAM THEORY

The mainstream theory of transfers to the poor is contained in the interpersonal equity condition for a social welfare maximum. The transfers, and the taxes to pay for them, should be lump sum, with the objective of equalizing the social marginal utilities of income across all people. The lump-sum transfers (and taxes) must necessarily be centralized since a government agency carries out the redistribution. The theory is indifferent, however, between cash and in-kind transfers. Any good or factor can be chosen for redistribution, so long as it is something that is commonly consumed or supplied by everyone in sufficient amounts. Therefore the transfers can certainly be in kind. But the income associated with a fixed factor or an endowment income could also be transferred until the interpersonal equity condition held for one of the goods or variable factors, in which case the transfers would be cash. Therefore, the theory is indifferent between cash or in-kind transfers, although one thinks in terms of transfers of income (cash) since the lump-sum taxes that are also required to satisfy the interpersonal equity condition are almost certainly going to be levied on some source of fixed income. Finally, the taxes and transfers are necessarily targeted to individuals; they have to be to equalize the social marginal utilities of income.

Whether the mainstream theory is useful in practice as a guideline for reaching Bator's bliss point on the utility possibilities frontier is highly problematic. We saw in Chapter 5 that under the three assumptions commonly employed to apply the social welfare analysis – equal social welfare weights at equal incomes, identical tastes for all people, and diminishing private marginal utility of income – the social marginal utilities of income are equalized by leveling everyone to the mean, a result that almost no one supports. The implication is that the social welfare maximizing framework has to be considered in a setting with distorting taxes – recall Okun's leaky bucket – with the goal of striking the best balance between the gains from making the distribution of income more equal and the inefficiencies and other costs associated with distorting taxes and transfers. Still, the theory with distortions added implies that the transfers (and taxes) must be centralized, are likely to be cash rather than in kind, and targeted. As we will see below, the targeting of transfers gives rise to a number of practical difficulties. Therefore, the government may choose the more modest objective of trying to achieve the best trade-off between efficiency and equity with a broad-based approach.

PUBLIC CHOICE THEORY

The public choice theory of transfers to the poor is based on the altruism of the non-poor to the poor that takes the form of a consumer externality: Something about the poor affects the utility of the nonpoor. As with all externalities, the policy implications depend on the exact form of the externality. If the nonpoor worry that the poor do not have enough of some particular good, then we saw that the purchase of that good by the poor should be subsidized. The subsidy is the standard Pigovian subsidy. The transfers are in kind, decentralized, and targeted to the poor. If, in contrast, the nonpoor believe that the poor simply do not have enough resources and are concerned with their entire well-being, then the subsidies should be in cash and must be centralized. They are still targeted to the poor.

The only caveat occurs with the in-kind Pigovian subsidies. If the government chooses to set a limit on the in-kind subsidy for reasons of budgetary accountability or to prevent resales, then the subsidy is likely to be equivalent to a cash subsidy. It is still targeted, however. A broad-based approach is inconsistent with the notion of Pareto-optimal redistributions.

Overall, though, the guidelines for the design of transfers to the poor remain ambiguous in public choice theory. As noted in Chapter 10, it is not clear whether the nonpoor worry about particular goods that the poor consume or about their overall well-being – probably some of each. The guidelines are also somewhat ambiguous in mainstream theory as well. Given the ambiguities, policy makers have to turn to a narrower set of issues when deciding how to answer the three practical design questions noted above.

In concluding this overview, we would note that there are a number of other theories to explain charitable giving beyond the mainstream and public choice theories discussed in previous chapters. For example, one explanation is entirely self-serving, that people give to charities to confer status on themselves, as when they are listed as donors to symphony orchestras and art museums. Research has shown that a large majority of these gifts in each dollar range listed are at the low end of the ranges and this is offered as some support for the giving-as-status theory.

Another theory relates to the gifts by parents to their children. They are overwhelmingly in kind rather than cash, the majority in the form of paying for the education of their children. Why do parents pay large sums for their children's education rather than just giving them the equivalent amount in cash and allowing them to decide how to spend the money? One answer, first suggested by James Buchanan, is that parents are caught in the Samaritan's dilemma. They love their children and want them to succeed. If they give cash, the risk is that their children will waste the money having a good time and not prepare adequately for their futures. Knowing that their parents love them, the children will then go back to their parents for more money. The parents know this, and also know that they will not be able to resist. They are Samaritans when it comes to their children; they will continue to support them. To avoid this situation, parents tie their aid to education, thereby increasing the odds that the children will be able to succeed on their own in the future (Buchanan, 1975, pp. 71–5; see also Bruce and Waldman, 1991).

There are still other motivations for giving that have been discussed in the literature, and they may or may not have implications for the design of public transfers.

At the very least, they contribute to the ambiguity that theory offers policy makers on the design of transfer payments. To make matters worse, problems associated with private information can also influence the design of transfer payments, an issue we will explore in Chapter 17.

BROAD-BASED VS. TARGETED TRANSFERS

The need for policy makers to turn to a narrower set of issues when deciding how to design transfers to the poor is especially true regarding the third question above, the choice between broad-based and targeted transfers. A simple example by Browning and Browning (1983, pp. 276–84) illustrates some of the key issues in this choice. We have updated the numbers so that they are more realistic for the United States today.

THE CREDIT INCOME TAX

One of the main advantages of a broad-based approach to aiding the poor is that it is usually much cheaper to administer than a targeted approach. The cheapest broad-based approach is the so-called credit income tax; it can be administered by the IRS with little or no increase in costs relative to a standard income tax without a credit. Under a *credit income tax*, each taxpayer receives a credit or subsidy, S, and then pays taxes on every dollar of income earned. Assuming a single tax rate t on all income (a so-called flat-rate tax), the credit income tax is T = –S + tY. The credit would be refundable because the objective is to provide aid to the poor. That is, individuals would receive a check from the government if their tax liabilities are less than the credit. The credit income tax guarantees an income floor of S (with Y = 0).

Suppose society consists of equal numbers of four-person families in each of five income classes: $10,000, $20,000, $30,000, $40,000, and $50,000. Assume that the government's main goal is to ensure that the people in the lowest income group have incomes equal to the poverty line, which is approximately $19,000 for a family of four (2005). Therefore, it wants the $10,000 families to receive a net transfer of $9,000 under a credit income tax. To focus on the issue of income distribution, assume also that it wants the net taxes on the higher income classes to equal the net transfers to the lower income classes. In other words, the example is of a pure self-financed redistribution from the higher income to the lower income families. Tax revenue for other purposes is assumed to be collected by some other means.

A credit income tax that satisfies these goals is T = –$13,500 + .45Y, as illustrated in Table 11.1.

TABLE 11.1 Credit income tax

Income	$10,000	20,000	30,000	40,000	50,000
Credit (S)	−13,500	−13,500	−13500	−13,500	−13,500
Tax (.45Y)	4,500	9,000	13,500	18,000	22,500
Net tax (T = −S + .45Y)	−9,000	−4,500	0	4,500	9,000
Net income	19,000	24,500	30,000	35,500	41,000

TARGETING COMBINED WITH AN INCOME TAX EXEMPTION

The United States, along with many other countries, has eschewed the credit income tax despite its low administrative costs in favor of targeting aid to the poor. To ensure that the poor do not then pay the aid right back to the government in taxes, the income tax exempts low incomes from taxation. A self-financing targeted approach that can be compared with the credit income tax above is the following. The government transfers $9,000 to the families in the $10,000 income class. It then levies a 15% tax on incomes, with the first $20,000 of income exempt from tax. The income tax is $T = .15(Y − \$20,000)$. Table 11.2 indicates the incomes of the five classes net of taxes and the transfer.

TABLE 11.2 Targeted transfer with income tax exemption

Income	$10,000	20,000	30,000	40,000	50,000
Transfer	9,000	0	0	0	0
Tax (T = .15(Y − 20,000)	0	0	1,500	3,000	4,500
Net income	19,000	20,000	28,500	37,000	45,500

The $10,000 families reach $19,000, the poverty line, under each tax-transfer regime, but otherwise the two approaches have quite different effects. The credit income tax has two disadvantages relative to the targeted approach. First, the tax rate under the credit income tax is much higher than under the targeted transfer, 45% vs. 15%. This difference matters, because we will see in Chapter 15 that the inefficiency of a tax rises with the square of the tax rate. A tax with three times the tax rate has nine times the efficiency cost, and the efficiency costs of income taxes are considerable. The credit income approach may save on administrative costs but it can easily give back these savings, and then some, in inefficiency costs. The example highlights a truth that a broad-based approach to transferring substantial amounts of aid to the lowest income class requires very high tax rates. A second, and related, point is that the credit income tax has to raise much more tax revenue than the targeted approach to transfer the same amount of income to the poor. The targeted approach raises $9,000 in tax revenue to transfer $9,000 to the $10,000 income class. The credit income tax raises $67,500 to transfer $13,500 net. Also, $4,500 of the transfer goes to the $20,000 income class, which the government has no interest in aiding. In other words, the credit income tax is necessarily less target efficient in transferring aid than a targeted approach, a problem with all broad-based transfer schemes. Under broad-based schemes, some people who are not in need of aid receive transfers, sometimes the majority of the recipients, as we will see below.

The targeted approach also has a number of disadvantages, however, and our example illustrates one of them. One of the great success stories in the eyes of the public are the people who work hard to raise their families out of poverty. This goes along with the second principle of the 1601 English Poor Law, that able-bodied people are supposed to help themselves and not rely on government transfer payments. Consider, then, members of the $10,000 income class who work harder, or undertake more formal education or job training to improve their skills, and increase their incomes from $10,000 to $20,000. How much better off are they? Under the credit income tax, they are only $5,500 better off, with income of $24,500 versus $19,000. They have to give up 45% of their extra income in higher taxes, which is true of anyone who earns an extra $10,000 of income. The *marginal tax rate* (MTR), the proportion of additional income paid in taxes, is 45%, the credit income tax rate. A 45% MTR is a huge disincentive to work harder or enter training programs to increase one's income. But look at the $10,000 families who increase their incomes to $20,000 under the targeted transfer. They are only $1,000 better off for doing so; their net incomes rise from $19,000 to $20,000. Their marginal tax rate on the additional earnings is 90%, not because they pay more taxes – they still pay no taxes – but because they lose the $9,000 subsidy. Losing a dollar of subsidy by earning more income is the same on the margin as paying a dollar of tax on that income. Notice, too, that anyone else who earns an additional $10,000 pays only $1,500 in additional taxes. Their MTR is only 15%, the income tax rate. Therefore, the targeted approach has the ironic effect of placing the highest marginal tax rates on the poor, and the rates are extremely high. Who among the nonpoor would work harder, or undertake extra education or job training, if they knew that the rewards for their efforts would be taxed at a 90% rate?

The 90% marginal tax rate in this example is not necessarily unrealistic for many of the poor in the United States. If they lift themselves out of poverty, they can lose not only their monthly benefits under one of the categorical public assistance programs, but also Housing Assistance, Food Stamps, and other social services they may be receiving while poor. The marginal tax rates on their efforts in the form of lost subsidies can be above 100%. The Earned Income Tax Credit (EITC) lowers the MTR as we will see below, but the poor and near poor in the United States still face the highest marginal tax rates, more than the 35% rate levied on the highest incomes under the federal personal income tax. In summary, the targeted approach keeps tax rates low on the nonpoor, but at the cost of hammering the poor who are trying to help themselves.

A NEGATIVE INCOME TAX

Nobel laureate Milton Friedman had long advocated a federal negative income tax, which combines the administrative advantages of the credit income tax with the target efficiency of the targeted approach. Under a negative income tax, the IRS defines a cut-off level of income, varying by family size, above which people are taxed and below which they receive transfers. The two portions of the negative income tax are entirely separable. The tax rates applied to the taxable incomes can be completely different from the transfer rates applied to incomes below the cut-off. But both portions would be administered by the IRS, just as the EITC is today, thereby saving millions of dollars in administrative costs relative to the current system of separate categorical transfer programs.

There are two additional features of a federal negative income that many people find appealing. First, it transfers income to all the poor, unlike categorical programs such as TANF and SSI. With a categorical approach, some poor people receive considerable support from public assistance and other poor people receive relatively little support. Also, by nationalizing the cash support of the poor, the negative income tax overcomes a troubling problem with the U.S. system, that the level of support the poor receive depends not only on their personal characteristics but also on where they live. Under TANF and SSI, there is enormous variation across states in the benefit levels to the poor, more than 6 to 1 under TANF (2003). Not surprisingly, the richer states tend to offer much higher benefit levels than the poorer states. (Medicaid also varies considerably across states, not only in the amount of support for certain medical services, but also in the income limits at which Medicaid ceases to apply.) A negative income tax would standardize the benefit levels nationwide.

Although reaching all the poor and standardizing benefit levels nationwide are attractive to many people, these two features go against two of the principles of the 1601 English Poor Law, that only the helpless among the poor should be supported and that public assistance should be local, not national. Consequently, Freidman's negative income tax proposal has not made much headway in the Unites States. It received its only serious hearing in the Nixon administration in the early 1970s, but a formal proposal was never presented to Congress. Even so, the variation in benefit levels across states did lead to the adoption of two federal programs – Food Stamps and the EITC – as add-ons to the existing public assistance programs. Also, SSI federalized the original OAA, AB, and AD programs and set a floor under the payment levels that was higher than what the lower income states had been offering. But the richer states add on to the SSI payments, so there remains considerable across-state variation in the benefit levels under SSI. The United States continues to adhere strongly to the principles of the 1601 English Poor Law.

PRACTICAL ISSUES WITH TARGETED TRANSFER PROGRAMS

Even if Friedman's federal negative income tax proposal had been adopted, it would still retain many of the problems of any targeted transfer approach, and they are considerable. We referred to one above, the high marginal tax rates on the poor, but there are other problems as well. We conclude the chapter with a discussion of the more important ones.

SATISFYING THREE GOALS

Americans have never been entirely comfortable with their targeted public assistance programs and they likely never will be. We believe a public assistance effort would be considered a success if it met three goals:

1. *Get "everyone" out of poverty.* President Johnson declared a war on poverty in 1964 with the goal of eradicating poverty. The war effort, sadly, is still ongoing. In 1960, there were 39 million Americans below the government-defined poverty line. Today the number is 37 million (2005). The population is much larger today, of course, so that poverty has declined in percentage terms, from 22% of the population in 1960 to 13% in 2004. There will always be some people in any year who fall below the poverty line, but 13% of the population is far above any reasonable percentage one might use to say that poverty has effectively been eliminated. The issue is not financial. Economists have devised a statistic called the "poverty gap," which measures the total income the poor would need to lift all of them to the poverty line. The gap is approximately $100 billion in the United States, a very achievable figure with federal, state, and local spending exceeding $4 trillion (2006). Of course, the gap would be much larger without the $1.6 trillion already spent on social insurance and public assistance, but an additional $100 billion would be easily managed.

2. *The public assistance effort cannot be too costly to the taxpayers.* This goal is particularly relevant when the federal government is running large budget deficits, as it did during the Reagan and the two Bush administrations.

3. *Preserve incentives to work and to keep families intact.* This principle goes back to the 1601 English Poor Law, that able-bodied people should not be supported by the government if possible. The U.S. taxpayers definitely do not want to play the role of suckers when it comes to public assistance.

Unfortunately, these three goals cannot be met simultaneously with a targeted approach to public assistance. Something has to give, which then leads to discontent.

The problems start with the formula for transferring aid to the poor (we will consider cash payments, although the same points apply to in-kind aid). The only sensible way to transfer money to the poor as the principal form of support is the way it is actually done.

The government defines a cut-off level of income, Y_C, below which people receive aid and above which the aid ceases. Y_C would vary with family size; we will assume a family of four in our examples. The government then offers a subsidy, S, equal to some percentage, X%, of the difference between the cut-off level of income and the actual level of income, Y_A: $S = X\%(Y_C - Y_A)$. The family's total income, Y_T, under this transfer formula is the sum of its actual income and the subsidy: $Y_T = Y_A + S$. X has to be a fairly high percentage to give a reasonable amount of support to families with very low incomes. We assume X% = 75% in our numerical examples below. Also, we set the poverty line at $20,000 for ease of computation.

The first issue is where to set the cut-off level on income. A natural point is the poverty line since the aid is targeted to the poor. (In fact, the states and the federal government set the cut-off well below the poverty line under TANF and SSI because of the existence of the other in-kind programs and the EITC.) Setting Y_C = $20,000, the subsidy formula in our initial examples is $S = .75(\$20,000 - Y_A)$. A formula of this kind is said to provide guaranteed minimum level of income, the total income received by a family with zero income. Setting $Y_A = 0$, $S = .75(\$20,000) = \$15,000 = Y_T$ under our formula. Families with incomes between 0 and $20,000 receive some subsidy and their total income exceeds $15,000:

$$Y_T = Y_A + S = Y_A + .75(\$20,000 - Y_A) = \$15,000 + .25Y_A$$

How well does the subsidy formula meet the three goals above? The answer is not well at all. Consider the first two goals. The formula fails the first goal absolutely. Any family in poverty before the subsidy remains in poverty after the subsidy. To see this, suppose a family is $1 short of the poverty line, at $19,999, so that it qualifies for a subsidy:

$$S = .75(\$20,000 - 19,999) = \$.75$$

$$Y_T = \$19,999 + \$.75 = \$19,999.75$$

Including the subsidy, therefore, all families have total incomes in the range from $15,000, the guaranteed minimum, up to but not including $20,000. They all remain in poverty.

With a formula of this kind, the cut-off income has to be set at 1/X times the poverty line, where X is a decimal fraction, to get everyone out of poverty. To see this, compute the subsidy for a family with zero income, the guaranteed minimum. The subsidy is

$$S = X(\$20,000 (1/X) - Y_A) = \$20,000$$

with $Y_A = 0$. At X = .75, Y_C would have to be (1/.75)($20,000) = $26,667 (approximately) to get everyone out of poverty. This formula transfers aid to the nonpoor and removes some of the taxpayers from the tax rolls, costs that taxpayers may find excessive. These problems are magnified the lower is X.

The disincentives to work under this formula have been suggested above when we compared the credit income tax with targeted aid. Let's now take a closer look using our example to see just how strong the disincentives can be. Return to the cut-off level of income of $20,000 and look again at the formula for a family's total income above:

$$Y_T = \$15{,}000 + \$.25Y_A$$

The formula shows that for every extra dollar the heads of poor families earn, they get to keep only \$.25. The MTR is \$.75 because for every extra dollar earned, the family loses \$.75 of subsidy. To give one example, suppose the head of a family works harder and increases her income from \$12,000 to \$16,000, an increase of \$4,000. The subsidy received falls as a result by \$3,000, from $S = .75(\$20{,}000 - \$12{,}000) = .75(\$8{,}000) = \$6{,}000$ to $S = .75(\$20{,}000 - \$16{,}000) = .75(\$4{,}000) = \$3{,}000$. Therefore the family's total income rises only from $Y_T = \$12{,}000 + \$6{,}000 = \$18{,}000$ to $Y_T = \$16{,}000 + \$3{,}000 = \$19{,}000$, an increase of \$1,000. Thus \$3,000 of the extra \$4,000 has been lost to the reduced subsidy.

In general, the MTR is X% under this subsidy formula. X could be lowered to reduce the marginal tax rate, but then the formula either falls further from the goal of getting everyone out of poverty with Y_C = the poverty line, or Y_C has to be set even higher to get everyone out of poverty and the program becomes more expensive. The work disincentive issue is in a trade-off relationship with each of the other two goals under this formula.

WORK INCENTIVES UNDER THE LABOR-LEISURE MODEL

The labor-leisure model of labor supply leads to the expectation that people will work less, if anything, under the standard formula, in violation of the principle that the able-bodied poor should work hard to pull themselves out of poverty. Figures 11.1 and 11.2 illustrate the difficulties of maintaining work incentives under transfer programs.

Figure 11.1 begins by illustrating the standard economic analysis of a wage subsidy. The individual receives utility from two goods: the income (Y) earned by working, which is used to buy goods and services, and the hours of leisure time (Leis) when not working. The individual's preferences for income and leisure are given by the utility function $U = U(Y, Leis)$, which is represented in part by the indifference curves I_0 and I_1 in Figure 11.1. The individual has 16 hours to spend working or taking leisure time (8 hours is for sleeping) and the wage is originally W_0 before a subsidy. The budget line is

$$Y = W_0(16 - Leisure) = -W_0 Leis + 16W_0$$

with a slope of $(-)W_0$. The individual is in equilibrium at point A, the tangency point of the budget line and indifference curve I_0. She earns Y_0 of income and takes $Leis_0$ hours of leisure time.

Suppose she then receives a wage subsidy, s, that increases her effective wage to W_s:

$$W_s = (1 + s)W_0$$

This is not the subsidy under the subsidy formula above but it provides a useful baseline case for thinking about the effects of the subsidy formula and other possible options. The wage subsidy rotates the budget line upward as indicated in Figure 11.1. The slope of the new budget line is $(-)W_s$ and the individual moves to point B, the tangency point of the new budget line and indifference curve I_1. The new equilibrium is $(Leis_s, Y_s)$.

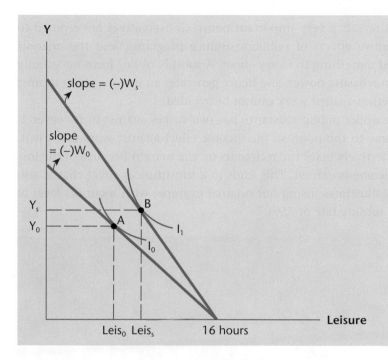

Figure 11.1

The question of interest is whether $Leis_s$ is to the left or right of $Leis_0$, that is, does the individual work harder or less hard with the subsidy? In Figure 11.1, she takes a bit more leisure time and works less hard, but in general the effect on work effort is ambiguous. It depends on the substitution and income effects of the wage increase, and they tug in opposite directions on work effort.

The substitution effect is a relative price effect of the wage increase. At the higher wage, the cost of taking an extra hour of leisure rises from W_0 to W_s in terms of lost income; leisure has become relatively more expensive. Alternatively, it takes less sacrifice of leisure time to earn an extra dollar of income; earning income has become relatively cheaper. Therefore, the change in relative prices is in favor of income and against leisure. People tend to work harder. The substitution effect moves them along their indifference curves towards more income and less leisure.

The income effect is an absolute price effect, a purchasing power effect. With the higher wage, the individual's purchasing power over income and leisure increases, as indicated by the higher budget line (unless the individual chooses not to work at all). Assuming that both income and leisure are normal goods, with more purchasing power the individual consumes more income and more leisure. But more leisure means less work. Therefore, the income effect induces her to work less hard.

The effect of the subsidy on work effort depends, therefore, on the relative strength of the substitution (in favor of work) and income (against work) effects. The income effect wins in Figure 11.1, but it could go the other way (Leis decreases) or be a tie (no change in Leis).

The baseline analysis reveals a very important point. Conservatives are reputed to worry about the disincentive effects of public assistance programs, and the analysis shows that there is indeed something to worry about. A subsidy of *any* form necessarily increases the recipient's purchasing power, and hence generates an income effect against work effort. The income effect against work cannot be avoided.

The standard formula under public assistance has two strikes against it, however. It provides more total income to the poor, so the income effect against work is present. But we saw that it also effectively taxes the recipients on the margin because of the loss of subsidy when more income is earned. This leads to a substitution effect that is also against work. Figure 11.2 illustrates, using our original example with a cut-off level of income of $20,000 and a subsidy rate of 75%.

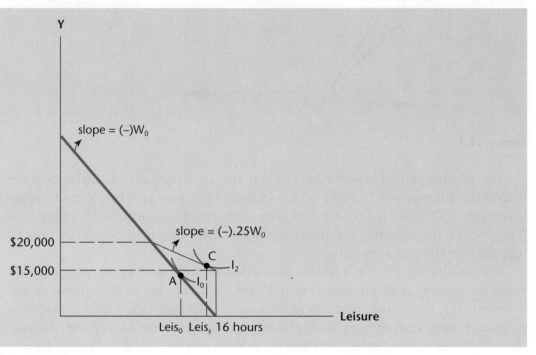

Figure 11.2

Recall that the guaranteed minimum income is $15,000, the subsidy the family head receives if her income is zero. Therefore, the new budget line is $15,000 above the horizontal axis at Leis = 16 (no work). Then, because the family head loses $.75 of subsidy for every extra dollar of income earned, her effective wage *decreases* from W_0 to $.25W_0$. The budget line rotates in the opposite direction from the subsidized line in Figure 11.1 until total income reaches $20,000, at which point the original budget line applies. The individual moves from point A to point C, the tangency point of the new budget line and indifference curve I_2. Leisure time has increased from $Leis_0$ to $Leis_S$, which is the expected result because the substitution effect against work now adds to the income effect against work. With the decrease in the wage from W_0 to $.25W_0$, taking an extra hour of leisure time sacrifices only a quarter of the amount of income; taking leisure has become relatively cheaper. Alternatively, earning an extra dollar of income now requires four times the sacrifice in leisure time; earning income has become relatively more expensive. The relative price effect favors leisure and the individual works less hard. In conclusion, the standard formula generates the maximum possible disincentive for the able bodied to work.

THE STICK APPROACH

In the early 1980s, President Reagan recommended and Congress agreed to give up almost entirely on preserving an incentive to work. The formula under the AFDC program (that TANF replaced) raised X to 100% beyond the first few months of earned income that the formula disregarded. Setting X = 100% is fine in terms of the first two goals, assuming that the cut-off level of income is set at the poverty line (as noted, the states set the cut-off below the poverty line). It gets everyone out of poverty and it is not too costly. The total additional subsidy is equal to the poverty gap, a relatively small amount. But it completely destroys work incentives within the range of poverty incomes because everyone winds up at the poverty line no matter how much income they earn, even zero. The guaranteed minimum is the poverty line. Therefore, the only way to induce work effort is through a stick approach that was called *workfare*. States were asked to force people to receive formal education or job training or to work as a condition for receiving any benefits. Most states made only half-hearted efforts to enforce workfare, however, since the federal government did not adequately subsidize states to provide the education and training required to prepare most recipients for jobs that paid enough for them to escape poverty. The success of workfare also depends on the state of the economy. Firms have to be willing to hire these new labor force entrants and in 1981–82, the economy was mired in the deepest recession since the Great Depression.

Workfare became the centerpiece of the new TANF program in 1996, however, and it was effective this time because the states had to require recipients to work if they could as a condition for receiving any federal aid. The aid was now given lump sum as a block grant to the states, out of which they had to finance the monthly payments to recipients as well as the work and training and job search programs. The combination of a booming economy, the ability to kick recipients off the welfare rolls after two years, and the establishment this time of more effective education and training programs, along with childcare programs for working mothers, had the effect of reducing the TANF caseload over 40% by 2001. The program was widely viewed as a success for this reason.

A stick approach does not rest comfortably with everyone, however, because under TANF the stick is being applied overwhelming to single women with children. There can be no doubt, though, that the majority view about single-parent, female-headed families had changed from 1935 to 1996 with the breaking apart of the nuclear family. In 1935, the majority believed that single women with children should be at home raising the children. By 1996, the majority believed that these women should be working if they are able to, with the children placed in childcare facilities.

THE EARNED INCOME TAX CREDIT (EITC)

As indicated in Figure 11.1, the best the government can do to preserve work incentives is to offer recipients a wage subsidy. The subsidy formula would be $S = X\%Y_A$, with $Y_T = Y_A + S = (1 + X\%)Y_A$. A subsidy of this form turns the substitution effect in favor of work because on the margin an individual keeps whatever wage is earned plus X% of the wage.

EITC is a wage subsidy of this kind. Workers with very low incomes receive a substantial subsidy on their wage income up to a cut-off level of income. The subsidy is 40% of earnings up to $11,350 of income for a family with two children (2006; the income limit increases each year with the increase in the CPI). The EITC subsidy was increased in the 1990s to offset somewhat the total disincentive to work under the categorical public assistance programs, and it is effective in this regard. Still, EITC-style subsidies have their own set of difficulties.

In the first place, a subsidy of the form $S = X\%Y_A$ cannot be the principal form of public assistance because a family with no income would receive no subsidy, and presumably starve to death. This is why the formula described above that bases the subsidy on the shortfall relative to a cut-off level of income is the standard formula. At best the wage subsidy can be used in addition to the standard formula, exactly as the EITC is used.

Second, an EITC-style wage subsidy suffers the most severe form of what economists call the notch problem. The *notch problem* refers to the disincentive effects that can arise at the cut-off level of income, the notch, at which aid ends and tax liability may begin. The transition from transfer recipient to taxpayer has to be managed carefully to prevent extremely high marginal tax rates that can be well in excess of 100%. This is true of all targeted transfer programs, but particularly true of EITC-style wage subsidies.

Suppose a person earns the cut-off level of income, $11,350 under the EITC, and the subsidy ends at the cut-off. The maximum subsidy is 40% of $11,350, equal to $4,536 (.4 · $11,350 = $4,540, which the IRS adjusted to $4,536), for a total income of $15,886 (= $11,350 + $4,536). If the person then earns another $100, raising her wage income to $11,450, she loses all her subsidy. Her total income is now $11,450 as opposed to a total income of $15,886 with a wage income of $11,350. Earning an additional $100 of income lowers her total income by $4,436, a marginal tax rate of 4,436%! Clearly the government wants to avoid that kind of penalty for work effort.

The government avoided the notch problem by applying the EITC to two more income ranges. In the second range, wage incomes from $11,350 to $14,850, the maximum subsidy is held constant at $4,536. For wage incomes above $14,850, the third range, the subsidy is phased out (reduced) by 21 cents on each additional dollar of income earned until the subsidy reaches zero, which it does at an income of $38,348.

Adding these two income ranges to avoid the notch problem is not costless in terms of work disincentives, however. In the second range, a worker experiences only the income effect of the subsidy, which is in favor of leisure and against work. There is no substitution effect because the subsidy is just the lump-sum amount of $4,536 at all income levels in this range. Workers in the final range, those earning between $14,850 and $38,348, face an additional MTR of 21% on their earnings beyond whatever their personal income tax rate is (either 10% or 15% for the majority of these workers), because they lose 21 cents of the maximum $4,536 subsidy for each additional dollar earned. They remain subsidized in total but are taxed on the margin. Thus, there is both an income and a substitution effect in favor of leisure and against work effort, just as with the standard subsidy formula under the categorical programs that we depicted in Figure 11.2. Moreover, workers in the 15% tax bracket have an MTR that is higher than the MTR of the highest income taxpayers, 36% (= 15% + 21%) vs. 35%. The disincentive effect on these workers is especially disconcerting since many of them are the ultimate success stories: They have pulled themselves out of poverty by increasing their earnings. Finally, the majority of the income transferred under the EITC goes to workers in the second and third income ranges who do not live in poor families or are not themselves poor. The EITC is grossly target inefficient as an antipoverty program.

In conclusion, the EITC does sharply reduce the work disincentive effects of the lowest income workers even though it by no means eliminates them. With a subsidy rate of 100% in the standard formula, the 40% EITC subsidy reduces the MTR on the lowest incomes only to 60%. The EITC also transfers a substantial amount of income to the people with the lowest incomes. But it has a number of very undesirable properties as a targeted antipoverty transfer program, all of which arise to avoid an otherwise horrendous notch problem. The government certainly does not want to generate disincentive effects to work for people with incomes between $11,350 and $38,348, nor does it want to provide substantial amounts of transfers to these people, but it has no choice with a wage subsidy.

There appears to be no way to bring "everyone" out of poverty, at minimal cost to the government, and in a way that preserves work incentives for people with low incomes. Figure out a way to reach all three antipoverty goals and you will be famous.

CHAPTER 12

Social Insurance: Social Security

The provision of social insurance has become the most important function of the federal government in the United States. In FY 2005, the $860 billion of expenditures by the Social Security system alone, which provides monthly pensions to retirees and their dependents, monthly payments to disabled workers, and medical care to the elderly under the Medicare program, far exceeded the $495 billion of defense expenditures. Approximately 40 million retirees and their dependents receive Social Security pensions and another 8 million disability payments, 16% of the U.S. population. And Social Security does not include a number of other social insurance programs that add $150–200 billion to federal expenditures, principally retirement pensions to federal employees who are not covered by Social Security, unemployment insurance, veterans' benefits, and price supports for farmers.

The Social Security pensions ("Social Security") and Medicare are of special concern to the American public because of the impending retirement of the huge baby boom generation born between 1947 and 1964. The trustees of the Social Security system make 75-year projections of expenditures, given current benefit schedules and various assumptions about the economy, including increases in health costs and life expectancy. Under their intermediate assumptions, they project that expenditures under these two programs will rise from 7% of GDP in 2004 to 14% of GDP by 2040 and 20% of GDP by 2079. Historically, the entire federal budget has averaged about 19% of GDP (Palmer and Saving, 2005).

The revenue to finance the Social Security system is provided by a payroll tax on employers and employees. At the current tax rates, the projected revenues are nowhere near sufficient to finance the projected benefits over the 75-year period. The expected shortfall of revenues exceeds $4 trillion. Economists and others have offered numerous proposals to reform the Social Security system and place it on a sounder long-run financial footing, including privatizing at least part of the system. As of this writing, however, Congress has not been willing to make any changes.

Rather than consider a variety of reform proposals, the goal of this chapter is to understand the economic principles relating to social insurance, principles that any reform proposal would have to take into consideration. Once these principles have been established, we apply them to the Social Security retirement pensions as an example.

The primary economic question is why have social insurance in the first place. What are the market failures that drive insurance into the public sector?

THE DEMAND FOR SOCIAL INSURANCE

As noted in Chapter 10, social insurance is fundamentally different from public assistance. Public assistance is means tested, designed to transfer income or in-kind aid to people who have become impoverished. Social insurance, in contrast, is not means tested. Its goal is to protect people of all incomes from suffering a large decline in their consumption and standard of living when certain events occur that greatly affect their earning ability, for example retirement in the case of Social Security pensions, illness under Medicare, and a spell of unemployment under Unemployment Insurance. It is these events that trigger the benefits under the social insurance programs. Social insurance does protect low-income people from becoming impoverished when the events occur, but the majority of payments under social insurance programs go to the nonpoor.

PRIVATE INSURANCE

People's demand for insurance, public or private, is based on their desire to protect income and consumption in the face of life's misfortunes. Economists say that people want to smooth their consumption across various states of nature. The states of nature are the "good times," when the events being insured against do not occur, and the "bad times," when the events do occur. People are willing to give up some of their income and consumption in the good times by paying a premium to an insurance company in return for receiving a payment from the company when the bad times occur. In this way, consumption is much more equal – smoothed – between the good and bad times. Let's consider the demand for private insurance first before turning to the market failures that lead to the public provision of insurance.

Figure 12.1 shows the relationship between income and utility for a representative person. Notice that utility function U(Y) bows downward to the horizontal axis (U(Y) is concave, in mathematical terms). As such, it assumes that people have diminishing marginal utility of income (MU_Y), that the slope of U(Y) continuously decreases as income increases. An immediate implication of diminishing MU_Y is that starting from any income level such as Y_0, the loss in utility from a given decrease of income such as –a exceeds the gain in utility from the same increase in income: $[U(Y_0) – U(Y_0 – a)] > [U(Y_0 + a) – U(Y_0)]$. In other words, people with diminishing MU_Y are risk averse; they have a particular desire to protect themselves from decreases in income. Risk aversion is the basis for the demand for insurance, as illustrated in Figure 12.2.

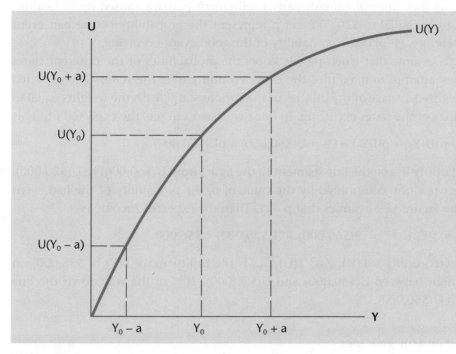

Figure 12.1

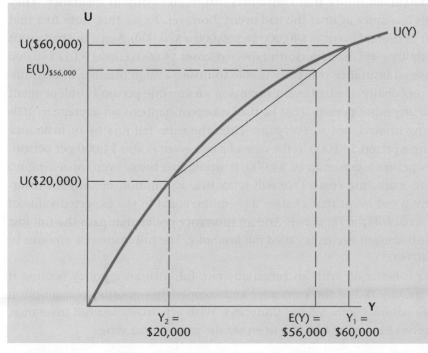

Figure 12.2

Figure 12.2 assumes that all people are identical and that there are two states of nature. In the good state, consumers earn income Y_1, equal to $60,000. In the bad state (ill health, a spell of unemployment, partial retirement perhaps caused by ill health), income falls to Y_2, equal to $20,000. Let p represent the probability of the bad event occurring; therefore, (1–p) is the probability of the good event occurring.

Economists assume that when people know the probabilities of the different states of nature, they attempt to maximize the expected utility over the states. The expected utility is a weighted average of the utilities in the various states, with the weights equal to the probabilities of the states occurring. In our two-state example, the expected utility is

$$E(U) = (1–p)U(Y_1) + pU(Y_2) = (1–p)U(\$60,000) + pU(\$20,000)$$

The expected utility lies on the line segment in the figure from U($60,000) to U($20,000), with the exact position determined by the value of p, the probability of the bad event occurring. The Figure 12.2 assumes that p = .1. Then the expected income is

$$E(Y) = Y_E = .9Y_1 + .1Y_2 = .9(\$60,000) + .1(\$20,000) = \$56,000$$

and the expected utility is $E(U)_{\$56,000}$. $E(U)_{\$56,000}$ is the utility above E(Y) (= $56,000) on the line segment between U($60,000) and U($20,000), 10% of the way down the line segment from U($60,000).

Actuarially fair and full insurance

$E(U)_{\$56,000}$ is the maximum utility that consumers can receive without insurance. They can do better with insurance against the bad event, however. To see this, note first that the loss as a result of the bad event is $40,000 (= $60,000 – $20,000). Since the bad event occurs with probability p = .1, each person's expected loss is $4,000 [E(loss) = (.1) $40,000 = $4,000). Suppose an insurance company is able to insure a large number of consumers, and that the probability of a bad event occurring for any one person is independent of it occurring for any other person. That is, the bad event happens on average to 10% of the people being insured, not to everyone. Then the expected loss to an insurance company of paying a person $40,000 in the case of a bad event is also $4,000 per person. If it charged each person a premium of $4,000, it would just break even, assuming no administrative and marketing costs. (We will relax this assumption below.) An insurance policy against a bad event that charges a premium equal to the expected value of the loss is called *actuarially fair insurance*. And an insurance policy that pays the full loss suffered when the bad event occurs is called *full insurance*. The full insurance amount in our example is $40,000.

The consumer is better off with an actuarially fair, full insurance policy because it removes the uncertainty facing the consumer and completely smoothes consumption over both states of nature. Figure 12.3(a) illustrates. With actuarially fair full insurance, the consumer receives income of $56,000 in either the good or bad state:

Good state: Y = $60,000 – premium = $60,000 – $4,000 = $56,000

Bad state: Y = $20,000 + insurance payment – premium =

$20,000 + $40,000 – $4,000 = $56,000

Because income is now certain to be $56,000 in either state, the consumer receives utility of U($56,000), the point on U(Y) above Y = $56,000. Furthermore, since U(Y) is concave, U($56,000) lies above E(U)$_{\$56,000}$, the expected utility without insurance, as shown.

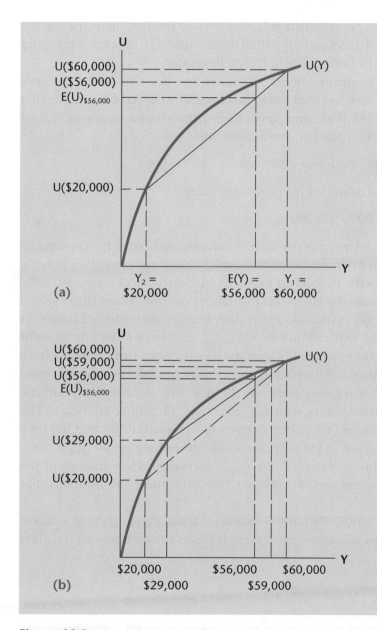

Figure 12.3

Notice that this result depends on consumers being risk averse, with diminishing MU_Y. If MU_Y were constant so that U(Y) was a straight line from the origin, then U($56,000) would equal $E(U)_{\$56,000}$ and consumers would gain nothing from the insurance. Consumers in this case are said to be *risk neutral,* in the sense that they are indifferent to risk. They gain nothing from an insurance policy that removes their uncertainty and so they accept the expected outcome under uncertainty as the best they can do.

Another very important point is that full insurance is the best outcome for the consumer. Partial insurance that covers only part of the loss in return for a lower premium is always dominated by full insurance. Figure 12.3(b) illustrates.

Suppose the insurance company offered consumers a policy that paid them only $10,000 if the bad event occurs, so-called *partial insurance.* The expected loss under that policy is (.1)$10,000 = $1,000. If the company charged the consumers a premium of $1,000, then the policy is actuarially fair. The outcomes are now:

Good event: Y = $60,000 – premium = $59,000

Bad event: Y = $20,000 + insurance payment – premium =

$20,000 + $10,000 – $1,000 = $29,000

The problem with such partial insurance relative to full insurance from the consumers' perspective is that it does not remove the uncertainty. The consumer receives $59,000 with Pr = .9 and $29,000 with Pr = .1, an expected income of E(Y) = (.9)$59,000 + (.1)$29,000 = $56,000.[1] Actuarially fair partial insurance does not change the expected income relative to having no insurance. But it does change the expected utility, as Figure 12.3(b) indicates. The expected utility, $E(U)_{\$56,000}$ now lies on the line segment from U($59,000) to U($29,000), which is above the line segment from U($60,000) to U($20,000) without insurance. E(U) rises because income has been smoothed somewhat. But since U(Y) is concave, any point on the new line segment must still lie below U($56,000), the certain utility with full insurance, including $E(U)_{\$56,000}$. The same is true of any partial insurance policy. It gives an expected utility that lies on a line segment that begins above U($56,000) and ends somewhere below U($56,000), and therefore must be below U($56,000). $E(U)_{\$56,000}$ increases as the amount of the partial insurance increases, but remains below U($56,000) until the insurance has become full.

The conclusion is that actuarially fair full insurance is the Pareto-optimal solution in the face of uncertainty for risk-averse consumers. It places the economy on its utility possibilities frontier.

The risk premium

One other view of the value of full insurance to consumers is useful before turning to a discussion of social insurance. When people are risk averse, they would be willing to accept a full insurance policy that is not actuarially fair. This willingness is what allows insurance companies to write policies that cover their administrative and marketing costs and earn an accounting profit after they have made all the required insurance payments under their policies. Refer to Figure 12.4, which continues our example.

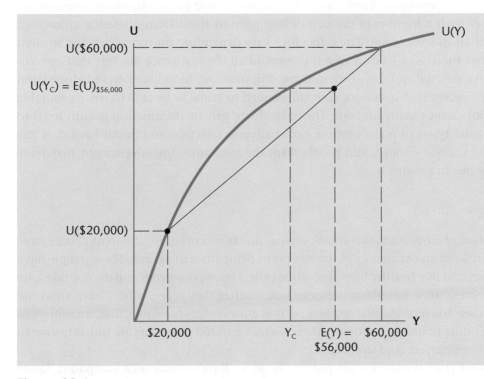

Figure 12.4

We have seen that consumers have an expected income of $56,000 and receive expected utility of E(U) $_{\$56,000}$ without insurance. Therefore, they would be indifferent between accepting that uncertain result and having a full insurance policy that guaranteed them a certain income of Y_C in the figure, and certain utility $U(Y_C) = E(U)_{\$56,000}$. The amount $60,000 – Y_C is called their *risk premium*, the amount they would be willing to sacrifice to turn a risky situation in a certain situation. The risk premium is the maximum premium the insurance company can charge consumers for full insurance, so that they have $60,000 less the risk premium under either state of nature. The risk premium is greater than the actuarially fair premium, which is why consumers gain with actuarially fair insurance. The risk premium is also larger the more risk averse consumers are, that is, the more concave (bowed downward) their utility function. The intuition is that the more risk averse consumers are, the more utility they lose from any given loss of income should the bad event occur. The risk premium is zero if consumers are risk neutral; they are willing to accept the risky situation and would not be willing to pay anything to remove it.

◼◼◼ SOCIAL INSURANCE

Since risk-averse consumers are willing to pay insurance companies a premium for full insurance that allows the companies to cover their costs and earn a profit, why is there a need for public provision of insurance? The answer is that private insurance markets are often beset with a number of difficulties that prevent them from operating efficiently, or even at all in some cases. The difficulties vary depending on the risks being insured against, but there is one factor that is present in all the insurance markets that governments have entered, private or asymmetric information. Individuals have information about themselves that insurance companies need to know to be able to write profitable policies but cannot easily find out. The individuals' private information in turn leads to two potential types of market failure called adverse selection and moral hazard. If the information is bad enough, and people want the insurance, the government may have no choice but to provide it.

Adverse selection

The problem of *adverse selection* arises because, unlike our example, different people have different risks of an occurrence of the bad event being insured against. Some people have good genes and live healthy lifestyles, while others have poor genes and do not take care of themselves. Some have long life expectancies after they retire, others have short life expectancies. Some blue-collar workers such as autoworkers have jobs that are subject to recurring bouts of unemployment, others such as tenured professors are unlikely ever to become unemployed. And so forth.

Different risks themselves are not the issue, so long as insurance companies know which risk class each individual belongs to. They simply charge different premiums for different risk classes. Automobile insurance is an example. Insurance companies have extensive data showing that young males have the highest accident rates, and so they charge them the highest premiums for automobile insurance. But if people with different risks have private information about their riskiness that the insurance companies cannot know, then insurance companies may not be able to write profitable policies.

The problem of private information becomes clear if we expand our earlier example to include two risk classes of consumers, with half the consumers belonging to each risk class. Assume, as above, that consumers earn $60,000 if the bad event does not occur and $20,000 if it does. Assume, also as above, that the low-risk consumers have a probability $p = .1$ of the bad event occurring. The high-risk consumers have the same tastes (same utility function) as the low-risk consumers, but a probability $p = .8$ of the bad event occurring. Their outcomes are pictured in Figure 12.5.

The high-risk consumers have an expected income of $28,000 [$E(Y) = (.2)\$60,000 + (.8)\$20,000 = \$12,000 + \$16,000 = \$28,000$] and an expected utility without insurance of $E(U)_{\$28,000}$. Their expected loss is $32,000 [$= (.8)\$40,000)$]. With full insurance and an actuarially fair premium equal to their expected loss, they receive $28,000 in either state of nature and a utility of U($28,000).

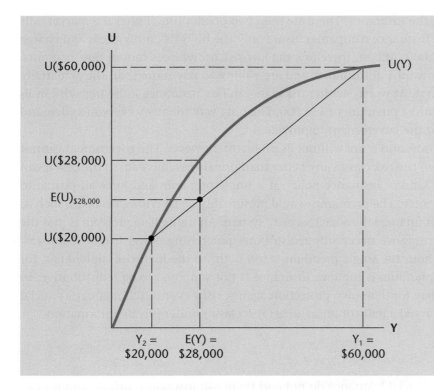

Figure 12.5

If insurance companies know which individuals belong to each risk class, then a company can break even by offering actuarially fair, full insurance to both risk classes, charging premiums of $4,000 to the low-risk class and $32,000 to the high-risk class (assuming no administrative and marketing costs). Private insurance achieves the Pareto-optimal solution that places society on its utility possibilities frontier.

Suppose, instead, that insurance companies cannot know whether an individual is high risk or low risk. Then their only choice is to offer the full insurance at a single premium. If they know that half the people are low risk and half high risk, then one obvious choice for the premium is $18,000, halfway between the expected losses of the low-risk and high-risk individuals: [(.5)$4,000 + (.5)$32,000 = $2000 + $16,000 = $18,000]. They will break even if both classes of individuals buy the policies. But the low-risk individuals may not be interested; $18,000 may be above their risk premium of $60,000 − Y_C in Figure 12.4. If it is, they are better off accepting the expected utility of the risky situation, $[E(U)_{\$56,000}]$.[2] In that case, the pool of the insured consists of only the high-risk individuals. They are quite happy to pay a premium of $18,000 to cover an expected loss of $32,000; that is better than actuarially fair insurance for them. The insurance pool becomes adverse for the insurance company, hence the name adverse selection.

Unfortunately, the gains to the high-risk individuals come at the expense of the insurance companies, who now lose money. They are charging an $18,000 premium to cover only high-risk individuals who have an expected loss of $32,000. Consequently,

219

they stop offering the insurance. There are then two possibilities. Either the market fails completely or the insurance companies insure only the high-risk individuals and charge a premium of $32,000. At best, therefore, the low-risk individuals cannot buy insurance even though they want full insurance and are willing to pay more than the actuarially fair price to obtain it. At worst, neither risk class can buy insurance if the high-risk individuals cannot afford a premium of $32,000. The only way to satisfy everyone's demand for insurance is for the government to provide it.

Government provision is not without its problems, however. The government cannot distinguish between the risk classes any better than private insurers can, so the best it can do is to offer one kind of insurance policy at a single premium and force all people to purchase the insurance. The premiums would presumably be paid for with taxes, such as the payroll tax that finances the Social Security system. An immediate problem is that the mandated social insurance necessarily redistributes purchasing power from the low-risk individuals, for whom the single premium is too high, to the high-risk individuals, for whom the single premium is too low. Insurance is not supposed to be redistributive; in principle, people pay for their own protection against risky events. But mandatory social insurance cannot avoid a redistribution across risk classes under private information.

Moral hazard

The problems with social insurance do not end there. All insurance, private and public, is subject to the problem of moral hazard under private information. *Moral hazard* takes two main forms, one direct and one indirect, and both entail efficiency costs. The direct effect is that individuals can influence the probability of the bad event occurring, unbeknownst to the insurer. For example, under retirement insurance, people have an incentive to retire early to begin collecting benefits. Under medical insurance, they have an incentive to choose unhealthy lifestyles. Under unemployment insurance, people are more likely to accept jobs that have a higher incidence of unemployment. When information is private, the insurer cannot know if the event being insured against happens legitimately or if people are simply gaming the system to collect the insurance. For example, are people retiring early because their health is poor and their job has become a huge burden or do they simply want to collect the retirement benefits and not work? Attempts to game the system in these examples clearly impose opportunity costs on society in the form of lost worker productivity and poor health.

The indirect form of moral hazard is that the increased incentive to accept the insurance increases the insurers' expenditures. Moreover, expenditures increase the most under full insurance, which is the optimal form of insurance absent private information. If the insurance is private, the increased expenditures force the companies to charge still higher premiums if the insurance is offered at all. A classic example is health insurance, for which full insurance lowers to zero the marginal costs to the insured of seeing their doctors or undergoing tests for medical conditions. People thus have the strongest possible incentive to go to doctors for even minor aches and pains, and for doctors to engage in defensive medicine and order tests that they know have a very low probability of yielding useful information. If the insurance is public, the increased expenditures require higher taxes and higher taxes can generate substantial efficiency losses. We will show in Chapter 15 that the efficiency loss of a tax rises with the square of the tax rates.

Implications for social insurance

The moral hazard costs of insurance have two important implications for social insurance. One is that the optimal level of social insurance is almost certainly not full insurance for any risk. The other is that social insurance may not dominate private insurance and other forms of self-insurance even if private insurance markets are so plagued by private information that only the very high-risk people are insured. Both implications turn on the point that once the private markets fail, the government is forced into what economists call a "second-best solution." Society cannot hope to reach its utility possibilities frontier in the provision of insurance under private information. The best the government can do is balance the benefits from the social insurance against the costs of the insurance. As always in economic analysis, the optimal amount of social insurance is the level at which the marginal benefits and marginal costs of the insurance are equal.

THE BENEFITS AND COSTS OF SOCIAL INSURANCE

Speaking purely in terms of the efficiency implications of insurance, and ignoring the inherent redistributions across risk classes, the benefits of social insurance are the opportunities it gives individuals to smooth their consumption across states of nature, just as with private insurance. One important determinant of the size of these benefits is the extent to which the social insurance crowds out what economists refer to as "self-insurance" against the same risks, which may or may not take the form of private insurance policies. For example, does the provision of a public pension induce people to save less from their own resources for retirement? Does the provision of unemployment insurance reduce precautionary savings that people would otherwise undertake for such temporary events as a spell of unemployment? Does the provision of public medical insurance induce people to substitute the public insurance for their own private medical insurance? To the extent that public insurance crowds out various kinds of self-insurance, the consumption smoothing benefits of public insurance are correspondingly reduced.

Regarding the costs of social insurance, the key factors in the size of the moral hazard costs are the ability and willingness of people to change their behavior to game the social insurance policies and the ease with which the government can detect gaming. Another important cost relates to the mandated feature of social insurance. Are people being forced to do something against their will? For example, do low-wage workers pay more in payroll taxes than the amount they would otherwise save for their retirements? If so, then this is another source of efficiency loss in addition to the efficiency losses from higher taxes.

The optimality of partial insurance

The two implications for social insurance turn on the marginal benefit = marginal cost test for social insurance. Regarding the nonoptimality of full insurance, we have seen that full insurance maximizes the consumption smoothing benefits of insurance but that it also maximizes the moral hazard costs of providing insurance. Therefore, as insurance moves from partial to full, the marginal benefits of further smoothing consumption decrease and the marginal cost of the moral hazard inefficiencies increase. The optimal point at which marginal benefits equal marginal costs is almost certainly less than full insurance.

Partial insurance usually takes the form of deductibles before the insurance takes effect or co-payments ("coinsurance") by the insured to cover part of the cost of a bad event. Deductibles and co-payments reduce the consumption smoothing benefit of insurance, thereby raising the marginal benefit. They also simultaneously reduce the marginal moral hazard costs by forcing the insured to bear some of the costs of the bad event. This in turn reduces the incentive to game the system and otherwise overuse the insurance.

No social insurance?

Regarding the desirability of having any social insurance at all, the problem is that partial social insurance may not pass the total benefit-cost test for particular kinds of risks at the level for which its marginal benefit and marginal cost are equal. The total net benefits (benefits – costs) are at their maximum when marginal benefits equal marginal costs, so if the net benefits are negative at that level, then the social insurance is not worthwhile. Social insurance is more likely to fail the total benefit-cost test the more that social insurance crowds out self-insurance and the higher are its direct and moral hazard costs. The crowding out effects and moral hazard costs of most social insurance programs are difficult to estimate with any precision, however. As a result, economists may well disagree on whether a particular social insurance program is worthwhile.

If social insurance does fail the overall benefit-cost test for a particular risk, the most likely fallback option is a means-tested public assistance program that is triggered by the event that would otherwise be insured against. The goal in this case is simply to help those whom the bad event would otherwise impoverish. Medicaid is an example in the market for medical care. Unfortunately, such means-tested programs are also subject to crowding out of self-insurance and moral hazard costs. David Cutler and John Gruber (1996, pp. 403–27) estimate that every dollar of Medicaid crowds out 20–50% of private medical insurance for low-income households. And those who qualify for Medicaid have the same incentives to overuse medical services as under any medical insurance program, private or public, that offers almost full insurance.

SOCIAL SECURITY PENSIONS

With the principles of social insurance in hand, we turn to an analysis of Social Security retirement pensions. The benefits and costs of social insurance described above are always present in any government insurance program, although their precise form varies from program to program. But there may also be other features of a particular program that are as important as the pure social insurance benefits and costs in considering whether or how to reform the program. Such is the case with Social Security pensions.

THE STRUCTURE OF THE SOCIAL SECURITY PENSION PROGRAM

To analyze Social Security pensions, you need to have an understanding of the structure of the program. It is fairly complex, with a number of design characteristics that are all relevant to an analysis of the program.

The Social Security Act of 1935 established a Social Security Trust Fund managed by a board of trustees that would take in all the income, pay out all the benefits that participants were entitled to, and invest any surplus in assets whose returns would be available for future benefits. The benefits originally consisted entirely of retirement pensions, but over time the Trust Fund added disability insurance (1956) and hospital insurance (1965, Medicare, and later other forms of medical coverage). The fund is often referred to by the initials OASDIHI. OAS refers to old age and survivors insurance, DI to the disability insurance, and HI to the hospital insurance under Medicare.

The following income and benefit features apply to the retirement pensions (OAS):

1. The principal source of income to the Trust Fund is the tax on the payrolls of covered employees, which now include almost all private sector workers. The tax rate is 15.3%, allocated as follows: 10.6% to OAS, 1.8% to DI, and 2.9% to HI (Medicare). The tax is split 50/50 between employers and employees, although as we will see in Chapter 19, the split makes no difference to the burden of the tax. Most economists assume that workers bear the entire burden of the tax, half because of their share of the tax and half because employers pay lower wages to cover their part of the tax. The tax for OAS and DI is payable up to a limit that increases each year with the average increase in wages during the year. It was $90,000 in 2005. There is no limit on the HI (Medicare) portion of the tax.
2. The pension benefits are in the form of an annuity, which is a stream of income payable each month from the time of retirement until the beneficiary dies. The benefits are also extended to the surviving spouses of deceased beneficiaries throughout their lifetimes. The benefits to which an individual is entitled are calculated by a two-step process:
   (a) The Trust Fund considers the income a beneficiary earned over the 35 years with the highest earnings. The earnings each year used to compute benefits are subject to the same limit that applied to the payroll tax in that year ($90,000 in

2005, for example). The earnings in a given year are increased (indexed) by the average growth in wages in each subsequent year until the time of retirement when the benefits begin, to put all the earnings over time on a commensurate basis. For example, wages earned 20 years before retirement are increased by the average rate of growth in wages each year during that 20-year period. The total wages over the best 35 years increased (indexed) in this way are then divided by 35, and then again by 12 to obtain the individual's average indexed monthly earnings (AIME) during the 35 years of highest earnings.

(b) The AIME is then multiplied by a percentage that determines the primary insurance amount (PIA), which is the monthly annuity that the individual is entitled to. The PIA formula is heavily weighted in favor of workers with low earnings. In 2005, it was 90% of the first $627 of AIME, 32% of the next $3,152 of AIME, and 15% of the remaining AIME up to the limit. The PIA is increased each year by the increase in the CPI – the Social Security annuities are inflation protected.

3. The spouses and dependents of a beneficiary are also entitled to an annuity (PIA), subject to a limit per family per month that is computed by a formula based on the beneficiary's PIA. A spouse who never worked receives 50% of the beneficiary's PIA. In two-earner families, the spouse with the lower AIME receives either her/his own PIA or 50% of the husband's/wife's PIA, whichever is larger. But if the spouse receives her/his own PIA, the combined PIAs are subject to the family limit, which is less than two times the highest possible PIAs. In other words, in two-earner families, the lower earning spouses can lose some or all of their PIA despite having paid payroll taxes throughout their working lifetimes.

4. The age at which individuals can retire and receive their full PIA entitlement is called the "full retirement age." The full retirement age was originally set at 65. The 1983 amendments to the Social Security Act provided for a slow annual increase in the full retirement age to 67 by 2012. Individuals can choose to retire and begin receiving benefits at age 62. Those who retire between 62 and the full retirement age receive reduced benefits that are actuarially equivalent to the lifetime benefits they would have received had they retired at the full retirement age. Workers who delay retirement until 70 receive actuarially increased benefits relative to retiring at the full retirement age. Also, to try to ensure that people who take benefits before the full retirement age are essentially retired and not just gaming the system, any income earned over $11,000 (2005) reduces the Social Security annuity by 50 cents on each dollar earned until the annuity reaches zero.

5. The Trust Fund has been accumulating a surplus every year since the 1983 reforms. The surpluses are invested entirely in U.S. Treasury securities, and the interest earned on the bonds is retained in the Fund to cover future projected payments to retirees. Ever since 2001, when the non-Social Security portion of the federal budget went deeply into deficit, the Trust Fund has in effect been lending to the federal government to finance its other expenditures. These loans have helped to keep the government's interest costs down.

A MODIFIED PAY-AS-YOU-GO SYSTEM

As noted above, government insurance programs often have features in addition to the standard benefits and costs of social insurance that are important in analyzing the program. The wrinkle with Social Security pensions, and it is a big one, is that the Social Security Trust Fund does not operate in the same way as a private pension fund. A private pension fund must be fully funded in order to remain solvent. That is, the fund must accumulate assets that, along with the returns earned on the assets, are sufficient to meet all the projected future payments to the current employees during their retirement.

A fully funded pension fund can set up either as a defined benefit or defined contribution plan. Under a *defined benefit plan*, the fund agrees to pay each retiree a lump sum or an annuity that is based on the retiree's earnings while working for the company. Usually the amount is based on the last year's earnings or an average of the last few year's earnings. The firm bears the risks of ensuring that enough of the firm's revenues are allocated to the pension fund each year so that the pension fund remains fully funded. The Social Security pension is set up as a defined benefit plan. Under a *defined contribution plan*, the firm and the employees contribute amounts each year to the pension fund that are allocated to each individual employee. These are often referred to as 401K plans because that is their designation under the federal personal income tax. The money available to an employee upon retirement depends entirely on the assets that have accumulated, with interest, to that employee in the fund. By definition, the pension fund is always fully funded, and the employees bear all the risk related to the amount of their pension wealth available to support them in their retirement. In the early years of private pensions, most were established as defined benefit plans. But since 1980, companies have been switching to the less risky (for them) 401K defined contribution plans, to the point that 63% of all private pensions were defined contribution plans by 2004 (Munnell and Sunden, 2006, Figure 3, p. 2).

In 1935, President Roosevelt envisioned that Social Security would operate as a defined contribution plan. But the need to support the retiring elderly at the time was so pressing that those plans were scrapped. Instead, the income that came into the Trust Fund from the payroll tax was immediately paid out to the covered retirees. The first Social Security check was paid to Ida May Fuller in 1940, a sum of $24.54. The Trust Fund never had any accumulated assets to invest beyond the first few years. Economists refer to this kind of pension system as *pay-as-you-go*, the opposite of a fully funded pension system.

The Social Security pensions remained on a pay-as-you-go basis until 1983, when the Reagan administration convinced Congress to build up a surplus in the Trust Fund in anticipation of the baby boomer retirement years. The two major 1983 reforms were an increase in the payroll tax and a reduction in benefits brought about by increasing the retirement age from 65 to 67 in a series of small steps from 1983 to 2012. As a result of the reforms, the board of trustees projected that surpluses would build up in the Trust Fund each year through the first two decades of the 21st century and then the assets of the fund would be steadily drawn down to zero by 2058, the end of the 75-year projection horizon in 1983. Beyond 2058, Social Security would revert to a pay-as-you-go basis without further reforms. For these 75 years, then, Social Security would be a modified pay-as-you-go system, still far short of a fully funded system.

The 1983 projections turned out to be too optimistic. By 2005, annual expenditures from the fund were projected to match the annual payroll tax revenues earmarked for the pensions in 2018, after which the government bonds that are the fund's assets would be drawn down each year until they reached zero in 2043. Beyond 2043, the Trust Fund would again be a fund in name only, with no assets. Indeed, the pension program would fall short even of pay-as-you-go; it would run deficits. Without further reforms, and there were none between 1983 and 2005, the projected payroll tax revenues each year after 2043 are insufficient to meet projected annual benefits, and the deficits would continue indefinitely. The pension program had projected unfunded future liabilities in 2005 in excess of $4 trillion.

THE ECONOMICS OF A PAY-AS-YOU-GO PENSION SYSTEM

The baseline OLG model

The long-run economic effects of a pay-as-you-go pension system are very different from those of a fully funded system. The simplest baseline model that economists use to guide their thinking about different kinds of pension systems is a so-called overlapping generations (OLG) model consisting, at a minimum, of two generations or cohorts alive at any one time, young workers and old retirees. All people have identical tastes and plan their consumption decisions over their entire lifetimes in accordance with the life-cycle hypothesis. They are not credit constrained, so that they can borrow and lend at different stages in their lives to smooth out their life-time consumption, as illustrated in Figure 12.6. The standard earnings pattern is that incomes, Y, rise through middle age and then fall sharply during the retirement years. Therefore, to smooth their lifetime consumption, C, they borrow when young and consume more than their incomes, then save during their middle ages by paying back their earlier borrowings and building up a nest egg, which they draw down in their retirement years to support their consumption. Given the assumption of diminishing marginal utility of consumption, consumers are interested in smoothing consumption over time, just as they are interested in smoothing consumption over different states of nature in an uncertain world. The baseline model assumes perfectly competitive markets so that the economy operates on its production possibilities frontier, and further that consumers have rational expectations over all future events, prices, and rates of return. That is, they are able to predict the future accurately on average, with no bias in their predictions. Finally, the timing of death is certain and there may or may not be a bequest motive to leave purchasing power to heirs after death. Assume for the moment no bequest motive.

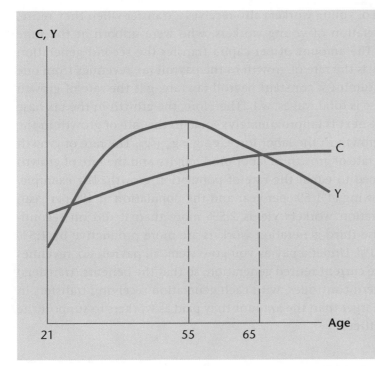

Figure 12.6

A fully funded, defined contribution plan

In this baseline model, the introduction of a fully funded, defined contribution public pension plan would have no effect at all on the economy. The essence of a defined contribution plan is that the government invests the funds contributed each year to maximize the utility of the contributors. Thus, the funds would be invested exactly as the consumers would have invested them had they kept the funds themselves. Therefore, consumers who had set their lifetime consumption and saving plans would simply reduce their private saving in an amount equal to the forced saving in the public pension. Personal saving would decrease by an amount equal to the increase in government saving, so that national saving would remain constant. There would be no effect on consumption or saving, or anything else, neither when the public plan is introduced nor at any time in the future.

A pay-as-you-go plan

The introduction of a pay-as-you-go system financed by a tax on wages is an entirely different matter, however. Assume for simplicity just two generations, elderly retirees and young workers. When the plan is introduced, the first generation, the retirees, receives a pure transfer, T per person, paid for by the second generation, the young workers. The retirees make no contribution to the plan.

The second generation of young workers also receives a transfer when they retire, paid for by the third generation of young workers, who were unborn at the time the plan was introduced. The amount of per capita transfer the second generation receives is $(1 + g)T$, where g is the rate of growth in the payroll tax revenues from one generation to the next. Assuming a constant payroll tax rate, g is the rate of growth in the tax base. The tax base is total wages, w.L. Therefore, the growth in the tax base from one generation to the next is (approximately) equal to the rate of growth in the wage, g_w, plus the rate of growth in the labor force, g_L. $g = g_w + g_L$. The rate of growth in the wage is equal to the rate of growth in labor productivity and the rate of growth in the labor force is assumed to equal the rate of population growth. For example, if labor productivity is growing at 1.5% per year and the population at 1% per year, then a tax on third-generation workers yields 2.5% more than it did on second-generation workers, because third-generation workers are more productive by 1.5% and are a larger cohort by 1%. Under a pay-as-you-go system, all payroll tax revenues are immediately paid to the current retired generation, so that the benefits (transfers) also rise by 2.5%. The pattern continues, with each generation receiving transfers in retirement that are $(1 + g)$ larger than the amount they paid as workers to support the preceding generation of retirees.

The redistribution across generations

It may appear that everyone gains from the pay-as-you-go pension, but this is not the case. The first generation of retirees each clearly gains an amount T when the pension is introduced, paid for by the second generation of young workers. True, the second generation of young workers receives an amount $(1 + g)T$ when they retire, an apparent gain. But had they been able to save the transfer T that was paid to the retirees, they could have earned the market rate of return, r, on T which, assuming no other taxes, is equal to the marginal product of capital. In the U.S. economy, the marginal product of capital r is larger than the growth in the payroll tax revenues, g. Therefore, the second-generation workers lose $(r - g)T$ on the forced saving T. The same is true of every subsequent generation. They earn a rate g on the payroll taxes paid to finance the pensions of the older generation but could have earned a rate r on these taxes had they been able to keep them. They, too, lose $(r - g)$ on their payroll tax contributions.

In essence, then, the introduction of a pay-as-you-go public pension constitutes an intergenerational redistribution in which the initial generation of retirees gains and all subsequent generations lose. It can be shown that the present value of the combined losses of generations two onward equals, in the limit, the transfer T given to the first generation in a world without taxes on income from capital.[3] When capital income is taxed, the combined present value of the losses of the subsequent generations is many times larger than the initial transfer T.

The increase in consumption/reduction in saving

In the baseline long-run OLG model of lifetime consumers, an intergenerational redistribution from younger to older generations reduces saving and increases consumption. This is most easily seen if we assume that there are no bequests, which is not a bad first-pass assumption since the vast majority of people leave little or no bequests.

The initial retirees who receive the transfer T have more lifetime resources, so they increase their consumption. If current and future consumption are both normal goods, then both will increase. That is, they may save some of the transfer for future consumption to smooth their consumption. The young workers (and all future generations) have fewer lifetime resources, so they reduce both their current and future consumption to smooth their consumption out of their reduced resources. But the older generation is nearer to the time of death, so they naturally have a higher marginal propensity to consume out of any change in lifetime resources than the younger generation, who have more years remaining to smooth their consumption. Therefore, the increase in consumption by the first generation of retirees exceeds the decrease in consumption by the second generation of young workers, and total consumption in the economy increases. Since the economy is at full employment on its production possibilities frontier, more consumption means less saving. Also, there is never a change in government saving because the total payroll tax revenues received are immediately paid out to the retirees. Therefore, total saving decreases (total consumption increases).

In the limit, the decreased consumption (increased saving) by all subsequent generations beyond the first generation of retirees would match the increased consumption by the initial retirees in present value terms. But since almost all the future generations are not yet alive, total consumption always remains higher and total saving lower following the introduction of a pay-as-you-go pension system.

An increase in consumption (decrease in saving) based on differences in marginal propensities to consume out of changes in lifetime resources may not seem like much to worry about, but it can have a huge negative effect on the economy in the very long run. The problem is that an increase in consumption (decrease in saving) implies a permanent decrease in investment in a full employment economy. A decrease in investment in turn leads to a smaller capital stock over time and a less productive economy, with lower output and wages. Alan Auerbach of Berkeley and Lawrence Kotlikoff of Boston University have constructed OLG baseline models to simulate the long-run effects of various government policies. In their baseline model without bequests, calibrated to the U.S. economy, they find that the introduction of a pay-as-you-go public pension that replaces 60% of average wages ultimately reduces the capital stock by 23% and wages before tax by 5.8%. The resulting loss in consumer welfare is equal to the loss consumers would suffer if their lifetime resources were reduced by 6.9% (Auerbach and Kotlikoff, 1987, p. 153). The macroeconomic consequences of a pay-as-you-go pension system through the induced reduction in saving are potentially very large indeed.

229

Other effects on saving

There are, however, both theoretical and practical reasons to believe that the effects of a pay-as-you-go pension on saving and the economy are likely to be much smaller in magnitude than the Auerbach/Kotlikoff simulations would suggest. On a theoretical level, Harvard's Robert Barro (1974) has noted that the addition of a bequest motive in the baseline model may lead to drastically different results. To see this, suppose that the elderly are altruistic toward their children and do not want them to be harmed by a government policy. They understand that a pay-as-you-go pension system represents a redistribution from their children to them. Therefore, they save the initial transfer so that they can return the transfer, with interest at rate r, to their children as a bequest. The children, knowing this, treat the payroll tax as a forced defined contribution plan, to which, as we have seen, they can fully adjust their own saving and consumption plans. As a result, there is no increase in consumption by the initial retirees, and since no subsequent generation suffers any loss in lifetime resources, there is no change in future consumption either. The intergenerational redistribution has no effect on the economy whatsoever.

Most economists believe that the no-bequest version of the baseline model is much closer to the truth than Barro's altruistic bequest version. Nonetheless, there are other practical reasons to question whether the macroeconomic effects of a pay-as-you-go system would be very large. One reason relates to the direct moral hazard cost of a public pension system, that it tends to lead to earlier retirements. The Social Security system almost certainly had this effect, because soon after the full retirement age was set at 65, the vast majority of workers began to retire at 65. Early retirement tends to increase saving for retirement simply because people expect to live more years as retirees. Also, by working fewer years, they have to save at a higher rate out of income in each working year to build up sufficient funds for retirement. Economists call this the *retirement effect on saving* of a public pension.

A second reason why consumption may not fall so much is that many consumers are credit constrained, especially those with low incomes. They cannot borrow and lend to smooth their consumption over their lifetimes. Instead, many are living from paycheck to paycheck and saving very little, if anything. For these consumers, the payroll taxes they pay may represent forced saving that they would not otherwise have undertaken. If so, then their consumption decreases by the full amount of the taxes; their marginal propensities to consume are one. This helps to offset the increase in consumption by the initial retirees.

A third reason for questioning the predictions of the baseline model is that the majority of people do not adequately prepare for their retirement even if they have sufficient lifetime resources to do so (see below for more discussion). They appear to place too much emphasis on the present and near future and too little on the distant future in planning their consumption over time. In any event, they behave far differently from the rational, life-cycle consumers in the baseline OLG model. Consequently, the implications of the baseline model may not be much of a baseline after all as a guide to policy reform.

In truth, empirical estimates of the crowding out effect of the Social Security system on private saving are all over the map. The best one can say is that the crowding out effect on personal saving would appear to be somewhere between 30 and 40 cents per dollar of payroll tax revenues (Gruber, 2005, p. 344). Add to this the high proportion of U.S. investment financed by foreign saving, such that a decline in a dollar of national saving leads to only a 40–60 cent decline in U.S. investment (Stiglitz, 2000, p. 370), and the macroeconomic effects of Social Security pensions may be far less than the Auerback/Kotlikof simulations suggest. And even if the effect on saving is large, the federal government can easily offset any decline in saving (increase in consumption) caused by the Social Security system by raising taxes to increase government saving. For instance, the two George W. Bush tax cuts in the early 2000s decreased government saving by more than any plausible estimate of the decrease in personal saving occasioned by pay-as-you-go Social Security pensions.

Social Security as a redistributional program

This is a good time to reflect for a moment on a point that is often overlooked in the public debate on reforming Social Security, that it is much more than a straight public pension plan. It is also by design meant to be a significant redistributional program, in two respects. The first is that it attempts to redistribute within generations by means of its PIA benefit formula, which replaces much more of low incomes in retirement than high incomes. The average replacement rate of the AIME for workers is approximately 40%, but as we have seen, it can be as high as 92% for low-income workers. The second is that the pay-as-you-go feature redistributes a substantial amount of lifetime resources across generations, as the baseline model indicates. The intergenerational redistribution is especially large in the United States because, from 1937 to 1983, the payroll tax rate was increased in a series of steps from its original value of 2% to the current 10.6%, and there was also a huge expansion in the number of workers covered. Since the resulting increases in payroll tax revenues were paid out immediately to the current retirees as increased benefits, all cohorts who retired before the 1983 reforms received positive returns from the system, meaning that the returns from their tax payments exceeded the marginal product of capital. It was not just the initial retirees in and around 1935 who gained, as in the simple baseline model. The losses began with the cohorts retiring after the 1983 reforms; except for the low-income workers, they have earned less on their tax payments than the marginal product of capital, and the losses to future retiring cohorts are projected to continue indefinitely.

Peter Diamond and Peter Orzag (2005, p. 16), who have been among the main contributors to the debate on Social Security reform, describe the transfers to the pre-1983 retirees as amounting to a legacy debt for the Social Security Trust Fund, in the sense that the tax collections to pay for the transfers were never made available as assets to the Trust Fund that could accumulate with interest. By 2005, the size of the missing assets, with interest, that future generations have to cover was $11.6 trillion, if Social Security is to be converted to a fully funded pension plan.[4]

Such large redistributions across generations may have some equity appeal if a nation values equality in line with the social welfare analysis of Chapter 5. Younger generations benefit from ongoing increases in productivity that make them richer on average than older generations, so that the Social Security transfers are intergenerationally equalizing. Even so, the potential reductions in saving, investment, productivity, and output from the transfers may be too large in some people's minds to justify the equalizing effect of the redistributions.

SOCIAL SECURITY AS SOCIAL INSURANCE

The macroeconomic effects of Social Security pensions are extremely important to one's view of the program, but they are not the only issues. The benefits and costs of social insurance described in the first section of the chapter come into play as well, along with some related issues that are often associated with social insurance programs. It is this set of issues that get to the heart of the question: Why have a public pension program?

Adverse selection

There are two fundamental uncertainties associated with planning for retirement. The first is the date of retirement. Workers can never know for sure when they will retire. Ill health, dislike of one's job, or loss of one's job late in life may precipitate a decision to retire, and these events are often difficult to foresee very far in advance of when they occur. The second uncertainty is the length of one's retirement, which depends on life expectancy. People cannot know how long they will live, and are unlikely to be able to predict their life expectancy with much accuracy until they are older and either near or in retirement. We saw earlier in the chapter that when people have private information about uncertain events, private insurance markets are subject to the problem of adverse selection. Adverse selection is at best a source of inefficiency in private insurance markets; at worst, it can cause the markets to fail altogether. It is the uncertainty associated with life expectancy that leads to adverse selection in private pensions, and it is centered on the market for annuities. The fact that social security benefits are in the form of annuities is not an accident.

The advantages of annuities

Private insurers do offer annuities to individuals for their retirement years and annuities are a sensible way to finance consumption during retirement. Suppose a person wants a smooth pattern of consumption during his retirement years at as high a level as possible, and does not want to leave a bequest. He has a choice between two types of assets. He can: (a) purchase an annuity from an insurance company that gives him a monthly stream of income until he dies; or (b) purchase a portfolio of safe nonannuitized assets such as government bonds and live off the interest on the bonds and the principal as the bonds mature. The insurance company can offer a higher stream of monthly income in an annuity for any given initial purchase price precisely because there is a possibility that the person will die each year in the future, after which the annuity payments stop. In contrast, the returns on nonannuitized assets continue even if the person dies. The higher income and consumption stream per dollar of investment offered by annuities is the essence of their attraction as a retirement asset.

Suppose, instead, the person wants to leave a bequest. The annuity still has the advantage that it is the cheapest way to finance the person's own consumption until death, which leaves more money for his heirs. It also ensures that the amount left to the heirs does not depend on how long he lives, and this should also be desirable to anyone with a bequest motive.

Adverse selection in annuity markets

Despite their attractiveness as a retirement asset, annuities are vastly underutilized in the United States, to the point that annuity markets are very thin and the annuities that do exist are expensive, with high administrative costs. Part of the thinness and expense is due to the problem of adverse selection. Insurers would like to be able to distinguish between people who have low and long life expectancies in offering annuities. From the point of view of the insurers, the low-risk people are those with low life expectancies and the high-risk people are those with long life expectancies. If they could distinguish between the two, they would offer annuities at a low price to individuals with low life expectancies and at a high price to individuals with long life expectancies. But life expectancies are far better known to individuals than to insurance companies, so they are forced to offer annuities at a single price. The single price is too high for the people with low life expectancies and they drop out of the market, leaving insurance companies with a more adverse pool of long life expectancy applicants, which in turn requires them to set higher prices for the annuities. The result is a very thin market in which only people with long life expectancies who are able to pay high prices for the annuities purchase the private annuities. The people with lower life expectancies would like to buy annuities but are shut out. The only recourse is a public pension program like Social Security, which offers annuities to everyone at a given age that are independent of their life expectancies.

One immediate problem with public annuities is that they necessarily redistribute purchasing power from the people with low life expectancies (low risk), who are paying too much, to those with long life expectancies (high risk), who are paying too little. Under Social Security, there are two main channels of redistribution through this route: (1) from men to women; and (2) from low-income retirees to high-income retirees, because people with high incomes tend to live longer. The redistribution from men to women supports the redistribution built into the PIA formula, since women tend to have lower AIMEs than men. The redistribution from low-income to high-income individuals directly offsets to some extent the intended redistribution in the PIA formula. The high-income offset happens to be doubly strong, because high-income individuals are more likely to marry, and the 50% benefit available to spouses redistributes in favor of married couples.

Other problems with private annuities

The redistributions notwithstanding, there are a number of reasons besides adverse selection to favor public over private annuities.

Paternalism: poor retirement planning

Peter Diamond (2004) argues that private annuity markets are so thin in the United States that there has to be more to the story than adverse selection. He believes that people just do not understand the advantages of annuities. Those who use them often make poor choices. One example is that people often purchase annuities with a 20-year guarantee option under which, if the beneficiary dies before 20 years, the annuity payments continue to the heirs for the remainder of the 20 years. This turns out to remove much of the cost advantages of a standard annuity; it is an expensive way to bequeath income to heirs. Most people do not purchase annuities at all, however, which Diamond believes is the primary explanation for the thinness of the annuity market. Suppliers are simply responding to a relative lack of demand.

The inability to understand the value of annuities is symptomatic of the more general problems that people face in planning for their retirement. Retirement planning is a complex process. People have to adopt an appropriate saving plan early on in their working years, they have to choose a portfolio of assets to purchase with their savings, and then, as they retire, they have to adjust their portfolios to provide for their own consumption during retirement and a bequest to their heirs should they choose to leave one. These are all difficult decisions, and the truth is that the majority of people are woefully unprepared for retirement. Only about half the people in the United States have private pensions, and the majority of the private plans are now 401K defined contribution plans that require employees to make choices about what assets to hold in their retirement accounts. Too many people carry portfolios that are not sufficiently diversified to protect them from risk, and too often they fail to make the maximum contributions available to them to ensure that they have sufficient savings for retirement. A recent study showed that the median value of financial assets in the United States held by people near retirement (55–64 years of age) in 2004 was less than $30,000 (Munnell and Sunden, 2006, Table 1, p. 2). A related problem is that by saving too little for retirement, people leave their spouses extremely vulnerable to poverty. Elderly widows have three times the poverty rate as the elderly generally.

One of the primary motivations for Social Security pensions in 1935 was simply paternalistic, that without a public pension too many people would not save enough for their retirement. The idea behind the pensions was to provide a foundation for people's retirement that would prevent them from becoming impoverished; it was not meant to supply all workers' retirement incomes. Diamond and others believe that the paternalistic argument is valid today for keeping Social Security intact. It protects people from the poor choices they make in planning their retirement, principally that they save too little and make too little use of private annuities. As such, it helps them smooth their lifetime consumption more in line with what a rational, life-cycle consumer would do. The argument has merit. In 2005, one-third of the elderly in the United States received 90% or more of their retirement income from Social Security, and two-thirds of the elderly received 50% or more (Diamond, 2004, Table 1, p. 2).

Paternalistic arguments of this kind are commonly used in support of social insurance programs. Economists generally avoid such arguments in most contexts in favor of the view that people are best able to make their own decisions and should be given the freedom to do so. But sometimes the evidence is quite strong that people are irrational, meaning that they do not act in their own best interests. Planning for retirement would appear to be one such instance, at least for large numbers of people.

Inflation risk

Another disadvantage with private annuities is that they usually offer no protection for inflation. The few that are indexed for inflation do so only up to low limits, such as 3% per year. Insurance companies cannot easily protect against inflation because it is a so-called aggregate risk that affects everyone. Insurers can profitably offer policies only against individual risks that are uncorrelated with one another. When risks are individual and uncorrelated, such as having an accident, insuring a large pool of people reduces the total risk experienced by the insurer. This is the risk-spreading effect of insuring a large number of people, and the source of the advantage of using insurance as protection against misfortunes. But since an aggregate risk such as inflation affects everyone in the pool the same way at the same time, the risk is the same to the insurance company as it is to any one individual in the pool. There is no possibility of spreading the risk. Indexing the Social Security pensions to the CPI without limit is something only the government can do.

Protection against market risk

Yet another argument in favor of defined benefit Social Security annuities is that they help people spread the market risk of their retirement portfolios. This is especially true now that the majority of private pensions are defined contribution plans. The one counter to this is that Social Security annuities are always subject to the political risk that the federal government may some day choose not to honor its obligations to future retirees, or at least cut benefits. But the political tea leaves of 2005 suggest that any reforms to pensions will at least have to leave the benefits untouched for anyone 55 or older.

Administrative costs

A final argument in favor of social insurance is that public insurance programs are typically much cheaper to administer than private insurance, and pensions are no exception. There

235

are enormous economies of scale in providing pensions and only public programs can take full advantage of them. Public insurance also avoids the marketing costs of the private insurers. The cost savings from these two factors are very large. The administrative costs of private annuities are on the order of 10% of the annuity, and the administrative costs of private pensions generally average about 6%. In contrast, the administrative costs of Social Security pensions are around .6% of the annual benefits (Stiglitz, 2000, p. 359).[5]

Moral hazard

We saw in the first section of the chapter that there are both direct and indirect moral hazard costs of social insurance. The direct cost is the ability of individuals to use their private information to game the system and increase the probability of using the insurance. The principal indirect costs are the inefficiencies associated with the taxes used to pay for the insurance programs.

The direct moral hazard cost of Social Security pensions is the incentive to retire early. Do people retire at 65 or 62 because of ill health or simply because they choose to collect a Social Security pension rather than work? The government is unlikely to be able to distinguish between the two motivations. As noted above, there did appear to be an early retirement effect associated with setting the full retirement age at 65. Beyond this, however, most economists believe that the option to retire between the ages of 62 and the full retirement age is sufficiently small so as not to be a major problem. This is so because of the actuarial reduction in benefits for those who retire below the full retirement age and also because of the 50% benefit reduction rate for earnings above a minimal amount.

The size of the efficiency costs of the payroll tax is controversial among economists. A key issue here is whether people see a direct link between the taxes they pay and the benefits they will receive when they retire. Taxes that are raised on the benefits-received principle are not viewed by economists as having a deadweight loss. They are similar to prices paid for private goods. Only taxes for which there is no direct benefit can lead to a deadweight efficiency loss.

Taken literally, only taxes paid on incomes earned in the highest 35 years of earnings have a direct link to the eventual pension benefits because only incomes in those years are included in the AIME calculations that form the basis of the PIA benefits. By that accounting, taxes paid by many young workers and older workers are likely to be on incomes outside the best 35 years of earnings, and therefore lead to no corresponding increase in benefits. As such, they could be a source of deadweight loss. Similarly, taxes paid by married men or women with low-paying jobs may never yield a return, if they end up taking a benefit equal to 50% of their higher earning spouse's benefit. The lower earning spouse may also lose benefits if the two PIAs exceed the family limit. Deadweight efficiency loss from the payroll tax is possible whenever the taxes paid on additional income earned are more than the resulting increase in benefits. For all these people, then, the payroll taxes could lead to a substantial amount of deadweight loss.

A less literal interpretation would say that people do see a connection between their payroll taxes and their eventual pension benefits, but only vaguely so. Many people, for example, probably do not know that only the highest 35 years of earnings count in computing their pension benefits. In any event, so long as people generally view the payroll tax as a benefits-received tax, the issue of deadweight loss is of less consequence.

Harvard's Martin Feldstein, who is a strong proponent of privatizing part of the Social Security pensions, believes that the deadweight losses from payroll taxes are very high. He estimates that each additional dollar of taxes that would have to be raised to maintain the current pension program on a sustainable basis costs $1.50 because of the deadweight losses associated with the higher tax rates (Feldstein, 2005, p. 9). This is on the high end of estimates of the deadweight losses of the payroll tax.

One other source of inefficiency loss is associated with the people for whom the payroll tax is a forced saving, in the sense that they would have consumed the tax revenues rather than saved them if they did not have to pay the tax. Forcing people to consume and save other than what they would have chosen to do clearly lowers their utility and represents an efficiency loss. Presumably the forced saving losses are experienced primarily by low-income earners. We are not aware of estimates of the efficiency losses from forced saving.

SOCIAL SECURITY REFORM

There have been a large number of proposals to reform Social Security pensions, ranging from maintaining the current system and adjusting the tax and benefit schedules, to privatizing some or all of the system by establishing individual accounts within the system that are in the nature of a defined contribution plan. Since none of the proposals have been adopted as of this writing, we conclude this chapter with some general observations that apply to any reform proposal.

Rate of return concerns

Social Security pensions caught the public's attention for two main reasons, the impending retirement of the baby boom generation and a sense that current workers could earn a much higher return on their savings than they will ever receive from their payroll taxes if they had the tax revenues back to invest for themselves. The impact of the former is commonly represented in the media by the projected decline in the ratio of workers to retirees and it is indeed dramatic. The ratio stood at 16/1 in 1950, fell sharply to 3/1 by 2000, and is projected to be only 2/1 by 2040 (Stiglitz, 2000, p. 365). Regarding the rate of return issue, the average rate of return on stocks in the second half of the 20th century was 5.5%. In contrast, the return to retirees from their payroll taxes averaged only 1.9% from 1973 to 2003 (Gruber, 2005, p. 341).

These numbers are dramatic, and there are a few points to keep in mind when thinking about their impact. The first is that the two issues are related. Recall that the rate of return available on a pay-as-you-go pension plan is equal to the rate of growth in the payroll tax base for a constant tax rate, which is the sum of the rate of growth in population and the rate of growth in labor productivity. Both fell sharply in the last 25 years of the 20th century, the former because of the unprecedented baby boom from 1947 to 1964 followed by the equally unprecedented baby bust for the next 10 years, and the latter because of a dramatic decline in productivity growth from 1973 to 1996 to about .9% per year on average. The population growth is expected to remain constant at about 1% per year. Productivity growth has increased to about 1.5% per year on average since 1996. If that trend continues, young people entering the labor force today can expect a return on their payroll taxes of 2.5% per year, assuming no further changes in the tax and benefit schedules.

However, 2.5% is still 3% below the average equity return of 5.5%, but the two numbers are not directly comparable because the 5.5% return on equity has a risk premium built into it. Investing in stocks is risky, so that investors require a higher return on stocks to compensate for the market risk. High-income people with high savings and diversified portfolios that include some risk-free U.S. Treasury securities are indifferent on the margin between risky and riskless assets. Therefore, the best estimate of the risk premium for them is the difference between the 5.5% average return on stocks and the average return on the ultra-safe U.S. Treasury securities, which has been about 3%. The risk premium would be less for small savers with nondiversified portfolios and nonsavers. In any event, the advantage to young workers today to be able to manage their own diversified investments rather than pay the payroll tax may well be closer to .5% than 3%, assuming that the government will meet its future Social Security benefit obligations.

Increased life expectancy and wage inequality

A second point is that the baby boom/baby bust phenomenon in the last half of the 20th century is a temporary phenomenon, although "temporary" in terms of Social Security planning horizons can last for 75 years. More lasting problems for the Social Security Trust Fund are the increase in life expectancy and the increasing inequality in wages and salaries. Life expectancy has increased by five years for women and four years for men since 1940 (Diamond and Orszag, 2005, p. 14), and the percentage of incomes above the limit under the payroll tax rose from 10% to 15% from 1985 to 2005 (Diamond and Orszag, 2005, p. 15). Both trends contribute to the projected long-run annual pay-as-you-go deficit in the Social Security Trust Fund. Revenues from payroll tax are projected to be insufficient to cover current benefits to retirees for the indefinite future after the baby boomers die under the current tax and benefit schedules. In conclusion, the Social Security pension system is troubling to people for a number of reasons and in need of reform.

The huge legacy debt

One big problem that all reform proposals must confront is that once a pay-as-you-go pension system is established, it is costly to reform. This is most easily seen by returning to the simple baseline OLG model above in which we introduced a pay-as-you-go pension system. The first generation of retirees gained at the expense of all subsequent generations. Suppose that the government subsequently decides to end the system. The last generation of retirees at the time the system ended would be big losers. They paid taxes into the system while they were working and now receive nothing from the taxes.

Less dramatically, we noted that the 1983 reforms to be able to support the baby boomers in their retirement abruptly changed the returns to social security from being greater than market returns for all retirees prior to 1983 to being less than the market returns for retirees thereafter. The point is that any reform that attempts to rescue the Trust Fund from its projected indefinite deficits after the fund is exhausted will place large costs on current and some future generations beyond the burdens they are already bearing to support the legacy debt of the pre-1983 retirees.

The $11.6 trillion legacy debt is so large that most reform proposals are not aiming to convert the Trust Fund to a fully funded basis. Instead, the goal is for sustainable solvency of the fund at the end of the post-reform 75-year planning horizon, meaning that the ratio of the surplus in the fund to annual expenditures is either constant or growing indefinitely. Placing the fund on only a partially funded basis has the advantage of spreading the legacy debt over all future generations rather than asking the next few generations to bear all the burden. For proposals that want to retain the Social Security system, this will require tax increases and benefit reductions in some combination. For those who favor allocating a portion of payroll tax revenues to private defined contribution accounts, people would have to be willing to increase their rate of saving to add to the fund. Otherwise the fund would be exhausted even more quickly. In either scenario, the rate of saving in the economy has to increase. Under the first scenario, it is government saving that increases and in the second scenario, it is personal saving. Either way, current and future generations have to save more and consume less for the Trust Fund to achieve sustainable solvency.

Maintain or replace the Social Security pensions?

As a general rule, those who favor maintaining the system as is with tax and benefit adjustments tend to:

- adopt the paternalistic view of the system that it protects large numbers of people from making poor retirement plans through the annuity feature of the benefits and the extra protection of spouses
- like the redistributions that occur both across generations and within generations
- believe that the moral hazard costs of the system are low, especially the deadweight efficiency losses associated with the payroll tax
- not be too concerned about the political risks to pensions.

On the other side, those who favor privatizing some or all of the system tend to:

- reject the paternalistic view in favor of the view that people are generally rational and should be given the freedom to make their own retirement decisions
- stress the higher returns that private savings can earn without being too concerned about the additional market risks of this strategy
- believe that a public pension should not intentionally redistribute beyond providing protection from poverty
- believe that the payroll tax entails substantial deadweight efficiency losses.

The good news is that the projected deficit problem is quite manageable, whichever strategy is chosen. The required increase in saving for sustainable solvency would be about 2.6% of GDP, which is approximately the amount that education expenditures increased when the baby boomers were children and, more recently, is about equal to the extent of the buildup in defense spending during the 1990s (Diamond, 2004, p. 1, fn 2). All economists agree that the sooner the Trust Fund deficit is addressed the better, because delaying simply increases the required burden on the post-reform generations to reach sustainable solvency of the Trust Fund.

Tax Theory and Policy

Tax Theory and Policy

CHAPTER 13

The Pursuit of Equity in Taxation

Part III of the text turns from public expenditure theory to tax theory. Chapter 13 begins with an overview of tax theory and policy and then considers the problem of achieving equity in taxation.

THE MAIN ISSUES OF TAX THEORY

There are two main issues in the mainstream theory of taxation, one normative and one positive. The normative issue is how to design taxes to promote social welfare, more narrowly defined as the public interest in efficiency and equity. The positive issue is the economic effects of the various taxes that governments use. The two most important positive questions are: What effect do taxes have on people's desires to consume, save, and supply their labor, or on firms' desires to invest? Who bears the burden of the various taxes? Public officials need answers to these questions in order to design taxes that promote social welfare.

Public choice economists have added a third issue to the tax literature. Recall that they believe people enter government service to promote their own self-interests, not the public interest in efficiency and equity. One form this self-interest takes relates to the behavior of the officials who manage the public agencies. They are self-aggrandizers, according to the public choice perspective; their primary goal is to try to make their agencies as large as possible. This leads them to pressure legislatures for ever more tax increases, and legislators may not offer much resistance. They, too, have an incentive to spend more on behalf of their constituents to increase their chances of reelection. Therefore, a major issue in tax theory for public choice economists is to design ways to limit a legislature's power to tax, such as by constitutional amendment, and thereby limit public spending. As always, our focus in part III will be on the two mainstream issues of tax theory.

THE SIX MAIN TAXES

Mainstream economists have naturally focused the majority of their attention on the six taxes that governments in the developed market economists have chosen to raise the majority of their tax revenues: personal income taxes; payroll taxes; corporation income taxes; excise and general sales taxes; property taxes; and value-added taxes (VAT):

- A *personal income tax* is a tax on the income received by individuals. It is levied on individuals, but typically collected from firms who withhold the taxes owed from their employees' paychecks. Individuals then file a tax return once a year to determine their annual tax liability, and they either receive a refund from the government if too much has been withheld from their paychecks or send a check to the government if too little has been withheld.

- A *payroll tax* is a tax levied on the wage and salary component of income. In the United States, revenues from the federal payroll tax are earmarked for the Social Security System to pay for retirement pensions, disability payments, and medical care for the elderly. Half the tax is levied on the employers and half on the employees but, as with personal income tax, the employees' portion of the tax is deducted from their paychecks and sent by their employers to the government. Many other countries use the payroll tax to fund social insurance expenditures.

- A *corporation income tax* is a tax levied on the accounting profits of corporations. In the United States, the accounting profits of partnerships and proprietorships are allocated as income to the various partners and owners and taxed under the personal income tax.

- An *excise tax* is a tax on the sale of a single product, levied on the firms that sell the product. The tax on gasoline is an example. *General sales tax* is a tax levied on the sale of a broad range of goods and services, usually with a single rate applied to all the taxed products. It is also levied on the firms.

- A *property tax* is a tax on the value of items of wealth, most commonly residential, commercial, and industrial properties. It is levied on the owner of the property. The value of the taxed property is determined by an assessment undertaken periodically by the tax authorities, and the assessed value may or may not be related to the market value of the asset. A common variation of property tax is the *estate* or *inheritance tax* levied on the value of the assets that pass from the deceased to his or her heirs. The tax due is levied on the assets of the deceased under an estate tax and on the heirs under an inheritance tax.

- A *value-added tax* is a tax on the value added of firms, the difference between their sales revenues and their purchases of intermediate products (material inputs). It is levied on the firms. There is an income and a consumption version of the tax. The income version is as defined above, so-called because the value added of a firm is its payments to the primary factors of production, labor, capital, and land, and therefore its value added to the national income. The consumption version allows firms to deduct investment from their value added in computing their taxable value added.

Since the only two kinds of final goods that can be purchased with the national income are consumption goods and investment goods, deducting investment from value added is equivalent to taxing consumption.

With the exception of excise taxes, these taxes are referred to as *broad-based taxes* because they tax either a broad range of products (general sales tax) or large numbers of individuals and firms (the other taxes). Governments in the United States make use of the first five taxes. Table 13.1 records the main sources of revenues for the federal (FY 2006), state (FY 2004), and local (FY 2004) governments.

TABLE 13.1 Revenue sources of federal, state, and local governments

A. Federal government (fiscal year, 2006)

	$ (billions)	Percent of total receipts	$ (billions)	Percent of total expenditures
Total Receipts: Tax Revenues and Charges			$2,407	(91%)
Personal income tax	1,044	(43)		
Contributions for social insurance	838	(35)		
Corporation income tax	354	(15)		
Other taxes and charges	171	(7)		
Surplus			(–)248	(9)
Total Expenditures			2,655	(100)

B. State governments (fiscal year, 2004)[1]

	$ (billions)	Percent of total taxes	$ (billions)	Percent of general revenue
Federal Grants-in-aid			$395	(33)
Total Taxes			590	(49)
General sales and excise taxes	293	(50)		
Personal income tax	196	(33)		
All other taxes	101	(17)		
Direct User Charges and Miscellaneous Revenues			209	(18)
Total General Revenue			1,194	(100)

245

C. Local governments (fiscal year, 2004)[1]

	$ (billions)	Percent of general revenue
Grants-in-aid	430	(40)

	$ (billions)	Percent of total grants
From federal government	51	(11)
From state governments	379	(89)

	$ (billions)	Percent of general revenue
Total Taxes	420	(38)

	$ (billions)	Percent of total taxes
Property tax	308	(73)
Other taxes	112	(27)

	$ (billions)	Percent of general revenue
Direct User Charges and Miscellaneous Revenues	244	(22)
Total General Revenue	1,094	(100)

NOTE:

1. Data for state and local governments were available only through fiscal year 2004.

SOURCES: *Budget of the United States Government, Fiscal Year 2008* (Washington, D.C.: U.S. Government Printing Office, 2007), Part Five: Historical Tables, Tables 1.1 and 2.1. U.S. Census Bureau, *State and Local Government Finances by Level of Government, 2003–04, U.S. Summary*, available on the Census Bureau's website.

Table 13.1 indicates that the federal government relies on the personal income tax, the payroll tax to finance the Social Security system, and the corporation income tax. The personal income tax is the largest tax in the United States, but over 75% of U.S. taxpayers pay more in payroll taxes than in personal income taxes. The state governments rely on the personal income tax (43 states) and the general sales tax (45 states) (some states have only a property tax). The property tax on residential and business property is overwhelmingly the most important tax for the local governments. Table 13.1 also shows that the state and local governments rely heavily on fees for specific services and grants-in-aid from other governments as sources of revenues.

Governments in Europe also make use of personal and corporate income taxes, payroll taxes to support their social security payments, and property taxes. But they differ from the United States in one respect. They have chosen to levy a value-added tax (VAT) on businesses rather than a general sales tax. In 2005, VAT accounted for 31% of all tax receipts in the EU (OECD, 2005, Supplement 1, p. 38).

A final broad-based tax that economists have given much attention to is the *personal consumption tax* (also referred to as a *personal expenditures tax*). A personal consumption tax, like a personal income tax, is levied on individuals. The difference between the two is that under the personal consumption tax, individuals can deduct their saving each year from income in calculating their taxable income. Since income can only be consumed or saved, income less saving is consumption. Unlike the other six taxes, the personal consumption tax is not commonly used. Nonetheless, it is featured in the tax literature because many mainstream economists favor replacing the personal income tax with the personal consumption tax. They think it is the better tax on both equity and efficiency grounds.

THE FIVE GOALS OF TAX POLICY

Economists have identified five properties that any broad-based tax should ideally possess: (1) ease of collection; (2) ease of compliance; (3) flexibility; (4) promotion of economic efficiency; and (5) promotion of end-results equity.

EASE OF COLLECTION AND COMPLIANCE

The first two properties, ease of collection and compliance, are essentially administrative requirements, the former from the point of view of Departments of Revenue (DOR) and the latter from the point of view of the taxpayers. Ease of collection means that the DOR can collect large amounts of revenue with the tax with relatively little expense and effort. All the major taxes used by governments meet this requirement; they have to or they would not be used. For example, the U.S. IRS collected $2.0 trillion of personal, payroll and corporate income tax revenues in FY 2005 with an operating budget of $10.2 billion, only 0.5% of the tax revenues collected (U.S. Government Accountability Office, 2005, p. 1; U.S. Government Printing Office, 2007, Table 1).

Ease of compliance means that taxpayers can compute their tax liabilities (comply with the tax laws) with reasonable amounts of time, expense, and record keeping. The compliance requirement explains why developing countries rely more on business taxes than on personal taxes. These countries have relatively low literacy rates, which means that a large percentage of the population is simply unable to collect and process the records and other information that would be required of them under a tax such as personal income tax. Nor could they fill out the tax forms.

The compliance property also has a behavioral component. People (and businesses) not only have to be able to keep the records required to levy taxes on them, but they also have to be willing to make those records known to the DOR. People often have private information about the things that are typically taxed, such as some sources of income or various items of consumption. If they can easily hide this information from the DOR, then taxes on these items are unlikely to be very effective at raising revenue. For example, it is said that Europeans are less willing to pay taxes than Americans are, which may explain why European countries rely much more on value-added taxes on business (VAT) and much less on personal income taxes than do the U.S. federal and state governments. In any event, the collection and compliance requirements are closely linked. If taxpayers are either unable or unwilling to comply with a particular tax, then the tax would be extremely difficult for a DOR to collect.

FLEXIBILITY

Flexibility is a macroeconomic property. Tax policy is the primary tool of fiscal policy used as a stabilization device to smooth the business cycle. Tax cuts are used to promote aggregate demand and pull the economy out of a recession, tax increases to slow down an overheating economy and prevent inflation from taking hold. Changes in government spending on goods and services (G) are typically too difficult to change in a timely fashion to be used for stabilization purposes, and individual transfer programs may affect only a relatively small portion of the population.

To satisfy the flexibility property, a broad-based tax must have two characteristics: the tax authorities can change the tax liabilities easily and quickly; and the changes in the tax liabilities quickly affect one or more of the components of aggregate demand. The U.S. federal personal income tax does fairly well by these requirements. The majority of adults pay the tax, most of the tax liabilities are withheld by businesses from people's paychecks, so that a change in the tax laws can take effect within a month or two of enactment, and changes in personal tax liabilities have a direct effect on people's consumption and saving decisions through their marginal propensities to consume and save (MPC and MPS). The only caveat is that the MPC of a tax increase or decrease is much lower if people perceive the tax change to be temporary rather than permanent, but the MPC out of temporary changes in disposable income is still large enough to have a significant impact on aggregate demand within a quarter or two of a change in the tax law.

ECONOMIC EFFICIENCY

The promotion of economic efficiency has a negative slant for most taxes. We saw in Chapter 3 that all economic agents must face the same prices for an economy to achieve a Pareto-optimal allocation of resources and be on its utility possibilities frontier. The problem with broad-based taxes is that they are distorting. They introduce inefficiencies into the economy by driving a wedge between the relevant prices faced by buyers and sellers. For example, under a sales tax, consumers base their consumption decisions on the prices of the goods and services that include the tax. Producers, in contrast, base their supply decisions on the prices net of the tax, because they must send the tax portion of the price to the DOR. Only the prices net of the sales tax are available as revenue to pay their factors of production and earn a profit. Similarly, under an income tax, the producers' demand for labor is based on the wages and salaries inclusive of the income tax, whereas individuals base their labor supply decisions on their take-home pay, their wages and salaries net of the tax. With buyers and sellers basing their decisions on different prices, the Pareto-optimal condition that MRS = MRT for all goods and services (and factors of production) cannot hold, and the economy moves below its utility possibilities frontier. The tax is said to generate a deadweight loss that no one can regain. The efficiency property applied to tax policy is therefore expressed negatively, to avoid inefficiency. The goal is to design a tax, or set of taxes, that raises a given amount of tax revenue with the minimum amount of inefficiency or deadweight loss.

END-RESULTS EQUITY

Finally, the design of tax policy to promote the goal of end-results equity goes hand in hand with a nation's transfer policies, simply because governments pursue end-results equity by taxing some people – the haves – and transferring to other people – the have-nots. Careful thought has to be given to both parts of the redistribution. Regarding the tax side, societies struggle with the question of what is the fairest way to collect taxes from the haves. Should they pay taxes in proportion to their incomes (or consumption, or wealth) or should those in the upper income classes be asked to pay a higher percentage of their incomes than those in the middle and lower income classes? Should people in the lower income classes pay any taxes at all? As with all matters of equity, these questions are fiercely debated in country after country, typically without any clear-cut resolution emerging.

TAX AND PUBLIC EXPENDITURE THEORY

Having discussed mainstream public expenditure theory in Part II, it turns out that we have already said quite a bit about mainstream tax theory. The truth is that much of the normative issue of how to design taxes is subsumed within public expenditure theory. Consider the taxes we have already discussed:

- the lump-sum taxes (and transfers) required to satisfy the interpersonal equity condition of equalizing the social marginal utilities of income (Chapter 4)
- Pigovian taxes (subsidies) to correct for externalities (Chapters 6 and 7)
- marginal cost pricing of decreasing cost services. These decreasing cost prices are called many different things – rates, fares, tolls, fees, and so forth – but they can be thought of as taxes since they are set by the public sector (Chapter 9)
- Lindahl prices (taxes) for nonexclusive public goods (Chapter 8).

Two points should be noted about these taxes. First, people tend to think of taxes as a necessary evil. But in those instances when public expenditure theory dictates the design of taxes, the taxes can only be a good, not an evil. They help society in its quest to maximize social welfare, to pursue the public interest in efficiency and equity. The last three taxes in the list promote economic efficiency. They help restore Pareto optimality in the face of market failures and bring the economy back to its utility possibilities frontier. The pattern of lump-sum taxes (and transfers) that satisfy the interpersonal equity condition for a social welfare maximum directly promote end-results equity. They bring society to Bator's bliss point on the utility possibilities frontier, the distributionally best point among all the possible Pareto-optimal allocations on the frontier.

The second point is a rather remarkable implication of the mainstream theory of public expenditure and taxation. Suppose the government *were* able to tax and transfer lump sum to satisfy the interpersonal equity condition. Then the mainstream theory of taxation would be *completely* subsumed within public expenditure theory. There would be no tax theory independent of public expenditure theory. The reason is as follows. Either public expenditure theory describes how to design a tax in a particular context, for example the three efficiency taxes above, or it does not, for example how to cover the subsidies of a decreasing cost service when price is set equal to marginal cost, or how to pay for a non-exclusive public good since Lindahl prices are impractical. If it does not, then we saw in Chapters 8 and 9 that the taxes needed to cover these expenditures simply become part of the lump-sum taxes and transfers needed to satisfy the interpersonal equity condition. The taxes have to be lump sum to keep the economy on its utility possibility frontier. Therefore, the only modification in the pattern of taxes and transfers for satisfying the interpersonal equity condition is that the taxes collected from people lump sum have to be sufficient to pay for the necessary lump-sum transfers to people to equalize the social marginal utilities of income plus cover these other public expenditures. There is nothing left for taxes to finance. Hence mainstream tax theory takes on a life of its own only because the broad-based taxes that governments are actually able to use are not lump sum, but distorting. They cannot keep the economy on its utility possibility frontier.

EQUITY AND THE MAINSTREAM THEORY

We begin our discussion of tax theory with the pursuit of equity in taxation because it is most closely related to the material of the previous chapters. We did not consider the possibility that taxes might be distorting in our discussion of public expenditure theory.

Our previous discussion of society's attempt to achieve end-results equity or distributive justice did not reach a satisfying conclusion. Recall that there was both good news and bad news. The good news is that the interpersonal equity condition for a social welfare maximum offers a simple and complete description of both the optimal distribution of income and the optimal redistribution of income through taxes and transfers if the original distribution is not optimal. The bad news is that it does not provide much practical guidance for tax or transfer policy. Chapters 4 and 5 described three serious difficulties in applying the theory. First, redistributing to reach the bliss point on the utility possibility frontier requires lump-sum taxes and transfers and, as just noted, no realistic broad-based tax is lump sum. Second, society has to agree on a set of ethical rankings of individuals that can be summarized by a social welfare function, but that agreement is unlikely to be reached, for three reasons. It is difficult for policy makers to know what the appropriate social welfare function is at any point in time, no one has made a convincing argument as to what the social welfare function should be within the much too broad limits of Rawlsian egalitarianism and utilitarian indifference to the distribution of income, and it is not at all clear that a social welfare function can evolve in a democracy (Arrow's General

Impossibility Theorem). Finally, economists have attempted to make the social welfare function operational by adopting Atkinson's three assumptions – equal marginal social welfare weights for people with the same incomes, everyone has the same tastes or preferences, and people have diminishing private marginal utility of income. But these assumptions lead to the conclusion that everyone should end up at the mean level of income, a conclusion that almost no one accepts.

The way out of this bind is symbolized by Okun's leaky bucket, the recognition that both taxes and transfers are costly. They are distorting rather than lump sum so they give rise to inefficiencies in the form of deadweight losses. They also entail administrative collection and compliance costs. Thus, as a practical matter, the optimal redistribution involves striking a balance between the gains from making the distribution of income more equal, as given by the operative social welfare function, and the costs of taxes and transferring, as suggested by Okun's leaky bucket. Incomes will remain unequal at the optimum because of the costs of redistributing. According to the mainstream theory, therefore, thinking about the pursuit of end-results equity in and of itself is not a sensible way to proceed. The distortions and other costs of taxing and transferring must also be taken into consideration.

The only other principle of equity in taxation that we met in the earlier chapters was taxing according to the benefits people receive from the various public services. The benefits-received principle is undoubtedly viewed as a fair way to levy taxes among the general public, but it has no standing as an equity principle in mainstream public sector theory. All issues related to end-results equity in the mainstream theory are incorporated in the interpersonal equity condition for a social welfare maximum. The benefits-received principle can be useful only for promoting efficiency, such as when it calls for marginal cost prices for decreasing cost services, or Lindahl prices for nonexclusive goods.

THE ABILITY-TO-PAY PRINCIPLE

As it happens, there is a long-standing alternative mainstream view of equity in taxation that dates from the writings of Adam Smith and John Stuart Mill in the late 1700s and early 1800s, almost 150 years before Bergson and Samuelson formulated their social welfare function. It is called the *ability-to pay principle*, and Smith and Mill conceived of it strictly as an equity principle, without reference to the efficiency costs of raising taxes. Smith and Mill's ability-to-pay principle has more than merely survived as an alternative to the social welfare view of tax equity. It is their ability-to-pay principle, not the social welfare view, that most often informs public discussions of equity in taxation in all the developed market economies.

In Smith and Mill's time, the benefits-received principle was the only widely accepted principle of equity in taxation. It dated from the feudal societies of Europe in the 14th and 15th centuries, when the noblemen would pay a tax to the king in return for protection of their fiefdoms from foreign invaders. By the late 1700s, however, the feudal societies had broken apart, population had grown and spread geographically, and governments were providing a wide range of public services. Smith and Mill realized that the link between taxes and public services was no longer tight enough to rely solely on the benefits-received principle. They saw the need for a second principle of equity in taxation based on the notion that people simply had to be willing to sacrifice for the common good. They should no longer expect a specific quid pro quo for their tax payments. Their sacrifice view of taxation gave rise to the notion of taxes as a necessary evil.

The question was how to ask people to sacrifice for the common good. Their answer: in accordance with people's ability to pay. In addition, they argued that the tax payments should honor two additional subprinciples: horizontal equity and vertical equity. *Horizontal equity* requires that two people who are deemed equal in every relevant economic dimension should pay the same tax. *Vertical equity* says that it is permissible for the government to tax unequals unequally.

These two subprinciples raise two immediate and difficult questions that a society must answer. First, in what sense are people deemed to be equal or unequal in terms of taxation? Both subprinciples require an answer to this question. Second, how unequally can unequals be taxed? This is just the time-honored question of distributive justice posed in terms of taxation. In the ability-to-pay tradition, the quest for horizontal equity is seen as the search for the ideal tax base, the item to be taxed. The reason is that any tax applies a (set of) tax rate(s) to the tax base. Therefore, two people with the same tax base necessarily pay the same tax, consistent with horizontal equity. Likewise, the quest for vertical equity is seen as the search for the ideal tax structure, which has two components. One is the rate or rates to apply to different values of the tax base and the other is the set of exemptions and other deductions from the tax base that taxpayers are allowed in figuring their tax liabilities. Common examples for personal income taxes are exemptions of the first amounts of income from taxation to protect low-income people from taxation and the deduction of extraordinary medical expenses from income when computing the income subject to taxation, called "taxable income". We will begin with horizontal equity, the search for the ideal tax base.

HORIZONTAL EQUITY: THE IDEAL TAX BASE

Neither Smith nor Mill made a convincing argument for any particular tax base in the quest for horizontal equity. The breakthrough came nearly 150 years later, in the 1920s and 1930s, from economists Robert Haig of Columbia University and Herbert Simons of the University of Chicago. Haig (1921) and Simons (1938) proposed a method of thinking about the ideal tax base that gained immediate acceptance among economists and remains the standard in the ability-to-pay tradition today. It consists of the following three principles:

1. *People ultimately bear the burden of taxation.* Governments may choose to tax businesses rather than people, such as under the sales tax, VAT, and the corporate income tax. But the relevant issue from the ability-to-pay perspective is which people bear the burden of these taxes. Can firms pass the tax burden on to their customers through

higher prices, or to their workers in the form of lower wages, or do the firms' owners bear the burden of the tax? Economists refer to the payment of the tax liability as the *impact* of the tax, and the ultimate burden of the tax as the *incidence* of the tax. We will see in Chapter 18 that although the government determines the impact of any tax, its incidence or burden depends on how markets respond to the tax. For now it is enough to note that the incidence or burden of the tax is the relevant consideration in determining the ideal tax base.

2. *People sacrifice utility when they bear the burden of a tax.* Modern economic theory expresses individuals' economic well-being in terms of the utility they obtain from their economic decisions, represented by a utility function. The burden of a tax is therefore the resulting loss in utility it entails. This led Martin Feldstein (1976) to propose a modern version of the principle of horizontal equity in taxation in terms of utility rather than taxes paid:

   ▪ *Horizontal equity (Feldstein):* Two people with equal utility before tax should have equal utility after tax.

   For future reference, Feldstein also proposed a corresponding minimal requirement for vertical equity, that taxes could not lead to reversals of utility:

   ▪ *Vertical equity (minimal requirement):* If person #1 has higher utility than person #2 before tax, then person #1 should have higher utility than person #2 after tax.

   Feldstein's interpretations of horizontal and vertical equity are widely accepted by mainstream economists.

3. *The ideal tax base is the best surrogate measure of utility.* Governments cannot tax utility, so the best they can do is tax whatever is deemed to be the best surrogate measure of utility. Here is where the disagreements come among mainstream economists. They all accept Haig and Simons' three principles for determining the ideal tax base, but they can disagree as to what constitutes the best surrogate measure of utility. The main contenders are income and consumption.

▬ HAIG–SIMONS INCOME

Haig and Simons argued that the best surrogate measure of utility is income, broadly defined as the increase in purchasing power during the year (assuming annual taxation). The increase in purchasing power is the sum of consumption and the change in a person's net worth or wealth. Therefore, Y_{HS} = consumption + change in net worth = $C + \Delta NW$, where Y_{HS} is Haig–Simons income, C is consumption, and NW is net worth. Consumption is the exercise of purchasing power and the change in net worth is purchasing power that has been deferred for consumption in future years. Using today's national income accounting terminology, the change in net worth arises from personal saving (S) out of income that adds to net worth and capital gains or losses (CG). A *capital gain* is the change, from the beginning to the end of the year, in the value of assets held at the beginning of the year. Therefore, $Y_{HS} = C + S + CG$. But the sum of consumption and saving is personal income (PI).[1] Hence $Y_{HS} = PI + CG$. *Haig–Simons income* is the sum of personal income and capital gains. Y_{HS} is often referred to as the "accretion standard," since income is defined as the increase (accretion) in purchasing power during the tax year. Another common designation of Y_{HS} is the comprehensive tax base, so common that it is denoted simply by the initials CTB.

The conclusion, then, is that two people with the same value of Y_{HS} are equals and should pay the same tax. Furthermore, since Y_{HS} is seen as the best surrogate measure of utility, horizontal equity is satisfied both in terms of tax payments (Smith and Mill's original interpretation) and utility (Feldstein's modern version). Two people with the same Haig–Simons income pay the same tax and sacrifice the same amount of utility. Two people with unequal amounts of Y_{HS} are unequals and may pay different amounts of tax, but how much different depends on society's interpretation of vertical equity.

Haig and Simons were persuasive. Their call for Y_{HS} as the ideal tax base was immediately accepted by the vast majority of mainstream economists. That Y_{HS} should have gained such widespread acceptance is remarkable since most matters involving end-results equity are filled with controversy. Yet the broad consensus held firm until the 1970s, when a number of mainstream economists began proposing consumption as the better tax base in terms of Haig and Simons' three principles. Today the majority of mainstream economists may well prefer consumption to Haig–Simons income as the ideal tax base. We will present the argument for consumption later on in the chapter.

Distinctions that should not matter

Once Y_{HS} is accepted as the ideal tax base, it has a number of strong implications for the design of taxes. For one, it requires the broadest possible personal income tax, a requirement that is never met in practice. The following are a list of distinctions within a personal income tax that should not matter, but usually do. The brief counterexamples in parentheses in the list below refer to features of U.S. federal income tax that violate the broad Haig–Simons income standard, features that we will return to in Chapter 14.

Sources of income

All sources of income should be included in the tax base:

- *Personal income vs. capital gains* – both components of Y_{HS} should be included in the tax base in their entirety and taxed at the same rate. (A portion of capital gains has almost always been excluded from the tax base.)
- *Earned vs. unearned income* – within personal income, all sources of income should be included in the tax base, whether they are earned income – wages, interest rates, and rents from supplying labor, capital, and land – or unearned income from the receipt of transfer payments. (Some cash transfer payments are not included in the tax base – public assistance transfers and a portion of social security retirement benefits.)

■ *Different sources of earned income* – all payments to factors of production should be included in the tax base. (Interest earned on accounts such as IRAs and 401Ks that are designated as retirement accounts are excluded from the tax base.) Also, it should not matter whether the receipt of earned income is in cash or in kind. (Many sources of in-kind income are excluded from the tax base, the most important being fringe benefits such as employer contributions to their employees' pension plans and medical insurance.)

Uses of income

The tax base reflects the increase in purchasing power during the year. It should not matter how that purchasing power is used:

■ *Consumption vs. saving* – the decision to consume or save out of income is irrelevant. (Purchases of IRAs and other financial investments designed to provide income for retirement are excluded from the tax base.)
■ *Various forms of consumption* – what people choose to consume should be irrelevant. (Taxpayers can deduct many forms of consumption from their incomes in computing their taxable income, such as extraordinary expenses for medical care, interest payments on their home mortgages, and contributions to charity.)
■ *Form of capital gains* – in the parlance of tax law, it should not matter whether capital gains (losses) are realized or accrued. Realized means that the asset was sold during the year, hence the gain (loss) was "realized." Accrued means that the asset continued to be held, so that the gain (loss) remained as part of the taxpayer's savings. Purchasing power increases in either case, so the distinction should be irrelevant. (Capital gains (losses) become part of the tax base only if they are realized.)

These distinctions get into the tax laws because once the tax exists, legislatures are tempted to use it to promote social ends (for example encourage saving for retirement, encourage home ownership, subsidize private charitable contributions, and provide tax relief for people who face large medical expenses). Also, some legitimate items in the tax base may be difficult for the taxpayer or the DOR to evaluate (for example accrued capital gains on real assets; how much did a house or a work of art that was not sold increase in value during the year?). Nonetheless, all these distinctions lead to the possibility of violating people's sense of horizontal equity once Y_{HS} is accepted as the ideal tax base.

There is only one legitimate deduction from Y_{HS} in computing taxable income: business expenses. *Business expenses* are expenses that are required by taxpayers to earn their incomes. As such, they subtract from the purchasing power available to taxpayers out of their incomes and should not be part of the tax base. An example is a uniform that a person is required to purchase as part of the job. Legal battles are fought over what constitutes a legitimate business expense. For example, the U.S. courts have ruled that commuting expenses from suburb to city are not a business expense but rather part of the consumption package of choosing to live in the suburbs. Nonetheless, the principle that legitimate business expenses should be excluded from the tax base is not in question.

A final point is that the tax base must be indexed for inflation, so that Y_{HS} income truly reflects an increase in purchasing power. Without appropriate indexing, people's real tax liabilities could be affected simply by inflation, and this is illegitimate. For example, suppose you purchased some shares of stock for $100 in 1982 and sold the stock in 2005 for $200. The capital gain subject to tax is $100 (= $200 – $100). But the price level doubled between 1982 and 2005, so that it took $200 in 2005 to purchase the same amount of goods and services as $100 in 1982. The $100 of capital gain did not represent an increase in purchasing power and therefore should not be taxed. The way to index for capital gains is to increase the purchase price by the amount of accumulated inflation from the date of purchase to the date of sale. This would increase the purchase price of the asset in our example to $200 and produce a capital gain of $0, which is the correct value of the increase in purchasing power that the asset yielded.

In summary, the ideal tax base under the Haig–Simons standard is Y_{HS} less business expenses, adjusted for inflation.

All other taxes are inappropriate

Once Y_{HS} is accepted as the ideal tax base, then all the other taxes that governments use – general sales taxes, VATs, property taxes, corporation income taxes, and so forth – are necessarily inappropriate. They are always open to the charge of horizontal inequity because they cannot guarantee that two people with the same Y_{HS} bear the same tax burden. In fact, many violations of horizontal equity are virtually certain to occur. The other taxes may also lead to reversals of before- and after-tax Y_{HS}, in violation of Feldstein's minimal requirement for vertical equity.

▬▬▬ HAIG–SIMONS INCOME AND UTILITY

Is Haig–Simons income a good surrogate measure of utility? This is a fundamental question in the ability-to-pay tradition because the willingness to accept any one tax base as an ideal to strive for depends on it being a good proxy for utility, by the third step in the Haig–Simons argument. Unfortunately, the answer is almost certainly "no."

The standard labor-leisure model can be used to show why income is unlikely to be a good surrogate measure of utility. Suppose people receive utility from income (Y) and leisure (Leis) according to the utility function U = U(Y, Leis), represented by the indifference curves I_0, I_1, and I_2 in Figure 13.1. They sleep 8 hours a day, which leaves 16 hours for work or leisure. The hourly wage rate is W, so that each person's budget constraint is Y = W(16 – Leis) = –W·Leis + 16·W, represented by the budget line in the figure. The slope of the budget line is (–)W.

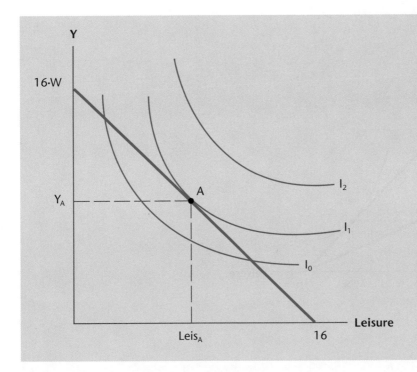

Figure 13.1

Whether income is a good surrogate measure of utility depends on whether people are identical or not. Suppose they are identical – same tastes, same skills, and same opportunities. In this case, Figure 13.1 applies to everyone. They all achieve maximum utility at point A, at which the budget line is tangent to indifference curve I_1, and earn income Y_A, which we assume is their entire Haig–Simons income. Y_A is a perfect proxy for utility since everyone does obtain the same utility. In fact, if all people were identical, then almost anything would be a good surrogate measure of utility, not only income but any item that everyone consumes, since everyone would purchase the same amount of that good or service.[2]

People are not identical, of course, and therein lies the difficulty. Figure 13.2 illustrates. Suppose two people have identical tastes, but differ in their skills and opportunities, with person #2 being the more highly skilled. This case is represented in Figure 13.2(a). There is one set of indifference curves for both people because they have the same tastes. But person #2 receives a higher wage, W_2 vs. W_1, reflecting his higher skills, and therefore has a better set of choices for Leis and Y along the higher budget line. Figure 13.2(a) assumes for the sake of illustration that person #2 takes all his gains in the form of higher leisure, choosing point B on indifference curve I_2. As in Figure 13.1, person #1 chooses point A on indifference curve I_1. Person #2 clearly achieves the higher utility but both people earn the same Haig–Simons income ($Y_A = Y_B$). Income in this case is a very poor proxy for utility. If they are taxed on the basis of their Haig–Simons income, person #1 is disadvantaged because she pays the same tax but is worse off before tax.

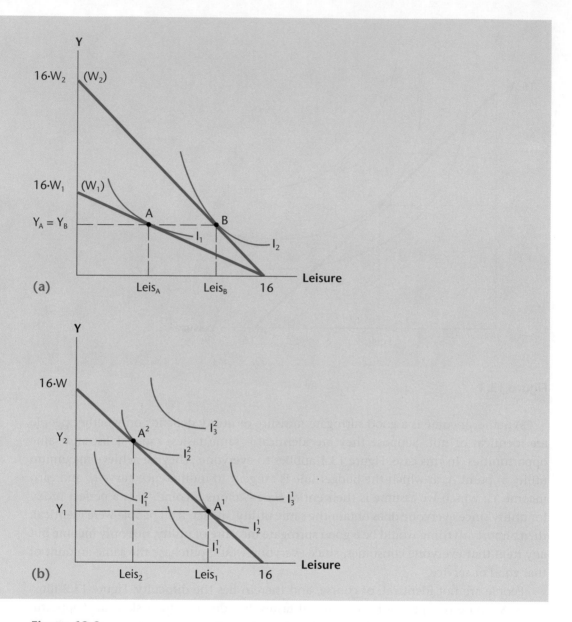

Figure 13.2

Figure 13.2(b) assumes that the two people have the same skills and opportunities, hence the same budget line, but different tastes. Person #1 a leisure lover, relatively speaking, with indifference curves I_1^1, I_2^1, I_3^1, and person #2 is a work lover, with indifference curves I_1^2, I_2^2, I_3^2. They are both in equilibrium on their second indifference curve, I_2^1 and I_2^2, to represent that they achieve the same level of utility. But they earn different incomes, Y_2 vs. Y_1, since person #2 achieves the utility by working harder and person #1 by taking more leisure time. Once again, income is a poor proxy for utility, suggesting that person #2 achieves the higher utility when in fact the utility levels are the same. If they are taxed on the basis of their Haig–Simons income, person #2 is likely to have less utility after tax even though they have the same utility before tax.

The problem when tastes, skills, or opportunities differ among people, as they surely do, is that income picks up only a part of what generates utility; it misses the leisure component of utility. Therefore income is unlikely to be a good proxy measure for utility.

The problem is not unique to Haig–Simons income, however. No matter what tax base is chosen, it will not include leisure time so that it, too, will capture only part of what yields utility to consumers. Thus, the ability-to-pay tradition is stuck with a nasty all-or-none problem in its quest for the ideal tax base. Either many taxes are perfect surrogate measures of utility if people are identical, or nothing is likely to be a good surrogate measure of utility if people differ. Unfortunately, the latter is the realistic case.

CONSUMPTION AS THE IDEAL TAX BASE

The equity case for consumption as the ideal tax base, which many mainstream economists now favor, adopts the same three Haig–Simons principles. It also recognizes that consumption may not be a perfect surrogate measure for utility. But it argues that consumption is a much better surrogate measure of utility than Haig–Simons income, by the following reasoning.

The first problem with choosing income as the best surrogate measure of utility is that the time frame is wrong. The utility that people achieve should be judged over their lifetimes, not on an annual basis, because people can temporarily have unusually high or low income (utility) for a year or two. Therefore, people's utility over their entire lifetimes is the best indication of how well off they are, both absolutely and relative to other people. (Think of graduate students on research or teaching stipends whose current incomes and utilities are much less than they will be, on average, over their lifetimes.) Second, the act of consumption most directly generates utility. Proponents of Y_{HS} as the ideal tax base have to think in terms of purchasing power as the surrogate for utility because of their annual perspective, since people can save some of their purchasing power today for future consumption. No such limitation applies in a lifetime context, however. The pattern of consumption over time is clearly the best surrogate measure of the utility they receive throughout their lives. Finally, the vast majority of people lead self-contained economic lives. They inherit little or no income and they leave only small or no bequests. The incomes they earn (plus any private or public transfers received) over their lifetimes are eventually consumed, so that the consumption generates all the lifetime utility that they receive. For those who leave substantial bequests, the bequest can be considered the final act of consumption and generator of utility.

For all these reasons, the proper interpretation of Feldstein's principle of horizontal equity is lifetime based: Two people with equal lifetime utility before tax should have equal lifetime utility after tax. Since consumption generates the utility, the principle in practice becomes: Two people with equal lifetime consumption before tax should have equal lifetime consumption after tax.[3] A tax on consumption meets this requirement.

A subtlety arises at this point. Suppose the DOR taxed on a lifetime basis by keeping track of tax payments over people's lifetimes. Then it would not matter if income or consumption were the tax base since everyone is subject to a lifetime budget constraint: Lifetime income must equal lifetime consumption (counting the bequest as the last act of consumption). If the DOR chose to tax income, it would adjust the last tax payment at the end of life to ensure that lifetime taxes were they same as they would have been had consumption been taxed. And the DOR certainly could keep track of the tax payments. After all, we saw in Chapter 12 that the Social Security administration keeps track of lifetime earnings to compute a person's pension in retirement.

But taxes are almost always levied on an annual basis without any attention to the pattern of tax payments over time. In this case, consumption must be the tax base to ensure that two people with equal lifetime consumption before tax have equal lifetime consumption after tax. The problem with taxing income is that two people with the same pattern of lifetime incomes could have very different patterns of lifetime consumption by choosing to consume and save differently year by year. Therefore, taxing income annually would lead to a different amount of lifetime taxes than taxing consumption.

The following simple two-period example illustrates the need to tax consumption on an annual basis. Suppose that two people each earn income Y in years 1 and 2. Person #1 consumes all her income in the period that it is earned. Person #2 saves all his income in period 1, and earns a rate of return r on his savings. Then in period 2, he consumes the income earned in period 2 plus the savings, with interest, from period 1. The pattern of consumption in the two periods is:

	Period 1	*Period 2*
Person #1	$C_1 = Y$	$C_2 = Y$
Person #2	$C_1 = 0, S_1 = Y$	$C_2 = Y + Y(1 + r)$

The lifetime consumption of the two people, discounted to present value at rate r, is

$$\text{Person \#1: } C_{PV}^1 = Y + \frac{Y}{(1+r)}$$

$$\text{Person \#2: } C_{PV}^2 = 0 + \frac{Y}{(1+r)} + \frac{Y(1+r)}{(1+r)} = \frac{Y}{(1+r)} + Y$$

The two people have the same (discounted) lifetime consumption before tax. If the government levies an annual tax on consumption at rate t, their (discounted) lifetime tax payments would also be the same. (Multiply the before-tax discounted lifetime consumption streams by the tax rate t.) The only difference is that person #1 would pay the tax each period, whereas person #2 would pay all his taxes in the second period.

Suppose, instead, they pay an annual income tax at rate t. One difference relative to the consumption tax is the way in which present values are calculated. The discount rate reflects the return to saving available to the two people. Since interest income is taxed under an income tax, the discount rate is the net-of-tax rate, $r(1-t)$. With this correction, the discounted lifetime taxes for person #1 are:

$$\text{Person \#1: } T_{PV}^1 = tY + \frac{tY}{1+r(1-t)}$$

Person #2 would pay tax on the income Y earned each period, just as person #1. But the return r on his saving in period 1, his income from capital, is also taxed. If we assume the tax on the interest is paid in period 2, then the discounted lifetime taxes for person #2 are:

$$\text{Person \#2: } T_{PV}^2 = tY + \frac{tY}{(1+r(1-t))} + \frac{trS}{(1+r(1-t))}$$

The amount saved in period 1 is the income after tax, $Y(1-t)$. Therefore

$$T_{PV}^2 = tY + \frac{tY}{1+r(1-t)} + \frac{trY(1-t)}{1+r(1-t)}$$

Horizontal equity is violated. The two people have equal (discounted) lifetime consumption before tax but different (discounted) lifetime consumption after tax because person #2 pays higher lifetime taxes.

The problem from the point of view of the consumption standard is the so-called "double taxation of saving." It is first taxed in period 1, such that the amount of saving is only the income net of tax, $Y(1-t)$. Then the interest income on the already taxed saving is taxed again in the second period.

Note for future reference when we discuss the incidence of various taxes in Chapter 19 that, in this simple example, an income tax can be made to be equivalent to a consumption tax by excluding income from capital. With the return to saving untaxed, the relevant discount rate is r not $r(1-t)$, and the final term in the tax on person #2 above is removed. Thus an annual income tax at rate t is equivalent to an annual consumption tax at rate t. Note also in our example that by excluding income from capital, the income tax is equivalent to a tax on wage income, the Y. In general, however, a wage tax is not equivalent to a consumption tax. To see this, think back to the OLG model of Chapter 12 that we used to analyze Social Security. A wage tax would be paid only by the younger generation of workers, whereas a consumption tax would be paid by both the younger generation and the older retired generation. The two taxes are not at all equivalent.

The other way to make an income tax equivalent to a consumption tax is to allow taxpayers under an income tax to deduct their saving in computing their taxable income. But this *is* a personal consumption tax, as described earlier in the chapter.

MUSGRAVE'S VIEW OF HORIZONTAL EQUITY

So which is the better tax base, income or consumption? Richard Musgrave (1990), the leading U.S. public sector economist in the last half of the 20th century, viewed the debate over this question as misguided. He argued that horizontal equity in taxation should be interpreted just as it is in a legal sense. Equal treatment of equals should mean nothing more than ensuring that taxes do not discriminate against people in inappropriate ways. People's tax liabilities should not depend on their race, religion, gender, or any other such personal characteristic. Beyond this, the search for the best surrogate measure for utility is a futile exercise. Income and consumption are both perfectly good tax bases in his view. Select one and then worry about vertical equity, the tax structure, especially the tax rates to be applied to different levels of income or consumption. Society's choices with respect to vertical equity have a far greater impact on the distribution of well-being than whether income or consumption is chosen as the tax base.[4]

Musgrave's position has merit, but it does not appear to have won the day, at least not in the United States. Debate continues apace about the fairness of replacing the federal personal income tax with either a personal consumption tax or a national sales tax. We will return to these debates in Chapters 14 and 19. The remainder of this chapter is devoted to the quest for vertical equity, which Musgrave viewed as the central issue.

VERTICAL EQUITY

The question of how unequally to treat unequals once the tax base has been determined is nothing more than the quest for distributive justice applied to tax policy. As such, it is hardly surprising that this question typically breeds strongly held opinions of all kinds, intense debate, and almost never a satisfactory resolution. People have no more success in deciding how tax rates should vary with income or consumption than they have in deciding what the optimal distribution of income should be. The United States is instructive in this regard. The tax rate applied to the highest incomes under the federal personal income tax has bounced around since the 1960s from 91%, to 50%, to 28%, to 33%, to 39%, to its current level of 35% (as of 2003) following the George W. Bush tax cuts. The pattern of allowable exclusions and deductions from the tax base is often changed as well. Issues relating to the tax structure never seem to be settled.

In truth, public discussions of vertical equity in tax policy almost never get beyond the rather broad question of whether taxes should be progressive, proportional, or regressive. Economists have devised many ways to define these terms, but the most common definition by far is in terms of the average tax burden. Assume for the sake of illustration that Haig–Simons income has been chosen as the ideal tax base. Then, for any tax, form the ratio of the burden of the tax for each taxpayer, T^h, to the taxpayer's Haig–Simons income, $\dfrac{T^h}{Y_{HS}^h}$. Ask how the average tax burden, $\dfrac{T^h}{Y_{HS}^h}$, varies with Y_{HS} as Y_{HS} increases.

If $\dfrac{T^h}{Y^h_{HS}}$ increases as income increases, the tax is said to be *progressive*. Higher income

taxpayers bear a higher proportion of their income in tax burden.

If $\dfrac{T^h}{Y^h_{HS}}$ remains constant as income increases, the tax is said to be *proportional*. All tax-

payers bear the same proportion of their income in tax burden. Higher income taxpayers bear a higher tax burden, but not a proportionally higher burden.

If $\dfrac{T^h}{Y^h_{HS}}$ decreases as income increases, the tax is said to be *regressive*. Higher income

taxpayers pay a lower proportion of their income in tax burden. They may or may not bear a lower tax burden in an absolute sense.

Notice that we have been careful to define T^h as the tax burden an individual bears for a given tax rather than the tax payment. Under an income tax, tax burden is often equated with tax payment, but this cannot be so under most other taxes. The sales tax, VAT, and corporation income tax are paid by businesses. As noted earlier, the burdens that individuals bear under these taxes depend on how markets respond to these taxes. The markets determine whether the tax burdens are borne by the firms' consumers, workers, or stockholders, which then determines whether they are progressive, proportional, or regressive.

Another point to note is that the way in which the average tax burdens are measured depends on the choice of the ideal tax base. If, as above, Haig–Simons income is seen as the ideal, then the denominator of the tax burden ratio should be Y_{HS}, and the average burdens should be measured on an annual basis. If, in contrast, consumption is viewed as the ideal tax base, then the average burdens should be measured on a lifetime basis, with discounted lifetime consumption (or income) in the denominator. Recall that the argument for choosing consumption as the ideal tax base relies on a lifetime perspective. Therefore, the determination of whether a tax is progressive, proportional, or regressive should also be made on a lifetime basis.

As we will see in subsequent chapters, people seem to have a fairly strong preference for proportional or progressive taxes over regressive taxes. Much less clear-cut, however, is whether the majority of people believe that taxes should be progressive or proportional, and for those who favor progressive taxes, just how progressive they should be. To say that a tax should be progressive does not go very far in pinning down the actual structure of a tax.

Chapter 14 analyzes the U.S. federal personal income tax and the call for a personal consumption tax from the ability-to-pay perspective developed in this chapter. The ability-to-pay perspective either explicitly or implicitly underlies almost all public discussions of these taxes, in the United States and elsewhere.

Applying Ability-to-Pay Principles: Federal Personal Income Tax

The U.S. federal personal income tax is an excellent vehicle for illustrating how ability-to-pay principles underlie public discussions of tax policy. It collects the most revenue of any tax worldwide and it is designed along the lines suggested by Haig and Simons because it taxes both personal income and capital gains. It also appears to be a highly progressive tax because it employs what is called a *graduated rate structure*: the tax rates applied to various ranges of income increase as income increases.

At the same time there are many slips from principles to practice. Not all components of personal income and capital gains are taxed, with the result that the tax base, called *taxable income*, is much less comprehensive than most taxpayers' Haig–Simons incomes. In addition, some of the components of personal income and capital gains are taxed at reduced rates. People see these differences between the federal tax base and the Haig–Simons ideal and it offends their sense of horizontal equity. These differences also happen to reduce substantially the progressivity of the tax at higher incomes relative to the progressivity implied by the graduated tax rates, and this offends some people's sense of vertical equity. The charges of horizontal and vertical inequities are all expressed in terms of the ability-to-pay principles developed in Chapter 13.

THE STRUCTURE OF FEDERAL PERSONAL INCOME TAX

The federal personal income tax (PIT) came into being in 1913 following the 16th Amendment to the U.S. Constitution, which permitted the federal government to tax income for the first time. The primary source of federal revenues before the income tax was tariff revenue on imported goods. The PIT evolved throughout the 20th century as a highly complex tax. The set of rules and regulations describing the tax, known as The Code, is now over 2,000 pages.

Fortunately, we need to understand only a few features of the tax structure to analyze the more important economic implications of the tax, particularly those that are the subject of ongoing policy debates. The features fall into two categories, the graduated tax rates and the main differences between the tax base – taxable income – and the ideal tax base of Haig–Simons income.

THE GRADUATED TAX RATES

An immediate complication in describing the set of graduated tax rates that apply to different levels of taxable income is that Congress could never decide whether it wants to levy the tax on an individual or a family basis. The compromise was to develop two sets of tax rates, one applying to single individuals and one applying to married couples. In the terminology of the U.S. IRS, single taxpayers file "separately." Married couples have the option of filing separately, with the tax rates applied to their own incomes, or filing jointly ("married, filing jointly"), with the tax rates applied to the combined incomes of husband and wife (but not the incomes of the children). Separate tax rates apply to each option, as indicated in Table 14.1. The rates in the table were those in effect in 2005, when there were tax rates ranging from 10% to 35%.

TABLE 14.1 Graduated tax rates: U.S. federal personal income tax (2005)

Married, filing jointly		Married, filing separately		Single person	
Marginal tax rate %	Income bracket	Marginal tax rate %	Income bracket	Marginal tax rate %	Income bracket
10	$0–$14,600	10	$0–$7,300	10	$0–7,300
15	14,600–59,400	15	7,300–29,700	15	7,300–29,700
25	59,400–119,950	25	29,700–59,975	25	29,700–71,950
28	119,950–182,800	28	59,975–91,400	28	71,950–150,150
33	182,800–326,450	33	91,400–163,225	33	150,150–326,450
35	over 326,450	35	over 163,225	35	over 326,450

SOURCE: Website of The Tax Foundation, U.S. Federal Individual Income Tax Rates History, 1913–2007, www.taxfoundation.org/publications/show/151.html.

A number of points should be understood about the graduated rate schedules. First, each range of taxable income to which a tax rate applies is called a *tax bracket*. Second, the graduated tax rates are referred to as the set of *marginal tax rates* because they are the rates that would apply to a taxpayer whose next dollar of income falls within a given tax bracket and would therefore be taxed at that rate. For example, a single taxpayer whose taxable income was $20,000 in 2005 faced a marginal tax rate of 15% because his next dollar of taxable income would be taxed at 15%; if his taxable income were $125,000, his marginal tax rate was 28%; and so forth. Third, the set of tax brackets with their own tax rates apply to all taxpayers, no matter how much income they have. For example, an individual with $1 million of income in 2005 and filing separately owed a tax of 10%

on her first \$7,300 of income, 15% on her next \$22,400 of income (= \$29,700 – \$7,300), and so on, with the 35% rate levied only on her last \$673,550 of income (= \$1,000,000 – \$326,450). Therefore, her marginal tax rate was 35%, but the average tax rate on her taxable income (tax liability divided by taxable income) was only about 33%.[1] Fourth, the boundaries of the tax brackets are adjusted for inflation; they are increased each year by the increase in the CPI during the tax year. Finally, notice that in comparing the tax brackets for married taxpayers filing jointly and single taxpayers, the first two tax brackets (10% and 15%) are exactly twice as wide for the joint filers and the single filers. Therefore, it would not have mattered in 2005 whether married couples with combined incomes less than \$59,450 filed jointly or separately. For the last four tax rates, however, the married, filing jointly tax brackets are less than twice as wide as the single tax brackets. This pattern is central to one of the ongoing public policy debates to be discussed later on in the chapter, the so-called tax penalty for married couples.

TAXABLE INCOME VS. HAIG–SIMONS INCOME

Recall that all components of personal income and capital gains should be taxed under the ideal Haig–Simons standard, and all at the same set of graduated rates. Neither category comes close to the ideal, with the result that taxable income under the federal PIT is much less than Haig–Simons income.

Personal income

Only about 40–45% of taxpayers' personal income each year is counted as taxable income by the U.S. IRS. The differences between personal income and taxable income fall into three main categories: personal exemptions, exclusions, and deductions.

- *Personal exemptions* are income that the IRS recognizes as potentially taxable income but chooses not to tax. In 2005, each taxpayer received a personal exemption of \$3,200. Married taxpayers filing jointly received a personal exemption for each spouse and each dependent child. Thus, a married couple with two dependent children received a personal exemption of \$12,800 (= 4 × \$3,200). The personal exemption is adjusted for inflation; it increases each year by the increase in the CPI.
- *Exclusions* are items of income that are recognized as personal income by the U.S. Department of Commerce when computing the National Income and Product Accounts but are not counted as taxable income by the IRS. The five most important exclusions are, in order: fringe benefits paid by employers to employees, principally contributions to employees' pension plans and medical and life insurance policies; transfer payments, including cash and in-kind public assistance payments (for example TANF, SSI, Medicaid, and Food Stamps) and part or all of the Social Security retirement pensions; non-marketed income imputed by the Department of Commerce, primarily the imputed

rental income received by homeowners to make homeownership comparable to renting[2] and the value of their own crops that farm families consume; purchases by taxpayers of financial assets designed to provide income for retirement income, such as Individual Retirement Accounts (IRAs) and 401Ks – the interest income on these retirement assets is also excluded from taxable income; and interest income on bonds issued by state and local governments, called "municipal bonds."

■ *Deductions* are items of consumption that taxpayers can subtract from their incomes in computing their taxable incomes. The four most important deductions are: extraordinary medical expenses;[3] state income taxes[4] and local property taxes; interest payments on mortgages taken out on taxpayers' principal residences; and gifts to charitable organizations, of which the most important are contributions to taxpayers' religious institutions and colleges and universities.

Taxpayers who subtract these specific exclusions and deductions in computing their taxable incomes are said to "itemize." In lieu of itemizing, taxpayers are given the option of claiming a standard deduction ($5,000 for single filers and $10,000 for joint filers in 2005) that they can deduct from their incomes in computing their taxable incomes. Most taxpayers itemize for the first time when they become homeowners and can deduct the interest on their mortgages and their local property taxes. (They can also exclude their imputed rental income, but it is the two deductions that tip the balance in favor of itemizing. Even homeowners who choose not to itemize can exclude their imputed rental income.)

A final point to note is that one item of personal income, dividends, has received favorable tax rate treatment beginning in 2003. The maximum marginal tax rate applicable to most dividends was limited to 15%, no matter how large a taxpayer's taxable income. This tax rate limit is important because the vast majority of dividends are received by taxpayers in the top 20% of the income distribution, those whose marginal tax rates are much higher than 15%.

Capital gains

There are two important differences between the actual tax treatment of capital gains and their ideal treatment under the Haig–Simons standard. First, a capital gain is taxed only if it is realized, that is, the asset is sold during the tax year. The taxable income is the difference between the sales price and the purchase price of the asset, no matter when the asset was purchased. Gains each year that simply accrue on paper and thus remain part of a taxpayer's savings are not taxed, even though they do represent an increase in purchasing power and are therefore part of Haig–Simons income. Second, capital gains are almost always taxed at favorable rates. In 2005, the maximum tax rate applicable to capital gains was 15%, the same as for dividends, providing the asset had been held for more than one year (so-called long-term capital gains; short-term capital gains are those on assets held for less than one year and are taxable at the regular graduated rates). As with dividends, the vast majority of capital gains are taken by high-income taxpayers.

A final point is that capital gains and losses should be treated symmetrically under the Haig–Simons standard, but they are not. Taxpayers can subtract capital losses from capital gains without limit so long as the losses are less than the capital gains. But capital losses can be subtracted from all other sources of income only up to a limit of $3,000 in any one year. Losses in excess of $3,000 must be "carried forward" to be applied to income in subsequent years, also with a limit of $3,000 in any one year, against sources of income other than capital gains.

With this overview of U.S. federal personal income tax in hand, we turn to a number of issues of concern to the public. These issues tend to arise whenever income is taxed; they are certainly not unique to the U.S. federal personal income tax. The first issue concerns the many differences between taxable income and Haig–Simons income.

HORIZONTAL EQUITY AND THE TAXATION OF PERSONAL INCOME

With less than half of personal income subject to taxation because of personal exemptions, exclusions, and deductions, the federal personal income tax is wide open to the charge that it violates horizontal equity. But the charge of horizontal inequity typically is leveled against exclusions and deductions, not personal exemptions. The reason is that personal exemptions perform a very different function from that of exclusions and deductions, one that people tend to accept. Let's consider personal exemptions first.

PERSONAL EXEMPTIONS

The role of personal exemptions in an income tax is to protect the lowest income taxpayers and their families from taxation. As such, they are typically viewed from the perspective of vertical equity, not horizontal equity. Personal exemptions by themselves tend to make an income tax fairly progressive throughout the lower and middle income ranges and at least mildly progressive throughout the entire range of incomes. This would be so even if tax rates were not graduated.

People in the United States seem to be comfortable with this pattern of middle and low-end progressivity. For example, many people have proposed that graduated tax rates be replaced by a single rate, the so-called flat (rate) tax proposal. But proponents of the flat tax almost always include a set of personal exemptions that would offer the same low-income protection as the combination of personal exemptions and standard deductions do under the current tax.

Figure 14.1 illustrates that a flat tax with a personal exemption is a progressive tax. The figure assumes that the flat tax rate is 20%, with a personal exemption of $10,000 (for a single taxpayer). It also assumes that there are no exclusions and deductions in the tax base, so that the only difference between taxable income and Haig–Simons income is the personal exemption. Haig–Simons income, Y_{HS}, is on the horizontal axis and the average tax rate (burden), T/Y_{HS}, is on the vertical axis, where T is the tax liability. There are two marginal tax rates, 0% on income up to the $10,000 personal exemption and 20% on income above $20,000. The marginal tax rates are represented by the solid horizontal lines. The average tax rate, T/Y_{HS}, is 0 for incomes up to $10,000, and then begins to rise along the dotted line. It rises fairly steeply at first and then becomes much flatter, approaching but never quite reaching 20%. For example, at an income of $20,000, the tax is $2,000 [= .2·($20,000 – $10,000) = .2 × $10,000], and the average tax rate is 10% (= $2,000/$20,000 = .10 = 10%). At an income of $50,000, the tax is $8,000 [= .2·($50,000 – $10,000) = .2 × $40,000], and the average tax rate is 16% (= $8,000/$50,000 = .16 = 16%). At an income of $100,000, the tax is $18,000 [= .2·($100,000 – $10,000) = .2 × $90,000], and the average tax rate is 18% (= $18,000/$100,000 = .18 = 18%), close to the 20% marginal tax rate. The average tax rate rises much more steeply over the first $50,000 of income than over the next $50,000 of income, and after $100,000 it approaches 20% very slowly. But the tax is at least mildly progressive throughout the entire range of incomes. Without the personal exemption, the tax would be proportional throughout, with T/Y_{HS} = 20%, the flat (marginal) tax rate.[5]

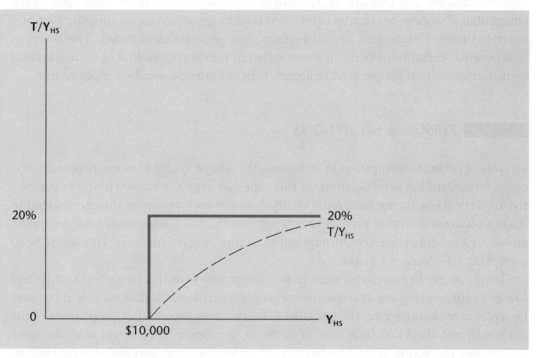

Figure 14.1

EXCLUSIONS AND DEDUCTIONS: THE LOOPHOLES

Legislatures place exclusions and deductions into an income tax primarily to encourage certain kinds of behavior that are considered to be socially desirable, such as contributing to charities, becoming a homeowner, and saving for retirement. Laudable as these goals may be, the exclusions and deductions tend to offend people's sense of horizontal equity. They see taxpayers with the same Haig–Simons income paying very different amounts of tax because they claim different amounts of the allowable exclusions and deductions. This is why the exclusions and deductions are commonly referred to as "loopholes," a pejorative term meant to indicate that the ability to reduce tax liability through these devices is seen as unfair.[6]

Assessing the horizontal inequities of the exclusions and deductions runs immediately into the difficulty that there are two notions of horizontal equity in taxation. One is that two people with equal Haig–Simons income should pay the same tax, which is the common interpretation of horizontal equity in public discussions of tax policy. The other is Martin Feldstein's economic notion of horizontal equity, that two people with equal utility before tax should have equal utility after tax.

If the IRS were to tax all of Haig–Simons income except for the personal exemptions, then the two notions of horizontal equity would both be satisfied. Two people with the same Haig–Simons income would pay the same tax. And, since Haig–Simons income is viewed as the best surrogate measure of utility, then by definition two people with the same before- and after-tax Haig–Simons income have the same utilities before and after tax.

Once the government allows exclusions and deductions into an income tax, however, the two notions of horizontal equity diverge. As noted, two people with the same Haig–Simons income may pay very different taxes, and the tax is viewed as violating horizontal equity. But, as Feldstein has pointed out, markets come to the rescue in terms of the second economic version of horizontal equity, assuming markets are competitive. Markets respond to changes in the tax structure, and they do so in such a way that the following two principles hold, one applicable in the long run and the other in the short run:

1. *The long run:* Once the market has fully responded to a newly legislated exclusion or deduction and reached its new long-run equilibrium, then two people with equal utility before tax must have equal utility after tax. The tax structure cannot be a source of horizontal inequity in the long run (Feldstein, 1986).[7]
2. *The short run:* Starting from a long-run equilibrium, any changes in the tax structure do give rise to horizontal inequities in terms of utility, but only temporarily in the short run until the market is once again in its long-run equilibrium

The markets for owner-occupied housing and apartment rentals are a good illustration of Feldstein's principles. The U.S. federal government has a long-standing tradition of promoting homeownership. In the 1930s, the government established and funded a separate savings and loans banking industry whose sole purpose was to supply low-interest mortgages to homeowners. In addition, Congress has made liberal use of the federal income tax to favor homeownership. Homeowners receive three large tax breaks relative to renters: The imputed rental income paid to themselves is excluded from taxable income, and homeowners can also deduct the interest paid on their mortgages and their local property taxes in computing their taxable income. Renters receive none of these tax breaks. These "loopholes" do promote homeownership relative to renting apartments, and they are not a source of horizontal inequity in the long run in terms of Feldstein's utility interpretation of horizontal equity.

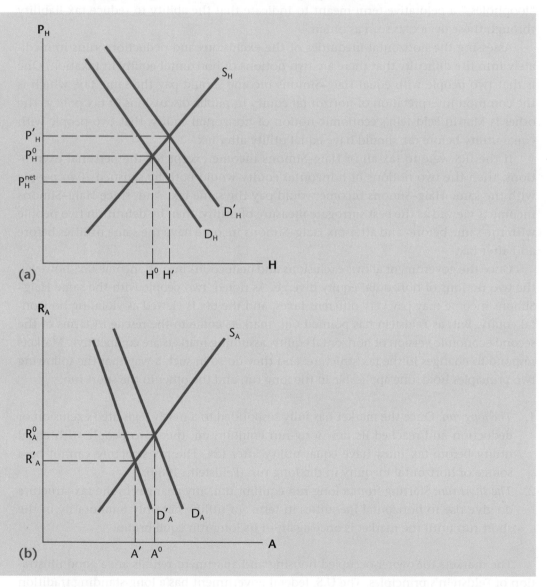

Figure 14.2

To see this, refer to Figure 14.2. Figure 14.2(a) depicts the market for owner-occupied houses and Figure 14.2(b) the market for apartments that offer comparable housing services to the houses in Figure 14.2(a). The number of houses (H) is on the horizontal axis and the annualized price (annual rental value) of the houses (P_H) is on the vertical axis in Figure 14.2(a). Similarly, the number of apartment units (A) is on the horizontal axis and the annual apartment rent (R_A) is on the vertical axis in Figure 14.2(b). The supply and demand curves before the introduction of the three tax breaks are D_H and S_H in Figure 14.2(a) and D_A and S_A in Figure 14.2(b). The pre-tax-break equilibrium is $\left(H^0, P_H^0\right)$ in the housing market and $\left(A^0, R_A^0\right)$ in the market for apartments, at the intersection of D and S in each figure. The annualized price of the houses, P_H^0, is assumed to equal the annual rent on the apartments R_A^0.[8] Both homeowners and renters are equally well off; they pay the same prices for comparable housing services.

The introduction of the three tax breaks drives up the demand for homes and lowers the demand for apartments, since owning a home is now more attractive. The demand for housing shifts up vertically by the value of the three tax breaks, from D_H to D_H'. Simultaneously, the demand for apartments shifts down from D_A to D_A' as people want to move out of apartments and into houses. The figures display the final long-run equilibrium. The post-tax-break equilibrium is $\left(H', P_H'\right)$ the housing market, and $\left(A', R_A\right)$ in the market for apartments.

The three tax breaks do increase homeownership relative to renting as intended by Congress. Homeownership increases from H^0 to H' and the number of apartments rented decreases from A^0 to A'. But the homeowners and the apartment renters are equally well off in the post-tax-break equilibrium, just as they were in the original equilibrium. The annualized price of houses may have risen from P_H^0 to P_H', but the relevant price to the homeowners is the price net of the tax breaks. That price is P_H^{net}, equal to P_H' less the value of the tax breaks, which is the vertical distance between D_H' and D_H. P_H^{net} is equal to R_A', the new equilibrium price of apartments. The equality of these two prices is no accident; it is the only possible outcome in the long-run equilibrium. If people paid the same (annualized) prices for comparable houses and apartments before the tax breaks, then they must also pay the same prices after the tax breaks. Once again, homeowners and renters are equally well off, paying the same prices for comparable housing services. Feldstein's economic version of horizontal equity is satisfied: The two sets of people had equal utility before the tax breaks and have equal utility after the tax breaks. There is no horizontal inequity in the new long-run equilibrium.

The equal utility outcome after the tax breaks is not peculiar to housing markets. It is the natural consequence of any competitive market. One of the defining characteristics of a competitive market is equal opportunity or equal access, which in turn generates horizontal equity – the equal treatment of equals – in any long-run equilibrium. A competitive market cannot be in its final equilibrium until equals are treated equally, because equals do not have to accept unequal treatment. They will keep adjusting until they are treated equally, in this example moving out of apartments and into houses until the two annualized prices are once again equal.

Another implication of this result is that competitive markets ultimately prevent Congress from favoring one subset of people among equals. The tax laws appear to favor homeowners over renters, but in the new long-run equilibrium both groups gain. They both face the same lower prices for comparable housing services, the homeowners P_H^{net} vs. P_H^0 and the renters R_A' vs. R_A^0. Favoring homeownership is different from favoring homeowners once the market achieves its new long-run equilibrium.

The short run is an entirely different matter, however. Suppose Congress suddenly removed the three tax breaks. The immediate effect is that homeowners are now worse off than the renters. They needed the tax breaks to justify paying the annualized price P_H'. The value of the tax breaks is said to be *capitalized* into the higher price of houses. With the tax breaks removed, homeowners are paying P_H' and the renters only R_A' for comparable housing services. There is now horizontal inequity, with equals treated unequally. But the horizontal inequity can only be temporary. People will respond to the price differences by moving out of houses and into apartments until the original pre-tax-break equilibria are restored, with the annualized prices equal to P_H^0 and R_A^0. The horizontal inequity ends once the prices are again equal.

REMOVE THE EXCLUSIONS AND DEDUCTIONS?

Since changing the tax structure generates horizontal inequities in the short run, does this mean that Congress should keep all the existing exclusions and deductions? The answer is "not necessarily," because the exclusions and deductions come with their own set of efficiency and equity costs. They also tend not to be the best way to subsidize favored activities.

The exclusions and deductions introduce two kinds of inefficiencies, one related to the specific markets that they affect, housing and apartments in our example, and one related to the income tax itself. We will see in Chapter 15 that a tax or subsidy that moves a market away from its natural supply and demand equilibrium generates a deadweight efficiency loss of value that neither the government nor anyone else can recapture. In our example, the pre-tax equilibrium quantity H^0 is the natural supply and demand equilibrium quantity of housing. By moving the markets to H', the tax breaks generate deadweight losses in the housing market. The essence of the problem is that in the housing market, houses are being supplied whose true marginal value, as measured by D_H, is less than their marginal cost, as measured by S_H. The second efficiency cost is that income taxes themselves tend to generate deadweight losses, and the losses rise with the square of the tax rate. If all the exclusions and deductions were removed from federal income tax, the tax base would be approximately twice as large. This means that the government could raise the same amount of revenue with a set of tax rates at only half their current values. With deadweight loss a function of the square of the tax rates, the deadweight loss from income tax would decrease by approximately three-fourths of its current value.

The equity cost of the exclusions and deductions is a potential violation of vertical equity. Returning to our example, housing markets tend to segment by income. Also, higher income people face higher marginal tax rates than lower income people with graduated tax rates. Therefore, the three tax breaks are worth more in tax savings to higher income people than to lower income people, which implies that the post-tax-break housing prices and rents fall more for higher income people than for lower income people. In other words, the three tax breaks reverse somewhat the progressivity of the tax embodied in the graduated rate schedule. This may offend people's sense of vertical equity.

The reduction of progressivity is inherent in all the exclusions and deductions with graduated tax rates. Consider as another example the deduction allowed for contributions to charity. The net price of giving $1 to a charity is $1(1 – t), where t is the marginal tax rate that applies to the donor. For example, every dollar given to charity by taxpayers in the 33% tax bracket saves them 33 cents in taxes because the charitable deduction lowers their taxable income by $1. The net price of the gift is 67 cents (= 1 – .33 = 1 – t). The higher the taxpayer's income, the higher is t, and the greater the value of the tax deduction.

One way to avoid the loss of progressivity is to use tax credits rather than exclusions or deductions to promote certain activities. A *tax credit* is given as a percentage of a taxpayer's tax liability. For example, a 10% tax credit reduces the taxes owed by 10%. But the 10% credit applies to all taxpayers, and is therefore independent of a person's income and tax bracket.

A tax credit leads to a proportionate reduction of taxes owed for all taxpayers because it is taken "below the line," after the tax liability on the taxpayer's taxable income is computed. In contrast, an exclusion or deduction reduces the taxes owed more than proportionally with income under a graduated rate structure because it is taken "above the line," reducing taxable income before the tax liability is computed.

The federal government has moved increasingly to tax credits in recent years. Nonetheless, the combined effect of all the existing exclusions and deductions removes much of the progressivity of the tax over the higher income ranges that would otherwise occur with the graduated tax rates.

A final difficulty with exclusions and deductions is that they can be an excessively costly way for the government to subsidize favored activities. A good example is the interest exclusion on state and local (municipal) bonds. It subsidizes state and local governments by lowering the interest payments on their debt. For example, suppose that the interest rate on a taxable bond, such as a corporate bond, is 10%, so that the annual interest on a $1,000 taxable bond is $100. (Bonds usually have a face value or principal of $1,000.) Suppose, also, that taxpayers in the 25% tax bracket and above buy the municipals. Taxpayers in the 25% tax bracket are indifferent between receiving $100 of interest on a $1,000 taxable bond and paying 25%, or $25 in taxes, and receiving $75 of interest tax free on a $1,000 municipal bond. They receive $75 in interest in either case. Therefore, assume that the interest rate on a municipal bond is 7.5%, three-quarters of the taxable bond rate. The subsidy to a state and local government by being able to issue a $1,000 tax-free municipal bond instead of having to issue a $1,000 taxable bond is $25, the saving on the interest payment ($100 interest at 10% versus $75 interest at 7.5%). The problem, though, is that taxpayers in the 28%, 33%, and 35% tax brackets also want to purchase the municipal bonds. If they purchase a $1,000 taxable bond, they would pay $28, $33, and $35 dollars in taxes, respectively, on the $100 interest, leaving them with $72, $67, and $65 after tax. Accepting the $75 of interest on a tax-free $1,000 municipal is a better deal for them. But it is a bad deal for the federal government, because the government has to sacrifice more than $25 in tax revenue from taxpayers in the top three brackets to offer a $25 interest subsidy to the state and local governments. Better to offer a $25 grant-in-aid directly to these governments, paid for with an additional $25 in taxes. The grant-in-aid would lower the total tax revenue the government has to collect, thereby lowering the deadweight loss from the income tax.

For charitable deductions, the issue is the price elasticity of demand for charitable contributions. If the elasticity is greater than one, then a 35% reduction in the price of charity for taxpayers in the top tax bracket generates more than a 35% increase in charitable giving. The government loses 35 cents for each dollar given to charity, but the overall giving to charity rises by more than 35 cents. In contrast, if the elasticity is less than one, then the government loses more in tax revenue than the increase in charitable giving.

In conclusion, the common perception that exclusions and deductions give rise to horizontal inequities is not correct, according to the utility version of horizontal equity. Nonetheless, one could argue that the gains in efficiency and vertical equity from removing these loopholes may well be worth the temporary pattern of horizontal inequities that would result. True, the supported activities would no longer be subsidized, but direct subsidies are usually the better option anyway if Congress wants to support these activities.

THE FAVORED TREATMENT OF CAPITAL GAINS

As noted earlier, federal personal income tax favors capital gains in two ways relative to the Haig–Simons standard. The maximum tax rate on capital gains is 15% (2005) and capital gains are taxed only when they are realized (an asset is sold) rather than year by year as the gains accrue. The reduced tax rates are typically justified by the need to stimulate saving, even though there is little evidence that personal saving in the United States responds much, if at all, to increases in after-tax rates of return. The failure to tax capital gains until assets are sold is typically justified by the need for symmetrical treatment of financial and real assets. The accrued gains (losses) each year on financial assets are easy to keep track of, but not so the accrued gains (losses) on many kinds of real assets. How much did that painting hanging in the den increase in value last year? How much value did the house gain or lose? It is impossible to know for sure unless the painting or the house is sold. The gains (losses) on the real assets could be estimated each year for tax purposes, with an adjustment when the asset is sold. But then taxpayers may be forced to sell the asset to pay the tax on an accrued gain, and people tend to view this as unfair. The problems with evaluating real assets appear to be decisive in the United States; Congress has never seriously considered taxing capital gains on an accrued basis.

The failure to tax capital gains on an accrued basis is, in effect, an exclusion from the tax base relative to the Haig–Simons ideal, with the same efficiency and equity effects as the exclusions and deductions from personal income. It distorts capital markets by favoring assets whose returns come in the form of capital gains. It also reduces the progressivity of the tax system. Taxing capital gains on a realized instead of an accrued basis places the government in the position of giving interest-free loans to taxpayers, and the value of the loans rises as income rises with graduated tax rates.

To see the interest-free loan, suppose that a taxpayer in the 25% tax bracket buys an asset for $100 and holds it for two years. Assume for simplicity that the value of the asset grows by 100% per year over the two years: It would become $200 at the end of year 1 and $400 in year 2 without any tax.

With the tax levied on a realized basis, the taxpayer pays the tax at the end of year 2. The capital gain over the two years is $300 (= $400 – $100). The 25% tax on the $300 gain is $75, leaving the taxpayer with $325 after tax (= $400 – $75) at the end of year 2.

If the asset were taxed on an accrued basis, the $100 capital gain at the end of the first year would be taxed ($100 = $200 – $100). The tax at a rate of 25% is $25, leaving the taxpayer with $175 net of tax ($200 – $25). The $175 then doubles in value to $350 by the end of year 2. The taxpayer pays a tax of $43.75 in year 2, 25% of the $175 capital gain (43.75 = .25 · $175). The value of the asset net of tax at the end of year 2 is $306.25 (= $350 – $43.75), which is $18.75 less than the value of the asset net of tax when the asset is taxed on a realized basis ($325 – $306.25 = $18.75).

The increased value to the asset holder by taxing on a realized basis results from not having to pay the $25 in tax on the capital gain in the first year. The $25 is in effect an interest-free loan from the government at the end of year 1. To see this, assume that the government did lend the taxpayer $25 at the end of year 1, and required repayment of the $25 at the end of year 2, but no interest. The taxpayer would invest the proceeds of the loan in an asset yielding 100%, so that the value of the asset doubles to $50 at the end of year 2. The gain on the loan-financed asset during the second period is $25 ($50 – $25), on which the taxpayer pays a tax of $6.25 (= .25 · $25). The taxpayer also returns the original $25 loan to the government at the end of year 2, without interest. The sum of the tax payment and the loan repayment is $31.25 (= $6.25 + $25), which leaves the taxpayer with $18.75 (= $50.00 – $31.25), exactly the tax saving from paying taxes on a realized rather than an accrued basis.

The value of the interest-free loan, and the tax saving, rises with the tax rate in the range of tax rates from 10% to 35%, because the avoided tax is higher in the first period the higher the tax rate. Therefore, taxpayers with higher income receive larger loans, which reduces the progressivity of the tax.

INFLATION AND THE TAXATION OF INCOME FROM CAPITAL

According to the Haig–Simons standard, the tax base should be adjusted for inflation to prevent real tax liabilities from varying with the rate of inflation. In fact, the U.S. federal personal income tax is only partially adjusted for inflation. The main items that are indexed to the CPI are the income limits of the tax brackets, personal exemptions, and standard deductions. The most important omission is the failure to protect income from capital from inflation.

Income from capital needs special protection from inflation because inflation has two effects on capital but only a single effect on wages. The return to capital is a product of the value of the asset, a stock variable, and the rate of return on the asset, a flow variable, and inflation affects both variables. In contrast, a wage or salary is affected only once by inflation since it is a single flow variable. Consequently, income from capital is taxed more heavily than wage income if it is not indexed for inflation.

The first effect of inflation on capital is that the nominal value of assets rises by the cumulative amount of inflation since the assets were purchased. If prices have doubled in the past 10 years, then the value of houses will also double in value, on average, as will the value of financial stocks. Bonds are also affected by inflation because it will take $2,000 in loans to buy a machine that cost $1,000 10 years ago. And so on.

The cumulative effect of expected inflation on the value of assets corresponds to the cumulative effect of inflation on wages, since nominal or observed wages also rise over time with the expected rate of inflation. When managers and workers bargain over wage contracts, they base their labor demands and supplies on the real wage, W/P, not the nominal wage. Therefore, if an inflationary process doubles the price level over a five-year period, then wages should also double to maintain the real wage. Real wages should rise approximately with the increase in labor productivity over time, but not as a result of general inflation.

The second effect of inflation on the return to capital is its effect on the rate of return. Assume for the moment that there is no income tax. In this case, the annual rate of return to capital rises point for point with the expected annual inflation.[9] To see why, think of two people or institutions engaged in a borrower–lender relationship, which is how many financial securities come into being (for example corporate and government bonds, home mortgages, and bank deposits). Suppose in a world without inflation, a one-year loan contract worth $1,000 would have an interest rate (rate of return) of 5%. The lender is willing to part with $1,000 today if she receives the $1,050 back in one year, the original $1,000 loan plus 5% on the $1,000 (.05·$1,000 = $50). The borrower is willing to pay the 5% interest if he agrees to the loan. Suppose, instead, that both the borrower and lender expect the rate of inflation over the coming year to be 10%. In this case, the lender will insist on an interest rate of 15% to make the loan. She wants a 5% increase in purchasing power one year from now, but with 10% inflation, she will need an interest rate of 10% just to protect the purchasing power of her $1,000. She expects that it will take $1,100 one year from now to buy what $1,000 buys today. So she adds the 10% inflation to the loan rate to achieve a 5% increase in purchasing power one year from now, and requires an interest rate of 15% to make the loan.[10] The borrower also thinks in terms of the purchasing power he has to sacrifice one year from now to take out the loan today. He knows that an interest rate of 15% when inflation is expected to be 10% involves the same sacrifice of purchasing power one year from now as an interest rate of 5% when there is no expected inflation. So he accepts the 15% interest rate on the loan.

The effect of inflation on expected returns to capital when there is no income tax is summarized by the Fisher equation, named after economist Irving Fisher:

$$i = r + \left(\frac{\Delta P}{P}\right)_E$$

where i is the nominal or observed interest rate (rate of return), r is the real interest rate (rate of return) that measures the increase in purchasing power, and $\left(\frac{\Delta P}{P}\right)_E$ is the expected rate of inflation. The nominal or observed rate of return on an asset rises point for point with the expected rate of inflation.

There is no further effect of inflation on wages that corresponds to the effect of inflation on the rate of return to capital.[11] Consequently, if neither income from capital nor wages are indexed for inflation, income from capital is taxed more heavily than wage income.

The way to protect capital income from inflation depends on the form that the returns take. We saw earlier that for assets whose earnings are in the form of capital gains, such as houses and stocks, the purchase price of the asset should be increased by the cumulative inflation, since the asset was bought before subtracting it from the sales price to compute the taxable capital gain. For interest-bearing assets, the rate of inflation should be subtracted from the nominal or observed interest rate in computing taxable interest income (assuming that the expected and actual annual inflation rate is the same over a time horizon of one year or less).[12] This adjustment follows from the without-tax Fisher equation. If the real rate of return before tax is r, then the real rate of return after tax at rate t should be r(1 − t). From the Fisher equation, $r = i - \left(\frac{\Delta P}{P}\right)_E$ without a tax. Therefore $r(1 - t) = (1 - t)\left[i - \left(\frac{\Delta P}{P}\right)_E\right]$. Taxable interest should be net of the annual rate of inflation.

Instead, the entire nominal or observed interest income is subject to tax. Suppose the nominal interest rate continues to adjust point for point with inflation. Then, from the Fisher equation, the real rate of return after tax is $r = i(1 - t) - \left(\frac{\Delta P}{P}\right)_E$; the real after-tax rate of return is less than r(1 − t). For example, if i = 16%, r = 4%, $\left(\frac{\Delta P}{P}\right)_E = 12\%$, and the tax rate is 25%, then the proper after-tax real return is r(1 − t) = 4%(.75) = 3%. The real after-tax rate of return would be 3% if $\left(\frac{\Delta P}{P}\right)_E$ were subtracted from i in computing taxable interest income: [.75(16% − 12%) = .75·4% = 3%]. But with all of the nominal interest subject to tax, i(1 − t) = 16(.75) = 12%, and $r = i(1 - t) - \left(\dfrac{\Delta P}{P}\right)_E = 12\% - 12\% = 0.$

The real after-tax rate is zero. Income from capital is too heavily taxed. Furthermore, the real rate of return after tax fluctuates with the rate of inflation, whereas it should always be 3%. For example, if the inflation rate were to rise 4% to 16% and the nominal interest rate also rose by 4% to 20%, then taxing all the nominal interest leads to a real rate of

return of $r = i(1 - t) - \left(\dfrac{\Delta P}{P}\right)_E = 20\%(.75) - 16\% = 15\% - 16\% = -1\%.$[13]

These examples are indicative of the heavy tax burden that income from capital bears when inflation rates are high. In the late 1970s, when inflation reached double digits in the United States, the real after-tax rates of return on many assets were negative. Wage earners suffered no such heavy burden since the tax brackets, personal exemptions, and standard deductions were indexed to inflation.

GRADUATED TAX RATES

Congress chose graduated tax rates over a single flat tax to increase the progressivity of income tax. But graduated rates raise a number of concerns that would not arise under a flat tax. We have already discussed one of them, that exclusions and deductions from the ideal Haig–Simons tax base inherently reduce the progressivity of the tax implied by the graduated rates because they are worth proportionately more to higher income taxpayers.

INCOME AVERAGING

Another concern is the need to allow taxpayers to average their incomes over time to preserve horizontal equity. Consider two taxpayers, one whose income is constant and the other whose income fluctuates widely. Person #1 has taxable income of $50,000 per year over two years and person #2 has taxable income of zero in the first year and $100,000 in the second year. Since both earn $100,000 over a two-year period, horizontal equity requires that their tax payments be the same over the two years.[14] With graduated tax rates, however, person #2 is likely to pay much higher taxes over the two years. For example, under the 2005 tax structure, person #1 would pay $8,415 in taxes each year, whereas person #2 would pay $19,706.50 in year 2, or $2,876.50 more tax over the two-year period: ($2,876.50 = $19,706.50 − 2 × $8,415 = $19,706.50 − $16,830). The way to correct for this is to allow person #2 to compute his tax liability in year 2 by averaging his income over the two years, so that he is assumed to have taxable income of $50,000 in each year. The United States used to allow income averaging over a number of years but no longer does so. Therefore, taxpayers with highly variable incomes are at a disadvantage.

THE MARRIAGE PENALTY

A within-in year version of the averaging problem is the so-called marriage penalty, which is a perennial issue in the United States. It arises from a combination of the graduated tax rates and the government's indecision over whether to tax on an individual or a family basis. The government wants to give a tax break to married couples so, as we have seen, it allows them to file jointly using a widened set of tax brackets relative to those that apply to single taxpayers.

When the option of filing jointly was instituted, the government had in mind the typical family at the time in which the husband worked and the wife either worked part time or not at all, so that the husband usually had by far the higher income, and often the only income. Widening the tax brackets somewhat gave married couples with very different incomes a tax break relative to a single taxpayer with the same income as the combined incomes of the couple. The break was justified by the greater needs of families relative to single individuals.

The advent of two-earner couples changed the view of this policy from a tax break to a tax penalty. When two people with similar incomes marry, filing jointly can increase their tax liability relative to their combined tax liabilities if they had remained single and filed separately. This happens because the filing jointly tax brackets are not twice as wide as the filing separately tax brackets after the first two brackets. Consequently, combining their incomes pushes the couple into a higher tax bracket than if they were able to file separately and pay taxes on their own incomes.[15]

For example, compare the following situations for two high-income couples with $800,000 in taxable income under the 2005 tax rates and brackets. First couple: one spouse has $800,000 of taxable income and the other has no taxable income. Second couple: both spouses have $400,000 of taxable income. The first couple is the one that Congress had in mind; they gain about a $6,000 advantage relative to if they were single and filing separately. They gain because much more of the $800,000 is taxed at lower rates with the wider brackets. In contrast, the second couple suffers approximately a $13,000 penalty by marrying and filing jointly. They lose because more of their combined income is subject to higher tax rates. The pattern in this example is inescapable with graduated rates and different tax brackets for married couples and single taxpayers. Spouses with quite different incomes tend to gain from filing jointly and spouses with similar incomes tend to lose. The problem is avoided only by taxing on an individual basis so that it does not matter whether people marry or not. All family members would continue to pay taxes on their individual incomes with a single set of tax brackets. The only other way to avoid a marriage penalty is to have a single flat-rate tax.

TAX CONSUMPTION RATHER THAN INCOME?

As noted in Chapter 13, many economists favor replacing the federal personal income tax with a personal consumption tax. The Reagan administration seriously considered switching to a personal consumption tax in its deliberations leading up to the Tax Reform Act of 1986, the largest single reform ever of the federal personal income tax. But in the end, the administration decided to stick with the income tax.

The Treasury Department proposed a virtual textbook version of an income tax. It asked Congress to remove almost all the exclusions and deductions so that taxable income would approximate Haig–Simons income except for personal exemptions, which would be retained (U.S. Department of the Treasury, 1984). Congress agreed with the administration about retaining the income tax, but decided in the end to keep most of the existing exclusions and deductions. Nonetheless, many economists and politicians continue to support some form of consumption tax, either a personal consumption tax or a national sales tax, to replace the personal income tax. We will discuss the personal consumption tax since it would remain a tax on individuals. A national sales tax would be levied on businesses and represent a more radical departure from personal income tax.

There are three points to keep in mind in thinking about replacing the personal income tax with a personal consumption tax. The first is the rather dramatic trade-off between efficiency and equity that would be involved, at least in principle. The second is a whole host of administrative issues to be resolved in switching to a personal consumption tax. And the third is the hybrid nature of the current U.S. federal personal income tax; it already has many features of a consumption tax.

███████ THE EFFICIENCY–EQUITY TRADE-OFF

Economists usually compare the efficiency and equity implications of tax reforms by building simple, perfectly competitive, OLG models of the economy, of the kind we used in Chapter 12 to analyze the macroeconomic effects of the Social Security system. The models are adapted to include different kinds of broad-based taxes, and simulated over a very long period of time, often 150 time periods covering many generations. Thus, they are particularly well suited to analyzing the impact of various tax reforms on long-run economic growth. The taxes analyzed are typically represented in their idealized forms, such as an income tax whose tax base is Haig–Simons income.

Taxes influence the long-run growth of an economy through their effects on saving, investment, the evolution of the capital stock over time, and factor productivity.

The effects on these variables of switching from an (ideal) income tax to an (ideal) consumption tax are nothing short of astonishing in these simple OLG models. By removing saving from the tax base, saving and investment eventually increase substantially, leading to a much larger capital stock and a much more productive economy. The result is that output and consumption per person in the new long-run equilibrium are higher by 10% per year and even more in many of these OLG models.[16] Ten percent of U.S. output is $1.2 trillion (2005), an increase in output of $4,000 per person per year, a truly enormous dynamic efficiency gain for the economy.

There is one drawback to this reform, however, a troubling equity issue: The current elderly generation at the time of the switch to a personal consumption tax suffers huge losses. The problem for the elderly is that their savings for retirement over their working lifetimes were already taxed twice under personal income tax. Their savings were undertaken with after-tax dollars and then the returns to their savings were taxed each year (recall the example from Chapter 13). Had the income tax remained, they would have been able to draw down their savings tax free to support their consumption during the retirement years. With the switch to a personal consumption tax, however, they are taxed a third time as they consume their retirement savings.

Societies are going to be reluctant to penalize their current elderly in this way, especially the United States. Over the last half of the twentieth century, the federal government substantially expanded its support of the elderly, primarily through increases in Social Security pensions and the establishment of Medicare. As a result, the poverty rate of the elderly fell considerably during this time; it was much higher than the national average in 1960 when the federal government first measured poverty, and then became less than the national average by about 1990. U.S. citizens do not want to reverse these gains, which may be the primary reason why the personal consumption tax has not been adopted despite its enormous efficiency gains.

There appears to be no way out of this efficiency–equity dilemma. Auerbach et al. (2001) experimented with various ways to lessen the burden on the elderly when switching to a personal consumption tax. They concluded that the burden could be reduced, but only by removing most of the dynamic efficiency advantages of the personal consumption tax.

ADMINISTRATIVE ISSUES

There are always a number of difficult administrative issues associated with any large tax reform. We will highlight a few that have figured prominently in the public debate on replacing a personal income tax with a personal consumption tax.

A reduction in complexity?

Tax reformers are almost always looking for ways to reduce the complexity of tax systems. Unfortunately, taxes invariably become complicated when they tax income from capital, largely because of the many different forms that assets and their returns can take. At the very least, taxpayers often face a considerable compliance burden of keeping accurate records of their income from capital. A personal consumption tax would appear to have a big administrative advantage over a personal income tax because savings are not taxed, but the gains on this score are illusory. The problem is that a personal consumption tax would likely be operated on a cash flow basis, with the tax base – consumption – computed as a residual. Asking taxpayers to keep track of their consumption directly would require a daily recording of all their consumption transactions, an exceedingly burdensome task.

Instead, taxpayers would be asked to keep records of their proceeds from all sources such as income and loans, and all forms of saving undertaken from these proceeds. The savings would include any purchases of assets and any returns on existing assets that are allowed to accrue as additional saving, which is an important component of income from capital. Consumption would then be computed as the difference between a taxpayer's proceeds and savings, and would be taxed. These are virtually the same set of records that taxpayers are required to keep under an income tax; only the computation of the tax base is different. Hence, switching to a personal consumption tax would not appreciably reduce the complexities of complying with the tax laws.

Is a personal consumption tax regressive?

Some people oppose consumption taxes because they believe that they are regressive. The ratio of households' consumption to income falls as income rises within any one year, so that a tax on consumption would appear to be a regressive tax if viewed on an annual basis. We will consider this issue more closely in Chapter 19 on tax incidence. For now it is enough to note that a personal consumption tax need not be regressive at all even if it is viewed on an annual basis. The government can institute a graduated schedule of tax rates on consumption just as it does on income, so that higher income taxpayers pay proportionately more in consumption taxes than lower income taxpayers. A graduated rate structure may cause difficulties for young people who are borrowing to increase their consumption as they make their lifetime consumption plans. But the point is that a personal consumption tax can be highly progressive if that is what society wants.

The taxation of real assets

A personal consumption tax does have one advantage over a personal income tax in the taxation of the consumption and income streams that arise from the purchase of real assets. The advantage lies in a difference in perspective. Proponents of an income tax take an annual view of taxation and want taxes to reflect the actual income earned by taxpayers in each year. That is, their view of the tax base is an ex-post view – tax the actual income flows that occurred during the year. Proponents of a personal consumption tax take a lifetime view of taxation. As such, they are willing to tax today on the basis of expected outcomes rather than actual outcomes over time, an ex-ante view of taxation. This is a particular advantage in the taxation of real assets.

Consider the purchase of a house as an example. In purchasing a house, the taxpayer is engaging in an act of saving to buy a real asset that yields a stream of housing services each year for as long as the person expects to live in the house. Under a personal income tax, the stream of housing services is viewed as imputed rent and should be taxed each year as part of Haig–Simons income. Under a personal consumption tax, the stream of housing services is viewed as part of imputed consumption and should also be taxed each year. But housing services are difficult to estimate, so the IRS has refrained from taxing them under the income tax. They are obviously just as difficult to estimate if the United States switches to a personal consumption tax, but now the government has an option. If the market for houses is in equilibrium, then the purchase price of a house equals the expected stream of housing services over time (discounted to present value).[17] Under an ex-ante perspective on taxation, therefore, it makes no difference whether the initial investment in the house or the stream of housing services is taxed. In other words, the government has the option of forcing taxpayers to prepay the tax on all real assets.

Therefore, for housing, the choice under a personal consumption tax is:

1. *Standard option:* Allow the taxpayer to deduct the purchase price of the house (a form of saving), and pay a tax on the imputed consumption of housing services each year (difficult to estimate).
2. *Prepayment option:* Do not allow the taxpayer to deduct the purchase price of the house (the saving is taxable), and do not tax the imputed consumption of housing services each year.

The two options are equivalent from an ex-ante perspective. In fact, taxpayers could elect the prepayment option (2) for financial assets as well.

People often borrow to finance assets, especially houses.[18] The treatment of borrowing and repaying the debt service (principal and interest) over time would be subject to the same options as the treatment of the assets that the loans finance under a personal consumption tax. To see this, consider an example in which a taxpayer borrows the entire purchase price of the house, and the repayment of principal and interest exactly matches the stream of the consumption of housing services over time. In this case, there is never any net consumption and thus there should be no tax. The initial proceeds of the loan match the saving represented by the purchase of the house. They are not available for consumption. And the consumption of housing services over time is matched by the saving represented by the repaying of the loan (reducing outstanding debt is an act of saving), so that net consumption is zero. Therefore, the two options above with debt financing become:

1'. *Standard option:* Allow the taxpayer to deduct the purchase price of the house from the tax base and count the loan proceeds as part of the tax base; count the imputed consumption of housing services each year as part of the tax base but deduct the debt service from the tax base.
2'. *Prepayment option:* Do not allow the taxpayer to deduct the purchase price of the house (the saving is taxable) and do not count the loan proceeds as part of the tax base; do not tax the imputed housing services each year and do not allow the deduction of debt service each year.

The two options are again equivalent from an ex-ante perspective.

Tax bequests or inheritance?

An issue that must be decided in switching to a personal consumption tax is whether to consider a bequest as the final act of consumption of the deceased or as a source of proceeds for the heirs. In the former case, the bequest is taxed in full at the time of death at the tax rate applicable to the deceased. In the latter case, the proceeds are taxed only if the heirs choose to consume them. The issue here turns on whether the government wants to tax on an individual or a family basis, an issue that the United States has never fully resolved. Taxing the bequest at the time of death is consistent with the individual perspective, in which the bequest is the final act of consumption of the deceased individual and completes her economic life. Counting the bequest as proceeds of the heirs is consistent with the family perspective, since consumption by the family unit occurs only when the heirs consume the bequest.

▆▆▆▆▆ THE HYBRID PERSONAL INCOME TAX

The OLG models compare the economic effects of an ideal personal income tax, whose tax base is Haig–Simons income, with an ideal personal consumption tax, whose tax base is an individual taxpayer's entire consumption. Whether these comparisons tell us all that much about the actual effects of switching from an income to a consumption tax is questionable, however, for two reasons. One is that the current federal personal income tax is far from the Haig–Simons ideal, as we have seen. The other is that we can almost be certain that the consumption tax would not be an ideal personal consumption tax. Regarding the existing income tax, it happens to be a hybrid version of the two pure taxes. It contains a number of features that are consistent with a personal consumption tax rather than an income tax. The two most important features are the taxation of savings for retirement and the purchase of a house.

As we have seen, any purchases of assets that are designed to provide income for retirement, whether undertaken by individuals or their employers on their behalf, are deductible from income. In addition, the returns on these retirement assets are also untaxed, provided they are used to purchase more of the assets. Examples are IRAs and 401K accounts. These assets are taxable only when they are sold during the retirement years or converted into pensions. This is exactly how they would be treated under a pure consumption tax, providing that the proceeds from the sales or pensions are consumed rather than saved.

Housing is currently taxed as it would be under prepayment option (2') of a personal consumption tax, with one exception: The interest portion of the debt service on a mortgage is deductible under the income tax. Suppose a new personal consumption tax retained the mortgage interest deduction for political reasons. Then the switch to a personal consumption tax would not make all that much difference to the majority of taxpayers, including many of the current elderly. Their wealth consists mainly of financial retirement assets and/or housing, and the tax treatment of these two assets would not change. Therefore, switching to a personal consumption tax may not have much effect on savings, investment, and long-run economic growth, nor impose large costs on many of the current elderly. The great trade-off between efficiency and equity in this particular tax reform may exist more in principle than in fact, at least in the United States.[19]

Taxes and Inefficiency: the Excess Burden of Taxation

When Adam Smith and John Stuart Mill introduced the notion of taxes as a necessary evil, they meant that taxpayers have to be willing to sacrifice for the common good. They have to be content with the knowledge that their taxes allow the government to provide a wide range of socially desirable goods and services that markets might not otherwise supply. This is so even if certain individuals disagree with some of the goods and services being provided – they still have to pay their taxes. The Smith/Mill sacrifice principle was in contrast to the long-standing tradition at the time of the benefits-received principle of taxation, in which tax payments are directly linked to the receipt of specific benefits from the government.

Taxes are a necessary evil in a narrower economic sense as well. The taxes that governments actually use invariably introduce inefficiencies into an economy. As a result, taxes impose an excess burden on individuals: Their loss in utility from paying taxes exceeds the direct loss in utility from the tax payments themselves. Economists refer to this excess burden as the *deadweight loss* from taxation. The goal of efficiency as it relates to taxation, then, takes on the negative slant of reducing the inefficiency as much as possible. Specifically, *the efficiency goal is to raise a given amount of tax revenue with the minimum amount of excess burden or deadweight loss.*

Minimizing inefficiency is only half the problem in designing taxes, however. Taxes also have to be in accord with people's sense of equity. Taxes and transfer payments are the primary means of redistributing resources to promote society's goal of end-results equity or distributive justice. As we saw in Chapter 5, mainstream economists assume that society values equality over inequality. But we also saw that the more the government redistributes in the name of equality, the larger the efficiency losses from the taxes and transfers – recall Okun's leaky bucket. Therefore, the design of taxes ultimately involves a balancing act between the goals of promoting equality and reducing inefficiency.

Chapter 15 begins with an analysis of the excess burden of taxation. Chapter 16 then shows how to collect a given amount of tax revenue with minimum efficiency loss, and concludes with a discussion of the equity–inefficiency trade-off in taxation.

THE EXCESS BURDEN OF TAXATION

The excess burden of taxation is easily demonstrated with a very simple model of the consumer. Suppose an individual uses a fixed endowment of income, I, to consume two goods, X and Y, whose prices without any taxes are P_X and P_Y. Assume that $P_Y = 1$, so that units of Y are the same as dollars of income. The consumer's budget constraint is

$$P_X X + P_Y Y = I, \text{ or, with } P_Y = 1, P_X X + Y = I.$$

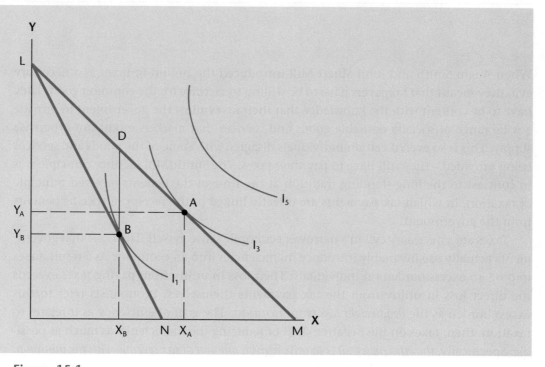

Figure 15.1

Refer to Figure 15.1. The consumer's preferences or utility are represented by the indifference curves I_1, I_3, I_5. The without-tax budget line is LM and has a slope of $(-)P_X$. The consumer is in equilibrium at point A, the point of tangency between the budget line and indifference curve I_3, and consumes (X_A, Y_A).

Suppose the government levies an excise tax at rate t on the consumption of X. The tax can be either an ad valorem or a per-unit tax. An *ad valorem* tax is specified as a percentage of the price, for example a 5% tax on hotel rooms or restaurant meals. General sales taxes are also ad valorem taxes. In our example, an ad valorem tax would raise the price of X to the consumer to $P_X(1 + t)$, with the tax equal to tP_X on each unit of

X. A *per-unit* tax is a tax on each unit of output, such as the federal and state excise taxes on a gallon of gasoline or a pack of cigarettes in the United States. In our example, a per-unit tax would raise the price of X to the consumer to $(P_X + t)$ on each unit of X. It makes no essential difference to the analysis of excess burden which form the tax takes. We will assume that the tax is an ad valorem tax, so that the price of X rises to $P_X(1 + t)$.

The higher price of X rotates the consumer's budget line inward along the X-axis to LN in Figure 15.1. The slope of the with-tax budget line is $(-)P_X(1 + t)$. The tax forces the consumer to a new equilibrium at point B, the point of tangency between the new budget line and indifference curve I_1. The consumer now consumes (X_B, Y_B). The tax paid by the consumer on X is DB, the vertical distance between the original and new budget lines at the new equilibrium point B.[1]

The tax has lowered the consumer's utility from the utility represented by indifference curve I_3 to the utility represented by indifference curve I_1. To see that this loss of utility is a burden to the consumer in excess of the taxes paid requires an income measure of the utility loss that can be compared directly with the taxes paid. The appropriate income measure is the parallel distance between the indifference curves I_3 and I_1. The parallel distance can be measured at any point along the curves, but the two standard and natural choices are at the old and new prices. Refer to Figure 15.2.

In Figure 15.2(a), the parallel distance is measured at the original, without-tax prices and is called the *Hicks' equivalent variation* (HEV).[2] It is the amount of lump-sum income the consumer would be willing to give up to return to the old prices, by the following argument. The tax places the consumer on indifference curve I_1 at point B on LN. Suppose the original, without-tax prices were restored, but in return the consumer had to give up income lump sum. If the consumer gave up no income, he would return to point A. By giving up income lump sum, however, point A is no longer attainable as the consumer's budget line shifts down parallel with the sacrifice of income. Still, the consumer is better off without the tax until the income sacrificed lump sum just equals the parallel distance between I_3 and I_1 measured at the original, without-tax prices. The consumer would be in equilibrium at point C on the dotted budget line OP. OP is parallel to LM. He is now indifferent between facing the new with-tax prices and facing the original, without-tax prices but sacrificing the income lump sum. He is on indifference curve I_1 in either case. Hence, the parallel distance between I_3 and I_1 measured at the original, without-tax price of X can be viewed as the income that the consumer would be willing to pay to have the tax removed. As such, it is an income measure of the consumer's loss in utility from the tax.

In Figure 15.2(b), the parallel distance is measured at the new, with-tax price of X and is called the *Hicks' compensating variation* (HCV). It is the amount of additional lump-sum income the consumer would require in compensation to be indifferent to paying the tax and facing the new with-tax price of X. The consumer was originally on indifference curve I_3 without the tax. Suppose the tax is imposed, but in return the consumer receives income lump sum to compensate for the tax. If the consumer received no income in compensation, he would be on indifference curve I_1 at point B. By giving him income lump sum, the consumer can achieve higher indifference curves than I_1. If he receives lump-sum income equal to the parallel distance between I_3 and I_1 measured at the new, with-tax price of X, he would be in equilibrium on I_3 at point F on dotted line QR. QR is parallel to LN. He is now indifferent between facing the original, without-tax price of X and the new with-tax price of X with the additional lump-sum income as compensation. He is on indifference curve I_3 in either case. Hence, the parallel distance between I_3 and I_1 measured at the new, with-tax price of X can be viewed as the compensation required by the consumer to offset the harm caused him by the tax. As such, it is a second valid income measure of the consumer's loss in utility from the tax.

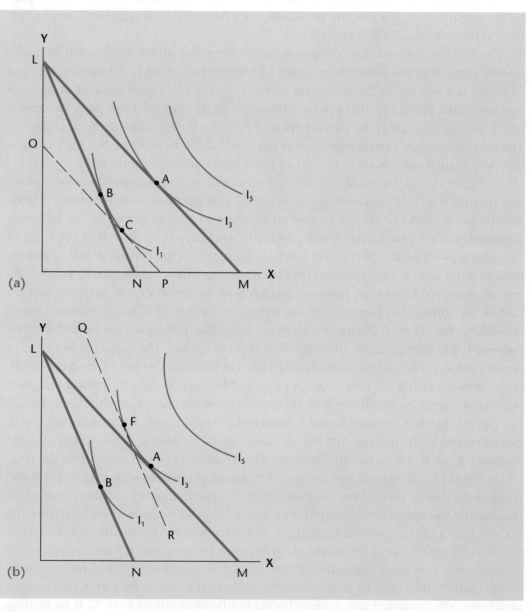

Figure 15.2

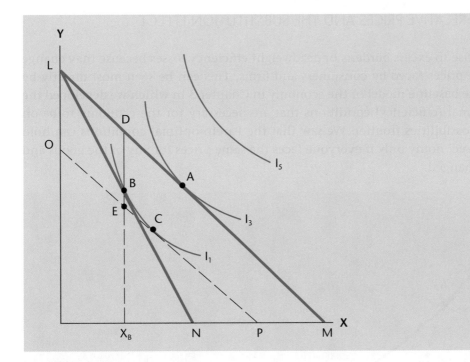

Figure 15.3

Either income measure of utility loss can be used to indicate the excess burden of the tax. We will choose the HEV because it can be compared directly with the actual tax revenues paid. Refer to Figure 15.3, which reproduces the without- and with-tax equilibria from Figure 15.1. The taxes paid by the consumer, as before, are given by line segment DB. But the HEV is the parallel distance between I_3 and I_1 at the original, without-tax price of X, the vertical distance DE measured at X_B. DE exceeds DB: The amount the consumer would be willing to pay to have the tax removed, the income measure of the utility loss, exceeds DB, the taxes paid. The distance BE is the *excess burden* from the tax, the loss in utility in excess of the direct loss in utility from the taxes paid, measured in terms of income. Alternatively, if the original, without-tax price of X were restored and the consumer received back the tax revenues DB, he could not return to I_3, the original utility level. He would need income equal to DE to return to I_3. The tax has clearly imposed a burden on the consumer in excess of the taxes paid.

The excess burden is the inefficiency or deadweight loss resulting from the tax. Of the total loss to the consumer equal to DE, the amount DB of taxes paid represents a transfer from the consumer to the government. But no one can recapture the loss in utility BE – it is simply a deadweight loss.

RELATIVE PRICES AND THE SUBSTITUTION EFFECT

Taxes give rise to excess burdens or deadweight efficiency losses because they change the relative prices faced by consumers and firms. This can be seen most directly by recalling the baseline model of the economy in Chapter 3 in which we developed the Pareto-optimal (efficiency) conditions that are necessary for the economy to be on its utility possibilities frontier. We saw that the Pareto-optimal conditions can hold in a market economy only if everyone faces the same prices for any of the goods and factors exchanged.

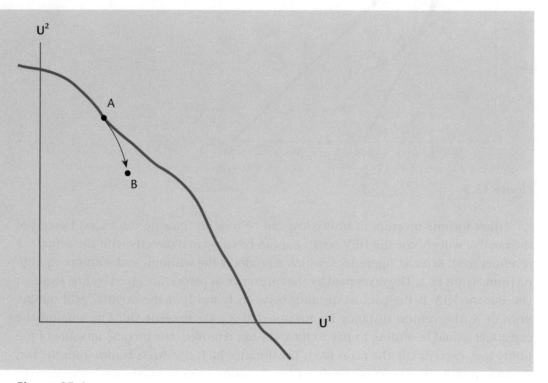

Figure 15.4

The problem with taxes is that they drive a wedge between the prices faced by consumers and firms, which prevents one or more of the Pareto-optimal conditions from holding and forces the economy below its utility possibilities frontier. In terms of our two-good example above, the relevant Pareto-optimal condition is that the marginal rate of substitution between X and Y in consumption must equal the marginal rate of transformation between X and Y in production: $MRS_{X,Y} = MRT_{X,Y}$. If consumers and firms face the same prices P_X and P_Y, and markets are perfectly competitive, then the condition does hold. Individuals consume X and Y such that the $MRS_{X,Y} = P_X/P_Y$, and firms supply X and Y such that their $MRT_{X,Y} = P_X/P_Y$ (recall that the $MRT_{X,Y}$ is the ratio of marginal costs, MC_X/MC_Y). But an excise tax on X drives a wedge, equal to the amount of the tax, between the prices faced by consumers and firms. The relevant price of X to consumers is the price including the tax, or $P_X(1 + t)$. In contrast, the relevant price of X to firms is the price net of the tax, P_X, since firms have to send the taxes, tP_X, to the government. They are left with only P_X on each unit of X sold to pay their factors of production and earn a return to capital. Consequently, consumers equate their $MRS_{X,Y}$ to the relative prices $P_X(1 + t)/P_Y = P_X(1 + t)$ with $P_Y = 1$, and firms equate their $MRT_{X,Y}$ to $P_X/P_Y = P_X$. $MRS_{X,Y} \neq MRT_{X,Y}$ and the economy moves below its utility possibilities frontier, as illustrated in Figure 15.4. The tax has introduced an inefficiency or deadweight loss in terms of lost utility that cannot be recovered.

The substitution effect

That the change in relative prices generates the deadweight loss from a tax implies that the substitution effect is the source of the loss. To see this, return to our simple consumer model and refer to Figure 15.5, which reproduces the before- and after-tax equilibria from Figure 15.1. The tax increases the price of X to the consumer and reduces the consumer's quantity demanded of X from X_A to X_B. Recall that economists divide the change in the quantity demanded that results from a change in the price of a good into an income effect and a substitution effect. The two effects are pictured in Figure 15.5. They combine to bring the consumer from point A on I_3 to point B on I_1.

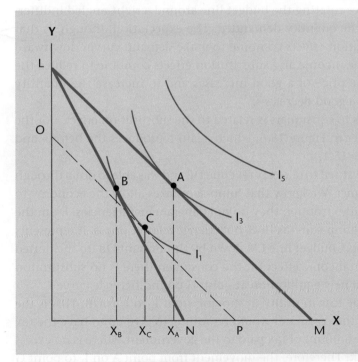

Figure 15.5

The income effect is an absolute price effect, also referred to as a purchasing power or real income effect. The increase in the price of X from P_X to $P_X(1 + t)$ reduces the consumer's purchasing power because he now has to spend more of his scarce income on each unit of X. It is equivalent to a reduction in the consumer's lump-sum income that would bring him to point C on the post-tax indifference curve I_1. Notice that C is to the left of A in Figure 15.5, indicating that X is a normal good. A decrease in the consumer's real income decreases the quantity of X demanded, from X_A to X_C. The income effect could be in the other direction, however. If X were an inferior good, then a decrease in real income increases the quantity demanded, and C would be to the right of A in Figure 15.5.

The substitution effect is a relative price effect. It says that consumers tend to substitute in favor of goods that have become relatively cheaper and away from goods that have become relatively more expensive. To isolate the substitution effect from the income effect, it is measured as a movement along a given indifference curve, such that utility is held constant. In Figure 15.5, the substitution effect of the increase in the price of X moves the consumer from point C on I_1 to point B on I_1, the after-tax equilibrium. Since the substitution effect is measured along one indifference curve, it is almost always negative in sign: An increase in the relative price of X lowers its quantity demanded and vice versa. B is to the left of C in Figure 15.5; the substitution effect further reduces the quantity of X demanded from X_C to X_B. The only exception would be if the indifference curves for X and Y were right-angled. In that case, the substitution effect would be zero, since rotating the budget line around a right-angled indifference curve does not change the quantity demanded. The expectation, though, is that both the income and substitution effects combine to make demand curves downward sloping. For normal goods, the income and substitution effects combine to reduce the quantity demanded when the price of a good increases and to increase the quantity demanded when the price of a good decreases.

The excess burden of taxes to consumers is related to the substitution effect, not the income effect. To see this, refer to Figure 15.6, which again reproduces the before- and after-tax equilibria from Figure 15.1.

Suppose the government wanted to raise tax revenue DB and was able to do so through a lump-sum tax on the consumer. We know that lump-sum taxes allow the economy to move along its utility possibilities frontier; they do not generate inefficiencies. From the consumer's point of view, the lump-sum tax does not change relative prices. It represents a parallel shift in the without-tax budget line LM down by the amount DB, to the dotted line ST. As such, it only has an income effect on the consumer; there is no substitution effect. The consumer reaches a new equilibrium at point G on indifference curve I_2.

The income measure of the loss in utility in moving from I_1 to I_2 is DB. This is the amount of lump-sum income the consumer would be willing to give up to have the tax removed. But DB is exactly the amount of tax paid to the government. There is no excess burden from the lump-sum tax. Therefore, the movement from point A on I_1 to point G on I_2 is the *unavoidable loss* from paying DB in taxes. Paying taxes clearly involves a loss of utility and DB is the measure of the burden of the tax payment. The burden can never be lower than the amount of taxes paid.

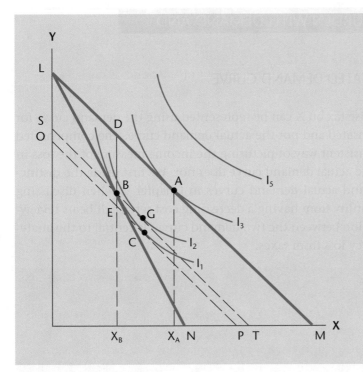

Figure 15.6

In contrast, the excise tax places the consumer on the lower indifference curve I_1 to raise taxes of DB from the consumer. The income measure of the consumer's loss is DE, larger than DB, the taxes paid. Relative to a lump-sum tax, the consumer bears an excess burden of BE, which is the *avoidable loss* in raising DB in taxes from the consumer. Moreover, the excess burden (avoidable burden) is entirely due to the substitution effect.

To see how the substitution effect generates the excess burden, suppose the government levied a lump-sum tax on the consumer that placed him on indifference curve I_1. The consumer would be on indifference curve I_1 at point C on the dotted budget line OP, and would pay an amount DE in taxes, the parallel distance between the without-tax (LM) and with-tax (OP) budget lines. As always with a lump-sum tax, the taxes paid would be equal to the income measure of the loss in utility from the tax. Because an excise tax is used, however, the price of X rises to the consumer and the substitution effect kicks in. The income effect of the price change is the move from A on I_3 to C on I_1. If that were the only effect, then there would be no excess burden from the tax. But the substitution effect then moves the consumer along I_1 from C to B. As it does, the amount of taxes paid drops, from DE at point C with the lump-sum tax to DB at point B with the excise tax. By further reducing the quantity demanded of X, the substitution effect lowers the taxes paid on X. But it does not lower the overall burden of the tax relative to an equal burden lump-sum tax because the consumer remains on I_1. Therefore, the taxes paid become less than the overall burden because of the substitution effect; there is an excess burden from the tax.

MEASURING EXCESS BURDEN WITH DEMAND AND SUPPLY CURVES

THE COMPENSATED DEMAND CURVE

The excess burden of the excise tax on X can be represented using the demand curve for X, providing it is the compensated and not the actual demand curve. The compensated demand curve provides a consistent way of picturing the income measure of the loss in utility from a tax, whereas the actual demand curve does not. We first made the distinction between compensated and actual demand curves in Chapter 9, when discussing how to measure the gain in utility from having a decreasing cost service. It bears reviewing here, because the distinction between the two demand curves is central to the analysis of the deadweight efficiency loss from taxes.

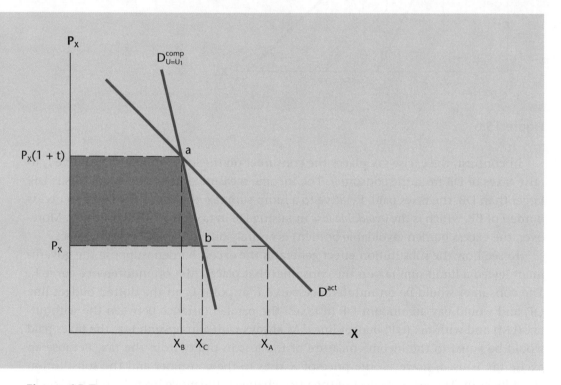

Figure 15.7

Figure 15.7 pictures the actual and compensated demand curves for X from our simple consumer model, and the with- and without-tax prices $P_X(1 + t)$ and P_X. The actual demand curve, D^{act}, shows the actual with- and without-tax equilibria from Figure 15.1. At $P_X(1 + t)$ the consumer wants to buy X_B; at P_X, the consumer wants to buy X_A. The compensated demand curve $D^{comp}_{U=U_1}$ is the amount of X demanded at each price, assuming that the consumer gives up income lump sum as prices decrease, or receives income lump sum as prices rise, to keep him at utility level U_1; U_1 corresponds to remaining on indifference curve I_1 in Figure 15.1. At the with-tax price, $P_X(1 + t)$, the consumer is on I_1 and wants to buy X_B. Since this is the actual with-tax equilibrium, the actual and compensated demand curves coincide at $(X_B, P_X(1 + t))$. The consumer would be willing to give up income lump sum to have lower prices, including the original without-tax level of P_X. The income given up at each price below $P_X(1 + t)$ is just enough to keep the consumer on I_1 and therefore at utility level U_1. But giving up income reduces the quantity of X demanded, assuming there is an income effect for X, so that the quantity of X demanded is less than on the actual demand curve. $D_{U=U_1}^{comp}$ lies to the left of D^{act} for all prices below $P_X(1 + t)$ (and to the right of D^{act} for all prices above $P_X(1 + t)$). The quantity demanded at P_X, along I_1 in Figure 15.6, is X_C, as shown on Figure 15.7. In other words, the quantities demanded along $D_{U=U_1}^{comp}$ reflect only the substitution effect of changes in the prices of X, whereas D^{act} reflects both the substitution and income effects. The two curves coincide only if there is no income effect for X.

The price along either demand curve equals the $MRS_{X,Y}$, the amount of Y that the consumer is willing to give up to consume one more unit of X. With $P_Y = 1$ as in our example, units of Y are the same as dollars of income. Therefore, the $MRS_{X,Y}$ indicates the income the consumer is willing to give up to consume one more unit of X, in the sense of being indifferent because she would receive the same utility from the trade of Y for X. Begin at the with-tax price $P_X(1 + t)$ and let the price drop to the without-tax price P_X in small increments that increase the quantity of X demanded by one unit. Each new price represents the income the consumer is willing to give up for that next unit of X.

The successive increments of income are comparable along $D_{U=U_1}^{comp}$ because the consumer is being held on the same indifference curve, the same level of utility. Therefore, the entire shaded area behind $D_{U=U_1}^{comp}$ to the price axis from $P_X(1 + t)$ to P_X, area $P_X(1 + t)abP_X$, is the amount of income the consumer would be willing to give up to have the price return to P_X from $P_X(1 + t)$. It corresponds to DE in Figure 15.6, the amount of income the consumer would be willing to pay to return to the without-tax price of X. It is a valid income measure of the utility loss from the tax. In contrast, the increments of income at each price along D^{act} are measured on different indifference curves, different utility levels, and therefore are not comparable measures of willingness to pay. Consequently, the area behind D^{act} to the price axis between $P_X(1 + t)$ and P_X is not a valid income measure of utility loss.[3]

Figure 15.8 illustrates the excess burden of the excise tax to the consumer using supply and demand curves. The supply curve, S, is assumed to be perfectly elastic at the without-tax price P_X. That is, the marginal cost is constant at P_X; firms must receive P_X to supply more units of X. The compensated demand curve is $D_{U=U_1}^{comp}$, indicating the quantity of X demanded, assuming that the consumer remains on indifference curve I_1 in Figure 15.6 (at utility level U_1). Because supply is perfectly elastic, the price rises from P_X to $P_X(1 + t)$ as above and the quantity demanded falls from X_C to X_B. Notice that the measure of excess burden uses the actual with- and without-tax prices but not the actual with- and without-tax quantities. The without-tax quantity demanded along D^{act} in Figure 15.7 is X_A, which is greater than

X_C. The income measure of the utility loss is the entire area behind $D_{U=U_1}^{comp}$ to the price axis from $P_X(1 + t)$ to P_X, area $P_X(1 + t)abP_X$. It corresponds to DE in Figure 15.6. The tax collected is area $P_X(1 + t)acP_X$, equal to $[P_X(1 + t) - P_X]X_B = tP_XX_B$, the actual tax paid by the consumer. It corresponds to DB in Figure 15.6. The excess burden is triangular area abc, the difference between the income measure of the utility loss from the tax and the tax paid. It corresponds to BE in Figure 15.6. Economists refer to area abc as the *deadweight loss triangle* resulting from the tax. It represents the portion of utility loss suffered by the consumer that is not captured by the government as tax revenue.

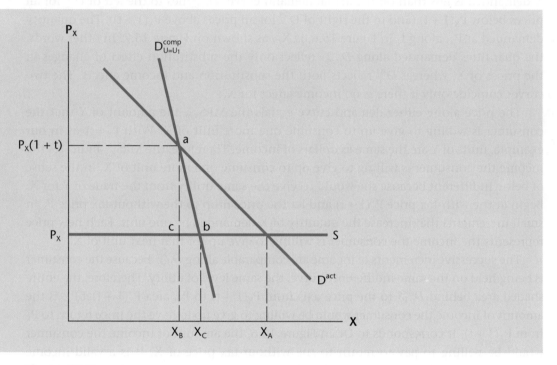

Figure 15.8

WHAT TO TAX?

The supply and demand analysis leads to a common prescription for tax policy: To reduce efficiency loss, tax goods and services (factors of production) whose demands (supplies) are inelastic. Ideally, the government would want to tax goods (factors) whose demands (supplies) are perfectly inelastic to avoid deadweight loss altogether. Figure 15.9 illustrates. It partially reproduces Figure 15.8, with the exception that the compensated demand curve $D_{U=U_1}^{comp}$ is vertical, that is, perfectly inelastic. This corresponds to the case in which the consumer's indifference curves are right-angled. There is no substitution effect of a price change.

The quantity of X demanded remains at X_C as the price rises from P_X to $P_X(1 + t)$. Consequently, the income measure of the utility loss, area $P_X(1 + t)abP_X$, the area behind

$D^{comp}_{U=U_1}$ between the two prices, equals the tax revenues collected, also area $P_X(1 + t)abP_X$ ($= tP_XX_C$). There is no efficiency loss from the tax.

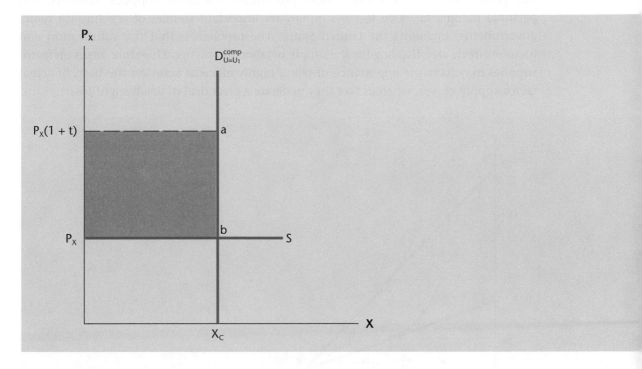

Figure 15.9

The danger with the policy prescription is that it is likely to be applied to actual demand (factor supply) curves rather than the appropriate compensated curves. Unfortunately, it is not necessarily true that taxing goods (factors) whose actual demand (supply) curves are highly inelastic avoids deadweight loss. The problem is that deadweight loss depends only on the substitution effect, whereas the actual demand (factor supply) curves reflect both the substitution and the income effects.

The prescription is probably reasonably accurate for goods and services, however. The substitution and income effects work in the same direction on the demands for normal goods and services. Therefore, if the actual demand elasticity is very low, close to zero, it is likely that both the substitution and income effects are small and a small substitution effect reduces deadweight loss. The only exception would be for inferior goods and services, for which the income effect is negative: A rise in price because of a tax reduces the consumer's real income and increases the quantity demanded. The income effect works in the opposite direction from the substitution effect. In this case, a small actual demand elasticity could be the result of offsetting large income and substitution effects, and a large substitution effect generates a large amount of deadweight loss. Not many goods are inferior goods, however, so that this possibility does not have much practical significance.

Factor supplies: labor

The policy prescription is much more problematic for factor supplies, however, and personal income taxes on factor supplies are important sources of revenue for many governments, including the United States. The problem is that the substitution and income effects are offsetting for the supply of labor and saving. Therefore, taxes on factor supplies may have the appearance of being highly efficient taxes on the basis of actual factor supply curves, when in fact they generate a great deal of deadweight loss.

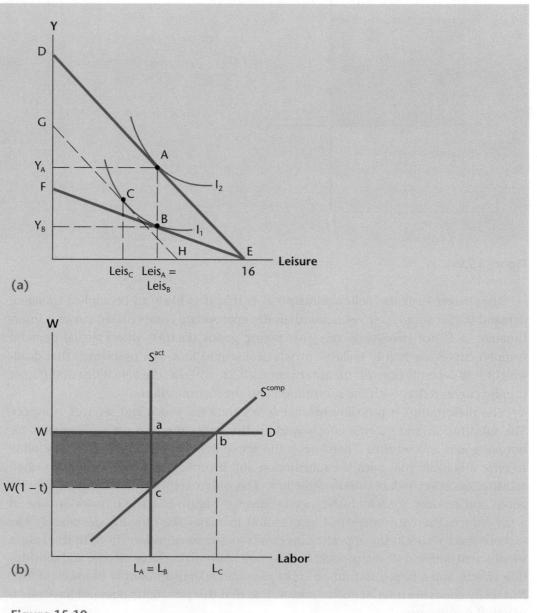

Figure 15.10

Figure 15.10 illustrates the nature of the problem. Figure 15.10(a) depicts the standard income-leisure model of labor supply that we have used a number of times in the text. The individual gains utility from income (Y) and leisure time (Leis), represented in part by the indifference curves I_1 and I_2. There are 16 non-sleeping hours to split between labor and leisure, and the wage is W. The budget constraint without taxes is Y = W(16 – Leis), or Y = –W·Leis + 16·W. It is represented by the budget line DE in Figure 15.10(a), and has a slope of (–)W. The without-tax equilibrium is point A on indifference curve I_2, at which the individual takes $Leis_A$ of leisure time and earns income of Y_A. A wage tax at rate t lowers the effective wage to the individual to W(1 – t) and rotates the budget line downward to FE, with a new slope of (–)W(1 – t). The new equilibrium is at point B on indifference curve I_1, at which the individual takes $Leis_B$ of leisure time and earns income of Y_B. Since there is no change in leisure time ($Leis_A = Leis_B$), the supply of labor in this example is designed to be perfectly inelastic, as illustrated by the actual labor supply curve in Figure 15.10(b). The supply of labor is L_A (= L_B) at the wages W and W(1 – t) (and all other wages). The actual supply curve, S^{act}, is perfectly inelastic.

A perfectly inelastic, or at least highly inelastic, supply of labor is not at all an anomaly, precisely because the substitution and income effects tend to offset one another. The substitution effect is a relative price effect. As the wage decreases from W to W(1 – t), earning income becomes relatively less attractive (taking leisure time tends to become relatively more attractive). For example, if the wage decreases from $10 to $7.50 because of a 25% wage tax, then earning $7.50 used to cost three-quarters of an hour of leisure time but now costs one hour of leisure time. Conversely, taking an hour of leisure time used to cost $10 of income but now costs only $7.50 of income. Taking leisure time is now relatively more attractive than it was before the tax. But more leisure means less labor. Therefore, the substitution effect of a wage change tends to make the labor supply curve upward sloping. A decrease in the wage lowers the quantity of labor supplied, and vice versa.

The income effect is an absolute price or purchasing power effect. With the wage lower because of the tax, the individual's ability to obtain income and leisure time is diminished. Her real income or purchasing power is less. With less income, people tend to buy less of all desired goods, so the individual takes less income and less leisure time. But less leisure means more labor, so that the income effect tends to make the labor supply curve downward sloping. A decrease in the wage tends to increase the quantity of labor supplied, and vice versa. The net effect of the substitution and income effects on the actual labor supply curve, S^{act}, is ambiguous. It could be upward or downward sloping, or perfectly inelastic, as in our example. Indeed, the overall supply of labor in the United States does appear to be close to perfectly inelastic over a wide range of wages.

The actual supply curve may be perfectly inelastic in this example, but the compensated supply curve is not. Refer again to Figure 15.10(a). The compensated supply curve between W and W(1 – t) is obtained by rotating the budget line along indifference curve I_1 from B, when the wage is W(1 – t), to C, when the wage is W. (The dotted line GH is parallel to DE.) This picks up the independent effect of the substitution effect on labor supply. Since the indifference curves are not right-angled, there is a substitution effect and it is negative, as expected. An increase in the wage reduces the quantity of leisure demanded/increases the quantity of labor supplied along I_1. The compensated supply curve is upward sloping.

Figure 15.10(b) pictures the upward-sloping compensated supply curve, S^{comp}, along with the perfectly inelastic actual supply curve, S^{act}. The demand curve for labor from firms, D, is assumed to be perfectly elastic at the without-tax wage, W. The figure shows that although the wage tax appears not to generate a deadweight loss when looking at the perfectly inelastic actual supply curve, S^{act}, it does generate a loss when measured with the appropriate compensated supply curve S^{comp}. When the wage decreases from W to W(1 – t), the compensated quantity of labor supplied decreases from L_C to L_A even though the actual quantity of labor supplied does not change. The excess burden or deadweight loss in terms of S^{comp} is measured analogously to the demand for a good. The income measure of the loss in utility from the tax is the area behind S^{comp} to the wage axis between W and W(1 – t), shaded area WbcW(1 – t). The taxes paid are [W – W(1 – t)]L_A = tWL_A, area WacW(1 – t). The excess burden or deadweight loss is the difference between the income measure of utility loss and the taxes paid, triangular area abc.

MIT's Jerry Hausman was one of the first economists to develop a method for untangling the separate income and substitution effects of the federal personal income tax from econometric estimates of the actual supply of labor. In a celebrated paper published in 1981, he showed that the almost perfectly inelastic supply of labor in the United States was the result of offsetting income and substitution effects that were both fairly large, on the order of .3. Based on the estimated substitution effect, he concluded that federal personal income tax generated a deadweight efficiency loss equal to approximately 29% of the revenues collected from the tax. Prior to the publication of his article, many economists had assumed that the tax was likely to be a fairly efficient tax simply because the actual labor supply elasticity was so low (Hausman, 1981, Table 3, p. 54). Some estimates of the loss following Hausman have been smaller, some larger, but the consensus is that personal income taxes lead to quite a bit of deadweight loss.

ADDING THE SUPPLY SIDE

So far we have been assuming the supply curve for good X is perfectly elastic. In fact, the supply curves for most goods and services are upward sloping, even in the long run. With supplies upward sloping, producers cannot raise their prices by the full amount of an excise tax, as in our example above. Consequently, they are forced to bear some of the excess burden of the tax. Figure 15.11 illustrates.

The equilibrium before the tax is (X_0, P_X^0) at the intersection of S and D. Here D is the actual demand curve for X. The levying of the ad valorem excise tax t raises the firms' marginal costs by tP_X at every unit of output, so that the supply curve shifts up vertically by tP_X to S′. Since P_X rises with X along the supply curve, the vertical distance between S′ and S increases as X increases. The new equilibrium is $(X_t, P_X'(1+t))$ at the intersection of

S' and D. After paying the tax tP_X^t on each unit of X_t, each firm is left with the price P_X^t to pay its factors of production and earn a return on its capital. The total taxes collected by the government are $tP_X^t X_t$, the rectangular area $P_X^t(1+t)bdP_X^t$.

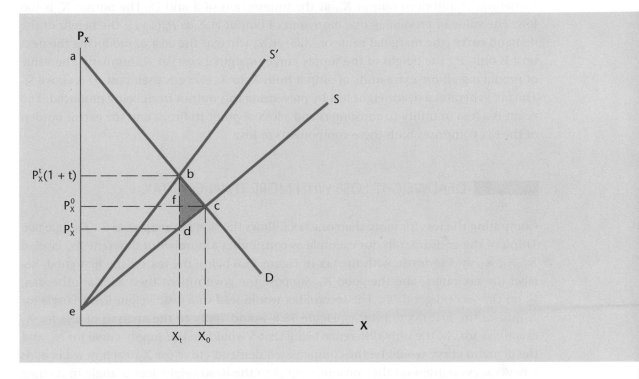

Figure 15.11

Notice that the tax simultaneously increases the price to the consumers, from P_X^0 to $P_X^t(1+t)$ and decreases the price to the firms, from P_X^0 to P_X^t. As a result, both sides of the market bear a burden from the tax. Assume for this example that the actual and compensated demand curves are the same for consumers – there is no income effect. Then at the original price P_X^0, consumers received a consumer surplus equal to acP_X^0, the area behind the demand curve down to P_X^0. The consumer surplus is the utility gain to consumers of being able to consume X at price P_X^0. The firms also received a producer surplus equal to the area ecP_X^0, which can be thought of as a pure economic profit, the difference between the revenues they receive, $P_X^0 X_0$, and the total costs of supplying X_0, equal to the area under S up to X_0.[4]

The tax causes both sides to lose some of their surplus as both the quantity of X and the relevant prices to each change. The consumers lose because they pay more for each unit of X and consume less of it. The firms lose because they receive less from each unit of X and sell less of it. The consumer surplus decreases to area $abP_X^t(1+t)$ and the producer surplus decreases to area edP_X^t. The combined loss in surpluses is the area $P_X^t(1+t)bcdP_X^t$. Some of the lost surplus is transferred to the government as tax revenues, area $P_X^t(1+t)bdP_X^t$. But the remaining lost surplus, triangular area bcd, is a deadweight efficiency loss, and it is shared by consumers and producers. The consumers' portion of the loss is area bcf and the producers portion of the loss is dcf.

The excess burden of the tax arises because the tax drives the market away from its natural equilibrium output X_0, at the intersection of S and D. The output X^t is too low. The value of producing one more unit of output at X_t is $P_X^t(1+t)$, the height of the demand curve (the marginal value or MRS) at X_t, whereas the cost of producing the next unit is only P_X^t, the height of the supply curve (marginal cost) at X_t. Similarly, the value of producing all the extra units of output from X_t to X_0 exceeds their cost (D is above S). The tax generates a deadweight loss by preventing this output from being produced. The result is a loss in utility to consumers and a loss of profit to firms, and the excess burden of the tax comprises both these components of loss.

DEADWEIGHT LOSS WITH MORE THAN ONE TAX

Computing the loss for more than one tax follows the same principles as for a single tax. Think of the consumer in our example as consuming a number of different Xs, labeled X_1, X_2, X_3, and so forth, with the tax in Figure 15.8 being the tax on the first good. Re-label the tax rate t_1 and the good X_1. Suppose the government then adds another tax, t_2, on the second good, X_2. The second tax would lead to a deadweight loss triangle for X_2 just as the first tax did for X_1. Figure 15.8 would apply to the analysis of loss for X_2 exactly as for X_1, the only difference being that S would be the supply curve for X_2, and the demand curve would be the compensated demand curve for X_2. Each new tax adds a new excess burden on the consumer equal to the deadweight loss triangle in its own market, computed exactly as in Figure 15.8.

But adding the second deadweight loss triangle does not capture the entire change in the excess burden on the consumer from adding the second tax. Excess burden is the income measure of the utility loss to the consumer from the two taxes less the tax revenue collected by the government. Suppose X_1 and X_2 are complements in terms of their compensated demands. Then the tax on X_2, by raising the price of X_2 to the consumer, reduces the compensated demand for X_1. Since X_1 is already taxed, the reduced quantity of X_1 demanded reduces the tax revenues collected on X_1 and increases the excess burden of the tax.

Figure 15.12 illustrates the reduction in tax revenues from X_1 as a result of t_2. Its starting point is the equilibrium pictured in Figure 15.8. $D_{t_1}^{comp}$ is the compensated demand for X_1 when the only tax is t_1. Tax t_2 is zero. The equilibrium is identical to that in Figure 15.8, with tax revenues $\left[P_{X_1}(1+t_1)-P_{X_1}\right]X_1^B = t_1 P_{X_1} X_1^B$, given by the rectangular area $P_{X_1}(1+t_1)acP_{X_1}$ in Figure 15.12. The deadweight loss is the triangular area abc. Since X_1 and X_2 are complements, the addition of tax t_2 shifts the compensated demand curve for X_1 down and to the left, to $D_{t_1+t_2}^{comp}$. The shift in demand does not change the prices for X_1, but it does lower the (compensated) quantity of X_1 purchased from X_1^B on $D_{t_1}^{comp}$ to X_1^D on $D_{t_1+t_2}^{comp}$. With the quantity reduced, the tax revenue collected on X_1 also declines. The new tax revenue is $\left[P_{X_1}(1+t_1)-P_{X_1}\right]X_1^D = t_1 P_{X_1} X_1^D$, equal to the rectangular area $P_{X_1}(1+t_1)deP_{X_1}$. Tax revenue has decreased by the rectangular area dace. Consequently, the excess burden from the tax on X_1 increases by area dace. The total deadweight loss in X_1 is now the area dabe, the original deadweight loss triangle abc plus the loss in tax revenue on X_1 because a tax was imposed on X_2. Had X_1 and X_2 been substitutes, the tax on X_2 would have increased the compensated demand for X_1 and increased the tax revenue from X_1. The deadweight loss in X_1 would have decreased by the amount of the increase in the tax revenue.

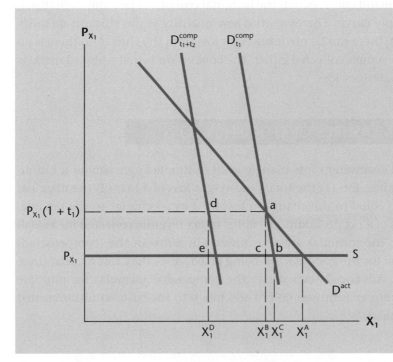

Figure 15.12

The method for computing the deadweight loss for two taxes applies to any number of taxes. Compute the loss as if the taxes had been added one at a time. The first tax t_1 leads to a deadweight loss triangle in X_1. Add the second tax, t_2. It leads to a second deadweight loss triangle in X_2, but may change the revenue collected on X_1. Add the tax revenue lost (subtract the tax revenue gained) from X_1 to compute the total loss from the first two taxes. Add a third tax t_3, and compute the deadweight loss triangle in X_3. Then add the combined tax revenue lost (subtract the combined tax revenue gained) from both X_1 and X_2 as a result of adding t_3. Continue in this manner until all the taxes have been included. Advanced texts show that it does not matter what order the taxes are considered. The total loss from the set of taxes is the same with any order, equal to the sum of the deadweight loss triangles in each taxed market plus or minus the tax revenue lost or gained in previously taxed markets as each new tax is added. This one-tax-at-a-time technique correctly computes the overall loss in utility to the consumer, measured in terms of income, less the tax revenues collected from the entire set of taxes.

One important implication of this technique is that losses cannot arise in untaxed markets, so long as the untaxed markets are competitive and not otherwise distorted by market power. This is true even if taxes in other markets increase or decrease demands in the untaxed markets because the taxed and untaxed goods are complements or substitutes. The intuition is that price remains equal to marginal cost as demands shift in the untaxed markets, so that the marginal value of the last unit exchanged after the shift, as measured on the new demand curve, equals the marginal cost of the last unit exchanged, as measured on the supply curve. Therefore, the new quantity is the efficient quantity exchanged in the market; there can be no deadweight loss from the shift. And there is no change in the total tax revenues collected either. The conclusion is that untaxed markets can be ignored in the analysis of loss.[5]

THREE ELASTICITY MEASURES OF EFFICIENCY LOSS

The supply and demand deadweight loss triangle leads to simple approximation formulas for three measures of interest: (1) the total deadweight loss of a tax; (2) the marginal deadweight loss of a tax, equal to the change in loss for a small change in the tax rate; and (3) the marginal loss of a tax per additional dollar of tax revenue collected for a small increase in the tax rate. The formulas are all expressed in terms of the (compensated) price elasticity of demand for the good (factor) being taxed. Also, they assume that there is only one taxed good. Advanced texts derive the comparable formulas for multiple taxes, but these more complex formulas do not add much to the basic intuition gained from the single-tax formulas.

THE TOTAL DEADWEIGHT LOSS OF A TAX

Refer again to Figure 15.8. The deadweight loss area abc is a triangle, so the formula for the size of the loss area is 1/2 base times height. The base is ΔX, the change in the compensated quantity of X demanded because of the tax, $(X_C - X_B)$. The height is ΔP, the change in price because of the tax, $(P_X(1 + t) - P_X)$. Therefore, the deadweight loss, L, is

$$L = \frac{1}{2}\Delta X \Delta P.$$

But $\Delta P = tP_X$ with an ad valorem tax. Therefore,

$$L = \frac{1}{2}tP_X \Delta X.$$

The compensated demand elasticity of X with respect to P_X is $E^C_{X,P_X} = \dfrac{\Delta X}{X} \bigg/ \dfrac{\Delta P_X}{P_X}.$

Therefore, to express the deadweight loss in terms of the compensated demand elasticity, multiply and divide L by X, P_X, and $\Delta P_X = tP_X$:

$$L = \frac{1}{2}tP_X\left(\frac{\Delta X}{X} \Big/ \frac{\Delta P_X}{P_X}\right)\left(\frac{tP_X X}{P_X}\right)$$

$$L = \frac{1}{2}t^2 E^C_{X,P_X} P_X X$$

where $E^C_{X,P}$ is the compensated demand elasticity of X with respect to P_X.

An important implication of the loss formula is that the excess burden or deadweight loss of a tax rises with the square of the tax rate. For example, cutting a tax rate in half reduces the deadweight loss of the tax to one-fourth of its value at the higher rate. Another important implication is that the loss rises in direct proportion to the compensated elasticity of demand, which in turn depends directly on the substitution effect of a price change.

THE MARGINAL LOSS OF A TAX

The marginal loss of a tax is the change in the loss for a small change in the tax rate. In other words, it is the derivative of loss with respect to the tax rate,

$$dL/dt = t\,E^C_{X,P_X}\,P_X X$$

ignoring the indirect effect of the change in the tax rate on the pre-tax tax base, $P_X X$. The marginal loss increases with the tax rate and the magnitude of the substitution effect.

MARGINAL LOSS PER DOLLAR OF ADDITIONAL TAX REVENUE

The total tax revenue, T, raised by the tax is $tP_X X$. The change in the tax revenue for a small change in the tax rate is the derivative of the total tax revenue with respect to t,

$$dT/dt = P_X X$$

again ignoring the indirect effect of a small change in the tax rate on the tax base $P_X X$. Therefore, the marginal loss per dollar of additional tax revenue is the ratio of dL/dt to dT/dt.

$$\frac{dL}{dT} = \frac{tE^C_{X,P}P_X X}{P_X X} = tE^C_{X,P}$$

the product of the tax rate and the compensated demand elasticity. This is a remarkably simple formula that leads to easy calculations of the deadweight loss implications of changes in tax rates. For example, if the compensated demand elasticity for some good or factor X is .4 and the tax rate on X is 10% (.10), then a small increase in the tax rate leads to an additional loss of $.04 [= (.10)(.4)] per additional dollar of tax revenue collected.

This completes the analysis of the excess burden or deadweight loss from taxation. The analysis in this chapter sets the stage for Chapter 16, which considers the trade-off between efficiency and equity in taxation when taxes are distorting.

CHAPTER 16

The Trade-off Between Equity and Efficiency in Taxation

In mainstream public sector theory, the government's ultimate objective is to maximize social welfare as given by the social welfare function. This is true whether the government is making certain expenditures to correct for market failures or designing taxes to pay for the expenditures. Regarding its tax policies, the government pursues both an equity goal and an efficiency goal as it attempts to maximize social welfare. The equity goal, discussed in Chapter 5, is to use taxes (and transfer payments) to promote equality. Inequality is costly in the mainstream model of maximizing social welfare. The efficiency goal is to raise whatever tax revenue the government needs to finance its expenditures with the minimum amount of deadweight loss. Unfortunately, these two goals are often conflicting, in which case the government must try to balance their conflicting claims. Chapter 16 begins with the principles for achieving the efficiency goal. It then discusses how to achieve the best balance between equity and efficiency in taxation in order to maximize social welfare.

MINIMIZING THE LOSS FROM TAXATION

The key to reaching the efficiency goal of minimizing loss for a given amount of tax revenue is the marginal loss per additional dollar of tax revenue, dL/dT, derived at the end of Chapter 15. The reason why is that the government should follow the equal marginal principle with respect to dL/dT to minimize loss: *Set tax rates to equalize the additional loss per additional dollar of tax revenue across all goods and factors.* To see that the ratios dL/dT must be equal, consider how efficiency can be improved if the ratios are unequal. Suppose dL/dT for good 1 is 2/1 and for good 2, 1/1. The deadweight loss for a small increase in the tax rate on good 1 is \$2 per additional dollar of revenue raised, whereas the deadweight loss for a small increase in the tax rate on good 2 is only \$1 per additional revenue raised. Whenever the ratios are unequal, the government can raise the same tax revenue with less deadweight loss by increasing the tax rate on the good with the lower ratio and lowering the tax rate on the good with the higher ratio.

In this example, the government should raise the tax rate on good 2 to raise one more dollar of tax revenue from good 2 and lower the tax rate on good 1 to raise one less dollar of tax revenue on good 1. There is no change in total tax revenue raised, but the overall amount of deadweight loss declines. By raising one less dollar of revenue from good 1, the deadweight loss on that good falls by $2. By raising one more dollar of revenue from good 2, the deadweight loss on that good rises by $1. Net, deadweight loss falls by $1 ($-1 = -2 + 1$).

The government should keep raising the tax rate on good 2 and lowering the tax rate on good 1 until the two ratios equalize. Suppose they equalize at 1.6/1. At that point, the ability to decrease deadweight loss with no change in tax revenues ends. Raising one dollar more revenue from good 2 raises deadweight loss by 1.6 units and lowering the revenue raised from good 1 by one dollar lowers deadweight loss by 1.6 units. There is no change in tax revenue or in deadweight loss. The overall deadweight loss is as low as it can be by taxing these two goods.

Furthermore, the ratios do tend to equalize by adjusting the tax rates in this manner. Recall that $dL/dT = t\ E^C_{X,P}$, where t is the tax rate and $E^C_{X,P}$ is the compensated demand elasticity of good X with respect to its price. Since dL/dT depends directly on the tax rate t, raising the tax rate on good 2 raises its dL/dT and lowering the tax rate on good 1 lowers its dL/dT, driving the two rates together at a ratio somewhere between 2/1 and 1/1. If the two ratios never equalize, then the good with the higher ratio should not be taxed. This would be the case if the compensated demand (supply) elasticity for one of the goods (factors) were zero, in which case taxing that good (factor) is equivalent to a lump-sum tax. All the required tax revenue should be raised from taxing that good.

Finally, what holds for goods 1 and 2 holds for all goods and factors. Overall deadweight loss is equalized when dL/dT, the additional loss per additional dollar of tax revenue, is equalized across all goods and factors.

THE INVERSE ELASTICITY RULE

The formula for dL/dT leads to two simple and equivalent prescriptions for minimizing overall deadweight loss. We have shown that dL/dT is to be equalized across all goods, and $dL/dT = t E^C_{X,P}$. Suppose the equalized ratio is the constant k. Then $t E^C_{X,P} = k$ for all goods, or $t = k/E^C_{X,P}$. The tax rate on each good should be set in inverse proportion to the good's compensated elasticity of demand. This is known as the *inverse elasticity rule* (IER), a rule for raising a given amount of tax revenue at minimum overall deadweight loss.[1] It says that tax rates should be higher on goods with lower demand elasticities and vice versa. The same intuition applies as in Chapter 15 for reducing excess burden or deadweight loss.[2]

THE EQUAL PERCENTAGE CHANGE RULE

An equivalent rule to the IER is the *equal percentage change rule*. Break out the compensated demand elasticity into its component parts:

$$tE^C_{X,P} = t\left(\frac{\Delta X}{X} \Big/ \frac{\Delta P_X}{P_X}\right) = k$$

But $\Delta P_X = tP_X$ with an ad valorem tax. Therefore, $\Delta X/X = k$. Tax rates should be set to generate an equal percentage change in the compensated demands for all goods in order to raise a given amount of revenue at minimum overall deadweight loss.

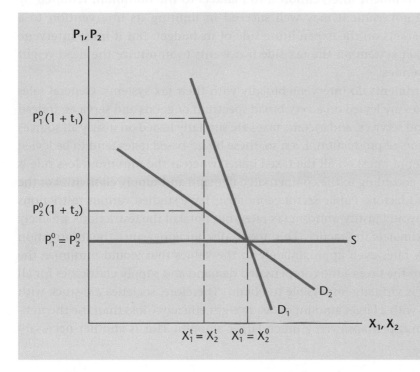

Figure 16.1

Figure 16.1 combines the messages from the two rules. It pictures the supply and demand for two goods, X_1 and X_2. The supply curve (marginal cost) S is assumed to be constant and equal for the two goods, horizontal at the without-tax price P^0. The compensated demand curves for X_1 and X_2 are D_1 and D_2, with D_1 being relatively inelastic and D_2 being relatively elastic. The figure assumes that the without-tax equilibria are the same for the two goods, (X^0_1, P^0_1) and (X^0_2, P^0_2), with $X^0_1 = X^0_2$ and $P^0_1 = P^0_2$. If the government needs to raise tax revenue, then the equal percentage change rule says the tax rates on each good should be such as to cause an equal decrease in the compensated quantity demanded of both goods. With their initial values equal, an equal percentage change in the two goods is the same as an equal change in the two goods. Suppose that the change to $X^t_1 = X^t_2$ raises the required revenue. Then the tax rate on X_1 should be t_1, to generate the with-tax price of $P_1^0(1+t_1)$ and the quantity demanded X_1^t, and the tax rate on X_2 should be t_2, to generate the with-tax price of $P_2^0(1+t_2)$ and the quantity demanded X_2^t. The tax rate is higher on X_1 because its compensated demand is relatively inelastic, in accordance with the IER. Taxing the goods in this manner guarantees that the overall deadweight loss is minimized for the given amount of tax revenue to be collected.

The IER and the equal percentage change rule have one uncomfortable implication for mainstream economists: If the government wants to minimize deadweight loss, it should tax almost all goods and services and factors of production, in general.[3] This is a highly intrusive tax policy that runs directly counter to the mainstream principle of keeping government intervention into markets to the minimum required by market failure. The government may well succeed in limiting its intervention to a small number of markets on the expenditure side of its budget. But it must intervene broadly in the market system on the tax side if it wants to minimize the deadweight loss from its tax revenues.

Of course, governments do intervene broadly with their tax systems. General sales and value-added taxes are levied on a very broad spectrum of goods and services, indeed "nearly all" goods and services, and income taxes are similarly levied on nearly all sources of income from factors of production. Even so, these broad-based taxes tend to be levied at a single rate (or set of rates) on all the taxed items, whereas the minimum loss rule is to vary the tax rates according to the compensated demand and supply elasticities of the individual goods and factors. Public sector economists have studied various restrictions on preferences that would justify uniform tax rates, but none of the restrictions are likely to hold even approximately in practice. This, too, is discouraging, since the information required to vary tax rates even approximately to the values that would minimize the deadweight loss from the taxes – the compensated demand and supply elasticities for all goods and factors – is virtually impossible to obtain. Therefore, societies are stuck with raising tax revenues with a larger amount of deadweight efficiency loss than the theoretical minimum amount, perhaps even a much larger amount. This is another necessary evil of taxation.

THE EFFICIENCY–EQUITY TRADE-OFF IN TAXATION

Minimizing inefficiency is only half of the problem in designing taxes. Taxes also have to be in accord with people's sense of equity. Taxes and transfer payments are the primary means of redistributing resources to promote society's goal of end-results equity or distributive justice. As we saw in Chapter 5, mainstream economists assume that society values equality over inequality. But we also saw that the more the government redistributes in the name of equality, the larger the efficiency losses from the taxes and transfers – recall Okun's leaky bucket. Therefore, the design of taxes ultimately involves a balancing act between the goals of promoting equality and reducing inefficiency.

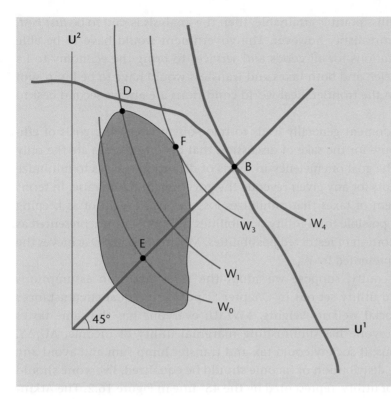

Figure 16.2

Figure 16.2 illustrates the nature of the trade-off in terms of the utility possibilities frontier and the social welfare indifference curves. Societies would love to be at the bliss point on their utility possibilities frontier, point B in the figure. The bliss point would achieve the highest possible level of social welfare, represented by social welfare indifference curve W_4 and there would be no conflict between efficiency and equity in choosing B. The bliss point is distributionally the best of all the efficient points on the frontier, reached through lump-sum taxes and transfers along the frontier.

Distorting taxes rule out the bliss point. The excess burdens or deadweight losses that distorting taxes generate force the economy to operate inefficiently at some point below the utility possibilities frontier. The taxes lead to a restricted set of utility possibilities, such as the shaded portion in Figure 16.2. The goal is still to achieve the highest possible level of social welfare as represented by the social welfare indifference curves, but the highest level must necessarily be less than the level of social welfare represented by W_4. Economists describe the attempt to maximize social welfare over a restricted set of utility possibilities as *second-best* analysis. Many features of an economy can make the quest for social welfare second best: distorting taxes; monopoly power in certain markets that the government cannot remove; legislated budget constraints; and asymmetric (private) information, to name a few. But they all share one trait in common – they prevent society from achieving the bliss point. Conversely, if condi-

315

tions are such that the bliss point is attainable, then the analysis is said to be *first best*. Those conditions are unrealistic, however. The government would have to be able to ensure efficient allocations for all goods and services to bring the economy to its utility possibilities frontier, and both taxes and transfers would have to be lump sum to keep the economy on the frontier. Real-world conditions are always second best to some extent.

A second-best environment generally leads to trade-offs between the goals of efficiency and equity. Suppose for the sake of discussion that distorting taxes are the only source of inefficiency. The goal of efficiency in terms of distorting taxes is to minimize the overall deadweight loss for any given revenue the government has to raise. In terms of Figure 16.2, the pattern of taxes that minimizes loss can be thought of as keeping the economy as close as possible to its utility possibilities frontier. This is represented as point D on the shaded portion of restricted possibilities. Moving to point D achieves the level of social welfare represented by W_1.

In thinking about equity, suppose we adopt the three Atkinson assumptions about social welfare and utility set out in Chapter 5: people in equal circumstances have equal marginal social welfare weights, $\Delta W/\Delta U$; everyone has the same tastes or preferences; and everyone has diminishing marginal utility of income, $\Delta U/\Delta Y$. Under those assumptions, if society could tax and transfer lump sum and avoid any efficiency loss, then the distribution of income should be equalized. Everyone should have the same income or utility, represented by the 45° line in Figure 16.2. The Atkinson assumptions render inequality costly; the ideal to strive for is equality. Suppose in the imperfect second-best world, the government can achieve equality, but only at point E on the 45° line. Moving to point E achieves the level of social welfare represented by W_0.

The highest level of social welfare society can achieve is point F on social welfare indifference curve W_3, at which W_3 is just tangent to the shaded restricted set of utility possibilities. Point D, the efficient loss-minimizing choice, is not as good as F because it generates too much inequality. Point E, the equalizing choice, is not as good as F because it generates too much inefficiency. Point F is the best possible compromise between the efficiency and equity goals. It maximizes social welfare even though it satisfies neither goal.

Second-best environments almost always involve compromises of this nature, and tax policy is no exception. Economists have most often considered the best trade-off between efficiency and equity in taxation in two environments. One is when the government can tax (almost) everything, as is necessary for minimizing loss. The other is the trade-off involved if the government chooses to levy only one tax. The candidates for study are the more important taxes, most often the personal income tax because the trade-off between efficiency and equity is most directly evident when the tax is levied on individuals (or families). The government's goal is assumed to be the same in either case: It wants to design a set of taxes, or a single tax, to maximize social welfare, given that the government needs to raise a given amount of tax revenue.

Economists can solve problems of this type, but the analytical tools required to do so are beyond the scope of this text. Instead, we will provide an intuitive discussion of the solutions to each problem. Fortunately, the intuition behind the features that determine the design of taxes is fairly straightforward.

TAXING (ALMOST) EVERYTHING

As we saw in Chapter 15 and the first part of this chapter, the key to reducing the inefficiencies of taxes lies in the compensated demand (factor supply) elasticities, which measure the substitution effects of price changes. The government should tax most heavily those goods and factors with low elasticities. If all society cared about was efficiency, then the tax rates should be set in inverse proportion to the compensated elasticities according to the IER.

But society also cares about equity, and concerns for equity are incorporated into the social welfare function. With equity now in the mix, the goal is to maximize social welfare. The question, then, is what does the social welfare function add to the design of tax policy? How does it modify the prescription of the IER?

The answer becomes clear if the social welfare function is defined in terms of the individual goods and services that individuals buy. Write the social welfare function as $W = W(U^1(X_{11}, ,X_{1i},..,X_{1N}),..U^h,(X_{h1},..,X_{hi},..,X_{hN}),.. U^H,(X_{H1}...,X_{Hi},...,X_{HN})) = W(U^h(X_{hi}))$ with H individuals, h = 1,...H, and N goods, i = 1,...,N. Suppose the government levies a tax on good i, and assume that everyone buys the good. The tax tends to reduce everyone's consumption of good i, which reduces their utilities. The reduction of any one person's utility in turn lowers social welfare. Consider person h as an example. The chain of events from the tax to the effect on social welfare through person h is:

$$t_i \uparrow \rightarrow X_{hi} \downarrow \rightarrow U^h \downarrow \rightarrow W \downarrow$$

How much W changes depends on the ethical weight society places on person h, which we summarized in Chapter 5 by person h's social marginal utility of income, SMU_Y^h.

Recall that $SMU_Y^h = \left(\frac{\Delta W}{\Delta U^h} \right) \left(\frac{\Delta U^h}{\Delta Y_h} \right)$, the product of the marginal social welfare weight $\left(\frac{\Delta W}{\Delta U^h} \right)$ and person h's private marginal utility of income $\left(\frac{\Delta U^h}{\Delta Y_h} \right)$.

In a first-best environment, the government would tax and transfer to equalize the social marginal utilities of income across all people. This is the interpersonal equity condition that is required to reach the bliss point. It would make no difference to social welfare who consumed the good since everyone would have the same SMU_Y. But in a second-best environment, the social marginal utilities of income remain unequal, so that it does matter who consumes the good. Suppose two people, person h and person 1, decrease their consumption of good i by the same amount in response to the tax, but person h has the higher social marginal utility of income. Then person h's reduced consumption of good i decreases social welfare more than person 1's equally reduced consumption of good i.[4]

In the pursuit of equity, therefore, the government should reduce taxes on goods that are consumed more by people with high social marginal utilities of income and raise taxes on goods that are consumed more by people with low social marginal utilities of income. This makes sense because the poorer people have relatively high social marginal utilities of income (high private marginal utilities of income and, possibly, high marginal social welfare weights) and the richer people have relatively low social marginal utilities of income (low private marginal utilities of income and, possibly, low marginal social welfare weights). So the policy prescription in the name of equity is entirely intuitive. It says: Keep taxes low on goods consumed relatively more by the poor and raise taxes on goods consumed relatively more by the rich.

In conclusion, the design of taxes on a broad range of goods and factors depends most importantly on two parameters in the combined pursuit of efficiency and equity in taxation: The compensated demand (factor supply) elasticities and the pattern of social marginal utilities of income. The former is the efficiency component and the latter is the equity component of tax design.

These two components may well be in conflict, leading to an efficiency–equity trade-off. A good example is the decision by U.S. state governments on whether they should exempt food purchased for home consumption from taxation under their general sales taxes. Forty-five states make use of the general sales tax; 26 states have chosen to exempt food purchased for home consumption and 19 have not.

The argument for taxing food purchased for home consumption is that it raises a large amount of revenue with low deadweight losses. The demand for food is highly (price) inelastic, on the order of .2 or less, and the compensated demand is likely to be highly inelastic as well. Food is a necessity, so much so that it also has a very low income elasticity of demand. A low income elasticity combined with a low actual demand elasticity implies a low compensated demand elasticity. Therefore, a high tax on food purchased for home consumption is called for on efficiency grounds. But the low demand elasticity for food makes it easy for suppliers to pass the burden of the tax on to consumers by charging higher prices for the food, a point we will discuss in Chapter 18. In addition, the ratio of food purchased for home consumption to income falls sharply as income rises, so that the burden of the tax falls disproportionately on the poor. It is a highly regressive tax. Since the poor have high social marginal utilities of income, the tax should be kept low on equity grounds.

The states are clearly split on how they have resolved the trade-off between efficiency and equity in this case. The 26 states that have chosen to exempt food purchased for home consumption were presumably more swayed by the equity argument. The 19 states that have chosen to tax the food apparently place more weight on the revenue-raising and efficiency arguments. Neither group is necessarily right or wrong; they have simply chosen to respond differently to a difficult efficiency–equity trade-off.

THE OPTIMAL INCOME TAX

Chapter 5 previewed the problem of determining the optimal amount of income taxation when society is concerned about both efficiency and equity. To review briefly, there were two individuals, a rich person R and a poor person P, whose utility depended only on their incomes. The social welfare function embodied the three Atkinson assumptions – equal social welfare weights for people with the same level of income, everyone has the same tastes, and diminishing private marginal utility of income, MU_Y. The ideal to strive for in terms of equity is to satisfy the interpersonal equity condition for a social welfare maximum at the bliss point on the utility possibilities frontier: equalize the social marginal utilities of income for everyone. Under the Atkinson assumptions, this is equivalent to equalizing the private marginal utilities of income. If lump-sum taxes and transfers are possible so that taxing the rich person and transferring the revenues to the poor person does not give rise to inefficiencies, then the marginal utilities of the rich and poor should be equal. MU_Y^P is the marginal benefit in terms of the increase in social welfare from giving a dollar of income to P and MU_Y^R is the marginal cost in terms of the decrease in social welfare from taking a dollar of income from R. The distribution is optimal when the marginal benefit and marginal cost of redistributing income are equal, or $MU_Y^P = MU_Y^R$. Since everyone has the same tastes, equalizing the marginal utilities of income implies that the rich and poor should have the same income, the mean income. All income above the mean should be taxed at 100%, and all people below the mean should have their incomes increased to the mean. Atkinson's assumptions establish equality as the ideal baseline to strive for in end-results equity or distributive justice. Conversely, inequality is costly in terms of the equity goal.

With distorting taxes, however, the marginal costs of transferring income are increased by the deadweight losses from taxing and transferring. These costs are symbolized by Okun's leaky bucket, and also include the costs of administering the tax and transfer programs and the costs to taxpayers and transfer recipients of complying with the tax laws and the requirements for receiving transfers. Label the marginal costs of Okun's leaky bucket MC_{OLB}. The optimal redistribution is still the point at which the marginal benefits and marginal costs of redistributing are equal. But now the full marginal costs of taxing and transferring income are $MU_Y^R + MC_{OLB}$. At the optimum, $MB_{redistribution} = MU_Y^P - MU_Y^R + MC_{OLB} = MC_{redistribution}$. This is the best compromise between the equity goal of equality and the inefficiency of taxing and transferring with distorting taxes and transfers: $MU_Y^P > X_1^t$, and $Y_R > Y_P$. The income redistribution stops short of leveling everyone to the mean. The inefficiencies of taxing and transferring are the justification for the remaining inequality. Review the discussion in Chapter 5 if these results are unclear to you.

THE FORMAL OPTIMAL INCOME TAX PROBLEM

The remaining questions concern the specifics: What parameters are the most important in determining how high income tax rates should be, and how much income should be transferred? The first economist to explore this question with a formal model was James Mirrlees, in 1971. His model of an optimal income tax was the primary basis for his Nobel Prize in Economics in 1996.

Mirrlees's model of optimal income taxation, and the many models that followed, all have essentially the same structure. One common ground is that they incorporate the three Atkinson assumptions, so that if lump-sum taxes and transfers were possible, then everyone should have the same utility. The simplest version of the optimal income tax problem contains the following elements.

The economy consists of a single factor of production, labor (L) that is used to produce a single, all-purpose consumption good C. There are H individuals who supply the labor and consume the good. They have a common utility function, U: $U^h = U(C_h, L_h)$,, h = 1,..., H. This is Atkinson's same tastes assumption. The social welfare function that society wants to maximize is the Atkinson social welfare function

of Chapter 5: $W = \dfrac{1}{1-e}\sum_{h=1}^{H} U(C_h, L_h)^{(1-e)}$, where e is society's aversion to inequality,

e = [0,∞], with zero representing utilitarian indifference to the distribution, and ∞ representing Rawlsian egalitarianism. Increasing values of e between 0 and ∞ represent increasing aversion to inequality.

The one difference among individuals is their skill level. The distribution of their skills is indexed by h in increasing order, so that person 1 is the lowest skilled and person H the highest skilled. The basic unit of labor L is called an efficiency unit of labor. A person with skill level h has hL efficiency units of labor, and all efficiency units of labor are perfect substitutes in production. The wage, W, is specified as the wage per efficiency unit of labor, so that person h receives income of $Y_h = WhL$. There is no saving, so all income available to individuals is used for consumption. Without taxes, $C_h = Y_h = WhL$, with the price of the consumption good equal to 1. Also, there is constant returns to scale production so that there are no pure profits to distribute to the individuals, who own the firms. The total revenues from the sales of C equal the total wages paid for the labor.

The government has to raise taxes to finance a certain amount of public consumption, R, undertaken to respond to allocational market failures, such as the provision of defense and public roadways. R also occurs in units of C. The simplest tax to use is the credit income tax with a single rate (described in Chapter 11). The tax paid by individual h is $T_h = -S + tY_h$. The provision of the credit S through the income tax is assumed to be the only transfer payment undertaken by the government. The government's budget

constraint is R = $\sum_{h=1}^{H} T_h$.

One immediate consequence of the tax is that it changes each individual's disposable income from $Y_h = WhL$ to $Y_h = S + (1 - t)WhL$. The individuals maximize their own utility by equating their marginal rates of substitution between consumption and labor to the after-tax wage (with the price of C = 1): $MRS_{C,L}^h = (1-t)Wh$. This response to taxation is the source of the deadweight loss from the tax, with the amount of loss determined by the compensated supply elasticity of labor, $E_{L,W}^{comp}$.

The government's problem is to set the two parameters of the tax function, the credit S and the tax rate t, to maximize social welfare. The two constraints that it faces are

the government budget constraint, $R = \sum_{h=1}^{H} T_h$ and the individuals' response to taxation

represented by $MRS_{C,L}^h = (1-t)Wh$.

The solution to this problem is beyond the scope of the text. Nonetheless, it is clear that the optimal levels of S and t depend on four factors: the revenue requirement of the government for allocational expenditures, R; the distribution of skills across individuals; society's aversion to inequality, e; and the compensated supply elasticity of labor, $E_{L,W}^{comp}$. Regarding the tax rate, it should be higher:

1. the higher the revenue requirement R. The more the government needs to spend to correct for allocational problems in the economy, the more taxes have to be collected.
2. the greater the dispersion of skills across individuals. The greater the inequality of skills, the greater the inequality of market income and the more gain there is to redistributing by raising t and S.
3. the higher is e. The more averse to inequality society is, the more costly is inequality and the more gain there is to redistributing.
4. the lower is $E_{L,W}^{comp}$. The compensated supply of labor is the source of the inefficiency from taxing (and transferring through S). If $E_{L,W}^{comp}$ is zero (the indifference curves for C and L are right-angled), then there is no tax inefficiency. Taxing and transferring is effectively lump sum and everyone should receive the mean level of utility after tax and transfer. The tax rate on all incomes above the mean should be 100%. As $E_{L,W}^{comp}$ rises from zero, the tax give rises to deadweight loss, and the amount of loss rises with $E_{L,W}^{comp}$. The tax rate t (and S) should be correspondingly lower to reduce the inefficiencies.

In these simple models, the size of the tax rate is particularly sensitive to e and $E_{L,W}^{comp}$, in fact, too sensitive to use these models by themselves as a guide to tax policy. There is simply too much uncertainty associated with the values of e and $E_{L,W}^{comp}$ to say with much confidence what the tax rate should be. Nonetheless, the optimal income tax models were used by many economists in the United States to support the reduction of the marginal tax rate on the highest incomes from 50% to 28% under the Tax Reform Act of 1986 (TRA86). At the time, the estimates of $E_{L,W}^{comp}$ were in the .1 to .4 range and the feeling was that society's aversion to inequality was fairly low (recall the discussion in Chapter 5 of Harberger's conjecture that e was less than .5). These values suggested a tax rate of around 30%, which is just about what TRA86 set on the highest incomes.

Since 1986, the tax rate on the highest incomes under the federal personal income tax was raised to 39.6% in the Clinton administration and then lowered to 35% under the George W. Bush administration. Suppose as a point of reference that the 28% rate was the correct highest tax rate in 1986. Should the highest tax rate have been raised since then? It is difficult to say.

On the one hand, estimates of the compensated labor supply elasticity have been creeping up recently, if anything. One reason is that women tend to have higher labor supply elasticities than men, and they have become a larger percentage of the overall U.S. labor force since 1986. Also, economists now believe that the costs of complying with the tax code, one of the costs of Okun's leaky bucket, are about 10% of revenues collected. No one paid much attention to compliance costs before 1986. Both of these trends increase the inefficiencies associated with the income tax and would argue for lowering the highest tax rate below 28%.

On the other hand, the distribution of income has become much more unequal since 1986. The Gini coefficient for income has risen steadily since the mid-1970s in the United States, from .397 in 1975, to .425 in 1986, to .469 in 2005. Concern for the increasing inequality also appears to have increased, suggesting that society's aversion to inequality may have increased as well. A higher e has an especially dramatic effect on the tax rate in the simple optimal income tax models. In addition, the revenue requirements R of the federal government increased substantially after 2003, primarily because of the Iraq War and the 2006 prescription drug benefit under Medicare instituted in 2006. All these factors would suggest that the highest tax rate should be greater than 28%. Which of the two sets of effects have dominated is unclear.

About the only point of agreement from all the optimal income tax studies is that there is only a modest gain in social welfare to having a graduated rate structure rather than a single flat rate, as in the model sketched above. This result provides ammunition for those who favor a flat tax on income.

Whatever the proper message one should take from the optimal income tax models, it is fair to say that mainstream economists prefer the optimal income tax framework to the ability-to-pay perspective in thinking about income tax reform. As we saw in Chapter 13, the ability-to-pay viewpoint considers the equity of the income tax without reference to the inefficiencies of the tax. Much of its attention is focused on the appropriate definition of the tax base, in the name of achieving horizontal equity. The optimal income tax framework differs in two important respects. First, it presumes that one cannot think about the equity of an income tax without considering the inefficiency of the tax. The two go hand in hand because the ultimate goal of mainstream public sector economics is to maximize social welfare and this requires achieving the best balance between equity and inefficiency in designing taxes. If inefficiency is ignored, the optimal income tax models prescribe a complete leveling of incomes to the mean to maximize social welfare, and hardly anyone is in favor of that. Second, the mainstream social welfare perspective follows Musgrave's advice in being concerned primarily with vertical equity, not horizontal equity, in designing the tax. The focus is on the appropriate tax rate (set of tax rates) rather than what components of income are taxed. The two views are not entirely detached, however, since mainstream economists who favor taxing income over consumption would presumably favor taxing Haig–Simons income, and not a subset of Haig–Simons income as the current tax does. Still, the focus of the optimal income tax literature is on the appropriate tax rate (set of tax rates), not the tax base, in the name of vertical equity.

Moreover, the optimal income tax models would have roughly the same formal structure no matter what the tax base was – Haig–Simons income, some component of income such as wages, consumption, or something else. The goal would still be to maximize social welfare; equality would be the outcome if the tax were lump sum; and the consumers' (producers) responses to the tax would be the source of inefficiency. The optimal tax rate (or set of tax rates) would be the one that generates the best balance between equity and efficiency in maximizing social welfare. The mainstream social welfare perspective offers a consistent approach to the theory of distorting taxation for all taxes.

Taxes, Transfers, and Private Information

Private or asymmetric information refers to information people have about themselves that others, including the government, cannot know, at least not without costly investigation and monitoring. As noted in Chapter 2, private information is itself a form of market failure and often a very difficult one for the government to overcome. Earlier chapters discussed two important examples of private information, one related to nonexclusive public goods (Chapter 8) and the other to social insurance (Chapter 12). Both examples illustrated how private information can prevent markets from forming, so that if people want public goods or some forms of insurance, the government has to provide them. In the case of public goods, private information leads to the free-rider problem, which prevents markets from forming because individuals have no incentive to reveal their preferences. In the case of insurance, private information leads to the possibilities of moral hazard and adverse selection, which may prevent insurance companies from offering profitable insurance policies against risks that people want insured. Unfortunately, government intervention continues to be plagued by the private information of citizens. The incentives to free ride, and the possibilities of moral hazard and adverse selection, do not disappear with government provision of public goods and social insurance. The result is that the government is unlikely to provide efficient solutions to these problems.

The public goods example also illustrated how private information can cause great difficulties for the mainstream view of government as agent, in which the government is supposed to respond to market failures in accordance with the preferences of citizens. The government cannot easily do this, however, if people can hide information about their preferences and have an incentive to do so.

The difficulties with private information are by no means confined to public goods and social insurance. The government's tax and transfer policies are often plagued by private information as well. The problem with taxes is that taxpayers may be able to hide part of the tax base from the government, which reduces the revenue raised from the tax. Examples are people hiding sources of income from the government under a personal income tax, or firms engaging in cash transactions with their customers and not reporting these sales under a sales tax. The more that income or sales are hidden from governments, the higher the tax rates must be to raise a given amount of revenue. As we saw in Chapter 15, the inefficiency or deadweight loss of a tax increases by the square of the tax rate.

The problem with transfers is that people may be able to exploit their private information to receive transfer payments that are not intended for them. An example is people with incomes well above the poverty line who are able to hide enough of their incomes to appear to be poor and thus qualify for various kinds of public assistance. Attempts by the government to prevent this behavior can significantly alter the design of transfer programs relative to what they would be under perfect information. More generally, the government's attempt to redistribute income in the name of end-results equity or distributive justice could be undermined if information about people's economic well-being is largely private. The government might not be able to tax and transfer to satisfy the interpersonal equity condition for a social welfare maximum even if it could use lump-sum taxes and transfers.

Chapter 17 considers these informational problems with taxes and transfers. We begin with taxation, using the personal income tax as an example.

PRIVATE INFORMATION AND TAXATION

Tax authorities distinguish between two very different methods that taxpayers can use to reduce their taxes: tax avoidance and tax evasion. *Tax avoidance* refers to taxpayers taking advantage of the provisions of the tax laws to reduce their tax liabilities, such as reducing their taxable income under the U.S. federal personal income tax by investing in tax-free retirement securities, and claiming deductions for charitable contributions or interest on their home mortgages. Tax avoidance is entirely legal. Indeed, Congress put these provisions into the personal income tax to encourage people to save for retirement, contribute to charity, and purchase their own homes rather than renting. It hopes that taxpayers will take advantage of the exclusions and deductions made available to them.

Tax evasion, in contrast, is illegal behavior. It refers to exploiting private information to reduce taxes, such as taxpayers choosing not to declare on their tax returns sources of income that they know are taxable, or claiming as a deduction charitable contributions that they did not actually make. The IRS tries to limit tax evasion by auditing a selection of tax returns each year and imposing severe penalties on cheaters, including heavy fines and even imprisonment in some cases. Its efforts are only modestly successful, however, primarily because it is able to audit only a small percentage of the returns. The IRS itself estimated that taxpayers were able to evade between $198 billion and $234 billion of tax liabilities in 2001 under the personal income tax, approximately 22% of the revenues collected (U.S. Government Accountability Office, 2005, Table, p. 1). Departments of Revenue everywhere struggle with the problem of tax evasion with all their taxes.

THE ECONOMICS OF TAX EVASION

Since tax evasion is criminal behavior, economists analyze it using variations of the standard economic model of crime first developed by Michael Allingham and Agnar Sandmo. Allingham and Sandmo (1972) viewed criminal behavior as the outcome of a straight economic expected value calculation. Think of robbery as an example. The idea is that a potential thief weighs the benefit of the crime, which consists of the utility received from the sum of money to be stolen, against the cost of the crime, which consists of the utility received under the penalty if caught. Both the benefit and cost are expected values, since they include the thief's estimate of the probability of being caught. The expected benefit is the probability of not being caught times the utility from the money to be stolen, and the expected cost is the probability of being caught times the utility under the penalty. Economists assume that in situations involving uncertainty, individuals attempt to maximize their expected utility. Therefore, a crime occurs only if the expected utility of the crime is positive or, equivalently, if the expected benefit exceeds the expected cost. Suppose that it does. Then the optimal amount of criminal activity is that which maximizes the expected utility or the expected net benefit, the difference between the expected benefit and the expected cost. The net benefit is maximized when the expected marginal benefit equals the expected marginal cost.

If potential tax evaders view evasion as strictly an economic decision, then tax evasion fits directly into the economic model of crime. Suppose a taxpayer earns income Y, and that Y is private information. The IRS cannot know Y unless it audits the taxpayer's return. To simplify the example, assume that the personal income tax is a flat tax, with tax rate t. If the taxpayer is honest, he declares all his income, pays a tax of tY, and has income $Y(1 - t)$ after tax.

A tax evader, in contrast, has to decide how much of Y to declare on his tax return, where Y_D is the declared income. The probability of being caught (audited) is p, which means that the probability of not being caught (not audited) is $(1 - p)$. If not caught, the taxpayer pays a tax only on the declared income, equal to tY_D. If caught, the taxpayer pays a tax on all his income at rate t, plus a fine f on the taxes that should have been paid on the amount of the undeclared income $(Y - Y_D)$. The fine is $ft(Y - Y_D)$. Therefore, the two possible after-tax incomes are:

Not caught: $Y_{NC} = Y - tY_D$

Caught: $Y_C = Y - tY - ft(Y-Y_D) = Y(1 - t - ft) + ftY_D$

with corresponding utilities

Not caught: $U(Y_{NC}) = U(Y - tY_D)$

Caught: $U(Y_C) = U(Y(1 - t - ft) + ftY_D)$

The tax evader's expected utility is:

$$E(U) = (1 - p)U(Y_{NC}) + pU(Y_C),$$

and both Y_{NC} and Y_C depend on Y_D, the amount of declared income.

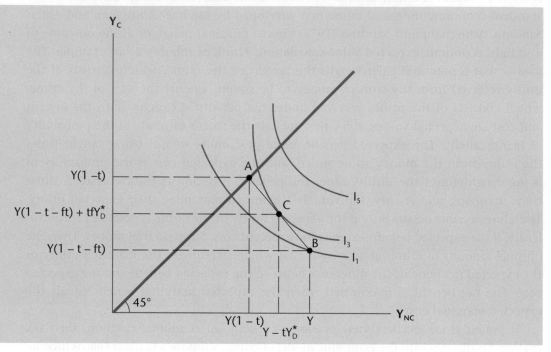

Figure 17.1

Figure 17.1 pictures the tax evader's decision problem. The income if not caught, Y_{NC}, is on the horizontal axis and the income if caught, Y_C, is on the vertical axis. The indifference curves are the different levels of expected utility for different values of Y_{NC} and Y_C. The 45° line is a frame of reference line for the honest taxpayer who declares all his income, so that $Y_{NC} = Y_C = Y(1 - t)$ for any level of income Y. The line segment AB indicates the different combinations of income available to the taxpayer for different amounts of declared income Y_D. It is constructed as follows.

At the given level of income, Y, the honest taxpayer who declares all his income is at point A on the 45° line, with after-tax income of $Y(1 - t)$. As the dishonest tax evader decreases the amount of declared income, the amount of after-tax income if not caught, Y_{NC}, increases and the amount of after-tax income if caught, Y_C, decreases. The taxpayer moves southeast from point A. The limit is point B, for which the taxpayer declares none of his income. If not caught, $Y_{NC} = Y$ at B. If caught, $Y_C = Y - tY - ftY = Y(1 - t - ft)$ at B. As the taxpayer decreases the amount of income declared, Y_D, between the end points A and B, the ratio of the change in Y_C to the change in Y_{NC}, the slope of AB, is constant at (–)f, the penalty rate. That is, AB is a straight line with slope –f. To see this, refer to the formulas for Y_{NC} and Y_C. If Y_D decreases by \$1, the taxpayer's after-tax income decreases by \$ft if caught and increases by \$t if not caught. Therefore, the slope, $dY_C/dY_{NC} = -ft/t = -f$, a constant. AB acts as the budget line for the evader in the decision on Y_D.

The evader's goal is to maximize his expected utility, reach the highest indifference curve, given the income opportunities available to him along the budget line AB.

The maximum expected utility occurs at point C, at which indifference curve I_3 is tangent to AB. The optimal amount of declared income is Y_D^*, generating income $Y_{NC}^C = Y - tY_D^*$ if not caught and $Y_C^C = Y(1 - t - ft) + tfY_D^*$ if caught. At C, the marginal rate of substitution between the two incomes, the slope of the indifference curve I_3, equals the slope of the budget line, the standard condition for a consumer to be in equilibrium. The MRS_{Y_{NC}, Y_C} is the negative of the ratio of the expected marginal utilities of the two incomes, equal to $-\dfrac{(1-p)MU_Y(Y_{NC})}{pMU_Y(Y_C)}$. The slope of AB is $(-)f$. Therefore, at the optimal Y_D^*,

$$\frac{(1-p)MU_Y(Y_{NC})}{pMU_Y(Y_C)} = f.$$

The equilibrium condition can also be interpreted as choosing Y_D such that the expected marginal benefit equals the expected marginal cost. As noted above, reducing Y_D increases after-tax income by t if not caught and decreases after-tax income by ft if caught. Therefore the expected marginal benefit of reducing Y_D by \$1 is $(1-p)MU_Y(Y_{NC})t$ and the expected marginal cost is $pMU_Y(Y_C)ft$. At Y_D^*, the expected marginal benefit equals the expected marginal cost, or $(1-p)MU_Y(Y_{NC})t = pMU_Y(Y_C)ft$. Since t appears on both sides of the equation, $(1-p)MU_Y(Y_{NC}) = pMU_Y(Y_C)f$. Dividing both sides by $pMU_Y(Y_C)$ yields the taxpayer equilibrium condition.

POLICIES TO REDUCE TAX EVASION

The IRS has two policy tools to reduce or eliminate tax evasion, either increasing the penalty rate, f, or increasing the probability of being caught, p, by auditing a higher proportion of tax returns. The two are not equivalent, however, because increased auditing requires more resources, whereas increasing the penalty rate is virtually costless to the IRS. At some point, the additional resources required to increase p may well exceed the additional tax revenues collected from the reduction in tax evasion. No such trade-off between resource costs and additional tax revenues exists for increases in the penalty rate.

Increasing the penalty rate

Figure 17.2(a) illustrates the effect of increasing the penalty rate. An increase in f increases the slope of the budget line, rotating it from AB to AB'. The new equilibrium is at point D, at which indifference curve I_2 is tangent to AB'. Since Y_{NC} decreases, and $Y_{NC} = Y - tY_D$, the amount of declared income increases.

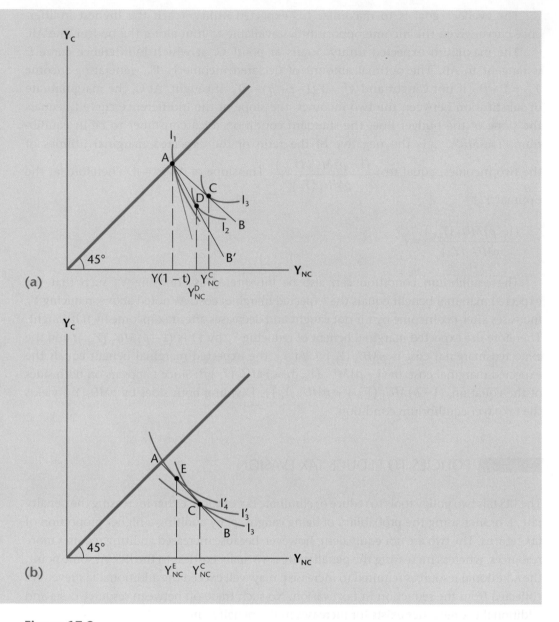

Figure 17.2

To eliminate tax evasion, the government has to increase the penalty rate f by enough to drive the taxpayer to equilibrium on the 45° line, along which $Y_D = Y$. To calculate the f that achieves this, note first that the equilibrium condition along the 45° line is that $MRS_{Y_{NC},Y_C} = -f$. But $MRS_{Y_{NC},Y_C} = -\dfrac{(1-p)MU_Y(Y_{NC})}{pMU_Y(Y_C)}$. Since $Y_{NC} = Y_C$ along the 45° line, the marginal utilities are also equal along the 45° line and the $MRS_{Y_{NC}=Y_C} = -(1-p)/p$. Therefore, if the penalty rate f, the (negative) of the slope of AB, is raised to $(1-p)/p$, then

$MRS_{Y_{NC}, Y_C = Y_{NC}} = -f$. (The gray line has a slope of $-f$.) The taxpayer is in equilibrium along the 45° line and declares all his income – at point A on indifference curve I_1 in Figure 17.2(a).

Raising penalties high enough can always eliminate criminal behavior in the economic model of crime, but the penalties may have to be quite severe. For example, suppose that the probability of an audit, p, is 2% (.02). Then $(1 - p)/p = .98/.02 = 49$. The penalty rate would have to be 49 times the taxes owed on the undeclared income. Society may well decide that such a high penalty violates the legal principle that the penalty must be appropriate to the crime. If so, then the IRS would have to bear the costs of increased auditing of tax returns to help reduce or eliminate evasion.

Increasing the probability of being caught

An increase in auditing activity increases p, which decreases $(1-p)/p$ and therefore also decreases MRS_{Y_{NC}, Y_C}, the slope of the indifference curves. That is, the indifference curves flatten at every combination (Y_{NC}, Y_C), as illustrated in Figure 17.2(b). Also, the indifference curve I_3' through point C represents a lower level of utility than the original indifference curve I_3, since an increase in p increases the proportion of expected utility accounted for by $U(Y_C)$, the after-tax utility if caught.

Point C on the flatter I_3' is no longer the equilibrium for the taxpayer. The new equilibrium is point E, at which indifference curve I_4' is tangent to the budget line AB. Once again, Y_{NC} has decreased, which implies that Y_D has increased – the taxpayer declares more income. As above, increasing p such that $(1 - p)/p = f$ eliminates the evasion, but this may require a prodigious auditing effort. For example, if $f = 2$, a fairly stiff penalty of 200% of taxes due on the undeclared income, then p would have to be 1/3 to eliminate

tax evasion: $[\dfrac{\left(1 - \dfrac{1}{3}\right)}{\dfrac{1}{3}} = \dfrac{\dfrac{2}{3}}{\dfrac{1}{3}} = 2]$. Raising the probability of being caught to 33% would

require a huge amount of additional resources, so much that the benefits of the increased tax collections may well be less than the increased resource costs. A combined strategy of steep penalties combined with modest increases in auditing resources that sharply reduces but does eliminate tax evasion is likely to be the best option for the IRS.

Changes in tax rates

A final point to note is that the tax rate t may also affect the amount of tax evasion. In our simple example, the slope of the budget line AB, $-f$, is independent of t. Therefore, changes in t cause parallel shifts in the budget line AB. An increase in t shifts AB down and a decrease in t shifts AB up.[1] Figure 17.3 illustrates the effect of an increase in t.

An increase in t shifts AB down to A'B'. The equilibrium is now at point F, the point of tangency between I_2 and AB'. The figure assumes that both Y_{NC} and Y_C are normal goods, so that both income levels decrease. The decreases in the after-tax incomes are due primarily to the higher tax rate. Whether declared income, Y_D, increases or decreases is ambiguous. Suppose that the tax rate increases from t to t'. On the one hand, a decrease in Y_D leads to a larger after-tax income, Y_{NC}, if the person is not caught, by the amount $(t' - t)\Delta Y_D$. The marginal benefit of tax evasion increases. On the other hand, a decrease in Y_D leads to a smaller after-tax income Y_C if the person is caught, by the amount $(t' - t)f\Delta Y_D$. The marginal cost of tax evasion also increases. Therefore, whether Y_D increases or decreases depends on the values of $(1 - p)$ and p and the marginal utilities of income at Y_{NC} and Y_C. Different penalty formulas may lead to nonparallel shifts in the budget line and have different effects on tax evasion. But in our specification of the tax penalty, changes in the tax rate can either increase or decrease tax evasion.

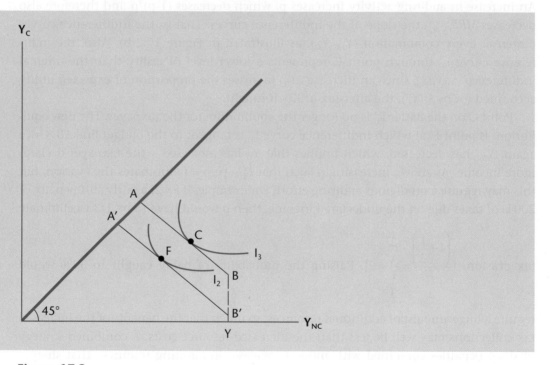

Figure 17.3

STRATEGIES FOR RAISING TAX REVENUES

Raising penalties and increasing auditing to reduce tax evasion would appear to be particularly attractive alternatives to increasing tax rates in order to raise more tax revenue. Raising tax rates sharply increases the deadweight loss of a tax, whereas the other two strategies penalize or deter cheaters in addition to raising revenue. The resource costs of the increase in auditing would have to be balanced against the resulting increase in tax revenues, and raising tax rates may be the only viable option if large amounts of new revenue are required. Nonetheless, stiffer penalties and/or increased auditing are certainly worth considering as revenue-raising options.

Before using these options, however, society has to address a prior question: Does it really want to deter or eliminate tax evasion? The answer is probably yes, but it is not entirely clear-cut. It depends in part on who counts in the social welfare function. Think of society as consisting of sets of people: honest people, labeled H, who would never evade paying their taxes; and dishonest people, labeled DH, who behave according to the economic model of crime and are quite willing to engage in tax evasion. Society may well decide that social welfare should depend only on the honest people, which we can represent by the social welfare function $W = W(U^H)$. Social welfare should not increase if the utility of the dishonest people increases because of the ill-gotten gains from evading their taxes. In effect, the dishonest people rule themselves out of society's consideration. Alternatively, society may decide that everyone should count, which we can represent by the social welfare function $W = W(U^H, U^{DH})$. Dishonest behavior is not necessarily condoned, but it does not ostracize people from the rest of society.

In the former case, there is no question that society would want to eliminate tax evasion. Eliminating evasion increases the tax revenues available to the government, thereby lowering the tax burden on the honest people. Moreover, the loss in utility to the dishonest people by the government's efforts to reduce evasion is of no consequence to social welfare. The government should raise the penalty rate sufficiently to eliminate evasion, to $(1 - p)/p$ in our simple model above. There is no need to worry about the penalty fitting the crime since the dishonest people do not count. Nor is there any reason to bear the resource costs of increased auditing.

The latter case is more subtle, however, and undoubtedly the more realistic one. People are forgiven for past transgressions after they have borne their punishment. The difficulty here is that there is now a social welfare trade-off between the honest and the dishonest people. As noted, the honest people lose from the tax evasion of the dishonest people because they have to pay more in taxes to meet the government's revenue requirements. By lowering their utility, the tax evasion lowers social welfare. At the same time, however, the dishonest people are better off if allowed to evade their taxes. Indeed, the ideal from their point of view is to be able to evade all their taxes. By raising their utility, the tax evasion raises social welfare. Therefore, allowing tax evasion would raise social welfare if the utility gains of the dishonest people increase social welfare by more than the utility losses of the honest people lower social welfare.

There are two cases for which social welfare might increase under tax evasion:

1. A high percentage of the population is dishonest. At some point, societies can reach a tipping point in which the notion that "(almost) everyone cheats" becomes a reality. Trying to stop cheating may be futile once cheating has become the norm.
2. The people who cheat are primarily poor. The poor have relatively high social marginal utilities of income, so that their increases in utility from cheating get more weight in the social welfare function, perhaps much more, than nonpoor honest

taxpayers. One thinks of the underground economy, in which transactions for labor services are often in cash and cannot be traced by the tax authorities. Underground economies are no doubt beneficial to many poor people, although certainly not exclusively to the poor.

The incentives to form underground markets for products legal and illegal cast the market system in a completely different light. The mainstream perspective is that the market system is good, not bad. Government intervention is justified only by market failures; otherwise, well-functioning markets should allocate goods and services. When markets go underground, however, they become a problem for the government, no matter how efficient they may be, precisely because they make it difficult for the government to collect tax revenue. How big the problem is depends in part on whether the people who engage in underground transactions are counted in social welfare and, if so, with what social marginal utility weight.

One suspects that for most of the developed market economies, the proportion of people who evade taxes is sufficiently low and sufficiently concentrated among the nonpoor to justify efforts by the government to reduce tax evasion. This is just a guess, however. Reliable data on evasion and underground markets are obviously difficult to obtain.

TAX AMNESTIES

Penalties and increased auditing are the stick approaches to reducing tax evasion. The gentler carrot approach is the tax amnesty, in which the Department of Revenue (DOR) grants tax evaders a few months' time to declare and pay taxes on previously hidden income without penalty. Whether tax amnesties are effective or not is problematic. Their intention is to entice risk-averse taxpayers who are afraid of being audited to come forward and admit their past evasions. Even better if these taxpayers subsequently mend their ways and cease evading taxes. But there are disadvantages to amnesties as well. Less risk-averse tax evaders may confess once, but then continue to evade taxes if they believe that the DOR is likely to have another amnesty period at some future date. Paying taxes later is better than paying taxes now if you can get away with it. Also, some honest taxpayers are likely to resent such lenient treatment of tax evaders. Worse yet, they may become tax evaders themselves if their resentment is strong enough, leading to the worrisome possibility that a tax amnesty could increase overall tax evasion.

The empirical analysis of tax amnesties is not encouraging. One well-known study by James Alm and William Beck (1993) looked at income tax collections in Colorado preceding, during, and following a tax amnesty granted from September 15 through November 15, 1985. They found that the amnesty had no effect on tax collections, not even during the amnesty period. Perhaps some of the honest taxpayers did rebel and begin to evade taxes, although Alm and Beck had no way of testing for this possibility.

PRIVATE INFORMATION AND TRANSFER PAYMENTS

The mainstream theory of transfer payments under perfect information has two main strands. One is the notion of Pareto-optimal redistributions, which came to the theory through the public choice perspective (discussed in Chapter 10). The other is the interpersonal equity condition for a social welfare maximum to promote end-results equity or distributive justice (discussed in Chapter 4). Let's briefly review each theory.

Pareto-optimal redistributions are transfers made to promote efficiency and bring the economy to its utility possibilities frontier. They arise if the nonpoor are altruistic towards the poor, such that the utility of the nonpoor depends on some characteristic of the poor. In effect, the economic deprivation of the poor confers a consumption externality on the nonpoor. The form of the transfers depends on what it is about the poor that bothers the nonpoor. If they view the poor as lacking in resources to purchase adequate amounts of life's necessities – food, clothing, shelter, medical care – then the transfers should be in cash. If they view the poor as lacking in a particular good, such as having insufficient food, then the transfer should be in the form of a subsidy of the poor's consumption of food. In this case, the transfers to support these goods can be *decentralized*; the market for food continues to operate as before, with the government reimbursing the poor for their purchases of food at the subsidy rate. Being able to decentralize in-kind transfers is desirable from the mainstream perspective because it reduces the government's intervention in the economy relative to cash transfers, which must be provided by the government (that is, *centralized*).

The mainstream theory agrees that Pareto-optimal redistributions are necessary to bring the economy to the utility possibilities frontier if people are altruistic, but that they are not sufficient in and of themselves. Society must also reach the best point on the frontier, the bliss point, to satisfy end-results equity or distributive justice. This requires an additional set of lump-sum taxes and transfers until the social marginal utility of income is equal for all people. (The transfers must also be lump sum to keep the economy on the frontier.) If these equity-based taxes and transfers sufficiently reduce the economic gap between the nonpoor and the poor such that the altruistic impulses of the nonpoor towards the poor disappear, then the Pareto-optimal redistributions would not be necessary.

THE BLACKORBY–DONALDSON MODEL OF HEALTHCARE

Private information can have dramatic implications for both strands of the mainstream theory. One implication for Pareto-optimal redistributions is that the decentralized provision of in-kind aid through subsidies may not be the best strategy. Government rationing of the aid may be preferred to decentralized subsidies. The other implication is that the government may not be able to establish the set of taxes and transfers needed to equalize the social marginal utility of income across all people even if it could tax and transfer lump sum. The source of the problem in each case is the same: With poor information about people, the government may not be able to prevent some people from claiming subsidies that are not intended for them if it adopts the perfect information policy prescriptions. Economists say that the perfect information transfer policies may not be implementable. Their desirable properties are irrelevant if the government cannot implement them as intended.

One of the first models of transfers under imperfect information was by Charles Blackorby and David Donaldson (1988). It is a very simple model of the provision of healthcare to medically needy people that illustrates how both strands of the mainstream theory are vulnerable to private information. It also serves to illustrate the *mechanism design problem* – how to design transfer programs so that people have an incentive to reveal the truth about themselves. In this case, the issue is whether those who claim to be ill really are sick and in need of medical care.

Blackorby–Donaldson assume that the economy consists of two groups of people, the healthy (H) and the ill (I). People within each group are identical, so they are represented by a single individual within the group. The economy produces two goods, an all-purpose commodity Y and medical care Z that can improve the health of those who are ill. The healthy people gain utility only from Y, whereas the ill people gain utility from both Y and Z. Their utility functions are:

$$U^H = Y_H$$

$$U^I = Y_I - e^{(1-Z)}$$

Notice that Z cannot cure the ill, only reduce the severity of their illness. If they purchase or receive no medical care, $Z = 0$, and they bear the full brunt of their illness. Their utility decreases by e, which is approximately equal to 2.8. As they purchase more medicine, the utility loss from their illness decreases. At $Z = 1$, the loss in utility is reduced to $-e^{(1-1)} = -e^0 = -1$. If Z is greater than 1, then the exponent becomes negative and $e^{(1-Z)}$ becomes less than 1.

The production side of the economy is extremely simple. The economy has 6 units of a resource that can be used to produce either Y or Z. The production possibilities frontier is $Y + Z = 6$. Alternatively, since Y goes either to H or to I, $Y_H + Y_I + Z = 6$.

The first-best, perfect information case

Suppose the government had perfect information about the two groups of people, so that it could reach the utility possibilities frontier. This is referred to as the first-best frontier, to distinguish it from the more restrictive second-best frontier under private information.

The first-best utility possibilities frontier is easy to characterize because the model is so simple. There is only one Pareto-optimal condition that must be satisfied for the economy to be on its frontier; the marginal rate of substitution and marginal rate of transformation between Y and Z must be equal. The MRT_{YZ} is the slope of the production possibilities frontier, equal to –1. One more unit of Y implies one less unit of Z, and vice versa. The $MRS_{Y,Z}$ applies only to I, since only he gains utility from Z. The $MRS_{Y_I,Z}$ is the ratio of his marginal utilities of the two goods, MU_Z/MU_Y. The MU_Z is

the derivative of U_I with respect to Z. The derivative of the function $e^{V(Z)}$ is $e^{V(Z)}\dfrac{dV}{dZ}$,

the function itself times the derivative of the exponent with respect to Z. Therefore

$\dfrac{d-e^{(1-Z)}}{dZ}=-e^{(1-Z)}(-1)=e^{(1-Z)}$. The $MU_Y=1$ – one more unit of Y_I increases I's utility by one

unit. Thus $MRS_{Y_I,Z}=MU_Z/MU_Y=e^{(1-Z)}$. The $MRS_{Y_I,Z}=MRT_{Y,Z}=1$, only if $Z=1$. Therefore, Z must equal 1 for the economy to be on its first-best utility possibilities frontier.

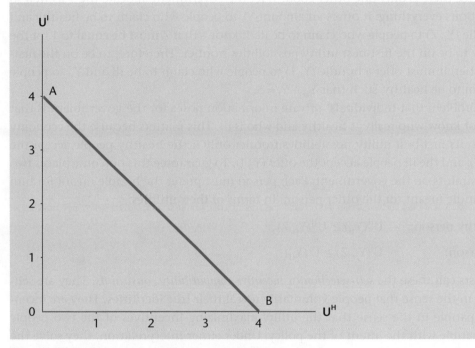

Figure 17.4

If $Z=1$, then society has 5 units of the resource to distribute between H and I for the purchase of Y. The first-best utility possibilities frontier is illustrated by Figure 17.4 for the different allocations of Y. H's utility is on the horizontal axis and I's utility is on the vertical axis. Suppose $Y_H=0$. Then $U^H=0$ and $U^I=5-e^{(1-1)}=5-1=4$. I's utility is always one less than his allocation of Y_I with $Z=1$. Point A (0,4) is one end point of the first-best frontier, the point of maximum gain for I. The opposite end point B (4,0) occurs if H receives 4 units of Y: $U^H=4$ and $U_I=1-1=0$. Between A and B the slope of the first-best frontier is –1, since a one-unit decrease in Y_I implies a one-unit decrease in U^I and a one-unit increase in Y_H implies a one-unit increase in U^H. Therefore the first-best utility possibilities frontier is the straight line segment AB.[2]

The second-best private information case

Suppose the government has very poor information about people, to the point that it does not know who is healthy and who is ill. This is very bad information indeed, the worst possible case, but it is the easiest way to illustrate the potential problems caused by private information.[3]

The first question to ask is whether the government can achieve parts of the first-best utility possibilities frontier in the face of its imperfect information. To consider this, suppose that the government chooses to ration the medicine through a government-run clinic. Since there is only one other good, Y, let the government allocate the Y as well so that it rations everything. It offers an amount Y_H to people who claim to be healthy and the bundle (Y_I, Z) to people who claim to be ill. It knows that Z must be equal to 1 for the economy to be on the first-best utility possibilities frontier. Therefore, to be on the first-best frontier, it must offer a bundle $(Y_I, 1)$ to people who claim to be ill and Y_H to people who claim to be healthy, such that $Y_H + Y_I = 5$.

The problem that individuals' private information poses for the government is that it does not know who really is healthy and who is ill. This matters because the economy can be on its first-best utility possibilities frontier only if the healthy people accept the offer of Y_H and the ill people accept the offer (Y_I, I). To guarantee this outcome places two new constraints on the government: Each person must prefer the bundle meant for him to the bundle meant for the other person. In terms of their utilities:

Healthy person: $\quad U^H(Y_H) \geq U^H(Y_I, Z)$

Ill person: $\quad U^I(Y_I, Z) \geq U^I(Y_H)$

Economists call these the *self-selection* or *incentive compatibility constraints*. They are self-selecting in the sense that people voluntarily reveal their true identities. They are incentive compatible in the sense that the utility-maximizing incentives of the two people are compatible with the intent of the policy. Under either interpretation, they solve the mechanism design problem because they ensure that people will tell the truth about themselves.

Consider the self-selection constraint of the healthy person. H cares only about Y; she has no use for Z. So she will accept Y_H over (Y_I, Z) only if Y_H is at least as large as Y_I. With $Z = 1$ along the first-best frontier, there are 5 units of Y to be split up between H and I. The self-selection constraint implies that H must receive at least half of the Y, or that $Y_H \geq 2.5$. Therefore, $Y_H = U^H = 2.5$ is one limiting value of the first-best utility possibilities frontier obtainable given the private information, point A (2.5, 1.5) in Figure 17.5. H could be given less then 2.5 units of Y, but then I must also be given less than 2.5 units. With $Y_H + Y_I < 5$, $Z > 1$ and $MRS_{Y_I, Z} \neq MRT_{Y,Z} = 1$. The economy would be on a second-best utility possibilities frontier to the left of $U^H = 2.5$, as illustrated in Figure 17.5.

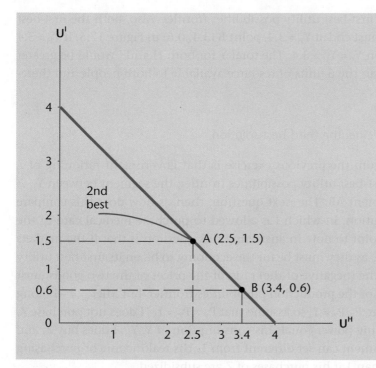

Figure 17.5

Consider next the self-selection constraint for I. I would like to have some Z to improve his health, but he will accept Y_{II} over (Y_L, Z) if Y_H is sufficiently greater than Y_I to overcome the lack of Z. This establishes an upper limit on the amount of Y_H to ensure that I tells the truth about himself and the economy is on the first-best frontier. At the upper limit

$$U^I(Y_I, 1) = Y_I - e^{(1-1)} = Y_H - e^{(1-0)} = U^I(Y_H, 0)$$

$$Y_I - 1 = Y_H - e$$

But $Y_I + Y_H = 5$, or $Y_I = 5 - Y_H$. Therefore

$$5 - Y_H - 1 = Y_H - e$$

e is approximately 2.8. Therefore

$$2Y_H = 4 + e = 4 + 2.8 = 6.8$$

$$Y_H = 3.4$$

If I takes H's allocation of $Y_H = 3.4$, his utility is $U_I = 3.4 - e = 3.4 - 2.8 = 0.6$. With $Y_H = 3.4$, $Y_I = 1.6$. If I instead accepts the allocation intended for him (1.6,1), then his utility is $U_I = 1.6 - 1 = 0.6$, the same as accepting Y_H. Therefore I must receive at least 1.6 units of Y for the economy to be on its first-best utility possibilities frontier. Any less and he pretends to be H. Since H also claims to be H for any $Y_H \geq 2.5$, no Z is produced and the economy cannot be on its first-best utility possibilities frontier. Also, both the first-best and second-best frontiers must end at $Y_H = 3.4$, point B (3.4, 0.6) in Figure 17.5. If $Y_H > 3.4$ and I pretends to be H, then $Y_I = Y_H > 3.4$. The total Y for both H and I would be greater than 6.8, which is more than the 6 units of resource available to both people and therefore not feasible.

Subsidies to purchase medicine: the third-best solution

One conclusion to draw from the previous exercise is that government rationing of Z can generate part of the first-best utility possibilities frontier, the segment between $Y_H \geq$ 2.5 and $Y_H \leq 3.4$, line segment AB. The next question, then, is how does this compare with the decentralized solution, in which I is allowed to purchase medical care in the private market? The first point to note in answering this question is that if the markets for Y and Z are competitive, as they must be for the economy to be on its first-best utility possibilities frontier, then the (negative of the) ratio of the prices of the two goods must equal the $MRT_{Y,Z}$, the slope of the production possibilities frontier. But $MRT_{Y,Z} = -1$ along the entire frontier. Therefore $P_Y/P_Z = 1$, so assume that $P_Y = P_Z = 1$. H does not purchase Z. His real income or purchasing power equals his consumption of Y, Y_H. I does buy Z, and at a price q that the government can set different from 1. His real income or purchasing power is $Y_I + qZ$. q is less than 1 if his purchases of Z are subsidized.

Notice, first, that q must equal 1 to be on the first-best utility possibilities frontier – Z cannot be subsidized. This follows because consumers set their MRSs between two goods to the ratio of the goods' prices to maximize utility, and I's $MRS_{Y_I,Z}$ must equal 1, the MRT, to be on the first-best frontier. With $P_Y = 1$, the price of Z to I must also be 1, so that q must be 1.

The no-subsidy result is peculiar to Blackorby–Donaldson's simple model. The healthy people show no altruism towards the ill people and thus there is no reason to subsidize I's purchases of Z. A richer model with altruism towards the ill would call for a subsidy to be on the first-best utility possibilities frontier – a Pareto-optimal redistribution from H to I.

More importantly from an informational standpoint, the self-selection or incentive compatibility constraint in the presence of a subsidy for Z requires that H and I must have the same purchasing power. In other words, the constraint is that $Y_H = Y_I + qZ = 3$, no matter at what value the government sets q. The reason is that if the purchasing power were unequal, everyone would claim to be the person with the higher purchasing power. For example, suppose I had higher purchasing power than H. Then H would claim to be I. Since the government cannot know who is healthy and who is ill, it also cannot know what the rich would do with their purchasing power. H could claim to buy Z and receive the subsidy, but in fact spend all her purchasing power on Y_H. Alternatively, if H has the higher purchasing power, I would claim to be H and use some of the Y_H to purchase Z.

The equal purchasing power constraint implies that only one point on the first-best utility possibilities frontier is possible under the decentralized policy. With $Y_H = Y_I + qZ$, and $q = 1$ and $Z = 1$ on the first-best frontier, the allocations are $Y_H = 3$, $Y_I = 2$ and $Z = 1$. The utilities achieved are $U^H = Y_H = 3$, and $U^I = Y_I - e^{(1-1)} = 2 - 1 = 1$. In Figure 17.6, point C (3,1) is the only point on the first-best utility possibilities frontier obtainable under a decentralized subsidy policy.

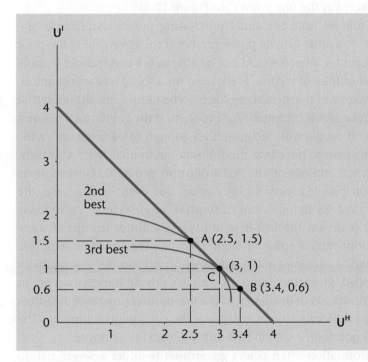

Figure 17.6

Other allocations of utility can be achieved by subsidizing Z ($q < 1$) to favor I, or by taxing Z ($q > 1$) to favor H.[4] They are shown by the line through point C in Figure 17.6 labeled 3rd best. These allocations cannot be first best because $q \neq 1$. They must also be below the second-best frontier, as drawn, because the constraint of equal purchasing power is more stringent than any of the constrained areas on the second-best frontier. For example, suppose a subsidy of Z led to $Y_H = U^H = 2.5$, at the juncture of the second-best and first-best frontiers. Under the rationing policy, Y_I also equals 2.5 and $Z = 1$. That cannot be an equilibrium under the subsidy policy because I has more purchasing power than H. H would claim to be I. Therefore, when $Y_H = U^H = 2.5$, under the subsidy policy, $Y_I + qZ$ would also have to equal 2.5. That can only happen if $q < 1$, $Z > 1$, and $Y_I < 2.5$, which places I below the utility he achieves under the rationing policy.[5]

Two important implications follow from the model. The first is that government rationing of medical care is preferred to a decentralized subsidy of medical care except for the one case in which resources are equalized across the healthy and the ill. This is not so far-fetched. Think of unscrupulous doctors in the United States who submit invoices to Medicare, Medicaid, and private insurers for medical services they never performed.

Suppose the government cannot easily monitor doctors and patients to determine whether medical services are actually provided, and false claims became widespread. Then it might be cheaper for the government to provide the medical services itself through government-run clinics rather than subsidize patients for the services. The government's information in the Blackorby–Donaldson model is so poor that government rationing of the medicine is the preferred alternative (except at the one point C in Figure 17.6).

The second implication follows from the equal purchasing power result under the decentralized option. It points to a more general problem, that if the government has poor information about people's incomes, then it would not be able to tax and transfer income to equalize the social marginal utilities of income as required for a social welfare optimum. The issue is not that real-life taxes and transfers are unlikely to be lump sum, although that is true enough. It is a more fundamental informational problem. If the government cannot know people's incomes, then all people with incomes high enough to be taxed under the redistribution program would claim to have low enough income to qualify for a subsidy. The government simply cannot implement the redistribution program. Governments do have some information on people's incomes, of course. But even in that case, the Blackorby–Donaldson model suggests an important truth, that the government is unlikely to be able to reach the bliss point on the first-best utility possibilities frontier if some people have private information about some of their income. The government's tax-transfer programs would have to be cognizant of the self-selection or incentive compatibility constraints that must be satisfied, given the nature of people's private information about their incomes. Adding these constraints to the design of the tax-transfer program guarantees that the bliss point is no longer achievable if one or more of the constraints is binding. The government is then limited to points on a second-best utility possibilities frontier.

In conclusion, private information often places governments under a severe handicap as they try to promote the public interest in equity and efficiency. Free riding, moral hazard and adverse selection, tax evasion, and restrictions on the nature of transfers – the list of difficulties is long and covers a number of the more important market failures that governments in capitalist nations are asked to overcome.

CHAPTER 18

Tax Incidence: Theoretical Issues

Public sector economics is still commonly referred to as public finance, which was the original name of the discipline. The British economists following Adam Smith who studied the government sector, and who had the most influence on U.S. economists, focused almost exclusively on tax theory and policy until the middle of the 20th century, when public expenditures began to receive equal attention and the title public finance began to give way to public sector economics.

One of the central issues of public finance has always been the question of tax incidence: Who bears the burden of a particular tax or set of taxes? Economists distinguish the *incidence* – the burden – of a tax from the *impact* of a tax, which refers to the agents on whom a tax is levied, the agents who write the tax checks to the government. The incidence and impact of a tax may differ because governments tax market transactions or marketable commodities, so that markets naturally respond to taxation. For instance, a sales tax is levied on business firms; they write the tax checks to the government and thus bear the impact of the tax. But they may be able to avoid some, or all, of the incidence of the tax if they can pass the tax on to consumers in the form of higher prices. If so, then the consumers bear some, or all, of the incidence of the tax even though they do not literally pay the tax. The ultimate interest in economic analysis is the incidence of a tax, not its impact.

The professional literature on tax incidence is voluminous, perhaps the largest in all of public sector economics. It is a difficult literature for students to tackle, and not only for it sheer size. It also happens to contain many different approaches to measuring incidence, both empirical and theoretical, and this is bound to be confusing at first pass.

The study of tax incidence is ultimately an empirical exercise. Its goal is to determine the burden of the various taxes that governments use so that public officials can make reasoned equity judgments about them. Does a particular tax help or hinder society's quest for distributive justice? The answer to this question requires knowing the incidence of the tax. Yet there are sharp disagreements in the professional economics literature on the incidence of some of the major taxes. One of the more famous examples relates to corporation income tax. Two of the leading public sector economists in the last half of the 20th century, Richard Musgrave and Arnold Harberger, conducted independent studies of the incidence of U.S. corporation income tax (Krzyzaniak and Musgrave, 1963; Harberger, 1962). Musgrave concluded that the tax was passed on more than 100% to consumers, whereas Harberger concluded that the burden of the tax fell almost entirely on corporate stockholders. There are sharp differences of opinion as well among respected economists on the incidence of sales taxes, Social Security payroll tax, and property tax.

The differences in the empirical literature arise in part because the theory of tax incidence is far from settled. Economists have proposed different measures of tax incidence that are not necessarily consistent with one another. They also disagree on the appropriate design of a tax incidence analysis, including such issues as whether the incidence of a tax can be considered independently from the rest of a government's budget and whether incidence should be measured on an annual or a lifetime basis. Different choices can lead to quite different conclusions about the incidence of particular taxes.

Chapter 18 discusses the theory of tax incidence. It considers the various approaches to tax incidence in the literature, and demonstrates some of the inconsistencies among them. The primary goal of the chapter, however, is to emphasize the principles on which economists have reached a consensus, even though the principles may not be entirely consistent with one another. A conventional wisdom of sorts has evolved on the theory of tax incidence. Chapter 19 then considers the empirical analysis of the incidence of the six major taxes: the personal income tax, payroll tax, sales tax, corporation income tax, property tax, and value-added tax.

SUPPLY, DEMAND, AND TAX INCIDENCE

A good place to begin is with the analysis of tax incidence that can be found in most principles texts. The usual example is a per-unit excise tax levied on the sale of a good produced by firms operating in a perfectly competitive market. Common examples of per-unit excise taxes are the taxes on each gallon of gasoline or pack of cigarettes sold. The supply and demand analysis of the tax is useful for demonstrating how markets respond to taxation and it leads to a number of important principles of tax incidence. Fortunately, choosing to analyze an excise tax on some good or service is irrelevant. The same principles to be developed below apply to all taxes levied on goods or factors of production. Also, there is no important analytical difference between a per-unit tax and an ad valorem (percentage of price) tax. The effects of a per-unit tax are just easier to show precisely on a supply and demand diagram.

Refer to Figure 18.1, which depicts the perfectly competitive market for good X. The quantity of X is on the horizontal axis and the price of X is on the vertical axis. The market equilibrium without the tax is (X_0, P_0), at the intersection of D and S, the market demand and supply curves. Suppose the government levies an excise tax on the sale of

X equal to t dollars per unit of X. Since the tax is levied on firms, they bear the impact of the tax and are the first to respond to it. Recall that the supply curve S indicates the marginal cost of supplying X to the market at each unit of output. Now that firms have to a pay a tax t on every unit of output, their marginal cost of supplying each output has also increased by t. Consequently, S shifts up parallel by exactly t at every output, to S'. Their willingness to supply X has decreased. The new market equilibrium is (X_t, P_{gt}), at the intersection of D and S'. P_{gt} is called the *gross-of-tax price* because it includes the tax. After paying the tax t on each unit of X_t, firms are left with P_{nt} per unit of X, the *net-of-tax price*: $P_{gt} = P_{nt} + t$, by the definition of the two prices. The tax revenue collected by the government is tX_t, the rectangular area $P_{gt}abP_{nt}$.

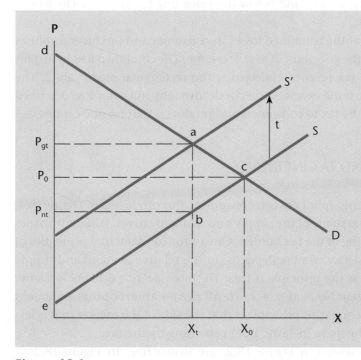

Figure 18.1

Firms may bear the impact of the excise tax, but the incidence or burden of the tax is spread between consumers and firms in this market. Markets can spread the burden of a tax to both sides of the market because a tax generates two prices, whereas before there was only one price. Before the tax, consumers and producers both based their demand and supply decisions on P_0. After the tax, consumers base their demand decisions on P_{gt}, the price including the tax. In contrast, firms base their supply decisions on P_{nt}, because that is all they have left per unit of X sold to pay their factors of production and offer a return to their investors. Because of the tax, therefore, the effective price has simultaneously risen to consumers, from P_0 to P_{gt}, and fallen to firms, from P_0 to P_{nt}. Consumers lose because they pay more (P_{gt} vs. P_0) per unit for less output (X_t vs. X_0), and firms lose because they receive less (P_{nt} vs. P_0) per unit for less output (X_t vs. X_0).

The losses to consumers and firms can also be represented by the standard consumer and producer surplus areas. The only caveat is that the demand curve must be the compensated demand curve, which it will be if there is no income effect on the demand for X. Consumer surplus is not a valid measure of welfare loss behind the actual demand curve.[1] The consumer surplus before the tax was area dcP_0, the triangular area below the demand curve and above the price line P_0 up to X_0. As a result of the tax, the consumer surplus decreases to daP_{gt}, the triangular area below the demand curve and above the price line P_{gt} up to X_t. The loss of consumer surplus is area $P_{gt}acP_0$. The producer surplus before the tax was area ecP_0, the triangular area above the supply curve and below the price line P_0 up to X_0. As a result of the tax, the producer surplus decreases to ebP_{nt}, the triangular area above the supply curve and below the price line P_{nt} up to X_t. The loss of producer surplus is area P_0cbP_{nt}.

A final point to note is that the combined losses in consumer and producer surpluses are only partially captured by the government as tax revenue. The combined loss in surplus is the area $P_{gt}acbP_{nt}$, and the tax revenue collected is the rectangular area $P_{gt}abP_{nt}$. The difference, triangular area abc, is the excess burden or deadweight efficiency loss described in Chapter 15, the burden of the tax to consumers and producers that no one captures.

ELASTICITIES AND TAX INCIDENCE

The tax incidence is fairly evenly split between consumers and producers in Figure 18.1, but this is a consequence of the shape of the supply and demand curves. Different shapes would lead to a different sharing of the tax burden. One of the fundamental principles of tax incidence is that the incidence of a tax depends on the relative demand and supply elasticities. One way to express the principle is this: *The more inelastic demand is relative to supply, the more consumers bear the burden of a tax.* All permutations of that statement hold as well.[2] The intuition behind this principle is that the side of the market that is less willing to respond to price (the more inelastic side) gets stung by the tax.

Two limiting cases, represented in Figure 18.2, are instructive. In Figure 18.2(a), demand is relatively inelastic because it is *perfectly* inelastic, vertical, within the relevant range of prices. When S shifts to S' by the amount t as above, the market price rises by the full amount of the tax t from P_0 to P_{gt}. The quantity X_t remains at X_0, and the net-of-tax price P_{nt} remains at P_0. Firms bear the impact of the tax but none of the incidence of the tax. They are able to pass the entire tax burden on to consumers in the form of higher prices. Firms always try to pass the tax on to consumers in the form of higher prices, an attempt represented by the shifting of the supply curve up by the amount of the tax. But they succeed only if the market price rises by the full amount of the tax, as in Figure 18.2(a). The market price usually rises by less than the full amount of the tax, as in Figure 18.1, however, in which case their attempt to pass the burden on to consumers is only partly successful.

In Figure 18.2(b), supply is relatively inelastic because it is *perfectly inelastic*. Firms are willing to supply X_0 no matter what the price, at least within the relevant range of prices. Now S and S' coincide; a vertical curve cannot be shifted upward. Consequently, the market equilibrium is unaffected. X_t remains at X_0 and the market price P_{gt} remains at P_0. The consumers bear no burden from the tax. They consume the same quantity at the same price as they did without the tax. Conversely, P_{nt} falls by the full amount of the tax, t, so that the firms bear the full burden of the tax.

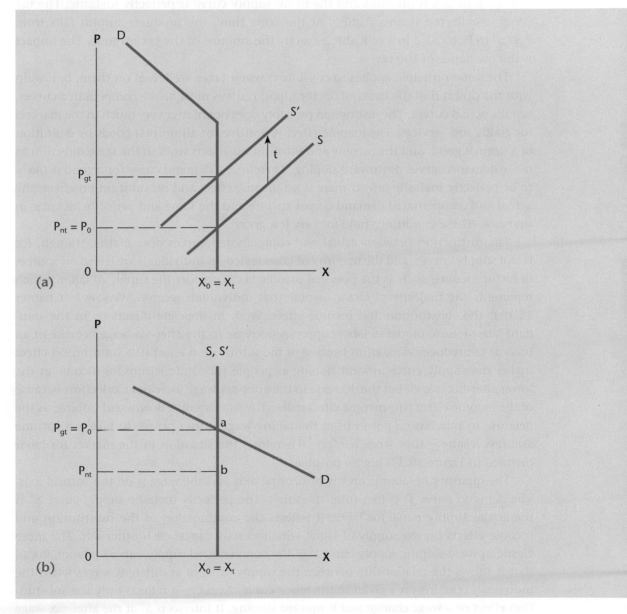

Figure 18.2

WHEN DOES IMPACT EQUAL INCIDENCE?

A second principle of tax incidence follows from the analysis of perfectly inelastic supply in Figure 18.2(b): *If the side of the market on whom a tax is levied has a perfectly inelastic supply (demand) curve, then the impact of the tax is the incidence of the tax. That is, the tax revenues collected represent the burden of the tax.* In Figure 18.2(b) the impact of the excise tax is on firms and the firms' supply curve is perfectly inelastic. The tax revenue collected is area P_0abP_{nt}. At the same time, the producer surplus falls from P_0aX_00 to $P_{nt}bX_00$, a loss of P_0abP_{nt}, exactly the amount of the tax revenue. The impact is the incidence of the tax.

The same principle applies to consumers when taxes are levied on them, but again with the caveat that the demand (factor supply) curves must be the compensated curves, not the actual curves. The distinction probably does not matter very much in the markets for goods and services. The income effect is positive for all normal goods by definition of a normal good, and the income and substitution effects work in the same direction to make demand curves downward sloping. Therefore, a demand curve for a good is likely to be perfectly inelastic only if there is no income effect and no substitution effect; the actual and compensated demand curves are one and the same and perfectly inelastic in that case. These conditions hold for very few goods.[3]

The distinction between actual and compensated curves does matter, though, for factor supply curves, and the majority of taxes levied on individuals are levied on sources of factor income, such as the personal income tax. Consider the supply of labor, which represents the majority of factor income that individuals receive. We saw in Chapter 15 that the substitution and income effects work in opposite directions in the standard labor-leisure model of labor supply. A decrease in the after-tax wage because of an income tax reduces work effort because of the substitution effect (the substitution effect makes the supply curve upward sloping as people substitute leisure for income at the lower after-tax wage). But the decrease in the after-tax wage increases work effort because of the income effect (the income effect makes the supply curve downward sloping, as the decrease in purchasing power from the falling wage causes people to take less income and less leisure – they work harder).[4] Therefore, the situation in the market for labor pictured in Figure 18.3 is highly possible.

The quantity of labor is on the horizontal axis and the wage is on the vertical axis. The demand curve D comes from the firms. The perfectly inelastic supply curve S^A is the actual supply curve for labor. It reflects the combination of the substitution and income effects on the supply of labor, which exactly cancel each other out. The more elastic upward-sloping supply curve S^C is the compensated supply curve for labor. Recall that it shows the relationship between the supply of labor at different wages when the individual remains on a given indifference curve. As such, it reflects only the substitution effect of a wage change and is upward sloping. It intersects S^A at the after-tax wage $W_0(1 - t)$, assuming it represents labor supply along the after-tax indifference curve in the labor-leisure model.

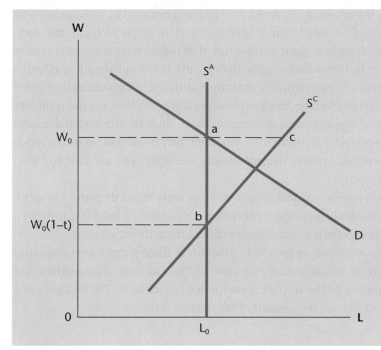

Figure 18.3

The market equilibrium before the tax is W_0, at the intersection of D and S^A. A tax on wage income levied on individuals at rate t lowers the wage to individuals from W_0 to $W_0(1 - t)$. (Here we assume an ad valorem percentage of wage tax because that is how income taxes are levied.) The individuals' willingness to supply labor shifts up by the amount of the tax, tW, at each quantity of labor supplied. Since the actual supply curve is vertically elastic it cannot shift. The market wage paid by firms remains at W_0, and the wage to individuals falls to $W_0(1 - t)$. The actual labor supply remains at L_0. The burden of the tax falls entirely on individuals as firms continue to hire L_0 workers at a wage W_0, exactly as before the tax. Furthermore, it appears that the impact is the incidence of the tax when measured using the actual supply curve S^A. The tax revenue collected is tW_0L_0, equal to the rectangular area $W_0abW_0(1 - t)$. The individuals' surplus before the tax, measured on S^A, is the rectangular area W_0aL_00, the area under the wage line W_0 up to L_0. In other words, it is the total labor income, since the opportunity cost of supplying labor is zero, with S^A perfectly inelastic. The individuals' surplus with the tax is $W_0(1 - t)bL_00$, the area under the net-of-tax wage line $W_0(1 - t)$ up to L_0, the after-tax wage income. The loss of surplus as a result of the tax is the difference in the before- and after-tax surpluses, area $W_0abW_0(1 - t)$, equal to the tax revenue collected. The impact is the incidence by this measure.

Using S^A to represent the loss of surplus from the tax is not legitimate, however. The loss has to be measured using the compensated supply curve, S^C. As discussed in Chapter 15, the correctly measured loss in worker surplus is the area behind S^C to the wage axis, area $W_0cbW_0(1 - t)$, which exceeds the amount of tax revenue collected by area abc. The burden of the tax exceeds the revenue collected (the impact) because of the deadweight loss from the tax, area abc. The conclusion above holds: The impact equals the incidence of a tax on individuals only if their compensated demand (factor supply) curves are perfectly inelastic. That is, impact equals incidence only if the substitution effect is zero. A zero substitution effect in turn implies that the indifference curves for that good (factor) are right-angled, so that changes in a price (wage) have no effect on the quantity demanded (labor supplied) along a given indifference curve. And, for the actual demand (factor supply) curve to be perfectly inelastic, the income effect must also be zero. Goods (factors) for which the substitution and income effects are both zero are said to be in absolutely fixed demand (supply).

Unfortunately, very few goods and factors are in absolutely fixed demand (supply). The supply of land may be the only important exception. Other than a land tax, however, the incidence of a tax on individuals almost always differs from its impact.

Note, finally, that taxes on goods or factors in absolutely fixed supply are lump-sum taxes, because no decision by taxpayers in response to the tax can change their tax liabilities. Therefore, a corollary to the impact-is-incidence principle is: *The incidence of a lump-sum tax is the impact of the tax, the amount of tax revenue collected.*

THE SIDE OF THE MARKET TAXED IS IRRELEVANT

The supply and demand analysis of a tax reveals another fundamental principle of tax incidence: *The side of the market that the legislature chooses to tax is irrelevant to the incidence of the tax. The incidence of the tax is the same whether buyers or suppliers are taxed.* Returning to the example in Figure 18.1, suppose instead of levying a per-unit excise tax of t on the firms, the Department of Revenue sent tax agents to sit just beyond the cash registers in retail stores and collect a per-unit tax t on good X from the consumers of X. Refer to Figure 18.4.

The before-tax equilibrium is (X_0, P_0), the intersection of S and D as in Figure 18.1. Since the impact of the tax is now on consumers, they respond by shifting their demand curves down by the amount of the tax t to D'. Their willingness to pay for the last unit of X consumed declines by the amount of the tax at every output. The new equilibrium is (X_t, P_{nt}), at the intersection of S and D'. If the tax rate t is the same in both diagrams, then the after-tax equilibrium is also the same. Firms receive price P_{nt} from consumers. After paying the tax, the gross-of-tax price to the consumer is P_{gt}, and $P_{gt} = P_{nt} + t$ as before. With the prices and quantities the same for both sides of the market as with the excise tax on firms, the incidence of the consumer-based tax is identical to the incidence of the excise tax. The only difference is that the market price, the price paid at the cash resister, is P_{nt} under the consumer-based tax instead of P_{gt} under the excise tax. But what matters for tax incidence is that the prices the consumers and firms base their demand and supply decisions on are identical under both taxes.

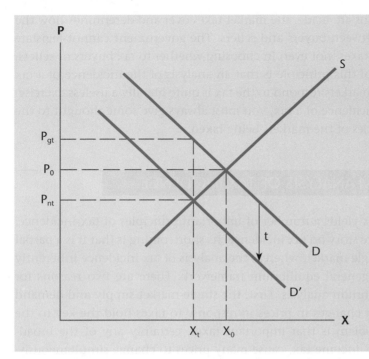

Figure 18.4

Practical considerations may well lead governments to prefer to tax one side of the market, however. A consumer-based tax on the purchase of goods and services is more costly to collect than an excise tax on firms, which explains the preference for excise taxes on the sale of goods. Regarding taxes on factors, a personal income tax on consumers can be modified fairly easily to take into account the personal circumstances of the taxpayers. For example, the government might want to exempt low-income taxpayers from the tax. It might also want larger families to pay lower taxes than smaller families with the same incomes because larger families have greater needs. Both goals can be met by means of a personal exemption to an income tax. Offering such low-income and larger family protection from taxation cannot be done so easily with a factor tax on firms such a payroll tax or a value-added tax. To protect low-income taxpayers and larger families might require establishing a separate transfer program to return some of the taxes collected to them, which is administratively more difficult than protecting them through a personal income tax. In principle, though, the incidence of a tax levied on one side of a market can always be duplicated by a tax levied on the other side of a market.

THE MARKET DETERMINES THE INCIDENCE OF A TAX

Still another fundamental principle of tax incidence follows from the relative elasticity and side of the market principles: *The market, not the legislature, determines the incidence of any tax.* True, it matters what goods and factors a legislature chooses to tax and at what rates, but after those decisions are made, the market takes over and determines how the burden of a tax is spread between buyers and sellers. The government cannot legislate who bears the burden of its taxes, not even in choosing whether to tax buyers or sellers. An immediate implication of this principle is that an analysis of the incidence of a tax that does not consider how markets respond to the tax is quite literally a useless exercise. When thinking about the incidence of a tax, you must always give some thought to the supply and demand elasticities of the markets being taxed.

GENERAL EQUILIBRIUM ANALYSIS OF TAX INCIDENCE

Supply and demand analysis yields a number of important principles of tax incidence, but it can hardly be the entire story on tax incidence. Its shortcoming is that it is a partial equilibrium analysis of a single market, whereas the analysis of tax incidence inherently requires an economy-wide general equilibrium framework. There are two reasons for insisting on a general equilibrium analysis. First, the single-market supply and demand analysis has established that changes in prices in response to taxes hold the key to the incidence of a tax. The problem is that important taxes, certainly any of the broad-based taxes such as personal income tax, cause many prices to change simultaneously. Focusing only on the single market in which the tax is levied ignores how the other price changes might affect individuals and firms. Second, the circular flow diagram of economic activity from the principles textbooks reminds us that an economy is a closed, interdependent system (except for the leakages of exports and imports). Tax revenues collected from individuals and firms do not just disappear; they remain in the economy and further affect individuals and firms. Consequently, a tax incidence analysis has to consider what the government does with the revenues. Let's consider the disposition of tax revenues first because it dictates how one thinks about incidence in an economy-wide framework.

THE DISPOSITION OF TAX REVENUES

A number of different assumptions can be made regarding the disposition of tax revenues, none of them entirely satisfactory for an analysis of tax incidence.

Balanced-budget incidence

One obvious option is to note how governments actually spend the revenues they collect from a tax or set of taxes and consider the incidence of the entire tax and expenditure package. Economists call this approach *balanced-budget incidence* to indicate that the expenditures are assumed to equal the revenues collected, so that all the revenues are accounted for. This approach is analytically sound and clearly realistic. But since it inherently ties the incidence of the tax to the expenditures financed, it precludes one from thinking about the incidence of the various taxes in and of themselves. Moreover, the incidence of many types of public expenditure is difficult to determine. For example, it is not obvious how to allocate the benefits of a nonexclusive public good such as defense, or of some decreasing cost services offered free of charge such as public highways. Also, most taxes are not earmarked for particular expenditures, so the balanced-budget framework is not so useful for thinking about the incidence of a single tax. It is best used for analyzing as a package the entire set of taxes that a government uses to collect its revenues. For these reasons, economists typically have not chosen the balanced-budget incidence framework to think about the incidence of individual taxes.

Benefits-received taxes

The balanced-budget incidence framework has led to one principle of tax incidence that is widely accepted by economists, however. It concerns taxes collected on a benefits-received basis. Suppose a tax is earmarked for a particular expenditure and covers the entire expenditure. An example would be an average cost price set for a decreasing cost service, such as a toll on a highway that covers the full cost of constructing and maintaining the highway. Only the people who benefit from the highway pay the toll. In this case, the tax (toll) has been set according to the benefits-received principle of public pricing and taxation. The principle regarding benefits-received taxes is this: *Taxes set in accordance with the benefits-received principle of taxation are not candidates for an incidence analysis.* The justification for this principle is that benefits-received taxes are not a burden to the taxpayer. On the contrary, people pay a benefits-received tax only if they receive a net benefit from the services being taxed. They are just like market prices in this respect; economists do not concern themselves with the incidence of the price of hamburgers.

The benefits-received principle can potentially have fairly wide application, depending on one's point of view about particular taxes. One example is the payroll tax that finances the U.S. Social Security system. The payroll tax is often viewed as a broad-based tax whose incidence is of interest because individuals' tax payments are not accumulating in an investment fund to pay for their future retirement pensions, as they would under a private pension program. Most of the revenues collected in any given year are paid to current retirees. But suppose employees view their payroll taxes today as implicitly committing the government to a promise that payroll taxes will be levied on future generations of employees at rates sufficient to pay for the public pensions of the current employees when they retire. In this case, the current employees may well view their tax payments as essentially earmarked for their own pensions and therefore as a benefits-received tax. If they do view their taxes in this way, then the conventional wisdom is that the incidence of the payroll tax is not an issue. The payroll tax would not be part of an incidence study of the overall U.S. tax system.

Another example is the local property tax in the United States, which some economists view as a broad-based tax and others view as a benefits-received tax earmarked to pay for local public services. Under the latter interpretation, the incidence of the local property tax is not an issue.

Single tax incidence

How can one think about the incidence of a single tax in a general equilibrium framework, assuming it is not earmarked to particular expenditures? Arnold Harberger (1962) proposed a method in the 1960s that has gained widespread acceptance among economists. He argued that the best way to consider the incidence of a single tax was by means of the following conceptual experiment. Build a general equilibrium model of an economy in which the government levies a tax on one of the goods and factors. Then assume that the government spends the tax revenues exactly as individuals would if they had been able to keep the revenues collected from them. This is equivalent to returning the tax revenues lump sum and letting consumers spend them. (If a tax is levied on firms, the lump-sum transfer goes to the owners of the firm.) In other words, Harberger's method is a conceptual balanced-budget incidence exercise involving a tax and a simultaneous lump-sum transfer to individuals. It considers the incidence of the combined tax with lump-sum transfer package.

Harberger's method is not without its difficulties, despite its general acceptance. An immediate problem is that it does not even approximate reality. Governments almost certainly would not spend the tax revenues as individuals would have. Individuals are unlikely to buy nonexclusive goods because of the free-rider problem, or provide the same amount of transfers as the government does in the form of public pensions, insurance, and assistance to the poor. Nonetheless, Harberger's conceptual method is the cleanest way to take account of the tax revenues while retaining the focus on the incidence of any one tax, which explains its acceptance among economists.

A deeper theoretical problem is that Harberger's conceptual experiment raises questions about what exactly is being measured. To see the issues, return to the two-good example in Chapter 15 in which we developed the concept of the excess burden or deadweight loss from a tax. Recall that the consumer buys two goods, X and Y, and the government levies an ad valorem tax t on the individual's purchase of X. The price of Y equals 1, so that units of Y are equivalent to units of income. Figure 18.5 reproduces the before- and after-tax equilibria in Figure 15.1.

LM is the budget line without the tax. Its slope is $-P_X/P_Y = -P_X$. The tax on X raises the price of X to $P_X(1 + t)$ and rotates the budget line to LN. The consumer is in equilibrium at point A on indifference curve I_3 before the tax, consuming (X_A, Y_A). The tax places the consumer in equilibrium at point B on indifference curve I_1, consuming (X_B, Y_B). The tax revenues collected equal DB, the vertical distance between the before-tax (LM) and after-tax (LN) budget lines above X_B.

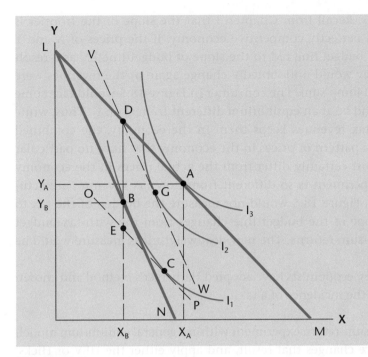

Figure 18.5

In Harberger's conceptual experiment, the government returns the tax revenues to the consumer lump sum. The lump-sum transfer shifts the after-tax budget line LN up parallel by the amount DB, the tax revenues, to the dotted line VW. (VW is parallel to LN.) The consumer would be in equilibrium at point G on indifference curve I_2. What is the burden to the consumer of the tax with lump-sum transfer? The answer is the excess burden or deadweight loss of the tax. Using the Hicks' equivalent variation (HEV) measure of loss, the overall loss from the tax is the parallel distance between the before-tax indifference curve I_3 and the after-tax indifference curve I_1 measured at the before-tax prices, distance DE. This is the amount of income the consumer would be willing to give up lump sum to return to the original prices. It exceeds the tax revenues actually returned by the amount BE, so that BE is the excess burden of the tax. In other words, Harberger's conceptual experiment equates the incidence of a tax with the inefficiency of a tax. It has to, because with the tax revenues returned lump sum, the loss to the consumer is only the loss resulting from the increase in the price of X, and this is the deadweight loss.

There are a number of difficulties with equating incidence with inefficiency in this way. In the first place, Figure 18.5 is a partial equilibrium analysis that misses how prices would actually change in a general equilibrium setting under Harberger's conceptual experiment. What is true for any one individual is not necessarily true for all individuals combined. Suppose the government levies a tax on every individual and returns the revenues collected lump sum, individual by individual. Any large tax and transfer operation moves the economy along its production possibilities frontier and changes relative prices. Recall from Chapter 3 that the slope of the frontier is the ratio of the prices in a perfectly competitive economy. If the prices of X and Y changed from the slope of budget line LM to the slope of budget line LN as a result of the tax being levied, they would undoubtedly change again as the revenues were returned to each individual lump sum. The consumer in Figure 18.5 would face some price line other than VW and be at an equilibrium different from G on I_2. Thus, while Harberger's return of the tax revenues keeps them in the economy, the combined tax/transfer would lead to a pattern of prices in the economy that have no particular standing. They would almost certainly differ from the actual prices in the economy because the conceptual experiment is so different from how tax revenues are actually spent. Moreover, BE in Figure 18.5 would not measure the burden of the tax to the consumer once the slope of the budget line changes from the with-tax budget line as a result of the lump-sum returns. The new deadweight loss measure would be something different.

Despite these ambiguities, economists have adopted Harberger's method and chosen one of two ways to describe the incidence of a tax:

a. Run the tax-with-lump-sum-return experiment within a general equilibrium model, note the pattern of price changes that result, and apply either the HEV or Hicks' compensating variation (HCV) to measure the incidence of the tax resulting from the price changes. The HEV asks how much the consumer would be willing to pay to return to the original no-tax prices. The HCV asks how much compensation each individual would require lump sum to be as well off at the new prices as at the original prices.

b. Run the tax-with-lump-sum-return experiment in a general equilibrium model, note the pattern of price changes that result, and make informal, heuristic statements about who gains and who loses because of the price changes. This was Harberger's choice, as we will see in Chapter 19 when we describe his analysis of U.S. corporation income tax.

A second difficulty with Harberger's method is it does not seem to be entirely in the spirit of incidence analysis because the lump-sum return of the tax revenues completely removes the payment of the taxes themselves from consideration. The only source of the burden is the resulting price changes. While this may seem odd, it is a sensible choice for considering the incidence of a tax, given that something has to be done with the tax revenues. At the same time, it is completely at odds with one of the other accepted principles of tax incidence, that the impact is the incidence of a non-distorting lump-sum tax. Harberger's method can only be applied to distorting taxes, those that generate an excess burden. To see this, suppose the consumer in Figure 18.5 paid a lump-sum tax that placed her on indifference curve I_1. Since a lump-sum tax shifts the before-tax budget line down parallel by the amount of the tax, the consumer would be at point C on I_1. If the tax revenues were returned lump sum, she would return to point A on indifference curve I_3 and there would be no burden at all. What is true for one consumer is true for many consumers. If the government levied a lump-sum tax on everyone and returned the revenues lump sum, nothing at all would happen. The economy would remain at the original equilibrium and no one would be burdened.

Therefore, economists have adopted two conflicting principles for measuring the incidence of a tax, one for distorting taxes and one for non-distorting (lump-sum) taxes:

1. *Distorting tax*: Conduct the Harberger tax-with-lump-sum-return experiment and measure the incidence by (a) or (b) above.
2. *Non-distorting (lump-sum) tax*: Impact equals incidence. Measure the incidence of the tax as the amount of tax paid. In the former case, the tax revenues are taken entirely out of play; in the latter case, they are the entire measure of incidence. This is the conventional wisdom on tax incidence among economists, despite the inconsistency. [5,6]

Differential tax incidence

A final approach to tax incidence is to consider the incidence of substituting one tax for another tax that collects the same amount of revenues. This is referred to as *differential tax incidence* and it is appealing because governments sometimes do make equal revenue tax substitutions. It would also appear to solve the problem of what to do with tax revenues, but this is not the case. One has to know the incidence of the first tax and the incidence of the second tax to know how the incidence changes. Therefore, if the taxes are distorting, the tax substitution is equivalent to a two-step Harberger experiment: Collect the first tax and return the revenues lump sum, and then collect the second tax and return its revenues lump sum. Measure the incidence each time and see how the incidence changes from one tax to another. Indeed, Harberger's approach can be thought of as a differential incidence experiment in which a distorting tax substitutes for a lump-sum tax. The lump-sum tax has no effect on the economy once the revenues are returned lump sum. So the incidence of substituting a distorting tax for a lump-sum tax is equivalent to levying a distorting tax in the first place, using the Harberger method.

THE EQUIVALENCE OF GENERAL TAXES

The two common measures of incidence for distorting taxes, (a) and (b) above, lead to another principle of tax incidence: *Two distorting taxes that give rise to the same pattern of relative prices throughout the economy have the same incidence.* The principle necessarily holds for the relative price measure (b), since tax incidence is based entirely on the changes in the pattern of relative prices caused by the taxes. It holds for the incidence-is-excess burden measure (a) as well. Excess burden depends only on the substitution effects of price changes, which are in turn based on movements along a given indifference curve as relative prices change. If two taxes give rise to the same changes in relative prices, they result in the same movement along any one indifference curve. Hence the excess burden of the taxes must be the same whether using either the HEV or the HCV of welfare loss to compare the tax revenues collected when measuring excess burden.

The relative price principle leads to a very useful baseline theorem regarding the equivalence of general taxes. A *general tax* has two properties:

1. If a tax is levied on one side of a market for a good or factor, then all transactors on that side of the market face the same tax rate (or set of rates, if graduated rates are used).
2. If the tax is levied on a number of goods or a number of factors, then (1) holds for each taxed good and factor and the tax rate (rates) is the same across all the taxed goods or factors.

Examples of general taxes are a sales tax on a broad set of goods and services levied on all suppliers and a personal income tax on all sources of income, such as on Haig–Simons income, levied on all individuals. Any tax that does not meet these two requirements is a *specific tax*. An example of a specific tax is corporation income tax, which taxes the accounting profits of corporations but not of partnerships or proprietorships.

Determining the incidence of the broad-based taxes is such a difficult task that it pays to have a baseline result to begin thinking about them. A useful baseline case is the incidence of these taxes in the simplest, fully specified non-trivial economy, consisting of the following four features:

1. identical consumers
2. perfectly competitive markets for all goods and factors
3. constant returns to scale (CRS) production so that there are no pure profits – total expenditures equal total payments to factors of production under perfect competition
4. a single time period, that is, a static economy with no saving and investment.

The baseline theorem on tax incidence for this economy is this: *In a perfectly competitive, profitless, static economy with identical consumers, the incidence of a general ad valorem tax on any subset of goods and factors can be duplicated by a general ad valorem tax on the remaining subset of goods and factors.*

A natural and intuitive way to think about this theorem is to divide the goods and factors into the set of goods and the set of factors. Let there be N goods and factors, X_i, i = 1,...,N, divided into G goods and the remaining N-G factors. The set of goods is $(X_1,...,X_g,...X_G)$ and the set of factors is $(X_{G+1},...X_m, ...,X_N)$. Assume that taxes are levied on consumers. A general expenditure tax at rate t on the goods purchased by consumers raises the goods' prices to consumers to $(P_1(1 + t),...,P_g(1 + t), ...P_G(1 + t))$, but leaves the factor prices unchanged. The theorem says that the incidence of this tax can be duplicated by a general tax t* on all the factors supplied by consumers. A general factor tax lowers the factor prices received by consumers (their take-home pay) to $(P_{G+1}(1 + t^*),$ $...,P_m(1 + t^*),...,P_N(1 + t^*))$, but leaves the goods' prices unchanged. (t* is negative for factor taxes – see the discussion below.)

Before describing how to make the two taxes equivalent, let's take a moment to consider the rather remarkable implication of the theorem. People in the United States vigorously debate the merits of substituting one broad-based tax for another, such as replacing the federal personal income tax with a personal expenditure tax, a national sales tax or a value-added tax on firms. But in this simple baseline economy, the theorem implies that all these taxes can be designed to have the same incidence. The theorem establishes the equivalence between a personal expenditure tax and a personal income tax. Also, since the side of the market taxed is irrelevant to the incidence of a tax, a personal expenditure tax paid by consumers is equivalent to a general sales tax paid by firms, and a personal income tax on consumers is equivalent to a value-added tax levied on firms' purchases of factors of production. Therefore, a general sales tax is equivalent to a value-added tax, so that all four of these broad-based taxes can be designed to have the same incidence.

The question, then, is how to design the tax rates to make them equivalent. To see how to do this, think about how a general expenditure tax and a personal income tax would affect the Pareto-optimal rule that the individuals' MRS between any two goods or factors equals the firms' MRT between the same two goods or factors. The MRT is interpreted as a marginal rate of transformation if the two items are goods, a marginal rate of technical substitution in production if the two items are factors, and a marginal product if one item is a good and the other a factor. The prices to the firms under either tax are the prices unadjusted by the tax rates: $(P_1,...P_G;P_{G+1},...,P_N)$. The firms set the ratio of the prices of any two goods or factors to their MRT. The prices to the individuals under the two taxes are:

General expenditure tax: $(P_1(1 + t),...,P_G(1 + t); P_{G+1},...,P_N)$

General income tax: $(P_1,...,P_G; P_{G+1}(1 + t^*),...,P_N(1 + t^*))$

The individuals set the ratio of the prices of any two goods or factors to their MRS.

Consider the three possible combinations of goods and factors:

1. Any two goods, say goods c and d. Under the expenditure tax, the individuals set

   $$MRS_{c,d} = P_c(1 + t)/P_d(1 + t) = P_c/P_d = MRT_{c,d}$$

   Under the income tax, neither c nor d is taxed. Therefore

   $$MRS_{c,d} = P_c/P_d = MRT_{c,d}$$

   Neither tax upsets the MRS = MRT equality between any two goods.

2. Any two factors, say factors h and m. Under the expenditure tax, neither h nor m is taxed. Therefore

$$MRS_{h,m} = P_h/P_m = MRT_{h,m}$$

Under the income tax, the individuals set

$$MRS_{h,m} = P_h(1 + t^*)/P_m(1 + t^*) = P_h/P_m = MRT_{h,m}$$

Neither tax upsets the MRS = MRT equality between any two factors.

3. Any one good and any one factor, say good c and factor m. Under the expenditure tax, the individuals set

$$MRS_{c,m} = P_c(1 + t)/P_m \neq P_c/P_m = MRT_{c,m}$$

Under the income tax, the individuals set

$$MRS_{c,m} = P_c/P_m(1 + t^*) \neq P_c/P_m = MRT_{c,m}$$

Both taxes upset the MRS and MRT equality between a good and a factor and are therefore distorting taxes. To ensure that they have the same effect on the economy, and therefore the same tax incidence, they must affect the equality in the same way. They do so if $P_c(1 + t)/P_m = P_c/P_m(1 + t^*)$, or $(1 + t) = 1/(1 + t^*)$. Equivalently $(1 + t)(1 + t^*) = 1$. For example, if the tax rate on the goods, t, = 1 (100%), then the tax rate on the factors, t*, must = $-1/2$ (-50%): $[(1 + 1)(1 - 1/2) = (2)(1/2) = 1]$.

The difference in the signs and values of the two taxes arise simply because of the way that goods and factor taxes on individuals are defined. Taxes in goods markets drive the price to consumers above the price to firms, whereas taxes in factor markets drive the price to individuals below the price to firms.

Figure 18.6 illustrates. Figure 18.6(a) shows the competitive market for good c and Figure 18.6(b) shows the competitive market for factor m. In the goods market for X_c, the individuals are the demanders and the firms are the suppliers. The tax t is defined relative to the net-of-tax price, P_{nt}, the relevant price to the firms. Therefore, if t = 100%, the price of X_c to the consumers, P_{gt}, is 100% above P_{nt} (that is, double P_{nt}). In the factor market for X_m, the individuals are the suppliers and the firms are the demanders. The tax t* is again defined relative to price that is relevant to the firms, but this time that price is P_{gt}, the gross-of-tax price. For example, the firms pay their employees salaries that include the tax. The relevant price to the individuals is P_{nt}, the price net of the tax, that is, their take-home pay. Therefore, if t* = -50%, then P_{nt} is half P_{gt}; the individuals' take-home pay is half their gross-of-tax salary. Furthermore, since total sales equal total factor incomes in this economy with no pure profits, a 100% sales tax on the net-of-tax price of all the goods yields the same revenues as a 50% tax on the gross-of-tax price of all the factors. The two distorting taxes t and t* are identical in every respect with $(1 + t)(1 + t^*) = 1$ and must therefore have the same incidence.[7]

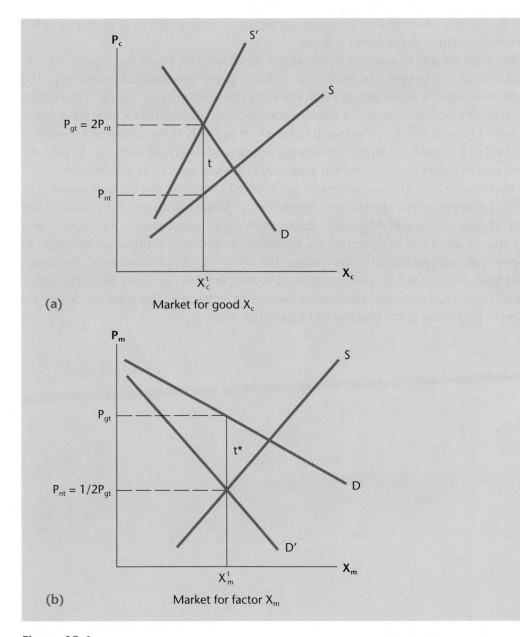

Figure 18.6

The difference is in the details

The baseline theorem on the equivalence of general taxes is just that, a baseline result from which to think about the incidence of broad-based taxes. In fact, the incidences of the four broad-based taxes covered by the theorem are unlikely to be equal, but the theorem reminds us that any differences among them must lie in the details. The details in this case refer to the ways in which an actual economy differs from the simplest economy on which the theorem is based.

We have already considered one example in Chapter 13 when comparing a Haig–Simons personal income tax with a personal expenditure (consumption) tax. The example assumed a multi-period economy with the possibility of saving, rather than the static one-period economy of the baseline theorem. We saw that a personal income tax would be equivalent to a personal expenditure tax only if the personal income tax excluded all income from capital. Otherwise, saving is double taxed under an income tax relative to an expenditure tax, which generates a different pattern of incidence.

We will consider other such "details" in Chapter 19 when we discuss how economists use the principles of tax incidence to determine the actual incidence of the broad-based taxes. The details include differences among individuals, non-competitive markets, and long-run vs. short-run perspectives on incidence, among many other possibilities. As suggested at the beginning of this chapter, the actual incidence of some of the broad-based taxes is unsettled; economists often have sharply different views about their incidence. They reach different conclusions because they disagree about which details are the most important to the incidence of a particular tax.

Tax Incidence: Applications

Chapter 19 describes how economists use the principles of tax incidence developed in Chapter 18 to think about the incidence of various taxes, with emphasis on the six major broad-based taxes. A natural place to begin is with Arnold Harberger's seminal analysis of the corporation income tax, which appeared in 1962 (Harberger, 1962). His paper on the incidence of the corporation income tax was the first formal general equilibrium model of tax incidence, and it quickly became the preferred template for tax incidence analysis among public sector economists.

THE HARBERGER GENERAL EQUILIBRIUM MODEL OF TAX INCIDENCE

Harberger's tax incidence model is a variation of the standard textbook two-good, two-factor general equilibrium model that we developed in Chapter 3. To review: There are two goods, X and Y, produced by two factors of production, labor (L) and capital (K), using the constant returns to scale (CRS) production functions $X = X(L_X, K_X)$ and $Y = Y(L_Y, K_Y)$. Individuals supply their labor and capital to firms in absolutely fixed amounts, with the aggregate supplies of labor and capital equal to $\bar{L}$ and $\bar{K}$. Individuals have identical tastes for X and Y, that is, identical utility functions over X and Y. The goods and factor markets are all perfectly competitive, so that individuals and firms are price takers in all markets. Also, perfect competition combined with CRS production implies that firms' revenues from sales of X or Y just equal their payments to capital and labor. There are no pure economic profits in production that would otherwise have to be accounted for in a tax incidence analysis.

The assumption of CRS production requires an additional assumption about production to have an interesting general equilibrium model, namely that the Y and X firms are unequally factor intensive. This means that they use different proportions of labor and capital when facing the same prices for labor and capital, P_L and P_K. We will assume that Y is relatively capital intensive and X is relatively labor intensive. Therefore, at a given price ratio, P_L/P_K, $K_Y/L_Y > K_X/L_X$. This assumption is necessary to ensure that the production possibilities frontier is bowed outward from the origin, so that the prices of goods and factors vary as the economy moves from one equilibrium to another along the frontier. (How the prices vary is described below.) If production of the two goods were equally factor intensive, the production possibilities frontier would be a straight line – constant cost – and neither the goods' prices nor the factor prices would vary as the economy moved along the frontier. The constant cost case is unrealistic, and also uninteresting for tax incidence analysis.[1]

The assumption of perfect competition has two immediate and important implications for the analysis of tax incidence. First, the labor and capital supplied to the market, $\bar{L}$ and $\bar{K}$, must always be fully employed in equilibrium. If, for example, some of the $\bar{L}$ were unemployed, then there would be excess supply in the market for labor and P_L would fall until the Y and X firms are willing to hire all of $\bar{L}$. Second, individuals have to receive the same wages for their labor and the same returns to their capital whether they are used in production of Y or X. If, for example, wages are higher in the X firms, labor would move from the Y firms to the X firms, driving the wage down in the X firms and up in the Y firms. The movement would continue until the wages to individuals are the same in the two industries.

▬▬ THE OPERATION OF THE MODEL

The analysis of tax incidence requires that we understand how the economy responds to any event that changes the equilibrium in the economy. It turns out that the two-good, two-factor model leads to predictable changes in the goods and factor prices as the economy moves along its production possibilities frontier. Figures 19.1 and 19.2 illustrate how the relative prices respond to a change in demand.

The economy is initially at point A on the production possibilities frontier in Figure 19.1. The slope of the frontier at A is the marginal rate of transformation between X and Y, $MRT_{X,Y}^A$, equal to the ratio of the marginal costs of X and Y. Under perfect competition, the prices of X and Y equal the marginal costs of X and Y, so that

$$MRT_{X,Y}^A = \frac{MC_X^A}{MC_Y^A} = \frac{P_X^A}{P_Y^A}.$$

Suppose the individuals' tastes change in favor of X, leading to an increase in demand for X and a decrease in demand for Y, as depicted in Figure 19.2. Figure 19.2(a) pictures the market for Y and Figure 19.2(b) pictures the market for X. The original equilibrium in the market for Y is (Y^A, P_Y^A) in Figure 19.2(a), at the intersection of the demand and supply curves D_Y and S_Y. Similarly, the original equilibrium in the market for X is (X^A, P_X^A) in Figure 19.2(b), at the intersection of D_X and S_X. (Y^A, P_Y^A) and (X^A, P_X^A) correspond to point A in Figure 19.1. The change in tastes shifts the demand curve for X up to D_X' and leads to the new equilibrium (X^B, P_X^B) at the intersection of D_X' and S_X in Figure 19.2(b). Simultaneously, the demand curve for Y shifts down to D_Y' in Figure 19.2(a), and leads to the new equilibrium (Y^B, P_Y^B), at the intersection of D_Y' and S_Y. (Y^B, P_Y^B) and (X^B, P_X^B) correspond to point B in Figure 19.1.

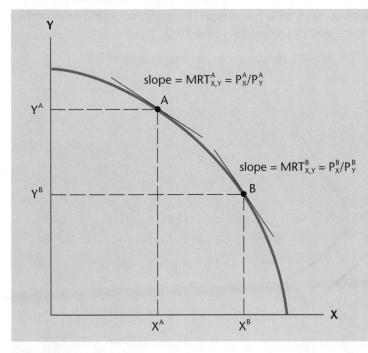

Figure 19.1

As expected, the change in tastes favoring X leads to an increase in the price of X and a decrease in the price of Y, as illustrated in Figure 19.2. The increase in the relative price P_X/P_Y is also shown in Figure 19.1. $MRT_{X,Y}^B$, the slope of the production possibilities frontier at B, exceeds the $MRT_{X,Y}^A$, the slope of the production possibilities frontier

at A. Therefore, $\dfrac{P_X^B}{P_Y^B} > \dfrac{P_X^A}{P_Y^A}$.

The change in relative prices occurs because of the change in the factor prices as labor and capital move from the Y firms to the X firms. The Y firms, faced with a decrease in demand, release some of the labor and capital, whereas the X firms, favored by an increase in demand, seek more labor and capital. But Y is relatively capital intensive:

$K_Y/L_Y > K_X/L_X$ at point A and the original factor prices $\dfrac{P_L^A}{P_K^A}$. Therefore, the Y firms release

more capital and less labor than is demanded by X firms. The result is excess supply of capital and excess demand for labor, which decreases P_K and increases P_L. As P_L/P_K rises, both firms become more capital intensive, and full employment of capital and labor is restored. Furthermore, since P_L is rising and the X firms use relatively more labor, the marginal cost of producing X rises, and so, therefore, does the price of X. Conversely, since P_K is falling and Y firms use relatively more capital, the marginal cost of producing Y falls and so, therefore, does the price of Y. The changes in marginal costs as the economy moves along its production possibilities frontier explain why the supply curves in Figure 19.2 are upward sloping. Also, with prices equal to marginal costs under perfect competition, P_X/P_Y rises, as indicated in Figures 19.1 and 19.2.

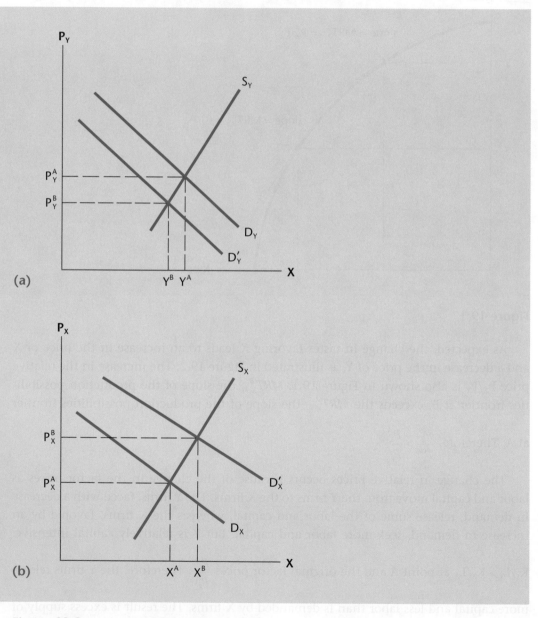

Figure 19.2

To summarize, as the economy moves along its production possibilities curve toward producing more X and less Y:

1. P_X/P_Y rises
2. P_L/P_K rises
3. Both firms become more capital intensive to maintain the full employment of labor and capital.

The reverse is true in each case as the economy moves along its production possibilities curve toward producing more Y and less X.

We are now in a position to consider the incidence of the various possible taxes in the simple two-good, two-factor model. The analysis of tax incidence in this model serves as a convenient baseline or first step in thinking about tax incidence before we add a number of real-world complexities.

▮▮▮▮ TAX INCIDENCE EQUIVALENCES

The assumption of absolutely fixed factor supplies establishes a number of immediate incidence equivalences among different general taxes in this simple model. Taxes levied on individuals on the wages earned from their supply of labor or on the earnings from their supply of capital, or a broad-based income tax levied on the combined income from their supplies of labor and capital (that is, their Haig–Simons income) are all lump-sum taxes. Recall that Harberger assumes that any tax revenues collected are simply returned to individuals with a lump-sum transfer.[2] But if lump-sum taxes are returned lump sum, then taxes and transfers have no effects whatsoever on the economy. The pre-tax/transfer and post-tax/transfer equilibriums are the same and no prices change. Therefore, the incidence of any of these taxes is assumed to be the impact of the tax, the amount of tax revenue collected. Adjusting tax rates so that each tax collects the same amount of revenue makes the incidence of the three taxes identical.

Furthermore, by the principle that the side of the market taxed is irrelevant, a payroll tax on all firms' use of labor is equivalent to an income tax on wages received, a tax on all firms' returns to capital is equivalent to an income tax on the earnings from capital, and a value-added tax on the payments to labor and capital by all firms is equivalent to a broad-based (Haig–Simons) income tax. These factor taxes on firms are also all lump sum. If revenues are returned lump sum, they, too, have no effect on any prices or allocations of factors between the Y and X firms.[3] Thus their incidence is assumed to be the revenue collected from each tax and can be made to be equivalent by a suitable choice of the tax rates.

In addition, the equivalence between subsets of broad-based taxes developed in Chapter 18 establishes the equivalence between an expenditure tax on both goods and a (Haig–Simons) income tax, both levied on individuals. Whether a tax raises the goods' prices to individuals by the same proportion or lowers the factor prices to individuals by the same proportion makes no difference. The incidence of the taxes is identical. Similarly, a general sales tax levied on both the Y and X firms is equivalent to a value-added tax on the payments to labor and capital by both firms. Furthermore, since the income and value-added taxes are lump-sum taxes by the assumption of absolutely fixed factor supplies, so too are the expenditure and general sales taxes. None of these taxes has any effect on the economy if the revenues are returned lump sum to individuals, as Harberger assumed. Therefore, the incidence of all these taxes is equal to the amount of tax revenue collected.

The only interesting taxes in this model, therefore, are specific taxes that are distorting and not lump sum. The most realistic candidates are taxes on the use of one factor in one of the industries, that is, a payroll tax on labor or a tax on income from capital paid by either the X or Y firms (but not both), and excise taxes on the sale of either X or Y. Harberger chose to analyze the corporation income tax, which taxes the returns to capital in corporations but not in proprietorships and partnerships.

THE INCIDENCE OF CORPORATION INCOME TAX

Harberger assumed that the corporate sector was the more capital-intensive sector. Therefore, let the relatively capital-intensive Y firms represent the corporations and the relatively labor-intensive X firms represent the non-corporate businesses, the proprietorships and partnerships.

Figure 19.3 shows the effects of corporation income tax on the prices of Y and X. Figure 19.3(a) depicts the market for Y and Figure 19.3(b) the market for X. The prices before the tax is imposed are P_Y^0 and P_X^0, at the intersection of the demand and supply curves D and S in Figures 19.3(a) and 19.3(b). The figures assume, for simplicity of comparison, that the pre-tax prices are equal: $P_Y^0 = P_X^0$. The tax on corporation income drives up the marginal costs of producing Y because capital is now more expensive to the Y firms. The supply curve for Y in Figure 19.3(a) shifts up from S_Y to S_Y', and establishes a new higher price for Y of P_Y', at the intersection of D_Y and S_Y'. Assuming Y and X are substitutes in consumption, the higher price of Y increases the demand for X. The demand curve in Figure 19.3(b) shifts up from D_X to D_X', and establishes a new higher price for X of P_X'.

The figures assume that the post-tax prices are also equal: $P_Y' = P_X'$. This outcome is possible because the tax on capital income in Y drives a wedge between the price of capital faced by the Y firms and the X firms. Since firms set the ratio of the factor prices, P_L/P_K, to the marginal rate of technical substitution of labor and capital in production ($MRTS_{L,K}$), the $MRTS_{L,K}$ are no longer equal between the Y and X firms, as required for production efficiency. Therefore the tax drives the economy below its production possibilities frontier, as would any selective tax on the use of a factor of production by any one set of firms.[4]

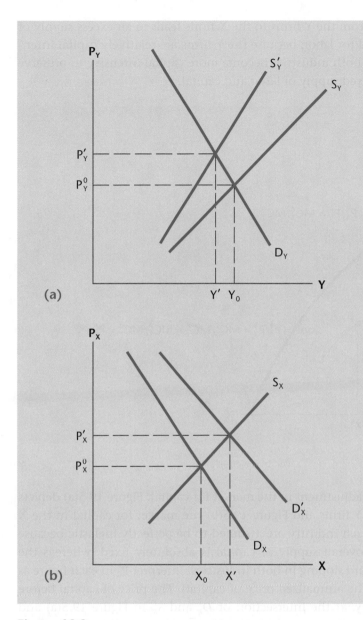

Figure 19.3

Figure 19.4 illustrates. The economy moves from point A before the tax to point B after the tax. According to the figure, the ratio of the marginal costs, which equals the ratio of the relative prices, is the same at A and B, consistent with the prices of Y and X before and after tax in Figure 19.3. In fact, Harberger assumed that the price ratio P_X/P_Y would not change, or at least would not change by very much, so that the effect of the tax on the goods' prices could safely be ignored in the incidence analysis.

The same is not true of the prices of labor and capital, however. They do change, and in the manner indicated in the previous discussion of the operation of the economy. The transfer of capital and labor from the Y firms to the X firms leads to an excess supply of capital and an excess demand for labor, because the Y firms are relatively capital intensive. P_K falls and P_L rises, and both industries become more capital intensive to preserve the full employment of the fixed supply of labor and capital.

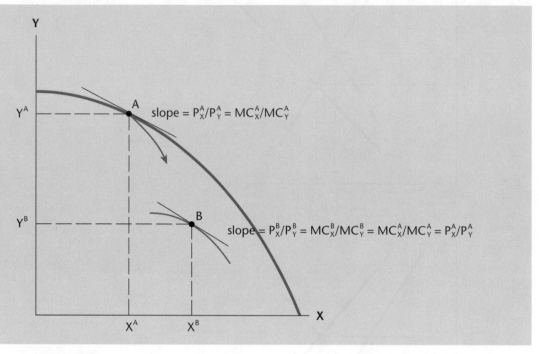

Figure 19.4

Figure 19.5 illustrates the adjustment in the market for capital. Figure 19.5(a) depicts the market for capital in the Y firms and Figure 19.5(b) the market for capital in the X firms. The supply curves to each industry are assumed to be perfectly inelastic because of the assumption that the overall supply of capital is absolutely fixed, whereas the demand for capital is downward sloping in both industries. Interpret P_K in each figure as an annual return to capital (the annualized price of capital). The price of capital before the tax is P_K^0 in each industry, at the intersection of D_K^Y and S_K^Y in Figure 19.5(a) and the intersection of D_K^X and S_K^X in Figure 19.5(b): $S_K^Y + S_K^X = \overline{S}_K$, the overall fixed supply of capital from the individuals.

The corporation income tax causes the demand curve for capital in Y to shift down by the full amount of the tax, from D_K^Y to $D_K^{Y'}$. Since the supply of capital to the Y firms is perfectly inelastic, the return to capital to the individuals who own the Y firms falls immediately to $P_K^{Y^{net}}$, at the intersection of $D_K^{Y'}$ and S_K^Y. This situation cannot last, however, since suppliers of capital are now earning $P_K^{Y^{net}}$ in the Y firms and P_K^0 in the X firms. They react by shifting their supply of capital from the Y firms to the X firms: S_K^Y shifts to the left and S_K^X shifts to the right. The shifting continues until the net-of-tax return to capital in the Y firms, $P_K^{Y^{net,final}}$, equals the (untaxed) market return to capital $P_K^{X^{final}}$ in the X firms.

The returns equalize at the intersection of $D_K^{Y'}$ and $S_K^{Y'}$ in Figure 19.5(a) and D_K^X and $S_K^{X'}$ in Figure 19.5(b).

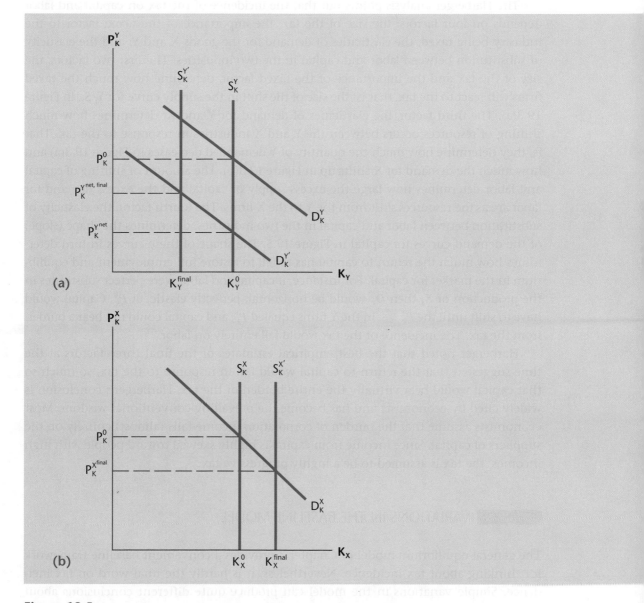

(a)

(b)

Figure 19.5

The adjustment of the supplies of capital shows that a legislature cannot isolate the incidence of a tax to the taxed sector. In our example, *all* suppliers of capital lose as the returns they receive decrease from P_K^0 before the tax to $P_K^{X^{final}} = P_K^{Y^{net, final}}$ after the tax. The legislature's intent to impose a burden only on corporate stockholders' income from capital is undermined by the operation of the competitive market system, which guarantees that individuals supplying a factor of production must earn the same return on that factor no matter where their factors are used.

The Harberger analysis points out that the incidence of the tax on capital and labor depends on four factors: the size of the tax; the importance of the taxed factor to the industry being taxed; the elasticities of demand for the goods X and Y; and the elasticity of substitution between labor and capital in the two industries. The first two factors, the size of the tax and the importance of the taxed factor, determine how much the taxed firms will react to the tax, that is, the size of the shift in the supply curve for Y, S_Y, in Figure 19.3(a). The third factor, the elasticities of demand for Y and X, determines how much shifting of resources occurs between the Y and X industries in response to the tax. That is, they determine how much the quantity of Y demanded decreases in Figure 19.3(a) and how much the demand for X shifts up in Figure 19.3(b). The amount of shifting of capital and labor determines how large the excess supply of capital and the excess demand for labor are as the resources shift from the Y to the X firms. The fourth factor, the elasticity of substitution between labor and capital in the two industries, determines the shape (slope) of the demand curves for capital in Figure 19.5. The shape of these curves in turn determines how much the return to capital has to fall to restore full employment and equilibrium in the market for capital. For instance, if capital and labor were perfect substitutes in the production of X, then D_K^X would be horizontal, perfectly elastic, at P_K^0. Capital would have to shift until the $P_K^{Y^{net,final}}$ in the Y firms equaled P_K^0, and capital could not bear a burden from the tax. The incidence of the tax would fall entirely on labor.

Harberger noted that the best empirical estimates of the final three factors at the time suggested that the return to capital would fall in response to the tax, so much so that capital would bear virtually the entire burden of the tax. Harberger's conclusion is widely cited by economists and has become the prevailing conventional wisdom. Most economists assume that the burden of corporation income falls (almost) entirely on the suppliers of capital. Since income from capital is highly skewed toward people with high incomes, the tax is assumed to be a highly progressive tax.

VARIATIONS IN THE BASELINE MODEL

The general equilibrium model of Chapter 3 provides a convenient baseline framework for thinking about tax incidence. Nevertheless, it is hardly the final word on tax incidence. Simple variations in the model can produce quite different conclusions about the incidence of the major taxes. We will briefly consider four such variations by way of illustration: variable factor supplies, non-identical individuals, mobile vs. immobile factors, and non-competitive markets.

Variable factor supplies

Relaxing the assumption of fixed factor supplies affects the analysis of tax incidence in both a static and a dynamic context. Regarding the static, one-time-period Harberger framework, the main difference in assuming that the supplies of labor and capital are variable and respond to changes in factor prices is that the major taxes are no longer lump-sum taxes. The Harberger methodology applies to all of them: levy the tax, return the revenues lump sum, see how the goods and factor prices respond, and draw incidence conclusions on the basis of the price changes. The incidence of these taxes is no longer their impact, the amount of the tax revenues collected. Variable factor supplies, with their presumed upward-sloping supply curves, also influence the amount by which the factor and goods prices change relative to their changes with the perfectly inelastic labor and capital supply curves of the fixed factors model. Variable factor supplies is, of course, the more realistic assumption.

But the biggest difference in tax incidence analysis that results from assuming variable factor supplies occurs in the long-run dynamic context. Consider as an example the long-run overlapping generations (OLG) model that we used in Chapter 12 to analyze a pay-as-you-go public pension system. Taxes on capital income in the OLG model have very different effects from those of the Harberger model.

Suppose that the incidence of a tax on some or all of capital income, such as a corporation income tax, is borne primarily by the suppliers of capital (owners of the firms) in the short run, as Harberger assumed. With the returns to capital decreased, the rate of saving by individuals eventually decreases. The decreased saving lowers the annual level of investment, which reduces the amount of capital available to future generations. The lowered capital stock in turn lowers the productivity of labor. Since the real wage equals the marginal product of labor in perfectly competitive labor markets, the real wage falls. Therefore, the decline in saving and investment necessarily shifts at least some portion of the incidence of the tax to labor in the long run, and perhaps the major portion. Labor cannot expect to escape the burden of taxes on capital income when the supplies of labor and capital are variable.

Non-identical individuals

Relaxing the assumption of identical individuals also affects the analysis of tax incidence in both a static and a dynamic context. In a static context, imagine a tax on good X that eventually increases the price ratio P_X/P_Y. Individuals who consume a higher proportion of good X bear a higher proportion of the tax incidence. Obvious examples are a tax on yachts and on food purchased for home consumption. Those with very high incomes bear almost all the incidence of the tax on yachts as the with-tax price of yachts increases and those with relatively low incomes bear a disproportionate share of the incidence of the tax on food purchased for home consumption as the with-tax price of food increases.

When combined with variable factor supplies, the most noteworthy effects of assuming non-identical individuals once again occur in a long-run dynamic context. The incidence of the major taxes change from their equivalent incidence equals the lump-sum tax revenues result in the simple static model. Again the OLG model of Chapter 12 is instructive. In the one-period Harberger model, the incidence of all the major taxes can be made to be identical by suitable choices of tax rates. This is not true in the OLG framework, as we already discussed in Chapter 13. To recall one example, a broad-based (Haig–Simons) income tax applies to income from capital for both the younger/working and older/retired generations and to the wages of the younger/working generations who are working. An expenditure tax applies to the consumption of both generations. Therefore, a switch from an income to an expenditure tax is not at all neutral, regardless of the tax rates. It places a very heavy burden on the older/retired generation who are living off their retirement savings accumulated during their working years. Under the former income tax, they saved out of post-tax dollars and paid taxes on the interest earned on their savings. Had the income tax remained, they would have been able to draw down their accumulated savings tax free for consumption during retirement. But with the switch to the expenditure tax, they pay taxes a third time as they consume their savings. In short, tax reforms can have very dramatic effects on the intergenerational pattern of tax incidence, effects that the single-period Harberger framework simply cannot consider.

Mobile versus immobile factors

Certain factors are much more mobile than other factors in some contexts. For example, capital is highly mobile from the perspective of states (provinces) and localities, much more so than labor. These differences in mobility matter for the incidence of state and local taxes because the relatively immobile factors generally bear the disproportionate share of the tax burdens.

In fact, the vast majority of the capital supplied to businesses in states and localities comes from individuals and financial institutions located beyond their borders, either in other states (localities) within the nation or even from foreign countries. As a result, the supply of capital to a state or locality has a kink in it, as illustrated in Figure 19.6. The upward-sloping portion of $S_K S_K$ in each figure consists of capital supplied from individuals within the community. Once the return to capital reaches the return available to the "world" beyond the borders, P_K^{world}, the supply becomes perfectly elastic. From the state or local perspective, they can have as much capital as they want so long as the return offered to suppliers of capital matches the return suppliers can get elsewhere. The individual state or locality is too small to have any influence on P_K^{world}. Beyond K_1, it is a price taker with respect to supply of capital.

The special supply condition for capital provides an exception to the principle that the effects of a tax, including the incidence, are the same no matter which side of the market is taxed. Suppose the state or locality decides to tax the income earned from capital by its own citizens under a state or local personal income tax. Figure 19.6(a) illustrates the effects of this tax. The demand curve for capital in the state or locality is D_K and the before-tax amount of capital is K_0, at the intersection of D_K and $S_K S_K$. The tax shifts up the upward-sloping portion of the supply curve, the part that applies to citizens, by the full amount of the tax. The citizens' supply of capital decreases from K_1 to K_2, but that amount of capital is simply replaced by the "world" suppliers, who are not affected by the tax. Therefore, the after-tax equilibrium remains at (K_0, P_K^{world}). The tax has no effect on the market for capital in the community. Nonetheless, the net-of-tax return to the local suppliers of capital falls by the full amount of the tax. They alone bear the burden of the tax because they are the relatively immobile suppliers of capital to the locality.

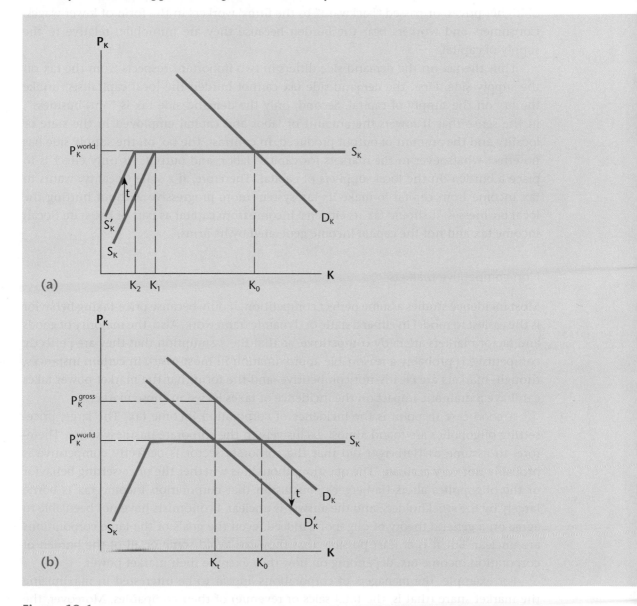

Figure 19.6

Figure 19.6(b) illustrates the effects of a capital income tax on firms within the locality, a tax on the demand side of the market. The tax shifts the demand curve for capital down by the full amount of the tax, from D_K to D_K'. The equilibrium amount of capital falls to K_t, at the intersection of D'_K and $S_K S_K$. The price of capital to the firms rises to P_K^{gross}, but the return to the owners of the firm, the suppliers of capital, remains at P_K^{world}. The capitalists cannot bear a burden from the tax because their return is set in the "world" market. This includes the citizens of the locality who supply capital to the firms. Instead, the burden is either passed "forward" to consumers of the firms' products in the form of higher prices, or passed "backward" to the firms' workers in the form of lower wages. Consumers and workers bear the burden because they are immobile, relative to the supply of capital.

Thus the tax on the demand side differs in two important respects from the tax on the supply side. First, the demand side tax cannot burden the local capitalists, unlike the tax on the supply of capital. Second, only the demand side tax is "anti-business", in the sense that it lowers the amount of labor and capital employed in the state or locality and the amount of output produced. In contrast, the tax on the supply side has no effect whatsoever in the markets for capital, labor, and output. Its only effect is to place a burden on the local suppliers of capital. Therefore, if a state (locality) wants to tax income from capital to make its tax system more progressive without hurting the local businesses, it should tax its citizens' income from capital as part of the state (local) income tax and not the capital income generated by its firms.

Non-competitive markets

Most incidence studies assume perfect competition, if only because price-taking behavior is the easiest to model in either a static or dynamic framework. Also, the majority of goods and factor markets are fairly competitive, so that the assumption that they are perfectly competitive is probably a reasonable approximation in most cases. In certain instances, though, markets are clearly not competitive, and the form that the market power takes can have a dramatic impact on the incidence of taxes levied in those markets.

A good case in point is the incidence of corporation income tax. The large, price-setting oligopolies are found almost exclusively in the corporate business sector. Therefore, to assume as Harberger did that the corporate sector is perfectly competitive is probably not very accurate. The question, though, is whether the price-setting behavior of the oligopolies alters Harberger's conclusion that corporation income tax is borne largely by the stockholders, and the answer is unclear. Economists have not been able to agree on a general theory of oligopoly. Indeed, even the goals of the large corporations are unclear. But it is at least possible that they can avoid some or all of the burden of corporation income tax, depending on how they exercise their market power.

For example, the managers of corporations appear to be interested in maximizing the market share (that is, the total sales or revenue) of their companies. Moreover, the stockholders appear willing to let them pursue this goal at the expense of maximizing profits in the short run, providing the managers earn a satisfactory level of profit. Figure 19.7 illustrates the difference between the goals of short-run profit maximization and maximizing market share: d is the demand curve of the firm, MR the associated marginal revenue curve, and AC and MC the average cost and marginal cost curves. To maximize profit, the firm selects the output q_{PM}, at the intersection the MR and MC, and sets the price P_{PM} on the demand curve. The profit is $(P_{PM} - AC)q_{PM}$, the rectangular area $aP_{PM}bc$. To maximize market share or total revenue, the firm selects the output q_{SM} at which MR = 0, and sets the price P_{SM} on the demand curve. The profit is $(P_{SM} - AC)q_{SM}$, the rectangular area $eP_{SM}fg$. This profit is necessarily less than the profit under profit maximization, but presumably the reduced profits are still satisfactory to shareholders.

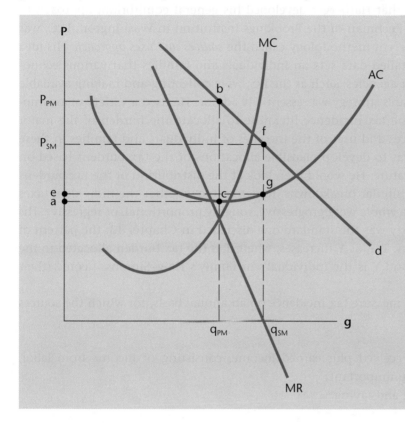

Figure 19.7

Suppose corporations are maximizing market share at (q_{SM}, P_{SM}) before the corporation income tax is imposed. The tax shifts up their costs. If the stockholders insist on trying to maintain profits at the satisfactory level $eP_{SM}fg$, managers would respond by raising price and reducing output, thereby moving closer to the profit-maximizing output and price (q_{PM}, P_{PM}). The after-tax profits could be as high as the pre-tax profits under sales maximization, in which case the stockholders escape the burden of the tax. It is borne either by the firms' consumers through higher prices or the firms' employees through lower wages as they hire fewer workers. In either case, the incidence of the tax is much less progressive than if stockholders bear the burden.

The market share-maximizing model could be used as a theoretical justification for Musgrave's empirical finding, noted in the beginning of the chapter, that consumers bear more than 100% of the burden of corporation income tax. In truth, though, the uncertainties surrounding the behavior of oligopolies make it difficult to know who bears the burden of the tax.

THE SOURCES AND USES ANALYSIS OF INCIDENCE

About the same time that Harberger developed his general equilibrium approach to tax incidence, Joseph Pechman of the Brookings Institution in Washington, D.C. was pioneering a very different methodology called the *sources and uses approach*. His idea was to exploit the detailed data sets on individuals and families that various economists and government agencies, such as the IRS, were collecting and making available to researchers. Pechman's strategy was essentially ad hoc. He used a variety of assumptions and results in the tax incidence literature to allocate the burden of the major U.S. taxes to the sources and uses of the incomes of individuals and families in these databases. The goal was to develop plausible allocations of the tax burdens based on the tax incidence literature. He would then look at the distribution of the tax burdens by income deciles, or similar breakdowns, to determine whether the individual taxes and the tax system as a whole were progressive, roughly proportional, or regressive. His measure of progressivity was the standard one discussed in Chapter 13: the pattern of the average tax burden, T/Y, as Y increases, where T is the tax burden allocated to the individual or family and Y is the individual's or family's Haig–Simons income (their pre-tax income).

Pechman chose to measure tax incidence on an annual basis, for which the sources and uses of income are:

■ *Sources:* transfers received plus earned income, consisting of income from labor, capital, and land (unimportant)
■ *Uses:* consumption and saving.

The allocation of tax burdens to the various sources and uses of income matters because, on an annual basis: transfers are received disproportionately by the poor; income from capital is received disproportionately by those with high incomes; and the ratio of consumption to income falls sharply as income rises. Therefore, tax burdens allocated to transfers and consumption tend to be highly regressive, and tax burdens allocated to income from capital tend to be highly progressive.

Pechman published two studies of tax incidence using his sources and uses approach with Bernard Okner, also of the Brookings Institution (Okner and Pechman, 1974, 1985). The Pechman/Okner monographs have been very influential. They are widely cited in the tax incidence literature and undoubtedly inform much of the public discussion of the incidence of the major taxes.

■■■■ THE MAJOR U.S. TAXES

Pechman and Okner's so-called central variant (most preferred) analysis of the five major U.S. taxes is as follows.

Federal and state personal income taxes

As a matter of convenience, Pechman/Okner assume that the supplies of labor, capital, and land are absolutely fixed, so that the impact of the personal income taxes is their incidence. We saw in Chapter 13 that this is not a proper assumption. The actual supplies of all these factors may be close to perfectly inelastic, but the compensated supplies of labor and capital are almost certainly not perfectly inelastic. The inelasticity of the actual supplies of labor and capital are the result of roughly offsetting substitution and income effects that may each be fairly large. The nonzero substitution effects imply that the income taxes on these factors generate deadweight efficiency losses, which should be counted as part of the burden of the tax.[5]

Pechman/Okner simply ignore the distinction between the actual and compensated supply elasticities in their analysis, and they are not alone in this. Many economists have published studies of the incidence of the federal and state (and local) personal income taxes under the assumption that the tax payments are the tax burden. In any event, under the impact-equals-incidence assumption, the federal personal income tax is highly progressive over the lower ranges of incomes because of the personal exemptions and standard deductions (refer to Chapter 14 for a discussion of the federal tax). The graduated tax rates continue to make the tax progressive over the higher range of income, but the progressivity built into the rates is undermined to a considerable extent by the various exclusions and deductions available to taxpayers who itemize (again, refer to Chapter 14). The result is only a mildly progressive pattern of burdens beyond the first few deciles of income. Overall, though, the tax is fairly progressive. Since most state income taxes imitate the federal tax, the same conclusions apply to state taxes as well.

Social Security payroll tax

The payroll tax to finance the Social Security system is levied on both sides of the market, and it has two separate components. First, employers and employees each pay a tax of 6.2% on every employee's wage and salary income up to a maximum amount that is indexed each year to the CPI. The maximum was $90,000 in 2005. This portion of the tax is earmarked to Social Security pensions and disability payments. Second, employers and employees each pay an additional tax of 1.45% on every employee's wage and salary income without limit. This portion of the tax is earmarked for payments under Medicare.

Since labor is assumed to be in absolutely fixed supply, the tax payments are also the tax incidence. The only wrinkle here is the attempt by Congress to split the burden of the tax between employers and employees. Unfortunately, the market does not allow the burden to be split. It falls entirely on employees (individuals and their families), as illustrated in Figure 19.8.

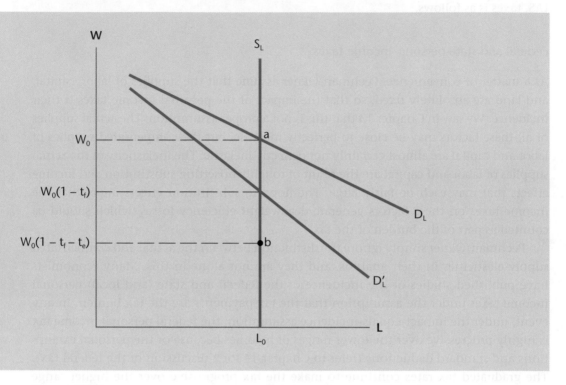

Figure 19.8

The demand for labor, D_L is downward sloping but the supply of labor S_L is vertical by assumption, perfectly inelastic. The pre-tax equilibrium is (L_0, W_0), at the intersection of D_L and S_L. The combined 7.65 (= 6.2 + 1.45)% tax on firms shifts the demand curve down by the full amount of the tax to D_L'. With S_L perfectly inelastic, the wage that employers pay to their employees falls by the full amount of the tax, to $W_0(1 - t_f)$, where $t_f = 0.0765$, the firms' portion of the tax. Then the employees' portion of the tax, also 7.65%, lowers the wage again by the full amount of the tax along the vertical S_L, to $W(1 - t_f - t_e)$, where $t_e = 0.0765$, the employees' portion of the tax. The net-of-tax wage to employees falls by the combined amount of the tax, 15.3%. The tax incidence is the combined tax payment, equal to the area $W_0 ab W_0(1 - t_f - t_e)$, and it is borne entirely by employees.

Under the Pechman/Okner fixed-supply-of-labor assumption, the Social Security payroll tax is highly regressive, for two reasons. First, the tax payments are allocated only to wage and salary income. This makes them somewhat regressive because the capital income portion of earned income escapes the tax. But the payroll tax becomes highly regressive because of the $90,000 income cut-off (in 2005) applied to the majority of the tax. Since T is constant above $90,000, T/Y falls steadily towards zero as income increases; the highest paid CEOs bear the same burden of the tax as employees earning $90,000. The income cut-off makes the payroll tax the most regressive of the five major U.S. taxes.

Corporation income tax

In their central variant, Pechman/Okner adopt the Harberger conclusion that the corporation income tax is borne entirely by corporate stockholders. Therefore, they allocate the entire burden of the tax to income from capital. Since capital income is highly skewed towards the rich, corporation income tax is viewed as a highly progressive tax.

States' general sales taxes

The states' general sales taxes are typically levied at a single rate on a broad range of manufactured goods. The one notable exception is that 26 states exempt food purchased for home consumption from the tax base. Some states also exempt purchases of clothing up to a given dollar amount. Only a few states tax services as well as goods.

Pechman/Okner's central variant assumption is that the supply of goods is sufficiently elastic in the long run so that it can reasonably be viewed as perfectly elastic. Under this assumption, although the suppliers pay the tax to the state governments, they are able to pass the tax on to consumers in the form of higher prices. The prices of the taxed goods eventually rise by the full amount of the tax. Refer to Figure 19.9.

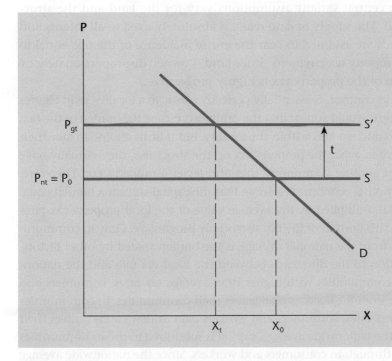

Figure 19.9

The demand curve for one of the taxed goods, X, is D and the supply curve before the tax is S, with S perfectly elastic. The before-tax equilibrium is (X_0, P_o), at the intersection of D and S. The sales tax t shifts the supply curve up by the full amount of the tax to S', and the new equilibrium is (X_t, P_{gt}). P_{gt}, the gross-of-tax price paid by the consumers of X, rises by the full amount of the tax. The net-of-tax price to firms, P_{nt}, remains at P_o. The full burden of the tax falls on consumers.[6]

Given the perfectly elastic supply assumption, Pechman/Okner allocate the burden of tax payments to the consumption of individuals and families. With the tax payments proportionate to consumption, $T = tC$, where t is a state's sales tax rate and C is consumption. Since C/Y falls sharply as income rises, T/Y also falls sharply as income rises and the sales taxes are highly regressive.

Local property tax

The local property tax is levied on residences and commercial and industrial properties within a community. In smaller communities with few businesses, the vast majority of the tax is collected from residences. The values of the properties being taxed are estimated periodically by a local tax assessor, and the assessment includes the value of the land and the structures on the land. The assessed values may or may not approximate the actual market values of the land and the structures. Then a single tax rate is applied to the assessed values. (Some communities have separate tax rates for residences and businesses, with all residences taxed at one rate and all business properties at another rate.)

The Pechman/Okner central variant assumptions vary for the land and the structures (capital) on the land. The supply of land really is absolutely fixed to all intents and purposes, so that landlords are assumed to bear the entire incidence of the tax, equal to the land portion of the property tax payment. Since land is owned disproportionately by the rich, the land portion of the property tax is highly progressive.

The supply of capital, in contrast, is essentially perfectly elastic to a locality, as in Figures 19.6(b) and 19.9. Therefore, it would appear that the capitalists escape the burden of the tax, passing it on to consumers and workers within the locality. But if firms choose to take their capital out of a community to avoid the property tax on the structures, they virtually have no choice but to locate in another community that also levies a property tax. Therefore, Pechman/Okner and most other economists assume that the capitalists bear a burden equal to the value of their capital multiplied by the average value of the local property tax rates nationwide, which makes this portion of the tax also highly progressive. Only in communities whose tax rates differ from the national average is the burden shared by other factors, and then only in proportion to the difference between the local tax rate and the nationwide average tax rate. In communities with higher than average tax rates, consumers and workers bear some burden from the tax as capital leaves their communities. In communities with lower than average tax rates, consumers and workers gain as new capital enters their communities. Relative to the nationwide average, capital is subsidized in these communities and the subsidy is passed through to consumers and workers. Since the nationwide average dominates in the incidence calculations, and the burdens and subsidies to consumers and workers essentially net out nationwide, the property tax is seen as a highly progressive tax, falling predominately on higher income landlords and capitalists.

Overall, the Pechman/Okner analysis views the U.S. tax system as a mixture of progressive taxes (personal income taxes, corporation income taxes, and local property taxes) and regressive taxes (Social Security payroll tax and the states' general sales taxes). Net, they conclude that U.S. taxes are not very redistributive. The T/Y tax burden ratios vary from 20.6% at the lowest decile of individuals and families to 27.1% at the highest decile, a pattern that they characterize as essentially proportional or at best mildly progressive (Okner and Pechman, 1985, Table 4.4, p. 48).

CAVEATS TO THE SOURCES AND USES APPROACH

John Whalley, in his 1984 Presidential address to the Canadian Economic Association, cautioned his fellow economists to be wary of the sources and uses approach to tax incidence (Whalley, 1984). He noted that the conclusions drawn from this approach can be very sensitive to the assumptions chosen to analyze each tax. By carefully choosing among different possible assumptions, each one plausible in its own right, a tax system can be made to seem either highly progressive or highly regressive. This is especially true if researchers mix annual and lifetime perspectives, which Whalley argues should not be done. He prefers adopting a lifetime perspective, for which the individual allocation assumptions are less important. Whalley illustrated his cautionary tale with an analysis of the Canadian tax system, which is very similar to the U.S. system.

Using Pechman/Okner's central variant assumptions, he found that the overall incidence pattern across deciles of Canadian taxes were much like U.S. taxes, mildly progressive. But by choosing different assumptions, Canadian taxes could be made to appear either highly progressive, with T/Y ratios starting at 11% at the lowest decile and rising steadily to 70% at the highest decile, or highly regressive, with T/Y ratios starting at 100% at the lowest decile and falling steadily to 16% at the highest decile (Whalley, 1984, Table 5, p. 666 and Table 7, p. 670). Possible variations of this magnitude are clearly troubling for the sources and uses approach.

The essence of the tax incidence games that one can play is this. If you want to make the tax system seem more progressive than Pechman/Okner's central variant case, adopt assumptions that either reduce the regressivity of the regressive taxes or remove them from the incidence analysis altogether and, if possible, make the progressive taxes more progressive. Conversely, if you want to make the tax system seem more regressive than Pechman/Okner's central variant case, adopt assumptions that either reduce the progressivity of the progressive taxes or remove them from the incidence analysis altogether and, if possible, make the regressive taxes more regressive. Here are some examples.

More progressive – the two regressive taxes are the states' general sales taxes and the Social Security payroll tax. To make the sales taxes less regressive, adopt a lifetime rather than an annual perspective. Since bequests are unimportant for most people, lifetime consumption is roughly proportional to lifetime transfers plus labor earnings. Therefore, allocate the burden of the sales taxes to lifetime consumption, which makes them roughly proportional rather than regressive. Furthermore, Browning and Johnson have argued that some transfer payments, notably Social Security pensions, are indexed for inflation. Thus they adjust automatically to increases in the prices of consumer goods resulting from the sales taxes, so that the transfer portion of lifetime resources escapes much of the burden of the tax. Since lifetime transfers are somewhat pro-poor relative to lifetime labor earnings, the sales tax may actually be slightly progressive from a lifetime perspective.

Regarding the Social Security payroll tax, assume that the current workers adopt the view that their payroll taxes effectively commit the federal government to providing them with the promised Social Security pensions when they retire. That is, the government is committed to continuing to tax the future workers at rates sufficient to pay the current workers' pensions. In essence, then, the current workers view their taxes as a benefits-received tax, which removes the tax from the incidence analysis.

On the other side of the ledger, personal and corporation income taxes can be made more progressive by noting that they both tax nominal returns to capital. There is no attempt to remove the portion of the returns that is due solely to inflation, which places a higher real tax burden on income from capital relative to labor income. Indeed, the real after-tax returns to capital can turn negative in periods of high inflation such as the United States experienced around 1980. Any adjustment that increases the relative burden on capital income increases the progressivity of a tax.

More regressive – two taxes that are highly progressive in the Pechman/Okner central variant are the corporation income tax and the local property tax. The progressivity of the corporation income tax can be reduced in one of four ways:

1. Assume that the supply of capital to the nation is perfectly elastic, so that the return to suppliers is determined on the world market. In that case, Figure 19.6(b) applies – the burden of a tax on the corporate firms' accounting profits cannot be borne by the capitalists. It is passed forward to the consumers of corporate products or backward to the corporate employees, both of which make the tax far less progressive, even regressive if most of the pass-through is to consumers.

2. Assume that the corporations are market share maximizers, as in Figure 19.7, so that the tax moves them closer to the profit-maximizing outcome and much, or all, of the burden is borne by consumers and employees.

3. Adopt the long-run argument that although the tax is borne by capitalists in the short run, the long-run effect is to reduce saving, investment, and the productivity of the economy, which lowers real wages and thereby shifts the burden to the wage and salary income.

4. Assume that the corporation income tax is a benefits-received tax, in this case a payment in return for the limited liability protection granted to corporate stockholders. If the firm goes bankrupt, the firm's creditors cannot go after the assets of indi-

vidual stockholders. Therefore, the corporation income tax is viewed by stockholders as a fee that they are willing to pay for this protection.

Regarding the property tax, assume that local property taxes are benefits-received taxes in the form of payments for local services. This view makes sense if people shop for localities on the basis of their tax–public service mix. For example, people choose to pay higher taxes for better schools and vice versa, just as they choose to pay more (less) for private goods and services of higher (lower) quality.

On the other side of the ledger, view the incidence of the states' sales taxes on an annual basis, which makes them highly regressive, and adopt the Pechman/Okner view that the Social Security payroll tax is just another general tax, and a highly regressive one because of the income cut-off.

Whalley considers still other assumptions that can make the tax system seem more progressive or regressive, but these examples are sufficient to capture the nature of the exercise.

THE LONG-RUN PERSPECTIVE

Many economists have criticized Pechman/Okner's annual perspective on tax incidence. They argue that tax incidence should be measured on a lifetime basis, in part because the income received by so many people varies considerably from year to year and in part because only a lifetime perspective can capture the full economic fortunes of any one person. In a lifetime perspective, the present value of the tax burdens allocated to an individual or family year by year would be compared with the present value of their income or consumption.[7]

Switching from an annual to a lifetime perspective affects the sources and uses approach in two respects that matter for tax incidence. First, the sources and uses of income differ. The lifetime sources of income come in three forms: inheritance, the annual stream of public and private transfers, and the annual stream of wage and salary income. The uses of income are the stream of annual consumption plus the final bequest upon death, which is important for only a small percentage of people. Likewise, the inheritance portion of income is important for only a small percentage of people. Notice that income from capital is missing from the sources of income. The reason is that savings grow at a rate of return that, on average, matches the rate of return that is used to discount future income to present value (see Chapter 20), so that there is no net increase in income from people's savings. All that income from capital achieves, on average, is to influence the pattern of consumption over time. Thus, it affects the uses side, not the sources side in allocating tax burdens.

Second, the two most important sources of lifetime income, transfers and labor earnings, vary much less than their annual counterparts. Most transfers are received when young and old, and many people who received them because they were poor in a particular year are not poor in a lifetime context. Similarly, the variation in lifetime earnings across workers is only about one-half to one-third as large as the variation in annual earnings. Turning to the uses side, most people eventually consume all their lifetime transfers and labor market earnings, which means that lifetime consumption also varies much less across individuals and families than does annual consumption. With the various components of the sources and uses of lifetime income much less variable than their annual components, the lifetime incidence of any particular tax is much less sensitive to how the lifetime tax burden is allocated among the sources and uses of income than is the annual allocation of the tax burden. Not surprisingly, most studies of the lifetime incidence of the U.S. tax system find that it is not very redistributive. They reach the same conclusion as Pechman/Okner's annual assessment: The entire U.S. tax system is essentially proportional to at best mildly progressive.

SOURCES AND USES VERSUS GENERAL EQUILIBRIUM MODELING

When Harberger developed his general equilibrium approach to tax incidence, formal general equilibrium modeling was in its infancy. Consequently, he was forced to use a very simple two-good, two-factor model and consider only a marginal change in corporation income tax. The 40-plus years since have brought enormous advances in general equilibrium modeling, to the point that the models can now accommodate such features as: discrete (large) tax changes; individuals belonging to a number of different income classes; many business sectors; and a more fully specified government sector, in which the government levies many different taxes simultaneously and uses the tax revenues to finance specific kinds of public goods and services and transfer payments.

General equilibrium models also have a distinct advantage over the sources and uses approach – they can measure the deadweight loss from the taxes and include them in the tax burdens. This matters because all the major taxes are distorting. Nonetheless, as with the sources and uses approach, these models rely on a large number of assumptions, in this case assumptions about the nature of the economy. These include assumptions about: the parameters of consumers' utility functions that indicate their relative preferences for private and public goods and for leisure time; the parameters of the production functions for the different industries in the model; and the competitiveness of markets for private goods and services (perfect competition in all markets is the standard assumption). Long-run models have to make further assumptions about how individuals and firms make predictions about the future, which economists know little about.[8] Unfortunately, the tax incidence results can often be quite sensitive to the choices made along all these dimensions.

In conclusion, economists have no best model for analyzing tax incidence. The sources and uses approach is sensitive to assumptions about the incidence of individual taxes and the choice between an annual and a lifetime perspective. The general equilibrium modeling approach is sensitive to assumptions about the structure of the models being used. It is fair to say that the general equilibrium modeling approach is now preferred by the majority of public sector economists who study tax incidence, and that the sources and uses approach still dominates public debate about tax incidence. One curious, and perhaps comforting, feature of the tax incidence literature is that the general equilibrium modeling approach tends to reach the same conclusion about the incidence of the overall U.S. tax system as does both the annual and lifetime sources and uses approach. For what it is worth, the consensus from all the approaches is that the U.S. tax system is somewhere between proportional to mildly progressive.

CRS, Unequal Factor Intensities, and the Production Possibilities Frontier

Under CRS production, production of Y and X along a straight line is always possible. Figure 19A.1 illustrates.

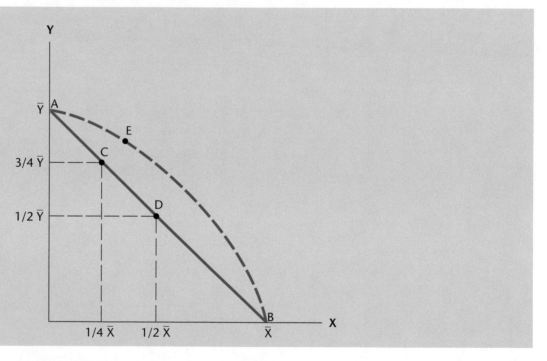

Figure 19A.1

Suppose all the labor and capital, $\bar{L}$ and $\bar{K}$, is used to produce Y. The economy would produce the maximum possible amount of Y, equal to $\bar{Y}$ at point A. Conversely, if $\bar{L}$ and $\bar{K}$ are used to produce only X, the economy would produce the maximum possible amount of X, equal to $\overline{X}$ at point B. Given CRS production, and starting at $\overline{Y}$, if a quarter of the labor and capital were reallocated from Y to X, then the economy would produce three-quarters $\overline{Y}$ and a quarter $\overline{X}$ at point C on line AB; if half of the labor and capital were reallocated from Y to X, then the economy would produce half $\overline{Y}$ and half $\overline{X}$ at point D on AB; and so forth. In other words, the CRS assumption allows production to lie along the straight line AB pictured in the figure. If the firms were equally factor intensive, then the proportions of L and K released from Y would be exactly the proportions of L and K that X would require to produce at least cost, and AB would be the production possibilities frontier for the economy. A linear frontier is a constant cost frontier; the marginal costs of producing Y and X are constant along the frontier. Therefore, with prices equal to marginal costs under perfect competition, P_Y and P_X are constant along the frontier. P_L and P_K are constant as well, since there is never any excess supply or demand for labor and capital to change the factor prices as resources are transferred from Y to X, or vice versa, along the frontier. The amount of capital and labor released by one of the goods is exactly the amount that the other good requires. Thus, there is no need for factor prices to change to reallocate the resources efficiently or to maintain full employment of labor and capital. Tax incidence analysis is uninteresting if no prices can change.

Return to the case in which, starting from Y, the Y industry releases a quarter of its capital and labor. Under CRS production, point C on line AB is a possible production point. But if Y is relatively capital intensive, then the economy can produce more of both goods by reallocating the capital and labor so that the Y industry has more than three-quarters of the capital and less than three-quarters of the labor, and vice versa for the X industry. By reallocating the capital and labor in this way, the economy can reach point E on the dotted line. The same argument applies to all points on AB as capital and labor are reallocated from Y to X. The dotted line is the production possibilities frontier for the economy and it is bowed away from the origin. The ratio of marginal costs along the frontier is the MRT_{YX}, the slope of the frontier, and it varies along the frontier. Therefore, the P_Y and P_X also vary along the frontier, as explained in the chapter. The excess supplies and demands for capital and labor as the economy moves along the bowed-out frontier also cause P_L and P_K to vary, as explained in the chapter. Consequently, taxes that lead to reallocations of resources between the goods cause the goods and factor prices to change, and the price changes become central to the analysis of their incidence.

Cost–Benefit Analysis

CHAPTER 20

Cost–Benefit Analysis

Cost–benefit analysis refers to the analysis of government investments, projects such as the construction of highways, bridges, tunnels, and waste treatment plants, the purchase of advanced weapons systems, and job training programs that teach people skills to make them more employable. Government cost–benefit analysis is akin to private firms' analyses of their own investments in plant and equipment. In both cases, government and firms are attempting to determine if proposed investment projects are expected to be worthwhile and should be undertaken. The analysis of government investments tends to be much more difficult, however, because it encounters a number of problems that tend to be absent in private investment analysis, both in principle and in practice.

DURABILITY AND THE PRESENT VALUE FORMULA

There is an immediate difficulty with both private and government investments that requires some attention before turning to the problems of cost–benefit analysis. It is that the investments represent an addition to the stock of private or public capital, and capital is durable. Capital purchased or constructed today is expected to be productive and yield a stream of net revenues or benefits for more than one year, often many years. For example, computers purchased today by private or government agencies are expected to last anywhere from three to five years before they are replaced by newer and better computers; other equipment such as desks, screens and projectors may last for ten years or more; and structures such as office buildings and highways are expected to last far into the future, perhaps forty years or more. The problem is that dollars received or spent in different time periods are not equivalent.

393

DISCOUNTING TO PRESENT VALUE

To see that dollars over time are not equivalent, suppose that someone offered you a dollar today or a dollar one year from now. You would surely take the dollar today, for a number of reasons: inflation will erode the value of the dollar received one year from now; the person may renege on the offer next year – the future is always uncertain. But suppose there is no inflation and you are convinced that the person would pay you the dollar one year from now. Nevertheless, you would still prefer the dollar today, even if you did not want to spend the dollar until next year. The reason why is that you, and virtually everyone else, have opportunities to save and invest at a positive interest rate or rate of return. Suppose the rate of return on a one-year certificate of deposit (CD) or a one-year U.S. Treasury note is 8%. CDs are insured by the federal government and U.S. Treasury notes are considered the world's safest financial securities, so that risk is not an issue with either one. If you take the dollar today and buy one of these securities, you will have $1(1 + .08)$ dollars one year from now, $1.08, equal to the dollar plus interest of $.08 on the dollar. Therefore, given the opportunity to save risk free at an 8% rate of return, you would be indifferent between receiving $1 today and $1.08 dollars one year from now; $1 today and $1.08 one year from now are equivalent in the sense of you being indifferent between them.

The same reasoning applies to the equivalence of dollars received (or spent) in all future time periods. Thus, $1 received today and invested at 8% for two years would increase to $1.08 at the end of the first year, and the $1.08 would increase again by 8% in the second year. The value at the end of the two years would be $[\$1(1 + .08)](1 + .08) = \$1(1 + .08)^2 = \$1.17$. Therefore, $1 received today is equivalent to $1.17 received two years from now. Since each year the value of the money grows by the factor $(1 + .08)$, $1 received today is equivalent to $\$1(1 + .08)^3 (= \$1.26)$ received in three years, $\$1(1 + .08)^5 (= \$1.47)$ received in five years, and $\$1(1 + .08)^n$ received n years into the future. More generally, $X today is equivalent to $\$X(1 + .08)^n$ received n years from now, assuming that money as it is received can always be reinvested at an 8% rate of return from then on. Computing the future value of current dollars is called *compounding to future values*, with the compound factor in our example equal to $(1 + .08)$ and the compound rate equal to 8%.

A second way to compare dollars over time is to compute the current value of dollars received in future years. Computing the current value of dollars received (or spent) in the future is called *discounting to present value*, and it is just the inverse of compounding current dollars to their equivalent future values. If $1 today is equivalent to $\$1(1 + .08)$ dollars one year from now, then $1 received one year from now is equivalent to $\$1[1/(1 + .08)]$ received today: $\$1[1/(1 + .08)] = \$0.93$. If you had $0.93 today and invested it for one year at an 8% return, it would be worth $1 one year from now: $\{\$0.93(1 + .08) = [\$1/(1 + .08)](1 + .08) = \$1\}$. Therefore, $0.93 is called the *present value* of $1 received one year from now. The term $1/(1 + .08)$ is called the *discount factor* applied to dollars received one year from now and .08 is the *discount rate*, 8%. Multiply by (1 + .08) to compound dollars from one year to the next in the future; divide by (1 + .08) to discount dollars from one year in the future back to the preceding year.

The pattern of discounting future values to their equivalent present value continues just as it does with compounding current values to the equivalent future values, with the discount factor replacing the compound factor. The present value of $1 received three years from now is $1[1/(1 + .08)^3] (= $0.79); the present value of $1 received five years from now is $1[1/(1 + .08)^5] (= $0.68); and the present value of $1 received n years from now is $1[1/(1 + .08)^n]$. More generally, the present value of $X dollars received (or spent) n years from now is $X[1/(1 + .08)^n]$ at a discount rate of 8%, assuming that money can always be reinvested at 8%. The two values are equivalent because if you had $X[1/(1 + .08)^n]$ today and invested it at 8%, it would increase to $X by n years from now: $\{X[1/(1 + .08)^n](1 + .08)^n = X\}$.

In conclusion, the process of compounding current dollars to some future year or discounting future dollars to their present value makes dollars over time equivalent, no matter when they are received or spent.

THE PRESENT VALUE FORMULA

Consider first an investment in a machine by a private firm, since analyzing private investments is more straightforward than analyzing public investments. Because the dollars invested in the machine are occurring today, a natural way to compare the projected future net revenues with the initial investment costs is to compute the present value of the projected net revenues. Let:

I_0 = the initial investment costs, incurred today. Assume that the machine is paid for with cash out of retained earnings.

R_i = the net revenues received in year i, equal to the revenues received from the additional output that the new machine allows the firm to produce, less any costs incurred in year i to operate and service the machine.

r = the discount rate, expressed as a decimal fraction (.08 in our example). The firm's managers are presumably promoting the interests of the stockholders. Therefore, the discount rate reflects the annual return that the stockholders of the company can earn generally on their savings. As such, the discount rate serves as the opportunity cost of capital when analyzing an investment.

N = the last year that the machine is projected to generate positive net revenue.

The stream of net revenues discounted to present value is $\displaystyle\sum_{i=1}^{N} \frac{R_i}{(1+r)^i}$ =

$\dfrac{R_1}{(1+r)^1} + \dots, \dfrac{R_i}{(1+r)^i} + \dots, \dfrac{R_N}{(1+r)N}$. This discounted stream can then be compared directly with the initial investment costs I_0, which are incurred today. If:

(a) $\sum_{i=1}^{N} \dfrac{R_i}{(1+r)^i} > I_0$, invest in the machine. The extra revenue generated by the

machine, discounted to present value, exceeds the initial investment costs.

(b) $\sum_{i=1}^{N} \dfrac{R_i}{(1+r)^i} = I_0$, the stockholders of the firm are just indifferent between the

following two choices: (1) having the managers invest in the machine; or (2) having the managers distribute the amount I_0 to the stockholders and letting them invest on their own at rate r. To see this, compound both sides up to year N by multiplying by $(1+r)^N$. If the stockholders receive the amount I_0 in cash today, by year N they would have $I_0(1+r)^N$. If the managers invest in the machine, and then distribute the net revenues received over time to the stockholders, by year N the stockholders would have: R_1 at the end of year one, which they would invest at rate r for N-1 years, obtaining $R_1(1+r)^{N-1}$ by year N; R_2 at the end of the second year, which they would invest at rate r for N-2 years, obtaining $R_2(1+r)^{N-2}$ by year N; and so forth, until they receive the last payment R_N in year N. This stream of returns by year N is $R_1(1+r)^{N-1} + ... + R_i(1+r)^{N-i} + ... + R_N$, which just equals $I_0(1+r)^N$. The stockholders do not care whether the managers invest in the machine or distribute the amount I_0 to them.

(c) $\sum_{i=1}^{N} \dfrac{R_i}{(1+r)^i} < I_0$, do not invest in the machine. Instead, give the sum I_0 to the

stockholders and let them invest the funds themselves at rate r.

Economists define the *present value of an investment*, PV_I, as the difference between the discounted stream of net returns and the initial investment costs:

$$PV_I = -I_0 + \sum_{i=1}^{N} \dfrac{R_i}{(1+r)^i}$$

The present value of an investment is also commonly referred to as the *present value formula*.

The investment rule in terms of the present value formula is that if:

(a) $PV > 0$, invest
(b) $PV = 0$, the managers are just indifferent between investing in the machine and distributing the sum I_0 to the stockholders for them to invest at rate r
(c) $PV < 0$, do not invest. Instead, distribute I_0 to the stockholders and let them invest at rate r.

If funds are limited such that the firm cannot invest in all the projects that have positive present value, then it should chose the combination of investments that yields the highest present value (including the value of any funds left unexpended and invested at rate r).

Some comments on the present value formula are in order:

1. The discount rate r serves as the opportunity cost of capital to the firm; it is the rate that stockholders can earn on their own investments generally. If the rate of return that stockholders can receive on their own savings changes over time to $r_1, r_2,...,r_i...r_N$, , then the separate discount rates $r_1, r_2,...,r_i,...,r_N$ have to be used for each year. For example, the discount factor for year one is $\dfrac{1}{(1+r_1)}$; for year two,

$$\frac{1}{(1+r_1)(1+r_2)}; \text{ for year three, } \frac{1}{(1+r_1)(1+r_2)(1+r_3)}; \text{ for year n, } \prod_{i=1}^{n}\left(\frac{1}{(1+r_i)}\right).$$

2. People often speak of "the rate of return on an investment." Economists refer to this rate as the *internal yield* on an investment, defined as the rate of discount, ρ, that just sets the present value of the investment equal to zero. That is, it is the rate of return that just makes a firm indifferent about undertaking the investment. The internal yield, ρ, is the solution to the present value formula when it is set equal to zero:

$$PV_1 = 0 = -I_0 + \sum_{i=1}^{N} \frac{R_i}{(1+\rho)^i}$$

The internal yield calculated in this way takes into account the timing of the returns. For example, consider two machines that generate a total of $10,000 in net returns, undiscounted, over 10 years. The first machine yields net returns of $9,900 in year 1, nothing for 9 years, $100 in year 10, and nothing thereafter. The second machine generates net returns of $100 in year 1, nothing for 9 years, $9,900 in year 10, and nothing thereafter. The first machine is a much better investment and has a much higher internal yield simply because the majority of its net returns occur early rather than later.[1]

Although it is convenient to characterize investment projects by their internal yields, care has to be taken in using the internal yield to rank investment projects. If funds are unlimited, then accepting all projects with an internal yield greater than the rate of discount is equivalent to accepting all projects with a positive present value. If funds are limited, however, which is the usual case, then ranking projects by their internal yields may select a different set of projects than ranking them by their present values. If so, then the ranking by internal yields is an error since ranking by present value is always correct.

The problem with ranking investments by their internal yields is that the internal yields ignore the scale of the projects, whereas the present value calculations do not. The following example illustrates why the scale matters. Suppose four projects are being considered, three small projects and one large project. The three small projects all have internal yields that are slightly higher than the internal yield of the larger project, but the internal yields on all our projects are well above the rate of discount. They all have positive present values. Having chosen the first three projects on the basis of their higher internal yields, there are not sufficient funds to finance the fourth project. So the remaining funds have to be invested at the lower discount rate. If the projects had been ranked instead on the basis of their present values, it is likely that the larger project would have been chosen along with one or two of the smaller projects, leaving fewer funds remaining to be invested at the lower discount rate. The overall present value from the combination of investments chosen would be greater, which is the desired outcome. The conclusion is clear: Always rank investment projects according to their present values.

3. Inflation makes no difference to the present value formula, since both the net revenues in the numerator and the discount rate(s) in the denominator of the discounted stream of returns increase by the factor $(1 + \pi)$ each year, where π is the annual rate of inflation. For example, in the first year inflation increases the net revenues to $R_1(1 + \pi)$ and the real discount factor to $\dfrac{1}{(1+r)(1+\pi)}$, the so-called nominal discount factor.[2] By year i, an ongoing inflation at rate π increases both the numerator and denominator by $(1 + \pi)^i$. With the numerator and denominator increasing by the same multiple term by term, the value of the discounted stream of returns is unchanged. Therefore, if nominal (actual) net returns are used in the numerator, use the nominal discount rate(s) in the denominator. If real net returns are used in the numerator, then use the real discount rate(s) in the denominator.

4. Initial investment costs often occur for a number of years, as they do in the construction of most structures. In that case, the initial investment costs that occur in years 1, 2, and so forth have to be discounted to present value along with the future net returns. A familiar example to students is their investment in a college education, undertaken so that they can earn higher incomes after college than they would have earned without the college degree. The investment costs of college are spread over the first four years, with the higher earnings occurring for the first time in the fifth year. Letting I_i be the costs of college in year i and R_i be the increase in incomes in year i starting in year 5, the present value of the education is

$$PV_{education} = -\sum_{i=1}^{4} I_i \left(\frac{1}{(1+r)^i} \right) + \sum_{i=5}^{N} R_i \left(\frac{1}{(1+r)^i} \right)$$

where N is the projected year of retirement.[3]

COST–BENEFIT ANALYSIS VS. PRIVATE INVESTMENT ANALYSIS

Using the present value formula to determine whether an investment is worthwhile is a necessary step in any investment analysis, private or public. But it is nothing more than a mechanical tool for ensuring that dollars received or spent over time are equivalent and therefore comparable. The interesting part of investment analysis comes in trying to quantify the elements of the present value formula, particularly the rate of discount r and the projected future stream of net returns, the R_i. Consider again the problems faced by managers of private firms in computing the present value of their proposed investments.

PRIVATE INVESTMENT ANALYSIS

For a private firm, r depends on the saving opportunities available to the firm's stock-holders, which the firm is unlikely to know for sure. Selecting an r that is too low generates two biases: (1) it accepts too many projects because it increases the stream of discounted net returns; and (2) for two investments with an equal undiscounted stream of future net returns, it favors the investment whose net returns occur farther in the future, because a too low discount rate does not discount the more distant net returns as severely. Conversely, selecting an r that is too high rejects too many projects, and it also favors those investments whose returns occur in the near future, other things being equal. Either mistake reduces the profitability of the firm relative to choosing the correct discount rate, and thus hurts the stockholders.[4]

Selecting the correct stream of net returns, R_i, is equally difficult, perhaps more so. No one can know the future with certainty, so the best any manager can do is estimate the R_i each year. There is likely to be an expected value and a probability distribution attached to each estimated R_i that depends on such things as the projected state of the economy in the future or perhaps legislation being debated in Congress that directly affects the firms. Examples might be a tariff on imports of the firm's product that would protect the firm somewhat from foreign competitors, or workplace safety legislation that would increase the cost of the firm's investments to ensure that they conform to the new tougher laws. So, for example, the projected R_i might be quite high if the economy is expected to be good over the life of the investment, the tariff passes, and the safety legislation is defeated. Conversely, the projected R_i might be quite low if the economy is expected to go into a recession, the tariff is defeated, and the safety legislation passes. The managers have to decide what they think are the probabilities of each of the three events occurring and adjust the expected R_i accordingly. There-fore, each possible outcome has a probability attached to it. As we saw in Chapter 12, uncertainty about the future reduces the value of the future net returns below their expected values.

COST–BENEFIT ANALYSIS

When analyzing government investment projects, public officials also have to choose an appropriate rate of discount and estimate an uncertain stream of future net returns, just as managers of private firms have to. The principles are somewhat different for public investments, but problems arise just the same. In addition, public officials face three difficult evaluation issues that are likely to be absent in private investment analysis: The inability to use market prices to evaluate some, or all, of the benefits and/or costs; concerns about the distribution of the benefits and costs; and political pressures that introduce bogus benefits and/or costs into the analysis. Before discussing these specific issues, however, we need to establish three fundamental principles of cost–benefit analysis.

THREE FUNDAMENTAL PRINCIPLES OF COST–BENEFIT ANALYSIS

The first principle relates to the expectations for cost–benefit analysis. In an ideal world, each cost–benefit study would be unambiguously correct in terms of economic theory. But to ask for this in the real world is to ask for the impossible. At best, cost–benefit analyses can only offer practical guidance to government policy makers. The reason why is that the desirability of any government investment depends on two factors: (1) the attributes of the project that give rise to its benefits and costs; and (2) the underlying economic environment in which the investment is undertaken. The problem arises with the second factor, because the underlying economic environment dictates how the benefits and costs of any project should be evaluated. It matters, for example, exactly how market prices are distorted by taxes and monopoly power, and whether the analyst considers the distribution of income to be optimal or not. We will see some examples of this below. Different policy analysts are likely to make different assumptions about the distribution of income, and no analyst can hope to capture all the factors that distort market prices in an economy.

The underlying theoretical ambiguities notwithstanding, most economists are convinced that the government, and society, would be well served by undertaking careful cost–benefit studies of all proposed government investment projects. The second principle, therefore, is that that policy makers should try to quantify the elements of the present value formula to the extent possible for all potential government investments. To this end, the three basic guidelines are:

1. identify all the sources of the true project benefits and costs
2. use state-of-the-art evaluation techniques to try to estimate the benefits and costs
3. avoid attaching bogus benefits and costs to the analysis.

Ideally, an agency of the government would oversee the various cost–benefit studies to ensure that the same evaluation criteria are being applied to all projects. Cost–benefit analyses that meet these guidelines are almost certain to inform public policy debates and improve government decision making.

The third principle is that cost–benefit analysis should assume that the economy is operating at full employment, unless specifically stated otherwise in the study. The main purpose of a cost–benefit study is to help policy makers determine the best use of society's scarce resources and the full employment assumption is best suited to that purpose. It underscores that each potential government investment project is directly competing for funds not only with other possible government expenditures but also with consumption and investment opportunities in the private sector. As such, the costs associated with any investment are properly viewed as opportunity costs, as required in economic analysis. If the economy happens to be in a recession with unemployed labor, then it is true that a particular project may benefit society temporarily by hiring some workers who are currently unemployed. But this would be true of other government expenditures, and of increases in private consumption and investment expenditures as well. A cost–benefit analysis would clearly have difficulty determining whether the employment effects of a particular government investment are necessarily larger (or smaller) than the employment effects of all the other possible increases in spending of the same magnitude. The prudent choice, therefore, is simply to assume full employment and concentrate on measuring the benefits and costs that are specific to each investment project being considered.

THE ELEMENTS OF A COST–BENEFIT ANALYSIS

With these three principles in mind, let's return to the specific elements of a cost–benefit study that go into evaluating the present value formula, beginning with the appropriate rate of discount.

THE PUBLIC RATE OF DISCOUNT

As noted above, the discount rate, r, in the present value formula for private firms serves as the opportunity cost of capital to the firm, the rate of return the firm's stockholders can earn on their own savings. Private investments have to beat that rate of return to be worthwhile.

The opportunity cost view

Some economists argue that the discount rate to be used in cost–benefit analysis, the *public rate of discount*, should be viewed in the same way as the opportunity cost of public capital. The opportunity cost in this case is the return that the funds used for public investment would earn if they were left in the private sector. Assuming that the values of imports and exports are equal, as they are (approximately) for most nations, then GDP is the sum of private consumption (C), private investment (I), and government spending (G): GDP = C + I + G. Under the additional assumption of full employment,

401

GDP = $\overline{GDP_{FE}}$, essentially a constant in a given year, so that any change in government spending comes at the expense of private consumption and investment: $\Delta\overline{GDP_{FE}} = 0 = \Delta C +$ $\Delta I + \Delta G$, or $\Delta G = -\Delta C - \Delta I$. Dividing by ΔG, $1 = -\dfrac{\Delta C}{\Delta G} - \dfrac{\Delta I}{\Delta G}$. The right-hand side gives the proportion of government investment that comes at the expense of private consumption and investment. The only question that remains is what constitutes the returns foregone from the loss of private investment and private consumption.

The foregone return from the decrease in private investment is the productivity of private investment on the margin. A government investment must at least match the productivity of private investment to justify taking funds away from private investment. The best single measure of the productivity of private investment is the average rate of return to capital before taxes, r_{BT}. Any taxes on the income from capital simply distribute the overall productivity of private investments between the private and public sectors. Therefore, each dollar decrease in private investment sacrifices $(1 + r_{BT})$ dollars of national income or output one year from now. As such, $(1 + r_{BT})$ measures the marginal rate of transformation between current and future output $\left(MRT_{Q_t, Q_{t+1}}\right)$.

The foregone return from the decrease in private consumption is the rate of return that individuals receive on their savings. A government investment must at least match the rate of return that people can earn on their savings to justify asking them to reduce their private consumption (increase their savings through taxes). The best single measure of the return to savings is the average after-tax rate of return to savings, r_{AT}. Each dollar decrease in private consumption sacrifices $(1 + r_{AT})$ dollars of someone's disposable income and possible consumption one year from now. As such, $(1 + r_{AT})$ measures individuals' marginal rate of substitution between current and future consumption $\left(MRS_{C_t, C_{t+1}}\right)$.

According to the opportunity cost view of the public rate of discount, therefore, the appropriate discount rate for cost–benefit analysis is a weighted average of the rates of return available to private investment and private saving, with the weights equal to the proportions that the funds for public investment come from private investment and private consumption:

$$r_{public} = (\frac{\Delta I}{\Delta G})r_{BT} + (\frac{\Delta C}{\Delta G})r_{AT}$$

Describing what the public rate of discount should be in principle is one thing; trying to estimate it for policy purposes is quite another. An immediate practical difficulty is that no one can know for sure what proportion of the funds for public investment comes at the expense of private investment and private consumption. This would not matter so much if r_{BT} and r_{AT} had roughly the same values but they do not, at least not in the United States. Income from capital is taxed quite heavily, first by the corporation income tax in the corporate sector and again by federal and state personal income taxes. Therefore, the marginal productivity of capital, r_{BT}, is much larger than the after-tax rate of return, r_{AT}, available to savers. The majority of estimates of r_{BT} range anywhere from 10–25% and of r_{AT} from 3–6% (these are real rates of return, net of inflation). An oft-cited estimate is by Martin Feldstein (1977, pp. 116–17), who believes that reasonable values for r_{BT} and r_{AT} in the United States are 12% and 5%. Even Feldstein's 7% difference between the two rates of return leaves an uncomfortably wide range of possibilities for r_{public}, given the uncertainty surrounding

the appropriate weights to apply to each estimate, $(\dfrac{\Delta I}{\Delta G})$ and $(\dfrac{\Delta C}{\Delta G})$.

One way around this problem is to discount the future net benefits of each public investment being analyzed with a number of different rates between 5% and 12%, with the hope that the present value formula is consistently positive or negative for all the different rates. This is unlikely to happen, however. As noted above, using higher discount rates tends to cause fewer investments to have positive present value and also favors investments whose returns occur earlier rather than later.

Other views

The view that the public rate of discount represents the government's opportunity cost of funds is by no means universal among economists. The most widely held alternative view is that public investments give rise to services that are ultimately consumed by individuals, such as driving on public highways. Therefore, all future consumption should be discounted by what society views as the appropriate marginal rate of substitution between present and future consumption. They call this rate the *marginal social rate of time preference*, $MRS_{t,t+1}^{Soc}$. $MRS_{t,t+1}^{Soc}$ corresponds most closely to $MRS_{C_t, C_{t+1}} = r_{AT}$, above, the after-tax rate of return to savers, and argues for a relatively low public rate of discount. Proponents of this view recognize that distorting taxes raise the opportunity cost of funds for investment. But they argue that the increased cost of funds should be reflected in the initial investment costs, I_0, in the present value formula, not in the discount rate. For example, suppose raising taxes entails a combination of deadweight efficiency losses and administrative and compliance costs equal to 40 cents per dollar of tax revenue. Then I_0 should be scaled up by 40%.

The opportunity cost and social rate of time preference views of the discount rate lead to very different values for the public rate of discount and, unfortunately, there is no clear way of deciding which is the better view. Different models of the economy tend to support one view or the other, and all models are by their very nature only partial descriptions of any actual economy. All we can do is offer some concluding observations:

1. Most economists would agree that society should discount future consumption at a lower rate than the rate that applies to private savings. That is, $MRS_{t,t+1}^{Soc}$ is less than $MRS_{C_t, C_{t+1}} = r_{AT}$. There are two of reasons for this. The first is that private savings have an externality component that savers ignore, namely that any future returns from their savings are taxed and used to supply public services or transfers to other consumers. Therefore, savings should be subsidized, as should all activities that give

rise to external economies. There should be more private and public investment, and a lower rate of discount encourages more public investment. The second reason is that current generations do not give enough weight to the well-being of future, unborn generations, especially those who will be alive far into the future. The best way to protect the interests of future generations is to assume a very low $MRS_{t,t+1}^{Soc}$. This argument is particularly compelling in the debate over global warming in which people are concerned about the state of the earth's climate in 100 years or more. Using anything but very low public discount rates in a cost–benefit analysis of strategies to combat global warming would essentially ignore the well-being of those in the distant future. For example, at a discount rate of 5%, Feldstein's estimate of r_{AT}, $100 of benefit received 100 years from now from a reduction in global warming has a present value of 76 cents. Note, finally, that proponents of the opportunity cost view of the public rate of discount would also substitute the lower $MRS_{t,t+1}^{Soc}$ for $MRS_{C_t,C_{t+1}} = r_{AT}$ in the formula for r_{public}.

2. One widely used theoretical model of public production in the presence of markets distorted by taxes generates a formula for the public rate of discount that is far more complex than either the opportunity cost or marginal social rate of time preference views described above. The model is well beyond the scope of this text. Suffice it to say that the opportunity cost view of r_{public} can be derived under a certain set of restrictive assumptions in that model. But other sets of restrictive assumptions can lead to very different results. One of the simplest outcomes occurs under the assumption that the supply of capital to a nation is perfectly elastic at a price of capital determined in the broader world capital markets. Under this assumption, any increase in the demand for capital by the public sector has no effect on any domestic prices or rates of return and, therefore, no reduction of private consumption. Therefore, all increases in public investment come at the expense of private investment, assuming full employment.

$\frac{\Delta I}{\Delta G} = 1$ in the opportunity cost formula, so that $r_{public} = MRT_{Q_t,Q_{t+1}} = r_{BT}$. r_{public} reflects

the marginal productivity of capital and is likely to be very high. This result is common in theoretical models, and the assumption that capital is supplied in any quantity at the rest-of-world rate of return may be a reasonable assumption for many smaller countries. Conversely, there are no simple and realistic assumptions in this particular theoretical model that generate $r_{public} = MRS_{C_t,C_{t+1}} = r_{AT}$ (alternatively, the lower $MRS_{t,t+1}^{Soc}$). Other theoretical models with tax distortions do support this result, however, and have been used to justify the marginal social rate of time preference view.

3. The disagreements among economists regarding the appropriate public rate of discount were highlighted recently by Martin Weitzman. Weitzman (2001) conducted a survey of economists asking them to give their recommended public rate of discount. He received 2,160 replies from economists in 48 different countries. The range of recommendations was from –3% to 27%, with the majority between 1% and 6%. The mean recommended rate was just under 4%. Economists have clearly not been much help to public policy analysts in pinning down the public rate of

discount. Perhaps the only choice available to cost–benefit analysts is to try a wide range of discount rates and present the various outcomes to the public officials who have to make the final decisions. The officials will simply have to use their best judgment as to which discount rate to accept.

4. For what it is worth, the Office of the Management of the Budget of the U.S. federal government, which is in charge of overseeing all the government's cost–benefit analysis, recommends using a 7% (real) discount rate for most public investments. The 7% rate would appear to be more in line with the opportunity cost view than the marginal social rate of time preference view of the public rate of discount. It also is strongly biased against investments whose benefits occur far into the future.

UNCERTAINTY

A full analysis of decision making under uncertainty is well beyond the scope of this text. We will only comment on one implication of uncertainty about future benefits and costs that is shared by private investment and government cost–benefit analysis. It is that the value of an uncertain discounted stream of future net benefits (revenues) is less than the expected value of the net benefits so long as people are risk averse. We made this point in Chapter 12 when considering an individual's demand for insurance.

Assume that all people are identical and view the net benefits of a proposed project in the same way to focus solely on the problem of uncertainty. Figure 20.1 reproduces Figures 12.2 and 12.4, reinterpreted to correspond to a cost–benefit analysis. It pictures a representative person's utility function in terms of income, $U(Y)$, and assumes diminishing marginal utility of income. That is, people are risk averse. Figure 20.1 assumes that there are two possible outcomes of a government project. The project would provide a discounted stream of net benefits to the person with a present value of $60,000 under the most favorable set of circumstances, which occurs with a probability of .9. But under another less favorable set of circumstances, which occurs with a probability of .1, the present value of the net benefits is only $20,000. The expected present value of the net benefits of the project is .9($60,000) + .1($20,000) = $56,000. The expected utility of the project, $E_{\$56,000}(U)$, is one-tenth of the way down the straight line connecting $U(\$60,000)$ and $U(\$20,000)$.

The person would receive the same utility as $E_{\$56,000}(U)$ with an income stream whose present value is Y_C, if Y_C were received with certainty. Therefore, Y_C is called the *certainty equivalent* of the uncertain stream of net benefits, and it is the value that should be placed on the discounted stream of net benefits in evaluating the present value formula. The expected present value, $56,000, overstates the value of the uncertain stream of net benefits when people are risk averse.

Alternatively, ($56,000 – Y_C) is the risk premium the person would be willing to pay to turn the uncertain stream of net benefits into a certain stream. As such, Y_C can be estimated by subtracting from the expected present value of an investment the premiums that people are willing to pay on standard forms of private insurance such as automobile or health insurance. They indicate how much people are willing to pay to avoid the uncertainty associated with automobile accidents or ill health.

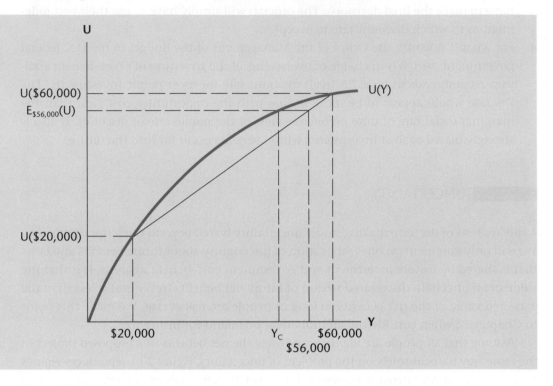

Figure 20.1

PROBLEMS IN MEASURING THE NET BENEFITS

Cost–benefit analysts confront a number of difficult problems in measuring benefits and costs that tend to be absent in private investment analysis. The general problem is the inability to use market prices to evaluate project benefits and costs. In private investment analysis, the standard assumption is that any one project is so small relative to the overall goods and factor markets that it has no effect on market prices. Therefore, both the revenues from selling the extra output produced by the project and the costs of producing, operating, and servicing the project are properly evaluated at the current and expected future goods and factor prices. Figure 20.2 illustrates.

The market for the output that a firm produces is initially in equilibrium at (Q_0, P_0), at the intersection of the market demand (D) and supply (S) curves. A firm is considering a project that would increase the output in the market. The additional output, Δq, increases the market supply to the dotted line S'. But Δq is so small relative to the market output Q_0 that the revenues from the projected output this year are appropriately valued as $P_0\Delta q$, and similarly for all future expected market prices. The same reasoning applies to using the equilibrium market factor prices in evaluating the costs of the project.

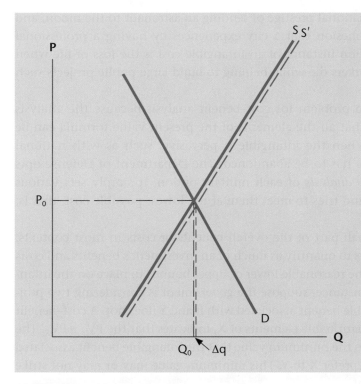

Figure 20.2

Matters are not so simple in cost–benefit analysis. The benefits and costs of public projects are often of a kind that makes it either impossible or inappropriate to use equilibrium market prices to evaluate them. In these instances, cost–benefit analysts have to use their ingenuity to develop alternative methods of evaluating benefits and costs. The four most common attributes that require alternative evaluation methods are that:

1. some of the project's benefits or costs are *intangible*
2. the project is *lumpy*, meaning that it is large enough to cause prices to change in one or more markets
3. some of the project's benefits or costs are *not marketed*: either benefits are provided free of charge or resources are drafted (conscripted)
4. market prices are distorted by taxes or monopoly elements, meaning that consumers and producers face different prices for various goods and factors. When markets are distorted, as they certainly are, then the evaluation of public project benefits and costs requires the use of special prices that economists refer to as *shadow prices*.

Intangibles

Intangibles are project benefits or costs that cannot be given a quantitative value in any obvious way. Examples of intangible benefits include the national security provided by a nation's armed forces, the national prestige of sending an astronaut to the moon, and the community spirit and cohesion that a city experiences by having a professional sports team. An all-too-common instance of an intangible cost is the loss of life when one or more construction workers die while helping to build large public projects such as dams and bridges.

Intangibles clearly pose a problem for cost–benefit analysis because the analysis is useful only to the extent that all the elements of the present value formula can be given quantitative values. When the intangible is pervasive, such as with national security, cost–benefit analysis has to be abandoned. The Department of Defense opts instead for a *cost-effectiveness analysis* of each military option. It simply sets various national security objectives and tries to meet them at the lowest possible cost, that is, in a cost-effective manner.

Intangibles are only a small part of the overall benefits or costs in most contexts, however. In these cases, it pays to quantify as much of an investment's benefits and costs as possible to give a sense of the reasonable lower or upper bounds to place on the intangible benefits and costs. For instance, suppose the government is considering two projects X and Y; X has an intangible benefit associated with it and Y does not. A cost–benefit analysis of Y, and of all the quantifiable elements of X, indicates that the $PV_Y > PV_X$. The difference, $PV_Y - PV_X$, indicates the minimum value that the intangible benefit associated with X must have in order to prefer X to Y. This minimum value may or may not strike people as a reasonable amount.[5]

Economists have debated among themselves whether the value of a life lost on construction projects, or of a life saved by reducing pollution, is or is not an intangible cost or benefit. A number of economists have proposed methods for placing a value on a human life that they believe are reasonable for the purposes of cost–benefit analysis. Consider the loss of life as an example.

A common proposal is to equate the value of a life with its economic value. The economic value is the present value of the lifetime earnings that a person would have been expected to earn had they lived, which depends primarily on a person's occupation and age at the time of death. The expected costs of a proposed construction project would then include an estimate of the probabilities that different numbers of construction workers will die, along with an estimate of the present value of lost earnings as a result of death. The U.S. judicial system has adopted this standard in awarding damages for loss of life in legal proceedings. Economists are called in to estimate the present value of the loss of income to the heirs of the deceased, which subtracts from the lost lifetime earnings the expected annual consumption of the deceased had he or she lived.

Some economists argue that the loss of life should also include an estimate of the pain and suffering experienced by the family and friends of the deceased, a point of view that is also accepted practice in the U.S. judicial system. In cases involving loss of life, the jury can add to the economist's estimate of the economic value whatever value they deem appropriate for the pain and suffering of the survivors.

Other economists adopt the view that construction workers who take on dangerous jobs such as building dams have already considered the risk of losing their lives. If the construction firms offer higher wages because of the risk of death, then the expected loss of life is already factored into the wage costs and no further adjustment is necessary. Mishan (1971) has argued that only unanticipated exposure to the risk of death should be added to the normal project costs.[6]

Still other economists, most notably John Broome (1978), argue that the loss of life is a true intangible and cannot be valued. He points out that a cost–benefit analysis necessarily adopts an expected value, ex-ante view of the loss of life since the projects being evaluated have not yet been undertaken. In his view, however, the proper stance for the government to take is an ex-post view, by the following argument. Suppose, on average, that two construction workers die when the government builds a dam. People who choose to work on the dam do so with an ex-ante view of the probability that they will lose their lives. They accept the job in part because the probabilities of them dying are low. But this is irrelevant according to Broome, because the government is fairly sure that two people will die and it should not care who those people are by the principle of impersonality. Therefore, the government's perspective is properly ex post. It is equivalent to being able to identify in advance the two people who are going to die. Presumably, no amount of money (or, at least a huge sum of money) would be sufficient to convince these two people to work on the dam if they knew for sure that they would die. Broome recognizes that the ex-post view could lead to the position that any project that is almost certain to involve the loss of even one life should never be undertaken; conversely, any project that is projected to save at least one life should be undertaken. Since he believes both positions are absurd, he concludes that the value of a life is truly an intangible that cannot reasonably be valued.

Lumpy investments

Government investment projects such as hydroelectric dams and mass (rail) transit systems are not the marginal additions to their markets that most private investments are. They are considered *lumpy investments* because they significantly increase market supply and change the going market prices. A new dam tends to lower the price of electricity for an entire region; a new mass transit system lowers transportation costs for many of the city's residents.

Figure 20.3 illustrates the problem of evaluating lumpy investments. Refer to Figure 20.3(a). The initial equilibrium in the market before the public project is (Q_0, P_0), at the intersection of the market demand curve D and the original market supply curve S^0. The project increases the market supply to S^1 and establishes a new equilibrium (Q_1, P_1). The increase in output resulting from the project, $Q_1 - Q_0$, cannot be evaluated using either the original price P_0 or the new price P_1. Instead, as noted in our discussion of decreasing cost services in Chapter 9, the proper measure of the benefit is either the Hicks' compensating variation (HCV) or the Hicks' equivalent variation (HEV), which are areas behind the compensated demand curves between the two prices. Figure 20.3(b) illustrates using the HEV. D^A is the actual market demand curve from Figure 20.3(a). D^C is the compensated demand curve in which the consumer is held at the new utility level when the price is P_1. The shaded area is the HEV, the amount of lump-sum income the consumer would require to return to the original price rather than face the new lower price. It is an appropriate measure of the benefit to the consumer of the increase in quantity, $Q_1 - Q_0$, made possible by the project.

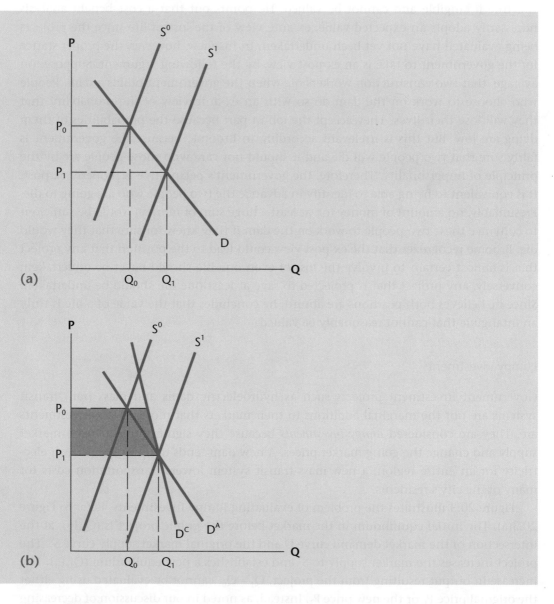

Figure 20.3

Economists prefer the HEV to the HCV for evaluating lumpy investments because the government might be considering a number of projects that would increase supply in this market. Since the HEV always measures the benefit at the original prices and the new utility levels, comparing the HEVs of the different projects gives a consistent ranking of the projects. The HCV, in contrast, measures the benefit along a demand curve that is compensated at the original utility level and the new price with the project. With different projects generating different prices, the prices used to measure the benefits by the HCV change each time and can lead to inconsistent rankings.

Non-marketed benefits and costs

Some or all of the benefits of public projects are not marketed at all; they are simply given away. This is hardly surprising, given the nature of the activities that governments become involved in, such as decreasing cost services and activities that give rise to technological externalities. Regarding decreasing cost services, the marginal cost of another person driving on an uncongested highway or visiting an uncongested beach or park is essentially zero, so the efficient price is zero. Regarding externalities, the building of a dam to generate electricity creates lakes suitable for fishing and swimming and often provides irrigation to farmlands, all external benefits typically given away by the government. Similarly, environmental policies that reduce water and air pollution confer benefits on individuals and firms for which no market exists – water and air are common use resources.

If the demand curves for these services and benefits were known, then the analyst could construct the appropriate HEV (or HCV) measures as described above under lumpy investments. But economists often have little or no direct knowledge of the underlying demand curves. For example, there has never been a toll on most rural highways; the price has always been zero. No other point on the demand curve has been observed. Similarly, individuals and firms have never been asked to pay for the benefits of cleaner air or water. In all these instances, therefore, cost–benefit analysts have to use some ingenuity to try to estimate the benefits. We will briefly mention three such attempts.

Evaluating the source of the benefits

Consider the rural sections of a new superhighway network such as the U.S. interstate system. Relative to the roads people used to drive in these regions, the interstate is safer and reduces travel time. Therefore, the analyst can try to estimate the reduction in accidents, both fatal and non-fatal, and then estimate the value to individuals of the reduction. The average medical costs associated with non-fatal accidents might be used to evaluate the reduction in non-fatal accidents, but evaluating the reduction in fatal accidents begs the question again of how to value a life saved. The savings in time could be evaluated by using some average hourly wage, or a multiple of the wage if the time savings are considerable. Presumably wages represent the value of the last (marginal) hour of working; inframarginal hours would have a higher value. In any event, the reductions in accidents and travel time are surely part of the reasons why people travel on the superhighways. As such, they are at least part of the preferences lying behind the unknown demand curve for superhighway travel.

Hedonic price estimation

Economists have made use of a statistical procedure called *hedonic price estimation* to try to uncover individuals' demand for cleaner air. The procedure is used in the context of purchasing a house. The idea is that a house is a so-called characteristic good – it has a number of attributes or characteristics that give rise to the demand for the house. The characteristics include: the attributes of the house itself (size, style, age); the attributes of the property (size, view); neighborhood characteristics (location in a residential or commercial area, safety, proximity to public transportation); community characteristics (quality of schools, property tax rate); and the amount of pollution at the property site. By collecting these characteristics on a large number of properties, economists can then estimate the independent effect of each characteristic on the price of a house. The estimation is called "hedonic" because hedonic refers to the pleasure received from each of the characteristics and hence people's willingness to pay for them.

The estimate of the independent effect of cleaner air on the price of a house is then used to compute the marginal value for cleaner air at each level of air quality. The estimated marginal value is assumed to be the price people are willing to pay for cleaner air in the usual sense that prices reflect marginal values. These prices are then combined with data on the individuals who purchased the houses, such as their incomes and personal attributes, to estimate a demand curve for cleaner air.

One important drawback of hedonic price estimation is the implicit assumption that when individuals buy a house, they are buying exactly the bundle of characteristics they want. That is, they are in equilibrium with marginal value equal to price for every characteristic, including the air quality at the house site. This may be true for the options associated with the purchase of an automobile, another characteristic good, since people can choose each option they want when purchasing a new car. But it is highly unlikely to be true for the purchase of a house. Suppose, for example, that a buyer wants both close proximity to the city and pristine air. If pristine air is available only 50+ miles from the city limits, then something has to give. The buyer cannot be in equilibrium with respect to both characteristics. Nonetheless, hedonic price estimation does give some sense of the value of cleaner air to consumers.

Contingent valuation

Still another technique to discover the value of non-marketed benefits is to conduct a survey of people and ask them directly. This technique has been used in an environmental context when there is no market at all that can be used even indirectly, such as a housing market, to estimate the benefit. Examples are the amount people would be willing to pay to avoid oil tanker spills that foul beaches and shorelines, or to preserve wilderness areas that they may never actually visit. The survey technique is called *contingent valuation* because the respondents' answers are contingent on the exact circumstances that they are asked to consider. The surveys also collect personal information on the respondents, which economists can use along with the answers to the questions posed to develop estimates of the demand curve for cleaner water or air.

Economists are sharply divided on the value of the information contained in the surveys. Some believe that they do give reasonable values of the willingness to pay for cleaner water or air; others do not. Yet there may be no other way to estimate the social cost of oil spills or the value of wilderness areas. In any event, courts in the United States accepted contingent valuation estimates when assessing damages to Exxon for the *Exxon Valdez* oil tanker spill off the coast of Alaska in 1989, and they have since been used in similar court proceedings.[7]

Shadow prices

One of the more difficult practical problems for cost–benefit analysis is that the evaluation of benefits and costs should take into account the various tax and market distortions that cause individuals and firms to face different prices for the same goods and factors. We saw an example of this above with the opportunity cost view of the public rate of discount. Because the returns to capital are taxed, the appropriate discount rate is a weighted average of the before- and after-tax returns to capital under one set of restrictive assumptions within a commonly used model of public production with distorting taxes. The same rule, within the same model and restrictive set of assumptions, applies to the prices of all goods and factors that are used in public projects. That is, for all markets distorted by taxes, the price that the government should apply to all marketed project inputs and outputs is a weighted average of prices faced by producers and consumers, with the weights equal to the proportions of the use of the good or factor that come at the expense of private production and consumption. Economists refer to these weighted average prices as *shadow prices*.

The intuition for why the government should use shadow prices in cost–benefit analysis is the same as the intuition behind the method of computing the deadweight loss of a given tax that we discussed in Chapter 15. We noted there that the computation of deadweight loss for a tax on, say, good X must include any changes in tax revenues that result in markets for goods that are substitutes or complements to X. The reason why is that the deadweight loss from a tax is the loss in consumer and producer surplus less any revenues collected by the government. The tax revenues are simply a transfer from consumer and producer surplus to the government, not a deadweight loss to society. Similarly, any change in government purchases of inputs and/or supplies of outputs that comes at the expense of the private production and consumption of goods and factors necessarily changes the tax revenues collected in those private markets, and therefore affects the overall loss to the economy from the distorting taxes. These gains or losses in tax revenues have to be taken into account in assessing the present value of any proposed investment. As with the public discount rate, the only simple shadow price occurs in the small country case for which the prices of goods and factors are set in world markets. Then the relevant price is a market price, the price faced by producers. This is the gross-of-tax price for inputs and the net-of-tax price for outputs. But also as above, this result applies for a set of restrictive assumptions in one particular widely used model of government production with distorting taxes.

The need for shadow prices is discouraging in a practical sense since almost all private markets for goods and factors are distorted by taxes of some kind. Therefore the need for shadow prices to evaluate government inputs and outputs is pervasive, and not reserved for a small subset of goods or factors. In addition, models that employ still further distortions between producer and consumer prices caused by market power would lead to different formulas for shadow prices than the weighted average formula described above. In general, the appropriate shadow price for the government evaluation of costs and benefits is the producer price plus an adjustment that indicates the change in deadweight loss from a marginal change in government production. The weighted average interpretation applies strictly under only one set of assumptions. Whatever the proper shadow price should be, it is obviously model sensitive.

Unfortunately, no model is going to give an accurate account of all the various market distortions that exist in an economy. At best, the cost–benefit analyst may be able to adjust a few factor and goods' prices for expected changes in tax revenues and see whether these adjustments have much of an effect on the present value of the investment.

THE DISTRIBUTION OF BENEFITS AND COSTS

When analyzing investment projects, should the government take into account the distribution of the benefits and costs or simply compute the present value of the aggregate benefits and costs? This is perhaps the toughest question of all for cost–benefit analysis.

A pragmatist would surely like to ignore the distribution of the benefits and costs, for two good reasons. One is that incorporating a concern for end-results equity in a cost–benefit study raises all kinds of difficult issues, to be discussed below. The other is that equity concerns can easily overwhelm the efficiency implications of the various projects being considered, which are generally thought to lie at the heart of a cost–benefit analysis. After all, most of the investment projects undertaken by government are in response to allocation (efficiency) market failures such as externalities, nonexclusive goods, and decreasing costs. Therefore, should not the choice of investment projects in these areas be made strictly on efficiency grounds, that is, in terms of aggregate benefits and costs?

Unfortunately, theory suggests that the answer is "no." It is almost certainly appropriate to consider the distribution of project benefits and costs. This is too bad because the pragmatists have a point. Cost–benefit analysis would be much simpler, and less subjective, if it could ignore distributional concerns.

The pragmatic approach of ignoring the distribution of benefits and costs can be justified theoretically by means of a very strong assumption: The government is continually redistributing income with lump-sum taxes and transfers to equalize the social marginal utilities of income across all individuals. Recall from Chapter 4 that the social marginal utility of income for person h is a product of the marginal social welfare weight society attaches to person h and person h's private marginal utility of income:

$$SMU_Y^h = \left(\frac{\Delta W}{\Delta U^h}\right)\left(\frac{\Delta U^h}{\Delta Y_h}\right).$$ Recall, also, that equalizing the SMU_Y^h, all h = 1,…,H, is the inter-

personal equity condition for a social welfare maximum. With this redistribution occurring behind the scenes, the distributional implications of any government decision made for allocational reasons, including government investments, are irrelevant. Any unwanted redistributional implications will be corrected. Suppose, for example, that a project's benefits accrue disproportionately to the rich and the project's costs are borne disproportionately by the poor. Think of a proposed superhighway from a city into the nearby mountains that would allow the rich within the city easier access to their ski chalets, but at the same time would displace a number of low-income city families from their houses because the highway goes through their neighborhood. The redistributions that satisfy the interpersonal equity conditions would take these unwanted distributional effects into account were the highway to be built.

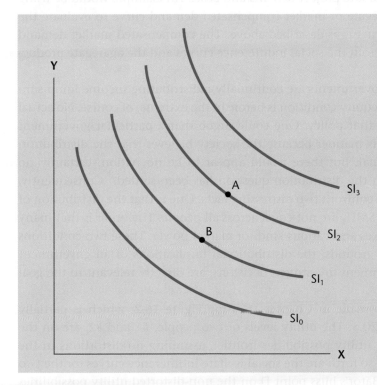

Figure 20.4

Another immediate implication of this assumption is that the economy is essentially equivalent to a one-consumer economy. Aggregate amounts of goods and services can be ranked according to a set of social indifference curves, as illustrated in Figure 20.4. The axes are the aggregate quantities of two goods, X and Y. The social indifference curves, SI_0, SI_1, SI_2 and so forth rank the various possible bundles of aggregate X and Y according to society's preference and indifference, just as an individual's indifference curves rank the individual's bundles of X and Y. For example, we can say that A on SI_2 is socially preferred to B on SI_1 so long as X and Y are both desired, because A contains more of X and of Y. This would not necessarily be true without the underlying interpersonal equity assumption. Suppose the distribution at A is inferior in society's view to the distribution at B. It may be inferior enough to override A's advantage of having more of both goods than B, in which case B would be socially preferred to A. A set of consistent, transitive social indifference curves in terms of aggregate X and Y is no longer possible to construct.

Furthermore, under the interpersonal equity assumption, the social indifference curves lead to aggregate demand curves for X and Y just as individual indifference curves lead to individual demand curves for X and Y. The aggregate production function (production possibilities frontier) for X and Y takes the place of the individual budget constraints. Therefore, the cost–benefit analyst can use aggregate demand curves (and factor supply curves) to evaluate project benefits and costs. An example would be using the HEV based on an aggregate or market compensated demand curve to evaluate the benefits of a lumpy investment, as described above. The compensated market demand curves can also be derived from the social indifference curves and the aggregate production function.

The assumption that governments are continually redistributing income lump sum to satisfy the interpersonal equity condition is heroic in the extreme, of course. No actual governments are pursuing that policy. One could argue that a particular government does not redistribute in this manner because the society believes that the distribution of income is already optimal. But there would appear to be no nation, certainly no capitalist nation, for which the distribution question has been settled.[8] Consequently, cost–benefit analysis has to confront two distressing facts. One is that the distribution of income is not optimal; the SMU_Y are not equal across all people. The other is that many markets are distorted by taxes and various kinds of market power. These two conditions imply that, on theoretical grounds, the distributional implications of all government decisions, including government investment decisions, are directly relevant to the goal of increasing social welfare.

This general point was made in Chapter 16 using Figure 16.2, which is partially reproduced here as Figure 20.5. The utility levels of two people, #1 and #2, are on the axes, the line U^1, U^2 is the utility possibilities frontier, assuming no distortions in the economy, and W_0, W_1, and so forth are the social welfare indifference curves for the two people. The ideal point is Bator's bliss point D on the non-distorted utility possibilities frontier, at which society reaches W_3. But the bliss point is unattainable because of the various distortions in the economy. Instead, the shaded area indicates the restricted set of (U^1, U^2) utility combinations that are possible, given the distortions.

Suppose the economy is currently at point A on W_0. The government is considering two investment projects: The first one would bring the economy to point B on W_1 and the second one would bring the economy to point C on W_2. The first project could be considered the better of the two on efficiency grounds, since it would bring the economy closer to the non-distorted utility possibilities frontier. It has the higher aggregate present value. But the second project is preferred because it leads to a higher level of social welfare. What it suffers on efficiency grounds it more than makes up with its superior distributional implications. Ignoring the distributional implications of the projects would lead the cost–benefit analyst to prefer the first project, and sacrifice some social welfare in doing so.

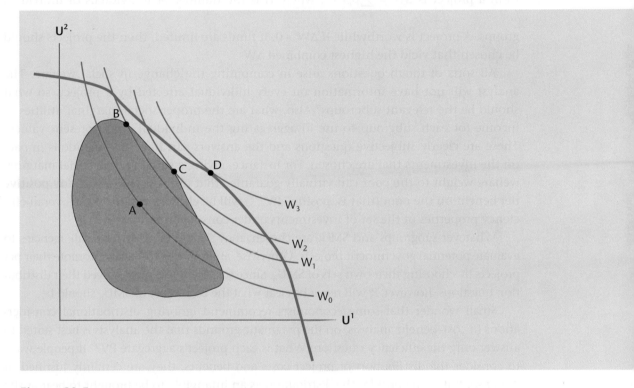

Figure 20.5

Unfortunately, cost–benefit analysis becomes much more difficult, and more subjective, once it takes account of the distribution of a project's costs and benefits. This is so for two reasons. First, the analysis can no longer rely on aggregates. The present value of a project's costs and benefits has to be calculated for each individual (or relevant individual group, say high-, middle-, and low-income people). The sources of the costs and benefits are the same as described above: The direct benefits (costs) of the project itself, such as the increased safety and reduced travel time of a superhighway or the benefits of a cleaner environment from an antipollution project; and the benefits or costs of discrete changes in prices in related markets as a result of the project, measured by the

HEV. But the HEV would have to be computed for each individual (individual group), based on their individual (group) demand and factor supply curves. To this we would add each individual's share of any pure profits or losses resulting from the project. An obvious example would be each individual's share of the taxes paid to cover the losses of a decreasing cost service that was priced at marginal cost or given away. These benefits and costs are clearly much more difficult to estimate than if the analyst can use the aggregate market demand and supply curves.

Second, the individual present values, PV^h, have to be aggregated by means of the individual social marginal utilities of income, $SMU_h = \beta_h$. The change in social welfare from a project is $\Delta W = \sum_{h=1}^{H} \beta_h PV^h$, where H is the number of individuals or individual groups. A project is worthwhile if $\Delta W > 0$. If funds are limited, then the projects should be chosen that yield the highest combined ΔW.

All sorts of tough questions arise in computing the change in social welfare. The analyst will not have information on every individual affected by a project, so what should be the relevant subgroups? Also, what are the proper social marginal utilities of income for each subgroup to use in aggregating the individual group present values? These are clearly subjective questions and the answers can have a tremendous impact on the investments that are chosen. For instance, giving a suitably high social marginal welfare weight to the poor can virtually guarantee that projects conferring any positive net benefit on the poor (that is, positive PV^{poor}) will be chosen, whatever the overall efficiency properties of the set of investments under consideration may be.

Whatever subgroups and SMU_h are chosen, they should be used across all agencies to evaluate potential government projects. Otherwise, analysts can too easily promote their pet projects by choosing their own sets of SMU_h. Since societies have not resolved their distribution questions, however, it will never be clear what the correct set of SMU_h should be.

Small wonder that some economists recommend ignoring distributional considerations in cost–benefit analysis, on the pragmatic grounds that the analysis is best suited to answer only the efficiency question: What is each project's aggregate PV?[9] If people want to consider the distribution of project costs and benefits, they are certainly justified in doing so. But then consider the distribution as an intangible to be brought to bear at the end, after the aggregate present values have been quantified to the extent possible; do not incorporate distributional judgments, the SMU_h, into the calculation of the present values. This may be good practical advice, but it is not appropriate on strictly theoretical grounds so long as the government is not optimally redistributing in the background to offset any unwanted distributional implications of the projects. And governments are surely not doing this.

AVOIDING SOME PITFALLS: BOGUS COSTS AND BENEFITS

Cost–benefit analysis is not immune to political maneuvering. Public officials often have a direct political interest in promoting, or preventing, certain projects. To this end they often trumpet benefits or costs that are not true benefits and costs. Whether they do this knowingly or are simply confused about the nature of the true benefits or costs is difficult to say. Whatever the reason, however, the focus on false benefits and costs can do great damage to public sector decision making. This is especially so because the bogus benefits and costs are often as large, even far larger, than the true benefits and costs. Therefore, if the bogus benefits or costs prevail in public debates over the advisability of the projects, they will usually be decisive. Here are some of the more common errors.[10]

REGIONAL MULTIPLIERS

Large public projects require a number of support services for construction workers while the project is being built and for those who operate the project once it is completed. They need food, clothing, places to live, entertainment services, and the like. As a consequence, new restaurants and supermarkets, clothing stores, hotels, homes, and movie theaters may come into being as a result of the project. An entire town may arise where none had existed for something like a hydroelectric project in a remote area. These additional benefits to the region are called the "secondary benefits" of a project. Since these secondary benefits are in the nature of a Keynesian-style multiplier resulting from the original investment, their combined value is likely to be many multiples of the direct benefits of the project.

Are these secondary benefits really net benefits to society, however? The answer is almost certainly "no." If the economy is already at full employment, as is the standard assumption in cost–benefit analysis, then the resources allocated to these new secondary ventures have to come at the expense of similar ventures elsewhere in the economy. The loss of these resources elsewhere leads to multiple secondary losses that have to be subtracted from the secondary benefits near the project site. Under full employment, the secondary benefits and losses should just about cancel one another.

If there is some unemployment in the region, then the project could lead to a net gain in secondary benefits over secondary losses. But *any* government expenditure of the same magnitude as the particular project being analyzed would probably produce the same amount of net secondary benefits. It would be difficult to argue convincingly that the net secondary benefits from any one project are necessarily greater than the net secondary benefits from any other government investments, or government consumption expenditures, of the same size. Therefore, it is best to ignore all such secondary benefits, whether assuming full employment or unemployment, and concentrate on the true, direct project costs and benefits.

THE LABOR GAME

A variation of the regional multiplier game is to count the total wages earned by construction workers and project operators as a benefit of the project. Politicians commonly point to the employment gains from a project as one of its main benefits. Indeed, governments often insist that any proposed government investment project include a study, called an economic impact study, that analyses the employment gains from the project. An economic impact study is quite different from a proper cost–benefit analysis, however.

In the first place, counting wages as a benefit is absurd on the surface since the wages paid to construction workers and operators are part of the project's costs, not its benefits. Move a large chunk of costs from the cost side to the benefit side and one can make almost any project seem worthwhile.

The one germ of truth in counting the employment gains is if the workers are currently unemployed and, importantly, *otherwise unemployable* in any other endeavor. Then the wages earned would count as benefits since the opportunity cost of hiring the workers would be zero. But this assumption clearly does not apply under the full employment assumption, and even if the workers to be hired are currently unemployed, they can undoubtedly be productive in other government projects or in the private sector. There are many ways to employ the unemployed – they are almost never otherwise unemployable. It is best, therefore, to count the wages as a cost, where they properly belong. Also, counting wages as a benefit leads to an unwarranted bias in favor of larger projects over smaller projects simply because they employ more workers. The same point applies to counting secondary benefits – they, too, are necessarily larger for larger projects.

DOUBLE COUNTING

Some cost–benefit studies engage in pure double counting. For example, suppose the cost–benefit analyst uses the hedonic price technique or a contingent valuation survey to estimate the losses suffered by people who live near a proposed new airport runway from the noise of the planes as they take off and land. In addition, the study includes as a cost the projected decrease in the prices of their houses if the runway is built. Adding the two together represents pure double counting. These people can either continue to live near the airport and suffer ongoing losses from the noise, or sell their houses at a loss to avoid the noise. If the housing market is in equilibrium with respect to the noise, then the decline in the prices of the houses must just equal the discounted present value of the ongoing losses from exposure to the noise. The present value of their loss is the same in either case. Since people cannot simultaneously stay put and move, adding the discounted stream of the ongoing losses to the decline in the housing prices is double counting the loss.

▬▬▬ CONCLUDING COMMENT

Crafting a good cost–benefit study is never an easy task. It requires a mixture of economic theory, ingenuity, and judgment. There are difficulties associated with the attempt to quantify every element of the present value formula, whether it be choosing the appropriate public rate of discount, measuring the value of benefits given away and the benefits or costs of discrete price changes in related markets, and selecting the proper shadow prices to evaluate project inputs and outputs. Accounting for the distribution of project costs and benefits multiplies the difficulties. It forces the evaluation of costs and benefits to be done at the individual rather than the aggregate level and requires choosing social marginal utilities of income to apply to each individual or group affected by a project. At best, cost–benefit analysts may have no option but to try different assumptions on each of these elements and see how they affect the ranking of the projects. Different assumptions will almost certainly lead to different project rankings, but at least it will be clear what is being assumed when a particular set of projects is recommended. And, when all that can be quantified has been considered, there are still likely to be intangible costs or benefits to be factored into the analysis.

These difficulties notwithstanding, most economists are convinced that public policy debates on government investment projects would be well served and informed by careful cost–benefit analyses that:

1. focus on true project costs and benefits
2. attempt to quantify the various elements of the present value formula
3. apply a consistent methodology to all potential projects
4. avoid the inclusion of secondary benefits, employment effects, and other bogus benefits and costs.

This is a tall order, but one well worth striving for.

PART V

Fiscal Federalism

CHAPTER 21

Fiscal Federalism: the Assignment of Functions among Governments

A *federal government* is a hierarchical structure of governments in which each government has some form of jurisdiction over governments in the level immediately below it, yet each government maintains control over its internal affairs. Many of the developed market economies have a federalist structure. The United States is an example, with its national government, 50 state governments (provincial governments in other federal countries), and over 89,000 cities, towns, and regional governmental bodies such as regional school boards and metropolitan district commissions. Economic unions among nations such as the E.U. add another tier, a supranational government with some jurisdiction over the nations in the union. An immediate implication of the federalist structure is that each person is simultaneously a citizen of more than one government, often three or more governments as in the United States and the E.U.[1]

A federal government gives rise to a number of economic problems that are absent when there is only a single government, as the text has been assuming so far. Chapters 21 and 22 focus on the two most important general problems. One is assigning the legitimate functions of government to the different levels of government in the fiscal hierarchy. The other is that people, and other resources, can move across the lower level governments in response to government tax and spending policies, which has a number of implications for society's pursuit of efficiency and equity.

Chapter 1 identified the legitimate economic functions of government in a market economy, all of which are based on different kinds of market failures. They can be thought of as requiring three distinct sets of government policies as suggested by Richard Musgrave: stabilization policies, which pursue macroeconomic goals such as full employment, low inflation, and long-run economic growth; allocation policies, which correct for inefficiencies arising from such problems as externalities, natural monopolies, and private information; and distribution policies, which redistribute resources to achieve end-results equity or distributive justice. Under a federal government, society must decide which level of government should perform each of these functions. This is a very important decision, because if the functions are not sorted properly among the levels of government, then different governments' policies could easily work at cross-purposes with one another. An obvious example is the redistribution of income. Suppose two people, #1 and #2, live in the same locality within a state. If both the state and its localities engage in redistributive policies, it could happen that the state wants to redistribute from person #1 to person #2, whereas the locality wants to redistribute from #2 to #1. Such incompatibilities must be avoided. More generally, in models with a single government, the mainstream view is that the government is attempting to maximize social welfare in its combined pursuit of efficiency and equity. The assignment of functions within the federal hierarchy must be done in such a way that the various governments are working in concert to maximize social welfare. The presence of a federalist structure cannot change the overall economic objective of the government sector. Chapter 21 discusses the appropriate assignment of the economic functions of government throughout the federal hierarchy.

The fiscal implications of people, and other resources, moving throughout a country arise because their movement is motivated in part by the public policies of the various governments. Consider the people who are searching for a new place to live as one example. Presumably most of them move into a state or province as a result of a job opportunity. Once the job decision is made, however, they then search among different localities for the one that suits them best, and one of the attributes they consider is the tax and spending mix within each locality. The quality of the local public schools and the amount of the property tax weigh heavily on people's decisions of where to live. Once people choose a locality, they then become one of the voters who will determine future tax and spending decisions. Just as people are able to enter localities whose policies they favor, they can also leave localities whose tax and spending decisions they dislike. Economists have shown that this movement of people, and other resources, into and out of communities, states, and even nations in response to public policies can easily undermine the government sector's pursuit of efficiency and equity. In addition, lower level governments have incentives to engage in competitions for resources through their spending and tax policies, and these competitions tend to be inefficient rather than social welfare enhancing. Just as people can move, so too can capital. The tax policies of states and localities can have a substantial impact on where firms choose to locate and invest. Chapter 22 discusses the more important implications of the movement of people and resources.

ASSIGNING THE FUNCTIONS OF GOVERNMENT

By the 1970s, mainstream economists had reached a consensus on the assignment of the legitimate functions of government throughout the federal hierarchy: Subnational governments could undertake many of the allocation functions of government but the national government should be assigned both the stabilization and distribution functions. The consensus has held firm since then regarding the stabilization and allocation functions, but has weakened somewhat regarding the distribution function. There are now a number of models in the literature that allow for state (provincial) and/or local redistributional policies along with the national policies. And, as a practical matter, many grants-in-aid from national to state and state to local governments are motivated by distributional concerns.

THE STABILIZATION FUNCTION

Economists assign macroeconomic stabilization policies to the national government as a matter of default. The thinking is that, as a practical matter, only the national government can hope to design effective policies to achieve macroeconomic policy goals such as reducing unemployment or restraining inflation. This is so even for the United States, whose largest and richest states are themselves very large economies. The argument in favor of national stabilization policies has three main components. We will use the United States as an example.

The first is the nature of the subnational economies. Imagine constructing a set of macroeconomic accounts in the manner of the national income accounts for the state economies and then for the local economies, with state (local) income (Y) equal to state (local) product. The state product consists of the expenditures by the state's (locality's) household sector (consumption), business sector (investment), government sector (government purchases) and foreign or rest-of-world sector (exports minus imports):

$$Y = C + I + G + (Ex - Im)$$

As we move from the national government to the state governments and then down to the local governments, the sector that naturally gains in importance as a percentage of the total is the foreign or rest-of-world sector. Many of the manufactured goods purchased by a state's households, businesses, and governments are produced by firms located outside the state's borders. They are imports from the state's point of view. Similarly, many of the goods that firms within the state produce are sold to households, businesses, and governments outside the state. They are exports from the state's point of view. And what is true for a state is even more true for the localities within the state.

In other words, the states and localities are similar to small nations who are surrounded by and trade with many large countries. But unlike small nations, they are fully exposed to economic events occurring beyond their borders. They cannot engage in commercial policies such as tariffs on their imports or subsidies on their exports to control the flow of goods into and out of the state. The Constitution of the United States forbids states and their localities from levying tariffs. Nor can states and localities control the flow of savings and investment across their borders; they are part of fully national financial and capital markets. In short, what happens to their economies is driven to a large degree by events happening beyond their borders, events over which they have almost no control.[2]

Their macroeconomic policy options are extremely limited in other ways as well.

The second component of the argument is that states and localities do not issue their own money, so they cannot engage in monetary policy to pursue macroeconomic goals. This leaves the states (localities) with only fiscal policy to pursue macro-goals, and the third component of the argument is that even here their policy options are too constrained to be very helpful. Unlike the national government, the states (and localities) cannot routinely issue debt to finance operating expenses, only capital expenditures. Most state constitutions require their governors to submit balanced operating budgets each year. Even if these provisions did not exist, however, Wall Street would enforce the balanced-budget requirement. States that persisted in running operating deficits would quickly find their debt reduced to junk bond status, with very high interest rates. So the best states can do to try to combat a recession in their economies is to make balanced-budget increases in expenditures and taxes. But with balanced-budget multipliers approximately equal to one, the budgetary changes necessary to have a significant expansionary effect on their economies are undoubtedly larger than what would be politically feasible to enact. In fact, state fiscal policies are usually procyclical rather than countercyclical. For example, the typical scenario when a state economy goes into recession is that tax revenues fall, leading to budget deficits. The states then must react with a combination of expenditure cuts and tax increases to remove the deficits, both of which are contractionary fiscal policies that make the recession worse.

State governors always talk a good economic game about policies to encourage economic growth and full employment within their states. But these policies most often consist of subsidies to attract businesses from other states in the form of tax breaks and industrial parks with subsidized rents and public utilities. These policies are unlikely to be very effective, however. Most states are playing this game, so that the policies are likely to be self-canceling, with only the businesses gaining. Also, the subsidies have to be financed with tax increases, which have a contractionary effect on the economy.

In summary, the combination of very open economies, the inability to conduct monetary policy, and severe restrictions on fiscal policy make it unlikely that the states can effectively pursue macroeconomic policy goals. What is true for the states applies even more so for the localities. Macroeconomic policy is therefore reserved for the national government.

The members of the E.U. face many of the same handicaps as the U.S. states in pursuing their own macroeconomic goals. They have removed all tariffs among themselves and most of the nations have adopted the euro and thus given up the possibility of conducting monetary policy. They do have more freedom than the U.S. states to pursue their own fiscal policies, but they have agreed to fairly stringent limits on the size of operating deficits they can run. In truth, the member nations that adopted the euro have given up most of their control over their own economies.

THE ALLOCATION FUNCTIONS

In the late 1950s, a congressional committee that was investigating the appropriate economic relationships among the national, state, and local governments invited

George Stigler of the University of Chicago to testify. As part of his testimony, Stigler (1957, pp. 213–19) wrote a monograph entitled "The Tenable Range of Functions of Local Government" that established a rationale for the assignment of the various functions of government among the three levels.[3] His rationale quickly became the consensus view of mainstream public sector economists.

Stigler took an axiomatic approach to justify the involvement of the state and local governments in the various allocation functions of government. He argued that people living in a modern liberal democracy would accept two principles relating to the economic responsibilities of the government sector. The first is a belief in participatory democracy, which has two implications. One is the government-as-agent principle described in Chapter 1, that in its economic policy making the government should act strictly as an agent of the people and follow their desires. The other is that the government-as-agent principle works best the closer the people are to the decision-making process. The ideal arrangement is the New England town meeting, in which each citizen votes directly on all governmental decisions, economic or otherwise. Larger towns, cities, and states require a representative form of government, for which a participatory democracy works best the closer the representatives are to the people. Local officials are likely to know the interests of their constituents better than state officials, and state officials in turn know the interests of their constituents better than national officials. As the geographic distance from the public officials to the people they represent increases, their knowledge about their constituents' preferences becomes less and less clear and undercuts the government-as-agent ideal.

The second principle is called "states rights" in the United States, the principle that people in individual states and localities have a right to establish policies in accordance with their own wishes and thereby to differ from other states and localities. This principle is a reaction to the fear that national provision would imply a standardization of services for all citizens. The states rights principle is also seen as permitting a healthy degree of experimentation across states and localities, as citizens in one state or locality learn about better and worse ways to solve economic problems from the approaches taken by other states and localities.

The combination of the belief in participatory democracy and states rights led Stigler to conclude that *economic decisions should take place at the lowest level of government consistent with the effectiveness of the decisions*. We just saw that macroeconomic policy cannot be effective below the national level. The same is not true of the allocation functions, however. Here Stigler's conclusion translates into placing the various allocation functions at the lowest level of government consistent with economic efficiency. Since most governmental economic activity undertaken for efficiency reasons centers on instances of externalities and decreasing costs/natural monopolies, the issue becomes the extent of the externalities and decreasing costs.

As it happens, for most natural monopolies, the costs stop decreasing fairly quickly, at either the local or at most the regional level. Think of the public utilities, bridges and tunnels, and recreational facilities such as parks and beaches. Only the decreasing costs associated with telecommunications and radio and TV broadcasting are likely to be national in scope. Therefore, the main assignment issue concerns the extent of externalities.

The geographic reach of external effects varies enormously depending on the source of the externality, from local (congestion on an urban highway) to international (global warming from carbon dioxide emissions). In light of this variation, Wallace Oates (1972, pp. 34–5) described the ideal assignment of externalities to the different levels of government as establishing a *perfect correspondence* between the extent of the external effects and the jurisdiction charged with correcting the externality. Matching the jurisdiction with the externality in this way gives the government sector the best chance of achieving an efficient solution to the externality. Jurisdictions that are set too narrowly or too widely are unlikely to achieve efficient outcomes.

The problems of combating pollution when there is an externality/jurisdictional mismatch are a good case in point. Suppose that three states border a lake, that some firms in each state produce the same products and are dumping pollutants into the lake, and that the responsibility for combating the pollution lies at the state level. Suppose further that only one of the states levies a Pigovian tax on its firms to reduce the pollution. This cannot possibly be an efficient solution because the firms in the other states continue to pollute without penalty. Furthermore, if the firms in the other two states are the main polluters, the attempt by the one state to reduce the pollution in the lake to safe levels would probably be in vain. The main effect of the one state's tax would be to put its firms at a competitive disadvantage relative to firms in the other two states. In this case, a regional antipollution policy that would tax all the polluting firms is the better option. A notable example today is global warming, which requires a coordinated effort by all nations to reduce carbon dioxide emissions in an efficient manner. The Kyoto Protocol is an attempt to do just that, but it is undermined by the fact that the United States, the largest CO_2 emitter, will not ratify the treaty.

By the same token, a jurisdiction that is much larger than the external effect can also be inefficient. The U.S. government's decision in the 1970s that all cars have to be equipped with antipollution devices is undoubtedly an unnecessary expense for many consumers and therefore a waste of resources. Automobile pollution is harmful only in cities and other densely populated areas where many cars are on the road at one time. Drivers in rural and other less densely populated states are paying $1,500 or so for pollution abatement equipment that probably has little to no benefit to anyone. A more efficient response would be a Pigovian pollution tax levied by states or localities for driving in densely populated areas. The computer technology exists now to levy such a tax fairly easily, but it did not when the United States mandated the antipollution equipment.

The assignment of the allocation functions roughly follows Stigler's prescription of providing allocation services at the lowest level possible. Libraries and local police and fire departments engage in activities whose external effects fall largely within the borders of their localities. States regulate the public utilities and establish metropolitan-wide commissions to provide rail transportation to cities and their suburbs and to operate and finance bridges and tunnels. Beaches and parks are either state or locally run, depending on where they are located. State police patrol the highways and handle criminal cases that spill across local borders. The main national allocation function is the provision of defense; a nation's security affects everyone in the country.

THE DISTRIBUTION FUNCTION

The traditional mainstream view among public sector economists is to assign the distribution function to the national government. Since the national government is also responsible for macro-stabilization policy, this means that the responsibilities of the state and local governments are limited to providing a subset of the allocation functions of government.

As with the stabilization function, the assignment of the distribution function to the national government is seen more or less as a matter of default. The traditional argument is that permitting state and/or local redistributional policies could easily give rise to two problems: policy incompatibilities among governments; and potentially destructive competition among lower level governments. Assigning the distribution function to the national government avoids both of these problems.

Potential incompatibilities

Recall that in the single-government model, the achievement of end-results equity or distributive justice begins with society articulating a set of ethical rankings of all the citizens. The rankings are summarized by the Bergson–Samuelson individualistic social welfare function, $W = W(U^h(Y_h))$, $h = 1,...,H$, where Y_h is the income of person h, U^h is his utility function, and H is the total number of individuals. Musgrave's distribution branch then (ideally) redistributes the incomes across the individuals with lump-sum taxes and transfers to satisfy the interpersonal equity condition for a social welfare maximum, that the social marginal utilities of income, SMU_Y^h, should be equal for all individuals.

Recall also that the $SMU_y^h = \left(\dfrac{\Delta W}{\Delta U^h} \right)\left(\dfrac{\Delta U^h}{\Delta Y_h} \right)$, the product of the marginal social welfare

weight $\dfrac{\Delta W}{\Delta U^h}$, the ethical judgment provided by the social welfare function, and $\dfrac{\Delta U^h}{\Delta Y_h}$,

each person's private marginal utility of income. These lump-sum redistributions bring society to the Bator's bliss point on the utility possibilities frontier.[4]

In thinking about how to model the distribution problem in a federal setting, assume that there are only two levels of government, the national government and many local governments. Having a third layer of state or provincial governments adds nothing of substance to the problems associated with lower level redistributions.

The first point to note is that the single-government modeling approach to the distribution question cannot be applied to a federal structure of governments. In particular, both the national and local governments cannot be assumed to have their own Bergson–Samuelson individualistic social welfare functions defined over the citizens in their jurisdictions. If they did, then the potential incompatibilities mentioned in the introduction to the chapter are very likely to rise. Figure 21.1 illustrates.

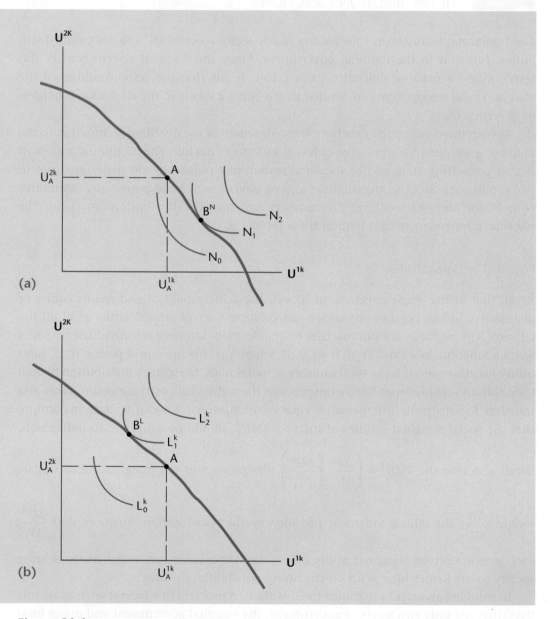

Figure 21.1

Let the national social welfare function be $N = N(U^h(Y_h))$, defined over all the citizens of the country, and $L^k = L^k(U_{hk}(Y_{hk}))$ be the social welfare function of locality k defined over its citizens, denoted by hk, person h living in locality k. Consider two people living in l, 1k and 2k. Figure 21.1 pictures the utility possibilities frontier U^{1k}, U^{2k} for two people. Society is at point A in each figure before any national or local redistributions occur. The curves N_0, N_1, N_2 in Figure 21.1(a) are the national social welfare indifference curves over the two individuals, based on the national social welfare function N. The curves L_0^k, L_1^k, L_2^k in Figure 21.1(b) are the social welfare indifference curves in locality k over the two individuals. The two sets of social welfare indifference curves are almost certain to differ because the national curves represent the ethical rankings of these two individuals as determined by the entire society, whereas the local curves represent the ethical rankings of these two individual as determined only by the citizens of locality k. The rankings in the figure differ to the extent that they call for incompatible redistributions. The national government wants to tax person 2k and transfer to person 1k to satisfy its interpersonal equity condition and reach its version of Bator's bliss point, point B^N in Figure 21.1(a). The locality requires exactly the opposite redistribution to satisfy its interpersonal equity condition and reach its version of Bator's bliss point, point B^L in Figure 21.1(b).

Potential incompatibilities of this kind ring true to Americans old enough to remember the civil rights struggles in the 1960s, when different national and state views of the appropriate treatment of whites and blacks led the national government to enforce the integration of public universities and other institutions within certain states. More generally, the potential for incompatibilities has to be avoided if society is to develop a clear sense of what it means to maximize social welfare.

The competition problem

When people are mobile, as they surely are in most countries, permitting local redistributions can also generate a destructive competition problem among localities. Suppose a city decides to redistribute by taxing its rich citizens and providing income transfers and social services to its poor citizens. Think of this outcome as resulting from a set of ethical rankings held by the middle class and the poor who, combined, outnumber the rich in a majority vote over the rankings. The rich do not have to accept this outcome, however. They can choose instead to escape to the suburbs and live among other rich people, thereby avoiding additional taxes to support the city's poor people. The city is left with a reduced tax base, which makes it even more difficult to support its poor.

This potential competition between city and suburb for the higher income people also rings true to Americans who witnessed the flight of the rich to the suburbs in the last half of the 20th century. The flight to the suburbs was especially destructive to those concerned with rising inequality, because it led to a wide disparity in the quality of public schools in the higher income suburbs and inner cities. These differences in educational quality tend to perpetuate the inequalities in succeeding generations.

Therefore, to avoid potential incompatibilities and the competition problem, the traditional mainstream solution is to assign the distribution function to the national government. This implies that the problem of achieving end-results equity or distributive justice must be viewed only from a national perspective, with the ethical rankings of individuals represented by the social welfare function based on the views of the entire citizenry. State and local governments are not permitted to express and act on distributional preferences. In his 1972 book, *Fiscal Federalism*, Wallace Oates underscored the traditional mainstream perspective on the distribution function. In addition to supporting national-only redistributions, he proposed as an ideal that the state and local governments would finance the allocation functions assigned to them by taxes set in accordance with the benefits-received principle. An example would be establishing Lindahl prices or taxes for local nonexclusive goods such as police protection (prices equal to each citizen's marginal benefit). Benefits-received taxes are ideal because they do not entail any redistribution from one taxpayer to another; everyone gets only the services they pay for. Any redistributions resulting from government tax and expenditure policies would come entirely from the national government, as intended (Oates, 1972, p. 150).

Objections to national-only redistributions

Letting only the national government redistribute may avoid incompatibilities and the competition problem, but it is an uncomfortable solution to the distribution question in a federal government. There are a number of difficulties.

In the first place, Oates' prescription to use benefits-received taxes to finance local services does not entirely work for the natural monopolies, which are surely meant to be provided by the state and local governments. Recall that the efficient provision of these services requires prices set equal to marginal costs, which leads to a deficit. The deficits are financed with lump-sum taxes, which become combined with the lump-sum taxes and transfers used to satisfy the interpersonal equity condition for a social welfare maximum. Since local governments do not have social welfare functions, they have to raise the taxes to finance the deficit in some other way, but there are no principles to guide them. One can argue that it does not matter, since any lump-sum payment will do to cover the deficit. They could elect a simple lump-sum tax such as an annual fee on all potential users, and let the national government correct any unwanted distributional consequences that result. An example might be that the elderly and students use mass rail transit disproportionately and they tend to have below average incomes. Therefore, an annual fee to use the mass transit system would be regressive and might have to be offset by the national government in its redistributions to satisfy the national interpersonal equity condition. That payment scheme would be efficient. Still, it is uncomfortable that the local governments cannot entirely finance their own services without having to rely on the national government to correct any distributional imbalances that may arise.

A more serious difficulty is that the ethical rankings of a government's citizens represented by the social welfare function are the only source of a political identity for the government in the mainstream public sector model, the only element that comes from the political process. Take away the social welfare function from the state and local governments and they have no role to play as separate, identifiable entities. They become purely agents acting on behalf of the people, with no input at all to the economic problems they are trying to solve. They merely collect data on people's preferences and the production functions for the services and then act accordingly. They have nothing to add as a government, per se, which is an unsatisfactory modeling approach for a federal government.

Finally, state and local governments surely do care about distributional issues related to their own citizens. There are fierce public debates about the incidence of state and local taxes, and states and localities provide income transfers and other social services to their poor. Recall from Chapter 10 that public assistance in the United States was entirely a state and local responsibility in the United States before the Great Depression, on the grounds that the local public officials would know far better than the national government who truly deserved public assistance and who was shirking. This is Stigler's participatory democracy principle applied to the distribution question. Although the growth of population by the mid-1930s rendered this justification problematic, the Social Security Act of 1935 nonetheless gave the states the administrative responsibility for the newly established public assistance programs, including determining the monthly benefit levels, with the national government restricted to setting some broad eligibility guidelines and providing financial assistance. Medicaid and TANF remain state administered to this day, and Medicaid is now larger than all the other major public assistance programs combined. In short, a model of a federal government that assigns all distributional concerns to the national government is not realistic, at least not for the United States.

An alternative model of fiscal federalism

In our view, a model of a federal government that denies a political identity and any concern for distributional issues to all governments except the national government simply does not capture the spirit or the practice of federalism. The lower level governments should be assumed to have a social welfare function that registers the ethical rankings of their citizens and to respond to those rankings with taxes and transfers that redistribute purchasing power among their citizens. At the same time, potential incompatibilities and the competition problem have to be taken seriously. One cannot assume that each government has a Bergson–Samuelson individualistic social welfare function defined over its citizens as in the single-government model. As we have seen, this would lead to the possibility of redistributional incompatibilities among the different levels of government and also to destructive competition among localities. There has to be some restriction on the social welfare functions at the different levels of government to avoid these problems.

The traditional mainstream model avoids these problems by denying the social welfare function to all but the national government. This restriction is too strong in our view, for the reasons given above. Instead, we believe that the following set of social welfare functions is more in keeping with the spirit of federalism. The lowest level, local governments have the standard Bergson–Samuelson individualistic social welfare function defined over their citizens. Define the subscripts and superscripts h, l, and s, where h stands for people, s stands for states, and l stands for localities. The social welfare function for locality l in state s is $L^{ls} = L^{ls}(U^{hls}(Y_{hls}))$, where hls = 1ls,..., hls,.,Hls, refers to all the citizens living in locality l in state s. The state (provincial) government honors the social welfare preferences of its localities. Its social welfare function is $S^s = S^s(L^{ls}(U^{hls}(Y_{hls})))$, where s = 1,...,S, the number of states, and L^{ls} are the social welfare functions of the localities within state s. The national government in turn honors the social welfare preferences of the states (provinces). Its social welfare function is $N = N(S^s(L^{ls}(U^{hls}(Y_{hls}))))$. Economists call this pattern of social welfare functions *dynastic*, after family dynasties in which the parents care for the utility of their children, who care about the utility of their children, and so forth through the generations.

The policy implications of the dynastic social welfare structure are as follows. The local governments tax and transfer resources lump sum to satisfy the standard single-government interpersonal equity condition of equalizing the social marginal utilities of income of their citizens:

$$\text{equalize } SMU_Y^{ls} = \left(\frac{\Delta L^{ls}}{\Delta U^{hls}} \right)\left(\frac{\Delta U^{hls}}{\Delta Y_{hls}} \right), \text{ all hls = 1ls,...,Hls,}$$

the people living in locality l in state s.

Then the state (provincial) governments transfer resources lump sum across their localities to equalize the social marginal utilities of income of all the states' citizens from the states' perspectives:

$$\text{equalize } SMU_Y^s = \left(\frac{\Delta S^s}{\Delta L^{ls}} \right)\left(\frac{\Delta L^{ls}}{\Delta U^{hls}} \right)\left(\frac{\Delta U^{hls}}{\Delta Y_{hls}} \right).$$

The lump-sum transfers within the localities ensure that the last two terms are equal, and the lump-sum transfers by the state across the localities assure that the entire SMU_Y^{hls} are equal.

Finally, the national government transfers resources lump sum across the states to equalize the social marginal utilities of income of all the nation's citizens from the national government's perspective:

$$\text{equalize } SMU_Y^N = \left(\frac{\Delta N}{\Delta S^s} \right)\left(\frac{\Delta S^s}{\Delta L^{ls}} \right)\left(\frac{\Delta L^{ls}}{\Delta U^{hls}} \right)\left(\frac{\Delta U^{hls}}{\Delta Y_{hls}} \right).$$

The lump-sum transfers of the localities and the states ensure that the last three terms are equal, and the lump-sum transfers by the national government across the states ensure the entire SMU_Y^N are equal for all the citizens.[5]

This dynastic social welfare structure gives each government an identity and a concern for the distribution of income among its citizens, while avoiding potential incompatibilities and the competition problem. There can be no incompatibilities in the redistributional policies of the different levels of government because each government accepts the ethical rankings of the governments immediately below it in the federal hierarchy. The competition problem could arise, but if so, it would be only because the higher level governments allow it to happen; it is not inherent in the dynastic structure. In the example given above, if rich city residents move to the suburbs to escape city taxes to pay for income transfers to the poor city residents, then the state could react by taxing the rich suburbs and transferring the revenues back to the city. This would undermine the incentive of the rich to leave the city.

Our alternative framework has an additional advantage over the traditional framework: It offers a distributional motivation for grants-in-aid. A *grant-in-aid* is a transfer from one government to another, as in our pattern of lump-sum transfers above from the national to the state governments and the state governments to their local governments. (The lump-sum taxes can be viewed as negative grants-in-aid.) Governments in the developed market economies make liberal use of grants-in-aid. In the United States, national grants to the states account for 32% of all state revenues and national and state grants to localities account for 39% of all local revenues (FY 2004). Furthermore, many of the grants do have a distributional motivation. U.S. examples include the national grants to the states to help finance their TANF and Medicaid programs, which account for 47% of all national grants, and the states' grants to their localities in support of the local public schools, which typically give additional resources to the poorer communities. The school grants are by far the most important of the state grants. In contrast, the traditional model with its national-only social welfare function offers no distributional motivation for grants-in-aid and little scope for any grants-in-aid at all. We will explore issues relating to grants-in-aid in Chapter 23.

What is the right federal government model?

Despite the advantages we see for our model of federalism over the traditional model, it is by no means clear that it is the right model, either theoretically or empirically. Economists who have explored the possibility of local redistributions have chosen many different models for their analysis. The most common choice is more in keeping with the traditional view: Either the national government taxes and transfers directly among all the citizens or the local governments tax and transfer among their citizens, but both levels of government do not redistribute. They do not assume that the structure of social welfare is dynastic. Furthermore, the distributional policies of the United States follow both the traditional model and our alternative model. We noted above a number of distributional grant programs that are consistent with our model. At the same time, we also described in Chapter 10 a number of national programs that redistribute resources directly to individuals without passing through the states or localities. Prominent examples include the EITC, run by the IRS, Food Stamps, and SSI. Also, most states do not require local participation in the Medicaid and TANF programs, so that these programs are essentially combinations of the traditional model and our alternative model.

U.S. citizens are no doubt reluctant to adopt our alternative model completely because they observe that, under the grant-supported programs, the poorer states and communities offer much less income and social service support to their poor citizens than do the richer states and communities. The grants-in-aid across states and localities have clearly not been sufficient to offset state and local resource imbalances. At a deeper level, some citizens may be skeptical of the ethical preferences that would be expressed within some states and localities and thus prefer the traditional approach of national-only redistributions. In any event, U.S. citizens have not been able to agree on the appropriate way to redistribute resources within a federal government in the quest for end-results equity or distributive justice.

CHAPTER 22

Efficiency and Equity Issues with Mobile Resources

In 1956, Charles Tiebout wrote an article praising the federal form of government from an economic perspective. The basis of his enthusiasm was the movement of people in response to the economic policies of the lower level governments in the federal hierarchy. He conjectured that people's ability to "vote with their feet," to leave communities (state/provinces) whose policies they did not like and join communities (states/provinces) whose policies they did like, would have two highly beneficial effects. One is that it removes the free-rider problem that would otherwise plague any nonexclusive goods that the lower level governments provide, such as police and fire departments. People have an incentive to reveal their preferences by moving to a more desired community. The other is that it leads to better matches between the nonexclusive goods that governments provide and people's preferences for these goods, since people with similar tastes tend to cluster in each community. The result is a more efficient provision of these goods (Tiebout, 1956).

Tiebout's conjecture spawned a huge literature on the economic effects of the movement of people within a federal government, and of capital as well. His influence on this literature was such that virtually all the economic effects resulting from people and other resources moving in response to government policies came to be described as Tiebout effects.

Tiebout's view of federalism turned out to be overly optimistic. Economists discovered that the movement of people and capital opens up new channels for potential inefficiencies to enter the economy. It can also make end-results equity or distributive justice more difficult to achieve. Worse yet, the movement of people in response to government policies may not even come to an equilibrium, in which case the efficiency and equity properties of a federal government are a moot point.

Economists have developed a staggering variety of models to explore the implications of people moving among states (provinces) and localities, mostly the latter. They vary along a number of dimensions, such as:

- the objectives of the governments (social welfare maximization, Pareto optimality with no concern for equity, maximize the profits of local developers or landlords who own all the land)
- the types of goods they provide (from nonexclusive goods to private goods)
- the taxes they use to finance their expenditures (property taxes, income taxes, lump-sum head taxes)
- the political process within the community (one-person, one-vote democracy, some form of representative government, landlords and developers make all the tax and spending decisions)
- the way people earn their incomes (earn wage income by producing goods within the community, earn rents from the ownership of land, earn profits from the ownership of capital supplied to the community or elsewhere, have endowment income that they take with them as they move)
- the existence or non-existence of a market for land (from land is so plentiful that it is free to land is scarce and commands a rent)
- whether moving is costless or costly
- how communities react to the policies of neighboring communities (from taking the other communities' policies as given when making their decisions to highly sophisticated decisions that take into account how the policies in all communities interact to affect the movement of people or capital).

Even this list is not exhaustive.

It would be impossible to present a representative sampling of all the possible modeling variations in this chapter. Instead, we begin with two of the better known models in the literature, one by Joseph Stiglitz and the other by Mark Pauly. The Stiglitz model shows that the movement of people can either be efficient or inefficient; roughly speaking, almost any outcome is possible. The Pauly model highlights the potential difficulties in achieving an equilibrium such that no one has any incentive to move to a different community. These two models also have quite different structures, so that they illustrate some of the enormous variation of the models in this literature noted above. They are also both models of local governments, which is true of the majority of models in the Tiebout literature.

THE STIGLITZ MODEL: ANYTHING CAN HAPPEN

The Stiglitz model belongs to the group of models that assume the localities lie in a fairly undeveloped region of a country such as a new frontier. Land is so plentiful within each community that it is assumed to be free, so there is no need to describe a market for land. (The houses people build on their land are simply one of the many consumer goods and services they choose to buy and are of no special importance. It is the market for land that matters in these models.) Also, people can move costlessly from community to community (Stiglitz, 1977).

Once people arrive in a community, they combine with all the other people there to produce output. Each unit of output can be used in one of two ways: either as an all-purpose private consumption good; or as a nonexclusive public good whose services are consumed equally by everyone. The public good has the property that it is nonexclusive within the community but exclusive to the community that provides it. That is, the public good provided by a community offers no benefits to anyone living in any other community. This is the standard assumption regarding locally provided nonexclusive goods. An example would be a local police force that can make arrests only within the community.

All the people in the region have identical preferences for the private and nonexclusive goods and the goal of each community is to maximize the utilities of each person. Finally, the public good is financed with a lump-sum head tax on each person and a tax on any pure profits from production.

It turns out that the frontier-type models with free land and lump-sum head taxes are the models most likely to generate an efficient equilibrium. Unfortunately, they are also capable of generating many different kinds of inefficient outcomes, depending on the exact structure of the model. We can see the various possibilities by describing the production function for a community and the preferences of the individuals.

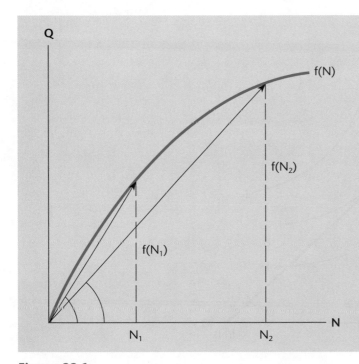

Figure 22.1

Let N = the total number of people in a community, each of whom works to produce output Q given by the production function $Q = f(N)$, pictured in Figure 22.1. Labor is the only factor of production, and $f(N)$ exhibits diminishing returns to labor. The marginal product of labor, the slope of $f(N)$, decreases as N increases – as more people arrive in the town and join in the production of Q, the additional output produced by each new entrant decreases. The average product of labor, $f(N)/N$, the slope of a ray from the origin to $f(N)$, also decreases as N increases. (The rays are drawn for N_1 and N_2.)

Q can be transformed into an all-purpose consumer good X or a nonexclusive good G on a one-for-one basis. But if X is produced, a unit of X is given to each person. Therefore, the production possibilities frontier for the community is $f(N) = NX + G$.

Each person consumes X and G and has a utility function over the two goods $U = U(X, G)$. The budget constraint for each person is 1/Nth of the production possibilities frontier for the entire community: $f(N)/N = X + (1/N)G$ or $X = f(N)/N - (1/N)G$.

Figure 22.2 pictures the equilibrium for each consumer, the utility maximum, when the number of people in the community is N. I_0, I_1, I_2 are the consumer's indifference curves for X and G and the budget line is $X = f(N)/N - (1/N)G$, whose X intercept is $f(N)/N$, G intercept is $f(N)$, and slope is $-(1/N)$. Each consumer maximizes utility at point A, consuming X_A and voting for the community to provide G_A of the nonexclusive good. Since the government's goal is to maximize the utility of the (identical) consumers, it will provide G_A. (This would be the outcome in a direct democracy with identical individuals.)

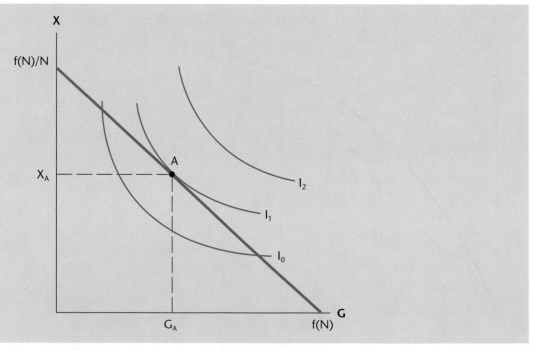

Figure 22.2

Figure 22.3 shows what happens to the maximum utility as the number of people in the community increases. The budget lines labeled (1) through (4) indicate the effect on each person's budget constraint as N increases. The intercept $f(N)/N$ decreases as N increases – recall that the average product of labor decreases. Therefore, the amount of X available to each person if G were zero decreases. The slope of the budget line $(-)1/N$ also decreases in absolute value. With $f(N)$ increasing in N, the total amount of G that can be provided if X is zero increases. There is, in effect, crowding out of the private good as N increases, but not of G. With this pattern of budget lines, the maximum utility available to each consumer at first increases, from A to B in Figure 22.3, but then decreases, from B to C and again from C to D. The initial increase in utility is due to the ability to increase the production of G. Eventually, however, the decrease in the ability to produce a unit of X for each person dominates the increase in G and utility decreases. In the terminology of the Tiebout literature, the production of the private good becomes increasingly congested.

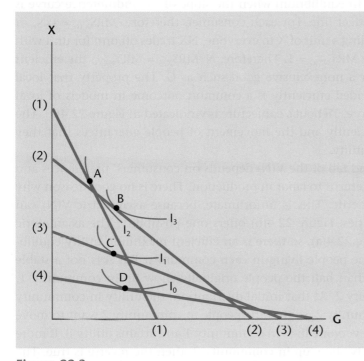

Figure 22.3

The way that utility increases and then decreases determines what happens as people move from community to community. To see the possibilities, assume that there are two communities each with a lot of free land available and that the total number of people who have to choose one community or the other is N*. Assume also that the production functions in the two communities are identical and, as above, that all individuals are identical. Since the people are identical, moving is costless, and land is free, the only possible equilibrium is one in which there is horizontal equity across the communities: People must receive the same utility no matter which community they choose. This must be so, since if the people living in one community have higher utility than the people living in the other community, those in the lower utility community will move to the higher utility community until everyone has the same utility.

Figure 22.4 pictures three possible outcomes. N_1 is the number of people living in community 1 and N_2 is the number of people living in community 2. N_1 increases from left to right, N_2 increases from right to left, and $N_1 + N_2 = N^*$, the total population. The curves labeled $V(N_1)$ and $V(N_2)$ give the maximum utilities achieved in communities 1 and 2 for each value of N_1 and N_2. $V(N_1)$ is read from left to right and $V(N_2)$ is read from right to left. The maximum utilities first rise and then fall, as described above.

In Figure 22.4(a), the V(N) rise and fall symmetrically over the entire population N^* and reach their peaks at $N^*/2$. Consequently, they lie one on top of the other. Half the people live in each community and each person receives the maximum possible utility.

Notice in addition that at the utility maximum described in Figure 22.2 for a given population, the consumer is in equilibrium when the slope of the indifference curve is equal to the slope of the budget line. For each consumer, therefore, $MRS_{X,G} = 1/N$, or $N \cdot MRS_{X,G} = 1$. Also, by providing a unit of X to everyone, NX trades off unit for unit with G in production. That is, the $MRT_{NX,G} = 1$. Therefore, $N \cdot MRS_{X,G} = MRT_{NX,G}$, the efficient Pareto-optimal condition for a nonexclusive good such as G. The property that local nonexclusive goods are provided efficiently is a common outcome in models of local governments. Overall, therefore, Tiebout's conjecture is vindicated in Figure 22.4(a). The public good is provided efficiently and the movement of people guarantees that they receive the highest possible utility.

The pattern of the rise and fall of the V(N) depends on consumers' preferences and the extent of the decreasing returns to labor in production. There is no good reason why the pattern should be symmetric. This is unfortunate, because asymmetric V(N) can generate all kinds of difficulties. Figure 22.4(b) offers one possibility. The asymmetric V(N) peak at $N^*/2$ as in Figure 22.4(a), so there is an efficient maximum utility equilibrium at point A, with half the people living in each community. But A is not a stable equilibrium. Suppose more than half the people originally show up in community 1, say N_1^0, with N_2^0 in community 2. At that initial distribution, the utility in community 1 exceeds the utility in community 2, so that the people in community 2 want to move to community 1. Eventually everyone lives in community 1 and attains utility B. If more than half the people originally show up in community 2, then the reverse is true. The utility in community 2 exceeds the utility in community 1 and everyone moves from 1 to 2. Eventually everyone lives in community 2 and attains utility B'. B and B' are the only stable equilibriums and they are inefficient. They yield less utility than if $N^*/2$ people lived in each community and received utility of A.

In Figure 22.4(c), the asymmetric V(N) each reach their peak before $N^*/2$. As a consequence, the only stable equilibrium is A and again people do not achieve the highest possible utility. Suppose N_1^0 people are originally in community 1 because that is the number that maximizes their utility, with utility equal to B. But then N_2^0 people are in community 2 and they receive lower utility than the people in community 1, so they move to community 1 until half the people are living in each community and receive utility of A. The same movement occurs if N_2^1 people are originally in community 2 because that number maximizes their utility, with utility equal to B'. Now the people in community 1 move to community 2 since they have the lower utility and again the equilibrium is at A, with half the people living in each community. A is the only stable equilibrium, and it is less than the maximum utility that each community is able to generate.

In sum, the movement of people can generate a stable, efficient equilibrium but it can just as easily generate one stable inefficient equilibrium or multiple stable and inefficient equilibria. Tiebout's conjecture that a federal government is efficient does not necessarily hold.

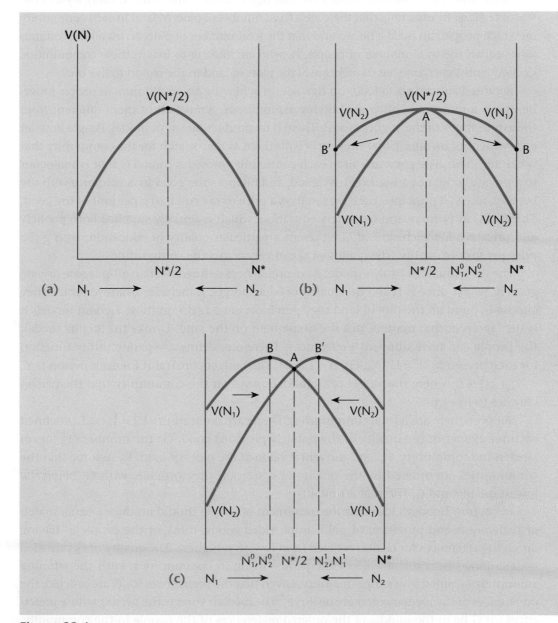

Figure 22.4

THE PAULY MODEL: IS THERE AN EQUILIBRIUM?

The Pauly model belongs to the group of models that lie on the other end of the geographic spectrum from the Stiglitz model (Pauly, 1976). The localities in his model are older, well-established communities situated in a densely populated region of the country. Land is scarce in the region and commands a positive rental value wherever it is located. The land rents, R, are equal within any one community but can differ across communities. Pauly stylizes the scarcity of land by assuming that there are a fixed number of plots of land in each community on which people can build a house, and that the total number of plots across all the communities equals the total number of people, H, who are looking to live in these communities. Consequently, everyone has to pick one of the plots of land in the region to live on.

Because Pauly wants to focus on the issue of achieving an equilibrium as people move, he makes a number of other simplifying assumptions, almost all of them different from the assumptions of the Stiglitz model. There is no production in his model. People have an endowment of income Y that they carry with them as they search for the community that is best for them. The government in each community provides a good G that is analogous to a private good, not a nonexclusive good, and finances the good in accordance with the benefits-received principle. Each person pays a price or tax equal to g per unit of the good. Think of G as primary and secondary education, which is actually supplied both publicly and privately. Let each unit of G represent a particular quality of education, with g the price per unit of quality. The quality of G can vary across the communities.

The individuals in Pauly's model have preferences defined over an all-purpose private good X, whose price is 1, and the quality of education G. X includes whatever house they choose to build on the plot of land they purchase; once again, in these Tiebout models it is the land rent that matters, not the house built on the land. Unlike the Stiglitz model, the people can have different preferences. Therefore, define a separate utility function for each person h: $U^h = U^h(X_h, G)$, h = 1,...,H. The budget constraint for each person is $Y_h = X_h + gG + R$, where the values of G and R depend on the community that the person chooses to live in.

Suppose there are L total communities. Then each community l, l = 1, ..., L is defined by three elements: the quality of the publicly provided good, G_l; the number of plots of land in the community, H_l; and the rental value of the plots of land, R_l. Assume that the communities are ordered by the quality of education they provide, with G_1 being the lowest quality and G_L the highest quality.

To capture Tiebout's idea that the movement of people should produce a better match of preferences and provision of publicly provided goods, think of the people as having different preferences for G, also ordered from lowest to highest. The quality of G_l provided is determined by a direct vote of the people living in community l, with the winning amount determined by a simple majority. Given that the preferences for G are ordered, the preferences of the median voter are decisive.[1] The median voter is the person whose preferences for G lie in the middle of the ordered preferences of the people in the community. Figure 22.5 illustrates the median voter outcome.

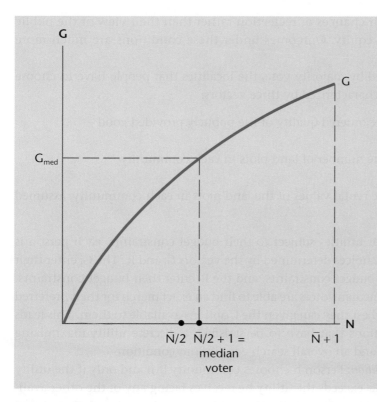

Figure 22.5

The people in the community are on the horizontal axis and their preferences for G are on the vertical axis. The curve G gives the ordered preferences for G, with the median voter's preference equal to G_{med}. If there are $\bar{N}$ +1 people in the community, with $\bar{N}$ an even number, then $\bar{N}/2$ people prefer a lower quality of G than G_{med} and $\bar{N}/2$ people prefer a higher quality of G than G_{med}. Consider a vote on G_{med} versus the next lowest quality of G, G_{med} – 1. G_{med} would win because it would capture the votes of the $\bar{N}/2$ people who favor a higher quality of G than G_{med} plus the vote of the median voter. This defeats the $\bar{N}/2$ people who would vote for G_{med} – 1 because they prefer a quality of G lower than G_{med}. In addition, a vote between any two qualities of G lower than G_{med} would always be won by the higher quality. Eventually, therefore, G_{med} would come to a vote against G_{med} – 1 and beat it. By a similar argument, G_{med} would win a majority of the votes against G_{med} + 1, namely the median voter plus the $\bar{N}/2$ voters who favor a quality lower than G_{med}. Also, in a vote between any two qualities greater than G_{med}, the lower quality would always win. Eventually, therefore, G_{med} would come to a vote against G_{med} + 1 and beat it.

The median voter model is overwhelmingly the political model of choice for Tiebout-style location models because it leads to a definite outcome. Matters become much fuzzier with representative governments whose legislators can engage in log rolling (if you vote for my project, I will vote for your project). Legislators may also cast votes to promote their chances of reelection rather than their view of the public interest in efficiency and equity. Outcomes under these conditions are much more difficult to predict.

With the G_l determined by majority vote, the localities that people have to choose from as a place to live are characterized by three vectors:

$\vec{G}_l = (G_1,...,G_l,...,G_L)$ the ordered quality of the publicly provided good

$\vec{H} = (H_1,...,H_l,...,H_L)$, the number of land plots in each community

$\vec{R} = (R_1, ...,R_l,...,R_L)$, the rental values of the land plots in each community, assumed equal within a community.

In trying to maximize their utilities subject to their budget constraints, each person is faced with a discrete set of choices determined by the vectors G_l and R_l. The G_l enter their utility functions and their budget constraints, and the R_l enter their budget constraints. No individuals except the median voters are able to find an exact match for their preferred G, so they search to do the best they can given the L options available to them. This leads to two equilibrium conditions that have to be satisfied, a discrete utility-maximizing condition for each person and an overall search equilibrium condition.

Utility-maximizing condition: Person h chooses community l* if and only if the utility he receives facing G_{l*} and R_{l*} exceeds the utility he receives facing any of the other available G, R combinations. Letting $V^h(G_l, R_l)$ be the utility person h receives facing G_l and R_l, person h chooses l* if and only if $V^h(G_{l*}, R_{l*}) > V^h(G_l, R_l)$, $l \neq l*$.

Overall search equilibrium condition: Everyone has to live somewhere. Therefore, the overall search equilibrium condition is that the number of people who prefer a particular community must equal the number of land plots in that community. Letting n(l) equal the number of people that prefer community l, the search equilibrium condition is that n(l) = H_l, l = 1,...,L. If the condition is not satisfied, then either the G_l, or the R_l, or both have to adjust until the condition is satisfied.

Unfortunately, there is no guarantee that the overall search equilibrium condition will be satisfied by adjustments in the G_l and R_l. The possible nonexistence of an equilibrium is what the Pauly model is designed to show. To see the problem, imagine that there is an initial equilibrium represented by the line segments in Figure 22.6. Each line segment represents one of the communities, and the G_l and R_l are the qualities of G chosen and the rental values of the land in each community. The communities are ordered by the G_l from lowest to highest. Recall, also, that the people in each community have different preferences for G. Presumably only the median voter in community l most prefers G_l. So think of the people as also ordered along each line segment by their preferences for G. Finally, the line segments have different lengths to represent that the number of land plots in each community can differ.

Suppose the residents of community 1 have a change in tastes and vote for a lower quality of G_1. The result could be a chain reaction affecting all the communities that may never settle back to a new equilibrium. The people who matter most in establishing an overall search equilibrium are those at the borders of the line segments based on their preferences for G. They are the ones who are closest to being indifferent to their current community and the one just above it (right-hand border) or below it (left-hand border). Suppose some of the people near the right-hand border of community 1 now most prefer community 2 after the reduction in G_1. Their attempt to move to community 2 could drive up rental values there. But with rental values now higher in community 2, some people near the right-hand border of community 2 might now want to move to community 3, with the result that rental values in community 3 now increase, and so on up the line of communities. Also, some people near the left-hand border of community 2 might now prefer community 1 after the rents rise in community 2. As the people reshuffle themselves through the localities, the votes on how much G to provide could also change, leading to still more movement. For example, if some "border" people do move from community 1 to community 2, and from community 2 to community 3, then community 2 now has more people who prefer a lower G than the original G_{med}, and fewer people who prefer a higher G than the original G_{med}. The identity of the median voter changes and presumably the quality of G in community 2 falls. Also, if the median voters consider how their votes affect rental values, then the change in rental values would change their votes even if the identity of the median voter in each community does not change. With both the G_l and the R_l changing in some or all of the communities, it is not clear whether a new overall search equilibrium can ever be achieved. The movement of people throughout the localities may end up in a perpetual state of disequilibrium in which at least one person always wants to move. This is certainly not what Tiebout had in mind.

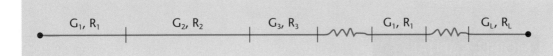

Figure 22.6

Whatever the outcome may be, Pauly's simple model points out two important features of a federal government. One is that when preferences over a publicly provided good differ, local decisions on the good can be expected to lead to a better match of people's preferences for the good than the alternative of having the national government provide one level of the good for everyone. People will sort themselves out among the communities by their preferences for the good. This is as Tiebout conjectured when people can vote with their feet.

The second feature is the central role of the market for land in establishing an equilibrium when people can move from locality to locality. Continue with the example of local public education, which does greatly influence people's choice of community. Suppose the set of people looking for a place to live consists of rich families and poor families, each of which has two school-aged children. The problem in establishing an equilibrium across communities is that everyone, rich and poor, wants to live with the rich families. This is so for two reasons. One is that children tend to learn more when surrounded by classmates from high-income families than by classmates from low-income families. The other is that most local schools are financed largely by property taxes on the value of both the land and the house, so that the rich families pay a disproportionate share of the total school budget because they buy larger houses.

Imagine that communities consist originally of only rich or only poor families. The poor families will try to move into the rich communities. If some succeed, then the rich families will want to move to another rich-only community. The poor will forever want to move to communities with higher percentages of rich families, and the rich families will be trying just as hard to escape living with poor families. The only way this scenario can ever reach an equilibrium is if the rich pay higher land rents in the rich-only communities than in the mixed rich–poor communities, and the poor pay higher land values in the mixed rich–poor communities than in the poor-only communities. The differences in land values must just compensate the rich for staying in the mixed communities, and also must just compensate the poor for staying in the poor-only communities. Whether an overall search equilibrium would ever obtain remains problematic, however, especially if the demand for education varies across the rich families and also across the poor families.

A final point is that the reliance on land markets to achieve equilibrium introduces another source of inefficiency into a federal government through local property taxes, which, as noted, tax both the land and the house values. The portion of the tax on the land is lump sum and therefore efficient, but the portion of the tax on the house distorts the market for houses and is therefore inefficient.

MOBILE CAPITAL

The difficulties caused by the movement of people in response to the lower level governments' tax and spending policies are not the end of the problems with a federal government. Capital is also highly mobile, even more so than people. Capital moves easily across local, state, and even national borders, and the movement of capital opens up another avenue of inefficiency.

Capital is sufficiently mobile that it is reasonable to assume that the supply of capital to a given locality or state is perfectly elastic at a return to capital determined in the broader national market. For economic unions such as the E.U. with its open borders, the supply of capital to any of the member nations may also be essentially perfectly elastic at the E.U.-wide or even world rate of return.

If the supply of capital is perfectly elastic to a locality (alternatively, a state or nation), then Figure 19.6(b) applies, adapted here as Figure 22.7. The demand for capital, D_K, comes from the firms within the locality and the supply of capital, S_K, comes mostly from outside the local borders. Therefore, it is perfectly elastic at the national (world) rate of return R_0. The initial equilibrium is (K_0, R_0), at the intersection of D_K and S_K. Suppose the government taxes the profits or returns to capital of its firms by means of a corporate income tax. D_K shifts down by the amount of the tax to D_K^1, and the new equilibrium is (K_1, R_0), at the intersection of D_K^1 and S_K. The cost of capital to the firm rises by the full amount of the tax to R_1. But since capitalists cannot suffer a reduction in their return to capital R_0 and still supply capital to the locality, the increased cost is passed through to consumers in the form of higher prices, or to labor in the form of lower wages. The result is that the government raises tax revenue in the amount R_0R_1ab, but at the costs of a lower stock of capital, less production, and a tax burden borne by its consumers and workers.

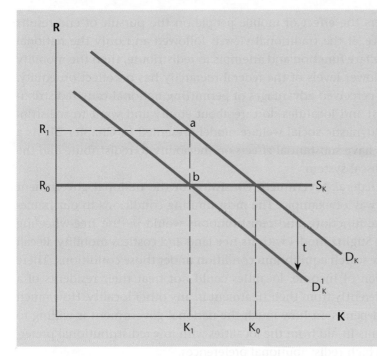

Figure 22.7

The losses from the tax give local governments an incentive to reduce the taxes on capital and raise the taxes on less mobile workers, which would have less effect on production. But this incentive ignores an important external benefit from the local tax on capital: The gain to other localities as their demands for capital increase and they attract the capital displaced in the community levying the tax, thereby increasing their production and employment. Since the overall losses are less than the losses perceived by the taxing community, each community has an incentive to set its corporate tax at an inefficiently low rate from the point of view of the state (nation, union) as a whole. The localities may even engage in a highly inefficient race to the bottom, setting ever lower tax rates to retain capital.

The corporate income tax had become a major issue in the E.U. by 2000. The nations with high corporate tax rates, primarily Germany and France, lobbied hard for a single rate for all the nations set by the E.U. at a high level, a so-called harmonization of the tax rate. Without harmonization, they feared their firms would be at too great a competitive disadvantage relative to the firms in the nations with low corporate tax rates, primarily Ireland and the 12 new members admitted in May 2004 and January 2007. Without harmonization, the nations may indeed all set their tax rates at an inefficiently low level. The calls for harmonization had not passed as this was written (2007).

MOBILITY AND EQUITY

Our final example considers the effect of mobile people on the pursuit of end-results equity or distributive justice. If the traditional view is followed and only the national government has a social welfare function and attempts to redistribute, then the mobility of people throughout the lower levels of the federal hierarchy has no effect on equity. This, indeed, is one of the perceived advantages of permitting national-only redistributions. But states (provinces) and localities do care about equity and want to redistribute, as represented by our dynastic social welfare model presented in Chapter 21. As a consequence, mobility can have substantial effects on the ability to redistribute and the progressivity of the entire fiscal system.

Consider a two-tiered federal government consisting of the national government and local governments by way of example. The most limiting conditions to our framework of local social welfare functions and redistributions would be the free-wheeling new frontier such as in the Stiglitz model with its free land and costless mobility. Recall that horizontal equity is the search equilibrium condition under those conditions. There can only be one distribution of income; localities could not treat their residents of a given income level any differently from their treatment in any other locality. How much redistribution takes place depends on how much the national government is willing to redistribute through its grants-in-aid from the localities with low redistributional preferences to the localities with high redistributional preferences.

For example, suppose there are two localities as in the Stiglitz model but that people have different amounts of endowment income as in the Pauly model. One locality decides to tax and transfer lump sum and level everyone to the mean income within the community, as suggested by the Atkinson assumptions of Chapter 5. The other locality decides not to redistribute at all. The leveling policy would attract all people from the other community who have less than that mean income level. Similarly, those residents in the leveling community with incomes higher than that mean income would move to the other community. This is the competition problem noted in Chapter 21.

The question, then, is how the national government will respond. If it lets the movement stand, then the average income in the leveling community would continue to fall, and all but the poorest people would eventually live in the other community. If the national government redistributes from the other community to the leveling community, then some people besides the poorest people would remain in the leveling community as the mean income in that community stabilized. The mean income in the leveling community could even rise if the national government distributed large amounts of income between the communities.

What the national government chooses to do depends on the preferences of all the people, the combined preferences of those living in both communities. If the national political process is heavily influenced by the middle class and the poor, then the government would redistribute quite a bit. The opposite is true if the rich dominate the national political process. Whatever the national decision, the leveling policy would serve to stratify the two communities by income level: all people with incomes initially above the final mean income live in the other community and all people with incomes initially below the final mean income live in the leveling community. It is not surprising that there is some stratification by income within the suburbs of metropolitan areas, although the stratification is by no means as complete as suggested by this model.

The conclusion is that local preferences over distributional policy could possibly have a significant effect on the overall distribution of income even under the horizontal equity equilibrium condition. Nonetheless, the influence of any one community whose distributional preferences are quite different from the norm is likely to be negligible if it is just one of many communities and contains only a small minority of the population. Its policies would likely be overwhelmed by the horizontal equity condition.

A local government's distributional preferences have more chance of being realized if mobility is costly, which it surely is to some extent. Perhaps costly mobility explains why metropolitan stratification is incomplete. Still, people in the United States do worry that the states have a powerful incentive to engage in a race to the bottom in providing public assistance, to prevent poor people from moving to the higher public assistance states. The traditional warning about the competition problem cannot be ignored. The desire of states (provinces) and localities to redistribute can pose serious difficulties for society's pursuit of end-results equity or distributive justice.

CHAPTER 23

Grants-in-Aid

Grants-in-aid are transfers of resources from higher to lower level governments in the federal hierarchy, such as from the national government to state (provincial) and local governments and from state (provincial) governments to their local governments. Public sector economists have a natural interest in grants-in-aid because they are an important feature of modern federal governments. In 2005 in the United States, national grants to states were 32% of total state revenues, and national and state grants to localities were 39% of total local revenues. In that same year, 36% of the expenditure of the E.U. central government were grants-in-aid to the member nations.[1]

There are two main economic issues associated with grants-in-aid, one theoretical and one empirical. The theoretical issue concerns the proper role of grants-in-aid in a federal system of governments. What problems are they supposed to address and how should they be designed to solve them? The empirical issue concerns how the receiving governments respond to grants-in-aid. The granting governments presumably have some goals in mind when giving the aid. Do the receiving governments respond to the aid in a manner consistent with those goals? The majority of the economic research on grants-in-aid has focused on these two issues.

THE THEORY OF GRANTS-IN-AID

The appropriate role for grants-in-aid depends on one's view of the appropriate economic functions of the lower level governments. Consider as examples the traditional view and our alternative view of how the economic functions of government should be assigned throughout the federal hierarchy.

THE TRADITIONAL VIEW

According to the traditional view, the state (provincial) and local governments should be assigned only certain allocation functions of government, the functions that they can carry out efficiently. This includes some of the decreasing cost/natural monopoly services and externality-generating activities, providing the external effects are contained within the jurisdiction of the lower level government. Since the functions of these governments are strictly allocational in nature, any role for grants-in-aid must also be allocational, to correct for any remaining inefficiencies that may arise.

The most likely candidates are the externality-generating activities. As noted in Chapter 21, Wallace Oates described the ideal assignment of these activities as establishing a perfect correspondence between the jurisdictional boundaries of governments and the extent of the external effects within the boundaries. If there really were a perfect correspondence for these activities in each instance, then there would be no role for grants-in-aid in a federal system of governments. Each government would simply attend to its own functions without any need for aid from any higher level government.

The need for grants-in-aid arises because the correspondences are likely to be imperfect for many externality-generating activities. Jurisdictional boundaries are set mostly for historical and political reasons, not so much by economic considerations. Governments typically respond to economic problems after the boundaries have been set. Consequently, externalities arising from activity in one jurisdiction are likely to spill over into other jurisdictions – industrial air and water pollution are obvious examples. When spillovers occur, the traditional view offers two options. One is that the decision-making authority over the externality-generating activity be assigned to a higher level government whose boundaries include the entire extent of the external effects. Examples would be a set of regional commissions to correct for the industrial pollution of rivers and lakes with borders on more than one state, or having the national government correct for industrial air pollution that has many sources and spreads throughout most of the country. If this option is chosen, then there is still no need for grants-in-aid.

This option has a potentially serious drawback, however. As explained in Chapter 21, the assignment of economic functions to lower level governments is motivated by Stigler's assumption of participatory democracy, that government decision making works best the closer public officials are to the people affected by their decisions. In terms of externality-generating activities, this implies that the public officials of jurisdictions in which the activities occur are likely to have a better understanding of the nature of the external effects and how to correct for them than the public officials in governments higher up in the federal hierarchy. If this is true, then the better option may be to leave the decision making at the lower level and have the higher level governments use grants-in-aid to influence the lower level jurisdictions to take into account the external spillovers of the activities within their borders. Indeed, correcting for external spillovers is the only important example of a role for grants-in-aid according to the traditional view.

The grants-in-aid to correct for the external spillovers would be designed exactly as described in Chapter 6 when there was only a single government. The relevant model in that chapter is the correction for a private activity that gives rises to an external effect. Recall that the efficient policy is a Pigovian tax (for harmful external effects, for example pollution) or subsidy (for beneficial external effects, for example public education) equal to the sum of the marginal external damage or benefit to all affected third parties. Ideally the per-unit tax or subsidy would be set at the amount of the aggregate marginal external damage or benefit, if the optimal amount can be measured. Furthermore, if the externality is an aggregate externality, then a single tax or subsidy is appropriate for all sources of the externality. If the externality is individualized, then a separate tax or subsidy is required for each activity that generates the externality.

These same principles apply to the spillovers across jurisdictions. The grants-in-aid should be Pigovian in structure. For beneficial spillovers, the jurisdiction should receive a grant-in-aid equal to the sum of the marginal benefits of the spillover to all other jurisdictions arising from the activity. The grant (subsidy) would be given on each unit of the activity and, ideally, would be set at the optimal amount of the spillovers. A single grant (subsidy) would apply to all jurisdictions if their spillovers are in the form of an aggregate externality. An example might be primary and secondary public education, assuming that all people in a democracy benefit equally from increasing amounts of education received by any one citizen. If the spillovers are individualized by community, then separate grants (Pigovian subsidies) are required for each community. An example might be the benefits of a highway or airport to people outside the jurisdiction in which it is located. The external effects are almost certainly specific to individual highways and airports – their location determines who is affected by them.

The same principles apply to harmful spillovers, but with a Pigovian tax (negative grant-in-aid) instead of a Pigovian subsidy. An example of an aggregate spillover that requires a single tax is industrial pollution of a bordering lake. In contrast, industrial air pollution is likely to be an individualized externality since the marginal external damage depends on the number of people affected by the pollution.

The problem with the traditional theory of grants-in-aid is that it has been almost entirely ignored by public officials. To give one example, Table 23.1 records the 10 largest national grant programs in the United States for FY 2004. These grants accounted for 80% of the total national grants-in-aid that year. Notice that only 2 of the 10 largest national grants-in-aid to the states in the United States are targeted to an allocation problem, the Department of Transportation (DOT) grants to support highway construction and maintenance and other miscellaneous projects. The other 8 grants are motivated by distributional concerns, to help states pay for income support and social services to poor and/or needy individuals and communities, mostly individuals.[2] Furthermore, the highway aid formula appears to be entirely unrelated to the estimated spillovers of the highways in each state to citizens of other states. The financial support for the interstate system is 90% for all states, regardless of the population density of the states. Support for other highways does vary somewhat from state to state, but the variation is due mostly to political bargaining between state and national public officials. To the extent economic considerations matter, they are specific to each state, such as the additional maintenance required for highways in the cold weather states because of frost heaves and the like. They have nothing to do with spillovers. Finally, the amount of funds available to each state is subject to an upper limit, whereas a Pigovian per-unit subsidy to correct for external effects should have no upper limit.

TABLE 23.1 The 10 largest federal grants-in-aid (fiscal year 2004)

Grant	Amount ($billions)
Medical Assistance Program (Medicaid)	183.2
Highway Planning and Construction	31.9
Section 8 Housing Choice Vouchers	22.4
Temporary Assistance for Needy Families (TANF)	17.2
Special Education Grants to States	10.1
Title I Grants to Local Education Agencies	8.3
National School Lunch Program	7.4
Head Start	6.6
DOT Miscellaneous Grant Awards	5.3
Special Supplemental Food Program for Women, Infants and Children	5.0
Total, Ten Largest Grants	297.4
Total, All Federal Grants	370.4

SOURCE: U.S. Census Bureau, *Consolidated Federal Funds Report: Fiscal Year 2004*, Detailed Federal Expenditure Data – United States 2/8/2007.

OUR ALTERNATIVE VIEW

Our alternative view of the appropriate functions of government sees the same potential allocational role for grants-in-aid as the traditional view, as an option for correcting the imperfect correspondences between jurisdictional boundaries and the extent of externalities. And the design of the grants to correct for the spillovers is identical in both views. In addition, however, our alternative view provides a distributional motivation for grants-in-aid; to correct at least partially for resource imbalances across lower level jurisdictions. In fact, the design of many grant-in-aid programs does appear to be motivated by distributional concerns in general and resource imbalances in particular. As noted in Table 23.1, 8 of the 10 largest U.S. government grants-in-aid help finance state and local redistributional programs. Moreover some of these programs give additional aid to the poorer states. For example, Medicaid, which is by far the largest grant program, reimburses state Medicaid expenditures with matching rates that vary inversely with a state's per capita income relative to the national average. The matching rates range from 50% for the richest states to 83% for the poorest states. Similarly, state aid to localities is typically adjusted by formulas that give additional aid to the poorer localities. Canada and many European countries also give substantial extra support to their poorer provinces through grants-in-aid. Giving additional resources to poorer states and communities through grants-in-aid is commonly referred to as *fiscal equalization*, and it is commonplace within the developed market economies.

Nonetheless, the actual design of distributional grants-in-aid programs is not entirely consistent with our alternative view either. Our model calls for lump-sum taxes and transfers levied by each government on the governments immediately below them in the federal hierarchy. The implication is that the grants to the poorer governments would be cash grants that the receiving government could spend as it wished. In fact, actual government practice departs from our prescription in three ways. First, grants offered as a form of fiscal equalization most often are *categorical grants*; they have "strings attached" – they have to be spent on certain goods and services (that is, within certain categories). The eight redistributional grants in Table 23.1 are examples. Second, the grants are often in the form of per-unit subsidies rather than being lump sum. The matching rates under Medicaid are an important U.S. example. Finally, grant-in-aid programs never (to our knowledge) levy taxes (negative grants) on richer communities. Instead, either all governments receive some amount of grant or the grant is set to zero for richer communities. Either way, the amount of fiscal equalization (redistribution) that results from these grant programs is necessarily limited relative to the pattern of positive and negative grants called for by our alternative model. The programs are still redistributive because the taxes levied to pay for the grants come disproportionately from residents in richer communities. But residents in poorer communities also pay some of the taxes to support the grants they receive, which limits the overall redistributional effect of these attempts at fiscal equalization.

Because the traditional view has no redistributional role for grants-in-aid, and our alternative view does not quite capture actual grant design, economists have developed a number of other models for designing grants-in-aid. We conclude the theoretical section of the chapter with two of the more popular models. One is a model of fiscal equalization in the spirit of our alternative model. The other is a motivation for grants-in-aid based on a cost disease that afflicts the services of lower level governments.

FISCAL EQUALIZATION

The fiscal equalization prescription in our alternative view is based on the social welfare functions of the state (provincial) and local governments. To make this prescription operational requires developing a proxy for the social welfare of the lower level governments that is easily measured and can be used in a grant formula. The literature contains many suggestions. Julian LeGrand (1975) was one of the first economists to propose a proxy measure of social welfare and it gained some influence not only among public sector economists but also in actual grant design. We will consider state grants to localities, with the goal of achieving some degree of fiscal equalization across the localities.

LeGrand proposed that the amount of grant a locality receives should be based on two factors: the purchasing power of its taxes; and the effort it makes to raise taxes to provide public services. Let:

T_i = the per capita taxes collected by locality i

P_i = a price index that reflects the costs of public services provided in community i

t_i = the tax rate that locality i applies to its tax base, presumably a property tax rate in the United States.

LeGrand proposed computing the purchasing power/tax effort ratio for each locality and using that as the basis for a grant formula. The purchasing power of the taxes is $\dfrac{T_i}{P_i}$ and the tax effort is the tax rate t_i. Therefore the purchasing power/effort ratio is

$\left(\dfrac{T_i}{P_i}\right)\left(\dfrac{1}{t_i}\right)=\dfrac{T_i}{P_i t_i}$. Before proceeding to his proposed grant formula, notice that the taxes T_i are a product of the tax rate times the tax base. $T_i = t_i Y_i$, where Y_i is the per capita tax base in locality i, presumably the average property value in the locality. Therefore,

LeGrand's purchasing power/effort ratio is $\dfrac{T_i}{P_i t_i}=\dfrac{t_i Y_i}{P_i t_i}=\dfrac{Y_i}{P_i}$. $\dfrac{Y_i}{P_i}$ is referred to as the

fiscal capacity of the locality, a measure of its ability to provide public services. Therefore, LeGrand's purchasing power/effort ratio is equivalent to the fiscal capacity of a community.

LeGrand proposed establishing a target level of fiscal capacity, $\dfrac{Y_T}{P_T}$, and then using a set of grants-in-aid to bring each community to the target fiscal capacity. Let G_i be the per capita grant given by the state to locality i. Then G_i is set so that

$$\frac{T_i+G_i}{t_i P_i}=\frac{Y_T}{P_T}.$$

Alternatively,

$$\frac{T_i}{t_i P_i}+\frac{G_i}{t_i P_i}=\frac{Y_T}{P_T}.$$

Next bring $\dfrac{T_i}{t_i P_i}$ to the right-hand side:

$$\frac{G_i}{t_i P_i}=\frac{Y_T}{P_T}-\frac{T_i}{t_i P_i}=\frac{Y_T}{P_T}-\frac{Y_i}{P_i}.$$

Multiplying both sides by $t_i P_i$ yields

$$G_i = t_i \left(Y_T \left(\frac{P_i}{P_T} \right) - Y_i \right).$$

The per capita grant for locality i depends on its tax rate (its effort) and the amount of resources that would be required to bring its tax base up to the target tax base. The latter amount depends in turn on its cost advantage or disadvantage relative to the target locality, the ratio $\frac{P_i}{P_T}$. The relative cost advantages or disadvantages would depend on cost factors beyond the control of local governments, factors such as population density, the average age of the housing stock, crime rates, the poverty rate, and the number of schoolchildren relative to the population. Higher population densities and an older housing stock raise the costs of a given amount of fire protection; higher population densities and higher crime and poverty rates raise the costs to the police of protecting the residents; and higher poverty rates and more schoolchildren raise the costs of providing a given quality of education to each child.

If LeGrand's formula allowed for both positive and negative grants (taxes), then his proposal is to level every locality to the target locality. This is similar to the interpersonal equity condition for a single government under the Atkinson assumptions described in Chapter 5, in which everyone is leveled to the mean income. More realistically, there will not be a complete leveling to the target fiscal capacity. Fiscal equalization grants are typically only positive and therefore apply only to localities whose fiscal capacities are below the target fiscal capacity. Also, the total amount of grant funding allocated to a fiscal equalization program is always limited, such that not all localities below the target fiscal capacity can be raised to the target. Therefore, the state has two decisions to make: Where to set the target fiscal capacity and how much of the fiscal capacity gap to close. For example, it could set a high target level and close only a small percentage of the gap for each locality, so that many localities receive relatively small grants. Alternatively, it could set a low target level and close a fairly high percentage of the gap for the few localities below the low target level. LeGrand's formula is only suggestive as a practical guideline.

Actual equalization grants do consider differences in fiscal capacities along the lines that LeGrand suggested. They take into account differences in local incomes or tax bases, such as the Medicaid formula described above. And they sometimes consider differences in the costs of providing public services and in local tax rates as well.

COST DISEASE

William Baumol and Wallace Oates have offered an entirely different rationale for grants-in-aid from any discussed so far (Baumol and Oates, 1975, pp. 243–66). It is based on two premises. The first is that lower level governments suffer from a cost disease relative to the private sector: The services they provide do not experience the cost-reducing technological change and productivity increases that characterize production in the private sector. As a result, public sector services become ever more expensive over time relative to private sector goods and services. The second is that higher level governments are better able to raise tax revenues because they can levy more progressive taxes. Therefore, one way to cope with the lower level cost disease is to have the higher level governments raise taxes and give grants-in-aid to the lower level governments to finance their services. This is likely to be a more acceptable strategy than having the lower level governments try to finance their ever more costly services themselves with their own less progressive taxes.

The argument that lower level governments suffer from a cost disease is certainly plausible. Schoolchildren are educated in the local public school classrooms much as they were 50 years ago. Fire departments fight fires in much the same way as they have since the advent of the modern fire truck. And although police forces make use of computerized technologies that were unavailable 30 years ago, they still need officers in patrol cars and on foot to protect the public. Technical change and productivity increases have not been nearly as important for local governments as for the private sector. (Roughly the same point applies to state-provided services as well.) Consequently, it becomes relatively more expensive to educate children and provide for public safety over time, and this puts enormous pressure on local budgets.

The cost disease problem can be demonstrated with a very simple model. Suppose an economy produces two goods (services), a public good G and a private good Y, using labor as the only factor of production. The total labor supply is L_0, and it is allocated either to the public good, L_G, or the private good, L_Y: $L_0 = L_G + L_Y$. The labor market is competitive, which implies that all labor is employed (the economy is on its production possibilities frontier) and also that workers must earn the same wage whether they work in the public or private sector. The production of Y experiences technical change that increases the productivity of labor over time at the rate of r% per year, say 3% per year. Therefore, the production function for Y over time is $Y_t = (1 + r)^t b L_Y$. The production of G experiences no technical change over time, so that the production of G in each time period is $G_t = a L_G$.

With these production functions, the production possibilities frontier for the economy is linear (constant cost) but shifts up over time at rate r% per year, as illustrated in Figure 23.1. The production of G is on the horizontal axis and the production of Y is on the vertical axis. The slope of the frontier at any time t is $(-)\dfrac{b(1+r)^t}{a}$.[3] As discussed in Chapter 3, the slope of the frontier is the marginal rate of transformation between the two goods, $\text{MRT}_{Y,G}$, and the $\text{MRT}_{Y,G}$ is the ratio of the marginal costs of the two goods, $\dfrac{MC_G}{MC_Y}$. Also, if the goods markets are competitive, the price of each good equals its marginal cost, so that the $\text{MRT}_{Y,G} = \dfrac{P_G}{P_Y}$. Since only relative prices matter, assume $P_Y = MC_Y$ = 1. Therefore, because the public good G experiences no technical change, its marginal cost and price increase relative to the marginal cost and price of the private good Y at the rate of r% per year, equal to the rate of growth of productivity in the private sector. This is the cost disease of the public sector.

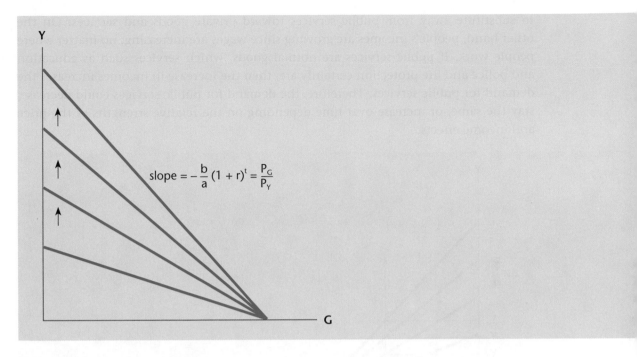

$$\text{slope} = -\frac{b}{a}(1+r)^t = \frac{P_G}{P_Y}$$

Figure 23.1

The intuition for the relative cost and price increase of G is that labor has to receive the same wage in either sector. With productivity rising at r% per year, wages also rise by r% per year. Private sector producers can cover the wage increase with the increased productivity of workers. Since productivity and wages are rising at the same rate, there is no change in private sector marginal costs over time and no change in price. In contrast, the public sector also has to offer wages that increase by r% per year to induce people to work there. But since the production of their services does not experience technical change, the only way they can cover the wage increase is to raise their prices by r% year. This is the same reason why tickets to plays on Broadway increase each year and are now well over $100, with no end to the increases in sight. The production of live theater is not subject to technical change; putting on a play always requires actors, a stage, and the various stagehands and set designers. Therefore, if the people involved in the production of plays are to be paid wages that keep up with wages generally, producers have no choice but to cover the wage increases with ever higher ticket prices.

Note, finally, that the increase in the costs and prices of public services *has nothing to do with inflation*. Our simple model assumes no inflation. Rather, the cost disease is a relative cost effect: The costs and prices of public services increase each year relative to the prices of private goods and services. This would be true no matter what the overall rate of inflation is.

An important question is what the cost disease does to the demand for government services. The answer depends on the price and income elasticities of demand. On the one hand, the increase in the relative costs and prices of public services induces people to substitute away from public services toward private goods and services. On the other hand, people's incomes are growing since wages are increasing, no matter where people work. If public services are normal goods, which services such as education and police and fire protection certainly are, then the increase in incomes increases the demand for public services. Therefore, the demand for public services could decrease, stay the same, or increase over time depending on the relative strengths of the price and income effects.

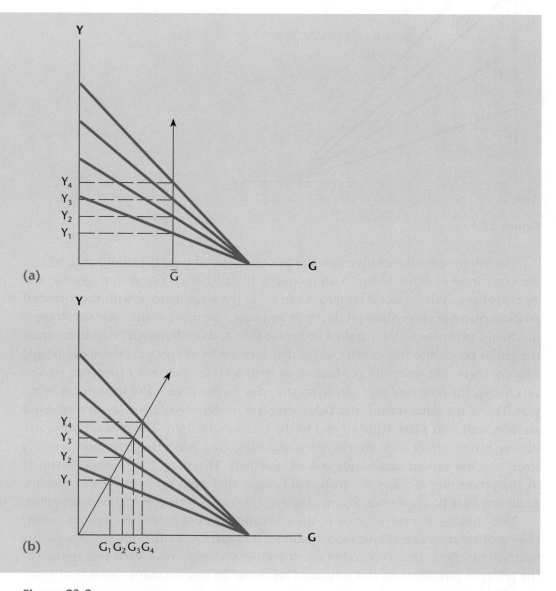

Figure 23.2

Figure 23.2 illustrates two of the possibilities. In Figure 23.2(a), the substitution and income effects cancel one another, so that people demand a constant amount of G over time. In Figure 23.2(b), people want more Y and more G over time, and in a constant proportion (for simplicity). Consider each of these cases.

G constant – With the amount of G constant, the labor allocated to G, L_G, is also constant. So, therefore, is the labor allocated to Y, L_Y. In addition, the ratio of total expenditures allocated to each good is constant. $P_G G$ and $P_Y Y$ both grow at an annual rate of r% over time, $P_G G$ because P_G is increasing at rate r and $P_Y Y$ because Y is increasing at rate r (with $P_Y = 1$). Suppose the local government levies a proportional tax at rate t on wage income to finance the expenditures on G. The tax revenues collected in each time period are $tW_t L_0$, and the total expenditures on G are $P_G G = w_t L_G$. Therefore, $tw_t L_0 = w_t L_G$, and

$$t = \frac{L_G}{L_0}.$$ The tax revenues rise at the rate of r% per year over time because w_t is increasing

at the rate of r% per year. Therefore, the government can raise the required revenues with a constant tax rate set at the ratio of the labor used in G to the total labor force. This should not cause problems for the government, although people might object to paying ever more in taxes over time for the same amount of public services (ever more taxes in real terms; remember, there is no inflation). Also, local governments in the United States use the property tax to raise almost 75% of their total tax revenue. The tax is levied on property values that are assessed by local tax assessors and adjusted periodically, every three years or so. People might object to having their property values (or their tax rates) continually revalued upward at an annual rate of r% just to meet the revenue requirement.

G increasing in proportion to Y – Matters are completely different if G is increasing over time, however. This appears to be the relevant case in the United States. Estimates of the demand for local public services typically find very low price elasticities, on the order of –.2 to –.4, and somewhat higher income elasticities, on the order of .7. The low price elasticities suggest that people have not reacted strongly so far to the cost disease of local public services. The income elasticities suggest that people view local public services as a necessity (income elasticity less than 1). The income elasticities have been sufficiently higher than the price elasticities so that the positive income effect on the demand for local public services has so far dominated the negative cost disease (relative price) effect on demand. The demand for state and local public services has grown steadily in real terms ever since World War II.

The effect of the rising demand for public services is dramatic. The only way that G can increase over time is if the amount of labor allocated to G, L_G, increases over time. Therefore, as time marches on, the amount of labor allocated to G must eventually approach L_0 in the limit, since the total labor supply is constant.[4] But even so, as Figure 23.2(b) indicates, the amount of Y produced can also increase indefinitely over time because of the continuous productivity increases in Y. Y increases so long as the amount of labor allocated to G increases each year at any rate less than r%.

Notice, however, the effect on local taxes. If the local government levies a proportional tax on income, the same formula applies as above. The proportional tax rate t is still equal to the ratio of $\frac{L_G}{L_0}$ in each time period. But with L_G increasing each year, the tax rate also has to increase each year. Eventually, t must approach 100% as L_G approaches L_0. People may well rebel at such steady tax rate increases over time, even though they have enough income after tax to buy increasing amounts of Y each year as well as pay the ever increasing taxes for the increased G. The cost disease is likely to dominate eventually and lower the demand for local public services with their relative prices rising each year.

This is where the tax advantage of the higher level governments comes into play, that they can levy progressive taxes more easily than local governments. For example, we have seen in Chapter 14 that U.S. federal personal income tax has graduated tax rates that rise from 10% on the lowest amounts of taxable income to 35% on the highest levels of national income. Baumol–Oates show that governments faced with cost disease can collect the required taxes in all time periods by establishing one set of graduated tax rates for all time. The demonstration of how to do this is beyond the scope of this text, but the intuition is clear enough. With graduated tax rates, the government automatically collects ever more tax revenues over time as people's incomes increase because the higher incomes keep pushing people into the higher tax brackets. Therefore, tax revenues increase more than proportionally with the increase in income, as required to finance public services afflicted with cost disease.

The Baumol–Oates argument is that people are more likely to accept ever higher tax payments if they happen automatically under a progressive tax system than if lower level governments have to keep increasing their tax rates. This is true even though people are equally well off with the lower or higher level financing. If Baumol–Oates are correct, then the best way to combat the cost disease and maintain a strong demand for local public services, such as education and police and fire protection, is to have higher level governments collect the revenues and pass them through to lower level governments with grants-in-aid. In their view, cost disease is a powerful rationale for grants-in-aid.

THE RESPONSE TO GRANTS-IN-AID

The empirical issue of import for grants-in-aid is how governments respond to the aid they receive. Public sector economists have devoted a huge amount of research effort to this issue without reaching any definite conclusions. They do agree, however, that the response to grants-in-aid depends on two factors: the formula by which the aid is offered; and the political process by which the receiving governments determine their tax and spending decisions. It is the latter that is difficult to model with much confidence.

GRANT-IN-AID FORMULAS

Grants-in-aid come in a number of different forms. The grant formulas vary along three dimensions: the grants can be unconditional or conditional; matching or non-matching; and open- or closed-ended.

An *unconditional grant* has no strings attached – it can be used by the receiving government for any purposes. The lump-sum distributional grants called for in our alternative model are unconditional grants. A *conditional* or *categorical grant*, in contrast, must be spent on a particular good or service. Most grants are conditional grants. Midway between these options is the *block grant*, which must be spent on a specific category of goods or services but can be allocated within the category however the receiving government wishes to do so. The U.S. grant to the states in support of the TANF public assistance program is an example. States must spend the funds on poor single-parent families, but otherwise they can do as they wish, such as provide monthly checks to the families, subsidize the education, training, and job search activities of the single parent, provide childcare, and cover the administrative expenses of running the various support services.

A *matching grant* is a per-unit or ad valorem subsidy to the services being aided. An example is the federal Medicaid grant to the states, which, as noted, pays anywhere from 50% to 83% of the state's medical expenses for people who qualify for Medicaid. A *non-matching grant* is a straight transfer of cash, such as the U.S. educational grants to low-income communities.

An *open-ended grant* has no limit on the amount of aid that is available to the receiving government. The Medicaid grant is an example. The federal government pays the matching percentage on all Medicaid expenses incurred by each state, no matter how large the expenses. A *closed-ended grant* places a maximum on the amount of grant funds available to the receiving government. Only matching grants can be open-ended in practice. If a non-matching grant were open-ended, the receiving government would use the grant to finance the entire amount of the aided service if the grant were a conditional or block grant, or the entire amount of its expenditures if the grant were unconditional.

Economists make use of consumer theory to think about how governments would react to the different formula options. That is, they think of the receiving government as if it were a consumer maximizing its utility subject to a budget constraint and consider how the formula options affect the budget constraint. As such, the effects on the government are the same as the effects of various kinds of transfers to an individual that we discussed in Chapter 10.

Figures 23.3 and 23.4 illustrate. In each figure, the receiving government is assumed to spend all its revenues on two services: education, E, and all other goods and services, O. The prices of E and O are each assumed to be one, for simplicity. The line AB in each figure is the receiving government's budget line from its own taxes and fees, before it receives a grant-in-aid. The government is in equilibrium at point H on indifference curve I_0 before receiving aid, spending E_H of its own funds on education and O_H on all other goods and services.

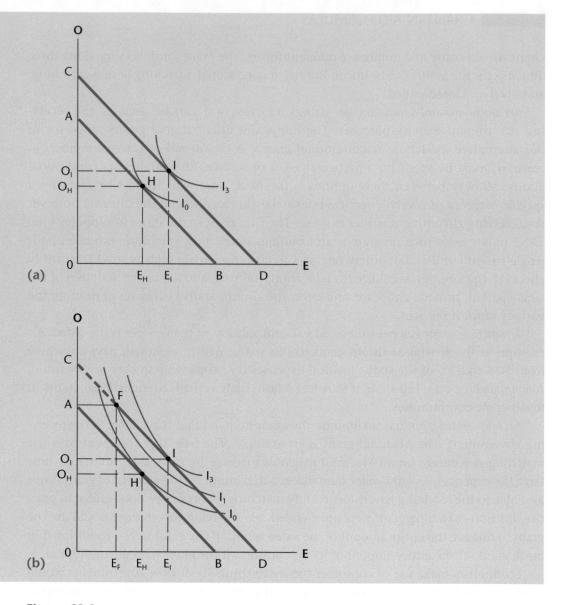

Figure 23.3

Figure 23.3 illustrates the effects on the budget line of an unconditional grant and a conditional non-matching grant. Both grants are necessarily closed-ended. In Figure 23.3(a), an unconditional grant shifts the budget line to the right (or upward) parallel to the government's own budget line AB by the amount of the grant. The new budget line with the grant is CD, with the amount of the grant equal to BD (or AC). The government's equilibrium with the grant is point I on indifference curve I_3 on budget line CD. It spends E_I on education and O_I on all other goods and services. I lies to the northeast of H, on the assumption that both E and O are normal goods.

In Figure 23.3(b), the government receives a non-matching grant conditional that it be spent on education. The amount of the grant is the same as the unconditional grant in Figure 23.3(a). The conditional education grant shifts the government's budget line to the right and parallel by the amount AF or BD. The only difference relative to the unconditional grant is that the rightward shift begins at point A, so that the new budget line with the grant is FD. The points on the dotted line CF, which were available to the government under the unconditional grant, are not available under the conditional grant. The most of all other goods and services the government can purchase with the conditional education grant is 0A, financed entirely out of its own taxes and fees.

Figure 23.3(b) illustrates two possible new equilibria, F on indifference curve I_1, and I on indifference curve I_3. Which equilibrium the receiving government chooses is easily revealed by its own spending. If it spends more than the grant funds on E, that is, uses some of its own taxes and fees on E, then the equilibrium is at I, the same as with the unconditional grant. The condition to spend the funds on E makes no difference to the government if it chooses to spend more than AF (= BD) on E. If, instead, the government spends none of its own revenues on E, then it is forced to the so-called corner solution F. But I is the relevant equilibrium under all the major U.S. grant programs, since governments always spend more than the amount of the grant funds on the aided services. In other words, receiving governments should consider the major closed-ended conditional grants as equivalent to unconditional grants of the same amount.

In Figure 23.4(a), the government receives an open-ended matching grant for E. The grant rotates its budget line from AB to AD as the matching rate lowers the effective price of E to the government by the amount of the matching rate. The matching rate is BD/0D. The government is in equilibrium at point J on indifference curve I_2, spending E_J on education and O_J on all other goods and services. The government spends LK of its own resources on E_J and KJ from the grant funds.

In Figure 23.4(b), the government receives a closed-ended matching grant for E. The matching rate is the same as in Figure 23.4(a). The budget line rotates outward from point A as in Figure 23.4(a), but only until it reaches the maximum allowable grant, assumed to be GF in the figure. Beyond F, the government has to pay the full price itself for each additional unit of E, so that the budget line becomes parallel to the original budget line AB. Therefore, the new budget line with the grant is line AFM.

At this point, the analysis is similar to the analysis of the conditional grant in Figure 23.3(b). If the government spends more on E than E_F, the maximum amount of E supported by the matching grant, then the grant is equivalent to the unconditional grant. The government is in equilibrium at point I on indifference curve I_3, spending E_I on education and O_I on all other goods and services. This is the same equilibrium as in Figure 23.3(a), given that the maximum grant GF is assumed to be equal to the unconditional grant BD in Figure 23.3(a). Neither the condition to spend on E nor the matching rate should have any effect on the receiving government relative to receiving an unconditional grant so long as the government exceeds the maximum allowable grant. In fact, governments always do exceed the maximum allowable funds under any of the major closed-ended grant programs.

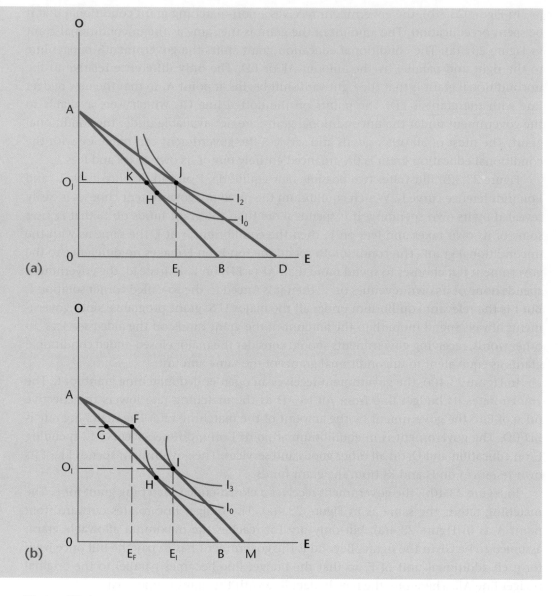

Figure 23.4

The intuition for the equivalence to an unconditional grant is that the matching rate has a price or substitution effect only if the matching rate applies on the *margin*, to the *last* units of E purchased. This would be true only if the government chose to be on the budget line segment AF, and receive less than the maximum allowable funds. Otherwise, the matching grant has only an income effect, the same as an unconditional grant. The price to the receiving government for additional units of E beyond E_F is one, just as with the unconditional grant.

To summarize, consumer theory suggests that receiving governments should react in one of two ways to the major grant programs. If the grant-in-aid is an open-ended matching grant, then the grant reduces the effective price of the aided service by the amount of the matching rate, and has both a substitution and an income effect on the government's demand for the service. If the grant is closed-ended, either non-matching or matching, and the government spends more on an aided item than the limit provided by the grant, then the grant should be viewed as equivalent to an unconditional grant of the same size as the maximum allowable grant. In fact, governments always spend more than the maximum allowable grant under all the major U.S. grant programs.[5]

THE POLITICS OF GRANTS-IN-AID

Trying to model how receiving governments respond to grants-in-aid requires much more than an understanding of the economic equivalences between different grant-in-aid formulas. The more difficult problem is deciding how governments determine their spending and revenue decisions in the first place. The decisions are arrived at through some kind of political process; they are not simply economic in nature. As such, a model that tries to explain governments' responses to grants-in-aid is only as good as its ability to model the underlying political process that generates their responses. Unfortunately, the political forces acting on spending and revenue decisions become numerous and varied once communities grow and move beyond the simplest one-person, one-vote direct democracies of the small village. No one model can hope to capture all the political nuances that come into play in large communities and state (provincial) governments.

Nonetheless, one has to begin somewhere, and the majority of economists have essentially chosen to begin with the small village. The most popular choice by far for developing empirical models of local (and even state or provincial) governments' decisions on spending, revenues, and grants-in-aid is the median voter model, which we introduced in Chapter 22. The fundamental assumption of the model is that a government's spending and revenue decisions are those that match the preferences of the median voter in its jurisdiction, the voter whose preferences on spending and revenues lie in the middle of the preferences of all the citizens. This assumption is most likely to apply, if at all, in the direct democracy of the small village. Economists know that the median voter is unlikely to be decisive on spending and revenue decisions in larger communities, in which the political process is some kind of representative government, not a direct democracy (and even less so at the state level). Nonetheless, the median voter model is chosen because it is the most tractable of the possible political choices for empirical work.

Having assumed that the spending and revenue decisions we see reflect the preferences of the median voter within a community, the question remains how to bring this assumption to the data. This is typically done by means of a second heroic assumption, that the median voter also has the median values of all the characteristics of the citizens that are likely to affect spending and revenue decisions, such as income, family size, educational attainment, and property values. This assumption is also a matter of convenience. For example, the U.S. Census Bureau publishes data for localities on their median incomes, family size, property values, and so forth. If it is assumed that the median voter has the median values of all these variables, then one can estimate a regression equation of the standard form for the demand for each public service because it is the demand equation of the median voter.

As an example, assume that the demand for education, E^d, is a function of all these economic and demographic variables, plus the relevant price of education and any grants-in-aid received by the government. Let's focus on price, income, and grants-in-aid and write the relationship to be estimated as

$$E^d = f^n(P_E, Y_{med}, A/N; \vec{Z})$$

where:

E^d = the demand for education defined by some education output variable, presumed to be the output preferred by the median voter

P_E = the effective price of the education output, reduced by any open-ended matching grants received from higher-level governments

Y_{med} = the income of the median voter

A/N = the per capita closed-ended grants for education received by the government to help finance the educational output; A is the maximum allowable grant received and N is the population of the locality

$\vec{Z}$ = a vector of other individual and community characteristics, with the individual characteristics equal to their median values and therefore assumed to apply to the median voter.

The two items of interest regarding grants-in-aid are the responses to open-ended matching rates, if applicable, and to the closed-ended per capita grants-in-aid. The effect of the matching grants can only be estimated if the matching rates vary across the receiving governments. They do for the Medicaid grants, but for many grants they do not. If they do, then they can be entered into the regression equation as an adjustment to the price term.

Regarding closed-ended grants, the analysis using consumer theory above is directly relevant because the equation is estimating the preferences of one of the consumers in each jurisdiction, the median voter. The theory tells us that, for the important grants, it should not matter whether the grants are conditional grants for education or conditional grants for anything else. All closed-ended grants should have the same effect on the median voter as an unconditional grant of the same size. Moreover, an unconditional grant should have the same effect on the median voter's demand for any public services as an increase in his or her income.

The only remaining issue is whether a dollar of a grant-in-aid per capita received by a government would be viewed by the median voter as equivalent to a dollar increase in her income, and the answer is almost certainly "no." Local governments rely on property tax for revenues. If the government receives a closed-ended grant-in-aid, the grant lowers the revenues that need to be raised through property tax. Therefore, the mean or average reduction in property taxes per person is the grant per capita, A/N.

But the distribution of property values within localities is skewed in the same way as the distribution of incomes. The median property value (income) is much less than the mean property value (income). This happens because the relatively few extremely high property values (incomes) at the top of the distribution increase the mean property value (income) but have no effect on the median property value (income), the property value (income) of the person in the middle of the distribution. Therefore the value of the per capita grant to the median voter is $\left(\dfrac{V_{med}}{V_{mean}}\right)\left(\dfrac{A}{N}\right)$, where V_{med} is the median property value and V_{mean} is the mean property value. $\dfrac{V_{med}}{V_{mean}}$ is less than one, which implies that an additional dollar of grant-in-aid per capita is worth less to the median voter than an additional dollar of income, Y_{med}. The coefficient estimate on A/N in the regression equation should be smaller than the coefficient estimate on Y_{med}.

The estimated responses to closed-ended grants-in-aid based on the median voter are much different from their expected values in two respects. First, governments appear to overrespond to grants-in-aid. The coefficient estimates on A/N typically exceed the coefficient estimates on Y_{med}, directly opposite to the prediction of the theory. Second, conditions on grants matter. Closed-ended education grants have a much greater effect on education spending than closed-ended grants for other services, and the same is true of conditional grants for all the other services. Theory predicts that the conditions should not matter, that all closed-ended grants should have the same effect on each spending category, no matter what services the grants are meant to support. Economists refer to this pattern of estimates as the *flypaper effect*, because money appears to stick where it hits. For instance, a closed-ended grant for education appears to stimulate spending on education beyond what it should. Moreover, the flypaper effect is estimated to be very large by most researchers.

The flypaper effect is no doubt encouraging to the granting governments. They presumably give conditional grants because they want to stimulate spending on the services receiving aid. Nonetheless, economists are puzzled by the flypaper effect and have offered many possible explanations for it, none entirely convincing. One problem at the outset is that the median voter is almost certainly not a very accurate model for most governments. On the one hand, the preferences of the median voter are not likely to be decisive within most jurisdictions. On the other hand, even if they were decisive, the median voter is not likely to have the median values of all the explanatory variables that relate to individual characteristics. To give but one of many possible examples, low-income people are less likely to vote than middle- and high-income people. Consequently, the median voter among people who vote undoubtedly has more than the median level of income or property value.

Another problem is that a fully rational response to grants-in-aid by any voter, median or otherwise, is a difficult decision. The people in a locality who benefit from a particular grant-in-aid are also citizens of the higher level government that gave the aid, which means that their taxes to the higher level government helped pay for the grant. Generally speaking, the citizens of higher income jurisdictions pay more in taxes to finance grant-in-aid programs than the amount of grants their jurisdictions receive from these programs, and vice versa for citizens in lower income jurisdictions. Almost all the estimates of grants-in-aid have ignored the need to pay for the grants-in-aid. But do voters ignore the higher level government's taxes that support the grants? If they do not, then the estimating model is not correct.

Whatever the explanation for the flypaper effect may be, it remains the most consistent and significant finding of the empirical literature on grants-in-aid. The effect is so large and so pervasive in the empirical studies of grants-in-aid that economists are convinced it exists, even if they are unsure why this should be.

A New Behavioral Public Sector Economics?

As modern economic theory developed throughout the 19th and most of the 20th century, economists simply took individuals' preferences over their goods and factors as a given. The given preferences are assumed to be well behaved and consistent over time, and can be represented by some utility function. In addition, people are rational. They attempt to maximize their utility functions subject to their budget constraints, whether in an annual or a lifetime context. These assumptions imply that people reveal their preferences through the economic choices that they make, and economic theorists developed techniques for recovering the underlying utility functions from estimates of individuals' demands for goods and supplies of factors. This is the theory of individual behavior that underlies mainstream public sector economics.

About 25 years ago, some economists began to question the long-standing assumption that preferences were a given. They turned to research by psychologists, sociologists, and neural scientists to learn about how preferences are formed and what can cause preferences to change. They then incorporated this information about preferences into their economic analyses. The study of how preference formation affects economic decisions and events became known as *behavioral economics*.

Interest in behavioral research spread rapidly, to the point that behavioral economics has become one of the new frontiers of economic analysis. The attraction of this new line of research is easy to understand – it is posing a stern challenge to the received mainstream theory. Behavioral economists are discovering that people often behave quite differently from the standard assumptions of modern economic theory. They exhibit many "biases" and "mistakes" relative to what would appear to be in their rational self-interests, and these biases and mistakes have potentially far-reaching implications for all the disciplines within economics, including public sector economics. The question arises: Are we possibly on the threshold of a new "behavioral public sector economics" that will replace, or at least substantially alter, both mainstream public sector economics and public choice?

RELEVANT BIASES AND MISTAKES FOR PUBLIC SECTOR THEORY

Three of the research findings of behavioral economics would appear to be especially important for public sector economics: social preferences, time inconsistencies, and the contextual nature of behavior.

Social preferences – The standard microeconomic textbook model of the consumer assumes that people are entirely self-interested. Their utilities depend only on their own goods, services, and factors of production, with no thought given to anyone else. This assumption had been relaxed on occasion by both mainstream and public choice economists. An example is the analysis of Pareto-optimal redistributions described in Chapter 10, in which the nonpoor exhibit altruism towards the poor. They care about the poor's consumption of certain goods or their overall well-being. When people care about other people, they are said to have social preferences.

Behavioral research has uncovered important nuances to the nature of people's altruistic impulses. For example, people appear to care not only about the economic fortunes of other people in certain contexts, but also about their character. The altruism described in Chapter 10 is called *pure altruism* since the character of the poor is not at issue. In contrast, behavioral research suggests that altruism most likely has an important reciprocal component. People appear to be both conditional cooperators and willing punishers. They cooperate with and care for others if they find that others behave the same way. Conversely, they are quite willing to punish people who behave selfishly and attempt to take advantage of others. People who take into account the character of others in this way are said to exhibit *reciprocal altruism*.

Inconsistent preferences – People often behave in a manner that implies that they have inconsistent preferences over time. The most common bias is to give far too much weight to immediate outcomes relative to the predictions of the standard model. For example, suppose people are faced with a choice of receiving an amount X at a given point in time or a much larger amount Y at some later date, say a month later. Y is sufficiently larger than X so that the discounted value of Y exceeds X at the time that X is offered. If the two dates are today versus one month from now, people often choose X, whereas if the dates are 12 and 13 months from now, these same people often choose Y. Y is always the proper choice according to the standard theory since Y has the higher discounted present value. It should not matter when the two options are offered.

People who choose X now are said to suffer from a *self-control problem*. They yield to the temptation of the immediate gain and they do so even though they regret the choice of X at a later date, as it becomes clear to them that Y would have been the better choice. Addictions to smoking, drinking, and drugs are common examples of this behavior. People with self-control problems are often described as having at least two selves, each with a separate set of preferences; an immediate self, who gives too much weight to the present, and a long-run self who properly weights all time periods and therefore understands what choices would maximize lifetime utility.

The contextual nature of behavior – Behavioral economists have discovered that people's preferences and their resulting behavior are often highly dependent on the situation or context they are in. For example, they respond differently to identical situations depending on how the options available to them are described or framed, and what other audio and visual cues they are receiving. We saw one instance of this in the public good experiments described in Chapter 8: The subjects contribute significantly more to the public good, against their narrow self-interest, if they are told that choosing the public good benefits the other subjects (positive framing) than if they are told that choosing the private good harms the other students (negative framing).

Another important contextual discovery is that people tend to compartmentalize decisions rather than seeing each decision as part of an overall decision process. This mistake appears to be especially common in the way that people view different assets in their portfolios. Suppose, for example, that housing prices are falling while the values of stocks and other financial assets are rising. Many people resist selling a house below a price that they think they should get for it, even though it is clearly in their interest to sell quickly, take the loss, and then partially or fully recoup the loss by investing in the assets whose prices are rising. Instead, they view the house in and of itself, rather than as one of many assets that they hold, which leads them to suffer even larger losses as they keep the house on the market.

IMPLICATIONS FOR PUBLIC SECTOR THEORY

The government responds to market failures in one of two ways in the mainstream public sector theory. It either takes over the particular service (for example defense, mass rail transit) or it leaves the failed market operating and tries to change individuals' or firms' behavior to achieve efficient or equitable outcomes. If it follows the second strategy, it attempts to change behavior either by improving information (for example providing information on product quality or monitoring safety in the workplace) or by changing individuals' or firms' budget constraints, that is, their incomes or profits or the prices they face (for example lump-sum taxes and transfers, Pigovian taxes or subsidies for externalities). Behavioral economics opens up a whole new set of policy options for influencing behavior that respond directly to individuals' or firms' behavioral proclivities. Here are a few examples of how social preferences, self-control problems, and contextual behavior can significantly influence the analysis of some important public sector issues relative to the standard mainstream analysis. As such, they can be viewed as examples of a new behavioral public sector economics.

SOCIAL PREFERENCES AND TAX COMPLIANCE

The standard mainstream analysis of tax compliance is presented in Chapter 17. It assumes that self-interested individuals will always try to exploit the private information they have about their incomes to hide income from the tax authorities and evade paying taxes. They would pay no taxes at all if they could get away with that. The way to reduce tax evasion is to audit some tax returns and impose penalties on cheaters so that it is in their self-interests to increase their compliance with the tax laws.

Suppose, however, that taxpayers exhibit the kind of reciprocal altruism suggested by the behavioral economists. This raises a whole new set of issues in thinking about tax compliance. In the first place, it is often noted that tax compliance is much higher than would be implied by the standard model, given the fairly low audit probabilities and fines imposed if caught cheating. This could be because people are conditional coopera-tors. They are quite willing to pay their taxes if they believe that other taxpayers are also so inclined and that the government is honest and attempting to promote the public interest in efficiency and equity. They are also willing punishers, however, so they would expect cheaters to be fined if caught. But the government has to be very careful in setting its auditing and penalty strategies. If it audits broadly and fines people for even minor instances of noncompliance, it risks giving the impression that "everyone cheats." This could turn the majority of people away from being conditional cooperators, to the point that they come to view their tax payments as something they have to do rather than something they are willing to do. Reaching this kind of tipping point could greatly increase the propensity to evade taxes. It may well be better for the government to audit relatively infrequently and impose fines only for relatively large evasions in order to maintain the public's goodwill as conditional cooperators. This possibility would not be considered from the perspective of the standard mainstream theory.

INCONSISTENT PREFERENCES, SAVING, AND SIN TAXES

The idea that people have time inconsistent preferences in the nature of temptation or self-control problems raises many economic issues. We will briefly consider saving for retirement and the sin taxes on cigarettes and alcohol as examples.

Saving for retirement

Among the more important economic problems facing the United States today (2007) is the remarkably low rate of personal saving. Personal saving out of income actually turned negative in 2005 and 2006, the first instances of negative personal saving since the Great Depression. The primary mainstream justification for government policies to promote saving comes from the macroeconomic perspective of growth theory, that increased saving would permit huge increases in average consumption per person in the long run.

When behavioral economists look at the low saving rate, they see a number of their research findings also coming into play in designing policies to promote saving. The most important is that large numbers of people probably do not save enough because they have self-control problems. They fall to the temptation of consuming too much today even though they will eventually regret their decisions. This explanation for the low saving rate certainly seems plausible, especially regarding saving for retirement. Recall from Chapter 12 that, in 2004, the median financial wealth of people near retirement in the United States, those between the ages of 55 and 64, was under $30,000. Surely a large number of people in this cohort near the median level of income could have saved more for their retirement and now regret that they did not. Recall also from Chapter 12 that one of the principal justifications for requiring people to save for retirement through the Social Security system was that they would not save enough on their own. For younger people with self-control problems, a government-mandated savings program directly increases their utility because it helps them overcome their temptation to consume too much. Similarly, providing tax-advantaged retirement savings securities such as IRAs and 401Ks, financed by taxes, has the advantage of offering large gains to those with self-control problems, while placing only relatively small second-order costs on those without such problems. The costs are the deadweight losses from the tax and asset allocation distortions that such programs generate.

Other findings from behavioral economics come into play as well in designing incentives to save. The experience with 401K plans shows that people are highly responsive to framing. The default option for 401K plans used to be nonparticipation; employees had to activate their own participation in their company's plan. When the default option was changed to participation (people have to choose not to participate in the plan), the percentage of people participating in 401K plans rose dramatically. This strong response to framing, combined with people's tendency to compartmentalize their asset allocation decisions, suggests that specific targeted attempts to promote savings such as through tax-advantaged IRAs and 401Ks may dominate a broad-based approach to encouraging saving, such as replacing the income tax with a consumption tax that leaves saving untaxed. IRAs and 401Ks may help people focus on the need to save more for retirement, especially when accompanied by advertising for these securities that underscores the advantages of saving for retirement. Providing such positive framing and cues would be more difficult with a replacement of the income tax by a consumption tax, precisely because it promotes saving in general and not just saving for retirement.

A final point is that any public policy designed to help people overcome self-control problems, whether to promote saving or otherwise, raises a difficult normative question. If people with self-control problems have inconsistent preferences described by an immediate self and a long-run self, which preferences are to count in assessing the social welfare effects of these policies? Do both selves count in the normative welfare analysis or only the more beneficial long-run self? If the former, what weights should be assigned to the two sets of preferences? If only the latter, then two further issues arise.

One issue is that there is now a clear break between the positive and normative sides of public sector analysis. The mistakes uncovered by behavioral economists suggest that economists should pay attention to the immediate self when designing policies to help these people, since the goal is to help them overcome their temptation. At the same time, however, economists evaluate the social welfare gains from these same polices in terms of the beneficial long-run self. In other words, positive economic analysis turns on the immediate preferences and normative economic analysis on the long-run preferences. A number of economists have adopted this position. In their view, the main advantage of behavioral research has been to improve the positive economic analysis of government policies.

A second issue is that basing social welfare analysis on the "true," beneficial long-run preferences places economists on a slippery slope of defining exactly what those preferences are. Unlike the standard theory, these preferences cannot necessarily be uncovered by the choices people make because, absent government policies to overcome the self-control problems, their choices tend to be determined by their harmful immediate selves. This leads one into the dangerous position of having to define what the true, beneficial preferences ought to be, and different people can easily reach different conclusions on this score. Who can really say with any confidence what people's true preferences are if they are not reflected in the choices they make? An economist might be tempted to say that the true preferences must be those described by the standard mainstream theory of the rational, utility-maximizing consumer. But if behavioral economists can show that people violate at least some of the assumptions of the mainstream model of utility maximization in certain important contexts, such as in the decision to save for retirement, why should one be confident that the other assumptions of the model still apply in these contexts? In short, the findings of behavioral economics tend to place normative policy analysis on very shaky foundations.

Sin taxes

Another example of a government policy that is placed in a different light by the findings of behavioral economics are the so-called sin taxes on cigarettes and alcohol. The traditional mainstream justification for these taxes has been an externality argument, a justification that has merit, given the dangers to nonsmokers of second-hand smoke and the highway accidents and fatalities caused by drunk drivers. Behavioral economists would also emphasize that cigarette smoking and alcohol are addictions that result from self-control problems, and this can change one's view of the taxes placed on them. For instance, one criticism of the sin taxes from the mainstream perspective, at least in the United States, is that they contribute to the increasing inequality of income because these two addictions disproportionately afflict people with low incomes. Yet if the taxes help people overcome their addictions, then they almost certainly make them better off. The utility gains reverse the perceived incidence of the sin taxes from the mainstream perspective, which views the taxes as making smokers and drinkers worse off.

THE IMPACT OF BEHAVIORAL ECONOMICS: SOME CONCLUDING OBSERVATIONS

To repeat an earlier question: Are we on the cusp of a new age dawning? Will behavioral economics eventually replace mainstream economic theory as the foundation of economic analysis for all the disciplines of economics, including public sector economics? It is still far too early to know.

Behavioral economics has its critics among mainstream economists. The following four reservations are commonly registered. First, and perhaps foremost, many economic theorists have noted that behavioral economics lacks the unifying theoretical foundation that it needs to become compelling as a general theory of economic behavior. At present, behavioral economics strikes them as little more than a set of explanations about behavior in a wide variety of specific contexts. It is nowhere near ready to replace the mainstream theory of the rational, utility-maximizing consumer. Second, many of the biases and mistakes described by behavioral economists, especially those related to social preferences, have been observed in laboratory experiments conducted with undergraduate students. There are a number of reasons to question whether the results of these experiments translate into real-world settings.[1] Third, although many people undoubtedly make the kinds of biases and mistakes described by behavioral economists, it is not clear that they have much impact in most market settings. So long as markets are reasonably competitive, and at least some people are the rational utility maximizers of mainstream theory, then the rational people will arbitrage away the biases and mistakes to their advantage. Whether people will continue to exhibit the biases and make the mistakes that put them at a disadvantage relative to rational people is problematic. Finally, as noted above, many mainstream economists have argued that the biases and mistakes uncovered by behavioral economists should not affect the normative, social welfare analysis of economic policies.

These criticisms notwithstanding, many mainstream economists concede that behavioral economists have uncovered patterns of nonstandard behavior that are common enough to be taken seriously. They would encourage further research along these lines, and they hold out some hope that further advances in psychology and neural science might uncover the theoretical foundations that are currently lacking. Regarding public sector economics, there is widespread acceptance that behavioral economics has had an impact on the design of economic policies from a positive perspective, as the examples above indicate. Also, the natural arbitraging away of biases and mistakes that occurs in competitive markets does not apply to the public sector. So, for example, if people are influenced by how issues are framed, then politicians might be able to gain acceptance for their policies more by how they present them than by how they might contribute to the public interest in promoting efficiency and equity. If there is indeed a new behavioral public sector economics, one of its main themes is likely to be the development of new institutions and mechanisms that help people in democratic societies focus on the content rather than the presentation of public sector issues and policies.[2]

Notes

CHAPTER 2

1. We will also see in Chapter 5 that social mobility itself can make it difficult for society to achieve its preferred distribution of income. In this case, process equity works against achieving end-results equity.

CHAPTER 3

1. These figures are for 2007.
2. Students who have taken intermediate microeconomics will recognize the $2 \times 2 \times 2$ model that we present in Chapter 3 because it is the standard model of an economy that appears in all the undergraduate microeconomic theory texts. The main results should be familiar, but be sure you understand them before proceeding to Chapter 4.
3. For example, suppose the marginal rates of substitution are equal at 2/1. They are indifferent to a trade of 2Y for 1X in either direction. If person #1 were to give up 3Y in exchange for 1X, then person #2 would be better off since he is willing to accept only 2Y in exchange for 1X. Person #1 is worse off, however, because she is willing to give up only 2Y for an additional X, but she is giving up 3Y for the 1X.
4. $I_1 = P_L \cdot L_1^* + P_K \cdot K_1^*$, where P_L and P_K are the market-determined prices for labor and capital, which person #1 takes as given. L_1^* and K_1^* are assumed to be fixed and independent of P_L and P_K.
5. We will ignore the minus sign from now on because it is only a directional marker, indicating that the consumer must give up X to purchase more Y, and vice versa, along the budget line. The MRS to which it will be compared is also a negative number, since X and Y must trade off along an indifference curve.

483

6. $MRS_{X,L} = \dfrac{\Delta X}{\Delta L}\bigg|_{U=\bar{U}} = \dfrac{P_L}{P_X}$ and $MRS_{X,K} = \dfrac{\Delta X}{\Delta K}\bigg|_{U=\bar{U}} = \dfrac{P_K}{P_X}$. Dividing $MRS_{X,L}$ by $MRS_{X,K}$

yields $MRS_{L,K} = \dfrac{\Delta K}{\Delta L}\bigg|_{U=\bar{U}} = \dfrac{P_L}{P_K}$ for all consumers. But $MRTS_{K,L} = \dfrac{P_L}{P_K}$ across all firms

for the economy to be on its production possibilities frontier, as demonstrated in the chapter. Therefore $MRS_{L,K} = MRTS_{K,L} = \dfrac{P_L}{P_K}$ for all consumers and firms.

CHAPTER 4

1. $\dfrac{\Delta W}{\Delta U^i} > 0$ implies that if ΔU^i is positive then ΔW is positive, and if ΔU^i is negative

   then ΔW is also negative.

2. The social marginal rate of substitution along a social welfare indifference curve is

   the ratio of the marginal social welfare weights, $\dfrac{\Delta W}{\Delta U_1} \Big/ \dfrac{\Delta W}{\Delta U_2}$.

3. The preferences are understood to be "right minded." People cannot be in favor of murder except possibly in self-defense.

CHAPTER 5

1. The annual survey in the United States is the Current Population Survey, which began in 1947. It currently surveys about 60,000 family households and unrelated individuals, which is a large enough sample to be representative of the entire population.

2. Notice that this result does not depend on Atkinson's even stronger assumption that the social welfare function is utilitarian. It would apply to any individualistic social welfare function that gave the same marginal social welfare weight to people with the same income.

3. U.S. Census Bureau, Current Population Survey, March 2005, Historical Income Tables, Households, Table H-4.

4. We choose distributions with equal means to focus entirely on the social welfare implications of inequality.

5. In the second case, if $e = 0$, then $W^A = HY_{ede}$. But W^A also equals $\sum_{h=1}^{H} Y_h^A = HY_M$. Thus $Y_{ede} = Y_M$.

6. For example, under complete mobility with all $p_{ij} = .2$, the population is spread equally over the five income classes after only one time period, no matter what distribution the government's policies have set in the previous time period.

CHAPTER 6

1. Government institutions are far from perfect, of course, so that government intervention may not bring the economy to its utility possibilities frontier either. Economists speak of government failures, meaning that governments are unable to undertake the policies necessary to correct market failures and achieve efficient allocations. As a practical matter, society often has to weigh the relative benefits and costs of government failures versus market failures when deciding whether government intervention is appropriate.

2. Alternatively, the equilibrium price equates the marginal rate of substitution (MRS) and the marginal rate of transformation (MRT), where the MRS and MRT are defined in terms of paper and another good whose price and marginal cost are equal to $1. Economists refer to this other good as the *numeraire good*. Since its price is $1, units of the numeraire good can be thought of as dollars of income. Therefore, the MRS measures marginal value as the income each consumer is willing to give up to consume one more unit of paper. The MRT is the ratio of the private marginal costs of producing paper and the numeraire good. With the marginal cost of the numeraire good equal to $1, the MRT is the private marginal cost of producing paper. As we saw in Chapter 2, equating the MRS and MRT between any two goods is one of the Pareto-optimal conditions required to be on the utility possibilities frontier if there are no externalities associated with the goods.

3. For example, if an unskilled worker can produce 21 units of output per hour and receives a wage of $7 per hour, then $\frac{MP_l}{P_l} = \frac{21}{\$7} = \frac{3}{\$1}$. The worker produces 3 units per dollar spent on the worker.

4. We could have used water pollution instead of air pollution in our example. Nothing in what follows changes by substituting water pollution for air pollution.

5. Think here of an even more finely targeted tax that is levied on the amount of harmful pollutants contained in the smoke emitted by the factory. Responses to a tax on water may also be highly variable, such as choosing different ways of disposing of solid and chemical waste products, or different ways of cleaning or cooling parts of the production process, or simply paying the tax.

CHAPTER 7

1. The price might not be P_p in a one-on-one bargain. One side may be able to take more of the consumer surplus from the exchange depending on relative bargaining power. For example, the person may be able to charge the firm the difference between MC and MB for each unit and thereby capture all the benefits from the exchange of the pollution rights. But the efficient amount of pollution PR* would still obtain, which is the essence of the Coase Theorem.

2. The series of taxes iterates to t_{opt} so long as the market is stable. Even so, the taxes could swing the market from outputs that are much too high to outputs that are much too low depending on the shapes of the demand and supply curves. In that case, it would take many iterations for the government to approximate t_{opt}. The government needs to be a bit lucky in following this strategy.

3. If t were set to the aggregate marginal damages of the pollution, then $t \cdot \dfrac{dP}{dq}$ would be the aggregate marginal damages of an additional unit of output at the optimum, and the right-hand side of the equation would be the full social marginal cost of pollution as indicated in previous diagrams. The tax is more likely to be set to meet a given pollution target, however.

4. Another possibility is to offer the subsidy $s\bar{P}$ to both the existing firms and all potential entrants. In this way, the potential entrants do not have to enter the industry to obtain the subsidy so the entry does not occur. The subsidy in this case is truly lump sum since it does not vary with entry. But identifying all potential entrants could be problematic.

5. This assumes that the subsidies are paid for by lump-sum taxes on other people. Recall that in these chapters on allocation problems, we are assuming that no other inefficiencies exist other than those specifically being discussed.

CHAPTER 8

1. The example in the text is from Tideman and Tulloch (1976).

CHAPTER 9

1. The total value to consumers at any output can be represented as the area under the demand curve to that output, and the total cost to the firm as the area under the marginal cost curve to that output. Therefore, the net value of the exchange, total value minus total cost, attains its maximum value at Q_{eff}, at the intersection of D and MC.

2. The United States has devised all kinds of names for the prices charged by the natural monopolies. We pay: electric *rates*; highway, bridge, and tunnel *tolls*; admissions and parking *fees* at beaches and parks; and subway *fares*. They can all be viewed as taxes whatever their name may be because they are publicly determined prices.

3. More generally, Friedman's distrust of public regulation was such that he thought private monopoly would be preferred to regulation in most instances of natural monopoly (Friedman, 1962, 27–30, 128–9).

4. We are assuming that the firm distributes the software by allowing consumers to download it from the Internet for a fee, since MC = 0. Distributing the program on CDs would raise the marginal costs and lead to a lower quantity and higher price than (Q_M, P_M).

5. The software firms would have to be able to effectively license and tag the software to individual computers to prevent consumers from giving or selling the software to other users. The potential for resales destroys the ability to make all-or-none offers, which is why all-or-none offers are usually limited to services. An example is cable TV, discussed below. Shirt manufacturers cannot make all-or-none offers to their customers.

CHAPTER 10

1. The federal government had established a pension fund for the military in 1911, and a separate pension plan for all civil service employees in 1920. The state and local governments also have pension programs for their employees.
2. Curiously, there was a program for the poor who were blind but not for the poor who were deaf, even though the blind fare much better economically than the deaf, on average.
3. An initial modest expansion of Medicaid to medically needy, low-income families who were not receiving public assistance had begun in the 1970s in some states, with federal approval and financial support.
4. The general purpose of insurance, private or social, is to smooth consumption over time. People sacrifice some income to pay premiums for insurance when their incomes are high in order to receive payments when the bad events insured against occur and would otherwise sharply lower their incomes. We discuss social insurance in detail in Chapter 12, including its consumption-smoothing properties. The focus of this chapter is the government's attempt to help the poor through its public assistance programs.
5. The taxes on the rich would have to be lump sum to keep the economy on its utility possibilities frontier.
6. The exception would be if the indifference curves were so steeply curved, for example right-angled, that the food subsidy and equal cash transfer place P on the same indifference curve. This is not the expected outcome, however.

CHAPTER 12

1. In general, with actuarially fair partial insurance, the insurance amount is $\frac{1}{p}$ times the premium, X. Therefore, the expected income is

$$E(Y) = (1 - p)(\$60{,}000 - X) + p(\$20{,}000 + \left(\frac{1}{p}\right) \cdot X - X) =$$

$$(1 - p)(\$60{,}000) + p(\$20{,}000) - (1 - p)X + p(\frac{(1-p)}{p})X =$$

$(1 - p)(\$60,000) + p(\$20,000) = E(Y)$ without insurance. $E(Y) = \$56,000$ with $p = .1$.

Under full insurance, $\left(\dfrac{1}{p}\right) \cdot X = (\$60,000 - \$20,000)$ and $Y = \$60,000 - X$ with certainty.

2. In terms of utility, they receive $U(\$42,000)$ with certainty under full insurance with an $18,000 premium. If their risk premium is less than $18,000, then $E(U)_{\$56,000} > U(\$42,000)$. The risky situation yields higher utility.

3. Discounting future dollars to present value is discussed in Chapter 20 on cost–benefit analysis if you are unfamiliar with the concept. It is the inverse of compounding current dollars to future values, as is done when calculating the value at some future time of an asset whose value grows over time at some annual rate(s) of growth. An example of compounding is the indexing of past wages described above in calculating the AIMEs at retirement that are used to determine Social Security annuities. For those familiar with present value discounting, the

combined losses of all but the first generation are $\displaystyle\sum_{t=0}^{\infty} \dfrac{1}{(1+r)^t}\left[\dfrac{(r-g)}{(1+r)}\right](1+g)^t T =$

$\left(\dfrac{1}{r-g}\right)(r-g)T = T$. When income from capital is taxed at rate t, r becomes $r(1-t)$,

which reduces both the numerator and denominator within the present value summation. The reduction in the denominator dominates, and increases the present value of the losses.

4. Diamond and Orszag's (2005) $11.6 trillion estimate includes the assumption that no one currently age 55 or older in 2005 would have their benefits cut, which appeared to be a binding political constraint at the time.

5. Medical insurance is another area in which the public sector has an enormous cost advantage. Public programs such as Medicare and the veterans hospitals have much lower administrative costs then private insurers, including the health maintenance organizations.

CHAPTER 13

1. Personal income not disposable income, because personal income measures income before the income tax is paid and is therefore the appropriate component of the tax base.

2. If two goods are perfect substitutes, then some people might consume one of the goods and other people the other good. An example is a house or an apartment that offers equivalent housing services. Then housing services, not houses or apartments, would have to be the tax base.

3. The lifetime utilities and consumption are understood to be discounted to present value so that the utilities and consumption over time are commensurate. The same

is true of lifetime income mentioned below. If you are unfamiliar with discounting to present value, read the first section of Chapter 20.

4. Equity is not the only issue in the ongoing debate between income and consumption taxes. Efficiency matters as well, especially in the long run. Economists study the long-run effects of taxes by constructing simple, stylized growth models and introducing various kinds of broad-based taxes. These models show that substituting a consumption tax for an income tax eventually generates very large increases in saving, investment, productivity, and growth because saving is no longer taxed. It may well be that the majority of economists who favor replacing income taxes with consumption taxes do so because of their long-run efficiency advantages and not because they view them as more equitable. We will return to the efficiency and equity implications of income and consumption taxes in Chapter 14.

CHAPTER 14

1. The average tax rate was 33.05% = (.10·$7,300 + .15·$22,400 + .25·$42,250 + .28·$78,250 + .33·$176,450 + .35·$673,550)/$1,000,000 = ($730 + $3,360 + $10,562.50 + $21,910 + $58,228.50 + $235,742.50)/$1,000,000 = (330,533.50)/ $1,000,000 = .3305 = 33.05%.

2. The imputed rent on owner-occupied homes is counted both as rental income to the homeowners and consumption of housing services in the national accounts to maintain the equality between national income and national product. Similarly, the value of the nonmarketed farm produce is counted as income and consumption.

3. Extraordinary medical expenses are defined as those exceeding 7.5% of what the IRS refers to as adjusted gross income (AGI), which is approximately equal to the taxpayer's income before personal exemptions, exclusions, and deductions have been subtracted.

4. Taxpayers have the option of deducting an estimate of the taxes paid under their states' sales taxes if it is a larger amount than their state income taxes.

5. The personal exemptions could be viewed as an issue in horizontal equity because married taxpayers who file jointly can take exemptions for themselves, their spouses, and their dependents, whereas single taxpayers can take only one exemption. But since needs increase with family size, the additional exemptions for families are seen to correspond roughly with their greater needs.

6. We ignore business expenses, the one legitimate deduction according to the Haig–Simons standard. The deduction for business expenses is not a loophole.

7. If the market is not competitive, then market power is the source of any horizontal inequities that may remain in the long run, not the tax structure (see Feldstein, 1976).

8. If people prefer houses to apartments, then the pre-tax-break price of the houses would be higher than the apartment rents to account for the relative attractiveness

of houses. But this would make no difference to the following discussion. Therefore it is easier to assume that the two original annualized prices (rents) are equal.

9. If interest is paid continuously, such as with most bank deposit accounts, then the instantaneous return to capital adjusts point for point with the expected inflation. The instantaneous return on a bank deposit is approximately equal to the daily return, the annual return divided by 360 (days). It is this daily return that is compounded continuously during the year and it adjusts point for point with the daily inflation rate.

10. The precise interest needed to increase her purchasing power by 5% is $(1 + .05)(1 + .1) = 1 + .15 + .005 = 1 + .155 = 1 + 15.5\%$. We are ignoring the last term that adds another 0.5% to the interest rate.

11. This is easily seen if inflation is viewed as a continuous process with the rate of inflation defined as an instantaneous rate compounded continuously over time. Then, with wages adjusted only annually, the wage adjustment would be the cumulative inflation at the instantaneous rate compounded over the year.

12. The interest rates and rates of inflation can be measured either as instantaneous rates compounded continuously or as annual rates. The examples that follow assume they are annual rates.

13. With different taxpayers facing different marginal tax rates, it is never clear exactly how nominal interest rates will adjust to changes in expected inflation. The nominal interest rate would have to rise to 21.333% to maintain an after-tax real return of zero in our examples when inflation increases from 12% to 16%.

14. For simplicity, we are ignoring discounting to present value because it is not central to the issue of income averaging.

15. Married couples can choose to file separately, but the tax brackets for married couples filing separately are all half as wide as the filing jointly brackets, so there is usually no advantage in choosing this option.

16. The switch from an income tax to an expenditure tax and many other tax reforms and fiscal policies are analyzed in Auerbach and Kotlikoff (1987).

17. The first section of Chapter 20 has a discussion of discounting to present value if you are unclear of this concept.

18. People also borrow to finance consumption, and the loan proceeds become part of the tax base if they are used to finance consumption.

19. If the mortgage interest deduction were not retained, then the personal consumption tax would increase the tax burden on housing.

CHAPTER 15

1. Along the original budget line at X_B, $Y_B^0 + P_X X_B = I$. Along the with-tax budget line at X_B, $Y_B^t + (P_X + tP_X)X_B = I$. Subtracting the two lines at X_B yields $Y_B^0 - Y_B^t - tP_X X_B = 0$ or $tP_X X_B = Y_B^0 - Y_B^t$. The tax paid is the vertical distance between the Y values on the two budget lines at X_B, distance DB.

2. British economist J.R. Hicks developed the two-income measure of utility loss represented in Figure 15.2.

3. The one exception is if the income effect for X is zero, in which case $D_{U=U_1}^{comp}$ and D^{act} coincide.

4. Recall that S represents the marginal cost of producing X at each output, so that the area under S up to any given X is the total cost of producing that amount of X.

5. Recall the homeowner, apartment example in Chapter 14, which referred to the efficiency loss only in the market for owner-occupied homes that receive tax breaks, but not in the market for apartments even though the tax breaks shifted the demand for apartments.

CHAPTER 16

1. The IER is also commonly referred to as the Ramsey rule after Frank Ramsey (1927), who first derived it.

2. Advanced texts show how to modify the IER to account for goods that are complements or substitutes to the good being taxed. The more complex rule does not change the basic intuition behind the single-good IER.

3. Since relative prices have to change to generate a deadweight loss, there must be at least one untaxed good or factor. Otherwise, taxing all goods and factors at the same rate would lead to no change in relative prices and no loss. For example, in our simple consumer model in the first part of Chapter 15, if the government set a tax rate of t on both X and Y, then raising both prices by (1 + t) is equivalent to reducing the consumer's endowment of income by a factor of (1 + t). [(1 + t)P_XX + (1 + t)P_YY = Income $\Leftrightarrow$ P_XX + P_YY = $\dfrac{Income}{(1+t)}$]. The tax would be equivalent to a lump-sum tax and there would be no efficiency loss. If there is no source of lump-sum income in an economy to tax, then setting a tax rate of t on all goods and factors would raise no revenue.

4. The tax on good i would also increase or decrease the consumption of goods that are substitutes and complements to good i, with further effects on individuals and social welfare. We ignore these additional effects since they do not change the intuition of how changes in utilities affect social welfare.

CHAPTER 17

1. Suppose t increases to t'. Then at point B, at which no income is declared and Y_{NC} = Y, Y_C shifts down from Y(1 – t – tf) to Y(1 – t' – t'f), a vertical shift of Y(t' – t + t'f – tf) = Y((t' – t)(1 + f)).

2. The first-best frontier continues beyond B to (5, –1), but we stopped at B on the assumption that the ill cannot have negative utility.

3. One patently unrealistic feature of this model is that the government does not know who is healthy and ill, but does know the utility functions of the two groups. The government's knowledge of preferences in models of private information is a common assumption in the literature. It is made as a matter of convenience to focus on the difficulties imposed by private information on other aspects of individuals such as their incomes or health.

4. The MU_Z, $e^{(1-Z)}$, ranges from e to 1 as Z goes from 0 to 1. For Z > 1, $MU_Z = \dfrac{1}{e^{(Z-1)}}$

   < 1. Therefore, I buys 1 unit of Z when $P_Z = q = 1$, more than 1 unit of Z if q < 1 (subsidy), and less than 1 unit of Z if q > 1 (tax).

5. With Z > 1, $MU_Z = \dfrac{1}{e^{Z-1}} < 1$, and $MU_Y = 1$. Therefore, I is worse off at Z > 1, $Y_I < 2.5$

   than at Z = 1 and $Y_I = 2.5$. I does not want to trade units of Y for units of Z since Z has the lower marginal utility.

CHAPTER 18

1. The distinction between compensated and actual demand (and factor supply) curves was discussed in Chapter 15 when measuring the deadweight loss from taxes. Recall that the actual demand (factor supply) curve reflects both the substitution and income effects of a price change, whereas the compensated demand (factor supply) curve reflects only the substitution effect. Consumer surplus is a valid measure of the welfare loss from a price increase only if measured behind the compensated demand curve. Review that material in Chapter 15 if you are unclear about these points.

2. For example, the more inelastic supply is relative to demand, the more the suppliers bear the burden of a tax.

3. The caveat on actual versus compensated demand and supply curves does not apply to firms' factor demands and goods supplies because there is no distinction between the two curves for firms. The actual factor demand and goods supply curves reflect only the substitution effect of price changes; there is no income effect.

4. Refer to the discussion in the section Factor supplies: labor in Chapter 15 if you are unclear on these points.

5. Harberger's balanced-budget exercise could be applied to the lump-sum tax in the following spirit: If the government spends the tax revenues in a way that has equal value to consumers as what they themselves would have done with the tax revenues, then there is no burden to the lump-sum tax.

6. To bring tax revenues into play with a distorting tax, one could assume that the government saves the tax revenues and thereby runs a surplus. But that assumption has its own price implications. Students familiar with the IS-LM model in macroeconomics know that an increase in taxes with no corresponding increase in government spending shifts the IS curve down. If national income remains on the production possibilities frontier because the economy is competitive and remains at full employment, then the interest rate has to fall. The decrease in the interest rate benefits some people and hurts others, so that it becomes part of the incidence analysis. There is simply no escaping the need to pay some attention to price changes, in this case part of the annual price (cost) of capital. Moreover, the interest rate would fall even if the tax were lump sum, so that the impact of a lump-sum tax would no longer be the incidence of the tax. In any event, economists have overwhelmingly preferred Harberger's lump-sum-return assumption to the assumption that the government saves the tax revenues in incidence analysis.

7. The theorem also holds if each subset contains a mixture of the goods and factors. The only difference is that if rate t is a tax on the goods in the first subset, then it is a subsidy on the factors in that subset, and similarly for t* on the other subset. Also, one subset can contain just a single good or factor. The implication is that the incidence of a tax or subsidy on one good or factor at rate t can be duplicated by a tax (subsidy) on all the other N-1 goods and factors at rate t*, with $(1 + t)(1 + t^*) = 1$.

CHAPTER 19

1. The Appendix to the chapter explains why unequal factor intensities cause the production possibilities frontier to be bowed outward even if the production function is constant returns to scale.

2. Equivalently, the government spends the tax revenues exactly as individuals would, had they received the revenues back lump sum.

3. Individuals own the firms, so it does not matter whether the revenues are returned to the firms or individuals.

4. If you are unclear about this point, review the discussion in Chapter 3 on why the marginal rate of technical substitution between labor and capital must be the same in both industries for the economy to be on its production possibilities frontier.

5. The deadweight loss would be the entire burden in a general equilibrium framework in which the tax revenues are assumed to be returned lump sum.

6. It may appear that firms bear some of the burden of the tax because their sales fall from X_0 to X_t. But the supply curve S represents the long-run marginal cost of supplying X. With S horizontal at P_0, the price of X received by firms continues to equal the long-run marginal cost of X, also equal to P_0. Costs are opportunity costs, so that the marginal costs of X equal the value of these resources in their next-best uses. With marginal costs constant, the resources freed up as X decreases to X_t are

assumed to move to their next-best alternatives, which are equal in value to their value (P_0) in X. Therefore, neither the owners of the firms nor any of the resources used by the firms bear a burden from the sales tax.

7. Chapter 20 has a discussion of how to convert a stream of annual values of a variable such as tax burden or income into a single lifetime present value. The present value of a variable is a lump-sum amount that, if received today, would be viewed by an individual or family as equal in value to the stream of annual values actually received.

8. Rational expectations is the usual assumption, meaning that people do not systematically over- or underpredict the future values of variables such as their incomes, their taxes, interest rates, and inflation.

CHAPTER 20

1. Advanced texts show that the formula used to solve for the internal yield may not produce an unambiguous solution. There could be one, many, or no values that set the present value equal to zero. We will ignore this complication and assume that the formula can be solved for a single ρ.

2. $(1 + r)(1 + \pi) = 1 + r + \pi + r\pi = 1 + i$, where i is the nominal or observed interest rate when the inflation rate is π. For example, if $r = .08$ as in our examples and $\pi = .05$ (5%), the nominal interest rate $i = .08 + .05 + .004 = .134$, or 13.4%. Often the interaction term is ignored and the nominal interest rate is represented as the sum of the real interest rate plus the rate of inflation, or 13% in this example.

3. U.S. college students will be happy to know that almost all studies find that the present value of a college education is very large. College is a good investment for most young people.

4. The uncertainties increase if the discount rate is expected to change in future years depending, say, or whether the economy is projected to be booming or enduring a long recession.

5. If the intangible associated with X is a cost, and $PV_X > PV_Y$ based on the quantifiable elements of X, then $PV_X - PV_Y$ indicates the maximum value that the intangible cost could have to prefer X to Y.

6. Mishan would also add in the expected pain and suffering of family and friends, in line with U.S. judicial practice in awarding damages.

7. See the articles by P. Portney (overview), W. Hanemann (for), and P. Diamond and J. Hausman (against) in the *Journal of Economic Perspectives*, Fall 1994, for different views on contingent valuation.

8. Arguing that the distribution of income is optimal would be a particularly tough idea to sell in the United States, given the oft-expressed concern for the increasing inequality that has occurred since the mid-1970s.

9. Among the best-known economists who take this view is University of Chicago's Arnold Harberger, who argues strongly for a pragmatic approach to cost–benefit

analysis. Harberger (1971) laid out his preferred set of practical principles in one of the more widely cited articles on cost–benefit analysis.

10. For a more detailed discussion of the pitfalls see R. Tresch, *Public Finance: A Normative Theory* (2nd edn) (San Diego: Academic Press, 2002).

CHAPTER 21

1. The opposite of a federal government is a unitary government, in which all governmental powers are vested with the central government. In fact, though, the local governments in countries with unitary governments do have many economic responsibilities, sometimes more so than the local governments in countries with federal governments. Therefore, the principles discussed in Chapters 21 to 23 apply to those countries with unitary governments as well. Among the 30 capitalist countries belonging to the Organization for Economic Cooperation and Development (OECD), 8 have federal governments: Australia, Austria, Belgium, Canada, Germany, Mexico, Switzerland, and the United States. The other 22 members have unitary governments.

2. The outside events include decisions by the national government. Many states are heavily dependent on defense contacts for military hardware and software, which ebbs and flows with the nation's defense needs.

3. Stigler (1957) meant by "local" either state or local, that is, any government other than the national government in the federal hierarchy.

4. We are assuming away the inevitable inefficiencies that arise when taxing and transferring, which complicates the optimal distribution problem. Assuming lump-sum taxes and transfers allows us to focus on the problem of assigning the distribution function to non-national governments in the simplest possible manner.

5. The localities may have to adjust their lump-sum transfers as they are taxed or receive transfers from the states, and the states may have to adjust their lump-sum transfers as they are taxed or receive transfers from the national government, but in principle the social marginal utilities can be equalized from each government's perspective.

CHAPTER 22

1. Assume there are an odd number of people in the community so that there is an identifiable median voter. This assumption avoids having to worry about tie votes.

CHAPTER 23

1. See Table 14.1 for the data on U.S. grants-in-aid. The data on the EU grants-in-aid come from the *European Union Financial Report 2005*, European Communities, Luxembourg, Office for Official Publications of the European Communities, 2006.

2. The Title I grants to local education agencies are targeted to low-income communities.

3. To see this, begin with the labor supply constraint, $L_G + L_Y = L_0$, and substitute for

    L_G and L_Y from the production relationships: $L_G = \dfrac{G}{a}$ and $L_Y = \dfrac{Y}{b(1+r)^t}$. Therefore,

    $\dfrac{G}{a} + \dfrac{Y}{b(1+r)^t} = L_0$. Multiply both sides of the equation by $ab(1+r)^t$: $Gb(1+r)^t + aY = $

    $L_0 ab(1+r)^t$. Solve for Y: $aY = -Gb(1+r)^t + L_0 ab(1+r)^t$ or

    $$Y = -\frac{b(1+r)^t}{a}G + L_0 b(1+r)^t.$$

4. The labor supply and population in the United States grow at about 1% per year. To account for this, think of the demands for G and Y in per capita terms and the results in the text carry through.

5. One other possibility not considered in the figures is a project grant that finances specific projects. The DOT Miscellaneous Grants and Head Start are project grants. Under these programs, the granting government receives proposals from the receiving governments for specific projects and awards grants to what it views to be the best projects until all the grant funds are exhausted. The share of the funding on each project by the granting and receiving governments is either specified by a formula or negotiable. In either case, these grants can be viewed as placing the receiving government at a corner solution such as F in Figure 23.3(b) since these are highly specific projects. The projects are usually undertaken only if they receive grant support. Therefore, these grants are not equivalent to unconditional grants of the same amount; the condition that the grant be spent on a specific project matters. Also, political considerations can trump purely economic considerations in the negotiations over the spending shares.

EPILOGUE

1. For a discussion of the strengths and weaknesses of laboratory experiments, see S. Levitt and J. List, "What Do Laboratory Experiments Measuring Social Preferences Reveal About the Real World?", *Journal of Economic Perspectives*, Spring 2007.

2. Readers interested in behavioral economics might begin with the following sources: D. Fudenberg, "Advancing Beyond Advances in Behavioral Economics," and W. Pesendorfer, "Behavioral Economics Comes of Age: A Review Essay on Advances in Behavioral Economics, both in the *Journal of Economic Literature*, September 2006 (balanced critiques of behavioral economics from two mainstream economic theorists); B. D. Bernheim and A. Rangel, "Behavioral Public Economics: Welfare and Policy Analysis with Non-Standard Decision Makers," Working Paper 11518, National Bureau of

Economic Research, July 2005 (another balanced critique of behavioral economics by mainstream theorists that is quite hopeful in tone; also contains detailed discussions of saving, addiction, and public goods seen through the behavioral lens); E. McCaffery and J. Slemrod, "Toward an Agenda for Behavioral Public Finance," Chapter 1 in E. McCaffery and J. Slemrod (eds) *Behavioral Public Finance* (New York: Russell Sage Foundation, 2006) (an excellent overview of the implications of behavioral economics for public sector economics; includes a more detailed discussion of the behavioral perspective on tax compliance than presented in the Epilogue).

References

CHAPTER 1

R. J. Gordon, "Where Did the Productivity Growth Go? Inflation Dynamics and the Distribution of Income," *Brookings Papers on Economic Activity*, **2**, 2005.

R. Nozick, "Distributive Justice," *Philosophy and Public Affairs*, **3**, Spring 1973.

J. Buchanan, "The Constitution of Economic Policy," *American Economic Review*, June 1987.

E. Fehr and S. Gachter, "Cooperation and Punishment in Public Goods Experiments," *American Economic Review*, September 2000.

CHAPTER 2

R. Musgrave, *A Theory of Public Finance: A Study in Public Economy* (New York: McGraw-Hill, 1959).

CHAPTER 4

W. Leontief, *Essays in Economics: Theories and Theorizing* (New York: Oxford University Press, 1966).

F. M. Bator, "The Simple Analytics of Welfare Maximization," *American Economic Review*, March 1957.

J. Rawls, *A Theory of Justice* (Cambridge, MA: Harvard University Press, 1971).

K. J. Arrow, *Social Choice and Individual Values* (New Haven, CT: Yale University Press, 1951).

CHAPTER 5

L. Thurow, *Generating Inequality: Mechanisms of Distribution in the U.S. Economy* (New York: Basic Books, 1975).

A. Okun, *Equality and Efficiency, The Big Tradeoff* (Washington, D.C.: The Brookings Institution, 1975).

A. Atkinson, *The Economics of Inequality* (2nd edn) (New York: Oxford University Press, 1983).

A. Atkinson, "On the Measurement of Inequality," *Journal of Economic Theory*, **2**, September 1970.

A. Harberger, "Basic Needs Versus Distributional Weights in Social Cost-Benefit Analysis," in R. Haveman and J. Margolis (eds) *Public Expenditure and Policy Analysis* (3rd edn) (Boston: Houghton Mifflin, 1983).

CHAPTER 7

R. Coase, "The Problem of Social Cost," *Journal of Law and Economics*, October 1960.

CHAPTER 8

E. Clarke, "Multipart Pricing of Public Goods," *Public Choice*, Fall 1971.

N. Tideman and G. Tulloch, "A New and Superior Process for Making Social Choices," *Journal of Political Economy*, December 1976.

J. Andreoni, "Warm Glow vs. Cold Prickly: The Effects of Positive and Negative Framing on Cooperation Experiments," *Quarterly Journal of Economics*, February 1995.

P. A. Samuelson, "The Pure Theory of Public Expenditure," *Review of Economics and Statistics*, November 1954.

E. Lindahl, *Die Gerectigkert der Berteverung*, reprinted in part in R. Musgrave and A. Peacock (eds) *Classics in the Theory of Public Finance* (New York: Macmillan, 1971).

CHAPTER 9

M. Friedman, *Capitalism and Freedom* (Chicago: University of Chicago Press, 1962).

CHAPTER 10

R. J. Gordon, *Macroeconomics* (8th edn) (Reading, MA: Addison-Wesley Longman, 2000).

CHAPTER 11

J. Buchanan, "The Samaritan's Dilemma," in E. Phelps (ed.) *Altruism, Morality and Economic Theory* (New York: Russell Sage Foundation, 1975).

N. Bruce and M. Waldman, "Transfers in Kind: Why They Can Be Efficient and Nonpaternalistic," *American Economic Review*, December 1991.

E. Browning and J. Browning, *Public Finance and the Price System* (2nd edn) (New York: Macmillan, 1983).

CHAPTER 12

J. L. Palmer and T. R. Saving, Trustees, *Summary of the 2005 Annual Reports, from the Social Security and Medicare Boards of Trustees*, March 23, 2005, www.ssa.gov/OACT/TRSUM/trsummary.html.

D. Cutler and J. Gruber, "Does Public Insurance Crowd out Private Insurance," *Quarterly Journal of Economics*, May 1996.

A. Munnell and A. Sunden, "401 K Plans are Still Coming up Short," *An Issue in Brief*, **43**, March 2006, Center for Retirement Research, Boston College.

A. Auerbach and L. Kotlikoff, *Dynamic Fiscal Policy* (New York: Cambridge University Press, 1987).

R. Barro, "Are Government Bonds Net Wealth?," *Journal of Political Economy*, November/December, 1974.

J. Gruber, *Public Finance and Public Policy* (New York: Worth Publishers, 2005).

J. Stiglitz, *Economics of the Public Sector* (3rd edn) (New York: W. W. Norton & Company, 2000).

P. Diamond and P. Orszag, "Saving Social Security," *Journal of Economic Perspectives*, Spring 2005.

P. Diamond, "Social Security," *American Economic Review*, March 2004.

M. Feldstein, "Rethinking Social Security," *American Economic Review*, March 2005.

CHAPTER 13

OECD, *OECD in Figures*, Statistics on the Member Countries, OECD Observer, 2005.

U.S. Government Accountability Office, *Internal Revenue Service: Assessment of the Fiscal Year 2006 Budget Request*, Statement for the Record for the Subcommittee on Transportation, Treasury, the Judiciary, Housing and Urban Development, and Related Agencies, Committee on Appropriations, 4/27/2005, p. 1.

U.S. Government Printing Office, *Budget of the United States Government, Fiscal Year 2008* (Washington, D.C., 2007) Historical Tables, Table 2.1.

501

R. M. Haig, "The Concept of Income: Economic and Legal Aspects," in R. M. Haig (ed.) *The Federal Income Tax* (New York: Columbia University Press, 1921).

H. C. Simons, *Personal Income Taxation* (Chicago: University of Chicago Press, 1938).

M. Feldstein, "On the Theory of Tax Reform," *Journal of Public Economics*, August 1976.

R. Musgrave, "Horizontal Equity, Once More," *National Tax Journal*, June 1990.

CHAPTER 14

M. Feldstein, "On the Theory of Tax Reform," *Journal of Public Economics*, August 1976.

U.S. Department of the Treasury, *Tax Reform for Fairness, Simplicity, and Economic Growth*, **I**, November 1984.

A. Auerbach and L. Kotlikoff, *Dynamic Fiscal Policy* (New York: Cambridge University Press, 1987).

A. Auerbach, D. Altig, L. Kotlikoff, and K. Smitters, "Simulating Fundamental Tax Reform in the United States," *American Economic Review*, June 2001.

CHAPTER 15

J. Hausman, "Labor Supply," in H. Aaron and J. Pechman (eds) *How Taxes Affect Economic Behavior* (Washington, D.C.: The Brookings Institution, 1981).

CHAPTER 16

F. Ramsey, "A Contribution to the Theory of Taxation," *Economic Journal*, March 1927.

CHAPTER 17

U.S. Government Accountability Office, "Tax Compliance: Reducing the Tax Gap Can Contribute to Fiscal Sustainability but Will Require a Variety of Strategies," Statement of David M. Walker, Comptroller General of the United States, before the Committee on Finance, U.S. Senate, April 14, 2005, Table, p. 1.

M. Allingham and A. Sandmo, "Income Tax Evasion: A Theoretical Analysis," *Journal of Public Economics*, November 1972.

J. Alm and W. Beck, "Tax Amnesties and Compliance in the Long Run: A Time Series Analysis," *National Tax Journal*, March 1993.

C. Blackorby and D. Donaldson, "Cash Versus Kind, Self Selection, and Efficient Transfers," *American Economic Review*, September 1988.

CHAPTER 18

A. Harberger, "The Incidence of the Corporation Income Tax," *Journal of Political Economy*, June 1962.

M. Krzyzaniak and R. Musgrave, *The Shifting of the Corporation Income Tax* (Baltimore: Johns Hopkins Press, 1963).

CHAPTER 19

A. Harberger, "The Incidence of the Corporation Income Tax," *Journal of Political Economy*, June 1962.

B. Okner and J. Pechman, *Who Bears the Tax Burden?* (Washington, D.C.: The Brookings Institution, 1974).

B. Okner and J. Pechman, *Who Paid the Taxes, 1966–1985?* (Washington, D.C.: The Brookings Institution, 1985).

J. Whalley, "Regression or Progression: the Taxing Question of Tax Incidence," *Canadian Journal of Economics*, November 1984.

CHAPTER 20

M. Feldstein, "Does the United States Save Too Little?," *American Economic Association Papers and Proceedings*, February 1977.

M. Weitzman, "Gamma Discounting," *American Economic Review*, March 2001.

E. J. Mishan, "Evaluation of Life and Limb: A Theoretical Approach," *Journal of Political Economy*, March/April 1971.

J. Broome, "Trying to Value a Life," *Journal of Public Economics*, February 1978.

A. Harberger, "Three Postulates for Applied Welfare Economics," *Journal of Economic Literature*, September 1971.

CHAPTER 21

G. Stigler, "Tenable Range of Functions of Local Government," in Federal Expenditure Policy for Economic Growth and Stability, Joint Economic Committee, Subcommittee on Fiscal Policy, Washington, D.C., 1957.

W. Oates, *Fiscal Federalism* (New York: Harcourt, Brace, Jovanovich, 1972).

CHAPTER 22

C. Tiebout, "A Pure Theory of Local Expenditures," *Journal of Political Economy*, October 1956.

J. Stiglitz, "The Theory of Local Public Goods" in M. Feldstein and R. Inman (eds) *The Economics of Public Services: Proceedings of a Conference Held by the International Economic Association at Turin, Italy* (New York: Macmillan, 1977).

M. Pauly, "A Model of Local Government and Tax Capitalization," *Journal of Public Economics*, October 1976.

CHAPTER 23

J. LeGrand, "Fiscal Equity and Central Government Grants to Local Authorities," *Economic Journal*, September 1975.

W. Baumol and W. Oates, *The Theory of Environmental Policy: Externalities, Public Outlays, and the Quality of Life* (Englewood Cliffs, NJ: Prentice Hall, 1975).

Index